MACHIAVELLI IN THE MAKING

Northwestern University
Studies in Phenomenology
and
Existential Philosophy

MACHIAVELLI IN THE MAKING

Claude Lefort

Translated from the French by Michael B. Smith

Northwestern University Press
Evanston, Illinois

Northwestern University Press
www.nupress.northwestern.edu

English translation copyright © 2012 by Northwestern University Press. Published 2012. All rights reserved. Originally published in French as *Le travail de l'oeuvre Machiavel* by Editions Gallimard, Paris, France, 2005.

10 9 8 7 6 5 4 3 2 1

Library of Congress Cataloging-in-Publication Data

Lefort, Claude.
  [Travail de l'oeuvre Machiavel. English]
  Machiavelli in the making / Claude Lefort ; translated from the French by Michael B. Smith.
      p. cm. — (Northwestern university studies in phenomenology and existential philosophy)
  "Originally published in French as Le travail de l'oeuvre Machiavel by Editions Gallimard, Paris, France, 2005."—T.p. verso.
  Includes bibliographical references.
  ISBN 978-0-8101-2437-0 (cloth : alk. paper) — ISBN 978-0-8101-2438-7 (pbk. : alk. paper)
  1. Machiavelli, Niccolò, 1469–1527. I. Smith, Michael B. (Michael Bradley), 1940– II. Title. III. Series: Northwestern University studies in phenomenology & existential philosophy.
JC143.M4L413 2011
320.01—dc23

                                                          2011036658

Contents

Translator's Note

In response to a note from me, in which I had emphasized the difficulty of translating the present work, Claude Lefort wrote (January 2, 2007): "I am sure my book is difficult to translate. My thesis director, Raymond Aron, vigorously criticized my style, which he considered to be Proustian, which was by no means a compliment! Since those days I have tried to be more concise." He went on to authorize my shortening and simplifying his sentences, which I have sometimes been able to do. But was Aron's allusion to Proust entirely negative? Did his ears hear all of what his lips were saying? And did Lefort's propensity for jovial self-depreciation deter a broader interpretation of the Proustian allusion? For although in this early (1972) thesis the sentences do indeed tend to meanderings and tucked-in afterthoughts (or what the French call "*repentirs*"), both authors thereby remain faithful to their mental movements' ranging through the depths of a meditation followed through to its reluctant release. A case in point: At the very beginning of his book, Lefort imagines a critic accusing him of the "perversion" of desiring to pursue the discourse (of Machiavelli) even beyond the silence that would hypothetically be imposed were one to stumble upon an interpretation that would end the discourse. And just as Proust inserts the origin of his text within the text of *Remembrance of Things Past* itself, so Lefort manages to foreshadow not only his technique of interpreting the oeuvre of Machiavelli, but his own interpretive work as well, as oeuvre of the oeuvre: he defers the end of Machiavelli's discourse "by freeing it from the fatal cycle in which it was lodged, by attaching it to the possibility of a new origin, by soliciting further survival in a reader." If I insist on this example, it is to emphasize that the fertile difficulty of Lefort's text is not just one of translation.

I have decided not to translate the term "oeuvre" in this book, because it is thematized—or even hypostasized—by the author in such a way as to warrant being left en bloc as a holistic phenomenon. Since a large portion of Lefort's book (particularly parts 1 and 5) is devoted to explicating this phenomenon (the original title of the thesis was "*le tra-*

vail de l'oeuvre Machievel," or, literally, the work of the work Machiavelli, as if Machiavelli [the name] were to be considered an oeuvre "worked" by time), it would be both presumptuous and redundant of me to elaborate on its characteristics here.

The original book was edited for translation by the author in order to produce a volume of more amenable dimensions. The portions of the thesis dealing with literary interpretations of Machiavelli were omitted. It is my sincere hope that those texts (for example Lefort's critical analyses of the interpretations of E. Cassirer, A. Gramsci, and L. Strauss) will be translated and published separately at a future time, along with Lefort's theoretical piece "The Field of Critical Literature." Indeed, what singles Lefort out among French sociopolitical thinkers is the breadth of his grasp of literary, aesthetic, and philosophical questions as well, putting him on an equal footing, mutatis mutandis, with his former friend and mentor Maurice Merleau-Ponty.

Lefort did his own translations from Machiavelli's Italian. My policy has therefore been as follows. I have compared his translations with the original Italian, and also consulted several current English translations of *The Prince* and *The Discourses.* I have followed Lefort's generally more literal translations whenever possible, but occasionally profited from Luigi Ricci's translation of *The Prince* (1903, revised by E. R. P. Vincent in 1935, published by The New American Library of World Literature in 1952). As for *The Discourses,* I followed the same procedure, consulting a variety of translations, particularly that of Leslie J. Walker, S.J., as revised by Brian Richardson (London and New York: Penguin Classics, 2003).

A note on the use of gendered pronouns. French continues to follow the practice of using "*il*" (he) for hypothetical persons of either sex. Since all nouns in French are grammatically masculine or feminine, grammatical gender is not as closely associated with sexual difference as it is in English. For example, the word "*personne*" (person) is feminine, as is the word "*sentinelle*" (sentry, guard), though about 50 percent of persons are masculine, and nearly all sentries are (although this may change). In cases where conformity with existing English requirements of nonsexist language could be attained without awkwardness or loss of clarity, I have made the appropriate changes. For the translator, there is a less obvious result of French assigning gender to all nouns. That is, indirectly, the reason it has often been necessary to break down the longer French sentences into several shorter ones in English. The use of "it" (to translate the French "*il*" or "*elle*" when referring to things or ideas) doubles the ambiguity of reference to the antecedent, thus rendering Lefort's often long, complex sentences untenable when translated without being broken down into shorter ones.

I take great pleasure in acknowledging the moral support of Judith Walz and Bernard Flynn in the completion of this project, as well as the ongoing encouragement of my Husserlian friend and editor Anthony Steinbock. The unusually high intellectual altitudes and frequent linguistic turbulence encountered during this intercontinental translation have made me keenly aware of how much I (and future readers of this volume) owe to the efforts of Northwestern's editorial ground crew, headed by Heather J. Antti: Martin T. Coleman and Susan Boulanger.

MACHIAVELLI IN THE MAKING

Part 1

The Question of the Oeuvre

This book was born of an attraction to an enigma—one that I myself cannot pretend to fathom fully. It is an attraction that, far from being diminished by an abundant critical literature in which both the position and the resolution of the enigma are poignantly repeated, has only grown stronger by a displacement: the receding of its object beyond the field in which, shrouded in its original obscurity, it seemed to lie.

Whoever may think that an interpreter is motivated by the desire to outdo his rivals and master a field of knowledge—as reflected in his "owning" the meaning of an oeuvre, and having the authority derived from it to win the favor of all future readers—will take it to be a simple refinement of that desire that I should undertake to direct this investigation to both the writer and his legacy in order to grasp the continuous movement by which the oeuvre eludes the grasp of its interpreters, and to reveal the complicity that makes up the substance of their conflicts, thus developing a new approach to that oeuvre. In this new approach, the oeuvre would remain at a distance, even at the most intimate moments of the dialogue, like someone we know to be speaking beyond the reach of our understanding, in a way that leaves us, along with the knowledge we obtain, a sense of uneasiness. It is as if, protracting the experience of doubt to the end, we were to waive the eventual fortuitous find that would put an end to further discourse. A refinement, perhaps a perversion even . . . Against such a thought it would be vain to defend oneself. But we may at least counter with the question: What judge can decide the issue? Who can pretend to separate himself from the desire for knowledge? To one who would bring the charge of perversion, what authority could support him that would be outside the field of discourse, a field that appeals to the other for support and maintains itself by speaking beyond the point at which the interlocutor falls silent—that is, by deferring the conclusion, by freeing it from the fatal cycle in which it was lodged, by attaching it to the possibility of a new origin, by soliciting further survival in a reader?

An enigma, I was saying. But it would be better to begin by taking stock of some questions that have sprouted into such an interrogative thicket that they must be thought together.

One of these is connected to the name Machiavelli itself. We hear it pronounced, we use it even before knowing where it came from. For at least four centuries it has been in the common language, with its derivatives—Machiavellianism, Machiavellian—to the point of constituting an irreplaceable signifier; and not just destined for political usage (though there it remains privileged) but suitable for designating an act that typifies the conduct of one human being toward another. It is an odd adventure, and an intriguing one, since even a cursory look at the history of the society in which Machiavelli lived, and a superficial reading of his oeuvre, are all we need to arrive at the conclusion that he was neither the practitioner nor the author of that political perversion that has been dubbed Machiavellianism. On the contrary, we would have to recognize, whatever our judgment of his actions and ideas, that he was a man of quality in both politics and letters—a politician more devoted to the state, more solicitous of Italy, more attached to freedom than were the masters he was obliged to serve and frequent, and a writer of great subtlety whose discourse, far from being reducible to a few irreverent maxims, unfolds along multiple and arduous paths, on a par with those of the most highly respected historians and philosophers—Livy, Cicero, Plutarch, and also Plato, Aristotle, Xenophon. He is indeed a writer who demands of the reader, both of his own era and of ours, an unusual degree of attentiveness and culture. Do the adventures of this term have any special significance? What sense are we to make of the fact that a proper name suddenly stops as if in a freeze frame, peels away from the person, and sets out to lead an independent life, taking up with a variety of dubious dialects and the most time-worn words, forgetful of its origins? Or better yet, what is the meaning of that remote decapitation of a proper name? By the pull of what power does it come to fall to the level of the common language—beneath the sway of what anonymous force to function as a sign?

A new sign of immoralism, so say some, imported from the oeuvre, from *The Prince* in particular; some expressions drawn from that source may have been repeated with delectation by certain readers, while horrifying others, till in the end, in total ignorance of the author, the oeuvre, and the exact wording of those sayings even, all that was left was the convenience of that word. But surely there has never been a shortage of testimony to immorality. The ears of mankind had heard enough bold utterances on the necessity of violence or the pleasures to be had from practicing oppression to be unimpressed by the effects of a discourse that not only cannot be reduced to such utterances, but ends with an appeal for the liberation of the Italian fatherland. For those who remember the arguments put in the mouths of Polos, Callicles, or Thrasymachus, there can be no doubt that opposition to the law in classical antiquity met with bold spokesmen. Further, the words of Callicles carry with them a defiance and invective of which there is no apparent trace in Machiavelli. Perhaps the adversaries of Socrates arouse less passion because they are paired with their refuter, or perhaps their outbursts lack real conviction. Could it be that these so-called breakers of idols never went beyond the level of make-believe? Was Socrates right to doubt their opposition to the laws and their disdain for the people, and to call them flatterers, going so far as to insinuate that they were more seduced than seducers, motivated, unbeknownst to themselves, by the desire of a *demos* they only think they dominate, enchained to a law they only think they are defying? And would it then be the case that Machiavelli introduces a protest of a totally different scope, one that the accusation of Machiavellianism disfigures, though not without designating it? Did Machiavelli not perhaps undermine the law in an entirely new and unknown way? Might he be the author of an effective transgression, the result of which was to upset, in his day, a certainty all the more fiercely preserved for being threatened by events; in such a way as to bring about the annulment, in a certain zone, of the established difference between morality and immorality? So serious that it could not be recognized? So grave that it was necessary to displace its object in order to condemn it?

For such a question to take shape, we must explore the end of Machiavellianism and research its beginnings, scrutinize the first milieus in which its usage spread—without forgetting that it continues to carry meaning at a distance from its origins, freed of the function or functions it originated to fulfill. We must avoid acquiescing too quickly to the explanations offered us. Can we be sure those very explanations do not participate in the movement that gave birth to it? We must take care not to replace one prejudice for another: to replace, for example, the idea that Machiavellianism can be deduced from the Machiavellian discourse, that it is its emblem put into circulation—for that other idea that it is the result of happenstance, the fallout of an unjust accusation, an unfortunate lexical accident swept up and assimilated into the language. In vain would we expect from such an enquiry an understanding of the oeuvre, for it is not from these effects that it permits itself to be thought. We say only that the effects are sufficiently troubling for us to see in them an admonition—the indication that something is involved to which it is not entirely alien.

But one question never springs up in isolation. Why pretend we do not know that in our day Machiavelli presents himself with the halo of a founder's reputation? With him, they say, political discourse came to be: not of course a reflection on the essence of good government or the art of governing, but a discourse that aims at politics as such, that circumscribes its domain and breaks all ties with metaphysics and theology.

That the irruption into language of the equivocal signifier "Machiavellianism" should be the effect of a first rupture in the order of thought, that that rupture, invisible to the vast majority, should nonetheless be silently recognized to the point of producing a slippage in the order of speech—now that would be of a nature to whet our curiosity. But still, it would be appropriate to wonder about the meaning we give the event, instead of rushing in to welcome a notion our contemporaries seem as sure of as they are that philosophical discourse began with Plato, scientific discourse with Galileo, or the discourse of history as such with Hegel and Marx. Now, scarcely do we hark to that notion than the discourse of others, of those individuals who make up Machiavelli's posterity, sweeps us up in a movement we are no longer the masters of—a continual source of astonishment, an astonishment that, though it may die out in each one the moment we have been able to form a judgment about that layer of posterity, spreads to the next, as if to keep open, beyond every question about the meaning of the oeuvre, a question about its identity.

Was Machiavelli the founder—the speaker—of a discourse radically new? The assertion that he was has its origin in a past more distant than one might be led to suppose by some modern commentators. If we consider his first opponents or his first defenders, they already share one certainty: something was written, for the first time, that either never should have been . . . or had to be. It is as if a liberty had been taken—intolerable or exultant—with the truth of books: that sort of truth that previously, from its own proper place, had sustained and constrained men's actions, organizing them, by the very virtue of its far remove, according to a secret logic. It is not the mere content of the statements that bears witness in the eyes of each party to an unprecedented daring, since the critical accounts of those statements on the part of the respective parties are immediately at odds; it is rather the movement of speech that seems to surprise, scandalize, or enchant, by the modification it introduces in the relation of the book to its object, and, at the same time, of the author to his reader. The desire to impute to Machiavelli the paternity of political discourse is accompanied in each reader by one sole representation of the oeuvre, the truth of which is affirmed by excluding as pure nonsense the truth of others. It is troubling to witness a belief so generally shared in the originality of a writer, and a disagreement enrooted so early in its posterity, so constantly maintained, about the meaning of the oeuvre.

When we begin to sound the literature that developed around this oeuvre, our first surprise is the degree of hatred of which it was the object, a hatred which, though it reached its zenith fifty years after its publication, never disarmed. But it is yet another surprise to discover that the defense of the writer, despite what is commonly said, dates as far back as his condemnation, and that it, too, has aroused the liveliest and most long-lasting passions. Still another surprise is to learn that in the name of objective knowledge, freed from the impurities of polemics, commentators have for centuries devoted their efforts to restoring the true figure of the writer—their own hatreds, loves, their professed neutrality still covering such a variety of interpretations that their motives have become anecdotal. But no less astonishing is the effort expended to discover an oeuvre known, studied, and discussed as few others have been in history, and to claim to condemn it or appreciate it adequately *for the first time;* no less astonishing the opportunity taken in each period of that discovery to proclaim a new truth about the present, as if by reading Machiavelli a veil were rent, as if the signs placed in *The Prince* or *The Discourses,* unknown, undecipherable till then because written for a future reader, awaiting a time that would reveal them, were to be jolted into vociferation by contact with the event; and no less astonishing the diversity of those whom the oeuvre fascinates, for it is not only philosophers, theologians, moralists, historians, who take up their pens: it is also politicians, or men whom nothing, apparently, had prepared to such an exercise and who, overcome with passion, convince themselves that there is an urgency involved in their alerting their contemporaries to the Machiavellian message.

Now, that there should be a discourse of posterity, or better, that that posterity should be ordered in the form of a discourse, and that that discourse should be articulated unbeknownst to its agents in the form of a trial (such that, although participants come and go, the same distribution of roles and arguments subsists, and beneath the emblem of a myth—identification, in its dual form, positive and negative, the resurrection of the author in its dual function of immortalization and execution, repeating itself as impervious to time)—this thought at once precipitates our questioning and broadens the field of enquiry. Indeed, how are we to understand that, from one era to another, the same differentiations or similar ones should reappear in the representation of the oeuvre, and especially that the ideological divisions to which we have become accustomed blur on contact with the oeuvre, that unexpected allies form, and well-established kinships come apart?

Doubtless these adventures already prompt us to reconsider the status of the oeuvre of thought, and to distinguish between knowledge of the oeuvre and ideology; doubtless they require of us to wonder about the nature of the Machiavellian discourse, to seek what it is in this discourse that makes such adventures possible, or even authorizes them. Perhaps they only take on their full significance on the condition that we reexamine our representation of the political discourse that is intertwined with that of the oeuvre. But might they not teach us something else as well, something about ideologies themselves? Ideology—or what we are quick to label thus, to give a name to a focal point of knowledge kindled and fed by the desire of a category of people to fashion and re-fashion the social order in conformity with the requirements of their own practice—is it not odd that we are prevented from measuring its efficacy, on an occasion in which one would expect—it being a question of the appreciation and exploitation of a political oeuvre—that it be manifested in the highest degree?

Might the oeuvre have some power to scramble the reference points according to which political power is organized, and to reveal—in the divorces and complicities formed apropos of it, on the hither side of commonly recognized opinions and values—an unknown play of opposi-tions that, not being within the range of our normal focus, persist there, sheltered from the variations of ideology?

Now these questions do not fade away when the attention shifts from the general field of Machiavellian literature to the more specific subcat-egory of its scientific criticism, that space in which knowledge is valued more highly than appreciation, and a tight rein is kept on the imagina-tion. There, faithfulness to the text predominates, upheld by a resolve to get at its meaning not only by the orderly comparison of discursive propo-sitions, the just assessment of their letter, and the proper adjustment of the conditions of coherence, but also by the reconstitution of what was at once the stage on which it was enacted as an event and its epistemo-logical milieu: the social and historical world of the beginning of the six-teenth century; even more specifically, within that world, Florence, such as it was defined in the chain of events that led it into servitude, in the context of class conflicts and political constitutions in which those events were framed, within the state of beliefs and knowledge that determined the relation of men to their milieu. Beneath the banner of science, the least that may be said is that no agreement is reached; the divergences become weightier with the work expended, and they are augmented by the costly labor that sustains them, far beyond the limits to which we are accustomed for works of reflection in general—which is already a mys-tery. Desire, being contained, wells up within the man of science—as if indifferent to the orderly reasoning of his critical discourse—to pass a final judgment on the meaning and value of the presumed Machiavel-lian message, and to act in consequence, be it indirectly, by averting its effects, in order to say or to insinuate a precious truth about his own day, and at the same time to castigate those who, having eyes, have not read the book, and have not read history.

But the scientific debate is of importance not only because of the divergences that can be seen repeating themselves within it, and because of the link that can be found there—the unbreakable link—between the critical intention and the political one. Such is its nature that it makes interpretation itself a mystery. In observing the movement by which rival theses develop—in every case on the basis of premises and in the direction of conclusions that differ, under the constant emblem of a restoration of the meaning of the oeuvre and in equal certainty of reclaiming the title to a knowledge hitherto usurped—we cannot help but wonder what governs it, what relationship is formed, beneath the level of declarations of method and of manifest judgments, between the discourse of the writer and that of the interpreter. In vain do we distinguish within interpretation the parts of knowledge and belief, in hopes of reducing its contingency to the effect of the dispositions of its author. However deeply we may situate their origin, whatever foundation we may assign to the values that command his reading, inspire his own questions and prepare responses, the separation cannot be made. The field of the scientific knowledge of the oeuvre—whether we measure it by the extent of the verifiable propositions it advances, the coherence of the system in which the argumentation is articulated, or the virtue of the principles that govern it—cannot be separated from the global field of interpretation, because the latter is itself symbolic through and through, because all determination of the elements is simultaneously a determination of the status of the oeuvre, of its insertion in time, in a history of thought, but also in a history of the world—a determination, in sum, of a *reality*, with respect to which and in the midst of which the critic is situated.

Thus I find myself prompted to interrogate the project that sustains interpretation as such. It is not only tempting to circumscribe the problematic that is engendered by reflection on the oeuvre, to unfold it in all its dimensions, that is, to investigate how the theses that focus on the meaning of the Machiavellian discourse comport with other theses on the meaning of history and politics. In addition, it has not escaped my notice that interpretation, by all it brings into play in laying claim to an understanding of the oeuvre, tends to replace it, and that at the moment it seems to take the oeuvre for its object, takes over as its own the intention that commanded the oeuvre, and focuses not on the oeuvre but what it focused on. Now, that the undertaking is taken up again and again and, in relation to its goal, always falls short, that the oeuvre indefinitely resists the movement of appropriation that it arouses, at the very moment when that movement shows the most decided submission to its ends, that the oeuvre withdraws at the very moment it is *re-produced*, at the very moment when the critic pretends to be self-effacing before it in order to let it speak—is there not in this more than the proof of an impossible access to objectivity? Is it not the sign that what we call objectivity forbids our thinking the essence of the oeuvre in relation with the power it has to found a critical discourse, to impose on others the dual necessity of taking the literal meaning of the document as its object and of writing in its wake on the very thing toward which its text points?

The question is not simply added to the one asked by the conflict of interpretations; it modifies its meaning. Let us begin by asking: Does this conflict shed light on the oeuvre? Is it not the oeuvre that secretly governs the conflict? In taking cognizance of what is at stake here, do we not take stock of the expanse of the field it opens up to political thought? Thus the astonishment we experience upon frequenting the literature of the Machiavellian critique puts us on the trail of meaning. But when we scrutinize one after another the writings of interpreters and discover, beyond the diversity of the theses, the repetition of an attempt whose object it is to banish all indetermination from the oeuvre, to fix the limits of its knowledge, to assign a status and function to it *in reality* (an attempt that presupposes in each one the assurance of a speech independent of the speech that makes it speak), another question arises to disturb our initial inquiry. The play of interpretations, I now begin to wonder—is it not structured by a lack of understanding of its foundation, the relationship between the critic and the oeuvre? To penetrate such an interplay—is this not to learn to discern the dynamics of that lack of understanding, the ruses by means of which the interpreter frees himself from this discourse of the oeuvre by turning it into a *thing said*, dissimulates the filiation that would reveal the nature of his debt, and, at the very moment in which he puts his own discourse in the place of the one to whom it owes its inception, makes bold to thrust aside the third party who would strip him of his right to have the last word, and pretends to forget the indetermination in which his own work begins and unfolds? Once more we go in search of meaning. It is true that these ruses are not gratuitous inventions: the ways of dissimulation navigate a space already structured by the singular oeuvre of Machiavelli: but it is one thing to receive what the oeuvre has inspired by way of thought in its posterity, and quite another to discover what that oeuvre becomes in the exchange of critical discourse, to discern the refusal to think in the oeuvre the power it possesses to inspire thought.

But these questions only speak to us because the oeuvre itself, in the first relation we develop with it—reading—puts us in a state of questioning. However banal this judgment about the oeuvre of thought may be (a banality, moreover, we must fight off in order to sound the truth it covers up), it is of the essence of the oeuvre to unfold within a relation such that he who becomes the agent of its manifestation asks questions. It is true that a book, determined by its limitations and the order of signs

articulated according to linguistic laws and the rules of discourse, is in
its entirety the substructure of a meaning that, intolerant of any sharing,
is the beaming forth of a presence—of the being of the oeuvre. But this
meaning is only promised. This presence is always a step behind what it
announces; the announcement and promise are inseparable from the
signs that the reader keeps going back to, to interpret, through a labor
that is his own: modulation and scansion of the discourse of the other,
but also apprehension and ordering of differences, also grasp and distribution of mass and value, terracing of levels, work—however felicitous—
the effect of which cannot deliver us from uncertainty, furnish us with
the ultimate guarantee of the truth of the discourse. The Machiavellian
oeuvre, an oeuvre of thought; if all we had to do was give it our patience
and our readerly faith, it would brush aside all questions regarding the
adventures, nay metamorphoses, to which history has exposed it. But
such is our encounter with it, at the assumed distance of today's reader,
that it escapes us at the same time it surrenders itself, and we recognize
the need for an effort on our part due to a doubt concerning its identity—a doubt that rebounds on ourselves, in that, from a specific place
in time, we were already attempting to think politics.

How it slips away, and commands the movement that, from one
reading to the next, increases our attraction and multiplies our questions—that is what I cannot say forthwith, because of the twofold impossibility of anticipating the idea of interpretation as a mode of interrogation, and interpretation itself as the unfurling of that interrogation.
The most I can do is think back on the time when—seduced as I was,
first by the freedom *The Prince* affords itself in ignoring the classical and
Christian distinctions between good and bad government, legitimate and
illegitimate authority (terms in an age-old debate), by its consequent
freedom in presenting power as the pawn in a struggle open to whoever
can best take advantage of the divisions within the civil society, freedom
to put the givens of political struggle into hypothetical form, to circumscribe, in the social field, a system of forces the combinations of which
are calculable, to assign to action rules whose validity is independent of
the nature of the goals to which the action is directed, and seduced by
the sparkle of a discourse whose rigor, concision, and lightness of movement seem to bear witness to the truth it designates—I suddenly doubted
whether I had understood, and even *followed,* given the views advanced
on the nature of the classes and the difference in their desires, on the
dependence in which the prince finds himself with respect to them, on
the necessity in which he finds himself simultaneously to oppress and to
limit his oppression, to make himself recognized by the people and to
maintain toward them a distance that preserves the difference between

the state and society, on the danger he faces, because of that very distance, of closing himself up in the illusion of security and omnipotence, on the risk, finally, that accompanies all action, since it is exposed to the hazards of the convergence or the divergence of events. Laden with this doubt, I glimpsed, at the very time during which these words let me glide from the idea of the rational to that of the irrational in politics, a depth of discourse, barely perceptible at first glance, a play of digressions, allusions, slippage of meanings, that destroyed my initial self-assurance.

Such is the first state of my interrogation. It bears on the name Machiavelli and the myth attached to it, on the characteristics of the political literature surrounding the oeuvre of the writer, on the scientific problematic of which it has become the object, on the meaning of *The Prince* and *The Discourses* and their significance, on the status of political writing in relation to political action. It bears at the same time on the essence of the reflective and the interpretive oeuvre. It is thus a multiple interrogation that propagates itself by division and risks languishing by an overabundance of branches. Thus we should not overlook the laws of the Schoolmen, and the interdict they raise against the mixing of genres. To each of the questions I have raised they would assign its proper domain: the history of ideas, the sociology of knowledge in several cases, political theory, epistemology, the philosophy of expression. But these questions, placed within their respective precincts, lose their just proportions. In isolation from one another, they are also cut off from the source from which they draw their being as questions. Either they become mere information questions, each one presenting itself in relation to a sector of the "real," bringing into view relations hitherto invisible but leaving in the shadows the act by which this sector is constituted and circumscribed as a zone of determinate operations; or else (and here it is the philosophy of expression I have in mind) the questions become unduly freed from the requirements imposed on the questioner by the relationship in which he stands to the oeuvre of a particular genre, leading him to lose sight of the conditions imposed on him, in his function as interpreter, by that oeuvre. It is true that to refuse to separate the questions from one another exposes us to the risk of forgetting our intent and goal. But if our interrogation is legitimate, it is because the questions that make it up are not simply related to one another within one movement of curiosity. They open onto one another. In our passing from one question to another, in allowing the enigma they reveal to unfold, we are at the same time led back to our situation as questioners, and confronted with the enigma of our identity.

When we ask "What is Machiavellianism?" we are not just trying to retrace the genesis of an idea, to clarify the conditions in which the term is used, or to satisfy the curiosity of the historian or the sociologist. The question is not to be settled by a response brought forth as a matter of fact. If it is important to us, it is because it sets us off in pursuit of a certain representation of politics—a representation whose characteristics are not just to be learned by observing a sort of behavior deemed blameworthy, but one that should rather dictate the characterization of such behavior. What is new in this representation is the conception of a perversion of social relations that triumphs by the application of a kind of knowledge reserved to the politician, by an assault on the law that would make him—the politician—the master of action. But our question, put in this way, already leads us away from the examination of that representation and toward the examination of the indictment of Machiavelli's oeuvre, and to what is at stake in it. We become aware of the complicity revealed in that indictment between those who, on the one hand, designate the writer as the first apologist of that perversion or accuse him of some error in reasoning that reduced him to it, and those who, on the other, pointing out the blindness, bad faith, and even real Machiavellianism of his adversaries, only want to legitimate his discourse. This is an invisible complicity if we limit ourselves to the letter of the opposing arguments, so nonplussed are we by the wide gamut of variegated allegations from either camp: the lability of an accusation in which the Machiavellianism of Machiavelli is taxed with Protestantism, Jesuitism, atheism, capitalist immorality, entrenched princely despotism, political cynicism, the spirit of revolution or of opposition; and the vicissitudes of a rehabilitation by which the writer regains a legitimate authority, as the theoretician of "reasons of state," patriotism, democracy, the logic of history, the foundation of a new science, or even an ethics of action that would base the necessities of Power on Christian imperatives. Only the assumption that the idea behind Machiavellianism is not accidental but concerns what is most profound in the political experience can keep us looking for a meaning in the apparent divagations of the discourse of posterity—locating among the theses advanced, however crude or sophisticated they may be, the signs of a conflict never clearly stated, only attested to by the repeated attempt to present the Florentine writer as the agent of an intolerable transgression or the guarantor of the restoration of law, the herald of a science either infamous or glorious.

But at the same time our first question concerns the nature of the question the oeuvre addresses to us. It prepares us to fathom what it is in the discourse of Machiavelli itself that lends itself to the constitution of the singular *imago* for which politics serves as a support. It is not enough to observe that that "image" became detached from its place of origin to the point that we speak of Machiavellianism without knowing anything about Machiavelli. We must also admit, conversely, that we cannot read *The Prince* or *The Discourses* without importing a certain idea of Machiavellianism. Worse yet: We cannot try to free the oeuvre from the popular representation with which it is associated by the majority of readers without in turn exposing ourselves to the subliminal determination it creates, without risking falling into the trap of denial and succumbing to the temptation of reestablishing the antithetical figure of a legitimate discourse. For such is ultimately the truth of the question: it not only opens onto other questions, but it points toward us. In interrogating Machiavellianism, we do not free ourselves from the meaning we gave it before the endeavor of reflection; we do not shed our belief in a political perversion; the term speaks, and goes on speaking; we catch ourselves using it as if it were impervious to the critical examination we subject it to. If it speaks, surely it is because it has been assimilated by language, and nourishes unbeknownst to ourselves the weave of our words; but it is also the sign of the obscure and enigmatic tribute we pay to the thought of others when we try to think for ourselves.

When we proceed to ask "Can that ever-proliferating literature of which Machiavelli is both origin and object instruct us?" that question already has its preamble. In the writings accumulated over several centuries—pamphlets, commentaries, interpretations—we divine the unity of a discourse in the form of a trial. But it is not enough to delve into its properties, to deliberate on the constancy of certain oppositions, the recurrence of certain themes, the general idea of the nature of the written oeuvre and the function of the interpreter subtending it, the repeated expression of the conviction that its author has been commonly misunderstood, the re-presenting of history that would illuminate the past. If the social and historical conditions appear incapable of furnishing the ultimate ground of the conflicts bedeviling posterity, they are at least germane enough to solicit our attention and require our reflection on the relationship critical discourse maintains with political discourse—as it seems to be modulated, moreover, according to the manifest order of theories or ideologies apparently assured of their definitions. We cannot, of course, give free reign to this reflection without going beyond the field of our current focus, but neither can we forget that at the horizon of our thoughts there stands a question touching the essence of political representation. If we consider, for example, the odd affinities that develop, as a result of contact with Machiavelli's oeuvre, between partisans and opponents of absolute monarchy, or the divisions that spring up in the eighteenth century among bourgeois ideologues, or in the twentieth century among Marxist ideologues, we must necessarily also have doubts about the meaning of certain oppositions that political leaders, our immediate experience, and the history of ideas lead us to think obvious. Only the study of the oeuvre would be able to elevate this doubt to the level of the interrogation it deserves. Thus doubt can do no more than announce such a study. But that study itself is introduced by the discourse undertaken by Machiavelli's posterity. The questions asked in that discourse take on their full meaning only because they designate the oeuvre as their point of origin. True, it is in vain, as I have said, that we should expect from their solutions a knowledge that would give us the meaning of the oeuvre. But it would be equally futile to pretend to close them off in such a way that Machiavelli's text is sheltered from their effects, preserved from any intermingling, held in reserve for the reflection of a pure reader. Even were one to take the position that the meaning of the literature devoted to Machiavelli is run through with nonsense from one end to the other, this nonsense would speak to us about the text that engendered it and on the basis of which it is structured, and would dispose us to receive what governs, in it, the forms of its degradation. But so tenacious is the prejudice of objective criticism that it inhibits our movements even when we think ourselves free of it. Since it is always possible to read an oeuvre in total or almost total ignorance of the commentary it has occasioned, since it immediately awakens a desire to know, and offers us a meaning at first glance, we are tempted to reduce the relationship we have with it to the one we have established with the text. Thus, no sooner have we admitted that the discourse of posterity introduces us to that of the author, than we deny the necessity of such a procedure. Having recognized that the oeuvre reveals itself through multiple interpretations, we still do not like to think it necessary to inhabit the space of criticism in order to learn to inhabit its own. So great is the force deflecting us from our predecessors to attach us to the writer, as if there were a direct communication between him and us, with no other obstacle between its truth than that of our honesty and keenness to know. Historicism or sociologism foresworn, the belief in a just deciphering of the signs inscribed in the book is renewed and, in secret collusion, the conviction that we thereby dominate the era in which the writer lived—which he himself could not have known entirely, being unaware of the meaning the future would ascribe to it. But what we discover in penetrating the critical literature are not travesties of Machiavelli's oeuvre, to be denounced in order to make the future reader ready receive it (revealing the temptation they were responding to, the hidden possibility in the primitive text they sought to exploit), preparing him for the sober representation of the original. That action and intention, justified perhaps by the concern to warn or demystify, would, on this view, have no other motivation than the edification of others, and it would be fair to say that they distract from the task of knowledge imposed by the oeuvre, which we respond to by our own efforts of reading and reflection. The truth is not only that the oeuvre already makes itself heard in the discourse of its posterity, but that we cannot spare ourselves the labor of their scrutiny; despite appearances, we are always permeated by them. To claim a freedom with respect to them that is denied us, we only increase the tribute that their heritage imposes. Indeed, to retain no more, in the course of our interpretive efforts, than the moment of reading, is to dissimulate the multifarious experience that sustains it and makes it last beyond what a knowledge of the language and the eye's alacrity command, and projects it beyond any assignable termination.

Let us observe already at this point that when the text is supposed to have a univocal meaning ready to surrender itself to the inspection of any attentive mind, it is forgotten that there would be little of it to grasp if we knew nothing of the time when it was written, if we could not awaken the power it had to shake established beliefs, if the horizons of its knowledge were totally obliterated, and the world of which it was a fragment were inaccessible. But let us leave aside that forgetfulness, and the fact that it is accompanied, among the most intransigent defenders of objective meaning, by a cult for biographical, historical, and sociological information, about which the least one can say is that it should raise a few problems and disturb the calm assurance about the possibility of any direct communication with the author. The oeuvre is assigned the status of a spiritual thing-in-itself—a thing that is what it is, independently of the representation of it elaborated by posterity. A fiction made all the stronger by the circumstance that all paths serve to lead us there. Indeed, it matters little whether we focus on the literal meaning to find the order of propositions adjudged most satisfying or to bring out what are called contradictions, or whether we claim to produce the hidden signifiers governing the discourse; it matters little that we discover the essence in a sum of judgments, an idea for which linguistic tropes may provide a metaphor, a conception of the world, a structure, a system, principles or categories that would command the possibility of the system: it is always by the same movement that we designate what is, what was waiting to be named, what in the said or unsaid of the text silently bore its identity, and that we magisterially brush aside the specious imagery disseminated by the turbulent cortege of commentators occupied with seducing their public. Perhaps it would be worthwhile to scrutinize this movement— to ask ourselves why vulgar realism, so energetically denounced by generations of philosophers when they have reflected on perception, science, or art, springs up intact in the theory of interpretation. Perhaps we should admit that the myth of thought's omnipotence, of which realism is a disguise, luxuriates precisely in the form of the interpretation, when the subject's discourse overlays the discourse of the other; when, beneath the cover of dialogue, the application of thought to thought creates the vertigo of perfect knowledge.

But without following up on these considerations here and now, if we simply take stock of the actual circumstances in which the work of the interpreter—our work—begins and is pursued, we will get a clearer sense of this fiction, we will see what is normally concealed, in order that faith in the *reality* of the oeuvre may be preserved. It does not suffice to observe that it offers a meaning before we acquaint ourselves with the commentaries with which posterity has burdened it, and that this first meaning arouses our curiosity and awakens in us a desire to know, and that this desire subsequently persists by the repeated reading of the text. The fact is, I do not decide—nor does anyone else—to write about an oeuvre of the past without inquiring into what has been written about it. The fact is also that the reading of interpreters not only gives us occasion to glean useful information, to save ourselves the time and effort of carrying out research already extant or to be certain of the originality of our theses, but that it introduces us to a debate in which what is at stake, as we focus on it more sharply, provides insight into what the oeuvre itself involves. Doubtless, to fully appreciate this fact we would have to inquire into the nature of the intellectual oeuvre and ask ourselves why it is irreducible to any specific representation we form of it, why it possesses the power to found an infinite commentary. But the fact itself teaches us a truth that it would be well to shelter, disengaging it from the psychological versions with which one is tempted to cover it. If I am invincibly inclined to explore the critical literature, it is not because I am giving in to the temptation of measuring my knowledge against that of others and keen for the glory of originality; it is because the oeuvre provides me ever more to think about in the space opened up for it by the thinking of others.

I learn to read an oeuvre in the wake of others. We all know this, whether we admit it or not. Between our first reading of the oeuvre (which, by the way, is not innocent, since it has benefited from the help, and been burdened by the invisible weight, of knowledge and beliefs wrought through contact with books) and those imposed upon it by the interpretive endeavor to which we are committed, the dialog is engaged with the commentators and has modified the relation it had instituted with the oeuvre. It has changed its questions, killing off some and giving rise to others. It has displaced the object of its desire to know.

Were we to try to reduce such an experience to the terms of a critique of critique, we would miss its specific virtue. It is not only, nor even mainly, hypotheses that are being examined—a series of witnesses summoned to appear before a court of reason to determine their objectivity; it is not an accounting established in order to open a new ledger of research. By our sojourn in the critical literature a certain power is acquired, a sensibility heightened by new organs is awakened, the effect of which is to increase the presence of the oeuvre beyond all expectations, to bring out of the text—like color, form, and depth in a canvas beneath the lingering gaze—a variety of movements, a profusion of unexpected signs. It matters little that the commentaries and judgments we encounter may appear outrageous or arbitrary, or that they may exhibit a partisan exploitation of the writer's words, retaining only what is likely to seduce or alienate the reader—they nonetheless create an inclination to take yet another look at the text, and to go more deeply into what we had slipped over superficially. It would be a mistake to reduce their effect to our assessment of their inexactitude. They affect us even though we may condemn them, transcending the criterion of true or false, awakening our minds to a heightened alertness. The injustice of which the oeuvre is clearly the victim is not the opposite of the promised justice. It is precisely in following the contours of those unjust assaults on it that we discover the network of defenses constituting its substance. It is because its adversaries or its partisans claim to contain it within the limits of their thesis or small number of theses that a glimpse of its essential complexity is afforded us. These procedures no longer allow us to be unaware of the expanse of the oeuvre's territory. It is even as if the polemic served the oeuvre's intention: in their headlong passion to isolate certain propositions and to read in them the truth of its teaching, both sides charge these moments of the discourse with the most meaning possible, restoring thereby the dramatic power that sustained it. In bringing out the extreme consequences of the writer's thought, they reveal that it in fact developed precisely beneath the menace of those very consequences, and that it steered its course in such a way as to avoid by a narrow margin those perilous points at which its critics thought to pin it down in order to destroy it. Such is the merit, for example, of the critical enterprise that consists in denouncing *The Discourses* as an oeuvre intended to deceive the reader, and in excerpting from *The Prince* the analysis of Cesare Borgia, finding that it is based on a few clauses which, taken literally, are the best suited to elicit blame, and concluding that the work is an apology for violence and oppression. It is not just because this enterprise is found quite prevalently, pressing writers of a variety of opinions into its service, that it matters for us. That operation, which involves mutilation, deformation, and extrapolation, and the object of which is to discredit Machiavelli's oeuvre, incites us to bring to light everything it places in the shadows, everything that we would otherwise have been unable to identify with such assurance; but above all it sensitizes us to the event, within the stream of Machiavelli's thought, of the Borgia phenomenon. It challenges us to come face to face with Borgia, just as the writer does in his reflections on politics—taking the full measure of his words, sounding his motives in depth, confronting the threat Borgia poses to the entire oeuvre.

It is impossible to unravel all the ties attaching the interpreter to both the writer and his posterity. True, it is the reading of the text that gives him his first and last powers. But if he is willing to bring to mind the least memory of the trials accompanying that reading, how can he not concede that it is far from remaining within the confines we like to set for it, once the work has been accomplished. It is true that there are limits imposed by the book or books of the author; it has a beginning, an end, a required progression or direction—and the most serious, the most widespread of errors, the effects of which I will have occasion to examine later, would be to misconstrue the meaning of a direction that has nothing accidental about it. But it is also true that the reading disregards both the order or the discourse and its limits, and both for the same reason. The book is in fact offered to the circulation of a look and marked throughout its length by all possible points of entry. No readers refrain from using them, or from going to wherever their reflection calls them or by chance they may alight—to dwell there, or from there to fly, insouciant of the imposed itinerary, forward or back to other parts of the text. And these movements it prompts are not of another order from those leading toward writings that concern it; it is because the oeuvre is not identical with the materiality of the book, because it gives itself implicitly in each fragment the reader's gaze detaches, that it manifests itself in the commentaries of others. The difference between the two texts, the writer's and the commentator's, is not what we imagine it to be at first, when we make the bluntly obvious observation that there are the real author's words and its translations, or when we cling to the naive idea of translation, for that difference assumes a first one, within the oeuvre. What we call distancing, to designate our movement toward the commentators—that is an experience we already have in reading the book. And this is the case not only because it is takes place in time, and because there is an externality of language in relation to ourselves, but because in each part of the text it is possible for a meaning to invest itself that commands the entire discourse; because, at each moment, there is a possible effect of anticipation and retroaction that confers upon it the value of an omen. It is true that the commentary of others comes from a different source than this discourse, and to some extent it is toward that source that we must return; and when we try to embrace the critical literature as a whole, the ordering principle we believe we have found there solicits our attention and orients it, as we have said, toward the play of political principles that govern it. But at the same time, that commentary, that literature, takes its place within the field we are exploring. The incessant modification to which the work of reading submits us goes hand in hand with the discovery of those instituted models—the theses of others. Those theses—we see them springing up in the interstices of the discourse; they echo our doubts, develop thoughts that perhaps would never have congealed, that surely would not have taken the direction they did, but that in any case at least germinated in us, and the fact of their having been formulated no longer allows them to be removed. Thus our reading grows with others we have already completed, and the text itself changes beneath the effect of a variation that realizes the continued passage from the implicit to the explicit.

A reading carried out by several people, one is tempted to say; but that would be to forget that, like the text of the writer, the commentaries only speak to us to the extent that we question them—and what is even more serious, they only speak to us to the extent that the text enables us to question them. If we did not find this power in them, we know very well that they would remain mute. Hence we would gain nothing in trading one fiction for another: by rejecting the idea that the text has its meaning inscribed within itself, therefore independently of the relationship it establishes with its readers, in order to assert that the meaning is borne by the manifold of the commentaries, that it is discovered upon the inspection of the system of properties presented by the critical literature. There is always a subject who stands as the guarantor of the advent of meaning. The only important thing is that we follow all the paths of meaning, and since we learn from others to understand the discourse of a writer, that we validate that experience entirely. Now we would distort and shut ourselves out from what it teaches us were we to imagine the domain of critical literature as the locus of a series of representations, each of which would allow itself to be appreciated independently of the others, and the domain of the oeuvre as a space truly separated from it, circumscribed by the borders of Machiavelli's books.

Such a separation does not have the status generally attributed to it. It appears in one perspective only to fade from view in another—while, it is true, it fades away to reappear. Of course it is inconceivable that the written work should have no identity. How, otherwise, would we be able to turn to it, to press it with our questions in hopes of hearing its responses—to return infinitely to the text seeking what it alone can teach us? But neither can we assert that it contains the trace of a thought that can be fully itself while standing at a distance from the thoughts of others.

For how, if that were the case, would it be possible to reach it, or, assuming it is somehow possible for its trace to communicate the thought per se, how could we possibly miss it? And why then would we seek a meaning in the variety of commentaries that apply themselves to ascertaining it? It is from that second observation that we first draw the consequences, without however forgetting the first. The self-restraint we impose upon ourselves in the interrogation of Machiavelli's texts is the consequence of our desire to welcome all that is capable of contributing to the dialogue to which they invite us. Convinced that the oeuvre only gives itself to us on condition that we give our thoughts to it, I am also persuaded that it never had any other existence than in an open exchange, that is, an existence of such a nature that the answer does not cancel out the question but requires new ones—by the institution of a collective discourse, at the heart of which the words of each are intertwined or articulated while at the same time mutually governing one another's advent; and thus—in questioning that exchange, that *institution,* at the very moment when my work in turn brings me to participate in it—it is already the oeuvre that I question.

The undertaking would be vain if critical literature furnished us, as some at times believe, with a multiplicity of images of the oeuvre-object. But the oeuvre is not designated merely as the object of judgments, commentaries, and interpretations; it is not just metamorphoses of its words that are offered us. And again we would be mistaken to add that the work of reconstituting or naming the ideas of the writer is accompanied in each commentator by an appreciation testifying to his or her own values. With that belief we prolong the definition of the work as a spiritual thing, a thing to be perceived and shown to others as it is. The truth is that the oeuvre only draws attention to itself because it opens up for its readers a path leading toward what it thinks. The truth is that those who turn to *The Prince* or *The Discourses* necessarily turn toward the world to which they give access, toward the main events of the life of the writer—from which he claimed to draw a truth that exceeded the limits of the present, in the institutions of his day whose differences and similarities he pointed out—toward the Roman past, the history of a state in which he found the laws of development of all states; and even when they do not stop to consider that world, it is nonetheless adjacent to it, or to fragments of it, that they think the political phenomenon. They think it in the oeuvre of Machiavelli and at the same time through it. It is in one and the same movement that they take care to ascertain what is said and that they are drawn by this "said" to what it says. Never is the possibility entirely given to us of distinguishing between what is truly being said and the truth of what is said, because the words of the writer are only understood by being forgotten, and when forgotten they continue nonetheless to govern the meaning into which they have thrown us. Thus it is by means of twin abstractions that we imagine the interpreter occupied with knowing the writer's thought: as if it were a substance whose properties were to be identified; or by thinking what he thought, as if this thing thought were itself an object that any mind, without stirring from its place and on its own terms, could appreciate. In either case, whether we posit Machiavelli's oeuvre as an object, or whether we forget it and posit what we take to be its object per se, we are condemned to miss the singular experience it institutes, the necessity to which it subjects us to question it in order to question the real, to discover—within its precinct—the political.

The unity of critical discourse emerges once these abstractions are dispelled, when we see, beyond the so-called representations of the oeuvre—themselves assumed to resist comparison with one another—a common opening onto the world, and beyond the so-called representations of the world, a common opening onto the oeuvre, when a space appears in which the lines reaching out toward the oeuvre and those extending toward the world converge indefinitely. Toward the oeuvre and toward the world, we say, but these terms can no longer, in light of our reflections, be understood in their usual sense, for when taken that way they express the original positivity attaching to them. The division to which they continue to bear witness is no longer exclusive of a certain indivision, since it is always in one and the same experience that the oeuvre and the world are given to us—the world in relation to the oeuvre, and the oeuvre in relation to the world.

Thus oeuvre and world are presented to others and ourselves. Admitting this, we must even recognize that the questioning of the discourse of posterity has its beginnings in the trial to which the writer's discourse submits us when—the moment we undertake to interpret it—the indetermination of the relationship we have with it is revealed. As long as we only grasp in the writer's discourse particular remarks, however profound they may appear to us, or however propitious to the exercise of our reflection, the question of the identity of the work does not come up. We may well meditate on one idea or another within the work, but in doing so forget what the work *is*. On the contrary, the intention of interpreting is accompanied by a general upheaval: there is henceforth not one passage that does not bear the trace of all the others, whose sense does not depend on the truth of the discourse to which it is attached; henceforth the presence of the work haunts all the thoughts awakened by the text; each one of these thoughts leads back to the past in which it was prepared, and draws us toward the future it announces; then and only then does the authority of the writer leave its mark on our own discourse, whatever may be the singularity of the experience that is ours, no matter how persuaded we are of having seized, in a world that is beyond all the signs the oeuvre brings with it, a meaning that has eluded it. The subjugation under which it places us scarcely surprises us, so natural does it seem to make of an oeuvre of the past a key element in the acquisition of knowledge. But the condition of interpreter is not inscribed in the constitution of the human mind. That we should focus, beyond all reference to significant statements that would accommodate themselves very well to anonymity, on the oeuvre as such, in order to find the assurance of a thinking we need in order to think; and further, that we should raise it to the level of an oracle, that we should elevate it in history as a moment that will dominate an entire landscape of knowledge, that we should make of the writer an author, that is, a guarantor—this attests to a form of culture in which writing, systematic knowledge, and authority can converge to form one sole power of competency. When the subject's desire to know is manifested in the relation to an author, and his writing refers to a first writing, he finds the terms of that experience instituted independently of himself. Interpretation presupposes in its practice that a model is already fixed, and that the statuses of author, oeuvre, and critique have already been formed. It assumes that there is, imputed to the author, a paternity in the generation of thought, and that with it the enigma of its origin arises; that an identity has been assigned to writings, the deciphering of which governs access to the meanings they disseminate; that a place and a task have been designated for a class of readers called to read and write, to listen and respond, and by the conjugation of these two operations in which their affiliation becomes manifest, to conserve and to transmit. At what time in history such a model was elaborated and what we can learn from it, to what degree it challenges the traditional conception of knowledge—these issues are not our concern. We only wish to expose the illusory nature of a relationship that would be reducible to the pure communication of ideas, and to recall the threefold enigma with which we are confronted in the form of the identity of the work, the presence of the author, and his or her authority; and to conclude that that amalgamated enigma refuses to allow itself to be broken down. Indeed, at one and the same time, the writings of *someone* appear to us in the form of an oeuvre, his name marks with its seal all his words, attests to the secret power to which they owe their meaning, and is designated as the locus of a posterity, in which he is recognized as the author, in which a task of knowledge is taken up, the origin of which is held to be the oeuvre. True, the real author is that writer who has the virtue of giving birth to a posterity, but it is also through the latter that the writer becomes an author; to whatever inner conflicts it may give rise, it maintains this strange *consensus* in which the oeuvre finds sustenance to maintain through time its power to make us think; it propagates the commandment that was promulgated within it to question it in order to question the things themselves; better still, the depth of these conflicts, in attesting to an irreducible distance between the oeuvre and all interpretation, results in reinforcing this power, in re-iterating this commandment. The questions, "What is an author?" "What is a work?"—we ask them when we read a text; they arise, for example, when we ask, "What intention governs the discourse of the writer?" "In what does his originality consist?" "What confers on his texts, despite all the differences we find in what he says, a community of meaning?"; but we only ask them because we have espoused the condition of interpreter, because they are part of a context and that condition, that context, are always determined; that is for us the condition of an interpreter of Ma-chiavelli, the context of the discourse of Machiavelli's posterity; we have learned our task—to interrogate Machiavelli and his oeuvre—from those who have become the support of his authority, and it is by scrutinizing the relation they have established with him that I begin to glimpse the meaning of my own endeavor.

When I devote myself to a small number of interpretations that seem worthy of particular examination by reason of their intrinsic qualities and the power they have, in being considered side by side, to reveal the variety of principles governing critical oppositions, this new research is imposed by the task I have undertaken of questioning the discourse of posterity; it has the same motivation, and no other significance than that of being carried out relative to the same questions—those posed by political discourse and the discourse of Machiavelli. Viewed as a series of critical studies, each of which concludes by rejecting the interpretation it scrutinizes, the endeavor might elevate, in the eyes of the reader, the omnipotence of the new interpreter; it might prepare him to appreci-ate the art such an interpreter showed in triumphing over the hardships to which others had succumbed, but nothing would save him from the charge of gratuitousness and arbitrariness. Why, it might rightfully be objected, take the time to focus on the discourse of others, hunt them down to their last retrenchments, ingeniously destroy their defense sys-tems, and produce the secret reasons that are decisive in their theses, if you are yourself already in possession of the key to the work? And why, if I claim to give an account of the divergences the work has engendered, pick, from among the many interpretations that recommend themselves for a scientific study of the text, these rather than others? But it has al-ready been noted that my purpose was not to decry errors to thematize a future truth—a truth no artifice can magnify—nor to offer an exhaustive treatment of the problems of critique. A few works have attracted my attention because in them we can best examine the project that haunts the interpretive project. Doubtless there are others capable of stimulating reflection in a similar way. It suffices that they offer a wide enough spectrum for us to discover in each of them, through the ever singular detail of an argumentation, how the relation established with the oeuvre is modulated, and to perceive, beyond what are normally called errors, the imaginary knowledge always outside the field of interpretation that allows the critic to assert his mastery over the oeuvre, to disengage from the questions it asked him, to seal it at last with the stamp of his judgment. Such is the path I have chosen; new, although prepared by the exploration of the Machiavellian literature. In pursuing it, I am challenged all the more imperatively to combine in the same interrogation a search for the meaning of the oeuvre and for the being of the oeuvre; and the enigma of my own condition of interrogator is thereby increased. Does not the freedom I assume in analyzing the interpreters mask yet another illusion? Does not my knowledge also have its blind spot? Does not reflection on critical discourse itself presuppose a body of principles that escapes its notice?

This doubt is not dispelled when we have recognized that all interpretation presupposes a bias caused by the identity of the interpreter, by the enrootedness of the subject in the being of which he speaks, and when we challenge the classical alternative of a thought that is pure adequation of self with self or a passivity that is a pure being affected by things, a privation of thought. We must go yet further, and conquer the right to go beyond the simple substitution of one interpretation in the place of another, of a simple shift in perspectives. This right—assuredly it is only in the exercise of the interrogation that it can be established. But we can at least say why the patient exploration of a few critical works puts us in a position to claim it. In considering closely their composition, we cannot be content with invoking the values of the author to explain the singularity of his or her theses. The very idea of value becomes equivocal. The concept of value is a very handy one as long as we are content with setting apart, beyond the logic of the discourse, the role of beliefs, which is to determine the exercise of that logic; but the moment we inquire into the structure of the critical argument itself, "value" is no longer helpful. When we have discovered, for example, that such and such an author is a Thomist, a liberal atheist, or a Marxist, we are still pretty much in the dark; the nature of their project remains hidden. It becomes clearer, however, when we can examine the articulations governing both the form he imparts to his writer's discourse—that is to say very specifically the selection of certain of his propositions and their rearrangement according to a significant order (the determination of a field of reality at the heart of which the work, considered in its entirety or in the series of "ideas" excerpted from it, appears as an event)—and the assertion of a systematic body of knowledge on the essence of politics. It may be that the interpreter wants to establish the coherence of the discourse and that he goes to some lengths to define the principle or the small number of principles that govern its entire course, or that he wants to bring out inconsistencies and find that they are based on underlying antinomies that the writer was unable to avoid; he may want to establish reality at a privileged level, or at several levels at once; or perhaps the event of the oeuvre is structured serially for him in keeping with the adventures of a life—for example, so that *The Prince* follows the order of personal tragedy of failure, exile, and dream—or that the event of the oeuvre is tied to the events that make up the history of an era, that it seems to bear a response to problems discovered within the makeup of the social milieu, or yet again that it finds its place only within universal history, or that it is considered the expression, or even to some extent the anticipation, of a profound change in human *praxis,* or even that it assumes its place, independently of all reference to the detail of the facts or the evolution of social relations, in the history of ideas. Again, it is possible that the interpreter maintains that there is an eternal truth of politics, or that its meaning, unintelligible till then, is revealed at the present end of history, or that the norms of political action are no different from those governing private morals. But whatever course the interpretation takes, it operates thanks to invisible pivots that assure the continuous passage from one plane of meaning to another; what it determines on one plane has its assigned place on another, but appears to carry its own self-evidence. The critic does not hold a discourse on politics and then submit it to the discourse of Machiavelli; that first discourse only unfolds in the wake of the second. Nothing of what he says—however firm the statement of its own principles at times may be—would he have said in those same terms, nor, perhaps, would he have been able to think, had he not meditated on the oeuvre of the writer. He does not hold a discourse on the history of Florence and Italy at the beginning of the *Cinquecento,* or on the origins of modern rationalism, or on the development of revolutionary ideologies, and then proceed to define the role of the writer or the function of his ideas against the background of the schema he has set up, for it is again from the reading of Machiavelli that he learns to analyze certain relations of general significance hitherto unknown to him. But neither is it true that the discourse on the oeuvre governs the other two; for what he retains of the oeuvre in order to circumscribe the essential, he only extracts because in it he finds signs capable of being articulated with other signs, traced elsewhere in the field of the supposed real, or capable of testifying to the truth of what he already thought. Now, the game is played in such a way that the communication between one order of meanings and the other engenders no indetermination—in such a way that on the contrary it produces the impression of a more and more rigorous determination that runs along the same rational concatenation. Indeed, once there is dissimulation, in each case, of the background according to which the knowledge of the writer's text, or that of reality, or that of politics is organized, one proposition is assured of encountering another in the course of the argument, as if it were not prepared by it, and of receiving a marvelous confirmation. Thus, provided that the interpreter proceeds with care, his work is bound to be coherent and destined (to such a degree is coherence viewed as an indication of truth) to gain our credence. When we read it, at first we marvel at the flawless argumentation, and if the idea we previously held of the work prohibits our full acquiescence, we at least concede that he offers a legitimate perspective. It is true that that conclusion is based on an odd equivocation. For when we allow ourselves to be drawn into the game of interpretation, we believe there is a meaning inscribed in the oeuvre—a meaning that preexists the operations of he who works at bringing it forth; we believe in a reality that is what it is outside the representation the critic makes of it, and we still believe in a truth that stays in its place and commands our recognition of it. That is the faith the interpreter communicates: faith in the meaning of the work, in the meaning of the world that bears it, in the meaning of the politics that it focuses on; faith in one sole meaning in which all these meanings come together; faith, it would be better said, in the reality of the oeuvre, in the reality of the world and in that of the Idea; faith in one sole reality offering one sole access. Now, such a faith does not tolerate the coexistence of several perspectives, because it tolerates no reservations with respect to what is—those reservations attested by the presence of a subject who would take a view of things, and disengage that view from the things in order to make it into his or her representation; for, once and for all, that faith requires a total and exclusive adherence to its object. Thus, we lie to ourselves when we concede the interpreter the legitimacy of his endeavor, while at the same time considering it odd, and holding open the possibility of other possible ones. We concede to him too much or too little—too much, because if the coherence he shows and the science we attribute to him are insufficient to eliminate our doubts, it is because the oeuvre, his object, exists for us, in its reality, outside his representation; too little, for if we consider his endeavor to be well founded, what it demands is much more than a certificate of legitimacy: that we surrender to its obviousness, that we make its object our object. If we consult Machiavelli's interpreters, there is not one who points out the limits of his endeavor, is satisfied with offering us a new perspective, or recognizes that others have a right equal to his own to compose a convincing representation of the oeuvre. Each one wants to say the truth about what is true. It is not for lack of modesty, or that values distort knowledge, or that the singularity of the situation occupied is forgotten. It is simply that they do not have any doubt that Machiavelli's discourse exists in reality, and that it has its meaning independently of the reading or commentary of others. It is in one and the same movement that they grant him the fullness of a thing of the world and of a thing thought, and that they claim to know him. The equivocation is thus at its height when we strike a compromise between adherence and reticence, giving our complicity to the interpreter, but claiming to remain available for a different knowledge. It is true that for the equivocation to last, we must refrain from interpreting in turn, for no sooner do we make it our business to discourse on Machiavelli than the discourse of others no longer suffers half measures. But then if we remained blind to the procedure of those from whom we claim to detach ourselves, if we did not question ourselves about the reasons that command rupture, that equivocation would not be lifted, our own interpretation would impose itself by the same willful act as that of our predecessors; we would have no other title to present than the coherence of the argument; we would put the reader before the alternative, yet again, of either giving credence to a legitimate representation or of seeking his object elsewhere.

How do we escape the hold of an interpretation? Why does the effect of coherence dissipate like a mirage when we ask ourselves whether what is said is true or not? In order to find out, we must be attentive to the relation that is established between the discourse of the interpreter and that of the writer—more precisely to our own experience of that relation when we take on the role of interpreter in the course of reading. The interpreter claims to let me know the truth of Machiavelli's oeuvre. If I am willing and able to understand him, it is because that work is present to me and further because it occupies my thoughts—without my being sure of its meaning, however. I approach the interpreter as a possible intermediary, in hopes that his work has enabled him to make that meaning available to me. Need I recall that his discourse is different from that of the author—with a difference that is not that of a translation from an original text, or a copy from a model, but one that attests to two nonidentical intentions, since one intends the other as an end? The fact that the interpreter also intends what the writer intends cannot make us forget that the former is turned toward the latter. I observe that the interpreter sometimes lets the writer speak within his own discourse, but (as I have already remarked) he quotes certain passages to the exclusion of others, and presents them in such a way that they acquire a meaning by that procedure that would not have occurred to us in reading the text. Sometimes these quotations proliferate, sometimes the reference remains indirect; in any case, the writer's discourse is designated as such the moment it is reproduced or alluded to—and the moment it is designated, it is condensed to the point of seeming reduced to its essence. I am tempted to recognize in that economy the sign of a gain; the discourse of the interpreter seems more faithful to the truth of the oeuvre than that of the author. In expurgating the latter of all he had let himself say unnecessarily, in delivering him from the accidents to which the first work of expression exposed him, does he not re-subject him more rigorously to the law of his intent? If he can claim this, it is not only because the oeuvre seems to be accomplished in the reflection of another—his own; it is also, as I have stated, because he can claim a knowledge the author lacked: he thinks he knows the reasons that make the author speak, the place from which he speaks, the effects of his word, the fate of his hypotheses; he knows what to think about politics by having learned from a history, past and present, which was Machiavelli's indeterminate future. Hence he is in a position to distinguish between the anecdotal and the essential, and, first and foremost, to fix in their reality the elements of the discourse of the writer. But this knowledge is itself brought to bear in a discourse, giving it the space necessary for its development; in part, it commands the operations that make possible the restructuring of the writer's discourse, and in part it is commanded by it. Paradoxically, the interpretation is carried out in the spirit of concision, in that it is devoted to getting at the essence, and it ends up with a profusion of arguments to make that economy effective. It erects a complex logistic apparatus to support the conquest of the presumed nugget of truth in the oeuvre. While it proposes to extract the principles and their articulations from the confused matter of Machiavelli's language, it spins out the threads intended to hold them together once freed from that ancient language. So extensive is that undertaking that it is not uncommon for the interpreter's discourse to be far longer than Machiavelli's. But however closely woven the new discursive fabric, however tight the knots with which the writer's discourse is bound, the latter keeps its own identity in my eyes. Everything the interpreter says is ordered according to the meaning imposed upon it by the original. I may admire the extent of his knowledge, the depth of his thoughts and even subscribe to his judgments: they only matter to me to the extent that they give me access to that meaning. Whether he speaks of the Renaissance and the various paths taken by modern rationalism, or of the struggles tearing Florence apart and the powerlessness of the dominant class to broaden the framework of democracy, or of the alliance being formed between the bourgeoisie and the prince against the nobility, or yet again of the ineluctable commandments of reasons of state, I only pay attention to these passages because they refer to something Machiavelli said, and open up a passage from the statement to its motivation, reason, or cause, and link it to something else said. Now, the *said* of Machiavelli, the meaning of which finds its guarantee outside itself, but which at the same time is the guarantor of the interpreter's knowledge—there is nothing to prevent its hollowing out, within the space of the interpretation, another space, and attracting me into it. The critic confines it within specific limits, in order to assign it the meaning his argument requires; but beyond these limits, the indefinite expanse of the discourse from which it has been extracted stretches forth. It is presented as a thing said—massive, intractable. But the interpretation, despite all its skilled maneuvers, does not supply it with the solid foundation that would give it its self-evidence; in order to do so, it is forced to produce the absent discourse of the writer as its own foundation. It cannot refuse to produce the body of that absence. For while it raises certain propositions or certain fragments of that discourse to the rank of essentiality, the labor of extraction and promotion that governs the result leaves visible marks. What it rejects, or lowers to the rank of anecdote, I discover or divine in the allusions, concessions, digressions, denegations, retractations, punctuating the argument. Thus the *said* on which the light is projected is disturbed by contact with the adjacent shaded area; it prompts me to look more closely at the discourse from which it has been taken, but the uncertainties that are raised in consequence reflect back on the passage in which it is quoted: however clear the meaning it at first appeared to have, I am soon forced to concede it is dependent on the legitimacy of a method that consigns whole portions of the writer's text to the domain of non-meaning. And the uncertainties are simultaneously carried over to the place in which this *said* was determined as event, in which the real was assumed to govern its meaning, and truth held to confer on it its value. It is as if the principles of the interpreter, which initially had escaped my scrutiny and determined my reading by sovereign decree, were now denounced by the oeuvre they had subjugated, and the interpreter, by an unexpected role reversal, were summoned to appear before the writer. The text I had read within the critical text now gave me the latter to read; that fragment of the oeuvre, rent as it were by the sword of an invisible science, and mended so as to leave no stitches showing, now found the power to break its threads and, in withdrawing, exposed the incision made by that supposed science. The interpreter had taken most of his references from *The Discourses* and used them to support the thesis that politics finds its only legitimate expression in serving a republic, a state that is at the same time a community, in which power goes hand in hand with the freedom and participation of all in public affairs. He spoke of *The Prince* and invoked its argument only to refer, within it, to a writing of circumstance—a sign, in his view, of the powerlessness to which exile had reduced its author, the hopes he had at one time entertained of having his post restored to him by the Medicis, his illusory belief in a providential authority, which enabled him to avoid having to recognize the inevitable decline of Florence. But the little hints he leaves behind are such as to arouse suspicion: for example, I learn from him, sometimes without it being his intention, that certain passages in *The Prince* announce *The Discourses,* that this first work is far from being reducible to a eulogy of tyranny, that the language of *The Discourses* is still on many occasions that of *The Prince,* that violence and cunning are always associated with the acts of those who govern. This doubt strikes the interpretation. From the shadows to which he has been relegated, a certain Machiavelli motions to us to test points on which the interpretation hinges. Is it certain that *The Discourses* proceed from a different intention than *The Prince*? Are the circumstances, when invoked, any less apt to account for one work than another? Does the monarchy/republic dichotomy, which appears obvious to the interpreter, furnish a reliable criterion with which to take the full measure of Machiavelli's thought? Does the so-called historical impasse in which Florence and Italy were at the beginning of the *Cinquecento* assign the oeuvre its status? Can the real be stated at the level of the series of events in which the historian recognizes a destiny in retrospect? Is the real what he constructs as such, at a distance from the time in which the present was being sculpted out of its future? Does that distance authorize the forgetfulness of one's own condition, and when he esteems that the space devoted to violence in *The Discourses* and *The Prince* attests to the writer's inability to conceive of the solution to the Florentine or Italian crisis, where does he get his assurance that it can be eliminated from history, and that it already represents nothing more than the sequel of past contradictions? These questions, of course, are ones that I ask: but I am only able to ask them because the oeuvre, the moment it escapes from the clutches of the interpreter, gives them to me to contemplate. To say that it escapes and that it charges me with these questions is to say the same thing. Now, how these questions proliferate as I circulate between interpretations, how the indetermination grows with the repeated experience of the determinations of which it is the object . . . The more I penetrate the field of scientific criticism, the more the foundation of reality and truth on which it was claimed to be based proves unstable. It is not that the reference points set up by the history of acts and institutions, by Marxism, *Kulturgeschichte*, or Thomism, are futile, but these reference points—the oeuvre has the power to set them in motion. The interpreter does not doubt their validity, because he does not doubt his knowledge, but the oeuvre knows nothing of the registers that have been drawn up and into which it is supposed to be inscribed (Machiavelli's oeuvre as well as any other, such as that of Marx, for example, which is similarly ignorant of the frameworks of Marxism). These registers—the oeuvre strips them one after the other of the so-called self-evidence in which they pride themselves, and exposes the conventions failing which they cease to serve in place of reality.

Thus the question I discover upon examining critical discourse changes in nature. First it is: What is the reality of the work? And in that first form it becomes twofold: What, I asked, is the real locus in which the oeuvre shows itself as it is, and what, within the oeuvre, is the real part of meaning? I take pleasure in thinking that I ask it explicitly, while others only designate it by their responses. But, in that form, the interrogation is still hidden. Whereas I denounce the interpreters' claim to reduce the writer's discourse to the limits of a thesis, and to the limits of the thesis of the world sustaining that thesis, I continue to maintain that claim, by sharing their faith in the reality of the oeuvre, in retaining the naïve idea that the oeuvre gives itself, and the reality with it, in representation; I merely transport elsewhere the privileged place that it behooves us to know. It is only when that faith loses its self-evidence that I confront the experience with which critical discourse confronts me. And it only loses its self-evidence when it appears to me as such, when I discover beyond the multiple theses of the oeuvre and the multiple theses of the world the same desire for determination. A desire that is a passion for the object: a useful passion, which protects the critic from the effects of the oeuvre, delivering him from the disturbance it produces in his thinking, preserving his integrity as subject. That faith is not given with the experience of the presence of the oeuvre and the world onto which it opens, it does not depend on the irresistible movement the advent of meaning commands, and we have not yet said anything when we have justified the intolerance of the interpreter by the willingness to be carried away that truth requires of him. He does not allow himself to be carried away; on the contrary he resists, avoiding the experience of the oeuvre by venerating the principle of objectivity. At the root of his intolerance there is the obstinate refusal to hear the other speak beyond the limits that make it possible to enclose his discourse within the confines of the certain. It is by a repression of all the doubts that would grant passage to an indetermination impossible to be rid of; it is in order to deny that there is in the oeuvre an excess of *thinking* over *that which is thought* that he closes himself up in a knowledge he will not allow to be challenged. Undoubtedly the paths of repression and denial are diverse. Criticism can tear itself apart, opposing, for example, the detection of the structure subtending manifest discourse to the recollection and classification of themes; the goal does not change by being moved. It is still a matter of subjecting the oeuvre to a representation, of assigning it to an order of reality in which a precise accounting of meanings is given. However different the procedures interpretation brings into play (difference, moreover, that is not negotiable and that is appreciated, if not for the value of the results, at least for the questions with which it charges us), they unite to produce the same effect—the strict suitability of the writer's thought to the measures applied to him or her—and to obtain it at the same cost: the rejection of the excessiveness the oeuvre brings us, which would shake the certainty of the foundation. It matters little that the critic may claim to remain faithful to the writer's discourse, to have no other concern than to clarify what the latter actually thought, to name his intention, banishing any explanation that draws on the social milieu or history—to the point of making himself be treated as an idealist by the adversary; or on the contrary, that he may claim the discourse to be nothing for him but the symptom of a truth pronounced outside its field, the echo of a collective voice or the trace of a force already sufficient of itself to produce its consequences in the actions of men—to the point where the accusation of sociologism seems legitimate. The conclusions are engendered on the basis of a work of objectification, presupposing the same will to undo the ties to which the reading had given birth at a moment when questioned and questioner were not distinguished—the same conviction that something is signified, by or in the writing, that can be labeled and imputed to a positive authority, that something has been acquired of which we must take delivery in order to state its price to the others.

What then is the oeuvre, that it slips the grasp of its interpreters, forces the repetition of the critical discourse, withdrawing every time from the representation in which we try to enclose it? Such is the question to which we must clear a path. That question is born of the dissatisfaction with which the interpretations leave us, but it only acquires its truth when from questions about meaning it becomes a question about the being of the oeuvre; when we require of ourselves to think at once the presence of the oeuvre, the evidence of its attraction, its absence in the representation, and its withdrawal from all reality in which we claim to file it away.

In an initial phase, we are tempted to believe that each interpretation furnishes its partial truth. Is it not, we ask, a series of "profiles" that criticism offers us? Would it not suffice to collate these views with one another to obtain a full appreciation of the oeuvre? But that temptation is vain. The "profiles" are incompatible; the different views denounce one another. The reality of the work cannot be in several places at once, because in each place it takes on a meaning that, in another place, is non-meaning. Thus skepticism awaits its chance, and to escape there is no other solution than to forget the attempts of others and to begin interpreting as if we had never heard of critical discourse before. A lie that we must pay for by knowing that for others our interpretation has already fallen into that discourse. But it is for lack of having understood it sufficiently that we turned away from that discourse; because we were in a hurry to arrive at a judgment, because we required of the critic his reasons in the same way he requires them of the writer—because we held the same idea of his work that he holds of the oeuvre, because we still thought of the latter as a simple object of knowledge. So indeed our only alternative was to accept or reject, and if we rejected, to go and gather from among the edifices in ruin a few stones that would serve in our construction. On the other hand, when we begin to examine carefully the dialogue connecting the writer to his posterity—that dialogue each one claims to conclude, and that is not interrupted, that is indefinitely launched anew as a result of new arguments, because no one, here, occupies the position of master, no one escapes, beneath the reader's eye, the oeuvre's response—the brutal alternative between meaning and non-meaning dissolves. It cannot be said that the others give us profiles of the work, but neither that they hide it. What they give us in every case is a certain absence, the contour of a certain hollow—something quite different in fact from what they claim to offer us: the work such as it is, the fullness of the work. But that is not nothing. The space ajar before us is not just any space; it is the one that is proper to the work, cut out for it as its own by the interpretation. Whither the oeuvre draws us we still proceed by a movement that transgresses certain limits, that must encounter them to transgress them. Nor can one say, and for the same reason, that when we pass from one interpretation to another, their views combine to form an ideal perception of the work, nor, when the opposite is the case, that they annul one other. The metaphor of vision is misleading. They are not views that are offered us; the work is not analogous to a thing, submitted to the eye of the mind, and we do not have the choice between perspective and illusion. The truth we draw from this experience is of a different order: a certain indetermination is followed by a different indetermination. Contrary to what one might expect, the exploration of scientific criticism does not produce the result of multiplying the determinations of the oeuvre: it increases its indetermination. This indetermination does not plunge the work into darkness, depriving us of any points of repair; on the contrary, the more the indetermination grows, the more it is determined; while as the responses thin out, questions are formed and interrelate, and further deepen the interrogation called for by the oeuvre.

Each interpreter, we were saying, wants to believe that the oeuvre is accomplished in his reflection, that it changes at last into its essence, that the knowledge that the oeuvre adumbrates is completed in his own knowledge. Our efforts would be vain if we in turn imagined it is enough to reflect the reflection of others in order to achieve fulfillment—that it is possible to reach the goal by assessing failure; that to unravel the knot gives us the power to retie it right. To whoever has applied himself to hearing the critical discourse, to begin to interpret is only legitimate on the condition of taking charge of the indetermination to which the oeuvre submits its reader.

When we interrogate the discourse of the writer—when, having returned to the silence of reading, we ask the text what it means—we are prepared for that task; all the questions we have asked have created within us an expectation, a disposition, to receive. There is nothing, or almost nothing, in what we read that does not resonate with a possible commentary and that we should not preserve from the effects of a possible commentary. There is nothing we do not try to open up to the greatest future, having measured the danger of a closure of meaning in partial statements. We know henceforth that in order to follow the path opened up by the oeuvre, we must not stop at the stations at which others believed they could take up fixed residence, that it is useless to put place-markers in a text after the manner of the critic-geometrician who then attempts to put them in the right order and have that order pass for the order of the oeuvre itself. To read Machiavelli, to write on Machiavelli, those two endeavors whose link we begin to intuit, now presuppose that we hold the meaning of his discourse—as long as it is in our power to do so—in suspense; that we lend it our thoughts in order to take in the full measure of what it proposes for our reflection; that we configure the space of a new discourse in which his continues to make itself heard, that is, to retain the virtue of making others speak. To interrogate Machiavelli entails, finally, that instead of extracting from his oeuvre answers to be submitted to our judgment and subjected to the answers suggested to us by the supposed problem of their origin, we perceive him as the man who questioned from his own place, and whose own place was a questioning, who, in destabilizing in his own day the foundations of established knowledge, carried the effects of that tremor further than either he or his readers could have imagined.

The circumstance that a reflection on the discourse of his posterity disposes us to receive the discourse of a writer does not mean that there is not a rupture between them. We do not follow a chain of questions the way one follows a chain of reasoning. The interrogation would be degraded if, under its cover, a form of logic analogous to that of a formal demonstration were practiced. When we directed our attention to the discourse of posterity, the discourse of Machiavelli remained on the horizon of our thoughts; we would not have been able to understand anything of the one if the other were not perceptible. When Machiavelli's discourse occupies our thoughts, the questions we faced are displaced without ceasing to alert us, and as they wait to be reconsidered, they do no more than sustain the question that captures our attention: that oeuvre—the oeuvre present in the text—what does it say? The enigma, we have noted, is that the work is at the same time in its text and outside its text, in the critical context from which he who wants to know it cannot turn away. But *at the same time* it is equivocal. The enigma is that the work gives itself *entirely* in its text and yet is only what it is by the relation that is established between this text and its readers. When we read it and it is important for us to understand it and have others understand it, to the point that we make the decision to write about it, a moment comes when all the thoughts we have pursued in the direction of criticism cease, when all the questions we have accumulated are laid down, not to fall into oblivion, but to constitute a soil beneath our feet. For us there is henceforth no other guide but the word of Machiavelli.

And so the mediators stand aside; the burden of the entire singular history carried by the oeuvre is reabsorbed. Each word sets us in what was its present, and we find ourselves as if alone, harkening to it, as if torn away from our time, transported without even the sense of a transition to that place. However fruitful our sojourn in the critical universe has been, it is impossible to take stock of what it has brought us and to know the passage that has led us from criticism to the writer's work. However certain we are of the power we have acquired—that power—we do not know how to define it. The capital of one experience is invested in another experience, but the investment cannot be measured in the trial of the interpretation. The oeuvre speaks henceforth to our memory; but it would not speak if we submitted it to a questionnaire of memories, if we were now to claim to be able to take from the discourse all we needed to answer its interpreters, drawing arguments from it to definitively rebuff their theses. For were we to do so, the presence of the oeuvre would vanish once again, that presence bearing testimony, as we assert, to the continuance of its words, of which we desire to institute ourselves as witness by opening the space of its influence.

To say that the writer's word becomes our only guide is thus to say that the earlier work has had no other effect than that of putting us in a condition to begin; that it has not relieved us of—but rather burdened us with—the task of sustaining, by ourselves, the relation of the reader to the work.

This beginning is such as to constrain us to confront the question yet again: What is the oeuvre? From *The Prince* and *The Discourses* we expect that they teach us how to read them, convinced as we are that there is no method that can determine what that reading should be. But the question of meaning would be blind if we did not know in what space we moved. And what gives our movement its proper direction is not only our knowing that the discourse must be held open beyond the limits to which it is confined by reducing it to a sum of statements, for however true that principle may be, no one can refrain from basing his or her thesis on certain statements at the expense of others. Now, the space of the oeuvre does not appear immediately when we enter into Machiavelli's writings. Perhaps it would be better to say that it hides itself. If it is true that every oeuvre of thought has the property of hiding itself qua oeuvre, that is all the more the case with a work like that of Machiavelli, because it speaks to us of the actual deeds of men within the context of society, of their motivations, of institutions, of the necessity to which these latter correspond; of events, their causes and effects; and of history and the order and disorder it conceals; because it speaks of a world that seems to preexist the discourse, to have for all the same identity, to be equally perceptible to anyone—the writer as well as his reader—who considers it from his own place. What we call thought in the oeuvre of thought, we do not think immediately as such; we think what is thought by it; something that is produced by virtue of an activity that is in fact singular, but that offers itself to us without betraying anything of that production. Something that is, as they say, pure meaning. And when that meaning is attached to familiar things, or things we believe to be such, because they already bear their name in common experience, it captivates us even more strongly. Let us consider, for example, the proposition with which *The Prince* begins. "All states and dominions which hold or have held sway over mankind are either republics or principalities." We do not think that proposition as such, that is, we do not think the act of thought that posits: "All states . . ." We focus on the meaning, which presents itself as indubitably as a perceptible object to our gaze. It matters little what judgment we will eventually make on the dichotomy republic/principality, or that we do not at the outset grasp its full significance, or that it only lets itself be comprehended in relation to other propositions. The fact remains that the moment we read "All states . . . ," the meaning takes possession of us, and that simultaneously the world thus signified is presented to us, the world denominated by state, dominion, sway, principality, republic—which is what it is, beyond what is written in the book and beyond the meanings I form.

Doubtless the reader not only yields to the institution of meaning and to the installation in the world organized by the oeuvre: he lends himself to it. And he not only brings his knowledge of the language, the words, and the syntax. If he perceives the meaning of the pair principality/republic, for example, it is because he is capable of summoning up apropos of these two terms a variety of forms of government and of seeing them ignored in favor of the new opposition. If he perceives the meaning of *sway* (*imperio*) it is because he can be astonished at the absence of other words in the first sentence in which the state is designated. In a general way, the meanings only affect him because he draws from within his own fund of knowledge the power to receive them, and to feel the divergences instituted in relation to other acquired meanings. If the world Machiavelli opens up to him becomes his world, it is again because he responds to the former incitement of the writer, to anticipate his next move, and make, from all he has learned about Rome or modern Italy, a concatenated series through which the thread of the discourse will pass. But however true it may be that the reader brings to his reading the treasure of his knowledge and experience, this treasure is in the sole service of the advent of meaning and the signified world. Whatever may be the conditions necessary for his transport to the place of the Other, it remains the case that it is the virtue of the oeuvre to solicit them, that all these secretly mobilized resources have no other effect than to allow the intellectual conversion they commanded to be accomplished. The fact remains that the most extensive systematic body of knowledge adds nothing to the reading, which it only carries to its highest degree the faculty granted to each to think what the writer has designated as an object of thought. That object, moreover, is not necessarily conceived of in the same way the writer conceived of it. The interpretation the latter gives to certain events, to certain sorts of conduct, or of the role of the prince, or of the conflicts tearing society apart, or of the nature of the state—he may well contest them, and substitute many other meanings; but at least he is placed before a certain world. It is these events, these sorts of conduct, class conflict, the role of the prince, that constitute *that which is thought*. The extent of his disagreement matters little. Whether, for example, he rejects the explanation of the failures of Louis XII in

Italy, judges the portrait of Cesare Borgia to be inaccurate, the condemnation of the condottieri system ill-founded, the model of Roman virtue anachronistic—whether he refuses to call the domination of a legitimate prince oppression: these disagreements presuppose a former adherence to the field circumscribed by the oeuvre. Borgia, Louis XII, the figure of the adventuresome captain, the Romans, the relationship to authority occupy his mind, as if they were naturally disposed to be placed in relation to one another and presented within one unified mental purview. Further, the freedom we have to think what the writer thinks differently from him increases the realist illusion. It is as if the writer had placed us beside him to show us a landscape we might not have been able to discover without him, but that, once revealed, would stand available to our own inspection; or as if, after having been introduced by him to a new group of people, we could take our leave of the intermediary and develop relationships with those close to him that owed nothing to his services. Such is the strange property of the oeuvre of thought: it causes itself to be forgotten forthwith in order to draw us toward its object; it operates in such a way that we only have eyes for it. It is pure prose, a language the whole merit of which is to be self-effacing before the things thought—before the things that bore their meanings before we named them.

This language, as it seems, is not different from the one we use every day. True enough, it does not convey opinion, orders, demands, or warnings, and in a general sense is not a simple mode of communication. But after all everyday language is not just that. Whenever we analyze a character, a situation, the concern for accuracy governs the disposition of our words. We oversee them in such a way that only the meaning is expressed, and the truth of the matter is made manifest. Whether our words are expressed in a conversation or in a letter, for example, the same law governs them. Indeed, when we go from the reading of *The Prince* to that of the correspondence of the author with his friend Vettori, we are not aware of changing registers. The letter of December 20, 1514, for example, comments on contemporary events and attempts to define the policy the pope should follow in the event of another attack on Milan. This writing doubtless owes its existence to a mere circumstance: Machiavelli is answering his interlocutor who wanted his advice, and it does not go beyond the framework of the current situation. But his analysis appeals to principles whose significance transcends the order of opinion. Judgments concerning the will of the people and of the prince, the fatal development of conquest, the dangers of neutrality, the difference between hatred and contempt, attest to a reflection on politics as such. That letter opens a window for us onto the Italy of 1514, onto a region of the world we have the freedom to know through other means, and simultaneously it brings us into the presence of meanings of a general order that we may adopt, reject, or rectify. The fact that *The Prince* has the ambition of treating a much larger issue, that it refers to a variety of events that are themselves a part of different historical periods, that it subordinates them to the logic of the argument, that it does not side with any particular actor, this in no way modifies the relation we establish through reading with the other writings of the author. Is the letter not an oeuvre of reduced size and small significance, restricted to the limits of a few facts and a few principles? Is not *The Prince* a very long letter, which uses its length to express in all its articulations an "idea" of politics, to give an account of the greatest number of facts possible or to test the outer limits of coherence? Is it not a matter of indifference that the interlocutor should be anonymous, a present reader or a reader from a future era? The writing that thought governs—whether a letter or an oeuvre, whether addressed to me or to a third party, or whether the addressee is without identity—when I become acquainted with it, does it not always make me the witness to the world whose meaning it expresses, and does it not consequently put me on the same footing as the author? If it requires my attention, is it not the case that what it thinks I am capable of thinking? Was I not already disposed in such a way that its object could become my object, and that its initiative sufficed to convince me to examine and to judge?

The sense of equality gives way when I come to doubt the author's word. Such was my assurance that I was unaware of it. I was carried away to the place he designated: the Italy in which Louis XII twice wins and loses Milan. I adopted or shunted aside the explanation of the French failures; I meditated on the proposition "One must note that men must either flatter or kill one another." Now I read: "Time drives everything before it, and is able to bring with it good as well as evil, and evil as well as good." That formula still has a meaning in isolation from its context; moreover, it brings to mind analogous ones by classical authors, and I find nothing surprising in it; but it importunes me to lead me back to a prior sentence that had caught my attention a little earlier: "The antiquity and long continuity of hereditary power extinguish the memories and causes of change." Does Machiavelli attribute to time the virtue of conservation, or is its essence change? Or are these two truths compatible, each in its place? Or is the discordance intentional? Does the author introduce the first term only to reverse it? Is this reversal definitive, provisional? Might it be a sign that signifies in turn through another sign? I discovered the hypotheses formulated in the first chapter, and, confident in the commentaries accompanying them, I awaited their examination one by one. Consequently I welcomed the first analyses devoted to the hereditary principalities and mixed principalities. Now, the fourth chapter establishes an essential opposition between the despotic state and the state ruled by a prince whose authority is limited by that of his noblemen. Is this a simple digression? Or did I take the wrong direction in following the first indications furnished? These doubts give another direction to the reading. The author surges from the shadows into which he had been relegated. It is now not only important to see what he designates, *hic et nunc*, nor to weigh each question asked. Over and above the questions that structured and continue to structure our reading, a new question is added: What are his reasons? Reasons conscious or unconscious, however we may decide the issue; but the transparency of his language is now a thing of the past. Those words that bowed out before their meanings, that seemed to be consumed in the act of reading, are reborn before our eyes. Those words that designated, perhaps they are hiding something; perhaps they only serve other words that must nourish themselves from them in order to signify. Perhaps they are neither innocent nor sly, but failed: signs that slip out, and whose discrepancy we must take by surprise if we are to know their origin.

Thus there occurs in reading something that happens in conversation. We were speaking of a third party; I welcomed without hesitation the remarks of the other person, I commented on them, and was completely taken up with describing and expressing judgments. Our words intertwined, the third party was their subject. And suddenly an utterance of the other's, the excessiveness of a term, the vehemence of the tone or an unexpected reserve, or an insistent question, raising suspicion, breaks the charm. It is my interlocutor, not the third party, who is revealed. Immediately his words become signs of an intention that had eluded me, and all that I had received speaks again a different language in my memory.

It is not the feelings of Machiavelli the writer that intrigue me, nor an intention he may have had toward the reader that I am, although nothing stands in the way of my imputing motives and designs in the development of his discourse. His is an oeuvre of thought. When I turn to it, it is his thoughts, then, that I come to think. No longer what it makes perceptible, but, within the place it allows me to uncover, the hints of a passage. I choose these hints by reason of their concordance. To think thought is, then, to think a certain order. Each punctual thought is henceforth a thought only in the relation it has to other thoughts, and its ability to be inscribed in a form. The form separates for me from that matter that the facts and generated meanings have become, and it is important to me, whatever may be the judgment I apply to them. But the form separates simultaneously from that matter that the language of the writer has become. The flow of the words that carried the reading has

stopped. Thought is outside the words. It depends on an invisible organization. However I may conceive of that organization, I imagine in it a
center, a hierarchy, a network of dependencies. Doubtless I can find in
the manifest organization of the discourse traces of that ideal organization; it may be that the manifest organization has itself the value of an
indication. But the ideal organization is ruled by a necessity that owes
nothing to the fact of expression. There thought finds its origin, an end,
its own articulations, of which I have, moreover, legitimate knowledge
through a language different from that of the author.

But the space of the oeuvre—do we recognize it when we think
thought in this way, or do we still not know the oeuvre of thought? Reading is discovery of the things of the world that the writer designates; it
is the appropriation of the meanings he establishes. These things—in
discovering them, we think them ourselves, just as, so we believe, they
should be thought. These meanings—we retouch them to make them
conform to what we judge to be the truth. Thus we are faced with certain
data that we subject to our reflection. When the thought of the author
becomes perceptible to us, we are faced with a new datum. We develop
the procedures that seem to us the most effective to make sure what that
thought is. That thought—we like to imagine it determined, to imagine
that it allows itself to be determined in its truth by the operation of cognizance. But what are these data? How can we say the work relates them
to one another? Are we really in the presence of the oeuvre when we
think the things thought, or when we think the thought that thinks them,
or when we pass from one object to the other? What is given to us is not
just discrete things—the conquests of Louis XII, the rise of the Borgia,
the crimes of Agathocles, the rivalries of the Italian cities, or such and
such a "fragment" of reality. Nor is it such and such a relation of essence
between phenomena—the credulity of the people and the oppression
by the Grandees, class struggle and tyranny. What is given—all at once,
though it can only be discovered little by little—is a world that Louis XII,
Borgia and Agathocles, the Romans of antiquity and the Florentines of
the *Cinquecento* all inhabit; a world in which they are so to speak turned
toward one another, taken up in the same family. What is given—all at
once, although the meaning springs up from successive meanings and
their difference—is the intelligibility of this world, this world reflected in
itself, and, by that reflection, positing itself as the real world. Now, what
is given in this manner is only given in virtue of the gift that was at its
origin—a gift by which that which was without attachment and without
voice gathers itself and begins to speak. Therefore it is to this gift that I
owe the ability to think what is thought by the work and to think it as I
think it. I was forgetful of it when I situated things and ideas in a space

itself; but I also forgot it when, wanting to define thought in its essence, I separated the form from the matter, for I did not yet know that Machiavelli's thought is that renewal of the world and that source of words that subjugates me to his oeuvre.

The domain the oeuvre causes to spring up seems strange, since it is its property, and yet no sign shows us where it starts or stops, since we explore it without knowing whether we are within its boundaries or without. If we scrutinize the designated facts or the writer's "ideas," we are clearly within the oeuvre, and yet we are imperceptibly borne without, for these facts and these ideas—the portrait of the Emperor Severus, or the proposition that unarmed prophets have always been defeated—do not need it to be what they are. Let us leave aside the details of the meanings to bring forth the architecture of principles constituting the thought in its essence, and again it is the oeuvre that provides the soil of our operations—but we leave it behind us as we advance. The whole landscape that emerged beside the pathways down which we pursued the discourse disappears; at best, all we retain of the expression are the artifices that would permit the functioning of the ideal machine called thought. But if the paradox stops us, is it not because we resist the experience to which the oeuvre subjects us, imagining a boundary where there can be none? Is it not because, having misunderstood the instigating movement of the discourse, the contingency of the origin that marks it throughout its length, the upsurge in it of the world of which it is the guarantor, we render ourselves incapable of receiving the indetermination into which the oeuvre projects us? This indetermination cannot be resolved in virtue of the object *reality* or of a determination of the object *thought:* it is the very nature of the oeuvre, which has no foundation other than itself.

When we speak of the space of the oeuvre, the term is convenient, but treacherous. For its space—we must understand that the oeuvre opens it, but also that it has no limits we can relate to other spaces, nor any form that we can circumscribe within other forms. Of what is opened we cannot know the contours; were we to desire to know them, we would no longer be open to what the work thinks, no longer stand within its opening. We might well examine, and multiply infinitely, the points of view: it would remain always flattened out on the plane of the sensible or the intelligible. Vain then is the search for that space. We cannot find it, we can only lose it. When we think what was thought for the first time by the author as that which must be thought for the first time, when we think, in these events which are the words that strike us, the advent of thinking, then we are in the space of the oeuvre—in its element. But that place is neither real nor imaginary; the world into which we are thrown is neither the private world of the one initiating it, nor the world of the facts he designates, facts visible to all. That place and that world are not in some place where one would like to situate them, and we ourselves, who find our direction in it, do not dispose of any external point of repair to advance. This is not to say that the oeuvre does not give us the occasion to think about the facts, ideas, and relationships manifested between many meanings. What would reading be if there were not a stop here and there, and a passing beyond what is presented? But the oeuvre as such only continues to exist if we feel the impossibility of taking our support from outside its orbit, if the necessity that governs the discourse is perceptible to us, and, even in its most erratic movements, maintains it in the same "tendency." The oeuvre only exists if, in the indetermination it makes us face, in a rigorous experience, the truth is pronounced—a truth that holds up in the perilous passage . . . Perhaps the first reading, which takes place beneath the emblem of discovery, astonishment, and expectation—in quest of a meaning nothing can stand in the way of till completion—is thus more faithful, more fully preserving of the presence of the oeuvre than the critical readings that follow; perhaps the last reading thus rejoins the first, when it professes to make that presence manifest.

But the term presence—is it not also treacherous? We say that one must take care to remain within the presence of the oeuvre, and that the latter disappears when one makes its thought into an object, when one unravels the discourse to extract the thesis that would be its essence. It appears to me in the experience of reading that every meaning is caught up in a weave of sense from which it cannot be detached completely without perishing; it seems to me that the writer's word consumes itself to further a power of words that has no sensible body; such is our certainty on this point that what we call the identity of the written work, the *Machiavellian* in Machiavelli, has no representation in the written statements themselves. But is this not to associate the present with the ineffable, to form a mystical relation with the oeuvre, and, for having wanted to defend language against the operations of science, to end up doing the opposite, lapsing back into the illusion of a beyond language? The answer to the question can be guessed: beyond the writer's words there would be a simple word governing them all—simple to the point of not being further decomposable into signs, such that all expression, however faithful it might pretend to be, would already degrade it; there would be a full word, so full it could flow into discourse, whose reflection discourse could do no more than mirror. This discourse should certainly be examined closely, but in it everything would be artifice, obligatory detour. *The Prince* and *The Discourses* would gravitate around an ineffable idea of politics. The analyses of Rome or of modern Italy, the judgments of fact or of value, the statement of particular truths or of universal ones, all would do no more than furnish support for that pure idea, merely develop its metaphor. Interpretation would thus be reduced to the invention, in immediate contact with the essence, of new artifices, to create a new sensible substitute to help others get to the place where the author is located; it would be translation determined to find in the text the translation that was already there. But when we speak of the presence of the oeuvre, the experience of that presence is tied to that of an essential indetermination. Now this is indeed the danger of indetermination, supposedly overcome by he who hypothesizes a point outside the sensible from which all the figures of discourse would radiate. According to that same hypothesis there would be a full word within the writer, and a coinciding of self with self, in such a way that the writer is assured in advance of what he cannot fail to find. We need not stop to remind the reader of the difficulties in which such a faith gets bogged down once the coincidence is seen to be restricted to the limits of the subject, nor of the fact that what is missing in the fullness of the word is the word of the other. It is better to observe that the certainty of the Idea shelters one from the vagaries of language. Whatever scruple of reading there may be, nothing can be read that is not envisaged as a testimony. The presence of the Idea is the presence of God, even if it is true that this god governs only a domain of the intelligible, and that it may be necessary to assign him his rank in the hierarchy of gods; the only legitimate task is to administer the proofs of his existence . . .

Thus, it is not the signs of an ineffable truth that we claim to gather, and we do not assign an extra-linguistic status to that ineffable. On the contrary, we affirm that the signs only refer to other signs; the differences are never annulled in favor of a sign that would finally be the pure sign of what it signifies; they are always postponed, the meaning always deferred; reading never gives us rest, but rather obeys the ever renewed commandment to leave any point it has reached—even if it is the end of the book, for it has no more than any other the privilege of closing—with the charge of new questions . . . But if we let ourselves be sent from sign to sign, at least we do not question the necessity of this movement. This movement is not in the signs, but neither is it in the difference; it is that through which there is, for us, sign and difference—sign instituted in difference, difference by signs. This movement has, no doubt, its conditions in the time of the reading, in the space of the book, and it is dependent on our initiative. But it is not in that time and in that sensible space, because it overturns them, and only has to do with us to the extent that we let it happen. In this movement the oeuvre is named as that of which neither the beginning nor the end are defined, of which neither the author nor the reader is master, as a place of passage and alliance. Just as the belief that the oeuvre reposes in itself in a non-transmissible formula, so the belief that it bears in the true part of itself a system of ideas or, independently of established meanings, a determined organ of production of knowledge, turns us away from this place, denying us passage and alliance. One must be in complicity with the author's word to be able to let oneself be *deeply moved* by the oeuvre and know the effect of being carried away that at once makes its presence perceptible and throws one toward the truth. And there must be such a conversion in order for all the author's words to be bound to one another, for them to speak the same language and at the same time for we ourselves to speak that language. It probably does not suffice to say of the movement that thus carries us along, to make it clearer, that it is interrogation itself. The word does not spare us the effort of thought. As long as what we understand by interrogation is the interrogative sentence or even the maintaining of the interrogative mood throughout the entire length of the discourse, as long as we see no more in it than the privation of affirmation, more generally a retreat from the sphere of judgment, we remain foreign to the truth of that movement. There is, moreover, a way of questioning, of distributing the question marks along the trajectory of an analysis, that does not challenge the status of the object, just as there is a way of affirming that unveils, outside the sphere of conventional meanings, a sense that destabilizes the notion of the real. But when one no longer flattens interrogation to the plane of interrogative enunciations, when one tries to appreciate its full measure and it proves to be both questioning of being and of meaning, then the experience of the inception of the relation to the oeuvre comes into view.

To investigate is of course to follow an itinerary, to go through stages, to unfold a discourse, but in such a way that no knowledge is gleaned that is not without its undercurrent of unknowing, so that each wave of words is accompanied by a reflux toward the same inlet, so that there is no reserve in each thing said that does not feed the same reserve of questions. To investigate is of course to scrutinize the world the other designates—the world toward which he clears a path—but in such a way that we know that he lives in it and that we live in it, that that world speaks and questions us through him, that the past itself questions our present. As long as we are faithful to that questioning, the work gives its presence, is in fact the place of *the same*. It is not, for example, that the author doesn't seem to have changed from one period to another of his production, or that we do not discover within one and the same book of his an essential variation, but the complication of the discourse is not for us the result of an inability to say the simple, nor his discordances the result of the immaturity of a part of his thoughts, or even a misunderstanding on his part of his true intention. Through that complication is revealed thought's coming to itself—not the signs of an inexpressible intuition, but neither the signs of an empirical genesis of thought that would teach us to delimit the part of the thought that has at last reached its destination—the "knowledge" part of the work—that advent as such, in all the modalities of the tearing away from the already-thought, in all the modes of the opening to the not-yet-thought, in the accumulation of reservations that is the source of meaning for the author and for the others, in the collection of all particular thoughts in the hollow of the same thinking, in the blind recognition of all thoughts by one another, and, with that experience, the re-launching of thought. Through that complication is simultaneously revealed the inexhaustible supply in which the oeuvre is rooted, the being of the world in its profusion, the being that cannot be held within any representation or measure, but is pronounced in the folding back, the meander, the immoderation of the word—ever at a distance and in excess of what has happened. Then, the place of presence, the place of the same, proves to be that of constant retreat, of constant differentiation. And it is one selfsame thing to say that we follow the movement by which a thought comes to itself and to say that we follow the movement by which it escapes. These two movements are only contrary in objective space, a space we do not inhabit, which is constructed in representation; they are but one when there returns to us in memory the implication of thought in being and the excess of being over all that *is*. Then we are no longer scandalized by the fact that the author's thought relates to itself in the moment in which we see it moving away from the point it occupied previously; or that the oeuvre is a collection and that it has no center, that it offers passage to whoever follows in its wake, and that its borders are invisible. Then is that violence denounced to which we would subject it by imposing a law upon it, by rejecting as waste the part imputed to influence or circumstance.

Beside the fact that no blow of the chisel will ever abolish the indetermination of the oeuvre,[1] that the criterion of influence or circumstance can be enlisted to serve any number of purposes, that it does not suffice to appeal to the factual history of a thought and to judge that the *after* discredits the *before*, that an author's disavowal would still constitute no more than an opinion, the value of which would not outweigh that of his writing, carrier that it is of a meaning of which he was not the sole master—the discourse of immaturity or of contingency does not reduce to meanings that will later or elsewhere be modified or disowned; it already has a demeanor that announces that of the "mature" discourse. Less self-assured or less free, it nevertheless allows, because the writer speaks a language no one else would have spoken in his place, the necessity of his endeavor to transpire. In the reading of Machiavelli, it is not the idea that *The Prince* and *The Discourses* differ in origin, or that the events and author's desires command or disturb his language, that can serve as our guide. To receive his oeuvre is certainly to perceive it in the entire gamut of its variations and in relation to the times, the society, the events concerning it, but it is, as much as it is in our power to decide this, to refuse to allow ourselves to untie the bond that subjects us to his word by letting it sink to the status of factuality; if it is true, for example, that the author's thought is influenced by his hope that a young prince will found a strong state in Italy, we must apply ourselves to hear what he says about authority in favoring this desire; or if it is true that he borrows from Xenophon or Aristotle, we must devote our attention to hearing how he makes them speak his own language.

It is hardly necessary to repeat that this resolution is no guarantee of faithfulness. We will not find security by the mere fact of designating the oeuvre in the interrogation and that interrogation in the oeuvre. It is not our putting ourselves in the presence of the oeuvre that can deliver us from doubt, since presence and indetermination are linked; it is not our renunciation of the solidity of the idea that assures our being positioned in what we now call the hollow or the opening of the oeuvre; it is not by taking up its questions that we can allow ourselves to forget that it is our taking up, and that our own words, from the first breath, determine those of the other; we must agree to let insecurity stop hiding behind the mask of mastery, admit that this is not the sign of a lack, and let it call itself by its true name. Indeed, how would the interpreter dream of contacting the oeuvre at its center, of recovering its discourse into a new discourse, or, short of that, draw conclusions about the impossibility of the encounter, since the work in itself is already outside itself, since its discourse occurs to itself, conquers its own identity in the very act of its enunciation? Assuredly he cannot but deviate from the oeuvre, but the deviation does not condemn him, because the oeuvre has already known an inner deviation; since the movement he executes—the oeuvre has already initiated it, and thus it cannot place him before the alternative of either possession or a privation of meaning. The encounter he is striving for is never certain, but at least he knows why this is the case, and that if he does attain it, it does not abolish distance.

But again it would be an error, and a forgetting of a part of the experience, to imagine that encounter and that distance as being those of two thoughts, one of which is related to the other only by allowing itself to be drawn, following its own movement, by the foreign movement that opens to it what is to be thought. If there is such an attraction, the fact is that it was within the horizons of a certain time that Machiavelli's thought was instituted, and that it is within the horizons of my own time that I think.

What is to be thought is never detached from the experience of the present. If the writer did not have the power, based on the experience his situation sets up for him, in a present, to engender thought about the world as such, I would not be able to join him; but that experience is not annulled at the moment of reflection; it does not slip away altogether, and I remain partially a stranger to him. I must simply concede that his experience contains the hollows of other possible experiences—just as there is in mine the wherewithal to let me be shifted toward his, toward the place from which he opens onto history, to the world in general.

The enigma we face is that the Open is not the anonymous space of a self-sufficient truth standing resplendent before all: the Open is conditioned by the opening of the oeuvre; the opening is conditioned by a present, and that opening—I cannot find it or re-execute it otherwise than from another present and in a new position. The enigma is that the author's name is irreplaceable, and yet I cannot think what it makes available to be thought except in my own name . . . We say the *open*, but here the term still risks betraying us, for whatever precautions are taken, it suggests exteriority and the determination of the visible. Of course every truly great oeuvre modifies the relationship of thinking to its element; it has results whose destinies are foreign to its own destiny. After Machiavelli, Rousseau or Marx bring about a new circulation of ideas. But it is also true that that circulation is carried out in misunderstanding the change that has taken place: the *open* has become invisible. It is only when we turn our attention to the oeuvre that we ask: What is open? Now, the open cannot then be circumscribed, like the space of a stage at which we might be a spectator, since it is nothing without a re-opening. We cannot even say without danger, "Machiavelli opened," because that event that we imagine was, at the moment it took place, contingent upon future events. The opening of the oeuvre is commanded, of course, by the first entrance that is its own, but it supposes other entrances as well; it is only because these entrances are multiplied in the course of time that it exists as such. It is legitimate to maintain that the writer Machiavelli speaks in 1513 of politics and history in such a way that centuries later, others, riveted to their condition, can hear him and speak in his hearing: and that he lives his time as he might live future times, of which he can know nothing, and that he thus prepares in advance a place for others. But we must also recognize as the other side of this power the quest for the word of the other; we must recognize that the writer of that word is missing, and that his oeuvre would not exist without that word. It supervenes in the repetition and variations of the discourse to which the oeuvre calls out. In this sense, far from closing before those who are deprived of the experience of its author, it does not cease asking for their collaboration. It is not Machiavelli's first readers, however intelligent they have been, well advised as to his intentions, and familiar with the world he speaks of, capable of grasping countless meanings that would later be missed—it is not the Guicciardini, Vettori, Buondelmonti, Rucellai, installed as they were within the same horizons as he, who are the best situated to give the oeuvre the opening it requires. It is those who live in a world the author could not conceive of, for whom his experience has become shadowy and who must withstand the test of the difference of places and paths. The more that difference grows, the greater the chances of the opening of the oeuvre. A simple chance, it is true, because the passage of time also brings with it the threat of the work's erasure or contraction. Moreover, it is possible that we may be mistaken as to its fate: we may think it dead, while the future may make it speak again. Or we may attribute virtues to it that it has in our eyes only, so that it offers us no more than an occasion to flesh out our fantasies. This doubt, let us repeat, is ineluctable. He who would revive a work always runs the risk, however great the author's reputation, of bringing forth a mere phantom, of sinking into an abyss of chimeras. But this doubt and this risk at least have the merit of reminding him of the condition of the writer, and of the impossibility, again in that ultimate test, of cutting his ties. For the writer after all did not know whether he was writing for a long time, however confident he may have been in his own strength. His imagination did not post him two or twenty centuries into the future to keep watch over the repercussions of his words; he spoke, as we said, in such a way that others far off could hear and speak in turn to his listening, from his own place; but there was no provision, no conjecture in that anticipation and no point of repair that could testify to the condition of the other. If he spoke in that way, it was without even being able to want to do so, precisely because that other, beyond a certain horizon, was absolutely hidden from him, and because in assuming the risk, in isolation, of putting the settled and accomplished again into play, of making his own condition the support of Being, in a certain region, he attracted to him all those who, later, in the neighborhood of the same region, would find themselves, in different conditions, exposed to the same indetermination.

Thus it would be futile to pretend to remove the oeuvre from the risk on which it is founded, to give it mastery over its domain. It awaits the risk of the other, expecting from him or her a new putting back into play that testifies to the first. Too much faith and reverence does not serve it. We are amazed, for example, that the writer had such great power to embrace his time, to perceive or foresee what escaped the attention of his contemporaries. But homage blinds: it is not that sort of power that makes the power of the work; and, moreover, we do not know what Machiavelli's was. Historians maintain that Guicciardini had more than he; if we are to believe them, he assessed events more accurately, had a better sense of the resistance of institutions, and was not one to let himself be deceived about the chances of a revolution in Italy. Should we challenge their view? But in that case what we should say is entirely different and almost the opposite: what is admirable is rather that the writer, rooted as he was in a certain milieu, a certain period, was able to disengage himself sufficiently to be able to think history in its essence. Now at this point the interrogation immediately reclaims its rights; the relationship of the writer to his time loses its initial meaning, and the strangeness of our own situation is revealed. Or else we marvel at a thought that was able to escape from the sensible world; we say that the work has succeeded in reaching eternity, that the truth it proffers is unattached to time and place; but it is a way of insinuating that one is nothing more in one's discourse than what one designates in it. In this case we keep silent about the fact that this presumed escape requires the active complicity of the interpreter, situated in his or her time and place; and no sooner do we identify that eternal part that we hold to be intrinsic to the work, and place that "truth" beneath the reader's gaze, than we rekindle the critical debate and find our opponents using against us what we used against them: unrecognizable in this new guise, again the eternal truth. The oeuvre we had contrived to shelter from time falls back beneath its sway in such a way that it makes us wonder now about its identity.

Yet it is evident that the oeuvre maintains its presence at a distance from the time and place in which its author wrote. But we cannot form a concept of that presence unless we set aside the conventions that govern the usual conception of time. The oeuvre is not present in the sense that, being a thing of the past, it is represented, and has that particular virtue in representation of making that to which it was formerly present appear; it is present in that it is not past. But if it is not past, it is not because it is timeless, and because there is in it no place for *passage* into the *passed*. We are not before the alternative of either envisioning the oeuvre as a discourse that was held in one place, at one time, and of determining in consequence what it was and what the world was that it named and the reality into which it inscribed itself, or of focusing, within it, on the "ideas" that increase the treasury of the mind. Nor is this alternative ever decided absolutely in practice. In actuality, whatever may be the stated intention of—and commentary made by—a particular practice, no one can retain one of the two terms of the alternative. Those who read Machiavelli as historians, and only want to resuscitate the past as the present it once was, unwittingly make the author's word emanate beyond the field in which they claimed to enclose it; those who believe themselves to be reading him as a philosopher and extracting from the dross of the discourse the nugget of meaning that time cannot tarnish are not unaware of his historical incarnation: not only is Machiavelli, in their eyes, a writer of the sixteenth century (and nothing they understand of him can be understood without knowing that before him and after him others had thought about politics), but it is by the experience of his singular discourse and within the horizons of the experience to which it is bound that it attains to what they consider to be the universal. Nevertheless, it is not a matter of indifference to recognize the impossibility of the alternative, for our reading finds its meaning in knowing that the same necessity reaches out toward Machiavelli's time and place and sustains a reflection on politics as such. That reading requires that we take upon ourselves the author's word as it occurs in the frequentation of things and other people, in its own world, in the actuality of a discourse that is dated and localized, and it requires at the same time that we receive a power of expression that surpasses all the particular modes of expression, that we discover in the work an origin that is not in time, behind us, but rather that of a task. But if it is true that the oeuvre is neither a thing of the past, nor outside time, there is nothing to be gained in deciding that it is both at once and that it would be appropriate to consider it from these two aspects. For it must be that it never had its full identity in time, since it has remained alive centuries after having been produced; just as it must be that it is not a stranger to time, since it can attract us, both by its language and by what it makes manifest, toward a region of the past. If it is still present to the distant reader, it is because it was never present after the manner of things, people, or words in the world, which are conditioned by their mutual demands; that it was, rather, instituted from a retreat; that this relation was not canceled, but itself held in abeyance, that its terms could no longer pass for present, certain terms, but were designated as substitutes for other possible terms—past or future terms that, themselves substitutes, had never been able to or would never be able to fit in to the closure of a relation. But to say that the oeuvre was instituted from a retreat does not mean that it is negativity itself. It is not just that it is always, in its retreat, engaged in a world from which it disengages itself, and that the relation it keeps in abeyance has a form to which it is subject; it is that it is still founded as a term—however different it may be from any particular term—and that it is still bound to a demand—however different it may be from all the demands by which exchange in the world is conditioned. A term that, the moment it is removed from the series of the terms of the world and becomes by virtue of that very fact a non-substitutable term, becomes the origin of an incessant return to experience, bringing in the principle of an indefinite substitution. A demand that, as soon as it is freed from any determinate demand—approbation, help, or merely response—as soon as the author's desire is abolished, becomes the interminable demand of a relation to itself of what occurs in time, of what will be given to others, and therefore an interminable demand of the discourse that will bear testimony to it. Thus, that fact that that this term cannot be identified, that this demand is without object, that the origin to which we refer is not located at any point of the intelligible or sensible world—this does not mean that we can turn away from it. The presence of the oeuvre in the coincidence of thought with itself is inconceivable; but the forgetting of the fact that, in the experience of the ever postponed difference, the being that is specific to the oeuvre is pronounced, would in turn proceed from a misunderstanding of time, from a flight before the enigma of instauration, in which past and future only separate to pass into one another. For once the oeuvre exists, it is its lapse into the past: the word that is proffered there is for everyone, beginning with the author, what has taken *place;* we will never be able to hear it save from this place. Its fall is even heavier than that of any word, because it is not joined to this place accidentally, but it hollows it out in naming itself there. And the oeuvre, as soon as it exists, is launched: it is always beyond what we can grasp of it; its word [*parole*] is not behind, but ahead; what we understand of it has not yet been understood, and is addressed, through us, to others yet to be born. And its launching is of a different order than that of words the most assured of a future, words of knowledge, because it is maintained—through the direct hardships of events, the mutations of practice, collective thought and sensitivity—in a time that exposes it to danger and forces it to continually demonstrate its power.

Doubtless among the innumerable writings that adorn themselves with the attributes of the oeuvre, there are few that possess the virtue of instauration. But those that do possess this quality modify our experience of time. With them, a dimension of the present ordinarily hidden is unveiled. As I return to Machiavelli's oeuvre, I encounter nothing that gives its limit to this movement, but I am myself turned back and subjected to its impulsion—without the latter delivering me from its attraction, however. I find myself caught in a loop such that I can only slide toward the past and, following the same direction, from the past to the future and from the future to the past. If the oeuvre is present for me, it is because its presence envelops me, because time is not abolished, but reflected, and because I am implicated in that reflection. In vain would I attempt to discover in the events of the past or the future the wherewithal to account for its appearance or disappearance; I would only succeed on the condition of dissimulating that I only think those events in already thinking the work itself. In vain would I affirm on the contrary that the oeuvre is in its essence indifferent to the events of history (that it does not age, as we like to say), I know very well that many propositions cannot be repeated as they stand, that even its language—I could not use it as is, in my time, and that, unless I were to retain only rather impoverished generalities, I must take some distance in order to restore to it its strength. The present that envelops me at once includes and excludes the difference of the past and the future, and I can think it only in this dual relation, that is, in knowing that history overruns the oeuvre, and when I attach myself to the work, in discovering history within it; in a more general sense, in knowing that the world is outside and in discovering it inside the oeuvre, to know at once the division of outside and inside and its obliteration. Thus inseparable from the reflection that the work inaugurates and that is never done being completed (at least so long as there are readers to take it upon themselves), a deflection takes place, which manifests the elusion of history or of the world: at the same time it offers itself as present, the work gives itself in its singular identity.

When we speak of the present of the work, we speak, then, of the present of history as well—of that history the oeuvre gives us to think within it and indicates outside it. The Italy of the sixteenth century is far away—defunct its institutions and the political mores that reigned at the time, as is the Roman Republic whose memory haunts *The Prince* and *The Discourses*. It is not true that I can recognize in the crisis of the Florentine regime or the conflict between the *popolo minuto* and the *popolo grasso* or between the patriciate and the plebs, or in the phenomenon of tyranny, the traits of a present-day experience. The concepts of class war, democracy, and totalitarianism that assist us in conceptualizing the politics of our time—we cannot apply them to the Greco-Roman period or the Renaissance without their losing part of their relevance. But however manifest the difference in societal forms and the passage in time from one to the other may be, the fact remains that, at least within certain limits, the past and the present, and the future as we imagine it in our time, retain a kinship; or more precisely there is, consubstantially to the time that passes, a time that does not pass, a trial that is reenacted in terms ever new—for example, of the division of classes, of Power and the Law, of the state and civil society, of the real and the imaginary. It is not that one can treat it as if, beyond the observed variations, there were in each case an essence, as if there were, composed of all these essences, one essence of the political. When we think we grasp it, we embrace a phantom; generalities declare themselves that are neither true nor false, because they apply to all situations and do not prompt us to think of any one in particular. But it is impossible to consider as strangers to one another phenomena that reciprocally illuminate one another, that, precisely because they are close to one another but do not overlap, array themselves in a symbolic field, taking their places opposite one other as signifieds and signifiers. It is their gathering in one selfsame place that the oeuvre makes it possible for us to conceptualize; however it may gather, it holds together, causes to gravitate in the same orbit, or rather, in the orbit of the Same, that which without it would not be. In this sense, whatever it may announce about history, it has us read a destiny in it; it has us read something in it that is to be read because it is written there, or writes itself there; something that does not have its condition in the Great Book or the Great Author, that even silently excludes faith in the infinite *logos*—so assured is the oeuvre to produce the true—since this is nothing without the contingency of the signs and of their difference, since, without being in time the way events or structures are, that only installs us in the present of history in allowing us to discover that present as still singular.

What a deliverance, indeed, if all we found in the oeuvre were thoughts born of foreign thoughts and bearing other thoughts, if it were only the stage representing the point of departure from which we leave to advance toward the truth—and if politics, of which the oeuvre speaks, allowed itself to be defined as a set of relations among others, which in every era had its form determined by being subjected to an instituted social system? Thus we would stand in the unlimited Openness of knowledge. Or again, what a deliverance, if we were completing our period of mourning for the being of the oeuvre and the being of history, and consequently had to be satisfied with the flight of meaning? But if it is impossible to be certain of the truth of the oeuvre and to give an account of the "knowledge" it contributes, or to evaluate even the power of knowledge with which it charges its posterity, it is no less impossible to doubt that it has an identity and that within it what is named is history—and, consequently, that meaning is what is at stake in interpretation.

To seek the meaning of the oeuvre, we said, is necessarily to seek the *being* of the oeuvre; it is to learn to discover the interrogation in the oeuvre and to confront the enigma of instauration, without ever being able to sidestep the risk that the word of the other initially assumed. But to question the being of the oeuvre is to desire to hear what is pronounced about being in the oeuvre. That endeavor requires that we apply ourselves to hearing what the writer hears during his era, as the yet unpronounced truth of the political discourse; that we attempt to reawaken the work [*travail*] that modifies, displaces, or ruins the already acquired meanings, in order to let what they cover up emerge; and, lastly, that we familiarize ourselves with the society and times that constitute the locus of the dissimulation and uncovering. And, in truth, what would it be to question the oeuvre of Machiavelli, if not to question the meaning of discourse and the meaning of the things it names? What would it mean to focus on the interrogation within the oeuvre, if not to discover within the discourse the meaning of that interrogation and in the world in which it is ordered the meaning of what is given to be interrogated? We are always brought back to the question of meaning, or, more accurately, we never cease confronting it. But it can only be rightly formulated if we remain within the space of the oeuvre, if we do not cease relating our position to a place, to a time of discourse, and continue to undergo the experience of its origin.

How odd our preoccupations must seem to the reader who expected us to proceed directly to the examination of our author's political ideas, and to state ours. All the more strange, in that politics seems to be the domain of action par excellence, so that one might expect it to communicate to the words that reflect it its own rapid and decisive movement. Let us leave aside, for the moment, the question of the precise sense in which politics is action, whether it has ever been able—whether it can ever dispense with speech, whether speech does no more than accompany it, clothe it, or disguise it; or even whether the very division between speaking and acting is as obvious as the majority of our contemporaries find it to be, satisfied as they are to convert the word into a complement—or, the most daring, into a conjunction—of action. I have only to refer the reader to Machiavelli to help him get over his surprise or find it more congenial. For there is no doubt that he speaks to the reader of politics; and yet, in *The Prince*, and even more so in *The Discourses*, how many meandering paths he discovers, or—to use a word that better names the enemy of the science of action—how much philosophy. On time, on the repetition and change that make up the substance of history, on the relationship of man with nature, on good and evil, *virtù* and Fortune, on reason and unreason, how many words that are free from the test of demonstration, whose only validity resides in their sustaining one another to flesh out the experience of being. And in the narration of events or the depiction of characters, that way of holding back the surprise, of presenting the argument in the form of a plot, of varying the tone of voice, of blending sobriety with irony, incitement with lyricism, of turning the grave and graceful phrase, of wielding metaphor, allusion, or ellipsis—how many signs of what the sociologist would today call literature.

No, it is true that Machiavelli does not reflect on the status of his oeuvre. But that is perhaps because he is writing during a period when thought still knows itself to be in the form of the oeuvre, in which the oeuvre is fully entitled to be the place of metamorphosis and instauration—a time in which the division between science and political philosophy, between art and demonstrative discourse has not yet become a trenchant opposition, such that thought is unaware of itself in what it thinks. He who, in the little town of San Andrea del Casciano, to which exile had relegated him, takes off his everyday clothes each evening and puts on his court attire before entering his study, and, once he is in the presence of the men of Ancient Greece and Rome forgets (so he tells us) even the fear of death—how can we doubt that he knows the threshold of writing and the scene the oeuvre opens up in the space of the world?

But because this knowledge is becoming increasingly obscured, what Machiavelli knew we can only know by means of a violent movement that pulls thought away from its degradation in the product of knowledge. All we can do is drag the question of the being of the oeuvre, which the oeuvre opened silently, onto the front of the stage. That violence is not without exposing us to a new danger. For such is the connotation today of the word *oeuvre*—and not only to others, but to myself as well—that we are tempted to understand that the *oeuvre* of thought is an *oeuvre* qua *oeuvre d'art*, or artwork, and, like the *oeuvre d'art* itself, we most generally only glorify it with one hand while subjugating it with the other to its power as fiction. We risk losing sight of the task it assigns us, the singular relationship to knowledge that is instituted under its authority. Yet this disturbance is still the effect of a naïve belief in the opposition between the real and the imaginary. It is not because we reject the realist reading of *The Prince* that we are left with the sole alternative of reading it as fiction. The situations of the characters that the work puts on stage—we know that they are not invented, we can know them through other testimonies than that of the author, and in them we look for historical truth. Our point is just that they only signify through one another: they are tied together in such a way that we can only relate to the real they designate in remaining caught up in their interconnections. Thus, we recognize that *The Prince* is symbolic the way a poem is, although that symbolism is not the same as that of the poem. Of course it is not insignificant for us to learn that the historical Cesare Borgia only partially resembles the Cesare Borgia described by Machiavelli; to the extent that we can be sure of the distortion to which the writer subjects his model, and if we are further capable of finding similar distortions in his work, we have a precious indication of the symbolic constitution of the oeuvre; but in vain would we claim to decry an error on the author's part on that account. The Cesare Borgia of *The Prince* is a Machiavellian hero who stimulates thought on the function of the prince, the relation between power and the people, the conflicts causing factions within the dominant class, and the limits of rational action. His traits are significant only to the extent that they differ from those of other Machiavellian figures, such as Giovampagolo Baglioni or Francesco Sforza, for example. If in the name of historical exactitude we made him into an imaginary hero, we would be forgetting that the supposedly real Cesare Borgia could teach us nothing about politics and history—or that in lending him a different voice, a different role than did Machiavelli, we would have to put him on a different stage, call in other actors, develop a different plot. Finally, it is not true that the Machiavellian hero is not that of history. He is historical in a different sense than the Duke who conquers Romagna; he opens a question whose roots go back to a time prior to his own, and that survives the disappearance of his undertaking. Thus we would also be wrong in thinking that the liberties taken by our author with known facts attest to the immaturity of the science of his era. For while it is certain that political thought is nourished by the historian's knowledge, that the historian does much more than bring subject matter to be reflected upon by the philosopher, and that he uncovers in the past a depth and a variety of determinations that modify the requirements of thought, by the same token we must recognize that that reflection and those requirements never give way before the ideal of so-called exact knowledge.

Do you believe, for example, that the discourse of Karl Marx, for having benefited from the political economy and history of his time, is less symbolic than that of Machiavelli? The Louis-Napoleon Bonaparte of the *18 Brumaire* is a Marxist hero and not a replica of the figure who dominated the French for twenty years and whose behavior, motives, and social role are the object of precise and in principle infinite historical inquiry. If he matters to us, it is solely, or even primarily, because we seek in him the faithful image of reality, and we are not done with him if we discover, for example, that the author has misunderstood the meaning of the political divisions that riddled the French bourgeoisie and aristocracy under the July Monarchy. He attracts us, and we are never done trying to decipher him, because he exposes the ambiguity of power, enrooted as he is in class society and sufficiently detached from it to mystify all groups; because, considering the space devoted to the illusions of the classes, in the accession of Bonapartism, we are led to doubt the possibility of reducing a political phenomenon to the sole framework of economic struggle; and considering also the status given to the event, as at once perturbation and acceleration of social development, we are also induced to reflect on the role of the rational and the irrational in history. The Marxist Bonaparte is one of the mediators we need to conceptualize the nature of the state and political bureaucracy, but, like the Machiavellian heroes, he speaks only within the world of the oeuvre, in the relationship he maintains with the other protagonists staged by Marx.

When the historian, in the realist perspective that is characteristic of him, accuses Machiavelli or Marx of turning their backs on the facts and betraying historical truth, he is wrong. He reminds us of the family member of a novelist who indignantly protests against the transformations made to the events, landscape, and characters from which the story draws its substance. True, his error is not the same: the family member does not understand the nature of the oeuvre; we do not hesitate to approve Proust's response to the reproaches of a furious woman friend who thinks she has been taken as the model. He decries the stupidity of socialites who think you "*fait entrer ainsi une personne dans un livre*" (put a person in a book that way).[2] But although it is risky to take the comparison too far, and to look at the Machiavellian Borgia or the Marxist Bonaparte the same way one does Odette de Crécy or Baron Charlus, still, the vice of realism perverts the reading of the oeuvre of thought just as it does that of the oeuvre d'art. There is an affinity between the philosophical and the literary modes of expression, and Machiavelli's characters and those of the novelist both have, to varying degrees, a symbolic function. The odd thing is that we are perfectly willing these days to accept that the oeuvre d'art is an oeuvre of thought, but not the reverse. We admit—nay, insist—that literature participates in the unveiling of being, but prefer to ignore the fact that the philosopher, and anyone who applies himself to reflecting on history and politics, is a writer, and as such never simply exposes things in their nakedness, but must give them the body of his or her language in order to show them.

In conceding this, it would seem we are giving up the solidity of the concept. But perhaps that fear conceals a different one: the fear of confronting the enigma of an oeuvre of thought that, in contrast with the oeuvre d'art, is an oeuvre only insofar as it calls upon the reader to question it, and not just to inherit in silence the motions of its discourse but to take the floor, to find within its precinct the voice of a critical discourse, to summon ever more readers to the debate of which it has become the origin and object.

Part 2

The Concept of Machiavellianism

Author's Note

The fortunes of Machiavelli aroused the curiosity of criticism very early, and an extensive literature is devoted to him. We have drawn most of our information from the works mentioned below. The list does not claim to be an exhaustive bibliography on the subject. Moreover, some additional works will be cited in the course of our analyses as they touch on particular points.

General Works

Artaud de Montor, A. F. *Machiavel, son génie et son erreur.* 2 vols. Paris, 1883.

Benoist, C. *Le Machiavélisme,* vol. 3, *Après Machiavel.* Paris, 1936.

Burd, L. A. *Il Principe.* Oxford, UK: 1891.

Croce, B. *Storia dell'età barocca in Italia.* Bari, 1929.

Derôme, L. "Histoire de la réputation de Machiavel, sa doctrine et sa mémoire d'après des documents nouveaux." *Correspondant* 127, 8–9. Paris, 1882.

Meinecke, F. *Die Idee der Staatsräson in der neueren Geschichte.* Munich-Berlin, 1924.

Panella, A. *Gli antimachiavellici.* Florence, 1943.

Procacci, G. *Studi sulla fortuna del Machiavelli.* Rome, 1965.

Sorrentino, A. *Storia dell' antimachiavellismo europeo.* Naples, 1934.

Tommasini, O. *La vita e gli scritti di Niccolò Machiavelli nella loro relazione col machiavellismo.* 2 vols. Turin and Rome, 1882–1911.

Villari, P. *Niccolò Machiavelli e i suoi tempi.* 3 vols. Milan: Ulrico Hoepli, 1912.

Studies on Specific Aspects

Alderisio, F. "Nuova Rivista Storica." *La critica straniera su Machiavelli nell' ultimo quindicenio,* 1940, 24, 1–2.

Battista, A. M. "Rassegna di politica e di storia." *La penetrazione del Machiavelli in Francia nel secolo XVI,* May–June 1960.

Bertini, G. M. "La fortuna di Machiavelli in Spagna." *Quaderni Ibero-Americani*, Nov. 1946–Jan. 1947.

Charbonnel, J. R. *La pensée italienne au xvie siècle et le courant libertin*. Paris, 1919. Geneva: Slatkine Reprints, 1969.

Chérel, A. *La pensée de Machiavel en France*. Paris, 1936.

Curcio, C. *Machiavelli nel Risorgimento*. Milan, 1953.

Elkan, A. *Die Entdeckung Machiavellis in Deutschland zu Beginn des 19 Jahrh.*, in *Historische Zeitschrift*, CXIX, 1919.

Meyer, E. "Litterarhistorische Forschungen." *Machiavelli and the Elizabethan drama*. Weimar, 1897.

Praz, M. *Machiavelli e gl'inglese dell' epoca elisabettiana*. Quaderni di Civilta Moderna 2, Florence: Vallechi Editore, 1930.

Thuau, E. *Raison d'État de pensée politique à l'époque de Richelieu*. Paris, 1966.

Waille, V. *Machiavel en France*. Paris, 1884.

Biographical Information

Artaud de Montor, A. F. *Machiavel, son génie et son erreur*. 2 vols. Paris, 1883.

Norsa, A. Appendix. *Il principio della forza nel pensiero politico di Niccolò Machiavelli*. Milan, 1936.

Santonastasio, G. *Machiavelli*. Milan, 1947.

Before reading Machiavelli, we have a certain idea of Machiavellianism. Although we may know nothing about the man and his work, we use the term without hesitation. It designates a character, a mode of behavior, or an action as surely as the word doorknob designates a certain object; embedded in the language, its derivation matters little: it serves. What Guiraudet wrote at the end of the eighteenth century, it seems that we can still repeat: "The name Machiavelli seems consecrated in all languages to recall or even to express the detours and heinous acts of the shrewdest, most criminal politics. Most of those who have pronounced it, like all the other words of a language, before knowing what it means and whence it is derived . . . must have believed it was that of a tyrant."[1] Whether Machiavelli deserves that reputation or not, whether it seems to be the result of a tragic misunderstanding or the just deserts of a despicable undertaking, all will nevertheless agree that we cannot equate the popular conception of Machiavellianism and the idea of the oeuvre. The idea has a meaning one can try to elucidate, but not of the same order as the one we will seek in reading the oeuvre. We understand it that much better by letting language do its work, by granting the term the power of expression it has prior to reflection, in common parlance, in the variety of its acceptations. As we apprehend it in this way, Machiavellianism is the index of a *collective representation:* what it evokes—it matters little whether we impute its origin to the Florentine writer, whether we admit it, validate it, deplore it, fight against it, challenge its foundation in reality—concerns our experience of politics and more generally human conduct. But as to the oeuvre, even he who thinks he can extract the doctrine of Machiavellianism from it is tied to it in such a way that perhaps no one else will share his conviction; his thought is exerted in keeping with a requirement of truth; he wants to know what is truly said, and whether the truly said is true or not.

The interpreters who apply themselves, the most seriously as can be, it seems, to demonstrating that the doctrine of Machiavelli was not Machiavellianism in the vulgar sense of the term, or that the use of the term is treasonous with respect to the oeuvre, are wasting their time. They cannot keep themselves from using it. Its use is so universally consecrated that no other term lends itself to fulfilling the same function. But if we are not empowered to abolish the popular conception of Machiavellianism, neither can we pretend not to know it. The fact that it was formed and has retained all its vitality for more than four centuries poses a problem we cannot avoid, because it concerns the prejudice of reading. It is all a matter of formulating it unambiguously, that is, without mixing at the beginning stages what we can learn from the examination of a representation and what we can learn from the reading of the texts. In considering the *imago* of Machiavelli in which certain beliefs about politics, the perversity of power and of man in general are condensed, we ask: What can that *imago* teach us about the sociological effect of the oeuvre?

What is that *imago?* What is Machiavellianism in the mythology of the modern mind? What is a Machiavellian personage? A Machiavellian undertaking or destiny? Although there are elements of treachery and bad faith in Machiavellianism, as Littré points out, neither of these two concepts accounts for it fully. Treachery can be cowardly, the man of bad faith uncertain about his goals: both of them lack, or at least do not necessarily entail, the conscious will to use treason or lying as a means to reach a deliberately set goal. Machiavellianism implies first of all the idea of a mastery of one's conduct. To be Machiavellian is to do evil intentionally, to put one's knowledge at the service of a design that is essentially detrimental to someone else. Hence one cannot be Machiavellian in the way one just *is* crafty or devious, by nature. If it includes ruse, it is a methodical ruse—if a crime, then one that bears the mark of an operation rigorously adjusted to the intention of the agent, or fully aware of what it is about.

Thus we see in common representation a certain number of traits that give it its originality. On first examination, we see the calculation of means intended to attain a certain goal, the foreseeing of whatever series of interrelated moves will ensure the success of a given undertaking, the anticipation of the conduct of the adversaries and how to foil it. In short, the Machiavellian is considered to be a strategist; but this strategist always uses stratagems. He acts in keeping with a plan known to himself alone, in such a way that his victims fall into the traps he has cunningly laid for them. In addition to calculation and ruse, the principle of secrecy commands his acts. He wears a mask that on all occasions hides from the eyes of others the movements of his soul. Better yet, he does not yield to those movements. He is entirely taken up with accomplishing his goals and allows himself to be distracted by neither hatred nor resentment, nor by any prompting that would risk putting him another's power. This last trait is essential: he is *sovereign*. Before him all men are naïve, ignorant of the roles reserved for them in the plot he has devised. He seems to have made it his rule of action always to treat others as means, thus demonstrating that he is of a different essence from the vulgar, removed from them by all the distance separating subject from object. But it must be further specified that this sovereignty does not derive from greater intelligence or wickedness alone. He wins it by the ways of acting that make his adversaries recognize him. Thus Machiavellianism, in our view, is not without a mise en scène that at the decisive moment brings to light the actor's total mastery, and not just his power or abilities with respect to his victims. Thus he does more than illustrate a criminal technique; he evokes an art, an activity destined to provide itself with the spectacle of its own success, enchanted with its own result. The Machiavellian takes pleasure in the complicated intrigue he has woven. When he could strike without delay, reach the goal directly, he chooses the oblique approach that will leave his victims time to appreciate the extent of his power and feel the full effect of their misfortune. He is the one who likes to play with his adversary, and not content with winning, maneuvers him into collaborating in his own downfall.

Malefic logic, trick after trick, serene perversity, the voluptuous enjoyment of crime—such are no doubt the components of a term to which we have grown accustomed through literature, the press, and everyday linguistic usage.

Let us consider that representation as I have described it, disregarding for the moment what the historical Florentine Secretary may have been like. Why, I ask, does this complex of traits remain stable over the course of centuries? Why does it strike the imagination of people of various countries and social strata so vividly? There is little use in arguing that certain sorts of behavior are simply Machiavellian, and that we are dealing with a category that subsumes actual experience. There are countless human types, but the stereotyping of characters through the mediation of literature has produced nothing like the Machiavellian type. If the latter fascinates us to such a degree that a word has come to implant its symbol within the nature of language and to consecrate its universal power of expression, that is an indication that its meaning is constituted at a deeper level than that of a typical association of psychological traits— in short, that the representation draws its sustenance from a source that maintains and renews its unity.

The political use of the term immediately comes to mind. It is apparently only one usage, a privileged one, among others. Though Machiavellianism characterizes preferably a kind of political conduct, it always seems charged with a more general meaning. If I hear it said of a statesman that he is Machiavellian, I understand that he is unscrupulous, mystifies his adversaries, stops at nothing to achieve his ends, and enjoys establishing his power on the wreckage of others. The statesman is thus discredited by a term also used by journalists to refer to a clever criminal, or by novelists to conjure up the wickedness of an ambitious woman. Bismarck, for example, is Machiavellian for the historian, as is Mme de Marneffe for Balzac: her criminal virtuosity, premeditated ruse, and artful way of leading Baron Hulot to his ruin earns her the appellation "Machiavel en jupons" [Machiavelli in petticoats].[2] But the accusation of Machiavellianism, the moment it is applied to a politician, takes on a special significance. For it is no longer just an individual as such that is denounced: his behavior seems to reveal an essential relation between man and man, to respond to something that is in the nature of politics, to translate a maliciousness inherent in the very nature of power. There are probably few heads of state, in the most diverse forms of government, who have escaped this accusation. It was leveled at Catherine de Médicis, Oliver Cromwell and Henry VIII, Henri III and Henri IV, Mazarin and Richelieu, Louis XIV, Napoleon I, Louis-Philippe and Napoleon III, Gladstone, Cavour, Bismarck, and a number of our contemporaries. It was even hurled at the Revolutionary Government in France in 1793, personified in its function as power-holder.[3] This points to the fact that, regardless of their individual personalities, politicians and men in power incarnate, in the eyes of their adversaries, at least for a time, the evil domination of man over man. They not only employ condemnable practices, a combination of bad faith, violence, and trickery: they appear as agents of an evil transcending the order of character and conduct, issuing directly from the function of governing itself. Machiavellianism is the name of this evil. It is the name given to politics qua evil; it designates what the common imagination likes to conjure up whenever power is perceived as something absolutely alien, possessed of an unknown and unknowable principle of action—an entity that, located at a distance that cannot be crossed, determines its life in common against its will and is the bane of its existence. As the converse image of men who are governed, doomed to ignorance, to submission, to the trial of an inscrutable destiny, there thus appears the symmetrical construct of the man who governs, knows absolutely what he is doing and where he is going, enjoys total possession of his goals, and takes pleasure in his power over the lives of others.

Thus it is not quite accurate to say with Guiraudet that Machiavelli represents the figure of the tyrant in the eyes of the common people, or that, as a recent critic writes, in the wake of so many others, he is an "incarnation of immortality," a "diabolical being escaped from the world of hell to bring about the perdition of the human race."[4] His traits are more clearly defined. If this were not the case, it would be impossible to understand—without presupposing the miraculous repetition of chance occurrence—why his name has retained through time the symbolic power we recognize in it. This name, the concept of Machiavellianism having been formed around it, confronts us with a differentiated representation that is part of the intellectual mythology of modern humankind. It is as such that it retains our attention, inasmuch as it affords a glimpse of a collective attitude stable through time with respect to certain problems, or, putting it in more neutral terms, a certain region of the real upon which this writer has touched. The myth of Machiavellianism carries with it an indictment of politics; this is what interests me and leads me to assume that it bears some relation to the oeuvre, since it is politics that constitutes the object of the latter.

Clearly the concept cannot be reduced to its political acceptation; it has, as previously stated, a polyvalent usage which, while enduring because of the vigor of its primitive symbolism, might be thought of as degrading it. Nevertheless, the extension of the term does not engender an indeterminateness of meaning. What might at first seem to be an abuse, or as purely accidental (as for example when one speaks of a Machiavellian suitor), only appears so to reflective thought. Mythical thought, on the other hand, maintains in its own way the unity of the representation. It is to the degree that its expressive power increases that the symbol sends its roots down, in its primary function, into the deepest level of meaning. When applied exclusively to politics, the term Machiavellianism can only refer to pernicious conduct or a certain system of traits characteristic of the bad governor, but in the extension of its usage, which seems to divert it from its political meaning, it gains a metaphysical dimension: political perversity absorbs the other modes of perversity; and the power that Machiavellian political conduct has to signify other modes of human behavior causes it to cease designating a particular one, and to take its place within the being of man.

"Incarnation of immorality"—Machiavellianism certainly is that, in all domains, but it changes the meaning of immorality: by lending immorality its face, it suggests the identification of immorality with politics.

As for the question that the myth of Machiavellianism brings with it, which is on the subject of politics (but that subject is hidden beneath various other, simultaneously proposed images), we are in a better position to hear it when we interrogate, along with the myth itself, the past, the period in which it was born; that is, the time following the publication and first dissemination of the oeuvre. One is no doubt astonished at first at the function of Machiavellianism in the ideological struggle. Far from having a univocal value, it only becomes determined by the interplay of antagonistic currents. It is true that what is called Machiavellianism designates Machiavelli's doctrine, which is a specific target that both Churchmen (preoccupied with restoring the authority of Rome) and humanists never tire of attacking—both Protestants and Jesuits; but that target only excites marksmen to the degree that the bolts directed at him ricochet off a living enemy, for the purpose of settling accounts. The enemies are Henri II or Henri III, accused of having made *The Prince* their bedside reading, Henri IV, guilty of having embraced the religion of Machiavelli for the sole purpose of reigning, and Catherine de Médicis above all, despised for having practiced the maxims of the man who was called her Florentine master.[5] But entrenched power turns the weapon against its adversaries, and while in France Machiavellianism is chiefly a symbol of the politics of intolerance, whose goal is to subordinate religion and make it serve the government, in Spain it is associated with the partisans of tolerance, those accused of disturbing religious unity for the sole purpose of ensuring the power of the state.[6] While to the Jesuits Machiavellianism is the breviary of the Reformation, for the Protestants it is synonymous with Jesuitism.[7] Machiavelli is himself the object of a universal hatred, denounced as a heretic, an atheist, a Mohammedan,[8] accused of all possible crimes by those who take turns striving to refute him (going even so far as to adjudge his doctrine more pernicious than the Protestant heresy![9]); but the evils of which he is accused of being the putative father are most often embodied in the present by others. The most famous of his contradictors, the Huguenot Gentillet, accuses him of "contempt for God, perfidy, sodomy, tyranny, cruelty, pillage, foreign usury and other detestable vices,"[10] but his work, destined long to remain the source drawn upon by anti-Machiavellians of every stripe, does not conceal its political intentions. Beyond Machiavelli, it targets the government; the condemnation of the author of *The Prince* is that of the instigators of Saint-Barthélemy.[11] In the course of the sixteenth century, the motivations of the polemics vary with the circumstances, so that Machiavellianism is made to merge in turn with each one of the ideologies that comes to occupy the historical stage and to mobilize a part of public opinion against itself: it is Anglicanism, Calvinism, atheism, Tacitism, Jesuitism, Gallicanism, Averroism; it is, according to Tommasini's formulation, "what events made of it and what hatreds wanted."[12] The figure of Machiavelli, as seen through the shadowy kaleidoscope of Machiavellianism, engenders at will the monstrous configurations of evil.

Enlisted in the cause of every hate, metamorphosing willy-nilly with events, Machiavellianism always presents this peculiar character of capturing men's imaginations and of embodying evil. Such indeed is the constant function that allows the diversity of acceptations of the term to appear in the sixteenth century. Machiavellianism is evil in the same way atheism or heresy is. It is not just the name of an atheistic or heretical doctrine, dreadful among others, or even more dreadful than others: it bodies forth an interdict that cannot be transgressed without exposure to damnation; it is, far more than a work of evil, the center from which malefic works and practices emanate. To fail to recognize this function would be to commit the error of seeing in it no more than a consequence of the ill repute of the author of *The Prince*, and in that ill repute nothing but the result of religious intolerance.

Intolerance and religious hatred—surely these must not be underestimated. Machiavelli's oeuvre, denounced as atheistic, offers in the mid-sixteenth century the occasion for a sinister emulation between Catholic and Protestant clans, vying for the merit of condemning it, and each attributing to the other its shameful paternity. A cursory consideration of the reception it received at the time of its appearance and the circumstances of its publication will serve to bring out the significance of the religious condemnation. At first, no apparent scandal. The pope authorizes the printing of *The Prince* and *The Discourses* through a Brief; a cardinal grants his protection, another accepts the author's dedication.[13] That is because Rome is not yet ablaze with the ardor to reform itself. The oeuvre of the Florentine is not indicted until the Church, condemning its own weakness, because of the progress of heresy, seeks to show dazzling signs of its power and purity. Thus, fifteen years after its publication, it becomes the object of the first attacks. An Englishman, Cardinal Reginald Pole, to whom Thomas Cromwell had ironically recommended the reading of *The Prince*, becomes incensed in vehement terms both over its diabolical words and the justifications furnished by his Italian interlocutors. He had scarcely approached the book when he recognized the hand of Satan. Satan reigning on earth would leave no other precepts to his son before turning the kingdom over to him.[14] The Italian Dominican Ambrose Catharin, otherwise open to modern ideas, denounces the atheism of *The Discourses* and places them at the level of books that Christians must abhor. A Portuguese bishop, Girolamo Osorio, finds that the second chapter of Book 2 of the *Discourses* is a scandalous apology for paganism.[15] These three attacks, which occur in the space of ten years, between 1540 and 1550, set the first features of the accursed doctrine that will be further embroidered upon by the relentless efforts of Christian polemicists, the first result of which will be the condemnation of the Council of Trent. Placed on the index, Machiavelli's oeuvre will henceforth be read prejudicially. As Antonio Panella writes: "Pole, Politi, Osorio, and Paul IV's index constitute a chain forged in the crucible of the Counter-Reformation."[16] Machiavelli appears to be the victim of a time in which the flame of religious intolerance consumes all works of thought, a time not suited to understanding, a time that, in the words of Lucien Febvre, "wants to believe," and clamors to confirm its faith.

But Machiavellianism is not just the product of that intolerance. Does not the oeuvre of the Florentine writer share the redoubtable honor of papal proscription with many others? And who are those who, during the second half of the sixteenth century, escape the accusation of atheism, however far they are from it being warranted? That accusation is at once the most violent one that can be made against an adversary and one of the most frequent, so restrictive have dogmatism and intolerance made the criteria for recognizing the faith of others.[17] To believe his contemporaries, Erasmus is an atheist; and Rabelais and even Luther—to mention only those who have attained international fame. "They were all impious," Lucien Febvre writes, "if we are to believe them—unbelievers and, finally, atheists, great and small."[18] Among the first to launch the term Machiavellian, using it in a pejorative sense that stuck, was Henri Estienne. He distinguished himself particularly by his zeal in precipitating into atheist hell the greatest minds of his day, some of whom were known for their excessive piety.[19] Father Garasse, a Jesuit to whom we owe the crudest and most spirited imprecations against Machiavelli, impassively maintained that Luther was a perfect atheist.[20] From this we must conclude that in a climate of such suspicion Machiavelli's oeuvre could not have been discredited merely by the fact of having been condemned by the chorus leaders of Catholicism and Protestantism.

It is true that to appreciate the significance of religious hostility, one must consider its motives, which are more serious in Machiavelli's case than those normally inspiring the condemnation of works adjudged to be impious or atheistic. From the most famous essays or treatises attacking Machiavelli, it transpires that he committed the crime of encouraging princes to govern without worrying about God, in the conviction that they need be accountable only to themselves for their own actions, and that they should expect no other punishment or reward than the failure or success of their temporal endeavors. These attacks are frequently connected to a critique of absolutism: it appears to go without saying that the sovereign freed from all duty toward God will know no further limits to the exercise of power. The same will be true of moral considerations: indifferent to religion, the prince cannot do otherwise than neglect virtue and find in vice the surest path to triumph. But neither the critique of despotism nor the defense of virtue is in itself a determinative motive. The proof of this is that the anti-Machiavellian Jesuits will not deny themselves the co-optation of precepts of government considered by others as most nefarious, introducing them into Christian instruction, taking care only to maintain the prince in his function as auxiliary to the divine will.[21] As long as the name of God is invoked and the prince appears to govern beneath his supervision, the greatest accommodations can be found with Christian morality. Machiavelli appears to be guilty of having broken that rule; he unleashed scandal as do all those who have had the audacity to violate a taboo.

But this is a violation of a taboo not only in the eyes of the priests, or more generally of men in charge of defending a dogma, whether Protestant or Catholic: denounced by them, his sacrilege mobilizes public opinion against him.

More generally, scandal is only brought about by the intervention of a public—only when a collective reprobation is aroused that sustains and justifies personal attacks. Now just such an anti-Machiavellian public is constituted, at least in France, the moment the work begins to be disseminated. By 1553, the date of the marriage of Catherine de Médicis and Henri d'Orléans, *The Prince* and *The Discourses* are distributed throughout the realm and read both at the royal court—where Tuscan is spoken fluently—and in cultivated milieus; a decade later, we know Machiavelli's reputation is solidly established.[22] At that time, none of the great anti-Machiavellian pamphlets has yet been written. La Boétie writes his *Contr'un* [*against one*] around 1550, which will remain unpublished until 1576; it is in that same year that Gentillet's *Anti-Machiavel* appears, the success of which was soon considerable. Thus Machiavelli's black legend was born, we may assume, before *The Prince* was solemnly condemned by the ideologues, before it became the object of learned and grave refutations; at the very least, it developed parallel to the history of literary anti-Machiavellianism. The origin of that legend is not only to be sought in hatred toward a breaker of idols: the scandal brought about by the image of the prince, governing however he likes, indifferent to Christian principles, absorbed in using his subjects to ensure his glory or pleasure has resonances other than strictly religious. Its strength comes from the fact that it challenges a traditional representation of society. It is not insignificant that popular anti-Machiavellianism was linked in France to an aversion to Catherine de Médicis and her entourage, and more generally to anti-Italianism. Accused of having made *The Prince* her Bible, of having passed its teachings on to her children and of having perverted the Kingdom of France, Catherine appeared to incarnate foreign power, being infinitely distant from her subjects, and having no other justification than the interests of the King. It matters little that the ascendency of absolutism already goes back a long way: once it is deprived of the cortège of justifications furnished by national tradition, power is suddenly perceived in its nakedness, as a system of oppression. But the name Machiavelli symbolizes not only the immoral domination of the foreigner and, in the deepest sense, that which is foreign in domination. It evokes more generally the Italian as one whose commercial, financial, and usurious activities single him out for prosecution and punishment.[23]

It is of course difficult to assess what the legend of Machiavellianism owes to the hostile feelings Italians aroused in Western Europe. But here I believe we touch on one of the sources of the myth. Anti-Machiavellianism brings with it an anti-capitalism that is fed by hatred of Italy and Italians. A rudimentary anti-capitalism, to be sure, but in keeping with an era in which social upheavals engendered by the rapid development of commerce and finance only partially change the traditional structure, in which the typically bourgeois means of production and way of life exist alongside archaic forms, in which the expressions of a modern mentality, however clearly defined they may already be, are just beginning to emerge from the shell of an essentially Christian language. There, where the businessman is still perceived as a grasping monopolist, where the pursuit of profit is called the sin of usury, where the misfortunes brought about by the new play of market forces are imputed to individual immoral practices, the imagination is prompt to project the responsibility for evil onto a specific human type.[24] The Italian merchant, twice guilty, as foreigner and speculator, is merely a scapegoat; but his image, in which the traits of the modern businessman, the implacable strategist whose calculations prepare the ruin of others, are deposited and crystallize, in turn determines the face of the Machiavellian, the cynical theoretician of cunning and exploitation. The unscrupulous political figure, the greedy shopkeeper and financier, the proud ideological apologist of power, are enveloped in one and the same reprobation, and seem to enjoy an equally perverse knowledge and satisfy a boundless appetite for power, the effects of which wreak havoc on society.

The echoes of that popular anti-Machiavellianism reverberate in the critical literature: Gentillet, in including among the crimes of the author of *The Prince* "foreign usury and pillaging," is simply repeating a theme familiar to the public, and that nothing contained in the oeuvre under attack could have led him to discover on his own. Machiavelli, who did not hesitate to write that he was a man who knew nothing of the art of wool, and who would later be criticized for his ignorance of industry and commerce, is only denounced as a theoretician of speculators because political practices and economic ones—the pursuit of power and that of profit—are to some extent merged in the public mind, both being reduced to an art of ploys and schemes that victimize the worthy man.

The best testimony to this representation is offered by the Elizabethan theater. Better than the written book, the play, presented as a spectacle, requires of the public, present and gathered into a group, a complicity with the writer—a sensitivity common to certain psychological and ideological situations. Machiavelli, evoked nearly four hundred times in the theater of Marlowe, Shakespeare, Ben Jonson, and minor writers, is the source of a hit theme the collective imagination never tires of.[25] His name has become such a draw at the beginning of the seventeenth century that it sufficed to include it in the title to win a publisher's favor.[26] What, then, does Machiavellianism symbolize? Atheism and the theory of political murder, writes Mario Praz; the ravenous hunger for power, hypocrisy, premeditated murder (preferably by poison), egotism, subtlety, the art of foresight and political astuteness, says Edward Meyer; Simpson had already pointed to self-awareness in crime. But to these diverse aspects rapaciousness and greed must be added. All agree in recognizing in *The Jew of Malta* the Machiavellian character par excellence.[27]

Perhaps we are distorting the face of Machiavellianism by making these anti-capitalist traits too salient. The satire of Machiavelli revealed in Elizabethan literature is a satire of politics as such. As Mario Praz remarks profoundly, the terms *politic, policy,* and *politician* are taken by the writers of that period in a regularly pejorative sense, while *politician* and *Machiavellian* turn out to be interchangeable.[28] The politician, now mercilessly derided, as in *Sir Politik-Would-be,* now depicted in tragic colors, is both the target of criticism and the fascinating figure on which the reflections of the modern evil are cast.[29] But that image of politics that becomes fixed and acquires its meaning in keeping with a certain representation of society and the myth of Machiavellianism thus condenses all the effects of the anxiety caused by the breakup of the old order. If violence, cruelty, and ruse appeared to the men of the times to be attributes of power, it was not because the spectacle of the immorality of princes was anything new. It was rather because such a spectacle was not a cause of astonishment as long as the relations between men and the status hierarchy seemed independent of the initiatives and actions of individuals. The function of each seemed established once and for all, and society regulated like an organism; the master's violence did not damage the dignity of his role;[30] the prince was cruel, and the tradesman greedy, but these vices were attached to conditions whose legitimacy was not questioned. But the behavior of the politician became an object of scandal, and politics itself threatening, when the rise of capitalism became sufficiently obtrusive to bring about an upheaval of the traditional social order. At that point the procedures to which the prince resorted in order to maintain and extend his power were no longer wrapped in the mists of idealization; they appeared suddenly deprived of the goal that justified them, as part of an activity without any redeeming spiritual dimension—as enigmatic as reprehensible.

The critique of power was inevitably expressed in Christian language. We can hardly be surprised. For centuries, the vision of society had been a religious one; Christian ethics inspired all speculations about social life; the relations between men and classes were never conceived otherwise than in reference to a divine plan for the governing of humankind. When the principle of that dispensation began to be questioned, it was through the old categories that the factors involved in the upheaval were perceived. In opposition to Machiavelli and his destructive teaching, the indignant ideologues lost no time in formulating—and in tirelessly reformulating—the duties of the virtuous prince, in their desire to reconcile the new requirements of power with the religious commandments. The anti-Machiavellians of all kinds found no better arm to oppose their adversary than the accusation of atheism, Satanism, and heresy. But the religious content of the criticism must not make us forget its social significance. What was unbearable was not only that society's interrelations seemed to have lost their moorings in the sacred, but that they had themselves lost their sacred character, that power appeared as the stake in a strictly worldly struggle, and that man became a stranger to man at the same time as his becoming estranged from God.

Machiavellianism as it was imagined doubtless signifies the negation of Christianity, but it is far more a sign of the subversion of the social order. The invectives directed at the Florentine writer by Catholic and Reformation theologians, the maniacal persecutions launched against him by the Jesuits, continuing more than a half-century after his death (his effigy was burned at Ingoldstadt in 1615) are what make up the essential of official anti-Machiavellianism;[31] but this only spreads to the extent that in large circles there has been a condemnation of the theory of "reason of state,"[32] pursuit of profit, and the breaking of the old ties of dependency in work. In the eyes of the majority, Machiavelli was the incarnation of the Satan. This is because evil can only be called Satan. Thus, people repeat that he has escaped from hell for the perdition of the human race; they like to present him as a spirit wandering from nation to nation to spread ruination; they torture his name to make it confess its demoniacal origin; in England his first name is confused with a nickname given to the devil; it becomes habitual to call Machiavellian what was previously called diabolical.[33] But that identification is not only the sign of the offense felt by religious consciousness. Satan is metamorphosed in the guise of Machiavelli. Evil becomes the work of man, of a new man, who, in the middle of this earthly existence, puts all his art to work to fool his fellow man, to turn him into his own creature, to enjoy his misfortune for the sole purpose of exercising power. Evil becomes the work of a human science, which disposes of the established rules, and turns the social order topsy-turvy. Everything that seems to contribute to the downfall of that order is Machiavellian—and therefore, as we have seen, all the ideological currents that in their adversaries' view destroy the spiritual unity of the old world, and therefore the conduct of individuals, whenever it is considered to corrupt human nature.

If, as Croce writes, Machiavellianism becomes at the end of the sixteenth century a ritual reference beneath the pen of the ideologues in all Western Europe, if the term assumes the value of a conventional sign appropriate to the designation of everything hateful in the domination of man by man,[34] the reason for this is that a new face of evil begins to reveal itself, at the very level of social relations—that there is an awakening of consciousness to a tragic situation of man in society or to malefic transcendence of power, and that a question about the being of society is in the process of formulation.

For lack of having succeeded in perceiving in Machiavellianism a collective representation, we condemn ourselves to see in the fortune of this term nothing but the result of the oeuvre's bad reputation, and in that reputation nothing but religious persecutions. The usage of the term, it seems, is too broad to get a fix on it. And, indeed, the fact that a character in Ben Jonson whispers into the ear of a wily woman, "*Do you hear, sweet soul, sweet Radamant, sweet Machavel*," tells us nothing about Machiavelli's oeuvre. The term is generally thought to be artificially grafted onto the oeuvre by men we cannot even be sure of having read it. The reputation of the Italian author, on this view, was fabricated by the Church finding itself in a momentary pass in which it needed to find a scapegoat—in short, for propaganda purposes. The alleged proof of this is that before 1545 the Church ignored the vices of *The Prince* and *The Discourses* and only denounced them after the Counter-Reformation offensive. Why, then, should we look for the first manifestations of anti-Machiavellianism? Because such an interpretation is only convincing if we concentrate our attention on the writings of a certain number of theologians, omitting all consideration of public opinion. However great the influence of the theologians, and however effective Rome's condemnation of the oeuvre, they do not give us the key to anti-Machiavellianism. Despite the affirmations of certain historians, that phenomenon came to expression very early in Italy itself. Bernardo da Giunta, in a letter to Mgr Gaddi (placed at the beginning of the first edition of Machiavelli's works) clearly alludes to the hostility that is directed at *The Prince* and *The Discourses*, and only solicits his support by offering an interpretation that already rejects the common representation of Machiavellianism.[35] The testimony of Busini, fifteen years later, is even more significant: everyone, he writes, hates Machiavelli, "the rich because he teaches the prince how to strip them of their goods, the poor because he teaches how to deprive them of their freedom; the bigots because he is a heretic, the good because he lacks forthrightness, the wicked because he is wickeder and more courageous than they."[36] In the complex of anti-Machiavellian feelings, heresy is mentioned by Busini only among other accusations. To the Italian public, Machiavelli is hateful because he formulates the theory of a power that is exercised at the expense of wealth and freedom, religion and ethics.

But beyond the content of these accusations, what is deserving of our attention is the precocity of a representation that, although it would be further enriched and circulate among various agents for specific ends, immediately achieved general value. In it, at a particular time period, the concrete and multiple expressions of collective aggression were invested; reduced to a common denominator, these constitute the figure of Machiavellianism. This operation shows that, following the lines of demarcation within the social and ideological space, aggression seeks a representation that will at once show and hide the principle of division. In a sense it comes up with this in the form of an image of the nefarious power of man over man: a generalized power, conceived of both as that of the prince over the rest of society, from which he is detached and which becomes his object, and a non-localizable power that arises across the entire range of society, and is the pivot of separation of the Subject, master of the wealth of power or of the new knowledge—of a good, whatever it may be, taken over by the violation of an interdict—and master of men who are at his mercy. And in a sense it is a question of a dissimulation, since the origin of the division is always assigned to *someone*. One is tempted to say that the fiction of Machiavellian power is at the service of a double intention, that of naming the loss of substance of society and of man, by giving form to the undoing of the bond between power and the totality of human existence, and that of warding off the threat of that loss by giving a form *within* society to the Subject whose presence guarantees by a destructive action the belief in its potential unity.

That the representation of Machiavellianism concerns not only a change in the status of politics at the time of the birth of modern society, but a change in the status of the Subject or, more strictly speaking, that it shows that the question of the status of politics and that of the status of the Subject are closely linked—perhaps we should see the surest sign of this in the fiction that opens the *Cartesian Meditations.* Must one not appreciate, in light of political myth, the hypothesis that founds the *cogito?* What is "a certain malignant demon, who is at once exceedingly potent and deceitful, has employed all his artifice to deceive me,"[37] if it is not the ultimate metamorphosis of the Machiavellian master? He has all his traits—the possession of omnipotence through the alliance between knowledge and lies, and the setting up of a plot that brings about the downfall of men by a work that is at the same time a game, since its sole effect is the spectacle of the fascinated dreamer ("I will suppose that the sky, the air, the earth, colors, figures, sounds, and all the external things that we see, are nothing but illusion and deception, by means of which he has taken my credulity by surprise"[38]). If the inauguration of the subject who knows scientifically must pass through the destitution of the Great Deceiver whose power is in depriving man of his bond with Being, is this not an indication of what is at stake in the myth? It is true that the evil genius is a figure of transcendence, while the Machiavellian politician represents the Other *within* society, man turned against man. But the Cartesian subject does not resemble the one of the medieval tradition: he borrows from a projection in the other world a new relation of man to man; in incarnating the *absurd* thought that the sovereign power is entirely deception, he points out a contradiction encountered in reality. And too little attention has been paid to the fact that the defeat of the hypothesis requires the identification of Descartes with the evil genius, that is, that he turns against himself and becomes the author of the division between thought and Being: "if, taking up an opposing side, I use all my efforts to fool myself, pretending that all these thoughts are false and imaginary."[39] Now we must remember the price we paid for the founding of science. With the impossibility of fooling ourselves, with the appearance of self to self, with the putting out of commission of the evil genius, which is not immediately his annulment ("and he may fool me as much as he likes, he can never reduce me to nothingness, as long as I go on thinking something"[40]), thought and existence remain joined, while the difference between inner and outer fades away. Power and knowledge are joined in the light of consciousness on condition that the operation of that fading away remains in shadow. The absurd thought thus resists destruction by bearing the trace of the omission that is covered up by the certainty of the *cogito*. Science keeps a secret link with the great deception—a link that the collective imagination does not cease reconnecting in the modern mythology, which is committed to the dichotomy between the good knowledge and power and their perverse counterparts, between the mastery of nature and Machiavellianism against nature. But if it may be said that the representation of Machiavellianism is thus seen as linked to the advent of the Subject, to the status of consciousness in modern times, it must not be forgotten that this status is defined reciprocally only in its relation to politics. The question of power, as power detached from society, and arising from within itself to confer upon itself a total exteriority in the representation it acquires of itself, that question, without being stated, sustains the movement that institutes the final guarantee of the operations of knowledge and that constantly seeks its legitimization by warding off an evil spell.

That the representation of Machiavellianism continues to exist, while the initial scandal that was attached to it has faded away—or better, that a term has been engendered, as if by the decapitation of the proper name, capable of introducing into the neutrality of language an inflection of the meaning of power—this phenomenon cannot be understood without appreciating all that it brings into play touching the relation of man to politics in the history of modern societies.

In anticipating such an appreciation, I must admit that reflection on the myth is not a matter of indifference with respect to understanding the oeuvre. Not that there is any reason to investigate the question of whether Machiavelli is or is not the author of a doctrine the gist of which is condensed in the concept of Machiavellianism. The myth and the oeuvre, as we have already observed, are incommensurable. But one can presume that the latter raised questions that inscribed their effect within a hiatus of social experience that touched common beliefs to the quick. And one can also wonder what grip these beliefs continue to hold on those who think themselves able, by the sole virtue of reading, to dispose freely of the questions.

Part 3

Reading *The Prince*

1

First Signs

It is in a letter addressed by the author on December 10, 1513, to his friend Francesco Vettori that we find the only irrefutable information on the relevant date and circumstances of the composition of *The Prince.* That letter—well known and oft quoted because of its depiction of his life in Sant'Andrea in Percussina, his place of retreat upon release from prison—reveals his schedule during the course of the last months of the year. He relates that in September he was up before sunrise retrieving thrushes from the snares he had set out the previous evening. "Since then," he writes, he has missed "that way of killing time." He continues: "I shall tell you about my life. I get up in the morning with the sun and go into one of my woods that I am having cut down; there I spend a couple of hours inspecting the work of the previous day and kill some time with the woodsmen who always have some dispute on their hands either among themselves or with their neighbors . . . Upon leaving the woods, I go to a spring; from there, to one of the places where I hang my bird nets. I have a book under my arm: Dante, Petrarch, or one of the minor poets like Tibullus, Ovid, or some such. I read about their amorous passions and their loves, remember my own, and these reflections make me happy for a while. Then I make my way along the road toward the inn, I chat with passersby, I ask news of their regions, I learn about various matters, I observe mankind: the variety of its tastes, the diversity of its fancies. By then it is time to eat; with my household I eat what food this poor farm and my minuscule patrimony yield. When I have finished eating, I return to the inn, where there usually are the innkeeper, a butcher, a miller, and a couple of kiln workers. I slum around with them for the rest of the day playing *cricca* and backgammon: these games lead to thousands of squabbles and endless abuses and vituperations. More often than not we are wrangling over a penny; be that as it may, people can hear us yelling even in San Casciano. It is with this lousy bunch that I have to surround myself to keep my brain from getting moldy, it is thus that I protect myself from Fortuna's wicked dealings with me, almost happy to see that she has brought me so low, and curious to see whether she will end up blushing over it. When evening comes, I return home and enter my study; on the threshold I take off my workday clothes, covered with mud and dirt, and put on the garments of court and palace. Fitted out appropriately,

I step inside the venerable courts of the Greeks and Romans, where, so-licitously received by them, I nourish myself on that food that alone is mine and for which I was born; where I am unashamed to converse with them and to question them about the motives for their actions, and they, out of their human kindness, answer me. And for four hours at a time I feel no boredom, I forget all my troubles, I do not dread poverty, and I am not terrified by death. I absorb myself into them completely. And because Dante says that no one understands anything unless he retains what he has understood, I have jotted down what I have profited from in their conversation and composed a short study, *De Principatibus*, in which I delve as deeply as I can into the ideas concerning this topic, discussing the definition of a princedom, the categories of princedoms, how they are acquired, how they are retained, and why they are lost. And if ever any whimsy of mine has given you pleasure, this one should not displease you. It ought to be welcomed by a prince, and especially by a new prince; therefore I am dedicating it to His Magnificence Giuliano. Filippo Casa-vecchia has seen it. He will be able to give you some account of both the work itself and the discussions I have had with him about it. But be aware that I am continually enriching and correcting it."[1]

Until this point, Machiavelli had never made the slightest allusion to a work in progress in his correspondence with Vettori. His most recent letter, which, like the preceding ones, discussed the current political situation, was dated 26 August. We may conclude therefore that he had not begun writing *The Prince* before the end of that summer. Clearly the work was not entirely completed in December, since the author contin-ued to correct and enrich it, but according to the judicious remark of a historian,[2] the lack of references to events after 1513 leads one to be-lieve no substantial revisions could have been made in 1514 or thereafter. Hence it must be considered probable that *The Prince* was composed dur-ing a period of three or four months. But we cannot conclude from that observation that it was summarily executed. The dating of the work, as best as we can establish it, does not tell us how much time the work that went into it took. That would be better estimated by our recalling the role Machiavelli had played on the political scene after 1498, since that is what prompted him to reflect on the nature of power and the behavior of those who possess it, the weakness of governments without a popular base and their similarities to one another, and on the power relations between states. It was in the pursuit of the public affairs in which he was constantly involved that the principles were formed that would guide his work as a theoretician. There is no reason to reject the author's testimony on this point. In his view, *The Prince* is visible proof of the experience he has acquired in his administrative and diplomatic functions. "If only it were read," he writes in the same letter, "it would be evident that the fifteen years I have devoted to the service of the state were spent neither in sleeping nor idle play."

On the nature of these functions, we are now sufficiently enlightened to know that although they did not make him one of the masters of the state, they did associate him with all the endeavors, all the negotiations, all the projects of Florence.[3] Far from being an underling, Machiavelli was in a sense the factotum of the Republic, now charged with giving definition to the decisions made by the city leaders and overseeing their application, now sent on a mission to sovereigns or foreign men of state, to plead the case of Florence or foil plots against her, now invested—during the government's last moments—with the authority of a high-ranking Commissioner of the Armies. Placed from the beginning of his career at the head of the Second Chancery, which specifically directed domestic and military affairs, he was also entrusted with the tasks pertaining to the First, which controlled foreign affairs, and then performed concurrently with that post the duties of the Chancery of the Ten, whose activities covered in large part that last domain. Such functions were all the more important because the members of the Signoria and the council did not always have a very thorough knowledge of public affairs and had to have recourse on many occasions to the competency of collaborators who were the only ones capable of ensuring the continuity of the governmental action. But in addition to this, these functions allow us to understand the singular nature of an activity that, however demanding it may be, since it is so essential to the life of the state and extends to many areas, nonetheless offers a well-informed mind a constant opportunity to critique the decisions made and to measure the tragic gap separating the determination of general political goals and their application in concrete situations. In addition to a flexibility of reasoning favored by the frequent change of occupations, we must add the power of taking a distance with respect to actions whose principles had been determined by an outside will, and a particular sensitivity to the problem of implementation. These qualities, meeting in Machiavelli the man of politics, as attested by his oeuvre, are clearly not the simple result of the ambiguous status to which he was attached during his career. Yet we may consider that he found in that status favorable conditions for an unusual freedom of reflection. Without participating directly in the decisions that committed the city's destiny, he had access to those who had that responsibility to the point of being listened to by them, if not followed in his opinions, and of becoming the chief collaborator of Gonfalonier Soderini. A man of offices, he did more than transmit the instructions of the leaders and check their application; he was often expected to translate them into precise terminology and to give specificity to a broadly outlined polity. Maneuvering on the terrain, whether of diplomacy or warfare, he was not content to obey, but in thinly veiled form and with a daring that often worried his friends, expressed his opinion, pushed the government to act, and put it sharply on guard against the dangers to which its hesitation exposed it. To read his Reports, he can even be seen at times playing a double role—writing orders he will have to apply as a delegate of the Signoria, and the summaries of the missions in which he puts them to the test. There is no doubt that this odd situation—which makes of him both the one dispensing the orders and the one submitting to them, at once the most knowledgeable party in the affairs of the city and the servant bound by the decisions of a weak and awkward Power, both actor and witness in any case—does not prepare him for an "objectification" of political conduct and for a mobility of perspectives that, however we may interpret *The Prince*, are undoubtedly part of its originality.

As for that experience acquired in action, we need not even imagine it, for it is written in the Reports, his mission summaries, the first texts of general significance in which his temperament as a writer can be discerned—lasting testimony, out of so many other writings that have been either lost or destroyed, to his reflection on men and events. It suffices to consider "On the Method of Dealing with the Rebels of Val di Chiana," the projected "Discourses to Be Pronounced before the Balia" (intended to justify the need for new public expenditures), the "Discourse on the Institution of the Militia," the two "Accounts" devoted to the affairs of France and Germany, his considerations on Borgia in his letters from Urbino and Imola, and even the "First Decennale"—a little poem recounting, in 1504, Italy's recent catastrophes—to be convinced that *The Prince* was the fruit of a long work of expression. The care with which these texts are composed, the rigor of the argumentation, the attention to giving these judgments a universal significance—whether he already brings together examples from ancient and modern times, or by devoting himself to isolating certain constant traits of the politics of states—already make him a theoretician. When Machiavelli, at forty-four years of age, undertakes to write *The Prince*, he is not only that man of politics that an already long career in the service of the state has prepared for reflection, he is a writer, familiar with literary exercises—and as such known, appreciated, and feared by his contemporaries. Despite an opinion commonly spread, it is even possible that during his active years he may have been able to assemble part of the documentation on which *The Prince* and *The Discourses* would be based, or even begin the project of a theoretical work, since, during the publication of the *First Decennale* (at the beginning of 1506) his editor Agostino Vespucci leads one to expect a work of a different nature: "This little work will not be a payment for what the author owes us," he writes, "but that will be earnest money on the more extended work that with no less secrecy he is hatching in his store."[4] Whatever the case may be, both in the main texts mentioned and in many official letters, studded with reflections on politics, some of the themes that will go into *The Prince* are referred to—references so substantial that it is not exaggerated to see in them a first draft of that work.

The critique of the politics of procrastination, dear to the "Florentine pseudo sages," is found throughout the letters that the Secretary addresses to the Signoria during his embassies to Catherine Sforza, Cesare Borgia, the king of France, and the emperor. It extends into that of neutrality, the danger of which is to put the city at the mercy of the victor, whatever the outcome of the conflict—an obvious criticism when an inevitable war between France and Milan breaks out, then between the King and Jules II, but not less significant when the author puts in the mouth of the Valentinois [Cesare Borgia] expressions that he will later adopt as his own: "There is no middle term; we must be either friends or enemies."[5] In the same spirit, already taking his lead from the example of the Romans in asserting that history always reproduces the same situations, he rejects half measures in the relations of a state to its rebellious subjects, recommending, according to the gravity of the offense, either total clemency or the destruction of the rebellious cities.[6] His estimate of the forces competing for the control of Italy, of which he finds the elements or verifies the accuracy during his foreign missions, is accompanied by a reflection on the nature and development of states. He brings out the stability of power in France, the merits of the hereditary monarchy, the nature of the ties that bind the barons to their sovereign, the servitude of the people, and the defects of the military organization.[7] His report on Germany contrasts the economic expansion of the main cities with the weakness of a political system undermined by conflicts between princes and communes, which puts the emperor in a position of dependency on both, forbidding him, despite his claims, to assert his authority on a part of the Italian peninsula. From his description of the ordering of Swiss cantons, he draws the model of a virtuous republic, able to ally a sense of independence to one of equality—invincible on its own territory, forbidding to the foreigner because it sends its own citizens into battle.[8] Lastly, his letters attest to his judgment on the decadence of the Italian states that, abandoning themselves to the mercenary system, are paving the way to servitude, and on the harmful role played by the Church, whose ambition and awkward plots have the effect of handing Italy over to the barbarians.

All these observations will make up a non-negligible part of the

subject matter of *The Prince*. But those who have read that work will recognize, additionally, in the first writings, some of the general ideas that
will dominate his analyses: that there is no good government that cannot
combine political wisdom with military power; that the same imperatives
are valid for republics and for princes, or more precisely there are no
good laws without good arms; that the relations between states are, at first
blush, relations of force; that it is not treaties, but arms that guarantee
the promises; that political morality is of a different nature than private
morality; that the obedience of the governed is only legitimate to the
degree that they benefit from the protection of governing bodies; that a
new prince must direct everything by himself, count on his own strength
alone, win over his subjects, attach his neighbors to him; that the virtue
of the great man is to know and seize the occasion; that the changeability of fortune overthrows all the undertakings that bear the mark of the
rigidity of human nature. All these propositions, introduced in the Letters and the Reports, usually tucked away in the meanders of a particular
commentary, in the form of simple remarks, announce *The Prince*, which
will give them their full meaning and articulate them within the dynamics
of its purpose.[9] It is true that we amply made the point, in opposition to
those who are satisfied with an inventory and classification of themes, that
the truth of this purpose remains beyond our grasp as long as we do not
know the oeuvre itself, as the experience of thought, and furthermore
we would be hard put to reconstruct it on the basis of information in the
Correspondence, if that were all we had left with which to do so. But the
Reports and Letters have the merit of affording us a glimpse of the long
preparation that went into the work completed in the space of a few
months, and help us restore its true temporal dimension.

But the idea that *The Prince* is a work that was improvised by the
force of circumstances is nourished from another source. From a sentence by the author, placed at the head of the second chapter—"I will
not here speak of republics, having already treated of them fully in another place"[10]—it has been deduced that he had already written part of
The Discourses when the hope of attracting the attention of the Medici
made him write an essay on tyranny. As for the possible unseemly opportunism of such a sudden change of direction, all those who desired
to minimize the significance of *The Prince* made the most of it, while the
others wondered about that odd turn. No one, until a relatively recent
date, questioned that this sentence belonged to the first writing of *The
Prince*, though in the absence of any manuscript attesting its authenticity
we cannot be certain of when it was written. Now, the scholarly study by
Hans Baron does more than just authorize doubt; it establishes the un-
likelihood of that commonly accepted hypothesis.[11] And as is the usual

case in such matters, when new light is shed, people are astonished that the erudite critics put up so long with such a confused view of the facts. Indeed, how could it have been accepted that Machiavelli was referring in 1513 or 1514 to a work the reader could not have been aware of since it had been neither published nor completed? How could it have been assumed that at that time he had already "fully" discussed republics, when it was known by contemporary witnesses that he wrote *The Discourses* at the request of a group of young bourgeois Florentines during or after conversations for which they gathered in the Oricellari Gardens, at a date that could not have been prior to 1515?[12] Lastly, how are we to understand that on a particular but important point—the value of the Swiss armies—*The Discourses* give an interpretation that is noticeably different from that of *The Prince*, if we do not recognize that during the interval separating these two works the battle of Marignan destroyed the belief in their invulnerability? Any well-informed reader should have been able to ask these questions. The response given by Baron is bolstered by an argument that should not be accepted without some reservations. Baron, considering that the analysis of *The Discourses* shows two stages of composition—a continuous, though somewhat loose commentary on Livy's texts on the one hand, and general considerations on Rome and Republics on the other—maintains that the commentary, only one part of which could have been written before 1513, could not by itself pretend to be a treatise on general politics. Furthermore, underlining the importance of the first part of Book 1, in which the principles of the history of Rome and of states are set forth, he points out that the model that inspires Machiavelli on this occasion, Book 6 of the Histories of Polybius, could not have been known to him before 1515, or even 1516 or 1517, the period during which its first translation into Latin appeared. The fact is that, even though we must have doubts about the hypothesis concerning the genesis of *The Discourses*, the conclusion, fully convincing, is that only fragments of it could have been written before *The Prince*, and that that work's reference to a work devoted to the overall question of the republics was doubtless added to the text at a time considerably later than its original version, either on the occasion of its presentation to Lorenzo de Medici in 1516, or even later. This conclusion confirms my view, then, that *The Prince* does indeed constitute the first moment of Machiavelli's political reflection, and that his "long experience with modern things and his continual reading of things from Antiquity" was manifested for the first time in this work. It suffices, further, to accept, once again, the testimony of the writer to be persuaded that his work at Sant'Andrea has no other object than *The Prince*—and it is by a strange aberration that an attempt has been made to dissociate his activity as a theoretician, occupied in reflecting on the politics of the Greeks and Romans and the preparation of *The Prince*, despite the fact that the letter addressed to Vettori linked them so rigorously.

Now, to recall once more the specific terms of that letter—"And because Dante says that no one understands anything unless he retains what he has understood, I have jotted down what I have profited from in their conversation [that is, of the men of Antiquity], and composed a short study, *De Principatibus*, in which I delve as deeply as I can into the ideas concerning this topic"—we must also recognize that the writer's express motive is not in the least to curry favor with the Medicis. True, he does observe that his work is well suited to being read by a prince, especially a *new* prince, and he announces his intention to dedicate it to Giuliano. But the fact that he expresses doubt that the latter would want to read it is sufficient proof that he did not undertake such a work solely for the purpose of submitting it to him. And if he mentions the need to address it to him, nowhere does he suggest that this is what was behind its creation. The sincerity of his tone and the freedom with which he addresses himself, as usual, to his friend Vettori does not lead us to suspect him of disguising his thoughts. But since taking the declarations of an author at face value always leaves one open to the charge of naïveté, his remarks to Lorenzo in the work's dedication may give a less equivocal confirmation of his relations with the Medicis. For indeed it is on that occasion, in which the object is to be pleasing, that Machiavelli could make a display of servility and make us believe his book has no other object than to procure the backing of a future prince. But such is the dignity of that epistle, the commentaries of his detractors notwithstanding, and the assurance with which he demands vis-à-vis Lorenzo his position as a master thinker that I find in it further evidence of the importance he attributes to his work. The fact that he should make the claim of giving Lorenzo "the power of understanding, in the shortest time, what he himself became acquainted with and understood during the course of so many years and at the price of such great difficulties and dangers"; that he should present himself boldly as a man of the most humble condition and find the authority to judge the nature of princes; that he should maintain, in effect, that his book is its own recommendation, because of the "*varietà della materia e della gravità del subjetto*"; that he takes pride in having banished the embellishments and artifices to which his predecessors had always had recourse: such language does not sound like that of a servant, but reveals rather a writer who is fully conscious of the novelty and value of his undertaking.

Still, the argument according to which *The Prince* was improvised on the spur of the moment, at the price of a sudden break in the course of a study devoted to Rome and republican institutions, had the advantage of furnishing a key to the work. Whether the determining factor was held to be the personal motivation that drove the writer to compose an essay on tyranny, or whether one imagined him stricken with an illumination in the aftermath of the fall of the government of Florence and discovering that only a prince could triumph over the chaos of Italy and snatch it away from servitude (two hypotheses that by the way were incompatible), a convenient story-line was offered the reader. From this point of view, the general considerations on the nature of man, society, and history were relegated to the background; however interesting, their role was seen to be that of supporting with varying degrees of success the practical project of *The Prince* and came from a meditation bearing no necessary connection to it. In rejecting this view—in recognizing that it is at one and the same time that the author interrogates the present and the most distant past, that he attempts to combine the experience of a man of action, the knowledge of a historian, and the reflection of a philosopher, to bind theory and *praxis*—we nonetheless also reject the simplifications that would prevent us from being receptive to the *varietà* of the material and the *gravità* of the subject. We now expect of the work itself that it teach us its order and the necessity in virtue of which its domain is circumscribed.

What the subject and the material of *The Prince* are does not initially seem difficult to say. Let us address ourselves once more to the letter in which the author presents his work to Vettori. The former says that he has asked himself "what sovereignty (*principato*) is, how many types of it there are, how it is acquired, how kept, and why one loses it." To Lorenzo, moreover, he says that he dared to conduct discourse on the government of princes and give its rules (*discorrere e regolare i governi di principi*). These words apparently agree with the plan revealed by a superficial reading. The first chapter enumerates the various types of principalities; the author announces, at the beginning of the second, that he will weave on this framework and explore how each type can be governed and preserved. The eleven chapters seem to correspond to that intention. The next three chapters are devoted to military politics, treating in a general sense aggression and defense; then the discussion proceeds successively to the relations that the prince must establish with his subjects—especially on the qualities he must show to establish and maintain his authority—and on his relations with his attendants and ministers. Lastly, three chapters portray the hardships of the present time, the respective powers of *virtù* and fortune, and the chance offered to a new prince to take over

Italy by delivering it from the barbarians. Limiting ourselves to this description, we might even think that the subject of *The Prince* comes from tradition, that it is but one more treatise on the art of governance. As for its material, we find it, if we are to believe the *Dedication*, in the actions of great men as revealed by knowledge of the past and of present times.

If we consider the text attentively, however, we cannot help but feel that there is something unusual about the author's project.

Indeed, the argument of *The Prince* reminds us neither of that of the scholastic treatises devoted to the same subject nor of that of works of antiquity to which it would be tempting to compare them.[13] The author does not situate the relations of the prince with his subjects in the more general setting of the relations of man with his fellow men, with Nature, or with God. He does not set out from a definition of the state or of the social relation; nor does he in any passage seem to care to give one explicitly. Nor does he compare the system of government based on the authority of the prince to other forms of political organization. Furthermore, he does not address a living prince to teach him what the good or useful is, nor does he resort to the fiction of a wise councillor discussing the best possible government with a prince whose face is familiar to him; finally, he does not describe the events of a specific era for purposes of edification, nor does he limit himself to comparing the actions of men of state from antiquity with those of their contemporaries. In other words, his approach is neither—at least if we take these terms in their conventional sense—that of the philosopher, nor the moralist, nor the psychologist, nor the historian. Clearly Machiavelli prompts our reflection on history, man, society, and the state, on the motivations of the prince, on good and evil; but at first sight the field of his reflection, the reality he intends, does not permit clear circumscription. While the questions relative to the art of governing were posed by his predecessors from a very well-defined point of view, in reference to traditionally recognized truths—whether founded on the authority of reason or religion—his questions seem to require no such presuppositions, and rather to command the movement of reflection entirely on their own. What does this movement delineate? This is indeed what we cannot avoid wondering as we move forward in our reading of this work. It does not suffice for us to say that the author brings new answers to old questions. The latter were shaped in reference to a certain image of the world; thus their way of being framed was unequivocal. But to state that you are going to discuss the government of princes and give the rules for them, that you will enquire into what it is (*che cosa è il principato*) and very prosaically how they are taken over, kept, and lost—this, despite the clarity of the words, raises questions the origin of which is obscure, questions that make us seek, beyond the answers they may bring, understood in their literal sense, their very meaning as questions.

Because we do not know from what perspective we can embrace the new domain offered to the reader's attention, we must suspend our judgment as long as possible. Rather than to precipitously define this domain as that of politics, at last promoted, as they say, to the dignity of being an object of science—as if that term, which we know to have been given, historically, very different acceptations, were sufficient to dissipate our uncertainty—it is better to consent to being astonished at the path on which the writer has set out, at a distance from his predecessors, and not to prejudge, on the strength of confidence in initial declarations and external commentaries, the true subject and the true material of his work, which can be revealed only by reading it. We will only have a chance of penetrating *The Prince*—we must begin by being persuaded of this—on the condition that we go back to the source of the demonstrations and considerations that seem to be self-sufficient in it, that we connect its manifest *subject* to the more ample discourse sustaining and organizing it, and that we understand why it is essential for it to remain on the hither side of expression. That requirement could doubtless be formulated with respect to all works of thought, for it is surely the case that we would never be able to understand them without perceiving what is not said in them, but remains at the periphery of what is said, either because what is unformulated carries with itself an obviousness that, in the mind of the author, can dispense with all commentary and yet has ceased being natural to us, or because it belongs to an experience from which language borrows its power but can do no more than point toward, and that must be awakened by other words in order for the authorial word to retain its primary function. But in the present case the motivations orienting my research are more pressing. In *The Prince* there is not only a visible order of ideas, about which we would have to inquire where it comes from, what is understood between the lines, how it frees itself from the principles that until then governed political reflection; that order, as soon as we pretend to reconnect it with the overall analyses, reveals that it covers over a strange disorder, so that one must either say goodbye to the coherence of the work, or undertake an exploration in depth to discover the meaning of what appears as order and as disorder.

Let us consider a bit further the writer's gait before following him in his thoughts. Our first impression is that he advances with a confident and rapid stride toward his goal. His work is divided into twenty-six chapters, some of which are extremely short, notably the first two, while the longest ones can be broken up into arguments the articulation of which is strongly underlined. The language is most of the time very concise, the exposition containing now and then formulations in which the truth of a development is felicitously condensed, sometimes with the force of maxims. At the beginning, several hypotheses are stated: it is a question of indicating in what conditions a prince is placed when he becomes the master of a state. These hypotheses then reappear, submitted to a systematic examination that brings out a few other, more particular ones. Each time, the difficulties connected with the taking of power and its retention are analyzed. The repeated use of the word *difficultà* already suggests that political action is to be treated as are the terms of a problem. It requires the use of a method thanks to which what appears at first difficult later turns out to be easily resolved. Indeed, the author shows with insistence, at the beginning of one chapter, how arduous it is to conquer a state; at the end of the development, we discover that a prince succeeds easily, provided he knows how to apply the appropriate rules. Generally speaking, the prince's failure is ascribed to errors of reasoning, his success to a precise knowledge of the facts, joined with a rigorous reflection on the principles. Thus, between the mechanism of action and the order of discourse a sort of equivalency is established, which cannot fail soon to strike the reader. The signs of logical thought are, moreover, multiplied in the course of the first analyses, not without ostentation. Machiavelli accustoms his reader to collapsing into one sole thought what is *ordinary, natural, necessary,* and *reasonable,* and to respect the *order of things.*[14] He deliberately prompts his reader to be astonished, for the sole purpose of then revealing the obvious to him. He places him before alternatives in which there is an inevitability of choice and the requirement of a rational decision. By the alliance of ancient and modern examples, he persuades him that the discussion is based on typical cases to which the diversity of facts can easily be reduced. Whether he seems to be deducing from a principle consequences of which history offers an illustration, or to induce from facts a rule of universal application, his exposition throughout the first eleven chapters is presented like a demonstration. At the end of it, Machiavelli announces that he will treat the military problem, in a general way. Thus the study of the initial hypotheses, which had continually confronted the reader with particular situations and concurrences of events, is apparently followed by a reflection on the constants of politics. It begins with the examination of the different arms at the disposal of the sovereign and the principles he must obey in all circumstances to defend the state; but it proceeds with the examination of the qualities he must manifest in the governance of his subjects. In the course of these two developments, the author begins with an enumeration: that of the arms (mercenaries, auxiliaries, mixed, and one's own), which is presented as exhaustive; and that, very extended, of the virtues and vices with which it is customary to gratify a prince. He then returns to each of these aspects mentioned in order to analyze them. It is at the very moment when he undertakes the methodical critique of the conduct of the prince that he attacks tradition and utopia, judging it to be more appropriate to "follow the actual truth of the thing than one's imagination."[15] This declaration, which eloquently confirms what is at stake in the coming discussion, sets the tone of the work. We have been put on notice: the necessity of true discourse orders the writer to say what the others have kept silent about, just as the necessity of action orders the prince to do what the ordinary man is incapable of accomplishing.

From the general examination of the politics of the prince, as embodied in the relationship he must maintain with his subjects and his entourage, there transpires an appreciation of the present situation of Italy and the challenges for a new prince. Whatever the judgment we are to make eventually on the meaning of these pages, it must be admitted that they offer, from a purely formal point of view, a conclusion that is perfectly articulated with the preceding analyses.

The theory, as it seems, merely finds its final point of application in the field of immediate practice. Furthermore, the assurance with which Machiavelli directs himself toward this conclusion inspires his reader with great confidence in the construction of his work. The beginning of Chapter 24 spectacularly ties back in with that of Chapter 2, which began the discussion. The second chapter accepted the common idea that a hereditary state is less difficult to keep possession of than a new one; then we learned that no difficulty could withstand the application of the method and that the surest guarantee of power resided in the prince's prudence; finally, the perspective is reversed; the virtue of knowledge replaces that of tradition: "If the admonitions we have given earlier are well applied by the prince," Machiavelli tells us, "they will make him seem old where he is new, and will make him in a nonce more confident and sure of his domain than if he were enrooted there *ab antiquo.*" Now, as we arrive at that final truth, the responsibility of those who failed to recognize it, and who, by weakness of mind and character precipitated Italy into the abyss in which it now finds itself, appears self-evident. In realizing their errors, we foresee the path that would unfold before the founder of a new state. After having invited us one last time to lift our gaze beyond the narrow horizons of the present world to persuade ourselves that man has the power to impose his will upon the course of things despite the vicissitudes of fortune, Machiavelli launches his final appeal for the deliverance of Italy.

Thus *The Prince* succeeds in passing for the most demonstrative of discourses. Reduction of empirical diversity to the givens of hypotheses; passage from the particular case to the general rule and vice versa; progressive extension of the inquiry from typical situations and circumstances to the constants of political behavior, and finally leading to the final image of the mastering of fortune—the composition seems to arrange for the most direct access to knowledge.

Perhaps it would be well to repeat that this impression is rendered all the more vivid by that fact that no effort is spared, at the beginning of the work, to assure the reader of the precision and necessity of the argument. The short time taken up by the first two chapters, one merely setting up the elements of a problem, the other delimiting the simplest case in order to move beyond it, is followed by the long time of the third, so adroitly modulated that it allows itself to be accompanied with the same ease, as if the sudden fullness of breath were regulated by what was to be said, without breaking the movement of the word. This chapter, the object of which is the first type of new principality—called *mixed*, because he who takes it over is merely annexing it to a state of which he is already the master—provides the best testimony to the logic of the composition. The author begins by underlining the difficulties such an undertaking necessarily encounters; he declares that he is supplying the universal causes of this. In the first movement, the example of the conquest of Milan by Louis XII is adduced in support of that explanation. The example in turn confronts us with two distinct cases, for the subdued people is, or is not, of the same stock and language as its invader. The two cases are studied successively; the simplest first; second, the one that exposes the invader to the greatest danger. The rules stated on this topic find their confirmation in the history of the Roman conquests. In a second movement, the examination focuses on the undertaking of Louis XII; it now appears that the conditions in which it developed promised him success, provided he knew how to avail himself of them, that is, how to apply the rational principles that dominated the politics of the Greeks and Romans. Echoing the first sentences of the chapter on the difficulty of creating a new state, we have the proposition, "let each one, then, consider how easy it would have been for the king to maintain his prestige in Italy if he had observed the rules we have given above . . ." The proof *a contrario* of the demonstration is furnished by the enumeration of the errors, numbering six, that determined the ruin of the king.

The conclusion follows rigorously. "King Louis therefore lost Lombardy for not following any of the teachings observed by others who conquered countries and wanted to maintain themselves in them. But there is no marvel in this: it is logical and normal." In the end, the gravest error of all informs the following principle, which must remain as a fixed point of repair in the rest of the work: "From this, a general rule can be drawn that never misleads, or rarely; it is that he who is the cause of another's becoming powerful precipitates his own downfall . . ."

But he who does not blindly trust the manifest signs of the composition and wonders whether the thought does in fact follow the course they seem to point out will not fail to discover a new facet of the work, so different from the one that presented itself to the first look that he will be reduced to becoming doubtful of the author's intentions.

The very definition of the initial hypotheses, as soon as one stops to consider them, elicits astonishment. Machiavelli, as we will recall, formulates two questions in his introductory chapter: "How many types of principalities are there, and by what means are they acquired?" In fact, he only retains one of them, the second, as if it determined the meaning of the first. While the title leads the reader to expect, by the way it is stated, a distinction in keeping with the spirit of the tradition, he immediately breaks with established usage, without giving his reasons, ignoring the specific characteristics of the different regimes and the ways in which sovereignty is exercised, and neglecting the classical opposition between legitimate and illegitimate power. It appears that the only thing that holds his attention and gives him the criterion for his classification is the taking of power. This power, we learn, either is received by the prince as an inheritance or he conquers it. Conquest is either partial or total, depending on whether he is already at the head of a state and is annexing a new domain, or his own enterprise brings him to the rank of prince; it makes him deal either with a people already accustomed to royal domination, or with a "free" people; it is carried out by means of one's own arms, or foreign arms; it is the work either of *virtù* or fortune.

The point of view of the monarch thus seems to be of the utmost importance; the various types of principalities being classified only in relation to the position he occupies at the moment of becoming master of the state. But the fact that the author leaves this perspective in the shadows already incites his interpreter to prudence. And in fact, although in naming it we obtain the most coherent image of discourse, it does not deliver us from all uncertainty. If Machiavelli does not wish to discuss any problems other than the taking over of power, is it solely for the sake of completeness that he mentions the inherited principality at the beginning to contrast it with various types of new principalities? And if that is his scruple, why does he neglect the case of the elective monarchy? Moreover, if he is speaking of an entirely new principality, and comparing the hypotheses of the foundation of the state and a radical change of regime in the state, why does he give us as a model Francesco Sforza, who did nothing but replace the tyranny of the Visconti with his own? To these difficulties a third is added. The distinction between one's own arms and foreign arms does indeed call for reflection on the means of action of the prince, but that of *virtù* and fortune is of a different order: man is not free to decide about the use of one or the other, as he is to choose an instrument or a method. Besides the fact that these two terms have, as opposed to the two preceding ones, a symbolic value still to be determined, they introduce a new dimension. In considering them, it must be admitted that the thinker does not necessarily coincide with the actor, although it is true that the actor may also be a thinker in reflecting on his own historical status: the prince is not only this subject who has the responsibility for his enterprise and his means of action, he is himself "represented," his work perceived as a result of either *virtù* or fortune.

Thus, the first Machiavellian definitions, despite their concision and the apparent rigor of their articulation, conceal a confused material. They seem to find their full meaning in the image of the prince, considered as the subject of action, but an imperceptible slippage within that image raises doubts about its coherence. Could it be that the reflections on the prince cannot be separated from those on the state and on the fate of human action? Having caught a glimpse of this question, we certainly are not yet in a position to know whether it was intended by the author to suggest it, or whether we should attribute it to a shortcoming of his method. But it is remarkable that at the very moment when, distancing his pursuit from the traditional philosophical considerations, he circumscribes the field of his investigation as being that of empirical operations required by the taking over of power, and prepares the reader to examine them one by one—as if that intent and that delimitation went without saying—we should be held back by an initial uncertainty.

Now, far from being dissipated, this uncertainty increases as we try to find in the first part of the work the development of the inquiry as announced. No doubt the first eleven chapters contain discussion of particular hypotheses the terms of which were posited at the beginning. But, visible from afar, the thread that should, as we believe, tie them together begins to stretch as soon as we try to seize and follow it; it becomes tangled or breaks. New themes appear all the while, new examples, new points of repair, and the relation between the actual discourse and the apparent plan proves increasingly loose, to the point where we have reason to wonder whether the plan is intended to assure us that we are on the right path or to lead us astray, and whether there is a path in the first place, or whether the *varietà* of the material is not swamping the one who claimed to bring order to it.

The two chapters that follow the introduction are devoted to hereditary principalities and to new principalities that are connected to the state of the conqueror. Thus the discussion corresponds to our expectations. We will soon understand, moreover, why the author considers this latter case before treating entirely new principalities. He is going from the easiest to the most difficult. Furthermore, the distinction made along the way between peoples who are or are not of the same stock as the invader felicitously finds its rightful place, as I have already pointed out, in the argument. In what comes after that, on the other hand, we are given a certain number of surprises. The fourth chapter is presented as a necessary digression, but considering the importance of the subject treated, we may be permitted to doubt that its sole function, as the writer would like to persuade us, is to do justice to an objection. Ostensibly, it is only a question of explaining "why the kingdom of Darius occupied by Alexander did not revolt against his successors after his death," and in a more general sense, why a new prince succeeds sometimes in maintaining himself without difficulty in a conquered country; in fact, the new hypotheses are confronted with a problem that, by its scope, greatly exceeds the framework of the initial givens. Machiavelli compares at length the monarchy of the despotic type with that of the feudal type, and, at the same time that he examines the question of the resistance they are capable of putting up against an eventual aggressor, brings out an essential difference between the two types of government, which concerns the mode of implantation of power in society. That this reflection is not announced in the first chapter might lead one to believe it to be accidental, but it is also permissible to see an artifice in the indirect way it is introduced. Chapter 5, it is true, appears to fit into the announced plan. As indicated by its title, the question concerns the way to "govern the cities or principalities that, before being conquered, lived under their laws." And in the first lines of the text, the author specifies "under their laws and in freedom." Nevertheless, the reader will recall, not without astonishment, that the writer had first contrasted states accustomed to living under a prince and those used to living in freedom; he observes therefore that this distinction is dropped; but the moment he is ready to admit that the attachment of a people to its laws is not the necessary consequence of its political organization, that all princes are not tyrants, that the term freedom probably only indicates the recognition of certain rights and the independence of the state, he must recognize that he is on the wrong track, since the continuation of the text reveals that one can indeed submit the subjects of a former prince to a new authority, once he and his descendants have been exterminated, but that one cannot overcome a republic without scattering its inhabitants and deciding to govern it in person, as "life, hatred, desires for vengeance and the memory of its former freedom" subsist in it after the conquest. How would the reader not be concerned about such twists and turns, and begin to lose confidence in the logic of the discourse? This upset increases with the reading of the two following chapters. The sixth treats new principalities acquired by one's own arms and by *virtù,* the seventh new principalities acquired by foreign arms and fortune. Thus we find associated criteria that the author had at first taken care to distinguish. In the first case, the example of Sforza is not mentioned, and is mentioned only briefly in the second and then set in opposition to that of Borgia. Moreover, we learn that first to be examined will be entirely new principalities, which experience at the same time the advent of a prince and the birth of a state. Sforza having done nothing but take over the duchy of Milan, it seems logical not to count him among the founders. But the fact that in the first chapter he embodies the type of the new prince, that he is for the second time designated as the one capable of taking over power by his *virtù* and his own arms and thus casts into the shadows the characters of less caliber who owed their crown to the favor of a foreign power, gives him an ill-determined status. This difficulty reveals another one: the two chapters we are considering seem to constitute an alternative, but beyond the opposition of terms, there circulates between them the same question: the foundation of the state. Borgia wanted to create a new principality in the center of Italy, thus taking up the task, the noblest of all, that bestows glory on the heroes of Chapter 6: the glory of giving a scattered people unity. Like them, he is thus in the strongest sense of the term a *principe nuovo,* and there is no doubt that in this respect his figure eclipses that of Sforza. Besides, Machiavelli tells us that he only depended on fortune and the arms of others at the beginning of his enterprise; in contrast with the kinglets created out of nothing by Darius, or the Roman emperors who owed their rank solely to the complaisance of a paid army, he acted in such a way as to depend on no one but himself and was able to provide himself with his own forces. It is by an exceptional *virtù* that he blazed a trail for himself to power; and although his failure can be ascribed to the malignity of fortune, to which he had been beholden at the beginning, since he was paralyzed by illness at the same time that the pope, his powerful protector, was dying, we may judge that that final concurrence of events would not have brought about his downfall if he had shown as much intelligence on that occasion as in the past.

Despite appearances, the same analysis is being carried out. From the image of the exploits of semi-mythological heroes to that of the Borgia's conquest, the meaning of what is to be understood by political *virtù* and the principles underlying the foundation of the state becomes more specific. The articulation of the two proposed themes (he who acts by *virtù* and his own arms has great difficulty in conquering, but not in maintaining the state—he who relies on fortune and the arms of others has little difficulty in becoming prince but much in remaining so) is doubtless not purely formal, but it is certain that it does not have the demonstrative function we were previously disposed to see in it. Are we to blame this on a defect in construction, or imagine that Machiavelli is deliberately muddying the waters, or yet again assume that his thinking is unfolding along several different paths at once?

These questions focus our attention, and now the development of Chapter 6 seems odd from more than one perspective. While Machiavelli says at the beginning that the founder's undertaking meets with the most serious difficulties, he says neither in what they consist, nor precisely how they can be overcome. True, he observes that they are connected with the introduction of new institutions (*nuovi ordini e modi*); but he also neglects to specify what they are. He names Moses, Cyrus, Romulus, and Theseus, without describing any of their actions. It is as if the empirical analysis that supported the reasoning up to that point were temporarily disqualified, as if the meaning were being established on a different level that had to remain hidden. In this context, the introduction of Savonarola completes our disorientation: neither prince nor founder of a state, this figure, who for a moment occupied the foreground to the political stage in Florence, never pretended to do anything but reform the government of the republic. Suddenly to set him, as unarmed prophet, in opposition to the armed prophets represented by the Greco-Roman heroes forces the reader, yet again, either to give up the image of a rigorously composed discourse, or to assume it to be governed by a hidden intention, or even to wonder whether the function of the state is its only or true subject.

Up to and including Chapter 7, the criteria advanced at the beginning have, it is true, been applied, and if we have already several reasons to doubt whether they really do perform the function assigned to them, at least we cannot deny that they appear to command the development of the discourse. But the same does not hold for what follows. Chapter 8 is titled "Of Those Who Have Attained the Position of Prince by Villainy," and Chapter 9 "Of the Civic Principality." Now, none of the hypotheses envisaged in them had been announced. We can no doubt find a justification for them: the author tells us they concern the study of a mode of advent of the prince that is neither the result of *virtù* nor of fortune, or requires no more than a certain mixture of those two powers. But if the first thread of the argument is not totally lost, it proves henceforth too tenuous for us to be satisfied with it. In reality, the two analyses that concern us treat phenomena that the classical writers took great care to define and describe: the usurpation of power by violent or pacific means.

Machiavelli, choosing a roundabout way to avoid mentioning those writers, gives the impression that he refuses the traditional point of view and calls upon the reader to examine his plan more closely. The questions that arise in the latter's mind vis-à-vis the text become more specific. Why does Machiavelli avoid speaking of both tyranny and usurpation? Why does he underline the criminal nature of a certain sort of takeover of power, since he has taken care until now to abstain from all value judgments in the statement of his hypotheses? Why, after having designated it as such, does he begin a discussion to determine whether it is just or not to speak of *virtù* in the case of Agathocles, a cruel hero of that policy, and why does he add to his response such reservations as to leave the reader in uncertainty? Finally, why does he chose the case of civic tyranny to introduce, for the first time, consideration of general significance on the nature of social classes and the relations a prince must establish with his subjects—considerations one is justifiably surprised not to have found in Chapter 6? Is it not the case that in the absence of any precaution or artifice, and if he went directly to the goal, it would appear that the figure of Agathocles is not substantially different from that of Sforza, who seized the duchy of Milan at the head of armed bands, abusing the confidence of the people? Further, would we not discover that the policy of the cruelest tyrant strangely resembles that of the glorious founder? Or are these precautions, these tactics, perhaps not of a purely tactical order? Should we not rather understand, in trusting the structure of the discourse, that there is at once difference and a similarity between the actions of either group, but that they are to be conceived in new terms, outside the categories of common sense?

Whatever the response may be that emerges after the text has been more thoroughly penetrated, it is already clear at this point that the first Machiavellian concepts do not ensure the work's coherence; it is rather the case that they make up a structure so thin and fragile that it is legitimate to ask whether it is not a pure and simple trompe l'oeil. Thus, the security that the image of the continuous demonstration provided at first gives way to insecurity. The solid ground on which we thought we were established has become quicksand. Digression, insinuation, elision, the game of double truth blur the argument and suggest an underlying subtext whose origin we do not know, nor whither it tends, but only that it is essential to identify it.

Let us consider, lastly, the two chapters that close the first part of the work. Chapter 10 presents itself as a digression of a general nature on the military problem. So at least its title, "How the Strength of All States Should Be Measured," would have us think. But again, the title does not convey an accurate idea of the subject treated. The fact is, Machiavelli distinguishes small and large states, and only treats the former. Considerations of a political nature are far more important than military ones, his main argument establishing that the prince's best defense is to not be hated by the people. Furthermore—and this is probably no accident—the only example proposed to the new prince is that of the German republics, which offer the best model of military organization. That example reminds us that already on two occasions the republic has been held up as a model. But until this point only the Romans were cited. For the first time it is toward the free cities of the present that our gaze is directed. In conclusion, for the first time as well, Machiavelli, amending his judgment on the basic perversity of man, gives credit to his nature: "for men," he writes, "are of such a nature as to be well disposed as much by favors they have bestowed as by those they have received."

As for Chapter 11, perhaps it is the one that holds the greatest surprise. Not only by reason of the subject treated, ecclesiastical principalities, which nothing previous led us to expect would be treated, but equally because a new prince could learn nothing of practical value from it. Indeed, Machiavelli offers no direct counsel here, either to a pope or a prince, and the analysis breaks with the principle that commanded it up to this point. Thus, when we ask ourselves what the meaning of this break might be, we are justified in wondering whether we are dealing with a simple digression, or whether, on the occasion of a new particular case, there is the deepening of a reflection about which we have already felt that it could not express itself without taking an indirect approach. What the principle of its working is we do not yet know, but the astonishing composition of the chapter once again challenges our curiosity. There is no difficulty involved in the ecclesiastic states, Machiavelli tells us on the one hand, except before the taking over of power; maintaining it presents no difficulty; this power is sustained by very ancient institutions "*ordini antiquati nella religione*"; only states of this sort are "secure and happy"; on the other hand, the advent of the prince of the Church, as opposed to that of the hero-founder, requires neither the intervention of fortune nor that of *virtù;* his state is not governed, his people not defended. Here we have before us on the one hand reasons that transcend human understanding and therefore forbid historical analysis; on the other, historical analysis teaches us that the rise of the Papal States is due solely to the very prosaic politics of Alexander VI and the help of Cesare Borgia. This artfully balanced passage, which concludes with an apology for the new pope Leo X, attests to prudence, but even more to irony, by means of a procedure that, easily recognizable here, is perhaps more discreetly used elsewhere for the same purpose. No doubt the author has not resisted the temptation of passing judgment on papal politics. But assuredly he had other means of doing this, which he uses, by the way, in other circumstances. The fact that he attracts our attention to the function of the *ordini anti-*

quati, which sustain the power of the Church, and thus reminds us, at the end of the first part, both of the words of the second chapter—the very ones that, dedicated to hereditary principalities, inaugurated the series of these hypotheses—and his considerations on the *ordini nuovi,* the creation of which he associated with the highest forms of political action; and also the fact that he should take the risk of evoking divine intervention, after having declared in Chapter 6 that it bore testimony to the *virtù* of Moses, this time to let it be understood that we have no need of such an image to interpret the politics of the popes and the history of their states—leads us rather to think that the exposition of this last case corresponds to a hidden intention and adds, on several points, a complement to the earlier analyses.

Thus, when we approach the work, the landscape changes; the borders, at first so clear, that circumscribed the fragments of the discourse become indistinct. First of all, we must give up the idea that the introductory chapter contains a plan, admit rather that it furnishes a substitute for one, and prepare to seek the meaning at once in the line of what is said and beyond it, in the still undetermined region it merely delimits. Second, the concepts according to which the argument is articulated prove themselves ambiguous. "New principality" is opposed to "hereditary principality," but subsequently splits in order to designate *new state* and *property of a new prince.* "Free people" is opposed first to "people accustomed to living under a prince," then connotes at once "people attached to its laws" (which can be under a prince), and "republic"; "*virtù,*" above all, radiates in several directions, forming with "fortune" a binary discriminator that has more than one meaning: being simultaneously a hinge within a reasoning (a piece necessary to the machinery of discourse), a simple trompe l'oeil, and a symbol whose content becomes richer and more differentiated little by little. And as the most apparent landmarks disappear, other possible contours of the work—and we must recognize that their concealment is probably not accidental—become perceptible. Thus, to the initial astonishment brought about by the beginning of the discourse, in which no space is given to the distinctions of principle between various types of states or political regimes, another astonishment follows: that of seeing them appear as the obverse of the "pattern," now having become the objects of study without being named, now exploited in the course of an argument that seems not to be aware of them, now simply mentioned without the author's wanting to exploit them: a series of oppositions among which we find the despotic regime and the feudal monarchy, the politics of foundation and the politics of annexation, military tyranny and civil tyranny, the state of small and of large size, the principalities founded or not on laws, the lay state and the ecclesiastic one.

Lastly, we discover little by little that the examination of particular hypotheses, which makes up the material of the first eleven chapters, constitutes a passageway for the expression of reflection on the present situation of Italy and on politics in general—on the relations between powers, the foundations of power, ways of governing, the nature of the People and the Grandees; its movement does not in the least follow that of the apparent demonstration, but seems controlled by the need to unveil, in a discontinuous way, the ideas to which a direct expression cannot or must not be given.

Doubtless it is sufficient to mention its first difficulties to get a glimpse of the problem posed by the reading of *The Prince*. But were one to consider with the same attention the continuation of the work one would encounter other, similar difficulties. Thus, Chapter 12 begins a development on military politics in terms that would lead one to believe one has moved from the particular to the general, whereas, as we have just seen, the analysis has already been focusing for a long time on questions concerning the essence of the state and the government. With this development, the theme of war is approached for the second time, since it had already been in Chapter 10; and it will be for the third time in Chapter 20, without our being able at first sight to understand the reason for this dispersion. At least we notice that, in this last chapter as in Chapter 10, the considerations on the arms of the prince are closely tied in with other considerations on the relationship he must maintain with his subjects, so that it is as if war would be clarified when placed vis-à-vis politics, and vice versa. It should also be noted that the author first recommends to the prince of a small state to rely on his fortifications and not to incite the hatred of his subjects, and then, when he comes back to the question, vigorously speaks out on the uselessness or even the danger of fortifications, and praises the arming of the people; we wonder whether he is getting caught up in a contradiction or deliberately following a winding path to reach his goal. The example of Sforza prolongs our hesitation; its function had already seemed equivocal in the first chapters, and now seems to serve opposite purposes, since here he appears successively presented as a vulgar oppressor who only got power by abusing the confidence of the Milanese, denounced with all those whose exploits had no other effect than the downfall of Italy, opposed by force of arms, passing from the condition of a private individual to that of a prince, and accused of having destroyed the power of his own House by having built a fortress in Milan that caused his name to be hated.

This being the case, we must either give up looking for a logic in the author's thought, or conclude that through the multiple figures of Sforza that are offered to us the true image of the prince toward which Machiavelli wishes to lead us can be found.

Finally, the way the discussion is introduced that will dwell at length on the government of the prince is no less a source of astonishment, because it was heralded by no prior indication. On the contrary, Machiavelli, in Chapter 9, after having underlined the necessity for the prince, however he may have come to power, to bind his people to him, cautioned the reader: "And the prince will be able to win them over in many ways, for which, since they change according to the subject, no certain rule can be given, and I will therefore omit speaking of it (*e però si lasceranno indietro*)." Similarly, at the beginning of Chapter 12, he specified that it now remained for him to treat, in a general way, war (*offese e defese*) as if that question were to close the discussion. "The main foundations of all states," he wrote, "the new, the old, and the mixed, are good laws and good arms. And since it is not possible to have good laws where the arms are worthless and if the arms are good it is necessary that the laws be good, I will omit speaking of laws (*io lascerò indietro el ragionare delle legge*) and will speak of arms."

If we refuse the idea that the work is the fruit of constant improvisation, we must no doubt admit that the new development in Chapter 15 corresponds to a necessity of the discourse. Is it, for the writer, a way to approach the most dangerous subject, to have others feel, or make oneself feel, the distance that separates it from those who, before him, discussed the "qualities" of the prince, or what he at first calls his "*modi e governi*," or perhaps to get a second wind in order to conduct the critique at a deeper level to its conclusion? The fact is that at this precise moment Machiavelli declares that he is distancing himself from the *ordini* of others, using the same term he used to refer to the principles that command the life of a state, thus positing himself implicitly as a founder, a new thinker who, without heritage, goes to the "*verità effettuale*" just as the prince who was capable of seizing the occasion goes straight to power. That truth—we have indeed good reasons to suppose that it has emerged in the course of the preceding analyses, but perhaps we should prepare ourselves to see it emerge in a different light. Just as the *nuovi ordini* of the prince did not let themselves be reduced to a body of institutions that could be described, similarly those of the thinker transcend perhaps a simple knowledge of conduct and facts. Perhaps, then, we should interpret the writer's caveat more closely: if he seems to preclude a general discussion on the politics of the prince, before suddenly introducing one in the form of an attack on tradition, is this not an appeal to seek beyond a certain representation of the *modi e governi* or the "*verità effettuale*" the foundation of a new thought? In any case, one is all the more inclined to presume that this procedure has a meaning since it is repeated several times in the course of the work, though we cannot assert that it reflects the same intention in each case. In Chapter 6, for example, Machiavelli observes: "And even though one should not speak of Moses, he having merely carried out what was ordered him by God, still he deserves admiration, if only for that grace which made him worthy to speak with God." A moment later he declares that the great founders of state did not act otherwise than did Moses, that they received no more than the occasion from fortune and only succeeded because of the excellence of their *virtù*. In Chapter 11, as I have said, he only first mentions the problem of ecclesiastical principalities by way of preterition: "But since they are governed by a reason that is higher than the human mind can attain, I will not speak of them (*lascerò il parlarne*) because, being exalted and maintained by God, it would be the work of a presumptuous and reckless man to discuss them." Immediately thereafter he seeks the causes of the rise of the Papal States. At the end of Chapter 18, he mentions "a prince of our time, whom it is not well to name, preaches nothing but peace and faith"; a few pages later he is not afraid of naming him: Ferdinand of Spain, we learn, has become the first king of the Christians by repeated wars; and in order to wage them, he used religion, expelling and robbing the Marranos with a *pietosa crudeltà* of which we know no example "more miserable and rare." Finally, in the middle of Chapter 20, remarking that a new prince finds the most reliable and faithful supporters not among his first devotees, but among those whom he first saw as suspect, he adds: "But one cannot speak very generally of that matter, for it changes according to the subject"; then, without transition, he specifies: "I will say only this thing . . ." and continuing with an expression that he uses frequently—"And since the material requires it I do not want to neglect to remind the prince (*non voglio lasciare indietro ricordare a' principi*)"—he gives the true reason for this. All these examples testify to the same meandering approach, which leads to the same result: the reader loses the feeling of being carried forward by the necessity of a chain of reasoning leading, as in geometry, directly from hypothesis to consequences; he must embrace several thoughts at once, stop at the threshold of a domain to assess the difficulty or danger in proceeding before finding himself in it, keep in mind the route already traveled and its direction as he takes an unexpected path, constantly wonder about the significance of the itinerary, accept little by little the complication of the material—its *varietà*, as the Dedication called it—which seemed at first to offer no resistance to the mind's inspection.

Finally, by comparing the composition of Chapter 3, which just now showed us a model of rigor, and Chapter 21, we will be better able to appreciate the distance separating the two modes of expression, and the difficulty in conceiving of the relationship between them. The latter is titled "How a Prince Must Act in Order to Gain Esteem." Machiavelli begins by citing the example of Ferdinand of Aragon, showing the hypocritical and cruel policies that enabled him to acquire glory and renown (*fama e gloria*); then he briefly mentions those of Bernabò of Milan, known to everyone as one of the most sinister figures among Italian tyrants, without recalling his crimes or entering into the detail of his actions. Upon which he begins, with no transition, a discussion on the danger of remaining neutral in a conflict, invokes in support of his thesis the conduct of the Romans, and, without fear of contradicting his earlier remarks on the perversity of human nature, observes that one can expect of a prince to which one is allied, even if his victory places you at his mercy, gratitude and love, alleging that "men are never so unseemly as to oppress you with such patent ingratitude." Then, using an expression that he had made a very different use of at the beginning of his discourse, he concludes that the *order of things* is such that "one can never flee one obstacle without running into another"; so that rational action now proves to be linked to an awareness of an ultimate indetermination, and the discovery of truth to be no longer the solution to a problem, the acquisition of certainty, but a seeking of the lesser evil. In the end, the prince is suddenly invited to encourage *virtù*, to protect his subjects in doing their work, win their confidence through his financial policy, reward those who contribute to the development of the city or state, and entertain the people with festivals and public games. From one theme to another, no logical connection is to be found. It is certain on the other hand that the final portrait of the *good prince* bears no resemblance to that of Ferdinand or of Bernabò. The readers, considering the argument and its strange conclusion, are left "satisfied and stunned," as were, the author told us, the subjects of Borgia on the day when Remirro de Orco, his minister, to whom the difficult task of pacifying the state by terror had been assigned, was cut in half by order of the prince in the middle of the public square at Cesena, with a block of wood and a blood-stained knife by his side . . .

Such then is the dual impression we get from a first reading of *The Prince*. At once that of rigorous discourse, whose movement carries us from the beginning to the end, without our being able to resist the eloquence of the demonstration, and that—increasingly strong as we advance in our examination of the text and focus our attention on it—of a thought adrift, breaking through suddenly on the occasion of a digression, drawing back or stopping at the moment it seems to throw itself freely in the direction it had set out for itself, and retracing its steps again and again, to modify or even reverse the meaning of what it has already said.

If I am right, this twofold play of writing must be accounted for. We must adapt our reading to it, ask ourselves why the author subjects himself to it, whether his thought is not simply organized simultaneously on two levels, especially whether the quest for a rationality immanent in political conduct does not go hand in hand with the discovery of its limitations, whether the conversion of an experience into an object of knowledge does not engender its own critique, whether the approach to reality, at the same time as requiring a growing determination of phenomena, does not expose one to a fundamental indetermination in relation to which the place of the knowing and acting subject is located. We must see to it that interpretation reserves as long as possible for the ideas of the writer, in the margin of their immediate meaning and punctual concatenation, the radiating space for the thought within the work to propagate.

2

The Logic of Force

"All States, all powers, that have held and hold rule (*imperio*) over men have been and are either republics or principalities." This is the opening statement of the first chapter of *The Prince*, the shortest chapter of all, as we have observed, in which in a few lines the hypotheses of an inquiry are enumerated. If we are astonished at the abruptness of this beginning, the contemporaries were even more so, for, instructed in classical and Christian tradition, they were accustomed to finding philosophical, moral, or religious considerations at the beginning of a political work. Furthermore, the author does not say why he omits these from his project. In neglecting to speak of the origin and the goal of the state, of the comparative merits of the various forms of government, of the function of the monarch in society, of the legitimacy and the illegitimacy of certain forms of power, he suggests by his very silence that these ideas have ceased being pertinent, or at the very least he invites his reader to wonder if they remain so, and in what sense. It is as if from now on one sole question governed political reflection—that question that he hastens to formulate the moment he has finished distinguishing several types of kingdoms: "to dispute by what means they can be governed and held on to." It is true that this question, understood its literal sense, is not entirely new. It may be found in *De Regimine principum* by Egidio Colonna, published in 1473, who, inspired by the Treatise of Thomas Aquinas, had tried to reconcile Christian principles with the practical requirements of the governing of men.[1] But the question arose in its time in a context that made it possible to delimit its scope with precision. The reader was first invited to explore in what the highest form of happiness (*felicitas*) consisted, toward what goal the actions of the prince are directed, what virtues they require, what passions may be enlisted in their service. He was to meditate on the conduct of man at various stages of life, and then consider, in its various aspects, how a prince should conduct himself toward his family—his relations with his wife, children, ministers, attendants, and close friends. Before finally getting to the examination of the politics of the prince, in times of war and in times of peace, the reader had to ask himself to what ends the community of the family, the city, and the state had been created by God (*propter quod bonum inventa fuit communitas domus, civitatis et regni*). It is true that Aristotle's *Politics* in Book 5, examined the means at the disposal of a Power, of whatever nature, to avoid the revolutions that threaten it, but the study was based on a definition of the state that left no doubt as to the author's intentions. It taught first of all that the organization of the state was subordinate to the principle of justice; that the good government ensured harmony between the various elements of the community; consequently, a government was defective and vulnerable to the degree that it abusively privileged one of these elements, and well organized and durable in proportion to its prevention of excessiveness. Hence the analysis of a tyranny, however daring it may have been in its attempt to establish the rules for its conservation, was unequivocally on the side of Good. If the prince's interest could serve to support him, it was because the essence of the state could be recognized even in its vitiated forms, and because the good of the tyrant and the common good could not be entirely dissociated without bringing about the downfall of the empowered.

On the other hand, the Machiavellian question, once it is reduced to its own terms, acquires an entirely new status. It is a question that does not arise from within an ordered discourse and world, in which he who asks it and he who is considered qualified to adjudicate would have only to recognize their respective assigned places, but rather it advances to meet fields of knowledge and operations destined to interrelate on their own, at the level of specificity that is characteristic of them, and to place the thinker and the doer in the function of a *subject* become the guarantor of his own activity.

Indubitably it is not by chance that Machiavelli announces that he will discuss the manner in which the principalities can be governed and retained (*come questi principati si possino governare e mantenere*). The turn of phrase is eloquent. We had already noted that the first hypotheses were organized in keeping with the perspective of a prince, although that perspective itself was not revealed. Here the language attests to an ambiguity that is inherent in the subject matter of politics, as begins to become evident to us. Governing and maintaining a state are operations that have their point of origin in the prince; thus, in order to determine exactly what they are, the best thing to do is take up his position, and to interrogate the place he occupies when taking control of the state, the conditions imposed upon him by the history of the governed people, whose master he has become, and the means of action he may employ. Conversely, however, in virtue of the very fact that the state exists, the prince is placed in one of the particular circumstances that we can observe, and must perform the functions imposed on him by his status. Hence in the first chapter neither the prince nor the state can provide us with the reference point of the origin, and it is up to us to take up an intermediary position, in a space created by the writer's movement from one pole to the other—a space that is in some respects indeterminate, and yet presented as the locus of the real. Machiavelli classifies all states, both ancient and modern, into two categories, and then distinguishes several sub-types of principalities; he does so only by adopting the point of view of a prince. But he does this in such a way as to avoid mentioning the circumstance of the founding of the state (though he will insist on this issue later), as a result of which the state seems to exist prior to the action of the political agent. On the one hand, the kingdom is conceptualized through a definition constituting it as the result of the operations of the acting subject. As opposed to Aristotle, Machiavelli is not content with seeking typical specimens within empirical space. On the other hand the prince, qua acting subject, is himself determined solely in relation to the place he occupies with respect to the object. Now, is it not Power, *imperio*, at once subject and object, introduced as a concept in the very first sentence of *The Prince*, that Machiavelli proposes for our consideration? Indeed, this *imperio*, if it is the word we use to designate the power that one person, or one group of people, exercises over others, and if it changes form according to circumstance, is also what stands above people, taken in their generality. It is that entity in virtue of which relations between people are ordered within the framework of the state—a dimension of (rather than a figure within) society: a dimension, the originative cause of which it would be as useless to seek in any particular human motivation as in a religious or metaphysical principle.

The fact that Machiavelli attempts, from the beginning of *The Prince*, to disengage his reader from a traditional image of the state is confirmed by his analysis of the hereditary kingdom. If he mentions this case at the beginning and discusses it before any other, it is, according to him, because it is the easiest one to resolve. Also, the brevity of his remark seems to confirm his minimal interest in it. But we have already learned that the introduction does not, properly speaking, give us a plan; it offers rather the suggestion of a method. The inquiry does not progress with any degree of regularity, at least not toward the most difficult part, since that aspect, the foundation of a state, is not approached until the middle of the first part. Moreover, how can we fail to note that the distinction between old and new principalities is not inherently obvious—that it is not more pertinent than the difference between the founding and the conquering of a state? Hence the decision to begin with the study of hereditary principalities has a different reason. By approaching things from this angle, the reader is first confronted with an example that political thinkers gave pride of place to since the Middle Ages; in their view, the hereditary prince was the one whose authority was considered legitimate, and who came to power by pacific means. In placing this example in a new light, Machiavelli destabilizes the commonly held opinion that he at first seemed to embrace—assimilating it to that of the conqueror, exemplified in this case Louis XII, who was himself a hereditary prince who chose to expand his state—a circumstance through which our author immediately associates the problem of peace with that of war.

At first blush, the analysis remains faithful to convention. He who holds power for having received it from his ancestors, Machiavelli observes, can do no better than to maintain the validity of the old principles of government (*l'ordine de' sua antenati*) and to play for time with respect to events; he need only show an "ordinary ability" to remain in power, and if an adversary succeeds, exceptionally, in ousting him, he will return the moment that adversary encounters difficulties. His subjects are used to his dynasty and not averse to obeying him. Machiavelli designates him, in accordance with established usage, as the "natural prince." Now there is no doubt that this term originally corresponded to a specific conception of the monarchy. The latter is "natural" since inscribed within custom, for custom is, in the Thomist view, a second nature. What has a stable form in time corresponds to the advent of a *habitus*, the place and function of which is inscribed within the hierarchy of beings—an idea ever present in the work of Colonna, and that Savonarola always echoed, though placing it, it is true, at the service of the republican cause, when he affirmed that the habits of the Florentine people now constituted their nature to the point of making it impossible for them to be subject to a monarchic form of government.[2] Even in the observation that the prince who has been driven out "by some very exceptional and excessive force" will be able to regain his power, it is possible to recognize an image from Aristotelian physics, according to which "every body is conceived of as possessing a tendency to occupy its natural place, and so to return to it, when removed by violence therefrom."[3] But these remarks merely prepare for a reversal of perspective. Indeed, the author's arguments refute the thesis they seem to support. If the natural prince enjoys security, it is, we are told, because he "has less cause and less necessity to give offense to his subjects (*offendere*)." It is also because "antiquity and the long continuance of hereditary rule obliterate, with the memories of their origin, the reasons for any change." He is, it must be recognized, more loved than a new prince, because it suffices, we are told, that he not make himself hated due to "extraordinary vices" for the *consensus* of his subjects to be maintained in his favor. Thus the truth is that his power benefits from a habituation to oppression. The permanence of the dominator weakens the resistance of the dominated, so that their submission may be obtained with less effort.

It is therefore through consideration of the opposition of the prince to his subjects that the picture of the most stable government emerges, and not with respect to a harmony based on the inner disposition of the social body. The reader was pleased to see in stability the result of a good form, the establishment of which would correspond to a design of Providence or a natural finality, and was ready to think it to the prince's credit that he was wise enough to become its instrument, as opposed to the tyrant, always involved in violence; but as it turns out, stability must be thought of in terms of a prior instability and violence, and the "old prince" merely has the privilege of exploiting the earlier triumphant struggles of a "new prince." Between the two regimes there is not an essential difference, but one of degree, deriving from their respective positions vis-à-vis the adversaries they have to subdue. To the conquest of power there corresponds a rapid and violent movement that must triumph over various forces of resistance; but to the degree that it has been successful, there comes a moment in which it is changed into a slow movement, tending to maintain itself on its own. It is this passage from one regime to another that may be thought of as *natural,* that is, *necessary* under certain conditions—as is, to use an anachronistic metaphor, the shifting of gears of a motor—not the motor, or form of political organization, itself. If I have correctly understood the closing statement of the chapter devoted to inherited principalities, there are not, according to the author, two specifically distinct moments—one corresponding to that of the social body proper, and another to its corruption. Rather, the same causes explain the permanence of power and the repetition of accidents. It is equally true that "antiquity and the long continuance of hereditary rule obliterate, with the memories of their origin, the reasons for any change," and that "one change always leaves a dovetail into which another will fit."

But perhaps I have too readily accepted the idea that the pedigree of old power alone suffices to guarantee the attachment of subjects to their prince. Perhaps it is no accident that Machiavelli, in evoking the figure of the hereditary prince, does not choose the example that would naturally come to anyone's mind, the king of France, master of a powerful and well-established state, but prefers to speak of the dukes of Ferrara, second-rate figures whom he knew (and this was common knowledge) to have reconquered their states in the same way they had lost them: solely on the basis of the vicissitudes of international politics. Indeed, we soon go on to learn that the stability of the government in France comes not from its origin but from the structure of a power divided between the prince and his barons. And we discover toward the end of the work, in a passage to which I have already alluded, that a new prince may be more firmly established and more secure than the heir to an old dynasty. We must assume, therefore, that the hereditary prince gives us but one point of repair; that he serves only to make us appreciate the distance it behooves us to take up with respect to popular opinion.

This hypothesis is immediately confirmed as we continue reading. Machiavelli had first considered that an old prince is "more loved" than a new one. By the beginning of the next chapter, it appears that the latter cannot conquer a state without soon being hated by all; not only by his former enemies, to whose interests he is detrimental, but also by his own partisans, whose appetites he cannot satisfy. Thus we are justified in being doubtful about the meaning of what the writer first called *love*, and wonder whether what he was thinking was *less hated* when he wrote: *more loved*. This doubt is all the more justifiable as he specifies that in all the new principalities the same difficulty arises—a *natural* difficulty, as he observes, because men are wont to change masters in hopes of improving their condition. Considering this disposition, we can scarcely continue to believe that time is on the side of the hereditary prince. Furthermore, a moment ago the natural prince seemed so firmly established in the state that he could not fail to retake it, if he happened, by an exceptional force, to be driven out; now, the history of the conquest of Milan reveals that the prince's return to power cannot be imputed to the nature of the re-gime, but is a consequence of the difficulties in which the occupier finds himself. Indeed, Ludovico il Moro ("The Moor"), discussed here, is not a natural monarch, but the son of a usurper, and it can by no means be said that the long history of the house of Sforza wiped away the memory of its origin. The truth is that Louis XII's failure has a universal cause: it derives from the fact that the victor cannot fail to arouse the hostility of his new subjects immediately following his success.

It is true that the distinction between the old and the new prince, between the order of custom and that of innovation, remains valid, but it cannot be understood in terms of the classical idea of nature, nor be translated into ethical terms. It leads rather to our imagining the field of politics as a field of forces in which power must find an equilibrium for the conditions. The case of conquest is, in this perspective, privileged, in that it immediately brings out the problem that the prince must solve if he wishes to maintain his position in the state: he must resist the ad-versaries his exploit has created, and establish himself within the field of forces that his own actions have modified, causing disturbances that tend to spread, to his detriment. Thus, his actions are determined by a state of war in which he finds himself confronting at once other monarchs and his own subjects; and his politics can be no more than a strategy analogous to that of a captain who, having captured a choice position on the battlefield, expends his energy in foiling the attempts of the enemy resolved to take it back from him.

What Machiavelli delineates is, then, a very general, schematic account of the situation, in which the protagonists (states, social groups) are reduced to the function of abstract agents, potential allies, or adversaries of the prince. But this schematic representation already introduces us to the complexity of the political play of forces. For it is not sufficient that the individual who has seized power should dominate his adversaries by violence; that same power threatens to turn against him by sparking their resistance, without allowing him to gain support—as may be observed in the early stages of a conquest, in which the hatred stirred up by an occupying army and the disappointment inevitably brought about by the policies of the new prince become the causes of his downfall. He must also act in such a way as to make the new power relations turn to his advantage, both within the state and beyond it. Politics is a form of warfare, and it is surely no accident that, in order drive this point home, Machiavelli chooses first to conduct his reasoning on the basis of the seizure of power by force of arms. But we should also recognize that this form of warfare obeys specific imperatives: it does not depend on pure violence, and the prince does not triumph solely because he is the strongest, since he must maintain himself, hold on over time, and coexist with those he dominates, imposing his authority day in, day out, and continually containing nascent discord. From the analysis of the situation in which he finds himself immediately after the conquest, it emerges that his actions have a double nature: they tend in the direction of both more and less violence. If the people whom the victor is going to govern are of the same language and mores as his own subjects, Machiavelli tells us, the rule is for him to make the former prince disappear and to exterminate his entire family, in order to preclude the return of the dynasty, while at the same time avoiding any change in the laws and taxation, that is, while limiting as much as possible the effects of his aggression. If the conquered people are different from his own, he must go and live there in person, in order to see to it that his delegates do not indulge in pillage, and that malcontents may find redress in him. Or else he must set up colonies there, for thus the only ones wronged will be the small number whose lands and goods have been pillaged, and who are placed in a situation of being incapable of doing harm; whereas the others, satisfied to be left in peace without the destruction brought about by an occupying army, have no reason to rebel. In both cases, two requirements are reconciled: that of overcoming by force, of immediately extinguishing the most dangerous centers of resistance, and that of winning recognition for that force, thus guaranteeing one's own safety by ensuring that of others. The author supplies us with the key to this policy in noting that men "must be either cajoled or killed"; but we are to construe this as meaning that the two terms of the alternative may be equally applicable according to the case at hand: in reality, some must be killed and others cajoled—and for the same reason, deriving from the logic of power relations. Machiavelli finds another way to convince us that things are indeed as he describes them: he ties in with the same analysis problems of domestic and foreign policy, reasoning as if the relations of the prince with his subjects were of the same nature as those obtaining between states, that is, between independent agents, whose conduct is solely determined by their respective interests. Indeed, in this last example as well, the power of the prince is solely determined by the field in which it is applied. He must at once impose his will and make compromises, in order to bring about a balance sheltering him from foreign aggression. He must, as the author points out, "become the leader and defender of his less powerful neighbors, and endeavor to weaken the stronger ones, and take care that they are not invaded by some foreigner more powerful than himself." This is a strategy that, as we can clearly see, is guided by no other consideration than the desire to maintain and or increase one's power.

This term, power, which Machiavelli uses repeatedly in the passage to which I allude, is taken by him, at least at this stage of his discourse, in a purely positive sense. Thus, it is appropriate to point out that if the image of the legitimate prince, governing for the good of his subjects, in keeping with a divine plan or the order of nature, is passed over in silence, it is not because it is replaced by an apology for power. The arguments of the classical philosophers, which attempt to supply a foundation for the idea of good government, are no less ignored than are those traditionally ascribed to their adversaries the Sophists. In one sole instance, in which the writer notes that "the desire to acquire possessions is a very natural and ordinary thing, and when those men do it who can do so successfully, they will always be praised for it, or at least they will not be blamed," he seems to want to justify the appetite for power. But that assertion itself only takes on its true meaning within the framework of an analysis that, from beginning to end, is placed beneath the emblem of pure observation. The fact that conquests are carried out and that, when successful, they are not criticized—this is all that need be taken into account, just as we were obliged a moment ago to admit that men change masters readily or that an old prince has less reason to offend his subjects than does a new one. These are phenomena that can be found throughout history, that present themselves to the eye of the observer, and that are intelligible because they fit in with other facts to which they are related as either causes or consequences, or both at once. It is this articulation that is stressed by Machiavelli, in such a way that we are always confronted with several terms at once and forced to conceive of them in terms of their relations, that is, in terms of the actions and reactions they exert on one another. For example, the idea that men are never satisfied with their condition does not have a value in itself: it must be understood at the same time that an old prince does not entirely cease to offend his subjects, even though they are used to his power; that every change creates the conditions for another change; that a foreign prince only imposes his power by violence and necessarily incites hatred; and finally that certain measures are capable of disarming opposing groups or individuals. Only the constellation of events is meaningful. We cannot consider the behavior of subjects otherwise than in relation to that of the prince, and vice versa, and it is the *fact* of their relations that constitutes the object of knowledge. Similarly, we cannot fixate on this last idea, according to which the desire for conquest is a natural thing, as if it contained a judgment on man that is sufficient in itself. For this desire is indeed natural, just as are the ones according to which the dominated want a change of domination, and weak states want to escape from the authority of a stronger one by means of the intervention of a foreign prince. Conquest cannot be understood in relation to motivation, which at a different level of being would mark its origin, but proves to be determined as one modality of political experience codetermined by the others, and that in turn codetermines them. Thus conquest is caught up in a network of necessity in which its success or failure is determined. Whence the significance of the fact that the formula that has captured our attention is only stated after an analysis of the politics of Rome and those of the king of France, in which that necessity is manifested, and the proof demonstrated that the conduct of the victor is inscribed in the order of things (*l'ordine delle cose*).

The question "What is power?" is therefore not important. What Machiavelli places before our attention, first and foremost, is only the conflict or conflicts between agents possessed of various degrees of power. What he esteems *natural or ordinary* are the relations established between them, given their respective degrees of power in the specific conditions in which they are placed. Thus, positing himself as a pure observer, he is thereby posited as a pure calculator, and his discourse gradually establishes an equivalence between what is natural, necessary, and in keeping with reason. To observe and to calculate are the same thing, because the empirical givens—the phenomenon "conquest of Milan," for example—can only be located and circumscribed to the extent that we recognize a combination of terms and relations, other examples of which are furnished by history. To describe the adventures of Louis XII is to give an

account of his mistakes, just as to describe the evolution of the power of
Rome is to show the operations that have led to the solving of a problem.
In both these cases, as in the Turkish example, the author discerns what
we have called, after him, an order of things, that is, not an order transcending experience, but an experience ordered in itself, the matter of
which, though always changing, since the situations do not repeat themselves, are distributed according to lines of force that remain constant.
Thus the prince appears as an actor whose conduct is determined by the
requirements of the situation, and consequently, whose own power is indissociable from his understanding the order of power relations involved:
he is, or is not, capable of recognizing that order, and if he succeeds in
doing so, it is because he has been able to rise above the confusion of
events, to resist the temptation of resorting to means that, though immediately effective, are bound to turn against him (for example, forming an
alliance with a foreign power that will inevitably become an enemy once
it has established itself in the country in which it intervenes), that is, ultimately, to free himself from the contingency of current circumstances
and from the very drives that prompt his actions.

Machiavelli, by placing the reader in this perspective, allows him to
discover that the position of the theoretician and that of the actor coincide. True, this coincidence is only partial. We must also admit that the
two take up different levels of rationality and are enabled at that level to
claim the truth of experience. Indeed, from one point of view, the theoretician seems to embrace history in its entire expanse: his field of representation encompasses all the combinations of power relations, every
possible status of the agent. Thus he ascends to the level of the idea of a
universal calculus, whereas the prince, at the very moment of successfully
resolving the difficulties confronting his undertaking, continues to move
within the finite horizons of a specific situation, and remains subject to
the immediate dependency imposed on him from without and the goals
he has set for himself. But from a different point of view, we see the theoretician condemned to reasoning about the past. If he has the power to
point out solutions, it is because the terms are already inscribed in the
real; the prince, on the other hand, has the advantage of thinking the
universal in the particular, of deciphering, within the present, the signs
of what will be the configuration of future conflicts. Thus he has, in
the practice of anticipation, the ability to test the infinite calculus, since
events will constantly confirm or deny the results obtained by it, and since
he must constantly factor in the effect of his own actions. Like a doctor
whose strength it is to formulate his diagnostic while the illness is still
at its beginning stages, he has the advantage, Machiavelli tells us, over
one who, the illness having already developed, disposes of all elements

necessary for certainty but is incapable of influencing its course. Still, it is theory that teaches us that theory and practice are not the same thing. In affirming the permanence of their conflict, in rejecting the idea that a political form carries stability within itself, the thinker recognizes the permanence of accidents, and consequently designates the function of the prince as that of a subject who conquers truth in a continuous movement of rationalization of experience. At the same time that he assumes the right to conceive of power relations in their generality, he teaches that they are always instituted by the empirical operations of agents placed in contingent situations. At the same time that he extracts from every situation the terms of a problem and makes us sensitive to the constraints of a method, he shows that the givens of this problem are always shifting, and that the solution is never supplied in advance. Thus the point of view of the thinker and that of the actor do not cancel each other out, or do not diverge from one another to the point of their relationship becoming unintelligible, and the antinomy run up against by the Ancients seems to be surmounted. Indeed, to the philosopher who claimed to ground Power in right it could be objected that by the very fact that he used language he was focused on the universal, thus becoming foreign, at the very moment he claimed to rejoin him, to the individual whom the claim to power closed up in the particularity and incommunicability of desire. Conversely, the moment an attempt was made to give form and feature to the universal, it became necessary to resort to the fiction of a government in conformity with nature, and give up seeking its inscription in empirical reality. Now thought has freed itself of the distinction between essence and existence, and we are no longer caught up in the alternative of a knowing that is affirmed in the forgetfulness of what is, or a doing that mocks any attempt to give it a name. There is nothing else in history but what *appears*, that is, the actions of men and the events around which they are interwoven; and a conquest, for example, is "natural" once it is ordinary, once it is a part to present and past experience. But what appears bears a meaning along with it, is immediately the material of a language, as we always grasp within it relationships, so that the existent ceases being that inert, unintelligible fact, defying thought—whether this be because thought, in order to maintain itself as thought, must turn away from it, or because in order to ground it in Being thought abandons its own norms and sinks into contingency. From now on we do not need to transfigure the prince to assign him a function within a rational system of the world; we apprehend him in his historical reality: he is Louis XII in Italy, or the Turk, or even—and this reference informs us that we must see in him the pure political agent—the Roman Republic. The identity we attribute to him matters little. Once we have given ourselves the image of him, he appears situated at the center of a network of relations as the bearer of a necessity that works to his benefit or detriment, depending on whether he proves capable of determining the actions of his adversaries or lets himself be determined by them. By his intermediary the real reveals itself as a field of operations: the frontiers of the real are those of the rational.

If we return once more to the first considerations inspired by the example of the hereditary prince, we can take stock of the distance traveled. It seemed that to maintain the state it sufficed to remain faithful to the old principles (*l'ordine de'sui antenati*) and to temporize with events (*accidenti*). Now it is the pseudo sages of Florence who are being criticized. They, as it seems hardly necessary to emphasize, are neither hereditary princes nor new princes—because they never stop recommending that we "enjoy the benefits of time" (*godere el benefizio del tempo*); "time," we learn, "drives all things before it, the good with the evil, the evil with the good." And while time's power to institute a form that would be worthy in itself and maintain itself independently diminishes, the subject's power to find an order in accidents and govern their course increases, as he places his trust exclusively in *virtù* and *prudenzia*. The image of the dukes of Ferrara, whose scant power is based on their dynasty's past, is replaced by that of the Romans, who built and maintained an immense empire because they were able entrust themselves to the future.

At the moment when the reader becomes cognizant of the political problem in the terms in which it presents itself to the prince, a digression invites him to conceptualize more clearly the limitations of individual action. This would appear to be nothing more than a further clarification, since the writer has already taken care to have us note that the failure of an invader, in the initial phase of territorial occupation, is attributable to universal causes. But perhaps that remark slipped by unnoticed, and the detailed criticism of Louis XII's errors suggested that the retention of power depends solely on the intelligence of the prince. Hence it seems well to meditate for a moment on the felicitous outcome of the conquests of Alexander, so that we may be persuaded that they only appear to constitute an exception, and that the objective conditions as well as the strategy of the agent determine the outcome of an enterprise. Indeed, if we consider the nature of peoples beneath the thumb of domination, we will conclude that while Alexander was able to impose his authority much more easily than were Pyrrhus or other invaders, it is not because they were of greater *virtù;* it is rather solely because their new subjects, having long been oppressed by a despot, were naturally disposed to obey. Nevertheless, the arguments used on this occasion are so important as to constitute in themselves a thesis whose significance we must grasp both from the point of view of its appearance at this particular point in the discourse, and from that of the indirect means through which it is introduced. Machiavelli, as he prepares to answer the question from a hypothetical objector who would be astonished at the ease with which Alexander conquered a part of Asia and passed that inheritance down to his descendants, suddenly classifies all the princedoms within the reach of memory into two categories: one comprising the states of a despotic regime, the other those in which the power is divided between a monarch and barons. This classification, which creates a surprise, the effect of which he is careful not to weaken by any justification, supplies him with the matter of his analysis; thus the reference to Alexander appears to have served merely as a pretext to proceed to the comparison of two types of power. The reader retains that the respective degrees of solidity of these two sorts of government may be assessed on the basis of their ability to resist foreign aggression. The despotic government at first seems the stronger, since in it authority is unified, and the ministers, rather than being long established lords of provinces with close ties to their subjects, do not have sufficient credibility to mount a rebellion that would pave the way for an eventual invader. In order to destroy the established power, then, they would have to rely solely on the power of arms. But the perspective is reversed the moment we consider the chances of the implantation of a new prince. The fact is, there would be no obstacle to his domination, once victory has been accomplished and the royal family exterminated. Having been held in slavery by their former master, the subjects are easily governed. In a country of mixed monarchy, on the other hand, rivalries will soon put his power at risk, and the factions that sustained him will turn against him. The groups he must oppress will rebel and seek foreign allies. On that hypothesis, it no longer suffices to "suppress the royal blood (*spegnere el sangue del principe*), as there always remain lords who will take the lead in new changes, and since one can neither appease nor suppress them, on the first occasion that comes along all the States will be lost." It must be admitted that the apparently most vulnerable form of government turns out, over to time, to be the most resilient, and the authority that makes compromises is stronger than unbridled domination. Thus we find, employed for a different purpose, an idea whose importance we have already had a glimpse of: power is to be assessed within the matrix of its relation to other powers. Now our reasons for appreciating the solidity of the French monarchy, the model of a government in which the power of the monarch is limited, are the same ones that governed our analysis of the relations between States, or our analysis of the policy of Louis XII in Milan. But we moved imperceptibly from a particular to a general point of view. Machiavelli is no longer describing just the logic of the operations of the prince. Henceforth he reasons about these systems of force that are incarnated in political regimes and that open a path to the study of social structures.

Still, the important thing is that this transition remains in the penumbra, that the writer's language does not present a surface amenable to moral assessments, and that the question of the nature of the state is consistently avoided. On these conditions, it even becomes possible to allude to the strengths of the republican form of government. An allusion, it is true, doubly cautious, since for one thing Machiavelli does not abandon the hypothesis of the conquest, and wonders merely about the difficulties a new prince would encounter in a city that was formerly free, to which he responds that the surest method would be to reduce it to ruin and scatter its inhabitants; and for another he intersperses, in the first part of the analyses, the case of monarchies accustomed to living beneath their rule and that of republics, as if the latter had nothing specific about them. But the new idea, advanced along with others that tend to dissimulate it (as on a battlefield the conquest of one position is accompanied by several operations of diversion), springs up in the following passage at the end of Chapter 5: the republics are the most solid regimes, the most resistant to the projects of an aggressor because the citizens are attached to them in freedom. This gives us to understand, since authority has not only limits, as in the feudal type of monarchy, but is largely dispersed among the citizens, that the logic of the relations of force plays in favor of a distribution of power and a system that would ensure an exchange between the governors and the governed.

At this point in the reading, the writer's approach has become manifest to us. In appearance, he restricts himself to the examination of the particular cases in which we can find the operations necessary for the takeover or maintenance of power; but by this means he introduces the first general considerations on the opposition between the prince and his subjects, the relations between states, and the relative strength of the various regimes. These are considerations that stake out the progressive movements of a thought for which it seems indispensable that it should remain on the hither side of expression—as if by delivering itself in the form of explicit knowledge it would either deteriorate or meet with the incomprehension of others—or, better yet, as if describing a meandering course—as if taking possession of truth only through a twofold and constant denial. Indeed, the idea of stability, touched upon for a moment in connection with the example of the hereditary monarchy, is countered with that of movement, understood as constitutive of all political experience; the idea of a time that preserves is contrasted with that of a time that drives all before it; the idea of a social nature defined as an order regulated by immanent or transcendent ends is countered with that of accidents whose concatenation is from cause to effect; the idea of a bond of love between the prince and his subjects is set in opposition to that of an oppression of varying degrees. But, simultaneously, from the image of a violence that is exerted endlessly and a force that draws advantage solely from its immediate superiority over the other, thought leads us back to that of an economy of power; in the face of the subject-slave condition, it finds a sense of "natural affection" for the nobleman on the part of a people who feel an attachment to his laws; a regime seems all the more solid to the degree that its power is more shared; and finally, the pure diversity of accidents allows relatively stable constellations to appear in historically typical situations, in political structures.

Where does this movement of thought lead us? Should we take hold of the positive truths that the discourse adumbrates and arrange them into the basic elements of a science of politics? Or seek, in the criticism of the images from which the common opinion takes its inspiration, the signs of a new status of experience and knowledge?

These questions are asked at the beginning of Chapter 6, devoted to the founding of the state. Now all indications are that with this hypothesis we are entering a new phase of the analysis. It is no longer merely a question of defining the operations that make it possible for the prince to govern and hold onto a conquered domain, nor to appreciate the impact of social and historical conditions on his undertaking. The action through which a subject takes power is now distinguished from all the others of the same sort, in that it institutes him as prince and gives a people its political unity. Thus we may assume that an examination of the conduct of the founder (for which, let us recall, the author had not prepared us) will occasion a reflection on the origin of the state. Furthermore, Machiavelli leads us to believe that his intention is not just to remain within the limits of a particular case, however privileged. While he announces that he is going to talk about "entirely new dominions, those in which the prince and the state are new," and does in fact treat this theme in the major part of the chapter, the title brings up another theme, that of dominions acquired by one's own *virtù* and arms. As the chapter progresses, he recalls the failure of Savonarola, the reformer who incessantly proclaimed his allegiance to the republican form of government, and ends with the example of Hiero of Syracuse, a simple captain who rose to become the head of the city by a coup d'état. Thus the hypothesis of the

founding of the state seems intended to enlighten us both on the nature
of the state and of power in general. It is true that on first reading, Chapter 6 does not fulfill our expectations. There is no answer to the questions
we asked; no response seems to be given. Machiavelli brings up the most
illustrious examples, those of Moses, Cyrus, Romulus, and Theseus, but
he does not analyze them, and we can hardly keep from thinking that
the politics of these glorious founders, whose memory comes more from
legend than history, eludes exact knowledge. On *virtù* and its relation to
Fortune, on the difficulty in introducing "*ordini nuovi*," on the authority
acquired by the prince once the initial obstacles have been removed, on
the happiness he derives from that victory and procures for his country,
we must be content with rapid and very general considerations, of which
the least we may say is that they are not backed up by a description of
the facts and that they leave us with a sense of insufficiency. The only
positive conclusion we can reach is that the founder must prefer force to
entreaties, that armed prophets triumph where the unarmed ones fail;
but in light of what we have learned that idea comes up short; for we
already know that the understanding of force, more than force itself, is
at the heart of politics. In short, the chapter now under consideration is
quite different from the previous ones, but not in the sense we expected.
While the careful examination of the politics of Louis XII or that of the
Romans led to a truth of universal significance, the author's remarks now
seem to float in a zone of indecisiveness where neither the weight of facts
nor that of ideas appears to count. But this disappointment comes from
the fact that we still want to take the statements literally, and perhaps we
should rather follow the lead of the prince to whom the past gives an object of inspiration rather than of imitation. Perhaps we should only use
the text as a springboard to reach the level of what it suggests to thought.
Indeed, the first lines of the chapter convey a message that seems to have
more than one meaning. Machiavelli asks his reader not to be surprised
if he adduces very illustrious examples: they offer, he says in substance,
the model of the highest political action, but it is neither necessary nor
possible that the new prince should identify with the founding heroes. It
suffices that he wants to resemble them, that is, not become their equal,
but move forward on the pathway they opened up. Prudence requires
him to remember the *virtù* of these glorious predecessors, not in hopes
of gaining it for themselves, but so that their own may get some tinge
of it. We learn that he is like the prudent archer who, to reach a distant
target, adjusts his aim in keeping with a point situated much higher than
his objective. Now we may reasonably doubt that an archer could ever
avoid bowing to this necessity, and that a founder of whatever merit could
ever have acted without role models, and we must observe that in aiming

higher the archer does indeed hit his mark. Hence we are inclined to the opinion that the figure of the hero is purely symbolic, or better yet, that the realistic function of the greatest examples is a symbolic function. In order to reveal this, we are ready to take a second look at the text. It occurs to us that Machiavelli himself proceeds as an archer, that his discourse follows the indirect path of the arrow, and that the general considerations in which we vainly seek meaning are perhaps simple points to find our range with rather than being the real target.

Thus, the movement of the discourse becomes more important than the apology of force, for it appears, once again, that Machiavelli presents us with the traditional image of political action only the better to mark a departure from it. Henceforth what attracts the attention is the gap between the idea the author starts with and the one he arrives at; what gives itself as meaning is not the meaning enclosed in each proposition, but the obvious discordance between the principles underlying the first and the second part of the argument. The creation of the state is first presented as the work of *virtù*. True, that *virtù* is defined as the antithesis of Fortune; it is the power of withdrawing from the disorder of events, of rising above time—which, as we have learned, *drives all things before it*—of seizing the occasion and thus of recognizing it, of introducing, in conclusion, according to the author's wording, *a form into a matter*. But for the first time it proves to be at the same time moral virtue: the founders are "excellent" men; Moses, of whom one should not speak, since he but "carried out what was ordered him by God," is adjudged admirable for that grace that "made him worthy to speak with God"; the others are no less so, since their conduct was no different than his; their glory is to have given unity and freedom to a people dispersed and oppressed, and their personal success is in keeping with the happiness and ennoblement of their country. But scarcely is that image adumbrated than it must be abandoned. Evoking the difficulties the prince will encounter at the beginning of his endeavor, Machiavelli suddenly employs a different language. It turns out that the founders are forced (*forzati*) to introduce new institutions (*nuovi ordini e modi*) in order to establish the state, and, the author adds, as if the two requirements blended into one, ensure its security. Of these institutions, we learn that nothing is harder to treat, nor more doubtful of success, for they do not benefit from any support within the society. A moment earlier in the text, the politics of the prince appeared to be an expression of the collective aspirations; now we are to understand that no one is on his side; his enemies are all those who derived profit from the old order and he finds but lukewarm supporters among those who would benefit from the new one, so strong is the incredulity of men in new things as long as no definite experience has demonstrated the solidity of the regime being established, and to such a degree does their changeability of mind prevent their being faithful to the cause that for a brief moment excited their passions. Again it seems that there the prince has no other problem than that of making his subjects obey; so that the position of glorious founder is brought closer to that of the invader, who, according to the analysis of Chapter 3, had to defend himself at once against his adversaries and his partisans. Thus it is not by chance that Machiavelli uses the same term to designate their action: *acquistare lo stato.*

Now it is at this stage in the discourse that faith and force are starkly contrasted, and the critique of the unarmed prophet is illustrated by the example of Savonarola—an argument that completes the destabilization of our first opinion. In the very terms in which the problem is posed ("it must be considered whether those seeking new things [*questi innovatori*] can do something on their own [*stanno per loro medesimi*] or whether they depend on others, that is, whether to succeed in their endeavors they depend on entreaty or force") the underlying schema sustaining the entire discussion may be found. The opposition between *virtù* and Fortune has changed into an opposition between the power to depend on oneself alone and subjugation to the desires of the Other, and this opposition in turn is changed into the opposition between the autonomy of man and dependence on God. It is true that Machiavelli seems to end with the apology of force, but this theme suddenly reveals its function, which is to deliver us from the myth of a history regulated by Providence. With it, the respect we had for the executor of the things ordained by God is brutally annulled. And while the figure of Savonarola is superimposed on that of Moses, the politics of the prince of the Jews is restored to its "reality." A moment ago we thought we had found within that figure the testimony of a divine grace by which other founders of States were unwittingly nourished; henceforth we must conclude to the contrary, that submission to God's decrees was nothing but appearance, and that the *virtù* of Moses is of the same sort as that of Romulus, Cyrus, and Theseus.

It is indeed true that in certain respects some uncertainty remains. To the questions, "What is the *virtù?*" and "What are the *ordini nuovi* to which the state owes its origin?" no certain answer, as I have said, can be given. But this uncertainty has taken on a strange weight. And of one thing there can be no doubt: Machiavelli invites his reader to a questioning of the foundations of politics, and begins by forbidding him to rely on the truths established by the humanist or Christian tradition. Now this questioning is so radical that one can judge that the case treated had no other function than to give it form. It was necessary, it seemed, to evoke the foundation of the state, the sacred that is attached to the highest political endeavor, the *virtù* of venerated heroes to give a glimpse, when these images come apart, of the true stakes of the discourse. How are we to conceive of the state, on what ground are we establish it, if the one who grounds it is alone, if there is no longer any arrangement in nature guaranteeing the endeavor, if men are not predisposed to grant it to one another, but rather resist the coming of their community; if, moreover, the idea of a providential ordering of society is a decoy? Such is the ultimate question that appears on the horizon, in the light of which all others pale. Machiavelli does not formulate it. He suggests it. He sends us in its direction. And he makes his suggestion in his own way—in a brief, light style, without the emphasis of a philosopher or a preacher, but a style about which there can be no mistake, especially given the name Savonarola, purposely placed, reminding us of a different call to the renewal of political thought and action.

The reference to the name Savonarola is more than a simple allusion to the failure of an unarmed prophet, more than an artifice intended to modify the image of the wisdom of Moses, and even more than an invitation to go beyond the fixed framework of the foundation of the state. Savonarola addressed the same interlocutors as Machiavelli, and already claimed to bring *ordini nuovi*. Thus it is the failure not only of his politics but also of its underlying principles that we are meant to appreciate fully, and it is toward a new practice, a new thought that we are to turn, in order to discover the road to a radical change—the way of thinking of a theoretician in the process of giving an accurate portrayal of the prince, and of substituting his own teaching to that of the defeated prophet. This substitution is betokened, to the desired degree, by an ironic paraphrase. Savonarola denounced the foolish and wicked who denied the possibility of governing by means of *pater noster*s, claiming to draw from the Old and New Testament proofs that cities had always been saved by prayer. According to Machiavelli, the fool is the one relies on prayer and forgets that Moses established his reign by force. According to Savonarola, it was the *unbelief* of men that was the source of Italy's woes; Machiavelli reemploys the same term with a different meaning: it is the lack of faith in the new things, not in the old image of a protective God, that is the obstacle to a political reform; and his irony has a twofold effect when he suggests that Savonarola failed because he was unable to force men to keep their faith, not in God, but in him. Savonarola distinguished the true princes (*veri principi*) whose only goal is the common good, from the tyrants who only desire to reign by force; Machiavelli insinuates that the best of princes, those who ensure the happiness of their country, have triumphed because they were able to impose their power against the will of all. Machiavelli's critique may be traced even in the image of the oppositions and resistances that the founder has to overcome. For, following the example of the prophet who went to war against the *tiepidi*, those who did not have the courage to fight for their faith, and who were no less guilty in his view than the *ostinati*, determined to remain in their blindness, the writer modulates the same term thrice—*tiepidi, tepidezza, tepidamente*—to designate those who appear to support the prince's action and be destined to profit from the new institutions, but abandon him for lack of being forced to faithfulness.[4]

But Machiavelli does not oppose the truth proclaimed by Savonarola with a different truth: only the urgent need to think politics at a certain level emerges from his discourse. It is in this connection that Chapter 6 marks a privileged moment; not, to be sure, because it makes it possible to glean new knowledge on the nature of politics, but rather because knowledge is now rooted in a not-knowing. This is the paradox fully illuminated by the analysis of the foundation—a foundation that was presented, however, as nothing more than one empirical example among others. At the beginning of *The Prince*, Machiavelli seemed to have set aside questions considered essential by those who had written on politics before him. He gave his research the air of a purely technical survey, as if it dispensed with all justification, as if it sufficed to consult experience to know by what means the state can be governed. But while the necessity that commands the actions of the prince in every situation is found in a few examples, it is the principle of that necessity itself, the status of the social as a field of forces, that of the government as a pure agent, and the relation of the reader to his object, that are elaborated in keeping with an increasingly specific critique of the images to which classical and Christian philosophy adhere, so that the requirement of scientific certainty and a determination of the real at once imposes itself as what gives the discourse its meaning and turns out to depend on the truth of a purely critical movement, bound in depth to the experience of an uncertainty with respect to the foundation of knowledge, or to that of an indetermination with respect to the very Being of the political.

Thus the repeated appeal to exact knowledge and to a practice that would be rigorously subordinate to it reverberates oddly, in a certain void—a void that the writer deliberately engineers, environing the new concepts of a theory of action, in the space in which thought formerly found reassurance in the presence of a divine or natural order.

3

The Social Abyss and Attachment to Power

Doubtless the foundation of the state is the most noble, the most perilous, and the most glorious enterprise that is offered to the reflection of
the theoretician, since it confers on a people its political identity and requires of the prince who ventures to undertake it the highest *virtù*. As for
this *virtù*, in which we have learned to recognize the power to rise above
Fortune, Machiavelli has given us to understand that it characterized the
best men (*eccelentissimi*). When we come to consider the action of those
who have taken over a state by guile or violence and seized, through a war
or a revolution, a title to which they had no right, it thus seems that we
sink to a level below politics. Neither Borgia, who, by the grace of Pope
Alexander and his French allies was able to seize the states of several despots of Romagna, nor Agathocles, the military leader who became the
king of Syracuse by having the directors of the City massacred at the opportune moment, nor the private citizen who is swept into power by the
struggle of one faction or class against another are by any means "excellent" men. These princes are what are normally called usurpers. But, as
I have said, the author abstains from calling them such, and his silence
on this point, we may surmise, has the force of a caveat. It is true that the
difference separating them from founding heroes is strongly emphasized:
such heroes have risen by *virtù* and their own arms, while usurpers have
done so by Fortune and foreign arms, or by some criminal path that is neither that of *virtù* nor that of Fortune, or yet again by a mixture of astuteness and luck. But from one group to the other the distance disappears
when we want to specify their figures and assess exactly what distinguishes
them. At first sight Romulus does not suffer comparison with Borgia or
with Agathocles; but analysis reveals intermediary figures that reveal their
kinship. First, Hiero of Syracuse, brought up in Chapter 6, immediately
after the examples of excellent men, as a glorious captain who, once in
power, did not recoil from the massacre of mercenaries in the service of
the City, in order to create a loyal militia; then Sforza, who has the merit
of becoming the duke of Milan by the force of his arms alone—both
being of such high *virtù* that they maintained without difficulty what they
had acquired at the price of the greatest dangers, but neither of whom

were founders, and they established themselves by violence; the second of them being assuredly more preoccupied with his own safety than with the interests of the state. Thus it is as if the opposition between the two types of political actors were only suggested to the reader in order to lead him to question its validity.

It is true that we have been prepared for this questioning. If, at least, we have understood him correctly, has Machiavelli not already taught us that the creator of *ordini nuovi*, at the very moment when he appears to be responding to the expectations of the people and acting on the promptings of Providence, has no other rule of conduct than that of seizing and holding onto power? How, then, can we be surprised now that despite the different conditions in which he is placed and the singularity of his goals, the tyrant should issue forth from a civil or military coup d'état? Perhaps it would be more appropriate to ask why the author surrounds himself with such precautions in the communication of this truth. But it is better to leave that question in suspense and to say that on the occasion of further analyses the relation of the prince to his subjects, left till now in shadow, will be clarified.

Such indeed is the direction taken by Machiavelli. Just as he discovered, in the glorious acts of the founders to which we normally like to ascribe the most noble motivations, the raw necessity of a power struggle, so he now reveals, where that struggle is immediately visible and its object fully exposed, the requirements governing it, the milieu of social coexistence in which the appetite for power is implanted.

The case of Borgia is the first presented for our reflection, and it is introduced in such a way that the reader is first inclined to belittle it. His destiny was, as it seems, in the image of those puppet princes (created in the past by Darius), who turned out to be incapable of maintaining their power, because it was to the Fortune of their fathers that they owed both their success and their downfall. But scarcely is this comparison established than, by a sudden reversal typical of him, Machiavelli begins to praise the duke and judge his conduct as exemplary. In enrooting himself in his states he had done everything—so we learn—that one may expect of a man who is *prudente e virtuoso*. Not only is it important to know how he set the foundations of his future power, but in considering his actions one will find no better precepts to guide a *principe nuovo*. The brief account of his exploits closes with an unqualified apologetic, and although the author deems it well to specify that he is addressing those who rose to power "by fortune and the arms of others," the final statement of the principles governing his politics has to all appearances a universal application. Thus the reader must admit that if Borgia was, at the beginning of his career, a creature of Fortune, he was never lacking in *virtù*. Better yet, all things considered, the support from which he initially benefited hindered as much as helped him. If we take into account the efforts he was required to make to free himself from the conditions in which he was placed, his merit is increased rather than decreased. But that truth obscures another: more important than the evaluation of Borgia the person is the image of *virtù* with which we are now confronted. While in the preceding chapter *virtù* could be interpreted as standing in stark opposition to Fortune, as princely power, dependent on itself alone, we now discover in it the exercise of a mastery that gradually draws man out of the present conditions and allows him to impose his will on the course of events. From one representation to the other, the same intent remains. Borgia's *virtù* does not seem, when we consider his political ascent, to be of a different essence than that of the heroes of antiquity, but a realist model has apparently replaced the mythic one of classical times. The general idea that the new prince must place his trust in neither luck, nor God, nor men, and rely on force alone, is succeeded by the description of a politics of *virtù* in which force is restored to its just place. Assuredly this passage is only possible because Borgia's endeavor, when judged in conjunction with the goal it would have achieved had it been able to overcome the last obstacles, bears similarities with that of the founders. Not content with profiting from the occasion offered him to take over territories of a few lords in Romagna, he applied himself to forging from the conquered peoples a new community, and his intention was to establish a great state in the center of Italy. He is the only prince of his times endowed with a sense of political creation and prepared to upset the equilibrium of forces instituted on the peninsula for centuries. Other contemporary endeavors pale in comparison: that of Savonarola, who did nothing but fulminate from atop a pulpit and proved incapable, for lack of force, of posing a serious threat to his adversaries, and even that of Sforza, who had only to set up his bands in Milan, and occupy Visconti Square. Thus the reader, once having seen the true proportions of the Duke's conquest, is more favorably disposed to accept the meaning of the lesson that emerges from it. In it he finds, first of all, translated in terms of military politics, the application of the already announced rule that the master of a state must act in such a way as not to have to depend on anyone but himself. Borgia's merit is to have been able to forge the instruments of a power that would soon make him the most feared prince in Italy. While at the beginning he owed his reputation to mercenary or foreign troops, to those with whom his father the pope had provided him or those of the king of France, he would not rest till an army entirely under his command had been formed. Judged in itself, this action should appear praiseworthy to all, but the art of the author is to present it in such a way as to as to make it indissociable from the politics of violence, cruelty, and trickery motivated by the drive to ensure the authority of the prince. Thus, he who contemplates the noble face of force must at the same time discover its dark face. Borgia, a political figure inspired by the most illustrious examples, is also one who makes terror reign in a vanquished country through the efforts a minister who was "expeditious and cruel," orders his execution when, the results having been obtained, his unpopularity might be a deficit, exterminates the lords whose domains he has seized, and especially—masterpiece of guile related with a complacency for which Machiavelli will not be forgiven—lures his lieutenants into an ambush and has them strangled.

This description forces us to open our eyes to the acts of violence that have always accompanied the birth of states and that the author had until now always prudently avoided. The moment we would like to think that the criminal use of force involves only Borgia, we cannot fail to recall that the politics of Moses was no different from that of other founders, and Romulus gives an outstanding illustration of it in murdering his brother. Of course we are inclined to think that, as distinct from the heroes of antiquity, the duke had no other motive than ambition. But the stark facts speak for themselves. And we may assume that if the duke had succeeded in achieving his goals, the blame attaching to his memory would have been wiped clean by the grandeur of the result. A plausible hypothesis, since his failure, identified at one time with the origin of his power and presented as therefore quasi inevitable, subsequently proves to be the consequence of an error in reasoning; a better understanding of his position within the Roman curia after the death of the pope would probably have allowed him to keep his states. But whatever our judgment of the duke may be, we cannot, when considering his politics, reduce them to an undertaking of violent domination and deny that it had already acquired, in the facts, a meaning going beyond the framework of his personal interests. Indeed, limiting ourselves to the description given by Machiavelli himself—and it matters little, in this case, whether or not it is accurate—the criminal acts that served him in aggrandizing his power were also those from which the conquered peoples benefited. In exterminating the lords of Romagna he delivered these peoples from terrible poverty and oppression, for they had, until then, "rather despoiled than governed their subjects," and abandoned them to disorder and robbery. In having the minister put to death whose cruelty at one time had been profitable to him—an execution, we are told specifically, that went hand in hand with the establishment of a civil court equipped with a wise president and the designation in each town of an attorney—he created confidence in the justice of law, previously discredited by a plea system. And

in doing away with the heads of the Orsini faction, his former lieutenants, he brought peace back to a state in which they had begun to sow
the seeds of dissention. In each one of these actions something different
from the espousal of the party of violence appears. Otherwise, we would
not understand the fact that before his fall "he had acquired the friendship of Romagna and all those peoples (over whom he had imposed his
authority) were won over to him for having begun to enjoy the good they
had received from him."

It is thus in vain that we may want to conclude with the simple
image of political *virtù*. If we seek our references among the enterprises
that the course of history accredits as legitimate, we encounter the use of
force, which, at the same time as it removes the prince from the caprice
of Fortune and opinion, sets him at a distance from the others in a sort
of citadel created for him by his position of dominance. But when we
examine the use of force in the most recent example of a great political
adventure and measure the violent acts that accompanied the prince's
ascent to power, we discover, as if shadowing his every move, the quest for
the people's consent, and the satisfaction given to the needs of the dominated. In one perspective, the obvious fact of the common good fades
before the spectacle of a use of force that appears an end in itself, and
in the other the prominence of acts of violence dims before the image
of the accomplished work.

It is true that this paradox might be deemed secondary. If Machiavelli shows that the same movement sweeps Borgia toward violence and
distances him from it, that is because, so some might say, in order to
suggest that it begins on the hither side of the vicissitudes of action, in
a knowledge in relation to which what we call good and evil has but a
purely positive status. And as a matter of fact, the enterprise of the Duke,
in the way it is presented, has the admirable quality of being seemingly
sustained from one end to the other by the same intention, of unfolding
as a methodically constructed work. But this answer changes the terms
of the problem rather than resolving it. For, whether the prince has the
power to posit himself as a subject of knowledge confronting the situation and to establish the program of his actions by calculation—a power
on which, as we have seen by the two examples of Louis XII and of the
Romans, political success depends—does not provide us with the key to
understanding the meaning of the relation binding him to his subjects,
nor why it is necessary at once to reduce them to obedience and win their
friendship, nor how, through this double bond, that unity of a particular
nature, the state, is instituted. Further, we are not the ones who project
into that work a question of which it has no awareness. Machiavelli, as I
have noted, designated the founders as "excellent men" and speaks of

the *virtù* of the prince, of the "good" of the people, of the "friendship" uniting them, and at the same time of "force" as what must be contrasted with "entreaty," of "cruelty" which presides over the pacification of a conquered country. What would this language mean if it were only a question of defining the technique of the taking of power? It must be confessed: If there was, at first, parallel to the critique of traditional ideas, a purely positive conception of action, the discussion has taken a new turn since the analysis of the foundation of the state created an opening in that other foundation that philosophical or religious thought assumes to lie at the beginning of political society.

But if we still had some doubts about the meaning of the debate, the considerations of the author on Agathocles's enterprise, and on that of Oliverotto da Fermo, his contemporary emulator, deliberately chosen from among Cesare Borgia's victims, would come opportunely to dissipate them. In designating as a crime the exploit by which they took power, exploring the relationship between *virtù* and villainy, bad and good cruelty, the necessity of providing for one's own security and that of seeking the confidence of the people, Machiavelli forces the reader to reflect on the meaning and value of political action. It would be imprudent for us to expect this interrogation to be immediately enclosed within a thesis. Perhaps it has no other purpose than to give us a better appreciation of the complication of the subject—which the Dedication to Lorenzo, as we will recall, termed the *varietà della materia*—and to forbid any containment of it within the limits of morality or science.

The truth is that at this point the discourse takes on a rapid, swirling movement that the reader can only follow in abandoning the various points of repair proposed along the way and in consenting to move forward into indetermination. Machiavelli first announces that he is going to speak of an enterprise conducted outside the paths of *virtù* or of Fortune, *"per qualche via scellerata e nefaria."* In thus designating it, and not in the positive manner a scientific observer would use in reference to a military coup d'état, he invites us to remember that the term *virtù* is never detached from a moral sense. But scarcely are we in possession of this recommendation than we must abandon it, since the author states that he will examine the actions of Agathocles and Oliverotto "without otherwise entering into their merit," adding that "it suffices for whoever would be forced (*necessitato*) to imitate them." Villainy is not recommended, but it is suggested that the criminal conquest of power being a fact of experience, it is better to understand how the prince accomplishes his ends, that is, enroots himself in his state, than to make a value judgment. Thus we are reminded of the remark prompted on the part of the author by Louis XII's attempt in Italy: "The desire to acquire possessions is a very natural and ordinary thing, and when those men do it who can do so successfully, they will always be praised for it, or at least they will not be blamed." Certainly the language used at present is not the same, and we may wonder whether the danger of assailing the reader too rudely is the only thing that prevents the author from using the same wording as before, or whether there may not be, despite the neutrality adopted by the observer, a difference between the action of a prince occupied in increasing his domain, and that of a private individual who overturns an established government in order to impose his personal tyranny. But whatever the case may be, the positive study of the facts is apparently all that matters. Now, this second suggestion is no more certain than the first, for we are immediately brought back to an evaluation of the behavior of Agathocles. The author observes that he is raised from the lowest condition to that of the head of the army, because he was able to add to his villainy a very great *virtù di animo e di corpo*, and presents his criminal coup d'état in relation to its consequences—the victory over the Carthaginians, which brought peace and security to Sicily by delivering it from foreign aggression. Agathocles's action is thus elevated, to the point where it may rightfully be asked whether he was in any way inferior to the princes whose *virtù* was admired a little earlier. It is precisely this question that Machiavelli asks, responding, it is true, in the affirmative, but not without a troubling reservation.

> Whoever considers well, therefore, his actions and qualities, will see few if any things which can be attributed to fortune; for, as stated above, it was not by the favor of any person, but through the grades of the militia, in which he had advanced with a thousand hardships and perils, that he arrived at princedom, which he afterwards maintained by so many courageous and perilous acts. On the other hand, it cannot be called *virtù* to kill one's fellow-citizens, betray one's friends, be without faith, without pity, and without religion; by these methods one may indeed gain some Lordship, but not glory (*imperio ma non gloria*). For if the valor (*virtù*) of Agathocles in braving and overcoming perils, and his greatness of soul in supporting and surmounting adversaries (*le cose avverse*) are considered, one sees no reason for holding him inferior to any other excellent captain (*inferiore a qualunque eccellentissimo capitano*). Nevertheless his barbarous cruelty and inhumanity, together with his countless villainies, do not permit of his being renowned among the most excellent men (*che sia infra li eccellentissimi uomini celebrato*).

We are no doubt sensitive to the opposition introduced between "excellent captain" and "excellent man." But considering the subject of the discussion and the author's previous comments, it is difficult to find in this his last word. Indeed, it was a question of discovering by what means Agathocles had succeeded in taking and maintaining power; now the reasons that explain his success are not limited to his military prowess; and, furthermore, we retain from the critique of Louis XII and the example of the Romans that the *virtù* of the great captains goes together with political intelligence. Machiavelli had very recently praised Borgia endlessly, though without classifying him in the category of excellent men. Thus, his refusal to apply that denomination to the tyrant of Syracuse does not suffice to settle the question. These reservations are, moreover, justified a moment later when the author, after having described Oliverotto's ascent to power, returns to the first case in order to ask a new question: "Some may wonder" he then writes, "how it came about that Agathocles, and others like him, could, after infinite treachery and cruelty, live secure for many years in their country and defend themselves from external enemies without being conspired against by their subjects; although many others have, owing to their cruelty, been unable to maintain their position even in times of peace, not to speak of the turbulent times of war." His response casts a completely new light on the preceding discussion. "I think this arises from cruelty being well or badly applied. Well applied may be called that cruelty (if it is permissible to use the word well of evil—*se del male è licito dire bene*) which is applied all at once, out of the need for one's safety, and which afterwards is not continued, but turned as much as possible to the benefit of the subjects."

This remark is all the more striking because of the fact that Machiavelli, in reporting the exploits of Borgia's lieutenant—who did not recoil from any means, not even the murder of his uncle and protector, to gain power—had just touched on the very lowest point of villainy in politics. With that example it was possible to grasp what he called "bestial cruelty and inhumanity," to such a point that it suddenly seemed incongruous to inquire into the *virtù* of Agathocles. Now, with no transition, the distance separating their enterprises is revealed. One unfolds entirely beneath the sign of violence; the other proves capable of being modified according to the imperatives created by the coexistence of the prince with his subjects. Machiavelli, it is true, refrains from comparing them: he leaves it to the reader to do so—not without facilitating his task, since, while saying nothing about Agathocles's end, he relates that Oliverotto, one year after taking control of Fermo, allows himself to be caught in the Sinigaglia trap (by simple-mindedness, as we learned in the preceding chapter), meeting there a death unworthy of both a great politician and a great captain.

But at the moment when the reader thinks he understands why and how a prince succeeds in maintaining the power he has won by the utmost acts of violence—in short, when he assumes he has at last penetrated the heart of the subject—it must be confessed that his image of political action is oddly jumbled. In vain we would like to praise those who, like Agathocles, put an end to terror and decide to act in the interest of their subjects. The insistence with which the author has spoken of his cruelty (the very use of this term, for which, let it be noted, it would have been easy for him to substitute a more neutral one), and the allusion to the parricide of his disciple forbid our forgetting or even minimizing the villainy, or even thinking that it could give way before the requirements of good government. But it would be equally vain to claim to hold to a blanket condemnation that would envelop in one sole opprobrium the continued exercise of violence and its metamorphosis in politics. This would allow, beneath the cover of moral intransigence, the meaning of a transformation to escape us—a transformation that, given its effects, must be recognized as essential. Machiavelli does not authorize our thinking that good wipes away evil, but neither does he authorize the opposite. To evil he obliges us to keep our eyes open even at the moment when he names the good, thus burdening us with an uncertainty felicitously summarized in the expression *se del male è licito dire bene.*

Nor can we free ourselves from this uncertainty by rejecting the underlying hypothesis, that is, by condemning the evil at its point of origin in order not to have to form judgments on its consequences, because it is not so much a question of sizing up the conduct of a man as of seeking out the meaning of a situation from which we can only turn away by leaving out part of the experience. Furthermore, the difficulty we have in reasoning within the framework of ordinary morality is not only tied to the analysis of a particular case. If the particular case makes us pass from the image of evil to that of a certain good, the examination of the glorious foundation had only confronted us with the image of the good to prepare us to receive that of as certain evil. We are the less likely to forget this in view of the fact that Machiavellian irony lets no occasion slip by to emphasize the passage from one perspective to another. After having learned that the heroes of antiquity (and Moses among them) entrusted themselves neither to men nor to Providence, we now discover that the criminal princes "can with the help of God and men (*don Dio e con li uomini*) find some favorable remedy."

Finally, there is nothing to be gained in assuming—all moral criteria being ruled out—that the surmounting of violence is the simple effect of necessity, that the same reasons explain the criminal politics of Agathocles at the beginning stages and his later efforts to give satisfaction to the people, because, quite to the contrary, the use Machiavelli makes of the term *necessità* until the end of Chapter 8 is so deliberately restrictive that it makes it impossible for us to situate them on the same level. First, the author speaks of the cruelties that are forced on the prince "by the necessity of his safety" (*per la* necessità *delle assicurarsi*), in pointing out their limit; a second time, he notes that the prince who takes power "must think of all the cruelties he must carry out (*quelle offese che gli è* necessario *fare*) and carry out all at once in order not to return to them every day, and by not doing so reassure men and win them over by his beneficence." A third time he specifies that he who acts differently "will be forced to always keep the knife in hand (*è sempre* necessitato *tenere il coltello in mano*) and can never depend on his subjects." This gives us to understand that the imperative of security and that of government are not of the same nature, or, better, being able to respond to the second frees us from the first.

Of course when the prince seeks a base in his subjects he is still responding to the need for self-preservation, but that endeavor gives politics an unexpected dimension. The direct struggle for domination is followed by an indirect one, involving the recognition of the self by the other. The power of death, from which action is deduced, is followed by that of life, which dictates that we consent to exchanges. Thus, after having observed that the prince must do evil in one fell swoop "to assure himself" (*assicurarsi*), Machiavelli adds that he must assure men (*assicurare gli uomini*) and win them over with acts of kindness, and concludes that in the absence of such a politics they would not be able to "assure themselves about him" (*assicurare di lui*). In this reversal of dependency a new sense of action is instituted. Now, the author discourages our seeking a moral interpretation in this, since at the moment when this transition occurs in the text he uses a deliberately cynical style, declaring: "Evil should be inflicted all at once, so that, tasted less, it may offend less; and the good, little by little, in order that it may be better relished." The truth is rather that necessity is suspended before reestablishing itself in a different register, at the point where the image that the prince projects of himself merges with the overlay of the one reflected back by his subjects. Thus, it is equally true to say that his conduct is dictated from one end to the other by the same determination, since we are led to understand by the beginning part of the conclusion of the chapter, that "a prince must in all things live with his subjects in such a way that no accident of good or evil makes him change," and that his merit consists in being able to break away from that determination at the right moment in order to take charge of the other's representation, as is taught by what immediately follows in the text: "for if the necessity [to change his behavior] occurs in times of adversity, there is no time to do evil [that is, to take severe measures], and if you do what is good, it will not profit you in the least because it will be thought forced (*perché è judicato forzato*), and you will not be thanked for it."

Now at the same time it must be admitted that the question that was raised about Agathocles's *virtù*—a question apropos of which we had not failed to observe that it was less about the tyrant of Syracuse than about the status of political action—was left in suspense. Indeed, if a moment ago we had good reasons for casting doubt on the validity of the opposition introduced between the *virtù* of the excellent man and that of the excellent captain, we are now disconcerted to see that the word has disappeared from the vocabulary of the discourse, now that what constituted the value of the political behavior of Agathocles has been specified. Perhaps we should consider that the question and the answer have been disjoined in such a way that the answer was understood only by those who were able to receive it. Perhaps, on the contrary, the risk of misunderstanding would have been greater if the author had daringly given the name *virtù* to Agathocles's decision to convert cruelty into action in the service of the subjects. But it is also possible that his reservations have a different motivation. When he wrote that one cannot call it *virtù* to kill one's fellow citizens, betray one's friends, be without faith, pity, or religion, because these means make it possible to acquire *power but not glory,* he was giving us a clue that we did not take into account, but that we are now better prepared to understand. In revealing that *virtù* does not go with glory, he was already implying that political action cannot be defined without taking into account the representation that men have of it. He was not, moreover, saying that *virtù* is incompatible with crime, lying, and lack of religion, but denying—and this is different—that those means of taking over power could be covered by using such a term. And no doubt it appeared that Agathocles had done something better than take hold of the *imperio*, since he repelled the Carthaginian invasion, took the war to Africa, and won the support of his subjects, so that we cannot deny that he won a certain glory . . . But that does not wipe away the mark of origin of his power—not his first crimes, which we know resembled those perpetrated by more noble politicians, but the fact that they were committed without justification or without disguise, by a man whom nothing but his own ambition destined to reign. If he cannot claim the glory of excellent men, or even that of Borgia, is it not because his rise to power was in the eyes of his subjects, and remains, in posterity's memory, that of a man—as Machiavelli was careful to point out—"*di infima e abjetta fortuna . . . nato d'uno figulo* (a simple son of a potter)."

Considering things in this way, we would understand better why the author contrives at once to compare Agathocles to illustrious princes whom he had held up as models and to distance him from them, to do away with the difference we expected to see and to shatter the identity we were then ready to be satisfied with. But the idea still leaves us unsatisfied and anxious to go further. In one way or another, we are led to situate the prince's action in the social milieu in which it acquired its specific meaning; but Machiavelli has not spoken of this milieu until now except in vague terms. The fact that the prince depends on his subjects, and that his conduct is only determined in relation to an opinion—these truths have now come to be superimposed on those stated earlier: that he must depend on himself alone and rely solely on force. We cannot as yet understand how these two sets of truths fit in with each other. Now, the analysis is suddenly rendered precise, embracing the political as well as the social relation, when a new hypothesis surges forth—the last, I believe—dedicated to the civil princedom.

No sooner has the author circumscribed the case he is going to examine, that of the assumption of power by a man carried by the favor of his fellow citizens, and observed that it is implemented at the instigation of the people or of the Grandees, than he declares: "For in all cities we find these two different humors, the source of which is that the people desire not to be commanded or oppressed by the Grandees and the Grandees desire to command and oppress the people: and from these two different appetites there arises in the cities one of these three results: princedom, liberty, or license."

Thus we are put in the presence of a judgment of universal application that sums up the teaching prudently insinuated in the preceding chapters and at the same time completes it. In retaining of the diversity of the types of government only these three, Machiavelli spectacularly abandons the traditional classifications characterized by the oppositions between governments that were legitimate or illegitimate, healthy or corrupt. This leads us to think that all that counts, in the eyes of the observer, is the way in which the class struggle is resolved. Either it engenders a power that rises above society and subordinates it entirely to its authority—as in the princedom—or it is regulated in such a way that no one is subject to anyone, legally at least—as in liberty—or it is powerless to resolve itself into a stable order—as in license. In this perspective, it matters little, in particular, to distinguish between the tyrant and the prince; but if it is permissible to confuse them, this is not only, as we might have assumed, because they must respond to the same problem of governance. The deeper reason is that the same causes explain their advent, because monarchy is always a result of the civil division. Henceforth, the factual conditions in which a man achieves tyranny make it possible to grasp the principle of the genesis of all princedoms. But at the same time light is shed on the question of the basis of princely power. Until now Machiavelli spoke in a very general way of the relation of the prince to his subjects. In Chapters 3 and 6 he alluded to the divisions brought about by the creation of *ordini nuovi*, but without specifying their nature. In Chapter 8, he merely noted in passing that Agathocles had had the senators and the wealthiest citizens put to death. Now, it becomes apparent that the concept of "people" blankets an opposition. Or to put it differently, within a people, a visible community to which the state assigns its identity, is found the masses of those without power—"people" in the precise sense that abstracts it from the fictive unity that political language projects onto it. It is indeed of an opposition constitutive of the political that one must speak, irreducible, at first blush; and not of a distinction made on the basis of the facts, for what makes the Grandees the Grandees and the people the people is not that they have by their fortune, their mores, or their function a distinct status associated with specific and divergent interests; it is, as Machiavelli clearly says, that one group desires to command and oppress, and the other not to be. Their existence is only determined by that essential relation, in the clash of two "appetites," in principle each one equally insatiable. Thus, at the beginning of princely power, and subjacent to it once it has been established, is a class conflict. Now to discover this means to prepare oneself to hear with a different ear that the prince must seek a base in his subjects, because the soil in which his authority is rooted appears henceforth to resemble the shifting terrain making up the flux of these two desires that can never completely extinguish one another. That is the reason why Machiavelli, when he brought up the example of the founders, first asserted that the prince can count on no one. Not only can he not find in men taken as a group stable support, since their community covers over a wrenching apart, but he cannot even rely on a part of them, since one class only exists by the lack that constitutes it opposite the other. The necessary search for a point of attachment passes through the experience of a void that no politics will ever fill—through the recognition of the impossibility of the state's reducing society to a unity.

But to admit that the attachment is always indirect is also to understand the nature of the political tie that it is appropriate to establish. When the prince is seen to arise like a third party at the heart of civil strife, at the instigation of one or the other of the protagonists, he becomes conscious of what his function dictates and of the necessity of choosing, between the two parties, that of the people. Indeed, the opposition between the Grandees and the masses implies an inequality: on one side the desire to oppress, and on the other that of not being oppressed: some call on him in order to "be able, in his shadow, to satisfy their appetite" (*sotto la sua ombra sfogare il loro appetito*); for others what is at issue is obtaining protection. If he decided to depend on those who command, he would expose himself to seeing his authority endlessly hampered. For it is only apparently that the Grandees bestow power on him. They only do so through fear of the people, to be strengthened in their status as oppressors. This strong power that they have decided to create must only be used against their adversary. They themselves are not in the least disposed to obey. In their view, the prince is not above the classes, an arbiter whose judgment is beyond question. He is their equal, and can neither command nor manage them as he wishes. Thus the attachment of the prince to the Grandees is necessarily converted into a personal relationship, although at the origin he is placed in a position of independence. As long as he has the support of the people—either because he was carried to power by them, or because he was able to switch parties opportunely—no resistance will be made to him; his action against the Grandees responding to the expectations placed in his government. The friendship of the people, Machiavelli writes, is easy to keep; they "demand nothing more than not to be oppressed." That is to say, "not oppressed" by the Grandees. Assuredly the prince oppresses in turn. If that truth is now left in the penumbra, at least the later analyses leave no doubt in that respect. But the violence of his power appears of a different nature than that of the Grandees, for in them the people encounter their *natural* adversary, the Other who constitutes them as the immediate object of its desire. From that relation the prince frees them, by the simple fact of not being a part of it, and by his presence he releases the Grandees from their claim to be the dominators. Doubtless that release is measured by the material protection drawn from him by his subjects, since he replaces the intolerable oppression that reigns within civil society with a lesser evil; but if it is perceived as such, it is because in its principle the power he exerts differs from that of the dominant class. The people can submit to his authority because his goal is not to command, but only not to be commanded. A refusal that is the basis of consent to a new commandment, the first visible effect of which is to withdraw them from the permanent embrace that holds them prisoner.

By an indirect path, which Hegel will later call "the ruse of reason," the desire of the people thus rejoins that of the prince. In attacking the Grandees, the prince is merely obeying his appetite for power, which will not suffer to be gainsaid by that of his equals. Conquering the people's favor, "he finds himself alone" (which is his goal), but that conduct presupposes that a limit be put on violence and satisfaction granted to the masses who seek security. Simultaneously the people, thinking to find in him a defender in the struggle against their class adversary, put themselves in the clutches of a new master and thus take up the cause of a submission that they loathed. Non-power and absolute power cling to one other in a darkness that it is essential to maintain.

Machiavelli succinctly lets us know in a turn of phrase that this ruse escapes the people's notice. They, he notes, lack the sharpness of vision and cleverness of the Grandees. And this remark, besides reminding us of the importance of opinion, suggests that there is still much to be said about the relationship between the prince and his image; but it suffices, for the moment, to steer the reader away from a misunderstanding. If we were tempted to define the agreement between the prince and his subjects in terms of a contract—one party bringing the benefit of his protection while the other in exchange commits itself to obedience—the reference to the people's naïveté would dissipate our illusions. Doubtless the masses find their best interests in serving a prince who guarantees security but, in lending him their support, they do not know what they are doing. While they struggle not to be oppressed, they are about to take on an oppression of a new kind. While they expect the good, they receive the lesser evil. While it may be that nothing better can befall them than to let themselves be duped—it is hard to say, since there is no way of telling what their fate may be in a republic—in any case they are not committing themselves by concluding a pact, but yielding rather to a wave of enthusiasm whose passing would end their attachment to the prince. Furthermore, how would their interests make them the partner in an exchange, since, reducible in the final analysis to the refusal of being commanded and oppressed, they admit of no definition in positive terms?

It is by the insistence with which he not only designates the class struggle as a universal and permanent phenomenon, but also reveals the essence of the people as the desire to escape the desire of the class Other, that Machiavelli turns away from an intellectualist interpretation. As long as the philosopher or historian limits himself to describing an originary state of insecurity in which each is a threat to his neighbor, it is permissible to imagine a moment when the renunciation of private individuals to power, in favor of one of them, coincides with the advent of an order that is profitable to all; as long as he speaks of civil division as a factual situation, without specifying its underlying dynamics, with the sole thought that inequality of conditions creates the division of antagonistic groups, the possibility of retaining that same image remains. But such an image cannot hold up to the discovery that an irreducible conflict rends society. True, this conflict may be adjudged modifiable by the intervention of the prince, but however valuable the change may be, since it creates or recreates the conditions of some form of coexistence, it cannot pass as a *solution*.

But this critique calls for another. The same reasons forbid presenting the relation that the prince establishes with his subjects as a contract and the retention of the terms of the analysis the author had outlined in the first place, when, connecting the problem of the takeover of power to that of military conquest, he reduced political logic to that of power relations. It is true that this perspective contains some truth, as is taught by the argument developed in favor of the thesis that the prince must have a base in the people. First, the power of the people is superior to that of the Grandees, since it is impossible to govern against the masses, while it is possible to impose one's authority over a smaller number; secondly, this smaller number has more daring, and it must always be feared that it might turn against his power, while the masses can do no more than abandon him; finally, the masses are always to be reckoned with, because the prince must of necessity live with the same people, whereas he can dislodge the Grandees in place and create others. But these arguments, however important, do not touch on the essential. It is not sufficient for the prince to form an accurate image of the forces he must master, for he will never discover, by stopping short at that distance from the phenomena, the *meaning* of the opposition onto which his power is grafted. In envisaging society as an object, he will miss the fact that the antagonistic classes are of a different nature, and that, incomparable in this respect to states, whose rivalry implies that they have the same identity and the same goals (whatever the inequality of their strength may be), the classes only exist in their confrontation surrounding those stakes which are for one group oppression, for the other the refusal of oppression. This truth is only perceptible to he who sees, beyond the immediate givens of conduct, the basic motivations to which they are attached, that is, *desire, appetite, demand*—terms that Machiavelli uses successively—by which the group posits itself as a political class. And there is no doubt but that when one takes this step in interpretation, one opens the way to making value judgments. Therefore it is not accidental that the author notes at this time: "besides that, one cannot satisfy the Grandees with honest dealings and without inflicting injury on others (*non si può con onestà satisfare a' grandi e sanza iniuria d'altri*), whereas one can satisfy the people in this way, for the aim of the people is more straightforward than that of the Grandees." This is a way of intimating that one cannot restrict oneself to the simple inspection of the facts. But moral appreciation is neither primary nor decisive. That the people are more honest than the Grandees only matters to the prince because he can draw a political lesson from it: the exercise of power proves to be easier if it can satisfy, in the least costly way, the needs of its partisans, that is, by sparing itself the use of violence and thus reducing the attendant dangers. Furthermore, it would be a mistake to depend on that honesty directly, as is proven by both ancient and modern examples: that of the Gracchi of Rome and of Giorgio Scali of Florence, who, having championed the cause of the people, thought they could rely on the support of the plebs when the hour of armed confrontation came, but were abandoned by them. The populace is only worthy of confidence when subject to the prince; to the man without governmental authority and force of arms, it offers deceptive support, even if the reformer gives expression to its desire. If there is such a thing as an honesty and faithfulness of the common people, it is only in relation to the action of a power that ensures its subjects against the oppression of the Grandees; it is only when the desire not to be oppressed, which in itself is powerless to grasp its object, to realize itself in the form of a power that would at the same time be a non-power, finds its counterpart in reality, in colliding with a third who inscribes it into the political reality.

Thus we can end neither with a factual nor a moral judgment. The truth goes beyond this, with the discovery of the being of the social, as it appears in the division of classes.

When Machiavelli attacks the detractors of the people—the commonplace opinion of them as epitomized in the saying, "He who builds on the people builds on mud (*chi fonda in sul populo fonda in sul fongo*)," he condemns two equally false images in politics, one of power, the other of human nature. It is in fact to commit an error with respect to the first to think that the prince can govern against his people by entrusting himself either to the force of arms or to that of a minority who brought him into power, and it is to commit an error on the second to despair of the support of the people under the pretext that they will abandon him when they should act. Such is doubtless the opinion of those pseudo sages of Florence, who were already mocked because they "have in their mouths from morning till evening to enjoy the benefits of time." If they are not named, at least we cannot help but mention them, knowing that the republican government collapsed beneath the threat of the Grandees, because it was unable to obtain popular support in time. And indeed the inability to build on the future and on the people, and the illusory confidence in the present and in acquired advantage, all have one and the same origin: the desire to forget that men and things are unstable, that time drives all things before it, that desire leaves no rest and that we can find no assurance unless it be in risk and by a movement that is in keeping with the agitation of the world. The critique of the people is naïve in that it assigns them an identity they do not have, and it is distorted in that it serves as an excuse for the weakness of the prince. It is true that the masses are more straightforward than the Grandees, since they want only to escape oppression, but that does not mean that this desire can be converted into power. If the men who put themselves at the head of the masses to advance the people's interests fail in that enterprise, it may be because the masses have an obscure knowledge of the impossible. But if the prince is willing to bring, not a solution, but the formula for a more tolerable order, they may rally to it, and if so, are capable of resolve. But he must be determined to impose that order and take the necessary steps for action, in order that the people have no doubts about his authority. Between confidence and force there is an exchange. The one is awakened by contact with the other and former is nourished by the latter.

Thus we understand why it is so important that the prince be confirmed as the sole master. If he waits to be forced by events to take all the power (*la autorità assoluta*), he will find no one at his side at the decisive moment. Those charged with governing will turn against him or will not be there, and his subjects, accustomed to a different commandment, will not be disposed to obey him. "For the prince cannot go by what he sees in peaceful times, when the citizens need the state, because then they come running, promising, wanting to die for him when death is far away, but in adverse fortune, when the state needs citizens, few are to be found." Thus states are in peril when it is necessary to go suddenly from one mode of government to another (*salire dall'ordine civile allo assoluto*). The just conduct is to foresee these difficulties by the institution, from the beginning, of a personal power, so that the people, placed in direct submission to the prince, feel the solidity of the bond continually.

Machiavelli had already noted, in the course of Chapter 6, "The nature of peoples is changeable, and it is easy to persuade them of something, but difficult to keep them in that persuasion. Therefore it is well to provide such good order that when they no longer believe, they can be made to believe by force." And at the end of Chapter 8: "A prince must in all things live with his subjects in such a way that no accident of good or evil makes him change." He now concludes: "A wise prince must think of a way by which his subjects, always and in all sorts of times, have need of the state and of him, and they will ever afterward be faithful." It seems that the lesson is always the same: the prince must act in such a way that his subjects depend on him and have no choice in the matter, in good times or bad. But the argument has become decidedly richer; henceforth force is connected with protection; the conditions of the security and power of the prince are also those of the functioning of the political society. The elements of brutality and excess in the critique of Savonarola is counterbalanced by a critique that tends in the opposite direction: his failure remains symbolic, for it is precisely that man who underwent, to his cost, the experience of the fickleness of the populace; his example, like that of the Gracchi, teaches that when death is near the masses fade away. But, simultaneously, it is revealed that his adversaries did not measure up to their task any better, for they who had scoffed at his seeking support with the people—they in turn fell for having turned their backs on them. They were doubly in the wrong, being neither prophets nor armed, and offering nothing, either to believe or to fear. And suddenly the significance of those *ordini nuovi* Machiavelli had spoken enigmatically about earlier is clear. We had learned that their creation meant being exposed to greater dangers, and met head on with the hostility of the partisans of the *ordini vecchi*, and found but timid defenders in those who were to profit from them, and that only force could be assured of success. Now we have every right to think that the daring of the founder consists in the fact of his overturning the established order, destroying the power of the Grandees, and, in order to build up his own, turning to the people. Force is no doubt necessary for him to overcome the "incredulity" of men, to convince those who, like the supporters of the Gracchi and of Savonarola, "do not believe in new things unless they have actually experienced them," but the principles of politics are not resumed in that of force. When the author writes that a prince who "by his courage and the institutions that he has created gives heart to the masses (*tenga con l'animo e ordini suoi animato lo universale*) will never be deceived by them and will indeed find that he has laid good foundations (*buoni fondamenti*)," we are to understand that these principles govern the alliance between the prince and the people.

To what does that alliance oblige the two parties? That is the question the reader raises. Machiavelli does not answer it—or at least does not do so in a way we expect. He observes in passing that the prince has many ways of winning the friendship of his people, but that no general rule can be given about it; so it is better not to speak of it. Yet we know the silence is provisional: he probably doesn't think the right moment to discuss it further has come yet. In any case, we are now accustomed to the twists and turns of the discourse, and are beginning to understand the reason for it. If it is true that nothing bears meaning by itself alone, if meaning is established in the relationship between one *thesis* and another, or (which amounts to the same thing) in the distance taken simultaneously from both—if it is necessary to establish points of repair, not in order to contain definitions but to make differences explicit—then on the contrary it is discontinuity that is required. The points of rupture decide as categorically as do the things said with respect to the truth of the discourse. And it is not linguistic ruse when the writer leaves the place where he was in order to place himself elsewhere. Or, better, the ruse does not come from

him, it is born of language, of the necessity of undoing fixed, independent representations to unblock the flow of the interrogative word.

At the point where political analysis stops, a discussion begins on the
military power of the prince. This subject, it is true, has already been
broached on several occasions: Louis XII's conquest of Milan and Cesare Borgia's conquest of Romagna gave occasion to the formulation
of a few principles: first, that the success of the prince presupposes a
precise calculation of power relations, not only as established at present,
but as they will be modified as a result of his own actions; second, that
the mercenary or auxiliary troops are never completely reliable, and that
one must have one's own armed forces. If Machiavelli revisits the question, it is, as we suppose, because it is now clarified with respect to the
preceding considerations on the relation a prince must have with his
subjects. Just as the examination of power relations introduced reflections on politics, so the requirements of an authority based on the
people, once uncovered, will be seen to command the idea of a specific
mode of government and a specific military organization. In reality, to
the problem raised at the beginning of Chapter 10, "How the strength
of all states should be measured" (the scope of which is immediately
reduced, moreover, since we learn that the issue is how a small state can
organize its defense), Machiavelli offers a response that is at once military
and political. Being of the opinion that a prince must be content with
fortifying his city and insuring provisions for it, without worrying about
the surrounding territory, he adds that potential assailants will hesitate
if he disposes of a well-protected location and *is not hated by his people.*
Thus the pursuit of the people's support is seen to be as necessary for
defense against outside enemies as it is for the consolidation of a stable
power within the city. Better yet: considering how little space is devoted
to strictly military considerations in this chapter, one might well wonder
whether they do not have as their main function to sustain a new political
argument. That Machiavelli speaks of "non-hatred," an expression he
uses twice, already attracts our attention. A moment earlier he recommended that the prince should win over the friendship of his people. The
term was a strong one, and somewhat surprising, since we doubted that
power ever allowed its subjects to forget their desire not to be oppressed.
But it was precisely from the relationship between *friendship* and *oppression* that meaning emerged. Now the concept of non-hatred is in turn
inscribed within a relationship; it is introduced at the moment when the
author proposes the model of cities of Germany, which are perfectly free
(*liberissimi*) despite the very small extent of their territory. Although it is

not the first time he has pointed out the strength of republics, since in Chapter 5 he had observed that they resist their aggressors with tooth and nail, and in Chapter 3 he had contrasted the thoughtlessness of Louis XII with the wisdom of the ancient Romans, the example chosen opens a new perspective. These cities, notes Machiavelli, "are fortified in such a way that everyone thinks it would be very tedious and difficult to reduce them, since they all have ample moats and ramparts, great quantities of artillery, and always in their public storehouses plenty to eat, drink and burn for a year. Besides which, in order to feed the plebs without loss to the common weal, the community always has in common holdings enough for a year to give them work in those crafts that are the nerve and life of the city, and by means of which the lower classes live. To conclude, they hold military exercises in great honor, and have many ways of maintaining them." And without transition he adds: "A prince therefore who has a strong city and does not cause himself to be hated by his subjects cannot be assaulted." This suggests that the problems to be resolved in a republic and in a princedom are not fundamentally different, that in any case it is necessary to link the material defense of the city with a domestic policy attentive to the interests of the lower classes, and that in sum a government in which the power is not hated is not without similarities to a free government. It is as if Machiavelli had only substituted non-hatred for friendship in order to go further, after that retreat, toward the conception of a state founded on the people.

That we have here a new step will soon be verified, as we proceed to see how he justifies the thesis that the resistance to an aggressor must be organized within the city walls. Refusing the arguments of those who fear that a prince might be abandoned by his subjects, when their lands are invaded and their properties despoiled, he raises in opposition this final observation: "And then all the more they come to unite with their prince. For men are of this nature that they are as much bound by the benefits that they confer as by those they receive." Such a formulation goes well beyond all that has been said heretofore. It is not just that the prince succeeds in convincing his subjects to trust him, so that he can trust them: the alliance is so firm that the very moment he falls to their mercy they discover in their freedom a new dependence: they are also bound by the help they proffer him. His prestige is such that it withstands the weakening of his power. Physical constraint has been transformed into social constraint; it has been internalized, so that the obedience obtained by the threat of arms has become consent, and consent obligation. This is a metamorphosis we can fully appreciate if we are mindful of the conclusion of the preceding chapter: men wish to die for the prince, Machiavelli said then, when death is far away, but in adversity there is scarcely anyone on whom he can rely; now, it is in the trial of adversity that the firmness of their attachment is revealed.

But the truth of this relationship appears at the level of military organization itself. Once admitted that there can be no good defense without popular support, he must again recognize that such a principle determines the nature of the good defense. The negligence of a prince in not procuring his own armed forces proves to be an error that reflects not only on power relations, as was thought until that time, but on politics. Thus, when a moment later, at the beginning of Chapter 12, Machiavelli distinguishes the problem of arms from that of laws, his intention is unmistakable. It matters little that he claims to limit himself to a critique of a strictly military order, announcing: "And as it is not possible to have good laws where there are not good arms, and where there are good arms it is reasonable that there should be good laws, I will leave off discussing laws, and will speak of arms"; we know that the foundations he now assigns to the state are not the deepest, and that the definition of arms, like that of laws, is rooted in a general conception of society and power. We need only understand that military tasks are in direct contact with the reality of the state, and are paramount for every government, whatever the nature of the regime.

In the critique of mercenary and auxiliary arms two arguments are thus intertwined, the second of which (which will be taken up again and carried to its conclusion in the most energetic terms) gradually establishes the need for a citizen army. It turns out on the one hand that the prince must make war in person, persuade the others of his power, and rely only on his own forces, for the troops of a condottiero or of an ally, not under his direct authority, are always ready, by the attraction of personal profit or at the instigation of an ambitious leader, to abandon him and turn against him. His own subjects, on the other hand, make up the only troops on which he can depend fully. Two complementary truths, indeed, but they are nonetheless established on different premises—so much so that in forgetting it we might even think them incompatible. And, indeed, if we went no further than the Machiavellian conception of power relations, as we find it summarized in this statement from Chapter 14—"between the armed man and one who isn't there is no comparison; and reason does not want one who is well armed to obey willingly one who is unarmed, nor that an unarmed man be able to be safe among his armed servants"—we would be unable to understand why an armed people would submit to a prince. Further: Is it not by virtue of a reasoning of this sort that the partisans of mercenaries condemn the idea of a national militia, being persuaded that they are among the dangers incurred by those in power, should they fall to the mercy of the citizens? To defend it, we must abandon the abstract logic of power relations, find the motivations determining the behavior of the actors—the prince, the people, the condottiero, the mercenary or auxiliary troops—and discover that politics has its own space in which antagonism is transformed into cooperation. That discovery—it is up to the reader to make it. As for the author, he limits himself to pointing out vices and praising the factual merits of two modalities of military organization, but he has given us all the elements necessary for reaching a conclusion. When, at the end of Chapter 10, he advanced the apparently paradoxical idea that men feel obligated by services rendered by them as well as by benefits received, he prepared the way for the welcoming of that other truth that the power of the people, far from removing it from the prince's authority, is a guarantee of their obedience.

The beginnings of a thesis of a citizen army echoes that of a state based on the people. And thus the movement inaugurated by Chapter 7, of which we said that it restores to power its social function, seems to be completed. But however convinced we may be from this point on of the author's intentions, we must still admit that a part of his discourse has been left in shadow. We cannot believe that the threads we hold in our hands make up the entire fabric, since, at the heart of the discussion on the prince's military power, there springs up before us—like a digression that is disconcerting at first glance—the examination of the ecclesiastical princedoms.

True, there are certain points of repair with respect to which the meaning of the new example chosen is determined. It is no accident, we may reflect, that the image of the German republics, models of well-governed and well-protected republics, follow those of pontifical Rome and of those princes of which Machiavelli writes: "Only they have territories and do not defend them, subjects, and do not govern them." Nor is it by chance that the historical creativity written into the *ordini nuovi* of a great politics is placed in contrast with the stagnation of a state governed by *ordini antiquati*. The meaning of a regime based on the understanding of power relations and the social relation is magnified by the contemplation of the non-meaning of a regime based on religion. The figure of the new prince dominates not only that of the hereditary prince, for whom it sufficed to refrain from transgressing the order of his ancestors and to temporize with events, assured as he was of the obedience of his subjects, if extraordinary vices did not excite their hatred—it shines by contrast with the figures of the ecclesiastical princes, of whom we now learn that they "stay in place however they may conduct themselves and live" and thus enjoy an immunity to history, whatever may be the extent of their misdeeds or their failings. Furthermore, it was important for Machiavelli to show, in passing, so we may surmise, that the expansion of pontifical Rome did not pose a problem for his theory of the state. And indeed it is that very demonstration that is presented with the argument that the temporal forces of the popes hardly counted in Italy until a recent date, and that it took the talent of Borgia and the circumstances of his fall for the Church to benefit from his labors and his trials (*fu herede delle sue fatiche*).

But however well founded these hypotheses may be, they leave us unsatisfied as long as we have not understood why the Machiavellian discourse, at this precise moment, requires such a digression, for until now that discourse, through its twists and turns, and at the cost of a deliberate complication in the first analyses, has not ceased deepening a conception of politics. Is it possible, then, that under the cover of examining a particular case, the writer wants to open a new perspective for his reader? The question is all the more legitimate because the considerations on the ecclesiastical princedom are not limited to Chapter 11. If that chapter seems, at first sight, to consist in an enclave in the discussion devoted to the military problem, a more attentive reading reveals that the critique of the politics of the popes is mixed with that of a system of defense characteristic of certain contemporary states. First, denouncing the vices of the use of mercenaries, Machiavelli explores its origins and brings out the role played by the Church in its institution. "You must understand that as soon as the Empire in its last days began to be driven out of Italy and the Pope had taken on greater temporal prestige, Italy was divided into several states, for most of the large cities took up arms against their nobles, who earlier, through the favor of the emperor, held them in oppression; and the Church supported these uprisings to increase its credit in the temporal realm; in many others, the citizens became the masters. Thus Italy having come practically speaking into the hands of the Church, and of a few republics, and these priests and these citizens being not in the least used to carrying arms, they began to hire foreigners." Thus it appears that the powerlessness of the states to form an army of citizens has something to do with the powerlessness of the Church, naturally destined to recruit its troops from outside. Then Machiavelli, as he lashes out a second time at the auxiliary troops—who, he observed, are even more dangerous than the mercenaries—turns his critical attention to Pope Julius II, whose plan to introduce the Spanish into the middle of Italy, "could not have been more ill-advised," showing that he had only chance to thank for not having fallen at their mercy. In both cases, the Church furnishes an extreme example of what one should not do and a perfect expression of weakness and inconsistency in politics; so that the spectacle of its powerlessness to conceive of the necessities of government and defense reveals the requirement of a politics based on arms and a military system based on a politics. But in both cases—and isn't this the main thing?—the critique of the Church abuts the contemporary situation and occasions a reflection on the conditions of a reform of the state in Italy.

It is true that Machiavelli had previously been able to choose historical examples that were recent, either supplying the subject matter of a long analysis, such as the case of Borgia, or being merely mentioned, as with the dukes of Ferrara, Francesco Sforza, or Oliverotto da Fermo. But one had the impression that such examples, like those of the great men of antiquity, or those of Louis XII, the Turk, or the German republics, had no other function than to illustrate general hypotheses or expose the multiple aspects of the political problem. Borgia was given as a model—offered to whoever might conceive of a plan and experience analogous conditions. On the other hand, the image of the pontifical state—a case among others, no doubt, but one that is no longer reducible to the dimension of a personal enterprise, since its characteristic traits derive from a constitution, itself historically determined—draws our attention in a new way. It is not for nothing that Machiavelli goes back over the merits of Borgia, in the framework of this analysis, and that he goes on to contrast his great politics with the adventurism of Julius II. With one, a future opened up in Italy that, with the other, closed. With one the just foundations of a new state were set; with the other the miserable enterprises that maintained and even precipitated the decadence of Italy were repeated. When the reader gauges this opposition—the weakness of the Church beyond its apparent progress, the significance of Borgia's actions, despite his factual failure—he receives the idea of a historical task, inscribed in the present. Whence an imperceptible transformation in Machiavelli's language. At first he seemed to espouse the prince's point of view exclusively; then the search for the conditions of power and security absorbed all his attention; then his status was seen to depend on the relation he established with his subjects; then the conception of the class struggle governed that of power; now the author leads us to consider that the interest of the prince is subordinate to that of the state, and this idea contains a judgment on Italian politics *hic et nunc*.

The argument turns in this direction during the critique of mercenary arms. In the first place, that critique does no more than confirm what is said in the preceding chapters. The prince, we are told, cannot rely on men who expect no more of him than some wages, for such a motivation, if it held them to obedience in times of peace, would not make them want to die for him; secondly, in giving up his command to a condottiero, he exposes himself to the greatest danger: either the latter does not have the military *virtù* and will bring about his loss, or he is capable of winning a war, and in that case there is nothing to prevent him from turning against his master and challenging his power. Those readers who would stop at these first propositions would conclude that Machiavelli translates in new terms the idea that authority is inseparable from force, and constraint from confidence. But the portrait he draws afterward of the condottiero is the product of a different intention. A personage without attachments, concerned solely with his prestige, incapable of supporting an infantry (because he does not have the territories that would make it possible for him to feed them), and who, making war a craft, has been reduced to transforming it into a masquerade and withdrawing it from the risks it must entail, he is judged on the basis of his function, and discredited accordingly. This critique would assuredly be illegitimate if the author were inquiring solely into the means of winning and keeping power, as is proven by the example, among others, of Francesco Sforza, who, a mercenary captain in the service of the Milanese, seized the duchy, once victory over Venice had been secured; hence if situations and actors are examined from a purely formal point of view, his enterprise is not condemnable. For it to be so, the function of the prince in the state would have to be taken into account, and the evolution of the state itself to the extent that the function of the prince is determined by that evolution. Henceforth success is no longer the only criterion by which the prince's action is assessed; or better yet, individual success is no longer confused with political success, the latter presupposing one is capable, besides taking and maintaining power, of responding to the problem posed by the edification of the state. Thus Sforza, a model of the ambitious military chief, having achieved princedom by the force of arms alone, and rising above his descendants on that score, is outclassed immediately as he shows himself to be incapable of establishing a bond with his subjects and of introducing *ordini nuovi*, that is, of creating a power that could live on without him. His conquest is appreciated, then, in the mediocre context of contemporary politics. Brilliant with respect to the dim luster of the interplay of republics and condottieri, his actions no longer excite admiration when it becomes apparent that not only did they not modify the status quo, but on the contrary reinforced its weakness. "The conclusion of such lovely prowess [that of Sforza and the other condottieri] is that Italy was overrun by Charles, pillaged by Louis, violated Ferdinand and dishonored by the Swiss."

There is no doubt but that the moment Machiavelli singles out Italy and accuses the mercenaries of having made it "enslaved and reviled" he is drawing our attention to a new object. But it emerges from considerations on the military power of the prince in such a way that there is no apparent break in the unfolding of the discourse. The critique of mercenary arms is privileged, in that it is deduced from the political principles formulated in the preceding chapter, and that it thus has, like them, universal significance, and at the same time puts us in the presence of a particular historical field, and forces us to gather the problems faced by the Italian states into one sole problem.

Thus the author can continue to be faithful to a technique he has used since the beginning of the work, which is to compare ancient and modern examples, in contrasting the military organization of Florence, Venice, and Milan with that of Rome and Sparta—which only the Swiss, *liberissimi* and *armatissimi,* have been able to take as their model. When he speaks of the three Italian states, they suddenly appear as accomplices in the same mistake, and promised to the same fate. Not only is it the case that they are equally weak. The truth is that they weaken one another, blocking one another's road to power. In their wars, their victories are false victories, their defeats false defeats. True, they did not invent the mercenary system and we must remember that in antiquity other states lost wars for having abandoned their own defense to the hands of strangers. But their case remains singular, since that institution acquired a generality in Italy hitherto unknown, to the point of dominating all political life. Or more precisely, born in specific conditions as a particular usage, it became a system that sustained itself, a parasite feeding off the substance of states and prospering as the host wasted away.

The reader, discovering the evils of such a system, has every right to suppose that its destruction would coincide with a restoration of the Italian states. But having arrived at this stage of the discourse, his uncertainty is still great. Are we to suppose that one sole authority would be imposed over the peoples hitherto dispersed or that the rise of a new state would force the others to modify their institutions and return to the path of political truth? The Borgia experience, clearly the most meaningful, does not allow us to decide, since his overly rapid failure prevents our knowing what would have been possible. To these questions another is added: What political transformations should accompany a reform of the military institutions? Of the too brief explanation proposed by the author of the weakness of the Italian states we can only deduce that a new politics would spare neither the power of the priests, nor that of the bourgeoisie, which turned its back on war to devote itself to private affairs. But in Chapter 13 Machiavelli offers one last indication. After having accused Louis XI of having debased the forces of the kingdom of France in replacing the national infantry created by his father with recruited mercenaries, he evokes the motive that inspired him to take that measure. Although he does not yet name it clearly, we can see that fear of the people lay at its source. Thus it is confirmed once more that the just idea of what a power may expect of his subjects, the risks that must be taken to inscribe them in time, the nature of true and false security, true and false foundations—these considerations are what must command the actions of the prince. The idea is insinuated that no new practice will be instituted in Italy as long as the *ordini nuovi* of political thought are not recognized.

4

Good and Evil, the Stable and the Unstable, the Real and the Imaginary

Machiavelli's discourse proceeds by a slow and methodical destruction of traditional political teachings. But those teachings are gleaned from more than one place. The tradition is not a unified one. It takes up several currents of thought. The principles governing opinion are manifestly drawn from classical antiquity, but also from Christianity, and they are derived, moreover, from a practice accumulated by earlier generations, in which one claims to read the truths of experience. No doubt, they are not averse to coming to terms with the accredited ways of seeing things by the Authors. Perhaps we should even consider that the accommodations are not accidental, that the alliance of apparently heterogeneous principles comes from a particular logic, and recognize, in the final analysis, the cohesion of the dominant political discourse. But whatever the truth may be about this hypothesis, the fact remains that critique is necessarily divided when it attacks inherited knowledge and the common opinion nourished by it. A deep division, since it tests the discourse of the oeuvre, which is occupied with conquering its identity in this critique, and is thus exposed, the moment it distances itself from a home in the Tradition, to allowing itself to be led back into the orbit of another home. The writer might try to protect himself from this danger by giving multiple warnings to his public, designating his adversaries at each step of the discourse, avoiding misunderstandings by repeated explanations on the nature of his intentions. But would that effort make it possible for him to overcome the reader's resistance? From where do inherited knowledge and common opinion derive their prestige, if not from their ability to relieve the reader of the risk of thinking, to disguise for him the unknown aspect of the *ordini nuovi*? If the political debate were one of pure ideas, the rigor of the argumentation would suffice; but it exceeds those limits. Just as power relations between political actors are inscribed within a social field, similarly power relations between ideas are inscribed within a field of ideas; the ideas only become operative in relation to an experience of the subject who is him- or herself never reducible to a concept. Thus the efficacy of the critique is assessed by the power acquired by the discourse of the oeuvre to modify that field, to work that experience to the point of opening it up to what was foreign to it.

Rather than closing his eyes to the nature of the multiple forms of resistance he must overcome and imposing his authority by the force of arms alone—by demonstration—the writer therefore tries another way; he ruses with these oppositions, adopting his adversaries' goals for the appropriate length of time, giving their beliefs their due, teasing out their contradictions, lending himself to the reader's expectations to the point of exhausting his resources and of preparing him for the *not yet thought*. But in doing so, let us not lose sight of the fact that he is not merely choosing a strategy of persuasion; he is also motivated by the requirements of his own discovery, since the path on which he sets his reader— he himself has blazed it in the struggle against his own prejudices, at the cost of many forages and retreats.

We have already observed that Machiavelli reveals his thought only gradually, and that despite the daring with which he sometimes announces propositions to which a reader accustomed to the *ordini antiquati* could not approve, the meaning of his discourse sometimes allows itself to be inferred by a relationship established between disconnected, or even contradictory terms. To the reasons we have already given for his attitude there should be added another, more precise one: his critique of the tradition must oscillate between two poles. He devotes his efforts at once to discrediting the classical and Christian conception of the state, and to condemning the unprincipled politics of the pseudo-sages of Florence. To the supposed knowledge of philosophy and religion he substitutes a not-knowing, in such a way that his analysis of power seems for a moment suspended in a void; but he opposes the ignorance of the pragmatists, satisfied with the glib sayings of the palace, with the lessons of history, the requirements of rational prevision, and the "order of things"—the order of the relations between forces and desires. This oscillation is a sign of neither confusion nor skepticism. The movement that carries him now in one direction, now in another, slowly delineates the figure of the new thought. Its contours are already sketched out; the critique of a thesis does not reestablish the one that was abandoned; the destruction of the earlier foundations of politics does not engender the retreat back into the limits of empiricism, nor does the refusal of it bring on the resurrection of traditional ethics. Thus, as his intentions become more clearly defined, he does not shy away from adopting the language of his adversaries, of rekindling their version of the way things are. On certain occasions, he corrected misunderstandings—declaring, for example, when he had praised the kindness and faithfulness of the people, that their qualities were derived from the fact that they possessed less cunning than the Grandees—now he gives rise to them, suddenly restoring to the reader the image of the good prince with which he is familiar, after having deprived him of it, yielding to his illusions, all the better to subsequently root them out.

This last intention is exemplified in the last chapter devoted to the military problem. In its beginning, it is all about the truth of power relations, and war definitely appears as the revealer of politics. "A prince should have no other aim or thought, nor take up any other thing for his study, but war and organization and the military discipline, *for that is the only art that belongs to one who commands,* and it is of such great power that it not only maintains those who are princes by race, but often enables men of simple condition to attain to that rank" [my emphasis]. Here is Francesco Sforza, designated once again as a symbol of the armed prince and contrasted with his descendants, who, because they forgot the necessity of war, fell from power. But scarcely is this argument launched, when the perspective is reversed: the portrait of the prince whose mind must never turn from war, and who only practices hunting to argue strategy before his men, reminds us of Xenophon's portrayal of Cyrus, till the invocation of this great model, in conjunction with that of Scipio, militates in the direction of the morality of government. "And anyone who reads the life of Cyrus written by Xenophon," notes Machiavelli in conclusion, "will recognize, in reading that of Scipio afterward, how many honors that example brought him, and how much Scipio, in chastity, affability, humanity and generosity tried to resemble what Xenophon wrote about Cyrus." Thus it is as if the harsh words on Agathocles, Borgia, and Sforza lost their force—as if the conquest of power had no other goal than to ensure the defense of the state and the vigorous development of good government.

Now, the reader is doubtless tempted to welcome this reassuring conclusion, however unexpected, as it completes an analysis that, taken all in all, has restored since Chapter 9 a certain idea of the common good. It turns out that the prince can and must obtain the love of his people and Italy be saved from its ills. Nor is there any doubt that this step is the preparation for a new departure, for the final abandonment of the old certainties; since, a moment later, Scipio's qualities will be adjudged weakness, the image of the "good prince" a myth, and the theory of the great Authors will be subjected to a radical critique. Between the end of Chapter 14 and the beginning of the following one, the change in tone is so noticeable that we cannot keep from thinking that the meaning of the discourse will be modified. Everything seemed to have been said, and yet it turns out that the most important still remains to be said. Reopening the question he had pretended to close, Machiavelli examines the relations that a prince must maintain with his subjects and friends, and, a bit bombastically, proclaims his break with the Tradition as if it had not already been carried out. "And as I know well that several others have written on the same topic, I fear that if I, too, write about it, I will be thought presumptuous if I depart, especially in discussing this issue, from the *ordini* of the others. But it being my intention to write something useful to one who understands it, it has seemed to me more appropriate to follow the actual truth of the thing than the imagination of it (*andare drieto alla verità effettuale della cosa, che alla imaginazione di essa*)."

But the opposition between actual truth and imagination, new from the point of view of the letter, is not new in spirit. It gives us a sense of what precedes just as much as of what follows. And when the author, condemning the danger of illusion, points out that "there is such a distance between how one lives and how one should live, that he who neglects what is done for what ought to be done will sooner learn to bring about his ruin than his preservation," we have only to recall the example of the illustrious founders, whose *virtù* was based on force, to understand the point being made. Better yet: when, after a long enumeration of the virtues and vices attributed to the prince, the conclusion is announced that "he need never hesitate, however, to incur the reproach of those vices without which his authority can hardly be preserved; for if he considers the whole matter carefully, he will find that there may be one line of conduct having the appearance of virtue which, if followed, would be his ruin, and another, seemingly that of vice, which will secure him safety and well-being," are we not brought back to a stage of the analysis prior to Chapter 9, which encouraged us to go beyond the stark opposition that had at one point been suggested between the imperatives of morals and security?

Thus, if we had to give up seeking in the portrait of good government—in Cyrus or Scipio—the ultimate meaning of the discourse, perhaps it is equally inappropriate to give full confidence to the rather sensationalist statements that open the second part of the oeuvre, and to imagine that the truth, adroitly veiled heretofore, will finally appear in its nakedness. The new beginning that is announced, as the first expressions used by the author lead us to understand, marks a return to the earlier meditation at a different level rather than the eruption of thought within a hitherto unexplored realm.

Machiavelli, the moment he declares that he departs from the principles of his predecessors, retains the terms of a question that in their view was essential. What should the qualities of a prince be? The discussion he initiates takes the scholastic treatises as its model, and it is apparently only by his answer that the teachings of the Tradition are contradicted. The Christian author[1] asserted that while it is of little importance that the action of the prince should turn to the immediate benefit of his subjects, it is blameworthy if its intention is perverse. On the other hand, Machiavelli contends that the virtue of the prince matters little if its effect is to make him lose the state. Inadmissible as it may be with respect to instituted morality, that response is still conventional. If we were to translate this to "the good is not the prince's business; he focuses on the useful," the thesis is well known, and the objection all ready. Or, considering the person of the prince, one may challenge that utility is, despite appearances, the end of his actions, to demonstrate that it yields before the requirement of happiness or salvation; or, reasoning on the state, one will object that there are at least two meanings of the word *conserve*, and to reduce the task of the governor to that of maintaining power is an abuse, and it is better, for example, to run the risk of defeat than to pay for success with a weakening of the body politic, the consequence of which would, in the long run, be the definitive ruin of the state.

But if the intention of the author were to substitute the idea of the useful for that of the good, or, better said, to superimpose on top of the values of ordinary morals, judged legitimate in private practice, those of political practice, one would not understand why that task requires a critical examination of the prince's virtues and vices. What difference would it make to establish concordances and differences between moral and political qualities if, definitively, it sufficed to stick with the latter to define the prince's conduct? The theory of empiricism would here seem to stand in for a factual empiricism ipso facto, without any justification. The fact that Machiavelli simultaneously rejects the traditional criteria of morality and seeks in what way the moral representation of politics interests the meaning of the latter forbids our reducing his thought to one sole dimension.

Already the study of military tyranny, based on the example of Agathocles, and that of civil tyranny invited us to read beyond the manifest meaning—how the prince should act, in determined conditions, to retain power—a question of a different dimension: What is political society essentially? What does it require of the prince? To what destiny does the state, once it exists, or the conditions of its existence are assembled, assign him? To ask questions in these terms, to think of the function of the governor with respect to the class struggles, in terms of a conflict that always takes the form, here and now, of a power relation, but draws its origin from the incomprehensibility or the incompatibility of the desires of men, this was to take up a position that was neither that of morality nor of political technique, and yet from which the meaning of both were to be unveiled.

It is true that now the qualities of the prince seem to lend themselves to a purely pragmatic definition, and that they are presented as *means,* the efficacy of which is measured on the basis a particular end: the preservation of the state. But there would be little to say about these means and this end if it were supposed that they were at the discretion of the prince, in feigned ignorance of the fact that the prince receives them as much as he chooses them. Now Machiavelli does not let us doubt for a moment the necessity out of which the prince is obliged to act beneath the eyes of his subjects and to compose the image of power they expect of him. The qualities of the prince, it is pointed out, are those that opinion recognizes in him. "I say that all men, when they are spoken of, and Princes more than others from their being set so high, are characterized by some one of those qualities that bring either praise or blame." And if he must know how to free himself from images that, innocently taken on, would bring about his downfall, his task is nonetheless to *appear* as others would like, not when they suspend the movement of their lives to lecture on good and evil, but when they abandon themselves to it in the pursuit of their goal.

No doubt Machiavelli is content first to observe that the prince must flee the "infamy" of the vices that would make him lose the state, and not fear incurring that infamy which is necessary to him in keeping it. But the repeated use of this term is sufficient indication that the conduct of the prince is inseparable from the representation elaborated by others. If there is at once an intolerable infamy and a tolerable one, it is, as we are ready to understand, because the traditional distinction between virtues and vices is both pertinent and inadequate. If there is "something that seems to be virtue" and engenders ruin, and "something that seems to be vice" and procures security, the fact is perhaps that what is perceived as such by a small number is not everyone's truth, or that what is perceived as such at the moment changes its features at length. In both cases, the criterion of utility ceases to be determinative, for the prince's goals are only defined with respect to a truth that has nothing to do utility, and in which the meaning of the social relation is stated.

Before the search for this truth, the objection we encountered a moment ago cannot stand. That there are several ways of understanding the preservation of the state, that is certain, and therefore one cannot restrict it to the idea that the prince must do everything to remain in power; but no more can one limit it to this other notion, that it requires the maintenance of good institutions, because in the passage from one to the other we would have accomplished no more than to substitute one conception of usefulness for another. Only the knowledge of what is, of the nature of power and of the society from which it emerges and in which it obtains, gives us the measure of utility—whether this be an appellation for the security of the prince or the common good.

Again, we must return to the letter of Machiavelli's discourse, omitting nothing, to discover the question. "My intention," notes the author at the beginning of Chapter 15, "being to write something useful to one who understands it, it has seemed to me more appropriate to follow the actual truth of the thing than the imagination of it." That is to say, the true commands the useful; but it is also to say that that truth is universal, and cannot be turned to the profit of one sole individual. The utility of the thing said, we are to understand, is not to be confused with what is useful to a particular person, even the prince; it gives itself to one who understands: not indeed to all, for the power of understanding is rare, but at least to whoever is able to receive the new word. Now, from this remark there may be drawn a consequence that we have the right to expect will be verified as the text goes on: If the Tradition teaches the prince rather to destroy than to preserve himself, does it not exercise as harmful an effect on the others, his subjects? To critique conventional moral politics—is that not, for them as much as for him, to prepare to discover a true relationship to the real? If that critique is intended for whoever understands it, is it not the case that a society in which it has become perceptible to a small number—those whose intervention is decisive— would have a different quality than the present one, under the fascination of its myths?

Among the qualities stated as those normally attributed to the prince, Machiavelli retains first and foremost—coupling them as the terms of a typical opposition—generosity and frugality, cruelty and kindness. Their examination provides the subject matter of Chapters 16 and 17, while the following one studies faithfulness to one's given word. The analysis implies, as had been announced to us, a return from the image of the thing to its actual reality. The image of generosity is replaced by the truth of rapacity, when we discover that to give one must take; that to sustain generosity one must pillage one's subjects—by crushing them under heavy taxes, for example. The image of kindness is replaced by the truth of cruelty, when we discover that the refusal to administer necessary chastisements at the appropriate time permits disorder, destructive of the city, to increase. Thus we become convinced that intention is judged by its results and that action finds its meaning over time. If the author criticizes conventional morality, it appears to be only to oppose its formalism with the demands of a concrete morality. He does not discredit the commonly admitted values. "I say that it would be well to be considered generous," he notes at the beginning of Chapter 16, and at the beginning of the following one: "I say that every prince must desire to be considered kind (*pietoso*)." At the end of these analyses, he seems to arrive at a factual meaning of generosity and kindness, as if he had rejected merely the immediate determination of virtue; the prince who does not give in to the temptation of generosity succeeds in meeting the financial requirements of the defense of the state and the other enterprises of power, so that in the end he can even show himself as generous toward his people. Similarly, he who turns away from kindness ultimately returns to it, like Borgia, who, after having behaved cruelly in Romagna, was able to bring peace to the country, give its inhabitants a sense of unity, and gain their loyalty. He who limits himself to this movement of thought must admit that it is not foreign to the spirit of classical philosophy. True, the language is new, and the reader may be surprised that so little weight is placed on the prince's intentions. What is more important than his desire to be good and the representation of the good in politics proves to be the concrete figure of his actions. But that there should be, for example, a false generosity, a purely formal virtue, which reveals itself, when submitted to the trials of factuality, to be associated with rapacity—Cicero had shown this in his *De officiis,* and the lesson had been lost neither on Thomas Aquinas nor his successors. On the other hand, the argument acquires another dimension the moment it is recognized that it is a question not of generosity in itself or kindness in itself, but the image of the prince characterized as *liberale* or *pietoso.*

This is the real reason why Machiavelli takes no interest in the intentions of the prince. In this way, he brings no new response to the moralist's traditional question, but rather changes the question itself, in taking as his point of departure a *phenomenon:* the prince such as he presents himself in the governing–governed relationship. He returns from the image of the thing to its actual truth only to decipher the meaning of the image inscribed in it. The terms in which the analysis of generosity is set forth are unequivocal: "I say that it would be well to be considered generous; nevertheless generosity, practiced in such a way as to make you considered as such, harms you. Because if you practice it virtuously and in the way it should be practiced, it will not be recognized, and will not spare you the infamy of its opposite. Therefore, for whoever wishes to retain the name of generous among men, it is necessary not to neglect any sort of sumptuousness. Thus, a prince of this nature will always consume in similar actions (*opere*) everything he has (*tutte le sue facultà*); and he will be obliged, in the end, if he wants to keep the name generous, to consume by such means all his resources, and will be at last compelled, if he wishes to maintain his reputation for generosity, to impose heavy taxes on his people, become extortionate, and do everything possible to obtain money. This will begin to make him hateful to his subjects, and having become poor, make him little esteemed by his subjects."

Now, what Machiavelli says of generosity, he repeats apropos of kindness and cruelty. It is the fact of *being considered* cruel, the *name* cruel, the *infamy* that the prince may or may not take on that Machiavelli wishes to discuss. And to object that all he is doing here is reversing the perspective of Christian authors (of Savonarola in particular, for whom the regard for reputation, the moment it begins to govern behavior, is the origin of evil, a reversal that would still testify to his dependency) is to misunderstand the meaning of his words. For in seeking the meaning of the *good* and the *bad image,* and the way the prince should position himself with respect to them, the writer would have us think through a truth that is irreducible to the terms of morality: what makes the prince be constituted qua prince in relation to his subjects, and the latter qua subjects in relation to the prince.

As for the critique of generosity, we are naturally inclined to interpret it in the terms of the tradition. Thus we think we understand that, to be generous, the prince must refuse to appear so, and that he becomes generous on the sole condition of using his own possessions and those of his subjects sparingly. But prejudice leads us astray. Machiavelli does not claim to return from appearance to being. He questions appearance in the certainty that the prince only exists for others, and that his being is *outside.* His critique unfolds solely in the realm of appearance.

The danger in generosity or kindness, he observes, is that the image of the generous or kind prince is unstable. It comes undone of necessity, with time, as a result of actions that aspire to maintain it. It is an attractive image that engenders a hateful one: that of the rapacious or cruel prince. The good image is not just the opposite of the bad one: it is contiguous with it, finds in it its immediate prolongation. One cannot form the first without prompting the upsurge of the second. The only way to escape this nefarious metamorphosis is to come to terms, from the very beginning, with a *not kind* image that is nevertheless not the worst: that of frugality, or of a certain sort of cruelty. Clearly these last two images do not coincide entirely: frugal (*misero*), the prince refrains from giving and from taking; cruel, he gives himself over to violence. In one case he accepts not being loved, while in the other he goes so far as to make himself feared. But they are in agreement in that cruelty, well conceived, presupposes an inner restraint: as the author notes, it should only be used with moderation (*in modo temperato*), prudence, and humanity. The prince should not allow himself to kill without justification and manifest cause, take care not to assault the property or honor of his subjects, and if he arouses fear, he should flee hatred. The image the prince must give of himself is not, therefore, the simple reflection of the one composed by the mass of men, always readily vacillating from one extreme to the other. It affirms itself rather in opposition to the gross representations that would strip him at either extreme of his identity. The others are predisposed to seeing in him an object of love or hate. But his look evaluates theirs. If he allows himself to be spellbound by the image they attach to him, his power is doomed. In doing so, he would become whatever they wish: concerned with being liked, he could not fail to become hateful; or, hated, he would resign himself to being hated, would become fearful of the fear of others—"he will frighten himself," notes Machiavelli—and will be precipitated into the catastrophic cycle of violence. To return to oneself: this does not mean to decide to ignore others in favor of obeying I know not what inner principle that would dictate some intrinsically just action. It does not mean breaking out of dependency, but rather modifying it. It means sounding the depths of the feelings that govern the good and the bad image, acting in such a way as to avoid their proceeding to either expression and thus crystallizing. It means improvising for those feelings a new outlet, stabilizing them in the form of an image that will validate their ambivalence by being at once *not good* and *not bad*.

But that formula, which suggests symmetry between the good and the bad image, remains equivocal, as long as we have not evaluated the respective power of love and hate. Is it possible that passion does not invest itself equally in both? It is a fact that the critique weighs more heavily on the first than the second. Of the latter, Machiavelli limits himself to saying that it is the object of hatred; on the contrary, he dwells on showing why the prince precipitates his downfall in trying to inspire or sustain love. Not content with observing that kindness degenerates into cruelty, and generosity into rapacity, he gives the reason for it, invoking once again the natural perversity of human nature. "Men," he says, "are ungrateful, fickle, simulators and dissemblers, anxious to avoid danger (*fuggitori dei pericoli*), and desirous of gain." Let us interpret this: They are not grateful to the prince for his generosity or for his goodwill, they are inconstant in their affection, simulate love and dissimulate hatred, steal away when their support is rightfully expected, and are never satisfied with what they are given. But we must not forget that the problem with the good image is that it elicits the bad one. Whether the prince is immediately the object of hatred or whether, in seeking to be loved, he cannot ultimately avoid it, it is still that hatred that is his downfall. It is true that the not-bad image does not restore the good one, no more so than the not-good one restores the bad. But the good and bad ones are not symmetrical, since the not-bad one is located at least in the vicinity of the good one, whereas the not-good one remains in any case at a distance from the bad one. How would we understand, then, this strange relation, if we had to stick with the idea of human perversity? Why would it matter, then, on that hypothesis, that the prince should regain, as a result of his frugality or a moderate cruelty, an appearance of kindness or generosity, and why would he find security in that appearance?

In the uncertainty in which we find ourselves, it is preferable to accept with some reservations the proposition that man is doomed to evil and consider that at this stage of the argument the meaning of the discourse is only partially transparent. This expectation disposes us to seek a response in Chapter 18; and indeed, the moment it begins, a new path is announced. The analysis of faithfulness seems built on the same model as that of generosity and kindness. But no sooner has the author contrasted ruse (*astuzia*) with honesty (*integrità*) and observed that the princes who have succeeded in outmaneuvering the minds of men (*aggirare e' cervelli degli uomini*) have surpassed those who based their actions on loyalty, he passes a new judgment on human nature. "One must therefore know that there are two ways to do battle; one by laws, the other by force. The former is appropriate to men, the latter to beasts. But since the former rather frequently proves insufficient, one must resort to the latter. This is why it is necessary to the prince to be able to use well both the man and the beast. That rule was taught to princes in veiled terms by the ancient authors who write of how Achilles and several others of these great lords of the past were given to be raised to the Centaur Chiron, to instruct them under his discipline. This means no other thing, thus having as tutor a half-beast and half-man, than that a prince must be able to use both the one and the other nature, and the one without the other is not durable. Since, then, a prince must be able to use the beast, he must choose the fox and the lion, for the lion cannot defend himself against nets, nor the fox from wolves. So it is necessary to be fox to know the nets, and lion to scare away the wolves."

This passage, an ironic paraphrase of Cicero, as has been justly pointed out,[2] completes the break with classical humanism. The two sources of injustice, as is asserted in *De officiis*, are force and ruse; one is characteristic of the lion, the other of the fox. Both constitute what is the most degrading for man, but the second is the most reprehensible, for there is no worse vice than giving the appearance of being an honorable man at the very moment one is doing evil. In reversing that opinion, Machiavelli daringly denies the conventional distinction between reason and passion, between man and beast. It is a distinction, moreover, that was taken over whole by the Christian authors, as attested by the treatise of Egidio Colonna.[3] Machiavelli demands that passion—the beast—be given its due; that the prince not imagine he can break with nature, that he is twofold, like his subjects, and that he dominates them solely by his power of knowing the motivations from which their actions follow—for the most part, blindly. But in placing the relation of the prince with his subject in this light, he declares at the same time the way his image is constituted. To know its foundation, it is decidedly insufficient to reduce man to his perversity and politics to pure force. True, the first illusion is to place one's trust in laws that presuppose total respect for commitments made, and therefore in human goodness. But the law exists and we must even admit that it is, as much as force, consubstantial with the relations of man with man. As for force, it is, in turn, effective only when connected with ruse. Now it is to take stock of that ruse that Machiavelli invites us in this new chapter, with the obvious intention of exposing the nature of power.

Ruse is presented by the author first as an attribute of the beast in man, such as the passion symbolized by the fox, just as the lion symbolizes force. Thus it is the art of escaping from the traps set by the adversary. We already recognize in this characterization of ruse the value of a self-splitting, a duplicity, allowing one to take up the point of view of others—the value of knowing his or her intentions and of canceling out their effect through one's own conduct. But Machiavelli evokes, in the same passage, another sort of duplicity: that of the prince who becomes at once lion and fox, and at a more basic level, man and beast, placed beneath the sign of the law and the sign of force. In this displacement of the meaning of duplicity, the theory of the ruse is delineated. Every man is twofold, both simulator and dissimulator, acting after the example of the fox, still beneath the dominance of passion. But the prince raises that duplicity to a different level: he is the *"gran simulatore e dissimulatore."* We should understand by this that he can disguise force as law, and also govern by the force of law, give the beast human form, and also repress the beast in man. At one extreme, ruse roots him in animality; and indeed he is moved by the liveliest passion, that of power. But at the other extreme, passion transcends animality, for the prince can only triumph over the ruse of others by understanding their machinations, by receiving their lies, and at the moment when he exercises his force, in agreeing with them and in harmonizing them in dissimulation.

That there are several degrees of ruse—the author persuades us of it, when he writes: "Men are so simple and obey so much to present necessity that he who fools always finds someone who allows himself to be fooled." Then, a few lines further: "That is why he [the prince] must have a mind ready to turn as the winds of Fortune and variations of things command him, and as I have already said, does not distance himself from the good if possible, but be able to enter evil, if necessary." The first proposition is disconcerting, since we know that man is changeable and always prepared to turn against the prince, after having sworn faithfulness. But it leads us to understand that there is a simple ruse, a disposition to betray when subjected to immediate need, which is satisfied at the instant of the other's failure; whereas it is the prince's prerogative to know the diversity of needs and situations, and conceive of all possible artifices for parrying them. While the vulgar crowd is unstable, in that it is always tempted to move from one position to another—in that, retaining no more than the appearance of the feeling that was a moment earlier his own, it suddenly acts according to the opposite feeling—the prince dominates man's natural fickleness, mentally embracing the variations of things, joining what is called virtue and what is called vice, and giving both their appropriate expression according to the event.

Thus, despite what is announced by the title of chapter—"How Princes Must Keep Faith"—it is not only, nor essentially, faithfulness to one's given word that is at issue. Doubtless Machiavelli's critique clashes on this point with the commonly held opinion; it suffices to evoke the recriminations it aroused to appreciate its impact. But whoever stops to examine this particular passage must admit that the audacity is more in the terms than in the thought of the author. If one were to translate it into more prudent language—were one to say, for example, that the prince proves more faithful to his mission in breaking a promise he cannot keep without damage to the state, that in wanting to keep it at all costs, it would soon cease being scandalous. In reality, Machiavelli only reasons on faithfulness, as he did earlier on frugality and cruelty, to expose a new dimension of politics. And in contrast with preceding analyses, this one is not satisfied with setting up an opposition between a real vice and an apparent one, the ultimate result of which would be to reestablish a certain good; its interest is to make an immediate connection between the vice that one could consider the most condemnable, since the prince risks losing his honor, the most dangerous since it attracts at once hatred and disdain, with the image of virtue. In replacing bad faith, the opposite of good faith, and treason, the opposite of respect for one's given word, with ruse, as the power of connecting law and force, reason and passion, and good and evil, the author brings us to consider the idea that power necessarily includes mystification. The prince can only sustain himself on the condition that he throws people off the track. "Never a prince," writes Machiavelli, "lacked legitimate excuses to *color* his lack of faith." And immediately recalling the example of those who were able to act successfully after the manner of the fox, he adds: "But there is a need to *color* that nature well."[4] Nothing can make us better understand that the ruse of power surpasses vulgar ruse, since the latter must itself be dissimulated; it is not born in view of a particular goal, nor is it defined as a means one might employ or not according to the circumstances. It is the art of attaching every particular action and every image to which it gives rise to a good image of the prince.

Of this theory, the first visible consequence is doubtless that it founds a politics of violence and deception. That the prince may act cruelly, make promises he has no intention of keeping—not only does Machiavelli admit it, but he shows on what conditions such a politics will succeed. This, however, is but one consequence among others. Ruse is not necessarily tied to the perversity of the prince. Provided he wants to, and the situation lends itself to it, he can be faithful and serve his subjects: ruse does not forbid his doing so, for that goodness still agrees with its opposite. It is but the felicitous moment of a factual coincidence between being and seeming, in which their difference is not at all obscured. Machiavelli says more. The prince will profit from having in fact the qualities he pretends to possess, if he is not a prisoner to them. This is to suggest that, to fully carry out his functions, the mask must not be foreign to the face it hides. "Therefore it is not necessary for a prince to have all the above-mentioned qualities, but he must appear to have them. And I may even dare to say that if he has them and observes them always, they are harmful to him; but pretending to have them, they are profitable; as to seem to be merciful, faithful, humane, sincere, religious: *and to be so,* but fixing your mind on this, that if it is necessary not to be these things, you can and know how to act in the opposite way" [my emphasis].

Now it would be an error to retain from the above merely a lesson in psychology. The bond between being and appearance is only intelligible if we go back to its origin: the relation of the prince with his subjects. If the prince must, willy-nilly, be deceptive, it is not only because his subjects are condemned to evils; it is more profoundly because they cannot put up with his spectacle, because they insist on the appearance of good. Acts of cruelty on the part of the prince, his treason—his subjects can put up with them as long as they are draped in veil of the common good. But if he throws off the mask and expresses himself as a cynic, there he stands, reduced to the limitations of his person, exposed to the eyes of all, like a man among others, and destined to hatred and disdain.

Thus we understand at present why the good and the bad image are not symmetrical; why the not-bad image reestablishes a good image, whereas the not-good image does not engender the bad. While the prince's subjects are sufficiently mean to deny his being good, they are not sufficiently so to see him as being the incarnation of evil. They would like to believe in his virtue, in a good image, and it is enough for them that he not make that belief impossible for them to be satisfied. In sum, if it is not difficult for him to mystify them, it is because that is their wish.

But is the term mystification the appropriate one? In retaining it, we must stick with the idea that the prince deceives, that his subjects are fooled, that they even fool themselves in allowing themselves to be fooled. Machiavelli authorizes this interpretation when, at the end of Chapter 18, he distinguishes the point of view of the small number who are capable of grasping the truth from that of the masses. "Men in general judge rather by their eyes than their hands, for each one can see easily, but few can feel. Everyone can see very well what you seem to be, but few have the feeling of what you are. And those few do not dare to contradict the opinion of the great number, who have on their side the majesty of the state to support them; and for the actions of all men and especially princes (for in their case no other judge can be appealed to), one considers what the outcome has been. If a prince, then, takes as his goal to conquer and to maintain the state, the means will always be deemed honorable and praised by all. For the vulgar crowd only judges by what it sees and what happens. Now, in this world there are none but the vulgar crowd, and the small number do not count, when the great number find support."

And yet, is it so easy to divvy up the roles between the deceiver, the deceived, and the third part which is reduced to powerlessness? Did not the critique of the Grandees in Chapter 9 propound that there is, between the prince and the people, a sort of connivance, a common interest in surmounting the reign of violence? Perhaps, then, it is not only useful to the prince that the people should stop at the level of appearance; perhaps it is precisely the condition necessary in order for authority to become differentiated from power. Perhaps the transcendence of authority—thanks to which the people gather in their unity and cease being simple matter for oppression—does not take place without the development of a collective structure of the imagination. If that were to be the case, it would have to be admitted that the prince obeys rather than commands by ruse, *that the reason for his ruse is inscribed in a ruse of Reason*, that his subjects are not altogether wrong in allowing themselves to be blinded by the majesty of the state, that the few seize only half the truth when they discover and denounce the vices of the prince. Furthermore, does it not suffice to give a name to that minority to assess its professed clear-sightedness? If they are the Grandees, we already know that they have enough astuteness to recognize that of the prince, manipulator of men and manager of wealth as they themselves are, but that they are incapable of rising above the immediate struggle against the Other. If by minority we mean the moralists, who, like the Savonarolists, claim to defend virtue in politics, we also know that they precipitate the ruin of the state and the servitude of the people by attacking the powerful without taking up arms to combat them. Both of them address only the particular: they grasp the motivations of conduct, the causes of an action, but not politics in its generality. They feel that the prince is different from what he appears to be; but because they come too close to him, they lose sight of the sense of his enterprise such as it is manifested in its results. How would the theoretician—he who focuses on the actual, effective truth—denounce the few, if he did not reject as abstract the conventional distinction between truth and falsehood, the imaginary and the real, if he did not intend to replace the point of view of Understanding with that of Reason, if he were not persuaded that error changes into truth as truth into error and that the imaginary necessarily inserts itself into the real? The vulgar, notes Machiavelli, only go by what they see and what happens (*il vulgo ne va sempre preso con quello che pare e con lo evento della cosa*); that is to say, their mystification is only partial. If they allow themselves to be blinded by appearances, it is not only because the prince is a "great simulator and dissimulator," it is also because he succeeds in triumphing over his adversaries and in maintaining the state. And as the author also observes, there is no criterion other than that success by which the politics of the prince can be assessed, nor any other judge but the vulgar crowd to evaluate it.

But this interpretation also leaves us with less than total satisfaction. If we admit that politics is never pure mystification, the fact remains that several forms of politics thrive in the shadowy relationship between the prince and his subjects; if we admit that the reality of power is linked to a collective system of institutional imagery, such imagery does not in all cases have the same substance to it. The example of Alexander IV "who never did anything but fool people," the allusion to a "prince of our time," Ferdinand, "who never preaches anything but peace and good faith . . . and is a great enemy of both," are there to remind us of the existence of a dark power. And indeed we know that neither of these men is in Machiavelli's view a great politician. Must one, then, give up making a distinction between an ambitious pope of the type of those who do not in the least defend their states, nor govern their subjects, and the glorious founder who brings happiness to his people with the introduction of *ordini nuovi*? Must we finally reach the conclusion that there is an ultimate ambiguity, and, because we have put the vulgar crowd in the position of sovereign judge, refrain from searching out the chances—let us not say of a good government, since the concept must be abandoned—at least of a politics that would be responsive to the requirements inherent in the social relation? Or, if such a search is not vain, is it possible to give a foundation to that politics?

Chapter 19 seems at first to bring a reassuring response to these questions. It is once more suggested that the interests of the prince merge with those of the people, and we can believe that the sad examples, invoked a moment ago, had but a limited significance. By a roundabout route, the reason for which, it is true, remains obscure, the author would rejoin the teaching of Aristotle; with that sole reservation, certainly important, that he is speaking of a prince, while his illustrious forerunner reasoned about the tyrant, there is between their remarks a striking resemblance. It is the very terms used by Aristotle that Machiavelli takes up several times, when he affirms that the prince must above all take care not to be *hated* and *disdained;* it is again of him that we must think when, evoking for the first time the danger of conspiracies—a subject to which Book 5 of the *Politics* gave so much space—he concludes that the best remedy is to satisfy the needs of the people. It is as if, beyond that, it sufficed for the prince to repress his passions and refrain from violating the honor and possessions of his subjects, for the state and its security to be preserved. Thus moderation seems to be the essential virtue of government—that moderation of which Aristotle judged that it made it possible to correct the excesses inherent in bad government, and to bring it back to the just measure that is the foundation of the good. Doubtless the author cannot say that the tyrant must give himself the image of a king, since he has wiped away the distinction between the legitimate and the illegitimate, but he declares that the opponents will back away before the image of a prince who is excellent and respected by his own people. And that observation has all the more weight, considering that the term excellent had not hitherto been applied to any but the glorious founder. Furthermore, the examples now proposed appear intended in all likelihood to soothe our anxiety. The first has something idyllic about it. The former lord of Bologna, Annibale Bentivogli, having been assassinated, the people, whose confidence he had been able to win, massacred the conspirators and their families, and, not content with having avenged him, inquired into the existence of one of his obscure descendants and had him come to Florence to turn the power over to him. The second seems to furnish a model of good government: the constitution of the kingdom of France is adjudged admirable, because the prince was able to constitute a Parliament, a "*tiers-juge*" capable of containing the ambition of the Grandees and of protecting little ones against their insolence; rising above the classes, he settled their struggle in such a way as to attach the people to him without exposing himself, by direct repression, to the rancor of the nobility. Now, with these considerations, the discussion on ruse seems to find a felicitous conclusion. In a sense, the Parliament is but an artifice intended to disguise the intentions of the prince; it is a screen he interposes between himself and his subjects in such a way as to shelter his person from hatred; the king of France makes use of it, just as Borgia, as related in Chapter 7, had made use of a minister to reduce the populations to obedience, thus disburdening himself of the unwelcome task that would have made him unpopular, by shifting that burden onto him. But in another sense ruse, becoming institutionalized, ensures the cohesion of the state; it transforms the class conflict; it delivers society from violence, quite as much as it does the prince from fear. "This institution (*ordine*)," notes Machiavelli, "could not have been better or more prudent, and there could not be a better means of insuring the security of king and kingdom."

This is a far cry from the vulgar deceits of Alexander, who never worked for anyone but himself and his family, or from Ferdinand, that prince whom it is not good to name, but of whom we will later learn that he only waged war and persecuted the Marranos to deflect his subjects from politics and hold them, mesmerized, under his dependence. Ruse, the power of which revealed itself in the spectacle of miserable enterprises, eventually finds its justification in the advent of an order to the benefit of all. And if it remains the case that the good image of the prince cannot be instituted from the recognized norm of the good regime, at least one can think that with it the wishes of society are realized.

But that conclusion, the moment it is advanced, is—not destroyed, but submitted to the harshest test. It must be recognized that the idea of non-hatred and non-disdain, like that of generosity a moment ago, only led the reader back to the vicinity of classic instruction to detach him or her from it the more completely. The peaceable movement of reconciliation is followed, once again, by the violent movement of rupture: Aristotle cannot, any more than can Cicero, be the corresponding figure for modern thought.

Indeed, the objection lent to an anonymous contradictor suddenly makes the efficacy of the good image problematic. "It will seem, perhaps, to many people," notes Machiavelli, "that if we give careful consideration to the life and death of several Roman emperors, they are examples contrary to that opinion of mine, alleging that such and such a one always lived perfectly (*egregiamente*), showing that spirit of great talent (*grande virtù d'animo*) and nevertheless lost the Empire or was killed by his own in a conspiracy." The author has shown sufficiently that the prince can bring about his own downfall in trying to be virtuous for us not to misinterpret the meaning of that objection. What is at issue is not virtue itself, but, from a new perspective, its image.

That princes have been able to act in the interests of the people, and that they have nonetheless perished beneath the blows of their adversaries—this is what must now be explained. It is not adequate to evoke exceptional circumstances. True, the circumstances in which they found themselves were not ordinary: "while in other princedoms, they only had to contend with the ambitions of the Grandees and the uprising of the people, the Roman emperors had a third difficulty, of having to withstand the greed and cruelty of the soldiers." The strength of the army, when it exceeds that of the people, has the effect of altering the relation between the prince and his subjects. It is impossible for the prince to resort to a mediator or to play that role himself, for the social struggle has already engendered a third party, a cruel and rapacious mass which, in contrast with the people and the Grandees, is content with disorder, and has no fear of the opposite class, and demands that its appetites be immediately satisfied. The prince must therefore act as he would in time of war— and we already know what necessity imposes on him. Machiavelli, when inquiring into generosity and cruelty, had in every case insisted on the singular relation that is established between the prince and his troops: "The prince," he wrote in Chapter 16, "who is leading an army that lives from pillage, from sacking villages, from ransom, and that enjoys the goods of others—that generosity is very necessary to him; otherwise he would not be followed by his soldiers." And in Chapter 17: "But when a prince is leading an army, with a large number of soldiers under his control—that is the time when he should not worry about being called cruel, for without that reputation an army is never unified or ready for any operation. Among the admirable things done by Hannibal, it is related that having a very large army, a mixture of an infinite number of nations and led to battle in a foreign country, there never arose the least dissention either among themselves or against their prince. This could not be due to anything but his inhuman cruelty, which, together with infinite virtues, always made him venerated and terrible before his soldiers." These remarks now seem to find a new application, without putting in doubt the principles of princely politics. But in judging thus, we would be forgetting that the predominance of the army presupposes a transformation of the social relation. As long as the army remains subordinate, its commandment calls for a particular conduct but does not discredit the ordinary relation between the prince and his subjects. On the other hand, when it becomes the main force, this extraordinary phenomenon forces us to rethink what was considered up to this point the norm. The power acquired by the army is indeed nothing but a consequence of the degeneration of the social body.

The question, however, goes far beyond the terms in which it is initially posed, with respect to the Roman example. It arises not only from an exceptional experience, that of an army out of control, but applies rather to a universal phenomenon, which is that of the corruption of society. Machiavelli lets this be clearly understood when he specifies: "When that community, whatever it may be—of the people, the soldiers, or the Grandees—that you consider necessary to you to keep your position, is corrupted, you must follow its mood (*ti conviene seguire il suo umore*)." It is true that corruption is an extreme or limiting state, but bearing in mind that its ferment is always inscribed in so-called ordinary conditions, that the class struggle always risks giving rise to immoderation, we may assume that the political response it elicits is of universal significance. In asking why power succeeds or fails in maintaining itself in the most perilous conditions, Machiavelli proposes, then, to discover its ultimate foundation. In other words, when he reasons on the problem of corruption, he continues to take his inspiration from Aristotle, who found in tyranny a limiting case amenable to clarifying the truth of politics; but the analogy of procedure brings out the difference of intention: for one, tyranny lets itself be thought in relation to the good regime: for the other, in relation to the extreme enormity of license.

If such is indeed the meaning of the discussion, if, beyond the apparent question, a question about the foundation of politics transpires, we certainly cannot stop with the first response given by the author. In saying that we must follow the corrupt masses since they are the most powerful, he merely sets a marker in the direction of the true response. Indeed, the examples chosen soon lead us to discover that the prince incurred as much danger in trying to satisfy as in frustrating their desires. In Rome, we learn, most of the succession of emperors since the reign of Marcus failed for one or the other of these reasons. Pertinax, who rose to power against the will of the army, strived to put an end to the license to which it was accustomed. The hatred he aroused, combined with the disdain brought on by his advanced age, did not allow him to hold onto the Empire. Alexander governed with goodness, so much so that in the fourteen years of his reign he never had anyone put to death without good justice. But his qualities did not suffice to preserve him from the army's hatred. Considered effeminate and dependent on his mother, he fell victim to a military conspiracy. On the other hand, Commodus, Antoninus, and Maximinus were *crudellissimi* and *rapacissimi;* "To content the soldiers, they did not forget a kind of injustice and outrage that could be exercised against the people." Now, they also knew a sad end. The first could not hold his rank, and derided the imperial majesty on many occasions, so that to the army's hatred was added that of the people. The second and third were of such great cruelty that they made themselves feared by everyone, including their family members. That fear turned against them and caused their downfall. One was of low extraction and therefore attracted disdain as well; the other, admired for his exceptional courage, was no more successful in escaping the blows of his adversaries. It is in considering the fate of Pertinax that Machiavelli launches the resounding maxim, "It must be noted that hatred is acquired as much by good works as by evil ones (*l'odio s'acquista così mediante le buone opera come le triste*)." But as we may conclude on examining the various ways of governing the Empire, it should not be understood in one sole sense, even though this sense is the first, to be retained and turned against the moralists. The proposition puts good works in doubt, but does not spare bad ones. Neither the best, nor the worst are always certain. In the extreme conditions of which license is composed, bad works do not suffice any more than do good ones in ordinary conditions. That is what the example of Severus teaches us—the most important piece in the analysis—which furnishes the second element of a response. Chosen *jure hereditario*, and thus originally under the thumb neither of the people nor the army, he fortunately succeeded in keeping civil peace, but did not face the difficulties that his successors had to confront. His power to rein in corruption is the sign of a state in which corruption had not reached its highest point. On the other hand, Severus is the black prince who triumphs in a black époque. He attains the singular merit of having succeeded in satisfying the army without incurring its disdain, and in oppressing the people without attracting their hatred. Now, this success has, apparently, but one explanation: the image of *virtù* came to cover the effects of cruelty and rapacity. "These virtues," Machiavelli observes, "made him so admirable in the eyes (*nel conspetto*) of the soldiers and peoples that the latter remained *quodammodo* [in a sense] astonished (*attoniti*) and stupefied, and the former reverential and satisfied." What the government of Severus was the author does not specify, but he at least gives us some indications of how he took power. His first act, while he was still a captain in Slavonia, was to persuade his troops to go to Rome to avenge the death of Pertinax, who had been assassinated by his Praetorian Guard. It was "under that color, without showing that he aspired to power," that he got the army to march. Then he offered Albinus, one of his two rivals, who commanded the legions of the West, to share the Empire, and under the cover of that allegiance, got rid of Niger, the other, who held command in Asia. Finally, by another trick, he got rid of the first, with the agreement of the senate, having accused him of hatching a plot against him. Thus his ploy was, on every occasion, to give violence the mask of legitimacy. It is in this that his personality differs sharply from that of the other emperors, and especially from that of his son Antoninus. This last, let us note, also proved to be a leader of quality, who aroused the admiration of the people and the army, but he abandoned himself imprudently to open acts of violence. To the corrupt army rabble he did no more than reflect its own image back to it, an image justly intolerable, that it had to destroy. While Severus was able to use that image cunningly, to respond to the army's *demand*, but not to the point of revealing its own nature to it—to make himself, among the soldiers, at once the same and the Other, the man of violence and of the law, maintaining the transcendence of power at the very moment he was using and allowing his immediate circle to use force. Severus appears great because he was double, as a prince must always be; better: because, in order to reign, he carries duplicity to its ultimate degree. He is not just a lion and a fox: he is "*ferocissimo leone*," and since he has to be, "*astutissima golpe*."

There is no doubt that the example of Severus invites us to reconsider the relations between what we have called the good and the bad image. It is true that the fact of the bad image's having been revalorized does not mean that the good image loses its efficacy thereby. Severus shows that he is cruel and rapacious, but does not forget what he owes to the majesty of the state; his politics still carry the mask of virtue and that dissimulation saves him at the same time that it keeps the masses from sinking into licentiousness. "His reputation," Machiavelli says, "always protected him from the hatred the people could have felt for him because of his pillaging." But the good image no longer returns the prince to the vicinity of goodness; the non-hatred does not change into a kind of love, nor oppression into the protection of the people, cruelty into a certain sort of kindness. Nothing, presently, allows us to suppose that the efficacy of the good image comes from a natural tendency of men to overcome their conflicts and come to agree with one another. It remains true that they cannot stand to see evil and that this repugnance binds them in the myth of the majesty of the state, thus furnishing the condition of their political coexistence. But that, as a result of this, power is stabilized and, simultaneously, that license is held momentarily in check, certainly does not mean that a durable order can be instituted, and even less that the prince's welfare is indistinguishable from that of the general welfare.

Now it would be futile to pretend to reduce the significance of this analysis on the pretext that the case of Severus is exceptional. Machiavelli reminds us of Borgia, of whom he already said that his subjects remained, beneath the shock of his politics, "astounded and stupefied"; Agathocles, who, he was careful to point out, was of low extraction and needed great "*virtù*" to escape the people's disdain; and, finally, the hero-founders themselves, as is attested by this conclusion: "Hence a new prince in a new princedom cannot imitate the deeds of Marcus, nor is it necessary for him to follow those of Severus; *but he must take from Severus what is expedient in order to give a good foundation to his States* and from Marcus the things that are suitable to maintain an already stable and well-assured seigneury with glory." The sad figure of Severus cannot, in the final analysis, be separated from the noble figure of Romulus: they cling to each other, as do the figures of all the princes Machiavelli passes in review. For, passing from one to another, what he has done is to go through the rules of syntax of a political language. And, so true is it that foundation cannot do without conservation, and the latter without a repetition of the foundational act, the last distinction itself must not fool us: the radiant traits of Marcus and the grimacing ones of Severus cannot be disentangled either.

Still, the regime of Severus is not that of Marcus, and the truth of politics is not contained in its entirety in that singular experience. The judgment passed by Machiavelli on a power inscribed within a space of unbridled freedom does not necessarily obliterate the one he passed a moment earlier on the power of the king of France, who reigned over a contemporary society efficiently ordered. Once it is recognized that there is no difference in essence between them, it is still necessary to ask on what common foundation they are established. If, in the final analysis, the principles of classical philosophy do not command the conception of the most well-ensured social order, does the example of Severus suggest others?

Severus acts within an arena in which disorder is at its height, and he succeeds in preserving the state and staying alive. He thus teaches us that at the frontier of the impossible a politics can still germinate. That politics does not seek illusory modes of recourse against insecurity: it is at the heart of instability that power is established, and in consenting to the movement that carries society to the extreme consequences of civil strife. On the opposite side, the conduct of Pertinax and Commodus concur in that they elude the difficulty: they are conducts of flight. Pertinax refuses violence; Commodus locks himself up in it: one makes himself into a rampart of law, the other a pillar of the Praetorian Guard. Both are incapable of confronting the contradiction that rends society: the fact that it is at once the space of coexistence and of the clash of competing appetites; that is to say, they are incapable of welcoming, accompanying, and mastering it. Both are therefore thrown back into the particular; they tumble into the common grave; one, because he lowers himself by fighting gladiators in the arena, the other for playing the role of a bourgeois family father; they are perceived as simple mortals whose cruelty or kindness is an impediment, men whom one can kill. Severus, for his part, thinks he is dealing cleverly with violence, placing it beneath the ensign of the law; and cleverness gives it a different *color,* it inscribes it within a different register. In that violence there lies reflected that of a corrupted humanity; but when reflected from the prince to the mass, it becomes unrecognizable. Men forget that Severus is one of them: "astonished and stupefied," or "reverential and satisfied," they are mesmerized by the *name* prince, which is indistinguishable, in their eyes, from the majesty of the state.

Such is the rampart of Severus, an invisible rampart that is neither the result of force nor that of good works: a *structure of the collective imagination (sua grandissima reputatione)*, which men construct themselves because he manages to make them want it. In Roman society, coming apart at the seams, in which law is faltering, there remains but the *name of the prince* to hold unchained appetites in check, and to ensure the metamorphosis of civil society into a political society. But based on this example we learn to read the truth of a universal experience, for, where disorder is less, where conflicts are centered on the opposition of the people to the Grandees, there remains the function of the collective, institutional imagination to cover over a pit that cannot be filled, to give an identity to what does not have one. Power always throws itself into a social void, and maintains itself only in movement—in that movement that alone holds society together.

Here we can assess the distance between Machiavelli and Aristotle—a distance that we may have been induced to forget, for a moment, by the portrait of a prince taken up with governing moderately and finding security in the protection he gives his subjects. For Aristotle, it is a place in which stability reigns. It matters little whether it is ideal: the regime that is in keeping with the essence of society has the accomplished form of any natural being. Of course, societies are subject to accident: accidental, for example, is the growth of the population, which upsets the relation between the whole and the part; the mixture of peoples; the opposition between rich and poor—and accidental also are the consequences stemming from it. Thus, the philosopher finds himself most often, if not always, in the presence of flawed regimes. But even in cases such as these—only the model of a well-ordered society allows them to be conceived of in their particularity. In this society each man is in his place, determined by the function assigned to him by his membership in the community. The form of the relations between individuals and to the governing institutional authority is justice; this last is translated by political authority, which, though it does not abolish natural inequality between individuals, relegates it to its proper place. Justice and equality are visible in the harmony of the entirety, and in its result, concord. The government that conceives the good regime possesses political wisdom; its efforts in maintaining it are guided by prudence, and the sign by which it is recognized is moderation.

In the absence of such a model, it seems illegitimate to adjudge one government better or less bad than another. To do so would be merely to counter the arbitrariness of violence with that of one's own preferences. That judgment is only founded if we are able to discern in certain traits of existent states a distortion of the good form in which the essence of the state is reflected, and thus assess the degree of the distortion. Then and only then does tyranny become the object of a critique, and with that critique there is posited the principle of a reform which, without denying the fact, reestablishes the conditions of a more suitable functioning of the state. When Aristotle recommends moderation to the tyrant in terms that are very close to those that Machiavelli will use, warning of the dangers of abandoning himself to violence, of violating the honor and possessions of his subjects, of disarming them, of losing his rank as prince to satisfy his whims—all acts that would bring him hatred or disdain—and of the profit he would derive from gaining their confidence by an able protection, he is doing no more than proposing a return from the lack of measure in which thought and action sink away, to the measure that regulates and preserves them.

To the Aristotelian description of tyranny Machiavelli does not propose a different one. He rather adopts it as his own, since it seems to him to apply to a typical experience of politics. But he grounds it on other principles, and sketches out a new ontology. It is not only that he rejects the distinction between the unjust and the just state, and, more profoundly, the distinction between subject and accident. For by judging that he wishes to know only defective regimes, or accidents, we would continue to reason in terms of classical philosophy and make his remarks unintelligible. If the diversity of situations must be thought in itself, and not confronted with an essence that would denounce them all as the effects of a *denaturation*, this is because society is, in principle, open to the event; and it is so because it does not relate to itself immediately, but is torn apart and indefinitely confronted with the task of repairing the breaches in which the appetites of classes and individuals are engulfed. It is not the event that causes disturbance; it is never but the point of encounter between the effects of incommensurable actions, the point where, in a manifest form, meaning is instituted or undone—a trace of that "time" that "drives all things before it, the good with the evil, the evil with the good." As long as one imagines society as the place in which all things tend to rest in the fullness of the natural form, the unstable, the moving, and the discordant are signs of a degeneration of Being. But Being, we are to understand, only allows itself to be grasped in relation to what happens, in the interconnectedness of appearances, in the movement that prevents appearances from becoming fixed, and in the incessant return of the already accomplished into what is once again at stake.

Thus it is not important to Machiavelli to account for the origin of the state. While in classical philosophy the question concerning the conditions of possibility of the state is reduced to the one concerning essence, both are now abandoned. Indeed, it is up to a mode of thought that experiences Being within time to take up the political relation, since no foundation supports it, in order to decipher it and deliver its meaning. There is no positivism of the fact here that would take the place of a positivism of essence. For the fact, provided we take it with all its ramifications, does not contain a meaning locked up inside itself; rather it slips between meanings, becomes the inducer of non-sense, of an indetermination that, assumed by a subject, opens up for him or her the space peculiar to political discourse. It is in the critique of what appears in the pirouette of appearances, in the conversion of a cognitive work that consumes all particular meanings into a *signifying* capital, that Machiavelli's book consists. It does not speak, nor can it, without demeaning itself, in the name of a truth *in itself;* it finds its legitimacy in the necessity of its exercise. There is no point in objecting that in the absence of a standard it is powerless to facilitate the passing of judgment on a politics, to implement comparison between various forms of power, because that objection is only valid when directed at a naïve empiricism that leaves the old ontology unchanged. It is true that Machiavelli cannot denounce the defects of a regime, since he has given up the model of a regime without defects, but this does not mean that empirical observation alone is valid, that in his view there is nothing but the failure of the prince, punished by the loss of power or death, the dissatisfaction of the people or the subservience of the state. In the critique of experience, he discovers that there is, in every situation, a *required* politics. In that politics the prince ensures his position, but it is not according to the criterion of his interests that that politics is measured. Otherwise, what image would be more satisfying than that of the pope destined to die peacefully in his own bed and to retain his States, despite his weakness and inertia? And why would reflection be focused, from one end of the discourse to the other, or nearly so, on the task of the new prince, to the point of making him, rather than the hereditary prince, the figure in which the truth of power is to be read? The required politics is the one that is in keeping with the being of society, welcomes opposites, is rooted in time, arranged in such a way as to stand alongside the abyss on which society rests, and to abut the limit constituted for it by the incompossibility of human desires. It is not even certain that this politics will favor the prince's fortunes, since Borgia, who managed to embody it for a time, came to a sad end, and (if it is true that his downfall was his fault) his destiny would surely have been more peaceful if he had not had such high ambitions. All that is certain is that the action of the prince is measured by the force of the requirement commanding it. This is, in the final analysis, the only trait held in common by the men of state who elicit Machiavelli's admiration (and the examples of ancient Rome and the German republics remind us that these are not always princes): the passion they have put into discovering the task inscribed in the situation given to them *hic et nunc*, the moment they devoted themselves to the conquest of power.

When the writer examines the actions of certain among them, he persuades us that they have made their way, by pathways rejected by traditional morality, toward moderation, so that his teaching seems to coincide, to some extent, with that of the Ancients. But that moderation is no longer inspired by the refusal of excessiveness; it is still the product of wisdom and prudence—terms whose repeated usage indicates that the author does not in the least renounce the claim of thinking the political, no more than did the classical philosophers. But now it is justified solely by the need that the ruling power has to resolve the struggle in which it is involved, and to find its limit in the relation to the Other—the people, the Grandees, the army. A universal necessity (was not Severus moderate toward Maximinus and Antoninus?), but also presupposing that the movement that, in society, begins again and again as a result of dissatisfaction is assumed and translated into a politics of risk. Between moderation and frenzy there is no incompatibility because the choice is not between Reason and Unreason, society in harmony with itself and society ravaged by passion. Reason includes Unreason; war and peace are two poles of social life; the conditions that ensure the cohesion of the state are also those that hurl it into a history.

Do not such principles, it will be asked, forbid our ever being able to transcend the limits of a particular situation and to judge that one type of government is superior to another? But to assert that there is in each situation a required politics is not tantamount to confining oneself to relativism, since these politics have a common foundation. It must not only be understood that the regime of Severus prevails over that of the emperors of his time, or that, in the present, the realm of France is better organized than the neighboring states. The truth is also that there are situations that are more or less rich, so that political action is of greater or lesser significance. *Virtù* opens up a career of greater or lesser breadth; society is more or less free and alive. In short, there are degrees of being.

Severus is the hero of a corrupt society, and perhaps he gives the right answer to the problem it poses. That answer enlightens us on the meaning of politics; but in wanting to reduce it to its particular terms or in claiming to grasp all truth within it would be to commit two equal and opposite errors. When death is very close, the field of the possible is reduced in the extreme; in such times the prince experiences the greatest difficulties, and it requires some genius on his part to keep the state alive; but then even if he succeeds, his politics remains severely limited. Where disorder is most extensive, politics soon ceases being inventive. Where class antagonism is incapable of developing a history, power cannot inscribe itself into time. Thus, when Severus disappears, we see his work collapse, and with Maximinus untrammeled violence returns. Despite appearances, the world of license is not the one in which movement is the liveliest; the world of license is, rather, the world of repetition. On the other hand, when civil strife groups men on either side around common objectives, when they are as concerned about the future as the present, a task of far greater dimensions comes into view.

Machiavelli does not let us forget that difference. Toward the end of Chapter 19, he observes that, in comparison with the Roman emperors "the princes of our time have less difficulty than did they, who were obliged to satisfy in an extraordinary degree their men of war." To listen to him, the empire of the Great Turk, the kingdom of the Sultan, and the Church are the only entities that still have to confront a similar situation. A simple digression, or so it seems, but one that announces the return to the problems of politics in the larger sense. Indeed, what is it that these three states have in common? They represent the modern forms of despotism. In them, the military or the ecclesiastical caste alone holds the power. It is such an ancient power that it has become uncontested. Thus the prince has nothing to do but let himself be carried along by it. License is, so to speak, crystallized in a regime in which all opposition has been crushed and the people have become accustomed to servitude. In these conditions politics becomes debased: the Turk is strong no doubt, but whoever conquers him with arms would encounter, as we have learned, no resistance on the part of his subjects—so weak is the society he dominates and so fragile his power. As for the pope, his power feeds on the powerlessness or timidity of the others, to the point where it is unnecessary for him to govern his people or defend his States. Modern despotism is assuredly of a different nature than that of the Roman despotism, and it may seem odd to speak of them in the same breath, since in one case power drifts like a frail craft on raging seas and in the other it seems to have found a port. But how better to communicate the idea that there is a form of security that has as little to recommend itself as the greatest insecurity—a security that is bought at the price of a diminished society and a wretched politics. And that, on the contrary, great politics is recognizable by its conquest of security in insecurity, in moving within the restless space of history, in recognizing the necessity of the Prince's having a mind ready to turn in all directions, and of his being prepared to ally himself to contrary forces instead of removing himself, and to coerce Fortune instead of avoiding her call [Chapter 18].

That politics—Machiavelli has given us on many occasions a glimpse of what it should be. But after his analysis of corruption, he can take one last step without running the risk of appearing to rejoin the truths of Tradition. Thus is clarified, in part, the figure of the prince. It is certainly not that of the good prince, accredited by Tradition, but at least we see that his situation does not imprison him in the lie of oppression, that on the contrary it provides the possibility of a relation of truth with his subjects and his neighbors.

Chapter 20 asks "Whether Fortresses, Citadels, and Several Other Things That Princes Make Every Day Bring Them Profit or Damage," and the following one asks "How the Prince Must Act to Acquire Esteem." What this amounts to, ultimately, is understanding what true security really is, and the truth about glory. Now Machiavelli suggests that there is a kind of security that is not just the product of fear, and a glory that is not solely nourished by weakness and the credulity of others. The first observation concerns the arms of the people. "There has never been a case, then, of a new prince disarming his subjects, but on the contrary, if he found them without arms, he always gave them arms." On this decisive aspect of the relation of the prince with his subjects, a conclusion to the argument left in suspense (deliberately, as we said) in Chapter 13 is reached. But such a proposition governs other, no less emblematic ones, and the most concrete ones, since they touch on the politics of the Italian states. First of all, the author notes, the prince cannot hold cities that have been subjugated by force alone or by struggle between factions, for it is not by putting others in a situation of insecurity that one can overcome one's own. Florence experienced this with the repeated rebellions of Pisa and Pistoia; and Venice, when, soon after its defeat of Vaila, it saw the provinces in which it had deemed well to stir up quarrels between Guelphs and Ghibellines turn against it. This remark does not, it is true, mean that peace is always propitious for the prince. Quite to the contrary,

"Fortune, mainly when it wants to make a new prince great [. . .] raises up enemies against him in order to give him occasion to overcome them, and, by the ladder his enemies have offered him, to climb higher" so that—one may think—a wise prince should sometimes create adversaries for himself, in order to give himself the merit of overcoming them. But accommodating divisions, allowing them to be established within the state, on the one hand, and seeking through that artifice the occasion to assert one's authority, on the other—these are two different things. Second, it appears to be in the prince's interest to win the support of those who, at the beginning of one's reign, showed themselves to be his adversaries. Just as he must arm his subjects to win their confidence, he must seduce the partisans of the previous regime to attach them to his cause, for, freed from fear, these last will be more faithful to him than his so-called friends, whose requirements—they being already persuaded of their rights—are impossible to satisfy. In both cases the appearance is deceptive, the first movement being the one dictated by fear; while the surest path reveals itself to be the most difficult, the one that involves risk. Third, fortresses are denounced as being an illusory recourse against insecurity. Conceived at once to protect the prince from a foreign aggression and to shelter him from the anger of the populace, they have no other effect than to increase, with his isolation, both internal and external danger, for the hatred felt by the people, in seeing the walls behind which power is enclosed, prompts it to revolt, and revolt opens the door to the invader. Among other examples borrowed from contemporary history, that of Milan upholds this truth, considered universal: "The castle of Milan, which Francesco Sforza built, has done and will do more damage to the House of Sforza than any other disorder or disruption that has befallen the country." Whence this lesson is to be drawn, "that the best citadel there is is not to be hated by the people." A conclusion we already saw in its nascent state, but that now has new weight, after the analysis of Severus, for it has become clear that he who states it is not a victim of illusion and knows the necessity of cruel oppression where corruption has destroyed the chances of an alliance between the prince and the people.

Finally, that the reputation of the prince depends, in certain situations, on his loyalty and his generosity, this is a last truth to be understood that completes the restoration of the image of great politics. But it does not in the least cancel out what has been said about ruse. If, in war, as we now learn, the prince must commit himself resolutely beside another state, declaring himself "true friend or enemy"—if he must, furthermore, protect his subjects, it is in the name of the same principles that govern his security, it is because risk is fecund, because generosity—on the imperative condition that it does not appear to be weakness or the substitute for another conduct impossible to pursue—permits the establishment with the other of an *extraordinary* relationship, distancing him from his own fear and inviting him to depart from himself, to bind himself in power, to risk, to give in return.

The argument in Chapter 21, as we may recall, seemed odd at first reading. There Machiavelli describes the cruel methods employed by Ferdinand of Spain to become *per fama e per gloria*, the first king of Christendom; then he evokes the somber figure of Barnabo of Milan, before drawing the portrait of a loyal and generous prince. But we now understand that there is a link between good glory and black glory. Who would doubt the blackness of Ferdinand in Machiavelli's eyes? His politics is but lies and cruelty; his wars succeed one another not for the good of the state, but to disarm the inner oppositions, to turn his subjects away from politics, to permit the exercise of personal power. Beneath the cover of religion, he drives out the Marranos and appropriates their goods. And for such an act, notes Machiavelli, there can be no example given that is "more worthy of commiseration and more singular" (*piu miserabile e piu raro*). Nowhere does the author pay him homage; he never pronounces, with reference to him, the word *virtù*. He silently traces out the portrait of the perverse tyrant of whom Savonarola said: "he wages and causes others to wage useless wars, that is, through them he seeks not victory nor to take possession of the goods of others, but does so only to keep the people hungry and strengthen his position in his state."[5] And in conclusion he associates his example with that of Barnabo, a little prince of abominable reputation who, moreover, perished by assassination. But on that occasion, as on others, irony sustains the intention of the discourse. The examples of Ferdinand and Barnabo prepare the reader to be receptive to another idea of glory than the one suggested by the fate of the lying and cruel prince, an idea that is and is not different, that opens out onto justice, while granting the extraordinary its place.

What brings glory, Machiavelli says in considering Barnabo's adventure, is the performance of something extraordinarily good or bad in the life of the state. There lies the true ambiguity: but the good and the evil are not two possibilities at equal distance from the prince. Beside the fact that they are always inscribed within a situation that gives them a different weight, it is permissible to think that what is called good is justified by transcending the limits of a private enterprise, by being inscribed within time, and by responding most amply to the *complication* that governs the history of societies.

In sum, nowhere is the royal road of politics traced out. And it is no accident if, to make us sensitive to the indetermination in which it moves, Machiavelli reasons on the relations between one state and another, which gave him the occasion, at the beginning of his work, to reveal the logic of force and to define the prince as the knowing subject. This perspective is not now discredited, but certainty is linked to the test of the uncertain and to the choice of the less uncertain. "Now, let no master of a state think he can ever choose an option that is certain; let him rather consider that he should take them all as being uncertain, for the order of things human is such that one can never flee one inconvenience without incurring another." This way of putting it gives us food for thought, beyond the immediate fact that motivated it. In it, does the argument not contain its conclusion? A conclusion that would maintain, in the response, a final question: that the prince must accept the indeterminate, and that, just so, if he accredits it, if he rejects the illusory security of a foundation, he is offered the chance of discovering, in the patient exploration of the possible, the signs of historical creation, and of inscribing his action in time.

5

The Present and the Possible

The great politics, as we have named it, presupposes taking up the charge of a task inscribed *here and now* in the being of the social. It would be fruitless to seek a definition of it in the model of a regime conforming to nature or a providential plan. In order to conceive of it, it would be better to reject the idea of such a model, and that the imagination renounce seeking support in Nature or in God. Then the necessity of the task may be designated by the fact that in it there seems to be accomplished the movement by which men tend—let us not say to agree, but to recognize in one another a common identity and history. Still, we should not allow ourselves to be misled by that image. If it is true that a task can be deciphered in things, how can we forget that power itself is inscribed within the register it deciphers? Power, no doubt, occupies its own space, and the prince is led, because he can distance himself from all the social agents, to take an overview of society. Hence he can believe that the terms of the problem to be resolved are posed independently of him, in the state of the relations of forces and a historical conjuncture. But the appearance of power is itself a moment in the institution of the social; it is to the extent that there is class division that a separate power is engendered. This last reproduces the division that it is its task to surmount. It is believed that it brings unity, but that unity is not effective; if it were, that power would immediately thereupon be reabsorbed into the substance of a community finally become itself as a result of its action. The truth is that power only offers a substitute for that unity. Now, if the power is efficacious, it is on the condition that the prince both depict and mask at the same time the division in question; that he find in the experience of separation, or, strictly speaking, in his own undertakings, in which that separation is signified, access to the real.

In the first chapters of *The Prince* the question that seems to dominate all the subsequent analyses—how to obtain and retain power—is justified precisely by what is not put into question: the existence of power as such. It is as if it were installed in the place from which the absolute reference has been expelled: the *imperio* is implicitly posited as what justifies the actions of the prince. The prince asserts himself, as it seems, as subject by situating himself at a distance from the mass, by treating the others as modalities of object-being, as forces whose interrelations he must know and whose workings he must calculate. In what follows, this moment of objectification is retained—and in fact it cannot be suppressed because in it is announced, in a preliminary form, the truth of the separation of politics; however, that truth denounces its abstraction; politics is not reflectively self-aware as long as it does not know what it is separated from, as long as it is not conscious of its own origin. It is by knowing the particular structure of the field of forces, by understanding why they are incommensurable, what, in their singularity, the desire of the Grandees and the desire of the people are, that the prince discovers the limits of objectification, and that he appears to himself as situated *in* society, invested with a power, charged with embodying the imaginary community, that identity without which the social body dissolves. In this reversal of perspective the truth of separation is realized: indeed, the prince learns that he cannot, without perishing, identify himself with the image that the dominators and the dominated compose of him; at the very moment in which he experiences his dependency, and in which he knows himself to be bound to the people, he must forbid himself to satisfy the desire of the people. He must keep this desire in suspense, in order to remain the third party, thanks to whom the civil order is instituted.

Now, in this situation, the ambiguity of politics is found. The prince embodies the imaginary that has been assigned to him by his function in society, but at the same time *he is caught up in it,* he is this desire for power and glory into which the desire of his subjects is metamorphosed. Here resides the blind spot of his task: that he can only rejoin the others through the space that they set aside for him as his own. The very conditions that ensure access to the real disguise it from him. Thus it is always possible that he may allow himself to become fascinated by his own image and that in assuming his role he may become estranged from the people—as dangerously as when he closes himself up behind the walls of a fortress. Such is the case of Ferdinand of Aragon, whose prestigious conquests are the result, ultimately, of the same delusion as the castle erected by Sforza in the name of a politics of power. Indeed, just as there are two degrees of power—at the first it is nourished from the weakness, and at the second from the strength of the people—there are, we discover, two degrees of the imaginary, a way for the prince to disarm the desire of his subjects and to alienate himself in his image, and a way of arming it and acting in such a way that his own image nourishes the imagination of the people, and his own desire that of the others. But no objective criterion allows him to distinguish these two forms of the imaginary, for nothing can cause him to detach himself from his desire for power and glory. As long as he does not come up against the manifest hostility of his people, at least, he can remain captive to an illusory power.

But this uncertainty is not nothing; if the prince recognizes the ambiguity of politics, he is already open to truth; in the absence of the power to conceive of the task that he must carry out, he has the idea that such a task exists. Machiavelli suggests that his reflection culminates in this discovery. The prince only asserts himself as such, as the political subject, by sustaining the indetermination that is constitutive of the real, by measuring himself in an enterprise whose meaning is not inscribed in things, independently of him, and that nevertheless is not produced by him, but rather passes through him—by constantly, time and again, putting his desire into play in the field of history. It is therefore not in objectification that he is truly the Subject, for the so-called objectivity masks his own position from him; it is in that specific interrogation that is imposed on him by the movement that makes him leave himself and return to himself, that reveals to him, at the heart of his project, the trace of a foreign necessity, and, in things, the reflection of his image.

That the prince's politics is the search for *what is*, and that what he is seeking is born of his action; that he must resist the fascination his image exerts on him, but that his imagination is nourished by that prohibition against himself and by becoming the image of a people; that desire and knowledge sustain one another, and keep one another from retreating into their respective selves; that, in the accepted risk of incessant founding, since there is never any foundation in itself, the legitimacy of power is affirmed: such is the conclusion brought by the last chapters of *The Prince*, which puts us back, at the same time, in a vis-à-vis with the contingency of *hic et nunc* action and the enigma of freedom.

The relationship that ties the prince to truth—we decipher it in the conduct he maintains with respect to his ministers. It is true that, as we have learned, he must be alone in holding power, and command in person in order to receive the obedience and confidence of his subjects. Thus, he could never shift the care of governance to the shoulders of his ministers. If he delegates authority to them, it is to give them a role unsuitable to him. The minister, we may have thought, is but an instrument in his hands, at best an intermediary intended to deflect the people's hatred from him. But now we see that he is just as important for breaking down the isolation in which the prince is tempted to enclose himself. In making his ministers simple executors of his will, he would deprive himself of knowing its effects; in condemning them to silence, he would surrender to the vertigo of his own word. Thus his task is twofold: the imperative of power demands that they be servants; the imperative of truth, that they be witnesses. The prince must see to it that his entourage does not form a barrier between him and his subjects, but that it be a milieu through which their demand is filtered. In this attempt, he gives up nothing of his power. That would be the case only if its sole measure were its might. If that were the case, the prince would be debased were he to reveal his dependency. But power is only what it should be if it is recognized by the people, if it responds to a disposition of the social body, and dependence is a sign of strength when it is instituted, not with respect to men, but to truth. With respect to men, suspicion and ruse are always de rigueur; therefore the prince must make sure that his ministers have no other interests than his own; give them the sense that they could not subsist without him; by the benefits he heaps on them, remove from them any desire to change regimes; by the way he welcomes their opinions, persuade them that the truth is useful. Further, he cannot allow everyone to speak as he wishes, and even less can he allow them to question his authority; he alone, then, has the prerogative of interrogation and the power of decision. But as long as these rules are observed, the requirement of knowing what is remains entire. With respect to truth, no reticence; here, confidence and modesty are necessary: the prince, Machiavelli notes, is *largo domandatore*, he must be *paziente auditore del vero*.

Assuredly truth comes through men, and thus the first task is to be able to choose sage counselors. But the wisdom that is demanded of them consists solely in their being able to fulfill their functions as ministers, that is, while remaining within the limits of obedience, not to hide from the prince what he cannot discover for himself and is necessary to his decision-making. If the prince needs them, it is because, as Lorenzo put it in the Dedication, "to have a good understanding of the nature of the peoples, a man should be a prince, and to have a clear notion of the prince he should belong to the people." It is because he needs the Other's *view* of himself, something he is dangerously deprived of when he is alone.

True authority, then, implies an exchange, but it would be erroneous to think that it is easy to institute it. Indeed, the conditions of power are such that the prince is always tempted to confuse reality with the immediate object of his desire and to evade the judgment of others. Thus, he is most often delighted to find himself surrounded with nothing but approval and praise, and by believing in his powers, he becomes prey to flatterers. The courts are full of these, Machiavelli notes, "for men are so self-satisfied, and flatter themselves in such a way as to save themselves from that plague with great difficulty." Thus the prince needs much prudence to distinguish between true and illusory authority and to discover that at the moment he imagines he owes nothing to others he is in fact dependent on them, condemned to perpetuate the image he claims to give himself, blinded by his own reflection, enchained to his past.

It is true that when Machiavelli speaks of the prince's ministers, we cannot help thinking of the author's personal situation, with respect to the regime that has just triumphed in Florence; perhaps the former secretary of the Republic, driven out by the Medici, wants to persuade them of the danger they incur as a result of the servility of their partisans and is pleading his own cause on this occasion. But taking this appeal as a vulgar offer of service would be to forget the relationship his work establishes with the new masters of power. The prince to whom Machiavelli is disposed to submit is the very one whom he institutes as *principe nuovo*, separating him from the miserable cohort of Italian tyrants to open up the career of founder to him; and when he asks him to be *paziente auditore del vero*, he is not only being the counselor who will do no more than answer questions asked him—he is the thinker who opens the path to knowledge.

Still, it would be another error to think that the prince can merely catch a glimpse of the task that it would be the role of the theoretician alone to conceive of in its entirety. The latter is not in possession of a knowledge he must partially suppress in order to make it accessible to the man of action. The best he can do is to lead him to question himself on the foundation of his power, just as he questions himself on the fundamental principles of political thought; he deprives him of the false assurance he gets from the strength and sacredness attaching to his function, just as he himself rids himself of the certainties passed down by the Tradition. He spreads out before the prince examples from the past, though not in order to induce him to submit to established rules, but rather so that he will remember that that past was a present, that it retains its "savor;" that is, in order that he may recover the taste for invention that is at the origin of the great historical enterprises.

Machiavelli does not teach the truth of politics; he institutes a relation to truth. As for truth itself, it is part of its essence that it occurs in the *hic et nunc* of action, and thus that it always partially eludes representation. From the discourse of the writer on politics, the prince cannot expect specific directions, or even models: all he can find there is an invitation, the best motivated and most pressing, to face the exigency of the present. The question asked on the foundation and the tasks of power cannot be resolved, for him, in a response that would then have to be translated into practice; it is converted into another question—a question the terms of which he alone, ultimately, can posit.

What must be understood, in sum, is that it is one and the same thing for the prince to seek the truth, to confront the present in its contingency, and to assume his freedom. These three requirements punctuate the development of the last chapters of the work. As soon as the author has announced the first, he inquires into the causes of the Italian decadence, and, rejecting all explanations of a historical nature, he reproaches the princes—among whom number, indubitably, those who held the fate of the Florentine Republic in their hands—for letting themselves be blinded by the image of their erstwhile might. The notion of the new prince thus acquires its full meaning in opposition to that of the mediocre tradition of political empiricism. The former is new, not only because he conquers his rank, but because he perceives the new, because there is no established order or hierarchy that can resist, in his eyes, the need to win the adherence of the people to his enterprise. And by succeeding in this, he builds a surer and more solid power than if he had long been established in the state. Furthermore, by constituting himself as new, he appears old: for men, becoming attentive to his enterprise, judge him on what he does; he acts beneath their eyes, and since they are more concerned with what is than what was, they forget the circumstances of his advent. The princes of Italy, on the contrary, perished or are perishing for having thought to find a shelter in the past. Confident in the antiquity of their institutions they were unable to look afresh on the society around them: they were able neither to forge the principles of a new military discipline, nor to win the confidence of the people, nor, when the latter were favorable to them, to subdue the Grandees. Incapable of imagining that the future was something different than the repetition of the past, they fled their state when times became adverse for them, with the sole hope of seeing their conquerors lost in turn by an excess of oppression. Such is the reason for their failure, which does not have specific causes: they never thought that the fate of the state depended on their own actions. And their misunderstanding of the political task is so profound that they cannot, even retrospectively, find the explanation for their defeat, and that rather than judge themselves, they accuse Fortune, as if, dispossessed of a power to which they attributed the solidity and permanence of a natural object, they had no other recourse than to imagine a superior power, soaring above human endeavors. This error, we said, is not at the level of facts; it is not an error of the understanding; it proceeds from a powerlessness of the Subject to mark his place in the social field. It is because that place seems to him already traced out, because power and glory appear to him to be his properties, and authority in his blood, that he is excluded from history. It is because truth, for him, is already named in heritage, in past institutions, that he cannot find access to it to assume the risk of its requirement of lending it his own name.

Therefore when Machiavelli wonders, in Chapter 25, about "The Influence of Fortune in Human Affairs, and How It May Be Counteracted," he is doing something other than slipping in, for the satisfaction of culti-vated readers, a noble theme of meditation, or claiming, for himself and for his prince, some title of high spirituality. The question, announced by a remark in the preceding chapter, proves to be the one dominating all political questions, and maintaining them in their truth qua ques-tion. It is true that if it were only a question of relating human action to a last condition of possibility, there would be little enlightenment in the assertion that man has the power to intervene in the course of the world and to impress his will into it. But more important than recognizing in man the partial mastery of his fate is understanding the meaning of his relationship with what he calls Fortune, what that name contains, let us not say in itself—for whatever he may say about it, it marks the locus of his ignorance, gives it a status in which he has no part—but in his experi-ence, why it is ineradicable, and how the Subject takes its bearings by its way of holding its meaning in suspense and experiencing, in the time of action and discourse, an intangible power that is neither totally his own, nor completely outside his control.

"I am well aware," Machiavelli starts out by saying, "that many have been and are of the opinion that the events of this world are so governed by Fortune and God that men, in all their wisdom, cannot change them, and that on the contrary there is no remedy whatever." That sentence alone, in associating God with Fortune, gives rise to a first doubt, for we do not know whether we should place Fortune under the sign of God, find in the incomprehensible agitation of the world the mark of an oc-cult power, or see in God no more than one of the masks our imagina-tion finds to adorn that mysterious confusion. But from this opinion, so convincing that, if we are to believe the author, he himself sometimes cannot resist it, it seems possible to recover by a judgment based on the experience of our free will. Although for the moment it merely posits a hypothesis, this judgment delivers us from the grip of the unknowable and ensures a first reduction of uncertainty. "In order for our free will not to be extinguished, I consider (*judico*) that it can be true that For-tune is mistress of half our works, but that *etiam* [nevertheless] it allows more or less the other half to be governed." Here only the term Fortune is retained, but the idea is not foreign to the Christian mentality, and the reader would be tempted to think that our freedom itself is a result of di-vine grace if the comparison, suddenly introduced, between Fortune and a tumultuous river, capable of unexpectedly overflowing its banks and devastating all in its passage, did not prevent his maintaining that image. Once again it is all as if the reference to the Tradition—in the present case, the allusions to the impenetrable designs of Providence—did no more than prepare the moment of rupture. The idea of an all-powerful being who would concede partial freedom to man is replaced by that of a nameless adversity. Fortune suddenly designates no more than the unforeseeable unleashing of natural forces—forces that can, no doubt, dominate man, but are certainly not without causes and consequently not unknowable to our understanding. Better yet: if we consider, as the author says, that men can make dikes and canals to regulate the river's flow and prevent the dangers of excessive flooding, should we not agree that Fortune ceases to represent a positive force, independent of man? For although it is impossible to predict the moment at which our enterprises will be threatened, it is not impossible to know the direction from which the threat may come, and to act in such a way as to set up resistance. The quotients of freedom and Fortune are not distinct as we were tempted to think; the latter, we learn, increases only as a result of our lack of foresight and inertia; but both are determined solely in relation to the idea we form of them. Thus, if we judge Fortune to be sovereign, it holds us in fact beneath its power, and we are dispossessed of our freedom; if we rely on our own strength, it diminishes, and the area of our freedom and knowledge increases. That is to say that beyond our actions, beyond our knowledge, there is nothing that can be defined as a real agent—a force or spirit that commands our personal destiny from a distance. We thought that Fortune designated an anonymous adversity. It would be better to say that it is only a name, that it refers to nothing, but simply points toward the limit of our freedom and that this limit itself depends on us. "If you consider Italy carefully, which is the seat of these revolutions (*variazione*) and which has given them their impulse, you will see it to be a true countryside without drawbridges or ramparts of any kind; now, if it were protected with appropriate *virtù* as are Germany, France, and Spain, either that inundation would not have caused such great revolutions, or *it would never have happened at all*" (my emphasis).

Thus the fire of reflection consumes the belief in an invisible power. The combat between *Fortuna* and *virtù* proves to be imaginary: man has no other adversary than himself, Fortune is nothing other than non-*virtù*, and *virtù* nothing other than mastery of the world and oneself. Now, we are all the better prepared to accept this as our final conclusion since Chapters 6 and 7 were devoted to precisely this antithesis between *virtù* and Fortune. Already, as we noted, the example of Borgia, presented as an illustration of a career placed beneath the sign of Fortune, became, in the course of the analysis, the support of a definition of *virtù;* his ultimate failure, initially ascribed to that unforeseeable event, the illness of Alexander, finally appeared as the consequence of an error of the understanding.

Still, this is not the last word, for if Machiavelli does not deny these first remarks, he does suddenly open up another perspective. What he has just said, he notes, suffices "as regards opposition to fortune in general," but when we have examined things more closely, when we get down to particulars, the picture changes. The strange thing is that in fact men reach the same goal by opposite means; or else while using the same means, and proving to have the same qualities, one fails where the other succeeds. It is true that this phenomenon is not in itself unintelligible, and Machiavelli immediately proposes an explanation for it. "I also think that the prince who is able to accord his conduct with the times will be fortunate, and unfortunate the one who does not proceed in accordance with them." Let us interpret this as meaning that there is no Subject who can posit himself independently of a factual situation, and that there is, therefore, no way of acting that is valid in itself; that the power of inscribing a form into matter can only be executed in keeping with what the matter itself demands. But the modification thus made to the preceding thesis does not leave the latter intact. It would not put it in difficulty if we were merely being directed to recognize the ever particular condition of the Subject. In that case we would say that it is always in a determinate social and historical field—*hic et nunc*—that the prince must conceive his action; and that he is able, on the basis of certain givens, to foresee the future, to weigh opposing forces, to impose and maintain his authority. But it must be remembered that this field and these givens themselves vary constantly, that time drives all things before it, and that consequently there is no certain conduct or method sheltered from the event.

Change—or what Machiavelli calls *variazione*—of which man is the victim—we thought at first that it was only a consequence of his powerlessness to decide his fate, the inverse of his inertia. But it now appears that there is another change, inscribed in being itself, which it is vain to oppose; and also that there is in human conduct, even when it is reflective and finds its present recompense in success, another inertia that exposes it to another danger. Machiavelli observes: "And there is not any man so wise that he will always be able to adopt to that [the fact that things and times change], either because he cannot readily deviate from the course to which his nature inclines him; or *etiam* [also] because, having always prospered by following one course, he cannot persuade himself that it would be well to depart from it. Which is why the cautious man, when it is time to act boldly, will not be able to do so, and this will cause him to fail; if his nature changed with the wind and circumstances, his fortune would not change at all." A given period requires a certain character and style of action; however, we forget the particular conditions and seek in the latter, in a personal principle, the explanation for success in politics. But let the conditions change and we are forced to admit that what used to be conducive to the greatness of the prince now precipitates his ruin. This is why the idea of Fortune is so vividly felt by us. Happiness and unhappiness are not exclusively our work; they are the fruits of an encounter. Although it is still up to us to seize the occasion, the occasion is a gift; and of this gift there is nothing to be said, nor anything to be known about its origin.

We imagined, a moment earlier, a subject capable of imposing his law on nature and of replacing the blind movement of the world with the controlled movement of his own will. Now, it is far more the opposite fiction that must be fashioned: that of a prince capable of changing himself, of seizing every opportunity, of lending himself to every gift, of equaling the variations of history with his own variations, of acquiring mobility, volubility, of always being attuned to the things of the world. A pure fiction, since man is determined at once by his temperament and by his enterprise; but at least it keeps us from misunderstanding what we call Fortune. We invoke it to express our adequation or non-adequation with the course of the world, and because neither can be entirely reduced to intelligible causes, because, if the principle can be thought, the fact remains impenetrable. The fact that we cannot obliterate the name Fortune does not mean that it is a positive principle, governing the world and tracing out individual destinies unbeknownst to them: the idea of a history in itself remains inconsistent, the convenient and superficial justification of our weakness or our ignorance, such that we must, for example, continue asserting that the disorder in Italy is not the work of an evil power, but proceeds from the incompetence of those governing it. We need only admit that it is impossible to divvy up neatly what is within our powers and what escapes them, and that the meaning of our endeavors is inscribed at the juncture of two equally indeterminate spaces.

Thus, to the uncritical belief of the vulgar in an occult power, Machiavelli opposes the *virtù* of action, and to the clever occultation consisting in a supposed knowledge of self, the irreducible unknown of fate. To the *perhaps* that emerges from the effort of mastery, he joins the *perhaps* arising from the irresistible drive of time, ever nourishing, ever devouring. But that ambiguity of the uncertain does not disarm us; on the contrary, it sustains us, since we are always implied in the hypothesis. Indeed, if, positing ourselves as subject, we cannot exorcise the image of an anonymous play of forces reflected back to us in the form of chance, no more can we withdraw from ourselves without measuring that loss, the degradation of our power. We are condemned to pursue our undertakings, with risk as our only assurance, and this is what ultimately imparts its style to political action.

While from the point of view of the pure observer nothing ever authorizes one mode of behavior's being privileged over another, from the point of view of the actor only daring can furnish the riposte to chance. "I consider," Machiavelli concludes, "that it is better to be impetuous than respectful, because Fortune is a woman, and it is necessary to beat her and knock her about." That is to say, in the absence of a sure knowledge of what the times demand, it is appropriate to act as if they were propitious, not only to seize the occasion, but to provoke it. And when he adds that Fortune is "always the friend of young people, as a Woman, because they have less respect, more ferocity and command her with more daring," he clearly gives us to understand that the political decision is not of those whose terms can be entirely weighed—that there is an ultimate darkness in passion and imagination that is secretly in connivance with that of history.

Doubtless this conclusion seems to bear the seal of the irrational; and those who prefer to see in *The Prince* no more than an attempt to objectify and rationalize the political field will have a field day denouncing its failure. But it has been apparent to us for a long time that the truth of politics does not admit of being reduced to terms of objective knowledge. Hence the reflection on Fortune merely makes explicit the idea that emerged from prior analyses, in particular that of the history of the Roman Empire: that the horizons of political thought are not themselves political, that the relationship of the prince with power is a figure of the relationship of man with time and Being.

It is from the conception of a positive rationality—a self-contained logic of the operations of the political subject—that Machiavelli turns away, but not at all in favor of a positive irrationality—the irrational of the theologians or the astrologers. It is rather to elicit—by maintaining their contradiction—the sudden emergence of the link between knowing and unknowing, technique and adventure, in which we always find the interweaving of the one who is called subject with what he or she calls object. Machiavelli's intention, here, not only survives the criticism of the formulations he has used to sustain it, but foreshadows the derisory nature of the devotees of the new science, who, having understood nothing of what is at stake, derive satisfaction from denouncing the weakness of the theory—as if they themselves, having proclaimed in writing the vanity of the myth of Fortune, did not, along with everybody else in the course of their lives, give the unknowable its due.

The Prince, as has sometimes been observed, could end with the chapter devoted to Fortune. There the writer's discourse seems to have come full circle, not in presenting us with a concluding thesis, but with a final question on the irrational and the rational in history. But from that interrogation Machiavelli brings us back, to conclude, to the consideration of the present, to what constitutes the object of the politics of a prince in that year of 1513 during which he is writing, as the Medici, reinstalled in Florence, must discover that the fate of the Tuscan state is bound up with that of all Italy.

Should we assume, then, that the work must justify itself by proclaiming a patriotic ideal, and that, brushing aside its fastidious reserve, it wishes to define in the most concrete terms the present historical task, as if it were part of the theoretician's job to point out to the prince the path he should pursue?

That Machiavelli should address the prince directly is nothing new. He has already done so on numerous occasions. But as we have seen, that prince was without definite identity. He was the political Subject, that Subject embodied by the man who professes to direct the state. Machiavelli addressed a faceless prince, and his discourse at the same time took on all of history's situations, all the ways of governing, and prompted thought on the essence of the social relation, human nature, time—in such a way as to engage the reader for whom the political is worthy of being explored, and to put each one of his readers on an equal footing with the prince. And yet this discourse, whose validity proved universal—we also came to see that it unfolded in relation to a particular experience, that it developed through the desire to shed light on the present political scene. Not only did the examples chosen constantly confront the Italian situation, but the critique of classical and Christian tradition, as well as that of empiricism, brought out a struggle against the living ideologies, the Savonarolists, the humanists, and the short-sighted politicians who had led the Republic of Florence to its downfall. If in a sense the goals of the work were the less determinable for being dictated in the final analysis by a search for truth that was its own goal, in another sense they revealed themselves as being the most particular, for that inquiry was nourished by the quest for a truth hidden in the present; or, better, the work was based on the circumstance that the truth of the inquiry was misunderstood here and now—and not only as the theoretical truth of a theoretical inquiry, but as the practical truth of a practical inquiry.

Therefore when Machiavelli makes his final exhortation, what is disconcerting is not that he calls on a new prince to create an Italian state and deliver the Peninsula from foreign oppression. The analysis of Borgia's exploits, which is evoked by a specific allusion in the last chapter, already contained an implicit invitation to follow the path he had cleared—an invitation, it is true, a bit equivocal, since it was equally possible to take from the example of Louis XII a lesson meant for a future foreign conqueror, but that ceased being so when the critique of the system of mercenary armies and hired warlords revealed the similarity of the Italian states, the origin of their common weakness, and, constituting them, so to speak, as the place par excellence of misunderstanding, identified along the contours of these defects the configuration of the conditions of a return to truth, to that of armies and politics, to that of an alliance between the governing power and the people founded on strength. From that point on we no longer doubted that theoretical speculations were inseparable from the definition of a task in the present. Furthermore, it seemed superfluous to invoke the author's patriotism to explain his concern to return from general considerations to the interpretation of the situation of Italy, for the latter was presented as a privileged stage of action. There we could observe the interaction of most of the historical actors, the concentration of most undertakings, the manifestation of the greatest instability and, in the contradiction between political weakness and material and spiritual strength, the urgent need for radical reform. Our astonishment comes from the fact that Italy's situation suddenly becomes the object of an emphatic exordium, and at the same time the prince takes on the traits of a Medici, while nothing is said of the obstacles that would stand in the way of his enterprise, or the reasons that would allow him to carry it out successfully. It is true that Machiavelli asserts that the Medici "with their *virtù* and their Fortune are favored by God and the Church," but he has sufficiently detached his reader from belief in Fortune or God and denounced the role of the popes in the Peninsula for us to have doubts about the seriousness of that argument. It is true that he establishes a precise parallel between the task of the new prince and that of the first founders, declaring: "And if, as I said, it was necessary in order to show the valor of Moses that the people of Israel should be captive; to discover the greatness of the spirit of Cyrus, that the Persians should be oppressed by the Medes; the excellence of Theseus, that the Athenians should be dispersed: so at the present time, in order to make known the valor of an Italian spirit, it was necessary that Italy should be reduced to the extremity in which we see it: that it should be more enslaved than the Jews, more oppressed than the Persians, more scattered than the Athenians; without head, without order, beaten, despoiled, torn, overrun by strangers; in sum, that it have endured every misfortune." But this comparison makes only more noticeable his silence on the difficulties accompanying the creation of *ordini nuovi*. While in Chapter 6 he warned the prince not to have to rely on anyone, he proclaims on the other hand that where there is great consent (*disposizione*) it is easy to succeed. Henceforth it is as if for the prince to reach his goal it sufficed to form an army of his own and to be convinced that the Swiss, the Spanish, and the French are not invincible, as if the examples of the founding heroes guaranteed the success of the enterprise.

However, that patriotic lyricism replaces reflection, that doubt disappears before hope at the precise moment when an interlocutor is designated in person and a goal is found in the empirical present—can we believe that these are not the result of an intention? Can we suppose that the Machiavellian discourse, so rigorously and prudently and ironically conducted, suddenly turns to passion? One sign, at least, cannot deceive us: in the space of thirty-odd lines, Machiavelli invokes the name of God six times. It was God, he suggests, who led Borgia until Fortune opposed his designs; God to whom all Italy prays that He will send it a redeeming prince; God who extends his protection to the Medici; God again who sends so many signs, to whom we owe these extraordinary, unprecedented deeds: that *the sea opened;* that *a cloud showed the way,* that *out of a rock water came forth,* that *manna* rained down. It would surely take a reader with a particularly thick skull to exult or be dismayed at such a return to the faith of the vulgar. How can we fail to see that Machiavelli "defers to others"? He reaches boldly into the arsenal of magic and religion and his eloquence goes beyond that of the preacher whose prophesies linger in everyone's memories. He is not speaking in his own name; he is providing the prince with the themes the latter should use to mesmerize his subjects; or, better yet, he composes before the prince the image he should try to engender in the minds of his subjects. He does not suddenly and inexplicitly exchange criticism for faith and patriotic passion; he passes from one register to another, from that of a way of thinking devoted to the search for meaning to that of propaganda, which considers meaning to be inscribed in things.

The ruse—for ruse it is—is to hide this passage. But does it not reflect the most just motivations? Is it even possible to name a task and a goal without reservations and afterthoughts? Does not the recourse to the eloquent use of language attest to the unbridgeable gap separating imagination from political reflection? We cannot, it is true, listen with the same ear to the long discourse ending with an interrogation on the powers of man and Fortune, and the pathos-laden exhortation of the last chapter, because it is not the same voice that speaks. But if the appeal to deliver Italy from the barbarians cannot be taken literally, is that a reason to deny it all truth?

To suppose, as some do, that it has no other function than to offer a cover to the ambitious enterprises of the prince, or to win the sympathy of the reader at the last moment, after having dealt roughly with him, would be to forget that it was already from the critique of political and military institutions that the idea of a reform in Italy emerged. It would be naïve, we said, to believe that Machiavelli, yielding to the inspiration of the patriot, suddenly bares his soul, but it would also be naïve to conclude, out of fear of being fooled, that he is fooling us. In taking too much or too little distance in relation to the discourse, we miss the movement of the word. Now, when we know how to receive it, the alternative disappears, and there is no longer any need to decide that the writer is either fooling us or himself. The truth is that he is voicing the passion of a subject who would prostrate himself at the feet of the prince for the noblest cause, and that of a prince sufficiently inspired to hear a message from the Absolute. It is assuredly a game: the tone attests to it. But this game is still a mode of expression. It signifies what could not be signified by a categorical discourse; it signifies it in such a way that giving it a status in reality is neither forbidden nor entirely allowed; it gives its sensible form to a *perhaps;* it causes it to blossom in the shadow of the law of Understanding, which knows only the true and the false, and excludes the third.

What does this *perhaps* tell us? First of all, that it could be that there is a prince to form the idea of an independent Italian state, conditions that are favorable to it, peoples who support it. No doubt, but yet something else; for should the hypothesis be vain, perhaps it would suffice that the prince be willing and able, in satisfying his appetite for power, to simulate the virtue of a founder and obtain the obedience of his subjects, in order for there to spring forth from this first trial the premises of a new politics. It might even suffice for both prince and people to feign to believe in one another's declarations—one with the intention of firming up his power, the other with that of escaping the oppression of the Grandees—for the goal to be reached; so true it is that there cannot be, in the present circumstances, a well-ordered government without the fiction of an historical task, nor an efficacious fiction that does not oblige its being undertaken.

Apparently Machiavelli does nothing other than to illustrate for a present prince remarks he has made on the relation of man to Fortune. It is for the prince to understand that there is no way to understand the limits of the possible, that they recede in proportion to his desire, that it is appropriate to act as if time fed his glory. But at the same time, he makes sensible, by his language, his own relation to Fortune. He pretends there is a prince to hear him, as if thought could find its prolongation in practice; as he advances beyond what it is permitted for him to know, he rejoins the threshold of action, he simulates the innocence of the prophet. Now in this game the status of thought is preserved. For if thought would derive glory from commanding a politics, it also ensures itself against failure by doing nothing more than lending itself to the imagination of the future. At the same moment that it accepts to link its fortunes to time, it makes us witnesses to that adventure and forbids our implicating thought entirely in it.

In sum, far from the passage to the imaginary signifying the renunciation to the real, it proves to be the last and most just way of making the limits of discourse sensible.

Part 4

Reading *The Discourses*

6

From *The Prince* to *The Discourses*

Even if we knew no more of Machiavelli's oeuvre than *The Prince*, we would have to affirm that it belongs to the lineage of great foundations. Although the first question taken up in that work seems to indicate a restricting of thought to the knowledge of operations necessary for conquering and retaining power, gradually, as the object of inquiry changes, the entire edifice of representations based on classical and Christian conceptions comes apart at the seams and a new relation to politics is introduced. The first remarks on the technique of action prove insufficient. Being brought to bear in order to circumscribe the conditions in which a well-regulated set of hypotheses and consequences is set forth, they do not contain within them the field of the political, but free up the inquiry from answers that block access to it and lead us toward its domain: the nature of power, the division of the state and society, the division of classes and of class aspirations . . . And since that domain can only be brought into view by overturning the reference points that regulate the experience of truth and falsehood, of the real and the imaginary, of being and time, the foundation of *The Prince* reverberates well beyond the frontiers of its place of origin.

But this assessment compels us to examine the significance of the project initiated by the *Discorsi sopra la Prima Deca di Tito Livio*, undertaken shortly after the completion of *The Prince*. Should we assume that the second work continues the work undertaken by the former, and that it develops the consequences as they would apply to a different subject matter—or rather that it marks a new beginning, taking some distance from the earlier work, even superseding it? Even had Machiavelli himself defined the relation between the two works, the question would not be moot, since we would still have to question his view of it. But we are all the more obliged to examine the issue because he did not do so, because *The Prince* is mentioned neither in the Dedication nor in the introduction with which the first book of *The Discourses* begins, and because his remarks in both those places are sufficiently discordant to make us wonder what his intent was.

At first reading, this introduction appears to define the objective of

the work unambiguously. The author wishes to convince his contemporaries of the necessity of extending the imitation of classical antiquity
to the political domain. That imitation, he points out, is presently practiced by artists, jurists, and physicians, but has had no appeal to those
charged with political action. Admiration for the classical authors does
not arouse in them the desire to turn to those authors for models of institutions and political conduct: "to found a republic, to maintain states;
to govern a kingdom, organize an army, conduct a war, dispense justice,
we find neither a prince, nor a republic nor a captain nor a citizen who
turns to the examples of the Greeks and Romans." Doubtless if such
negligence were due merely to "the weakened state to which the vices
of current-day education have reduced us . . . to the evils caused by that
proud indolence that reigns in most of the Christian states," there would
be no remedy. But, he specifies, it is more because of "the lack of a true
knowledge of the works of history, from which we are no longer able to
gather the fruit or appreciate the savor contained therein." Inclined to
seek in reading "no more than the pleasure caused by the variety of the
events," men become mere spectators of the historical setting, and do not
imagine that the history that plays itself out in it speaks to them of their
own history. Thus, "that imitation seems to them not only difficult, but
even impossible, as if the sky, the sun, the elements, and human beings
had changed orders, movements, and powers, and were different from
what they were in the past." The goal, then, being to arouse the desire
for imitation, the means of attaining it, we are to understand, is to re-
learn how to read. And for that, the works of Livy will supply the basis.
Anything that can contribute to understanding them along the lines of a
comparison between the events of Greco-Roman times and the present
day will serve to further the task.

Judging from these indices, the undertaking of *The Discourses* would
seem to be more limited than that of *The Prince*, since Machiavelli, despite
his intention to invoke modern examples to contribute to the knowledge
of universal history, limits his object to the analysis of texts by one author,
and the testimony to be extracted from them. Yet how can we accept without some reservations the appeal to imitation, after having discovered
the break that *The Prince* makes with the classical authors, particularly
Aristotle and Cicero? It is true that the first work sometimes used the Roman institutions and behavior as models, but it did so based on principles
that completely dismantled the Tradition. We may doubt that the writer
believes that the truths of politics are deposited in Livy. Our doubts are
confirmed when we observe that, already in the first lines of the introduction, he asserts the originality of his enterprise as if it were unprecedented. How could he compare himself to a navigator seeking unknown

seas and lands, how could he speak of the discovery of *modi e ordini nuovi*, how could he assert that he has decided to tread a hitherto unknown path if the continent—already known and admired by all—were *Rome*, if he restricted himself to restoring *ordini antiquati*, if he wanted merely to follow in the footsteps of the Greeks and Romans? The audacity of the formulations seem to suggest, this time, that *The Discourses* are, in the eyes of their author, the foundational work, and that *The Prince* was at best no more than a first attempt in the direction of discovery. But it is true that in order to maintain this hypothesis, one would have to understand why the appeal in favor of imitation and the announcement of new creation make their appearance in the same fragment.

Let us continue for a moment to harbor some doubt. Whatever the outcome, it is important to account for the lack of any mention of *The Prince* at the beginning of *The Discourses*. Now there is one possible explanation for this silence that would put an end to our questioning. As a matter of fact the author suggests this explanation in his dedication, by producing such an eloquent indication that we are immediately prompted to seize hold of it in order to determine the eventual fate of the two works. Addressing himself to Zanobi Buondelmonti and Cosimo Rucellai—one his former collaborator in the service of the Republic, the other the scion of a great bourgeois family, in whose dwelling a certain number of young people hostile to the Medici regime gathered to hear him—he drops the hint that he has abandoned vain hopes and changed interlocutors and parties. To appreciate the allusion, we must remember that he wrote to Lorenzo, "So may Your Magnificence receive this small gift in the spirit in which it was sent; in reading it and considering it attentively, He will recognize how unjustly I undergo a great and continual bad fortune." He declared at that time to his friends: "I may have been mistaken on many scores, but at least on one I have not been wrong: in choosing you before all others to address these considerations of mine to you. First, because in doing so I believe that I show a certain gratitude for the good I have received from you, and also because I believe myself to be departing, in this way, from the current usage among all writers. They never fail to address their works to some Prince and to award him, blinded as they are by ambition and avarice, the merit of all the virtues, when they should be blaming him for all the most shameful weaknesses. That is why, not wishing to commit that error, I have chosen not those who are Princes, but those who, by so many good qualities, would be worthy of being such."

Since it must be admitted that Machiavelli had not lost the memory of his former dedication when he made this declaration, it is tempting to suppose that he was inflicting a slight denial upon himself, intended to suggest a conversion. Thus the silence surrounding *The Prince* appears to be the sign of a disavowal. Repudiating the work dedicated to the monarchic form of government, perhaps the writer was transferring the services of his pen to the republican cause. Still, should we neglect to consider that the place of the prince is not obliterated in the address to Buondelmonti and Rucellai, since these two are told that they would deserve to occupy it? One must examine with prudence the words addressed to the recipients of dedications.

The fact that at a certain date Machiavelli decided to offer his services to Lorenzo is significant to the biographer, but for the interpreter of his writings that fact remains mute so long as the reader has not bestowed meaning on it. That reading, once accomplished, rules out the possibility of thinking that the substance of the work derives its meaning from the relation established with a particular interlocutor, or even that it is subordinate to our interest in the historical personage who has been determined to underlie a given political act. The work does, no doubt, give special importance to the point of view of the prince, but it is concerned with politics per se. It addresses here and there a possible prince, but in terms such that an actual prince, to assume the role, would have to give up the traits and beliefs traditionally attached to his condition. Furthermore, far from belittling the merits of the republican form of government, he suggests that it is in order to know them and to satisfy a certain number of democratic aspirations that a new monarchy should direct its efforts. Now, what we learn from the reading of the work confirms the impression given us by certain remarks in the offer of service to Lorenzo. Machiavelli, it seems to me, presented himself in the dedication at once as a humble servant seeking a favor and as an intellectual guide. He tells Lorenzo that he cannot give him any greater gift than that of making him understand what he himself, in the course of so many years and at the cost of so many difficulties and dangers, learned and understood *(tutto quello che io in tanti anni e con tanti mia disagi e periculi ho conosciuto e inteso)*. Far from shrinking before power, he proclaims his lowly condition in order to justify his boldness in discussing monarchic governance and in setting forth rules for it, arguing that it is appropriate to be one of the people to know the nature of princes. Why then should we believe that when Machiavelli upbraids himself at the threshold of *The Discourses* for having pinned his hopes on Lorenzo, he had to count himself among the flatterers? Assuming that he regretted his former gesture with respect to the young Medici, one still cannot conclude that the error or the illusion discredited the project of *The Prince*. Moreover, one has every right to wonder whether he is communicating his entire thought in the dedication of *The Discourses*, and why the allusion to his first project remains so veiled.

On further reflection, the indication does not seem to be such as to serve as the basis of a putative change of intent. In itself, it can hardly suffice to tell us in advance the relation between the two works. Its potential is, I repeat, dependent upon the actual reading of the text. A cursory attempt at substantiating it by a superficial examination of the argument of the first book suffices to make us admit that neither the interest in princely governance nor the assessment of his policies nor that of the comparison between the monarchic and republican character have vanished. We can, no doubt, read the study of the reigns of the first Roman kings at the beginning of *The Discourses* as a necessary part of a commentary on Livy, but if we assume that their object is the analysis of the republican model, how can we fail to be amazed to find a eulogy of the monarchy in the age of the good emperors, which would seem to be incompatible with the convictions displayed in the dedication? "The reader," Machiavelli does not hesitate to write, "will see that golden age when each can hold and defend the opinion he wishes. He will see, in short, the people triumphant, the prince respected and shining in glory, adored by his happy subjects." What is the underlying intention of this statement? We cannot know until its function at this stage of the discourse is clarified, but we must at the very least agree, taking it literally, that it contradicts the apparently universal characterization of corrupting princes and pandering courtier-authors. No less eloquent is Chapter 16, in which, in a long digression on princes who have incurred the hatred of their subjects (here pointedly called tyrants), the author reestablishes in condensed form a portion of the teaching of *The Prince*. And further on he continues to progress toward that restoration. In Chapter 26, in which he examines the case of an entirely new prince who does not want to conform to the customs of a royalty nor to those of a republic, Machiavelli recommends that he should do everything new, as he himself does, and he recommends the use of means that are *crudelissimi*, "contrary not only to all Christianity but to all humanity." On several occasions, in sum, he does not limit himself to comparing the merits of the prince with those of the people (as he does in Chapters 29, 56, and 59), but analyzes situations that are confronted by both a monarchy and a republic and require of power the same strategy (Chapters 30, 32, and 51); or else he defines the conditions requiring the establishment of one or the other form of government.

With respect to these first signs, the condemnation of those who address their work to a prince is not admissible without reservation. One is tempted to think that if its function is to suggest a break with the Medici, which it would be dangerous to speak of clearly, it serves mainly to cover up the silence surrounding *The Prince* by disarming the eventual hostility of the reader. This seems to be the astuteness of the allusion: the writer twice gives us to understand more than he says; without naming himself, he speaks in terms that can be applied to himself and that suggest that he regrets having sought the favor of Lorenzo; without mentioning the relationship between a work and the person to whom it is addressed, he allows one to suppose that *The Discourses* are as different from *The Prince* as its interlocutors, avid for science and freedom, are from a mediocre pretender to tyranny. In light of that artifice, we are inclined to reconsider the opposition pointed out earlier between the affirmation of the new and the appeal to imitation of the Greco-Roman classical authors. In making so forcefully his claim to originality for his undertaking, Machiavelli, it seems, awakens the curiosity of the reader and challenges him to the perils of following him down an unknown path. But it may be that he also frees his discourse from the liability of the reputation of *The Prince*, a work that boldly asserted the authority of the classics.

But then the question of the difference between the two works becomes even more pressing. If the teaching of the earlier one is taken up again in the later, what is the virtue of recommencing? Cannot the affirmation that *The Discourses* takes an entirely new direction retain a relative justification? Despite the appearances, the exploitation of the history of the classical period, and particularly the history of Rome, and even more particularly that of Livy—might they not supply the foundation of *The Prince* with the basis it still lacked? We hastened to make the observation that the object of *The Discourses* was more specific than that of *The Prince* in that it was limited to a commentary on one author and one historical fragment. Now, we must examine the concluding remarks of the Proem with as much circumspection as its plea in favor of imitation.

The fact of the matter is that an initial cursory reading of the text persuades us that it cannot be reduced to a commentary on Livy, even one that is enriched with modern examples. We find, even in the early chapters, a distinction of kinds of states and an appreciation of the role played by class conflict in their development that breaks with the way the classical authors saw things; particularly with that of the historian that Machiavelli seems to take as his mentor. The audacity of the interpretation is such that it is of no avail for us to try to take the initial considerations on the history of Rome as a simple preamble, and we cannot fail to see it as the announcement of a critique of the model presented by Livy. Moreover, the composition of the work, from the moment the foundation by Romulus gives Livy the first points of reference for his narration, proves confusing enough for us to wonder what Machiavelli's intention is. He follows more or less the chronological order of events, but on several occasions he interrupts it in order to bring out from the chain of events something that belongs to an earlier or later period. He mentions the same examples in various places in his work in order to give them a different commentary. He refers to episodes not covered by the First Decade, and on the other hand he omits entire passages from it that would seem to be laden with meaning in his eyes. It would be vain to try to base the order of ideas on the concatenation of facts that have taken place, because these latter seem to have been chosen on the basis of a principle of intelligibility brought by the author. On the other hand, it would be equally vain to try to identify this principle, to unlock the mystery of the logic of the argument, because these pronounced judgments are always interwoven in the story of remarkable events or acts, in such a way that their articulation seems to carry the mark of contingency.

Clearly there are, at the end of the first chapter, remarks relative to the composition of the work that are confirmed in the Preface of the second book and the beginning of the third. Machiavelli appears to have intended to study, first, measures of a public nature concerning the internal affairs of the City. Then he would proceed to the examination of Rome's foreign policy. In conclusion, he would analyze the role of individuals in the edification of the Republic and its empire. But these remarks, which would justify at most the empirical cutting up of the matter of the narration, turn out to be largely false. The first book gives ample room to the actions of the men who laid the foundations of the City and discusses the means available to ambitious men to get power or, if they already have it, to oust their opponents. The second book, while it deals principally with the wars and relations between states, contains a critique of the republican form of government and a decisive reappraisal of the image of Rome. At the same time, it casts a new light on the difference between classical and modern times. The third book presents unexpected considerations on the bases of the state and of religion, analyzes at length the phenomenon of conspiracy, often presents the conduct of enemies of Rome as exemplary, and seems more concerned with defining the modalities of action in the field of politics and war than with highlighting the contributions of great men to the upsurge of Roman power.

Thus *The Discourses* put their reader in a different position than does *The Prince*. The earlier work gave many indications, as we have said, of a rigorous organization. We thought ourselves assured, at the beginning, of the logical progression of the argument. It was only gradually that it became necessary to abandon the ostensible marks of the demonstration, accept the divagations of thinking, and reconcile ourselves with the necessity for it. In the second work, on the contrary, the path to be followed is so vaguely indicated, the glimpses of ramifications so plentiful, and the observations so equivocal that we must immediately become doubtful of the direction of the argument. The discourse presents itself to us as a mosaic, the fragments of which seem to have been assembled in such a way as to obscure the overall picture. And that first image that we remember from the beginning of the Proem, suggesting the discovery of an unknown continent, becomes all the more unsettling. It is true that the experience we acquired in reading *The Prince* encourages us to wait till we have explored the text in the expectation that it will furnish the means to interpreting it, and we may even think we have lost nothing in being deprived of the appearance of order. This is a tempting illusion, but it is also true that the signposts given to us did guide us, albeit in arousing our suspicion, whereas the appearance of disorder engenders perplexity.

Nevertheless, the difference in composition of the two works can direct us toward the answer we seek, for it prompts us to observe that the *manifest* object according to which the analysis unfolds in the two works does not lend itself to the same treatment. In making the *prince* the object, Machiavelli clarifies, in the perspective opened up by the mastery of power, the multiple elements of the political field. While his discourse comes to bear on the constitution of this field far more than on the function of the prince, which only becomes intelligible within it, it remains nonetheless the case that the political object continues to determine the movement of the inquiry. Even though we are led to scrutinize the division between the state and civil society, between classes and the class desires, between present and past, they are presented for our reflection according to the position of the object of the study. Even though that position has fallen away from the register of nature, to the point where that object seems only to be instituted by a displacement in relation to the locus of sovereignty henceforth recognized as imaginary, it is by keeping it constantly in focus that all the questions of the being of politics and history are revealed. By way of contrast, the manifest object *Rome* only regulates the discourse by constraining it to proceed on several planes simultaneously. Rome is not only the double subject matter of a narrative and a teaching. Thus conceived, it constitutes a state whose institutions and undertakings can be circumscribed in a space and time that is available to the historian's investigations. It lends itself to purposes of one who, with the intention of eliciting imitation, describes the situations in which the city or individuals attained distinction. Rome is also, as it appears at the beginning of the work, the incarnation of a socio-historical type, the traits of which are defined in opposition to those of other types. From this perspective, it is one element in a comparison, other elements being the states of ancient or modern times, particularly Florence. It appears that it is according to that comparison that the first possibility of a selection of signs capable of establishing the value of the Roman examples is based. Doubtless the reader will be inclined to think that the principle of comparison assumes a knowledge of the political—of the state and the difference between various forms of government, of classes and their conflicts, of authority and law—but he cannot fail to observe that the history of the Roman Republic reveals a remarkable relation between the different levels of authority within the political field that sheds light on its logic and would remain otherwise hidden; or, to speak in more general terms, that the order of the city is not dissociable from a style of becoming. Having made that observation, one must then agree that the object Rome, too, is irreducible to the function of a type. Its virtue is to make visible the distinction between types. It reveals, mixed in with characteristics that determine its singularity, other traits, inscribed within it and having the status of possibility, the realization of which is at the service of other configurations. In that perspective, it constitutes the privileged support for research into socio-political variations. The opposition of a given Roman institution to a Florentine one will appear less significant than their mode of advent, the singular *response* given by each to similar questions, the meaning of a choice—most often a tacit one—in keeping with which certain real possibilities are excluded. But it is still true that Rome, on the three registers in which the Machiavellian discourse is inscribed, remains the subject matter of Livy's narrative. The writer invites us to read the Roman text by constituting it through that of an author. If we are to believe the conclusion of the Proem of Book 1, his intention is to write, on the basis of what he knows of things ancient and modern, everything he judges to be necessary to a better understanding of the latter—and that, he specifies, in such a way that his readers may more easily draw from his own discourse that usefulness with an eye to which one should seek to know works of history (*la cognizione delle istorie*). Thus he presents himself as the interpreter of a work, suggesting at once that the work does not reveal its meaning immediately, and that out of this conquest of meaning there will arise a new disposition of the Subject— the conversion of a pleasure of the senses (*piacere di udire*) into a desire to do, that is, to imitate.

Although at this point we cannot yet determine to what extent the admiration shown for Livy is sincere or feigned (which is a legitimate question, since it is affirmed that the path opened up by *The Discourses* has not as yet been followed by anyone), one thing is certain. The object Rome does not allow itself to be disassociated from the representation of Rome. Rome—a fragment of a privileged history, an incarnation of a socio-historical type, a place in which the multiplicity of virtualities of the political are revealed—Rome presents itself to the reader simultaneously in reference to a unique discourse which must be experienced in order for the meaning of the past and the present to be determined. We must understand that there is a connection between the knowledge of a fact, the interpretation of a book, and access to the real, that is defined *hic et nunc* in action. How could we overlook the fact, in particular, that the object to be imitated is removed from the sensible plane, that it can be apprehended immediately neither in what can be testified to by perception, nor in the signs extracted from Livy's narration? Assuming that the concept of imitation is not meaningless, we can only understand it by freeing it from its normal meaning. The situation of the artist, the jurist, or the physician who discovers operations, rules, and forgotten forms in which the superiority of an ancient *techne* is manifested is totally different from the situation of the politician, who must blaze a path by new and untried means toward history, toward the discourse in which it proves itself to be true history, and conquer the possibility of imitation. One should doubtless not overemphasize an opposition about which Machiavelli is silent. The artist is not one who slavishly copies a fragment of statue. If he imitates, it is because the object is, through him, restored to its vital power, and, now that it has been converted into a model, it becomes, as an object from the past, more present than anything that belongs to the universe immediately given as present. But the difference between the present and the past is grasped by the politician in a special experience. Antique statuary may well remain, while giving new life to modern creations, a monument and an emblem of antiquity; but the Roman Republic is neither a monument nor an emblem. Through it the past takes hold of the present, and history, which is neither ancient nor modern, is revealed. Differences in the times are not abolished, but blurred, since the truth of antiquity is seen through the experience of the Florentine.

Let us return to the Proem. Imitation, we are told, seems difficult or even impossible to the contemporaries, "as if the sky, the sun, the elements, and human beings had changed orders, movements, and powers, and were different from what they were in the past." At first we think we are to understand that the laws of nature, particularly human nature, are immutable and differences in the times illusory. But as we consider the remarks introducing the interpretation of Livy, are we not rather to understand that differences in the times are doubly misunderstood by the Florentines? For, after all, if the laws cannot be grasped as long as the terms of the comparison have not been detached from the fictions of common experience, and if that comparison requires an entire project devoted to the *representation* of the past, we must conclude that the difference is falsely affirmed when the Romans are judged to be men of a different species, inimitable, and falsely denied when the present conditions that make them seem different are hidden, and the need for work being devoted to the signs of antiquity and modernity obfuscated.

We would be wrong, then, to see nothing in the plea for imitation but a ruse intended to calm the anxiety of the reader after the daring affirmation of discovery. Perhaps it has that function also, but Machiavelli fools only those who want to be fooled. From the Proem on, he uses the concept of imitation in such a way as to draw our attention. He does not limit himself, after having announced the path to novelty, to suggesting that it is a simple return to classical antiquity, but rather intimates that this return implies an elaboration of the subject matter hitherto identified as classical antiquity. In doing so he introduces an odd question, subordinating the requirement of imitation to that of knowledge, and the requirement of acting according to the image of the Roman to that of establishing a text in which that image becomes visible.

If I have understood correctly, must we not then be of the opinion that the silence with which Machiavelli passes over *The Prince* has itself more than one meaning—that it is not just the result of prudence, but that it marks the attempt to give political discourse its true beginning? It is true enough that *The Prince* brings us a new idea of history, with its mixing of deeds of antiquity and modernity, with its critique of common representations that underlie contemporary action and language, and with its implied critique of the great authors who are supposed to ensure the validity of these representations; but it leaves aside the locus of the temporal difference and (which is probably the same thing) that of interpretation. These two loci do emerge in the interrogation, beginning with the Proem of *The Discourses*. In taking up in his first work the task of exploring the field of politics from the perspective of power, Machiavelli is obliged to describe all the socio-historical relations as they relate to that point of view. Thus the depth of this field is indicated by signs located on the surface that is made up of the project of domination. *The Discourses*, on the other hand, destroy that surface (a violent operation, the first consequence of which is to deprive the reader of the general plan of their argument) and introduce a movement such that the exploration of social space and its subdivisions is simultaneously the exploration of time and its subdivisions, as well as of political discourse and its subdivisions. There is no reason to suppose that the paths explored in *The Prince* are abandoned. Rather we should think that in order to continue his enterprise the writer must lead it back to a point of origin that it lacked—to an origin that, as we intuit, cannot be situated on the political, the historical, or the theoretical plane, but that yields to the interrogation at their point of intersection.

I think that we have now sufficiently sounded the intent of *The Discourses* to undertake their reading. But as I think back on the signs that guided our first steps, I must admit that I have neglected to question one of them that should have caught my attention. Machiavelli denounces the powerlessness of his contemporaries to imitate, in the domain of politics and war, the *virtù* of antiquity; then he decides to instruct them by means a commentary on Livy, that is, by circumscribing the model of the Roman Republic. Yet he does not allow himself to think that the deeds of the ancient Romans are unknown to his age, since he notes in passing that countless readers of the things of history (*infiniti che le leggono*) take pleasure in the spectacle of their variety. Indeed, how could he fail to point out that interest? The readers of his day would lose faith in him, for they know how important a role the Romans play in political debates and the honor in which Livy, Cicero, and Plutarch are held. This is why he only says that that interest is vain, and that it does not carry with it a desire to know and to act. Now as long as we modern readers take his critique without considering the place Rome held in the minds of the Florentines, we will naïvely tend to adhere to the program of a return to antiquity, to subscribe to the notion of an opposition between the ancient and the modern, as if that were something new—to believe that Roman examples, actually abandoned, are to be restored by the author. But if we take note of the fact that he is addressing a public that maintains a remarkable relationship with antiquity, with Rome, and that the marks of their greatness are constantly renewed, we must weigh his words more carefully.

If it is too soon to specify exactly what that relationship is—if we must refrain as much as possible from anticipating our commentary on the discourse and from exploiting historical information that will be better used by letting that commentary require it—we cannot omit at the very least to observe that the Florentine humanists, at the beginning of the *Quattrocento*, glorified the institutions of the Roman Republic and the exploits of its heroes. Why does Machiavelli pretend to be unaware of their calls for imitation? It would be vain to propose that, under the Medici restoration, it was neither seemly nor without danger to refer to those who, a century earlier, had become spokesmen for the republican ideology, or that it was of no importance to evoke their actions during an age when they had lost their efficacy. To do so would be to forget that in the recent past of Savonarola and Soderini the Republic had reaffirmed its ties with the tradition of political humanism and it would be, above all, to deprive ourselves of the knowledge that Machiavelli, prudent enough to be silent about those who preceded him in praising the Roman Republic, found the audacity to do so on his own. It would be preferable to formulate another hypothesis. In affirming that no politician, no captain considers imitating the ancients, that the Roman model is unknown and that he himself will be the one to exalt it for the first time in its true form, the writer is no doubt letting it be known that he is preparing to subvert the Tradition that considered itself to be the guardian of an ancient heritage. In suggesting that the love of so many Florentines for Rome functions as a cover for their inability to confront the tasks of the present, he is no doubt letting the reader know that the significance of his interpretation of Livy and of Roman history is that of demystification.

Indeed, it is more justifiable to vindicate the audacity of his enterprise if, taking Rome as the basis of his reflections, his choice of Rome was not only dictated by the requirements of theory. By that choice, by means of the image of antiquity and Rome, Machiavelli succeeded in striking at the heart of the political illusions of his time.

7

Rome and the "Historical" Society

The opening sentences of *The Prince* strike the reader directly; they force him to reason about power without worrying about its foundation or goals, without distinguishing between legitimacy and illegitimacy. In *The Discourses*, on the other hand, the writer seems at first to receive him in the place of the *opinio communis*, where all political theses postulate the identity of the true, the good, and the useful. Its first words, all the more resonant by their contrast with the beginning of *The Prince*, associate the *virtù* of Rome's institutions and citizens, and the might of its empire, with the wisdom of its legislators. Thus Roman history announces itself as being transparent; from the founding of the state to its acquired greatness, from good causes to good effects, the order of events seems necessary, and he who is about to retrace its steps rightfully expects the approval of his public. The first and second chapters, in the largest part, appear to be of such a nature as to confirm this disposition. The author examines the conditions in which the cities are formed, then the first motivations prompting men to form groups and form a political organization, and finally the genesis of the constitutions whose respective defects turn out to necessitate the passing from one of them to another according to an order that is, in principle, immutable. It suffices, we are tempted to think, to observe the facts and apply good sense to assess the chances of the development of the states, especially the chances offered Rome, in relation to the traits fixed from the moment of its birth. A rudimentary familiarity with the identification and classification of cases of species in the scholastic tradition will enable the reader to identify the characteristics predisposing it to greatness. Let the distinction be made between cities founded by natives and those created by immigrants; the former proceed from the gathering of a population that has put its strength in common to preserve its security, the latter are subdivided into two categories: either their inhabitants remain dependent on their former country—because they have left it due to overcrowding, or because they are fulfilling the mission, for economic or military purposes, of maintaining a colony in a conquered land—or they enjoy independence, having deliberately fled their native soil, ravaged by some scourge. Again, let us distinguish between the cities established on fertile and on barren soil, the one group fated to work and poverty, and therefore protected from discord, but powerless to defend themselves against prosperous invaders; the others threatened by laziness and riches, but for the same reason prompted, if they wish to grow, to institute laws to check corruption. This classification introduces us to a definition of the state of Rome at the same time as it heralds its merits with respect to other states, both ancient and modern. Indeed, whether its foundation is imputed to a native or a foreigner—Romulus or Aeneas—it is certain, the author tells us, that it knew immediate freedom; and that, established on a soil propitious to its growth, it accepted, in assuming the risk of corruption, to impose upon itself the constraints that constituted its strength. Florence, in comparison, born beneath the authority of the Romans, whatever doubts there may be about its founders as well, proves to be marked by its original servitude.

Such, then, is the tableau sketched out beneath the sign of convention. The reader recognizes the familiar figure of Fortune, whose intervention decides the destiny of the state, and that of the legislator who, under favorable auspices has the power to apply his science. A line separates the *fastus* from the *nefastus,* and at the same time the rational from the irrational. On one side stands Rome, near the ancient kingdoms of Egypt, and on the other Florence, with Alexandria, which carry the stigma of their servile origin. The analysis of the different forms of government and of the specific characteristics of the constitution of Rome, in the second chapter, confirm the impression that the author does not deviate from the principles to which the men of his time subscribe, attached as they are to the classical tradition. Thus he praises the excellence of Sparta; he goes as far as to assert that it observed its laws without changing them for more than 800 years, attributes to Lycurgus the merit of having brought them all at once, and judges that there is no better state than one set in order at its origin by a prudent legislator. Of Rome he says only, at the beginning, that it cannot pretend to the same sort of perfection, because it belongs to those Republics that improve with the help of events. To demonstrate the value of its constitution, he establishes that it conforms to the model of the mixed regime elaborated by the philosophers. Though he does not quote them, his concern to connect his work with the Tradition is manifest. After having mentioned a few authors who wrote on politics (*alcuni che hanno scritto delle republiche*) to recall the classical distinction between three governments (*Principato, Ottimati, Popolare*), he sides with a few others, to whom, he notes, many ascribe more wisdom (*secondo la opinione di molti piu savii*) adding three other governments—corrupted variants of the former (tyranny, oligarchy, license). He paraphrases Polybius, to the point of concluding with him that all the states are taken up in a circle, destined to return to their point of departure, after having gone through the stages that conduct them each time from good to evil. And it is again from Polybius that he borrows the thesis that the state can be withdrawn from its mortal cycle, on the condition that it associate in one sole regime the three principles, monarchic, aristocratic, and popular, no one of which can win out over the others without degenerating, as he then illustrates with the two models of Sparta and Rome. The second then appears to the reader as shored up on the first; the truth of the Roman institutions being deciphered on the basis of the work elaborated by Lycurgus. If he can recognize that truth—admit that the Romans, in the course of their history have, in amending their institutions, corrected errors, it is because the science of the Spartan legislator discloses the solution to the political problem—a solution that the facts do not teach, since they merely testify to the blind succession of regimes. As Sparta embodies, par excellence, the archetype of the conservative state, the function of theoretical guarantor that Machiavelli has it play is furthermore of such a nature as to suggest that his remarks will be no less than revolutionary. Moreover, the critique of the instability of Athens, the condemnation of Solon, adjudged at fault for having created a constitution limited to the popular principle, weigh heavily at this point of the discourse. Rome announces itself through the image of Sparta, foreign to its democratic rival.

The effect produced by the last part of Chapter 2 is, consequently, extraordinary. "But let us come to Rome, which, in spite of the fact that it lacked a Lycurgus to constitute it at its origin in such a way that it could live free for a long time, yet knew such events (*accidenti*), born of the disunion that reigned between the plebs and the senate, that what a legislator had not done, chance did." Although in the text immediately following, the author continues to concentrate on showing, as he had announced at the beginning of the chapter, that accidents allowed the Roman Republic to forge a mixed regime, the emphasis placed on the conflict opposing senate and plebs—a conflict whose function is again stressed in the conclusion—modifies the meaning of the argument. It no longer suffices to observe that chance favored Rome: it must be admitted that what elsewhere was the work of a wise legislator was here that of class conflict. Introduced on the basis of premises furnished by the Spartan model, the Roman model thus brings about a reversal. The merit of Sparta as commonly recognized is to have formed, by combining the three political principles, a harmonious state; that is, to have eliminated discord and neutralized the possible effects of accidents. Now the *virtù* of the Roman Republic, we learn, is the result of the disunion of the senate and the plebs; the accidents serving Rome are therefore not deprived of intelligibility, but are determined by the struggle between the people and the nobility. Hence there emerges a totally new thesis: there is in disorder itself what is necessary to produce a new order; class appetites are not necessarily bad, since from their clashes the city may be strengthened; history is not the deterioration of a good primitive form, since it bears, in the modality of potentiality, the Roman creation.

This prompts us to reconsider the writer's first remarks, which seemed narrowly subservient to established opinion. Certain indications now lead us to consider that the author may not have fully shared his thought with us. His praise of Sparta and of Lycurgus seems excessive. In asserting that Sparta observed its laws for 800 years, and that the work of its first legislator was never questioned, he takes strange liberties with the known facts. No less surprising is his condemnation of Solon, for he cannot be unaware that his reforms spared the dominant class. The respect he shows for "the opinion of many," which gives credence to the distinguishing of six regimes, good and defective, make us suspect that he is not speaking in his own name. His exploitation of Polybius, moreover, is accompanied by a significant alteration of his theses. He omits mention, in his reconstitution of the genesis of societies, of his considerations on the family, thus deepening the opposition between the state of nature and the political state. He is careful not to assert, as does Polybius, that the changes of regime are necessarily regulated by a law of nature. And after having made mention of the cycle that all states are supposedly destined to run through, he hastens to add that given their short life span, one rarely sees the same forms of government repeated. Finally, he does not hesitate to say that all the regimes, "good" and "bad," are *pestiferi*, thus leaving us to think that the classical distinction is without pertinence. Now, this last observation extends the range of the suspicion. We may rightfully wonder whether the expression "mixed regime," which he praises vociferously, is in fact right in his eyes or if it merely provides him with an artifice to lead his reader in a new direction. Indeed, what virtue can we ascribe to the combination of regimes that are *pestiferi*? Does the work of Lycurgus, based on discerning good regimes, resist, despite appearances, the critique that assails them? Taking into account the distance covered from the beginning to the end of the chapter, must we not rather risk the following hypothesis? Machiavelli introduces, under the cover of classical theory—Aristotle's politics and Plato's laws—an interpretation of the history of Rome requiring new concepts. Enlisting the support of Polybius, he uses an argument that is the best suited to offer his reader a transition toward that interpretation, or to hide from him, provisionally, the distance taken from the Ancients. Polybius has the merit of deploying the Aristotelian schema within time, in order to inscribe within it the Roman model: a decisive operation, no doubt, since it entrusts to the fecundity of accidents what was reserved to the legislator's science, but leaves intact the idea that the essence of the state can be read in the principles of its constitution. Now the writer takes over this operation as his own, while eliminating the arguments he is uncomfortable with, to shift the locus of the political problematics, to lead the reader from the consideration of the form of the regime to that of the relations between classes, and at the same time from that of accidents (taken in their opposition to essence) to that of an historical logic.

If we accept this hypothesis, we must recognize that *The Discourses* are, from the beginning, the locus of a work of innovation—and not only despite the appearances, but in keeping with the movement that is born of appearances, that is, by means of a return to the origins of political thought, which forces a change of direction.

But are we not attributing to the author a confidence in his way of proceeding that is not there? If it is true that the function attributed to class conflict reverses the premises initially posited, must we believe that he has total consciousness of this reversal, and sweep aside without examination the idea that he advances new thoughts while holding to the conviction of remaining faithful to the classical theory? The reading of Machiavelli's ensuing chapters answers that objection, for besides the fact that they contain no reference to the cyclical theory of Polybius, the appreciation of the mixed regime is abandoned and we must admit that Machiavelli rigorously puts in place the themes of his interpretation, going so far as to explicitly downgrade the model of Sparta in the sixth chapter. The provisional conclusion we had reached, that Rome attains perfection thanks to the disunity between the senate and the people, is furnished with a basis in an argument showing the relation between law, liberty, and power.

Also worthy of note is the artifice that, at the beginning of Chapter 3, serves to introduce the discussion on the origin of law. Machiavelli again draws support from established opinion, before subverting the principles to which it appeals. "All the writers who have concerned themselves with politics" (*tutti coloro che ragionano del vivere civile*), as he begins by noting, "and history is filled with examples that back them up, agree in saying that whoever wishes to found a state and give it laws must assume in advance that all men are wicked and always ready to show their wickedness whenever they find the occasion." This judgment, which he implicitly makes his own, announces the object of the chapter, although its title did not make it possible to designate it. Indeed, in formulating the chapter as the response to the inquiry "What accidents led to the creation of the tribunes in Rome and how the Republic came out more perfect?"

the author suggested that he would describe a few of these so-called accidents to which Polybius attributes the felicitous effect of having modified the Roman constitution. Now, the play that is established here—and will be repeated on numerous occasions in the ensuing text—between the interrogative heading and its object, is effective. Beneath the promise of a story, Machiavelli prepares to advance an idea of universal significance; in taking hold of a theoretical statement that is largely given credence, he prepares to slip in an example that, rather than furnish an illustration of it, perverts its meaning.

Thus, enjoined to remember the classical opposition between the natural state and the political one, the reader finds himself immediately jarred in his prejudice, when he finds within the political state the proof of the natural wickedness of man, and to discover it in the behavior of the dominant class. Machiavelli, commenting on the events following the expulsion of the Tarquins, remarks that under their reign "the nobles seemed to have set aside all their pride," but that once they had been driven out, "they used all the less restraint with the people as they had previously been more constricted, and neglected no occasion to strike out against it." "It is," he adds, "a proof of what we are saying: that men only do good when forced, but that as soon as they have the choice of the freedom to commit evil with impunity, they do not fail to create turbulence and disorder everywhere." A strange proof, it should be remarked, if we bear in mind the meaning normally given to the initial proposition. Those who posit it draw on the hypothesis of a perversity of human nature to make the case that law is good per se. They thus avoid the whole question of social conflict. For them, law is the work of reason, and reason does not have its place in the empirical realm of civil society. Machiavelli, on the other hand, shows his indifference to the image of the natural man, that is, of a man who has not reached the level of the political state. An indifference that—let us observe in passing—prompts us to brush aside his brief paraphrase of Polybius on the origins of humanity. It is, he leads us to think, within the space of political society that it is fitting to inquire into the origin of law, and at the same time, the conditions in which law is made and unmade. It is in knowing the tendency that "naturally" leads the Grandees, *in society*, to give free reign to their appetites that we can get a glimpse of the link between law and the restraints placed on oppression.

Again, this commentary is insufficient. It must not escape our notice that Machiavelli, speaking of laws in this chapter, means for this term to designate something quite different than the network of obligations and prohibitions that is likely to arise in the mind of his reader. Thus, he finds the creation of the Tribunal to be exemplary in the institution of Roman laws. It is to the Tribunal that he attributes the merit of having put a limit to the insolence of the Grandees in the early times of the Republic. This *ordine*, as he calls it, was of course the product of a law, but we must consider that it was very different from the other laws, because it supplied the basis of the constitution. Considering, moreover, the comparison established, in passing, between the function of the tyrant and that of the tribune (both being capable of controlling the appetites of the Grandees), one is inclined to think there is no difference of essence between the prince's personal power and the anonymous power of the institution, and that both, after all, intervene as a third party to regulate the class struggle. But at this stage of the discourse, we must await further particulars. At the most, we may observe that such a comparison completes the discrediting of the classification of the regimes proposed earlier. The understanding of the political problem is not born of the appreciation of the principle of government—monarchic or tyrannical, aristocratic or oligarchic—but of that of the play of social forces that are organized within it. It is less important to define tyranny as a corrupt regime, we are to understand, than to discover that with it one form of oppression is replaced by another, that of the nobility—whose natural tendency is for a direct and unrestricted domination—by that of the prince.

The fact remains that the first light shed on the origin of the law provides no more than a brief clarification of the position of the nobility and the conditions that call for the repression of its appetites. Chapter 4, on the other hand, abandoning all reserve, designates the principle underlying the virtue of the Roman model. It cannot be considered accidental that its title introduces us directly to the argument, which the author emphasizes thrice at the beginning of the text with an *io*—an emphatic *I*—and that he speaks in his own name, and that, for the first time, he attacks the commonly held opinion (*contra la opinione di molti*). It is not true, he asserts in substance, that there is a good and a bad side of the Roman Republic: its good fortune and its military virtues, on the one hand, and its incessant unrest whose final consequence was to cause its downfall on the other. Its good fortune and its virtues are themselves to be attributed to the type of its institutions—what he calls its *ordine*—and the latter proceeds from the class conflict by which it was torn. "I say"—*io dico*, he writes, literally—"that those who condemn the outbursts of the nobility and the plebs blame what was the cause of the existence of Roman liberty, and that they are more attentive to the noise and cries occasioned by them than to the good effects they brought about." And further on he adds: "There is no longer the slightest reason to qualify as disordered a republic that was full of examples of such great virtue, for if it is true that such good examples are the result of a good education, and the latter the effect of good laws, it is the tumults, thoughtlessly condemned by the majority, that engendered those good laws." In making such a judgment, Machiavelli is surely doing no more than bringing the concluding remark of Chapter 2 to full expression. But it is henceforth impossible for the reader to escape from the violence of a thought that runs counter to the common faith in a *good society* in harmony with itself and pacific. The thesis, pushed to its extreme consequences, that Rome reached perfection thanks to the disunity between the plebs and the senate, may no longer be looked upon as being merely unusual; it takes on a scandalous significance. How can one accept without balking the proposition that the Roman virtues are the result of the disunity of its citizens, that the tumults are the *cause* of freedom, that good education and good laws flourish in the proximity of civil war? The sages of Florence go on repeating from generation to generation that the woes of the City come from the disunity of its members, who should treat one another as brothers; they maintain that the state prospers when virtue is honored, when good mores reign, when faithfulness to the old laws that presided over the education of the citizen is maintained. Now, here that lovely image of the state is eviscerated. Machiavelli does not allow us to think that the first order is the right one, since he makes the Roman *ordine* the product of a history; he does not allow us to think that law imposes this good order, by the sovereign intervention of a sage, since he roots it in social conflict; and he suggests that praise of the *unione* fosters the misunderstanding of class division, and that in desiring to mask it, we destroy freedom. Denouncing those who condemn the tumults of ancient Rome, he reproaches them for "not knowing that there are, in every Republic, two different humors, that of the people, and that of the Grandees, and that all the laws that are made in favor of freedom are born of their division." This formula forbids our circumscribing its interpretation to the history of Rome; it forces the reader to verify it with respect to the modern state as well, to question the political discourse held in one's own day. But it also brings us to appreciate the distance separating us at the present time from the model of Sparta. The suspicion we raised about the sincerity of the analysis in Chapter 2 was not idle: How could the image of concord instituted by Lycurgus resist the discovery of the *cause* of Roman freedom?

But once we have made that discovery we are still no more than at the midpoint of the journey. Let us already observe that Machiavelli no longer says only that *desunione* has led Rome to its perfection; he places it at the foundation of freedom. Now, the term no longer has the meaning given to it in Chapter 1, when, speaking of the origin of cities, the author contrasted freedom and servitude. Disunion, we are to understand, has not only preserved the independence of Rome; it has established freedom within it, that is, it has established a regime such that the power can be taken over neither by a man, nor by a faction. The regime of freedom therefore appears as the regime of law itself; or, strictly speaking, as the one in which the laws are related back to their foundation. Thus the comparison established between the Tarquins and the tribune is clarified. Apprised from the point of view of the threat that the Grandees pose for the people—and for the state—their function is identical; but the regime of tyrants proves to be profoundly foreign to the Republic, the moment we perceive in the one the full expression of the appropriation of the state by an individual, and, in the other, that of the anonymity of power. Henceforth Machiavelli forbids us to think that the institutions of the Republic play no more than the role of a third party in the class struggle: the tribunate in which the power of the law is expressed has the effect of impeaching the occupation of power by one person—whether of the prince or of oligarchs—and in this sense it is only effective as an organ of negativity. Doubtless, as was indicated at the end of Chapter 3, the tribunes play the role of intermediaries (*medii*) between the senate and the plebs, but they have no other reason for being, as we learned immediately thereafter, than to set up an obstacle to the insolence of the Grandees.

Now, these indications prepare us to accept the idea that is asserted in the last part of Chapter 4 and that will be reinforced in the following one by ample argumentation: at the basis of the law and of freedom is the desire of the people. Indeed, it does not suffice to dispel the illusion of the *unione*, to show the fecundity of the class struggle when it is expressed in broad daylight, for we could still give in to another illusion; we could imagine that the two adversaries occupy symmetrical positions and that their conflict is good *in itself*. The consequence of this would be the reestablishment, in a new way, of the image of a legislator who, placed outside the bounds of this conflict, would regulate its course, and the position of which would, by the way, coincide with that of the theoretician. It is therefore insufficient, in particular, to stop at the conclusion that all the laws favorable to freedom are born of the division of humors of the body politic. It must also be understood that it is within the social space, in the experience of class struggle itself, that law is instituted; and it is necessary to find the meaning of the movement that requires it. Machiavelli leads his reader there, by obliging him or her to abandon the position as a witness and to rejoin the cause of the people. First, he addresses the witness: "And if someone were to say: What extraordinary and almost savage (*efferati*) means; we see the people hurl invectives against the senate and the senate do the same against the people." But when the witness proceeds immediately to make only one of the protagonists the author of tumult and freedom alike: "I say that in every city"—he responds to the imaginary interlocutor—"there must be ways for the people to provide an outlet for their ambitions, and especially in those cities which count on the strength of the people, on important occasions. In Rome, there were such ways, so that when the people wished to obtain a law, either they acted as we have just said, or they refused to enlist to go to war, and consequently it was necessary, in order to pacify it, to appease it in some way." "The desires of a free people," he adds, "are rarely pernicious to freedom, for it is oppression that gave birth to them, or the suspicion that there would be oppression."

Such is the truth that the author prepared us to expect. Law cannot be thought beneath the emblem of measure, nor traced to the action of a reasonable authority, which would come to put a limit to the appetites of man, nor conceived as the result of a natural regulation of those appetites, imposed by the necessity of group survival. It is born of the excessiveness of the desire for freedom, which is doubtless linked to the appetite of the oppressed—who seek an outlet for their ambition—but does not reduce to it, since strictly speaking it has no object, is pure negativity, the refusal of repression. Hence, in what appears at first glance as release of the passion of the people, aggression against the state, "*modi straordinarii e quasi efferati*," we should read a different excess, that of desire over appetite, the only one being of such a nature as to found the excess of law on the actual order of fact of the City. Let us no longer be content with saying that in disorder there is the wherewithal to found an order; there is no order that can be established on the elimination of disorder, unless it is at the cost of a degradation of law and liberty. And disorder, in the true sense of the term, is not pure discord, the tumult in which particular interests clash, for that sort of discord accommodates itself very well, as in the case of Florence, with the appearance of order, that is, the acquired equilibrium of social forces; it is the operation of desire that keeps the question of the unity of the state open, and, in exposing it, forces those who direct it to put its destiny back into play.

Chapter 5 is devoted to developing this argument. But it is by approaching it from an odd angle, to which we could scarcely be too attentive, that the author arrives at his conclusion. Asking the question "On whom is the guardianship of freedom to be confided with more confidence, the Grandees or the People, and which of the two causes trouble most frequently, he who wishes to acquire or he who wishes to keep?" he seems at first to be limiting himself to comparing two equally convincing theses, one of aristocratic inspiration, the other democratic, as if these last remarks had not already made it possible to decide between the alternatives. But as we read on, we see that under the cover of neutrality he pursues the critique of the aristocratic thesis on the basis of its own principles. Moreover, we cannot help noticing that when he chooses the example of Rome, he speaks in his own name, introducing the argument with an "I say" (*dico*), while putting the defense of Sparta and Venice in the mouth of an undetermined interolocutor (*chi defende l'ordine spartano o Veneto dice . . .*).

Still, it is important to observe that the balance of the arguments is respected and that the first hypothesis on which the author dwells is based on an argument extraneous to the debate. In favor of the people, he reminds us that in contrast to the Grandees, whose desire is to dominate, their sole desire is not to be dominated, and he concludes that if the people are selected as the guardians of freedom, their concern will be, rather than to destroy it, to keep others from wresting it from them. In favor of the Grandees, he becomes the interpreter of the partisans of the established order, who deem it necessary to satisfy the ambition of the Grandees and dangerous to grant the turbulent plebeians an authority against which men in place, desirous of retaining their acquired positions, will not fail to rise in resistance. Resuming the debate in the alternative—Is freedom more threatened by those who want to keep or those who want to acquire—he shifts what is at stake in the issue and modifies its meaning in such a way that the answer now depends on the character of the state under consideration, which can give itself the goal of acquisition—like Rome—or of retention—like Sparta and Venice. This hypothesis introduces a relation between freedom and power, which awakens our curiosity; but we must admit that at this stage of the discourse it deprives the democratic argument of the scope it had, since it claimed to establish a universal truth. We must express our surprise, then, at the author's retreat in comparison with the preceding chapter. Indeed, only this surprise is capable of making us appreciate the importance of the following movement and move with it to its conclusion. That conclusion, applied to the alternative that we thought had been set aside, finally establishes that the desire of those who own is more dangerous, because the fear of losing incites the same acts of violence as the desire to acquire, and that besides this, the concern to keep prompts them to want to obtain ever more (*perche non pare agli uomini possedere sicuramente quello che l'uomo ha, se non si acquista di nuovo dell' altro*). The thesis of aristocratic inspiration is therefore entirely annulled, for it becomes manifest that it rested on a lie, that in fact the desire of the Grandees is not to keep what they have acquired, that it is insatiable, that it is itself the desire for acquisition—the latter not being the result of the destitution of the people, but bound up with the unlimited enjoyment of possession, power, and prestige. Thus we discover the mystification perpetrated by the conservatives, whose cleverness is to make it seem as if they are defending civil peace.

They affirm, in a first moment, that man is naturally wicked and that his appetites must be repressed; they obfuscate class division beneath the general division of nature and law, wishing to speak only of the essence of man and society; then, in a second moment, they reestablish the division between the Grandees and the people, and maintain that men whose appetites have been satisfied are naturally attached to the defense of law, that the good luck that has favored them makes them the guardians of order, from which society benefits as a whole.

Machiavelli counters them essentially with the notion that nature can be deciphered in society, that the violence of appetite is visible in the conduct of those who dominate, that they are naturally inclined to extend their power, and only submit to the law when forced to do so. Thus he cuts through the commonly established link between the moderation of the possessors and the order of law. But more important yet is to keep in mind—if we want to understand the rest of the discourse— the idea of desire that is insinuated in the analysis, for it prompts us to scrutinize its division. Not that there is desire to acquire and desire to keep; as for that division, we have just learned that it is fictive; the desire to possess is always the desire to acquire, and the fear of losing is not to be distinguished from the desire of having. But, parallel to the desire for something—power, goods, honors—there is the desire *not to be* oppressed. A division, however, that leaves desire, whether its coefficient be positive or negative, to the impossible conquest of its object.

Although it is too soon to take stock of the full significance of a theory of desire, we at least have a sense of its secret domination of the discourse in this very first part of the work. Machiavelli not only critiques the thesis of the conservatives; he establishes his own on premises that are incompatible with the vulgar democratic ethics. Thus he does not dissimulate, in passing, that the people themselves harbor envy and hatred, and therefore that their own desire is divided. His intention is to bring us to the recognition that the division of desire—as well as the class division, as he noted earlier—cannot be disguised with impunity; that political life presupposes the full development of its effects. This is, as we now assess it, the reason that made him advance the criterion of the power of the state before discrediting the conservative argument. His conclusion is reinforced by a principle that discredits that argument more efficiently than do its traditional adversaries.

One is immediately convinced of this upon reading Chapter 6, which reexamines the alternative of the state occupied with conquest and the state whose entire goal is to remain within its own borders. By placing the discussion on this terrain, the writer clearly makes his adversary's key concepts—power and security, concepts normally enlisted in the service of a theory that reserves authority for the Grandees—his own. But he works them in such a way that it is the Roman model that is decidedly founded, which is to say, the model of a state upheld by the people's desire for freedom.

One must indeed agree that the order of the City requires the expansion of the desire of men, in the double movement in which it opposes itself; that this order does not result in a repression of desire, imposed by the authority of reason, but is engendered in the bringing into play of division—repression being but a second effect of its expression, relative to one of its moments or, better, the index of its reflection; and that in one and the same movement power, law, and freedom are instituted.

Chapter 6 completes the process of persuading us of their connection by returning to the examination of the alternative that had only been sketched out between the state occupied with conquest and the state whose only goal is to maintain itself. Once again, the reader is submitted to an argument well suited to disconcerting him, since he is invited at some length to maintain the two solutions to the problem, despite the incidents that gradually undermine the prestige of the models of Sparta and Venice, and the fact that he must even receive a profession of faith favoring equilibrium and peace, before arriving at the conclusion. And, once again, we witness the rigor of a critique that exploits the other's arguments, lends itself to his way of representing things to make use of them to the end, and to give a new foundation to political thought. Machiavelli first displays the advantages of the Venetian regime, adept at excluding the people from public affairs, but he points out in passing that the effectiveness of the system depends on the small number of people dominated; launching a new encomium of Sparta, he makes the same reservation, adding that the City, in order to ensure its stability, had to close its gates to strangers. This suffices, in a first moment, to affirm that Rome would never have attained its greatness if it had not consented to the growth of its population and, taking on the risk of attendant troubles, taken the chances of power, "so that," he notes, "in Rome, to cut off the roots of its quarrels also meant affecting those of its power; for such is the fate of things human that one cannot avoid one drawback without lapsing into another." Supporting himself on this conclusion, he pretends to imagine the choice of a legislator, and recommends that he adopt one or the other of the two courses of action, according to the end he assigns to the state, and that he establish its implementation. "If someone wanted to found a Republic again, he should examine whether he desires for it to increase its conquests and power or close itself up within tight borders. In the first case, he should take Rome as model, and manage the outcome of its domestic quarrels (*dare luogo a tumulti e alle dissensioni universali*) with the least possible danger to his country; for without a great number of well-armed men, a republic cannot grow or maintain itself if it has grown. On the second supposition, organize it like Sparta and Venice; but, as conquests are the downfall of small republics, use the most effective means to keep it from growing." But the dilemma having scarcely been formulated, a stunning remark is added, for the author supports his last proposition on examples that discredit the image of Sparta and of Venice: suddenly designating with their case the model of a weak republic (*republica debole*), he observes that they have not resisted their attempt at conquest; of Sparta in particular he specifies that a "slight accident" suffices to destroy its empire and that in this way the weakness of its foundation (*il debile fondamento suo*) was exposed. As the accident mentioned is the revolt of Thebes, the reader has the right to wonder about the validity of the judgment that attributed to it earlier a stability of more than eight hundred years . . . Still, the denial is not explicit; and not only is the double hypothesis reproduced, but we must still recognize the excellence of a state preoccupied with preserving itself in order and peace. "And doubtless," writes Machiavelli, "I believe that where it is possible to maintain such an equilibrium (*potendosi tenere la causa bilanciata in questo modo*), there is the true way of political life and the true tranquility of a city." It is not until later that the dilemma is definitively resolved, and that the form of the Roman institutions—the *ordine romano*—is affirmed as being the only good one; that there is no middle ground between the two models of republics examined (*perchè trovare un modo mezzo infra l'uno et l'altro non credo si possa*). Now the demonstration is such that it consolidates the argument in favor of a *democratic* regime. It is futile, we learn, to raise security to the level of the principle of political action, for the effects of time cannot be mastered by anyone; necessity leads where reason did not wish to go; the state grows despite the decision of those who claimed to set its limits, or else if, by luck, it is sheltered from danger over a long period, the virtues of the people wither away, and their calculation is again foiled. In uncertainty, one must choose the party that is "the most honorable," that is, act in such a way that if it happens to expand, it can at least hold on to its acquisitions. It is therefore impossible to ground oneself in reasons of state to combat the desire of the people. What gives the state its reason are not the concepts of equilibrium, security, and conservation; it is the necessity in which it finds itself to face the accidents engendered within it by ambitions against its neighbors, or accidents others conceive against it. And it misunderstands that reason when, by artifices, it deprives itself of the force of the people.

"It is necessary," Machiavelli repeats at the end of the chapter, "to look at the divisions that existed between the senate and the people as necessary inconveniences to arrive at the greatness of Rome."

If we were to stop at this conclusion, one might think, it is true, that the power of the state furnishes political theory's ultimate criterion. But Machiavelli is not concerned here with defining the driving force behind the actions of states, and it is not important for him to compare their struggle with the one between classes in each state. His intention is to relate the authority of bodies of the political order, which it is customary to derive from reason or nature, back to desire. Hence we cannot be surprised that after having definitively established the superiority of the Roman world, he hastens to put the reader back within the walls of the City, in which the humors of the classes spread out and do battle with each other. If we fail to find this intention, the importance of the argument developed in Chapters 7 and 8 would elude us; and even more, its articulation in the final conclusions reached would be unintelligible: the theme of public indictment which makes up the substance of it would appear to direct the discourse unnecessarily toward a particular object. But at present, how could we doubt that the public indictment is far more than a singular and remarkable trait of the Roman constitution, that it allows us to discover, like the tribunate, although in a different perspective, the relation that law, freedom, and power maintain with desire?

Indeed, the institution that authorizes any citizen to denounce any other before an assembly of the people, a magistrate, or a council, is judged essential because of two consequences it brings about, the second of which, the only one directing commentary, allows us to see the remarks of Chapter 5 in a new light: "The first is that the citizens undertake nothing against the state, for fear of being accused, or if they attempt anything, they are immediately castigated, and without respect to persons; the second, that an outlet is thus offered to the humors that spread one way or another in the cities against such and such a one." The commentary is such as to immediately prompt us to reexamine the division of the desire of the people, the *signs* of which we have already observed. The people are worked by humors disposing them to aggression, at the same time that they are incited by the aggression of the Grandees to struggle for freedom. In a sense, it is therefore true that the body politic is in all its parts in effervescence and that all its members are susceptible to projecting onto the figure of an adversary the class hatred that lives within them. Furthermore, the desire not to be oppressed, which belongs in particular to the people, does not allow itself to be dissociated from the blind aggression that precipitates them against persons. The proof of this is adduced by the aptly chosen example of the attempted coup d'état by

Coriolanus. The people—having learned that he was advising the senate to take advantage of the absence of the army, occupied with fighting in Sicily, to take away all of their authority and bring them to the brink of starvation—were driven to tear their enemy to pieces, disregarding the law, so that without an intervention on the part of the tribunes civil war could have broken out. Now it is by sounding the depths of the violence of the people's desire and by being aware of the link that aggression against the other—his power, his possessions, his rank—maintains with the love of freedom, that one is led to reformulate the function of the law. How vain appear to be the artifices of the legislator who claims to be able to block the flow of humors of the body politic, if we judge them by their intention of maintaining a free, powerful, and orderly republic; or how deceitful, if we observe that repression is content with the domination of a small minority over the masses. Aggression persists beneath the interdictions, only it follows secret pathways—those opened to it by calumny—until it explodes in broad daylight and destroys the state, when a crisis suddenly weakens those who govern. Therefore there is no more effective institution than one that makes it possible to give humors a public outlet; that is, to both let them pass freely and to channel them. The Republic, which has been able to order itself in conformity with its principle, Machiavelli gives us to understand, is one in which all things are said, but in which the place, the pathways of discourse, are circumscribed by the authority that guarantees freedom of speech to all. Thus mistrust, envy, hatred, the moment a particular object awakens them, are named, and in being named, call for a response and, lending themselves to verbal exchange, find their endpoint in the need for a judgment. "Indictment and calumny," as we are told in Chapter 8, "differ in that the latter needs neither witnesses nor confrontations, nor precise circumstances to succeed and to persuade. All individuals can be calumniated by others, but all cannot be indicted—indictments, in order to be received, must be backed up by the most manifest proofs and circumstances that demonstrate their truth. Indictments are brought before the magistrates, before a people or councils; calumny is spread either in the public squares, or beneath arcades, and it is especially in the States in which, by a defect in the constitution, indictment is not allowed, that calumny is most practiced. Thus," he adds, "it is the duty of the legislator to give every citizen the ability to bring charges against another without fear of taking that action." But we must not, on reading this text, be led to believe that, beneath the necessity of judgment, the effects of aggression are wiped away before the truth. Machiavelli does not authorize this conclusion. After having related the episode that nearly cost Coriolanus his life and destroyed the Republic, and then having stressed its happy ending thanks to the public indictment launched by the tribunes, his commentary leaves no doubt as to the significance of the institution. "For if it happens, in these circumstances," he observes, "that an individual is harmed (*oppresso*) and has been wronged, the state suffers little or no disorder. Indeed, the operation is carried out neither by a private nor a foreign power—two powerful causes of the downfall of freedom—but solely by public authority which functions within specified limits, and does not transgress them to the point of causing the downfall of the Republic." And, he also notes, "let everyone consider the damage that the Republic of Rome would have sustained if Coriolanus had been killed in a riot, for that would have resulted in violence by a private citizen against another private citizen (*offensa da privati a privati*), which would have produced fear; fear seeks means of defense, calls for partisans; from partisans, factions (*parti*) arise in a city, and from factions comes the downfall of the state." What makes the virtue of the institution is not, then, that it eliminates error and injustice at the same time that it disarms instinct; it replaces private with public violence. Thus it is on purpose that Machiavelli uses but one term, *forza*, to designate both the actions of private citizens and those of the state. In the passage from private to public, violence remains, both because the institution draws its own power from that of the citizens, and because the state remains partially in the grip of the classes that communicate their humors to it. An individual can thus be the victim of the state's aggression; the essential is that the process of violence, which naturally leads to the dislocation of the body politic, be broken at one point, thanks to a level of authority that puts it in the service of its unity, by making us recognize the difference between the public and the private. Assuredly this level of authority—whatever the circumstances of its intervention, and the actual conduct of those charged with the exercise of public violence—is based on the desire not to be oppressed, which properly belongs to the people. Only this desire—which overawes the power of the private citizens, that of the Grandees whose existence is defined by an appropriation—is in fact of such a nature as to open up within society a public space—not that of public squares and arcades, which are simply places in which people encounter one another, where words always circulate between *one* person and *another*, but the anonymous space of the institution. It would be a mistake, however, to imagine an absolute break between the public and the private, just as much as it would be to want to delineate sharply between the desire not to be oppressed and the desire to acquire, or between the demand for freedom, and aggression. What is revealed by the analysis of the Roman institution, which Machiavelli makes the centerpiece of the republican system, is that the same force is in play in opposite terms: the public indictment is dissociated from calumny, but both feed on the malignant humors (*omori maligni*) of the City. If an outlet must be given to these humors—*sfogare i omori*—the reason is not only that it is less bad to let them flow away than to provoke, by their repression, an infection of the organism: it is also, and especially, that the desire for freedom is itself dependent on the stimulations of appetite and aggression.

Such a conclusion, however, defies both a naturalistic and a rationalist interpretation, in the classical sense. It is no doubt true that Machiavelli uses language susceptible of accrediting the former sort of interpretation. He speaks of humors and, seven times in the chapter devoted to public indictments, uses the term *sfogare* to indicate the operation of the institution that ensures their discharge. Thus, he suggests that political society is similar to the body, that it is subject to excitations and defined by natural functions. But he forbids using the metaphor to serve a thesis, since he elucidates the internal division of desire and the history, different in each state, which is instituted as a result of the fate of its effects in the class struggle. While he attaches himself—against a rationalist tradition—to undermining the image of the legislator, conceived as the sovereign master of the constitution of the City, he does preserve the idea of political choice, in comparing the destinies of Rome, Sparta, Florence, and Venice. And nowhere does he authorize the search for an empirical genesis of law in the analysis of class conflict and the desire of the people. To affirm, as I have been doing, that the foundation of law can be found in them does not imply that one can conceive of their anteriority in factuality, since with the social division the unity of the body politic is immediately brought into play, since the class struggle already bears the trace of their relations and the demand for freedom implies the transgression of the order of factuality.

Now, it is in rejecting the antithesis of political naturalism and rationalism, through the examination of the Roman institution of public indictments, that Machiavelli wins the power to lead his reader back to the consideration of the present, to teach him the cause of the corruption of modern republics and particularly of the Republic of Florence. It is no accident that, twice in the chapters we have been examining, mention of the crisis that swallowed up the regime of Soderini is put in tandem with a Roman example. For having been unable to provide an outlet for the humors, and thus allowing the desire of the people to flow freely, Florence, we learn, experienced nothing but violent acts between private individuals, generalized suspicion, calumnies, and factions, to the point where its government, incapable of tolerating the control of the people and of bringing justification to its acts, fell into disrepute, and it sufficed for Spanish troops to enter its territory for a foreign power to become the deciding factor in its conflicts. This weakness is neither the sign of a natural deterioration of its constitution (as is sufficiently established by observing that this befalls all states sooner or later), nor that of a legislation powerless to contain its citizen's appetites and prevent disorder. The Republic is not corrupt because the wickedness of man is irremediable, and Fortune alone can preserve the state for a time from its consequences, or because the primitive form of the City, good in itself, is misunderstood by men in the course of history; the corruption is its own doing, the effect of the continuous choice by which the City denies the truth of desire and aggression, rejects the conflict of the classes, forbids the people's demands, and covers up denial and repression with a discourse on order and peace. In other words, corruption is not a state of the body politic the opposite of which would be integrity; the same necessity governs the history of Florence and that of Rome, as it already governed that of Sparta. Recalling the progress of the discourse, since its beginning, the three cities are seen to compose merely different responses to one sole problem, and these responses each contain a developmental schema. In Sparta, the goal of the implementation of social relations is to remove society from the perturbations introduced by events; Sparta professes to exorcise the risks of history and its actual history is configured, up until its downfall, in keeping with its refusal of history. In Rome, the welcoming of conflict and the recognized dissymmetry of the classes end up opening society to the outside world and permitting, by the exploitation of accidents, its expansion; the differentiation of the political space attracts and governs change; Rome assumes the risks of history, and its actual history remains in connivance with the principle of the genesis of the state. In Florence, the artifices of the Spartan constitution are lacking; but the development of conflict, which brings its regime closer to that of Rome, leaves the actors incapable of forging the representation and the institutions it requires: Florence is torn between the refusal of history and the project of its growth, and its actual history bears the mark of that tension; deprived of the means of power by its interdict against the people's demands, but not renouncing its ambitions, it pays for its least-risk politics with the loss of its independence.

The Machiavellian interpretation of Roman history thus already offers a glimpse, in this very first part of the work, of the critique that strikes at once the present and past politics of Florence and the representation of politics to which the partisans of the republican regime remain bound. In speaking of Rome, the writer advances the theory of an *historical society*, which overturns the teaching of the Tradition, but simultaneously shatters an image that we have every reason to believe was effective in maintaining Florentine conservatism. Indeed, is not the image of the *good society of antiquity* that of a *Spartan Rome,* of a state—according to the opinion of the great authors—that attained to never-equaled greatness by the virtue of order and discipline, and despite the turmoil inflicted upon it by bad luck? And does it not show great audacity to sweep aside the model of Sparta and call for the recognition of a *Roman Rome:* a Rome that has nothing but its own history to stand on and whose greatness is linked to its excess?

8

Class Difference

The first eight chapters of *The Discourses* seemed to us to make up an introduction to the entire work. At the threshold of Chapter 9, we have a right to expect that the author, in keeping with this program, will take up an analysis of the work accomplished by the Romans within the City as the result of a public decision (*per consiglio publico*). In a sense, this expectation is satisfied, since, as his commentary returns to Livy's account, he approaches the first event, which was the foundation of Rome. This commentary, however, immediately proves to be subservient to an absolute distinction between good and bad princes and good and bad regimes that, by being too faithful to convention, again raises our suspicions. Machiavelli paints the portrait of the virtuous founder as public opinion likes to imagine him. Romulus not having refrained from the utmost violence to become the sole master of the state, it is presumed that his example is such as to bring out the specific character of political action and to disarm moralistic criticism. But his crimes are mentioned for the purpose of justifying them. Better still: while Livy had doubts about the purity of the motives prompting Romulus to kill his own brother and about the nature of the feelings he inspired in his entourage, to the point of hypothesizing that he was the victim of an inherited illness (*malum avitum*) — the passion to reign (*cupiditas regni*) — and that his despotism prompted the senators to make him disappear, Machiavelli passes over the questions of his alleged master in silence, and appears to wish to avoid leaving any disturbing element in his reader's mind. Romulus, so he teaches, had only good intentions. He did not act through ambition, but served the common good. It is not even enough to say that although the facts accuse him, the results excuse him (*accusando il fatto lo effetto lo scusi*): that way of putting it can leave some doubt about the virtue of the actor. Only necessity, we are given to understand, forced him to eliminate those who contested his rank, for necessity dictates that the state should be, at the time of its foundation, beneath one sole authority. Thus, no restrictions can be placed on the means used by Romulus, who, conscious of the goal he had set himself, had no choice in the matter. We must agree that his crimes, imposed, as they were, by the circumstances, served a just cause, and that he should, rather, be condemned had he not committed them. A first confirmation of this interpretation is given to us by Agis and Cleomenes, both of whom were determined to restore the state, re-instating the laws of Lycurgus—great reformers, then, dedicating themselves to a noble task. The first one failed, because he did not impose his will by force, while the other succeeded, because he decided at the opportune moment to have the ephors, who opposed his plan, massacred. In addition, Romulus's conduct itself, once he was installed in power, testified to the purity of his intentions, since he created a senate, involved it in his decisions, and thus laid the foundations of a free government, instead of exercising absolute power, like a tyrant. No doubt the language of Machiavelli may offend Christian sensibilities, since he does not hide the necessity of violence. But it is a moral language: the line between good and evil is drawn with rigor.

Now, not content with furnishing so appeasing an image of the beginnings of Rome, the writer seizes the occasion of this first analysis to persuade the reader of the nobleness of his convictions. It is an emphatic profession of faith, remarkable in its lack of relation to the presumptive subject of the discourse. Thus, he declares that men may be divided into two categories. On the one side there are the good, who are classified according to the quality of the enterprise: founders of a religion, founders of a state, great military leaders, writers; on the other, the wicked, *infami e detestabili,* "men who destroy religions, overturn states, the enemies of *virtù,* of courage, letters and arts that are useful and praiseworthy for the human species . . . the impious, the violent, the ignorant, imbeciles, the lazy, and the cowardly." The distinction seems so certain as to escape the conflict of opinions: "Wise or foolish, good or evil, there is no one who, having to choose between these two types of men does not praise those who are praiseworthy and blame the blamable." If wickedness is so widespread, it is therefore only because we allow ourselves to be "fooled by the appearance of a false good, of a false glory." This false good and this false glory are decried in politics beneath the guise of tyranny; opposite it, resplendent, stands the legitimate regime, be it a monarchy or a republic. Between the two a choice must be made. The founder must open up the career of vice or *virtù,* institute freedom or servitude, just as the new prince must ensure the reign of violence or of law. Machiavelli illustrates the necessity and results of this choice, using as his examples the destinies of Roman emperors, which he had already analyzed in Chapter 19 of *The Prince,* though there he derived a completely different lesson from them. There, he limited himself to evaluating the conduct of the successors of Marcus Aurelius. Marcus was an exception; his moderation had only served him, we are told, because the army was not yet entirely corrupt, and because, having come to power *jus hereditario,* his authority did not come from it. On the other hand, those who subsequently devoted themselves to wiping out corruption, Pertinax being chief among them, came to as sad an end as did the princes who indulged themselves without restraint. Only Severus, who had been able to maintain the *majesty of the state,* had succeeded in overcoming the difficulties of the times. At present, the reference merely invites us to divvy up the cortege into good and bad emperors. Pertinax and Severus become the exceptions— the former being fortunate, the latter unfortunate—destined to confirm the rule according to which security is the fruit of justice. History has become edifying, in the direction that flatters the common morality. It teaches that virtue is rewarded, that goodness, security, and glory are necessarily conjoined. It offers such an eloquent spectacle that it moves the witness to express himself in the accents of a preacher. "Let a prince cast his eye over the time that has passed from Numa to Marcus Aurelius; let him compare it to the times preceding and following it, and let him then choose the one in which he would rather have been born, and during which he would rather have reigned. On one side, under the good emperors, he will see a prince living in the most perfect security amidst citizens without alarm, justice and peace reigning in the world, the authority of the senate respected, the judiciary honored, opulent citizens enjoying their wealth in peace, virtue esteemed, and calm and happiness everywhere; also, consequently, all animosity, all licentiousness, all corruption, all ambitiousness extinguished. He will see that golden age in which each individual can assert and defend his position; finally, he will see the people triumphant, the prince respected and resplendent with glory, adored by his happy subjects. On the other side, let him examine one by one the reigns of those other emperors; he will see them bloodied by wars, torn asunder by divisions and just as cruel in time of peace . . ."

If we had to take what our author says literally, we would at least have to register our surprise at such a show of enthusiasm in praising the virtues of the Roman monarchy, since after all, the merits he was preparing to sing were those of the republic. And as for the golden age, we were not expecting to find it during a time when the people were subjugated. But we have every reason to think that the plea in favor of the good prince and the good regime has no function other than to win back the readers' confidence. If one portion of them, faithful to the old republican tradition, takes Cato's Rome as its model, is not the other more disposed by its culture, the mores acquired under the Medici, and its admiration for the new philosophy, to be enthused with the time of Titus, Trajan, or Marcus Aurelius? Chapters 9 and 10 are of such a nature as to seduce them. A new light has just been cast on the history of Rome, a light that is unbearable to the eyes of those who prefer to see in that city no more than peace and harmony realized under the aegis of wise governors: here, for a moment, the good image of the state has been restored to them.

While the writer resumes, in Chapter 11, the commentary on the outstanding events of the foundation of Rome, he first seems to continue in the same vein: he praises Numa for having recognized religion as the most necessary institution for civic life; he asserts that the Romans worshipped God more than did any other people in the world, that they feared breaking their oaths more than their laws. What is more, this prince seems to surpass Romulus in knowing how to create institutions without which the military virtues themselves could not preserve him. Such remarks are well suited to please conservatives who make religion, whatever the quality of their faith may be, the surest warrant of collective discipline. Still, we notice that they convey truths that it is not normally appropriate to say, and that they are then modified in such a way as to become intolerable to Christian ears and in the end to raise doubts about their sincerity.

In Chapter 11, the word God repeated with insistence is applied to pagan divinities; Numa is presented as an imposter, adept at feigning private conferences with a nymph; Savonarola appears to have used the same subterfuge, in persuading the Florentines that he conversed with God; a success all the more significant—so it is suggested—because he was involved with an urbane people, not brutish peasants, as was the founder of Rome. In the following chapter, praise of pagan religion lays the foundation for a merciless indictment of the Catholic Church, accused of having corrupted the mores of the people and causing the misfortune of Italy by keeping it from achieving its unification. True, it is noted in passing that if religion had been maintained in the beginnings of the Christian republic, according to the principles of its founder, the modern states would be more unified and happy; but the irony of the remark can hardly pass unnoticed, so certain is it that its function is appreciated in terms of political effectiveness. Still, even more than the critique of Christianity, the arguments invoked in Chapter 13 in favor of the ancient religion catch our attention. Previously Machiavelli had continually repeated that its virtue was to make men good. Observing that those very ones who do not believe in its truth must work to favor its success, if they are wise (*prudenti*) and know human nature (*sono . . . conoscitori delle cose naturali*), he let it be understood that the credulity of the people should be exploited in the service of the common weal. Now we discover that religion was used by the patricians to maintain their class dominance, and that they did not recoil from any cunning stratagem to discourage popular protest. Now, once recognized, the ploy to which the writer resorts to insinuate that truth puts us on guard against our own credulity. Indeed, the chapter is titled, "How the Romans Used Religion to Reorganize the City, Carry Out Their Enterprises, and Put Down Riots." If we are to trust that statement, we are favorably disposed to receive a new proof of the general utility of religion. But the text makes an eloquent terminological shift: instead of Romans, it speaks of nobles; and the examples it gives display the naïveté of the people, who, fooled by their manipulations, abandon their recriminations. Instructed by these stylistic maneuvers, we can examine more carefully the last two chapters devoted to religion, the manifest object of which is to demonstrate its importance in war. At first reading, we think we find in Chapter 14 an illustration of the thesis that an adroit captain must convince his troops that they are favored by the gods, and that if he lies about the result of the auguries, he must save the appearances by means of a stratagem. Indeed, the example that recalls the daring and cunning of the consul Papirius rigorously confirms the proposition announced in the title: "That the Romans interpreted the auspices according to their needs, and were wise enough to seem to observe religion when forced not to do so; and if anyone disdained it with effrontery they punished him." But if we compare this chapter with the next one, we cannot help but observe that the second leads to a conclusion that overturns the lesson of the first—a modification skillfully executed, since once again, the title of the argument, "How the Samnites Had Recourse to Religion as a Last Resort in the Conditions That Were Imposed Upon Them," does not lead us to expect it. The grand scheme, staged for the purpose of striking the Samnite soldiers with religious awe, turns out to be futile. The Samnites, notes the author, were defeated. Roman *virtù* and the fear engendered by past defeats were stronger than the strongest resolution they were able to muster by means of their religion and their oaths. Thus, after having recognized the efficacy of religion to sustain the discipline and morale of the armies, we are forced to discover its limitations and give first place to military virtue. But if we had any lingering doubts as to the path down which Machiavelli was leading us, one last sign would perforce convince us we are on the right track: four chapters further along, reexamining the succession of the first three reigns that marked the foundation of Rome, he reverses his judgment on Numa, the father of Roman religion, placing him among the weak princes, maintaining that he who would imitate him will be lost or saved according to the whims of fortune, and concludes definitively in favor of the superiority of Romulus.

Let us assess, by taking stock of the discussion of religion over five chapters, the work meted out to the reader by the author. First, religion is presented as the institution the best equipped to ensure the cohesiveness of the City; it has the power of engendering good mores, on which good laws and military virtue are based. What stands opposed to religion is not unbelief, but disdain for the customs inscribed in the representation of the gods, in the ceremonies and rites. The essence of religion is thus brought out through our consideration of the religion of the Romans. In contrast to the latter stands the religion of the Moderns, based on the power of a church for which only its private interests count, and consequently whose politics consist in dividing the states and weakening them. Then, the exploitation of religion by the Romans reveals the role it played in maintaining the domination of the patricians. The credulity of the people, associated up to this point with their goodness, becomes the mark of their subservience. Finally, the hypothesis that the religiosity of the Roman people is at the origin of their military superiority becomes doubtful, considering that their adversaries share it, and it does not shield them from defeat. The power of religion, maintained, no doubt, but downgraded, has ceased furnishing the explanation for the greatness of the state.

To appreciate the significance of the argument, it behooves us remember the prior state of the discussion. Machiavelli was attempting to isolate the elements that determine the good regime and the good prince; now, at present his governing principles are taking a beating, because of the displacement of the object of the discourse. Hence we are prepared for a fresh assessment of the distinction between forms of government, as it begins to take shape in the next three chapters.

These chapters are dedicated to the examination of the difficulties accompanying a regime change. We need hardly point out that this examination interrupts, with no apparent justification, the description of the beginnings of the Roman monarchy. But our surprise subsides the moment the historical analysis proves to serve the requirements of the interpretation. Evoking in Chapter 16 the circumstances in which the republic was instituted in Rome, Machiavelli begins by observing "that a people accustomed to living under the yoke of a prince retains its freedom, once liberated from the yoke, only with difficulty"; that its former subservience predisposes it to fall back into the clutches of a new tyrant; that it even has no chance of success if it has reached the last stage of corruption. The reader must admit, then, that the founders of a republic encountered the same problem as did the *principi nuovi:* they must exterminate the enemies of the new order and must not count on their own supporters. Moreover, the task of a free government seems more difficult, and to require more necessarily the use of violence. That the adversaries of the republic must be combated seems to go without saying: they are "all those who profited from the tyrant's abuses, who lined their own pockets with the prince's treasures. They have been deprived of their access to riches and power; they cannot be otherwise than very dissatisfied. They are forced to try every method to reestablish tyranny, which alone can give them back their former authority." On the other hand, the proposition that a republic makes no friends is based on an odd argument. It is, we learn, an intrinsic characteristic of this regime to engender ingratitude. Those who acquire honors and rewards attribute them to their own merit and do not think they owe anything to the state. The majority profit from the advantages of security and freedom without appreciating these benefits while they enjoy them. If authority must therefore establish itself in each case by analogous means, a new republic takes its rigor to the furthest degree: "There is no remedy more powerful, more effective, more certain and more necessary than to slay the sons of Brutus." One can, no doubt, hold that such a lesson does not yet change the representation of the free government. Its merits are, furthermore, strongly emphasized in passing. But, making the most out of this analysis, Machiavelli examines, in what he presents as a digression, the particular case of the foundation of a tyranny, that is, the case in which the action of power seems initially to arouse the most intense hostility on the part of the subjects. Then the picture changes: it no longer suffices to admit that all the regimes at the beginning must be founded on violence; we must also discover that the worst among them can only maintain itself by trying to resemble the best. While just a moment ago the free government was forced to neglect the people's backing, now the tyrant is forced to seek it. It is as if, facing common imperatives, in order to respond to them they had to switch the roles that the governed expected them to play. The one must resist the illusion that it is the expression of the collective will, while the other must resist the illusion that it is its arms that protect it. One must strike its children, the other win the recognition of its enemies as their father.

That a tyrant is not necessarily locked into violence, that the initial position of the oppressor does not determine the nature of his enterprise—in short, that the intelligence of the political game can overwhelm the immediate givens of the regimes—this is what already destabilizes the opposition of the good and the evil prince. Romulus was supposed to be praised for having wanted to institute a free government instead of a tyranny; at present the intention of the prince matters less than his actual conduct. And it may be said of the tyrant who can win the favor of his people, just as it can be said of the founder, that if the facts accuse him, the results excuse him. The concept of tyranny no longer designates a genus, closed in upon itself, distinct from the monarchy and the republic. Power seems to be defined in each regime in keeping with the answers to the question put to it by the conditions of its advent. Is it not the case, then, that these answers maintain a relationship between one another that the classical theory of the distinction between regimes overlooks entirely? It is true that Machiavelli does not advance along this path, but only opens it up. His purpose, moreover, is not to obliterate the opposition between the tyranny and the free regime; it suffices for him that he has modified the terms in such a way as to make that opposition uncertain. But in declaring that the tyrant must win the friendship of his people, he not only gives us to understand that satisfactions analogous to those procured by the republic can come to it. If that were the case, the reader could fall back on the teachings of Aristotle, and admit that the bad government has a chance of survival only if it corrects the excesses that distance it from the regime that is in keeping with nature: the idea of the good in politics would not thereby be distorted. On the contrary, Machiavelli's argument establishes that the republican regime is not of a different essence than the regime of overt domination, and that consequently a tyranny can adapt itself to the principles of its requirements. If the tyrant is willing to consult the desires of the people whose master he has become, "he will find," Machiavelli observes in effect, "that the people want two things: first, to avenge themselves on those who brought about their slavery, and secondly to recover their freedom." Entire satisfaction may be given to the desire for vengeance, we learn, by propounding that under the free government the Grandees oppressed the people, and that now the prince, in subjugating the former, liberates the people at the same time that he enslaves them. As for the desire for freedom, it is possible to respond to it partially by recognizing that the masses and the small number of men who covet the highest offices are acting on different motivations. Now, that is in fact the remark that casts a cruel light on the way republics function: the much touted freedom means for one group the chance to command and for the other security. "Indeed there is no republic, however governed, in which there are more than forty or fifty citizens who attain positions with authority to command. Now, since that is a very small number, it is easy to insure oneself against them, either by having them done away with, or by granting each one an appropriate share of honors or offices. As for the others, who ask no more than to live in security, they are easily satisfied with institutions and laws that reconcile the tranquility of the people and the power of the prince."

We have every right to suspect that these harsh remarks do not convey the whole of Machiavelli's thought. How can we forget the interpretations offered us in the first eight chapters? In them, the people's desire not to be oppressed could not be reduced to a desire for security; democracy brought us to recognize—and led to the flowering of—the truth of law, which aristocratic and monarchic regimes hid or suffocated.

Thus, while having to give up the image of the good regime, which had been introduced a bit earlier, one is not necessarily obliged to reduce the republic to the limitations imposed by a regime of repression. The reversal of perspectives does not authorize us to conclude that the latter is the only legitimate one. We need only admit that every society is divided between the dominators and the dominated, and that the external signs of freedom conceal a factual inequality, the consequences of which lend themselves to several arrangements. But the fact remains that if the difference between regimes is not obliterated, it does demand to be rethought. Just as it is important to avoid hastily concluding that they are all equivalent, for the sole reason that they all confront the necessity of ensuring the security of the people and all accommodate a small number avid for power and wealth, so it is equally important to relate the differences to the general conditions under which they are instituted, and to perceive the various governments relatively to each other as figures standing out against the same background. Therefore it is not by chance that Machiavelli, at the end of the chapter, chooses an example that completes the blurring of the conventional distinction from which he initially set out. Suddenly invoking the kingdom of France to praise a regime in which the power of the prince is felicitously limited by law and the people's security safeguarded, he leads us to consider that the good monarchy is a tyranny that has been able to extend beyond an individual career and inscribe an able project of domination within durable institutions. It becomes henceforth impossible to reduce the work of the tyrant to an ephemeral venture, the outgrowth of a republic in disarray. No doubt that is what in fact it most often is; but no criterion of principle makes it distinguishable from the enterprise of the founder who sets up the legitimate order of a monarchy.

Now, at the point where this movement of thought comes to an end, a new opposition abruptly arises—one we had formerly only intuited indistinctly. Judging that the Republic of Rome would not have been able to arise had not moral degeneration reached its ultimate degree under the Tarquins, Machiavelli suddenly makes corruption the touchstone of his political analysis. Freedom, as is specified in Chapter 17, can only be established where the social body is still healthy. A people that has let itself be corrupted by its princes cannot regain its freedom; or if by some unlikely circumstance a man of *virtù* has made it possible for them to seize it momentarily, they cannot remain free. It is therefore no longer to the intention of governments that we are to ascribe the nature of a regime; governments do no more than exploit the social and historical conditions that are thrust upon them, or else are doomed for failing to recognize the necessity of doing so. If the second Brutus failed where the first had succeeded, this is, we learn, because after Caesar the people no longer have the will to be free. If Caesar himself succeeded in subjugating Rome, it is because the war between factions under Marius and Sulla had perverted the republic. Whether we consider the present or the past, we are forced to reach the same conclusion: Milan and Naples are doomed to servitude and no revolution can deliver them from it. In vain did the Milanese people attempt for a short while to regain their freedom after the death of Filippo Visconti: they were unable to keep it. In vain, in classical times, did Epaminondas succeed in making Thebes a free city once again; with his disappearance it sank once more into dissoluteness. Moreover, the character of the republic is not to be properly understood by examining its laws, for "when the material is not corrupt, tumults and backlashes cause no harm; and when it is corrupt, the best laws can be of no avail, unless they are given by a man with enough power to enforce them until the material has become good."

Such is the power of corruption that one might even wonder whether there is any way of checking it before it has developed all its effects. As Chapter 18 says, reform is as difficult as a great mutation. In both cases it is no doubt possible to define the principle of action, but its application is in practice so difficult that it is even doubtful it can be carried out. He who must carry out a radical change in the institutions is forced to "resort to extraordinary measures, to violence, to arms; he has first to make himself absolute master of the state and be able to do with it what he will." Now, in actuality, a man who has a noble political plan is loath to use condemnable procedures, while a man determined to impose his authority by force is not inclined to use it for good. On the first hypothesis, the end prohibits the means that would be necessary; in the second, the use of these means deflects from the goal. As for he who must remedy an evil in a time when it is still possible to adapt institutions to the changes that have taken place in the city, his action presupposes the collaboration of men already in place. Now, in reality, if perchance an individual is in a position to expose vice at its source, the others remain deaf to his advice, being incapable of freeing themselves of acquired habits and transcending the horizons of the present. Furthermore, if they were capable of knowing the truth, corruption would not exist; for corruption begins to spread when democracy no longer carries men of merit (men capable of judging the public interest) to the foremost ranks but favors intrigue—when laws, intended in the past to ensure the selection of the best and to contain the ambitious, are made to serve the interests of this last group.

Pausing for a moment to consider these words—based on an analysis of Roman history that features the progressive degradation of mores as a result of security, the power acquired by the mighty and rich and the subordination of institutions (formerly the most effective in guaranteeing the exercise of democracy) to their interests—we should conclude that change escapes the action of individuals. When Machiavelli writes that "from all these causes together arises the difficulty or impossibility of maintaining freedom in a corrupt republic or of reestablishing it," he limits or even eliminates the practical application of the criticism. In theory, he judges, the republic can be saved by an intervention that reinforces the executive and protects it from the maneuvers of the Grandees. On the reformist hypothesis, as on the revolutionary one, "the government of the republic should be pushed in the direction of the monarchic state rather than the populist one, so that the men whose insolence makes them resistant to the yoke of the law can be curbed, so to speak, by the bit of an almost royal authority." In practice, the difficulty proves most often to be insurmountable. It is true that the pathway of action is not entirely closed; the writer even suggests to his reader at the end of Chapter 18, which we are now discussing, that it has another mode of access. After having recommended monarchization, he briefly adds: "To want to succeed in this in any other way would be completely cruel or completely impossible." An enigmatic reservation, though in encountering in this fragment the example of Cleomenes (introduced for no apparent reason), whose struggle against the corruption of Sparta was marked by the massacre of the ephors, we must wonder whether the restoration of a populist state would not require the extermination of the oligarchy.

But the allusion is too short for us to explore its significance at this point. It will be preferable to take stock once again of the itinerary covered thus far. At the end of Chapter 18, the opposition between the virtuous founder and the tyrant has not withstood scrutiny; the relationship between the various regimes with respect to the oppression of the governed masses has come to view; a new opposition has been established—the only one, apparently, to hold our attention—between the healthy and the corrupt regime, which coincides with that of the states founded on equality and those founded on inequality, and with that of young states and senile ones; simultaneously, the idea that the republic cannot in the long run be regenerated without its being oriented toward a monarchic form of government; but such an idea is accompanied by the gravest doubts about the chances of its being applied.

Prudence requires that we give a reserved reception to the writer's last remarks, because we have no assurance that they, in turn, will not be modified. At least we feel justified in asserting that the premises of the argument developed in Chapters 9 and 10 have been abandoned. It is not the intentions of the prince that determine the nature of a regime, nor is it the form of its institutions; it is the relation that the state establishes with the entirety of the subjects or citizens, and, more profoundly, the one they establish with one another, according to the degree of equality or inequality that has been achieved. True, these last ideas are still indistinct. And we must be content with learning that inequality is introduced when favor and credit, first, and later power and riches set a small minority apart, whereas equality reigns to the extent that distinction is engendered as a result of *virtù*. This view cannot make us forget the rapprochement between the tyranny and the republic, and the affirmation that the positions of command are always monopolized by an ambitious few. Perhaps it is more important to observe that at the moment when the phenomenon of corruption moves to the center of the argumentation, the author weighs the chances of a pacific versus a violent reform of the republic. Such a question seems well suited to suggest that the task of foundation—introduced a little earlier with the example of Romulus—is not limited in time to the empirical creation of the state, but that it sustains the action of the political Subject throughout its history.

The ensuing chapters flesh out this hypothesis while at the same time altering the heretofore uncontested representation of the origins of Rome. Indeed, while the author appears to follow Livy's narrative, his considerations on the reign of Numa and his successor Tullus take an unexpected critical turn, and open out in Chapters 25 and 26 onto a new discussion of the problems posed by regime change—ultimately leading to a conclusion that requires a new step forward on the reader's part.

First of all, the father of Roman religion, whom we previously saw to be preferred to Romulus, turns out to be a simple heir to the latter's efforts, a prince well served by chance and who was able to enjoy peace only by benefiting from the work of his predecessor. His politics, as Machiavelli notes, would have been the downfall of Rome if he had not been lucky enough to have as his successor a strong prince, who cared as much about arms as did the first founder. Tullus is now credited with the merit of having set the foundations of the power of the state. But his praise comes to a sudden end. Admirable in that he was able to draw the Romans away from the softening of their mores and to create—as every prince must, as once did Epaminondas and Pelopidas, and, just recently, the king of England—an army made up of his own subjects, he reveals that he has committed a threefold error in his relations with Alba, by putting the fate of Rome in the hands of the Horaces, by letting the fratricide of the winner go unpunished, and in believing that the adversary would be bound by having given his word. This was an error such as to discredit him, for he thus misunderstood the imperatives of war, violated the law he was committed to safeguarding, and yielded to the illusion that the sworn faith could prevail over reasons of state. This prince, we are told, by his ignorance of politics and of strategy, resembles those who abound in the modern world. True, the latter do not resort to the archaic practice of one-on-one combat; but if we consider the form rather than the content of war, their behavior appears analogous. Now, as in the past, Machiavelli asserts, it is an inviolable principle "that one must not risk one's entire fortune without bringing all one's forces to bear." Tullus, and Mettius his adversary as well, for that matter, ignored this in consenting to entrust the destiny of the state to the strength of three men. In doing so, "they could not have chosen a worse course." Modern strategists make the same mistake when they decide to occupy positions considered to be impregnable or to guard the pass of a possible invasion. Aside from the fact that in doing so they give the enemy the benefit of mobility and the initiative of attack, they make everything depend on the one battle without being able to engage all of their troops. In both cases they are blinded by the illusion of security: men are held to be invincible, fortresses impregnable, or passes impenetrable, whereas in fact there is no rampart against adversity. The law of war requires risk and a total mobilization of available forces. Mixing ancient and modern examples, Machiavelli thus brings early Rome out from legend. Without being concerned with knowing whether the facts recorded by Livy are historical or not, he puts them to symbolic use. By this approach, he modifies his readers' way of relating to Livy's narrative. They admire the mores of the first Romans; after having confirmed their admiration, the author points out to them that the *religiosità* and the *bontà* of the Roman people were not the basis of their power and that their boldest king lacked prudence. They are delighted with the exploits of the Horaces; he condemns the heroic conception of war and gives them to understand that the *virtù* of the strategist is of a different order from the bravery of the combatant. The compassion the people felt seeing the old Horace's tears moves them; he teaches that in a well-ordered state reward and punishment are never balanced one against the other, and that impunity in exchange for services rendered encourages sedition.

It is true that the critique of the Roman monarchy at this stage of the discourse brings out the merits of the republic. Chapter 20 establishes that Rome was delivered from the risks it had to run because of a weak or a bad king (*o debole o cattivo*), which is to say, we may surmise, a Numa or a Tullus. "The sovereign authority," the author writes, "was then vested in consuls, who owed it neither to heredity nor trickery nor violence (*ambizione violenta*), but rather came into that power through the free election of their fellow citizens; and they were always excellent men (*eccellentissimi*)." Adding that chance alone can bring about the succession of two *virtuosi* princes, he maintains that the voting law has the effect of ensuring the perpetual continuity of *virtù*. In Chapter 23, he again praises the Romans for the risks they took, under the Republic, in their defense against Hannibal. In Chapter 24, he shows the application with which they rewarded the exploits of their military leaders, however modest their means were, and punished the ambitious, even if they had formerly distinguished themselves in the service of the state.

We suspect, however, that the reason for such praises is to pave the way for a favorable reception of comments apt to undermine the image of Rome's good beginnings. The exaggerated encomium is a signal. Specifically, how are we to believe in its sincerity when faced with the assertion that the consuls were always *eccellentissimi*? A superficial reading of the first book has already taught us that they were sometimes blinded by their personal quarrels to the point of losing interest in the fate of the state. Now, this suspicion is borne out by the reading of the three following chapters, which cast a new light on the writer's intentions.

Without transition, Machiavelli returns to the conditions in which the Roman Republic was born, in order to draw the lesson that whoever would change the nature of the state, and install a regime that has the agreement of all, should preserve at least a semblance of the previous forms, in order that the masses do not perceive the fundamental changes that have been made to the institutions (*è necessitato a ritenere l'ombra almanco de' modi antichi, acciò che a' popoli non paia avere mutato ordine*). A necessity, he specifies, that would obtain even though in fact the new institutions may be entirely different from the former ones. The idea, illustrated by the decision made in Rome to maintain the former symbols of Roman authority and the religious ceremonies with which they were associated, is reinforced by the argument that "the universality of men feeds upon the appearance as if it were reality [and that] often the appearance strikes them even more than the reality." We cannot receive this idea without remembering that at the beginning of Chapter 16 Machiavelli spoke quite otherwise, asserting that a free regime does not make friends at its foundation, and that there is no surer way of strengthening it than by killing the sons of Brutus. No sign is given that would allow us to resolve the manifest contradiction; but does the contradiction itself not offer us a sign that we were supposed to interpret? Would not its terms cease contradicting each other if we admitted that beneath the name Roman, once again, the difference between the Grandees and the people lay concealed? On this theory, it is simultaneously true that those who profit from a new order are not predisposed to respect the laws that would curtail their new domination (so that Brutus or his emulators should turn against their supporters), and that the people only adhere to this new order as long as they do not perceive the face of the new master. This hypothesis brings to mind the remarks in Chapter 18 in *The Prince,* which are so close to those we are now examining that it is tempting to make use of them: "since the generality of men judge more by the eye than by the hand, because it is given to all to see you, but to few to come in touch with you. Everyone sees how you seem, but few can feel who you are . . ." This judgment was expressed in a fragment in which the author recommended to the prince to use every means necessary to accomplish his designs, with no other care than to color this nature well (*questa natura saperla bene colorire*) and to remain "a great hypocrite and dissembler." May we not assume that the founders of the Roman Republic are decidedly obliged to act according to the image of the prince—in the necessity of covering their enterprise with the good colors of the *majesty of state,* embodied in the ancient institutions, and of ruthlessly repressing the undisciplined Grandees whose excesses could lead to tyranny? If such is the truth that we are to understand, the praises addressed previously to the Roman Republic were indeed intended to offset its effects. They at once made the criticisms of the good beginning of the monarchy more acceptable and introduced those of the beginning of the republic. But the reader has an even more arduous challenge in store for him in the reading of Chapter 26: "A new prince, in a city or province conquered by him should organize everything anew." It is true that the question, already left in suspense in Chapter 16, remains unanswered: In a state in which corruption has reached its ultimate degree, is the establishment or reestablishment of freedom still possible? The hypothesis of a violent change by the intervention of a man who would not hesitate to use extraordinary means serves at present only to make evident the logic underlying the edification of an absolute power (*potestà assoluta*). But the broader significance of the argument clearly transcends the limits of the case being analyzed. He whose project it is to create that power must, we are told, "given that he is a new prince, establish all things anew like himself; thus, new names, new authorities, new men. He must imitate King David who, from the beginning of his kingdom *esurientes implevit bonis et divites dimisit inanes:* enrich the poor, impoverish the rich. He must build new cities, destroy the old ones, transplant the inhabitants of one place to another—in short, leave nothing in that state without some change, and nothing in it, neither rank, nor institution, nor form of government, nor wealth, that is not recognized as coming from the conqueror alone. He must take Philip of Macedon as his model. [. . .] These methods are cruel, no doubt, and contrary, I say, not only to all Christianity, but to all humanity; every man should abhor them and prefer the condition of simple citizen to that of king, at the price of losing so many men. Nonetheless, whoever has rejected the first two ways of good must resolve to take up the evil of the third."

Now there is already reason for surprise that at the end of the preceding chapter Machiavelli should introduce this development by announcing that he is going to speak of the absolute power called tyranny by the authors, since he treats an odd and extreme form of domination and not of the general model of tyranny. Further, the substitution, in the course of the analysis, of the term *principe nuovo* for tyrant is troubling. But certainly far more strange is the first example adduced in support of the thesis that the prince must renovate everything in the city. Is David not considered to be following a grand design in lowering the rich and elevating the poor? And is it by chance that the words that are ascribed to him come from the New Testament, in which they are attributed to Christ? Finally, the intrepid assimilation of the enterprise of the king of the Jews—placed, as it appears to be, under the authority of the king of the Christians—and of that of Philip of Macedon, casts doubt on the condemnation of the destroyers of "civic life," since the hero of the just cause uses the same violent methods as the cruel despot and since there is no crime in upending the established order if it proves to be devoid of legitimacy.

Thus, the last remarks of this chapter must be given their full weight. The means of such a tyranny are adjudged repugnant to Christian sensitivities and even to all human sensitivities; but are the product of a logic that it seems vain to try to escape. The reader, deprived of the certainty of the opposition between good and evil in politics, is challenged to recognize the necessity of action in a borderline case. This discovery, however, leads to a conclusion that, reinforced by the demonstration of the following chapter, opens a new perspective on the interpretation: "But men choose certain middle paths," Machiavelli finally observes, "that are the most harmful, because they know not how to be fully evil or fully good . . ." Now, what must be understood is not only that a lack of rigor brings about their downfall, but also that consequently they show themselves incapable of producing a work of historical significance. The example of Giovampagolo Baglioni, the tyrant of Perugia, persuades us of it. He, whose career, we are reminded, was studded with the blackest crimes, was not able to draw the consequences of his first choice. On one occasion, when the Pope imprudently had himself carried through the walls of Perugia in advance of his troops and was at his mercy, he backed away from the only crime that would have been meaningful. He "who thought nothing of incest or public parricide, knew not how—or better, did not dare—to avail himself of an excellent opportunity, in which everyone would have admired his courage, and which would have immortalized him; for he would have been the first to show prelates of the Church how little men are respected who live and rule as they do; he would at last have done something whose greatness would have far surpassed its infamy and risks." Hence it is impossible to limit one's considerations to the pure knowledge of the rules governing the violent play of politics. Politics itself is at the service of an appreciation of situations we invest with meaning. Baglioni is not discredited for a failure that brought about his personal downfall; the derision attaching to his adventure is judged on the basis of his inability to accomplish the task imposed on him by the circumstances. For if it is true that the Church is the main agent of division and corruption in Italy, he could, in striking it at the head, have changed the conditions of political action, and freed up new possibilities. That such an exploit, if he had accomplished it, might have obliterated parricide and incest, or even borne the trace of a political plan, cannot be assumed. Nor that it would have attained to truth by the sole fact that the necessity of the action agreed with the necessity inscribed within the situation. Now, it is indeed that conclusion that emerges from, and extends over, the entirety of the analysis and changes the image of the foundation accomplished by Romulus. There is no need to insist on the specific references contained in Machiavelli's discourse: they do not have a realist function. How can we not feel that in Chapter 26 the approach is ironic and symbolic? Ironic, because the examples of David and of Baglioni, by being linked contrary to reason, suddenly brings forth an unusual truth. Symbolic, because their only meaning is to return us to an idea of action that forbids the splice dividing good and evil, the order of morality and that of necessity, the possible and the impossible.

At the end of Chapter 27, Machiavelli no doubt thinks he has proceeded far enough to draw his reader into a new interpretation of the history of the Roman Republic, which constitutes, up until the end of Book 1, the main content of the discourse. In approaching it, we already know that the same principles govern the understanding of that history and that of the politics of modern states. It was necessary, we believe, to remove the twofold obstacle of the classical and Christian interpretations of politics, shatter the certitudes tributary to the distinction between good and bad regimes, good and bad princes, good and bad governmental modalities, cast doubt upon the excellence of the original institutions of the state, and introduce us to the idea of a logic of historical action, in order to make a critical reading of the history of the republic possible. Indeed, that reading is such as to make us recognize that neither the Roman state nor its citizens are good by nature; corruption is already at work during the regimes's earliest times; the dominating class is blinded by its egotism, and the people by their illusions and credulity; the best constituted republic is riddled with accidents analogous to those suffered by the decadent one, and shot through with the same weaknesses—and at the same time a certain ability to respond to events distinguishes Rome, giving it the possibility of mastering its history. Still, the discourse in this second part of the work does not feature themes that finally give us Machiavelli's thinking undisguised. The writer constantly compels the reader to wonder which path to take, constantly leading him back to familiar ground only to make him abandon it in order to discover the truth by means of disenchantment.

The decision concerning the goodness of the Roman Republic governs the argument of the first four chapters [I: 28–31] we are presently considering. Machiavelli hastens to assert that the state was less ungrateful in Rome than in Athens toward the citizens who had distinguished themselves in their service to it, and he finds the explanation for this in the fact that no one dared infringe upon its freedom in the first period of the republic. Thus he suggests that the origin of the goodwill of the regime was the virtue of the people, with all the classes mixed in together. The preceding analysis having been concluded with the proposition that men cannot be all good or all evil, cannot the reader go back to dreaming that in Rome, at least, faithfulness to just principles was maintained? Chapter 29 confirms him in this disposition, inviting him to compare the behavior of the prince with that of the republic. After having remarked that the republic is justified in mistrusting the ambitious who exploit their popularity to reduce it to subservience, he points out that the Romans did not strike down those who had aroused their concern and whom they had every right to condemn harshly; and, pointing out the exceptional severity of their attitude toward Scipio, he has us read and admire its motivation: the conviction that the authority of a citizen, however good, could not exceed that of the magistrates in office. Again, in Chapter 30, after having revealed that a republic has special difficulties since, unlike a prince—who can and must command his army in person—it has to delegate the authority to a citizen, the author recommends taking Rome as a model; while the following chapter goes so far as to stress the indulgence shown toward military leaders whose mistakes on the battlefield seemed to call for punishment. Now, it becomes quickly apparent that his praise for Roman kindness is accompanied by considerations that radically modify its significance. Availing himself of the reference furnished by the position of the prince, Machiavelli observes that he must, if he is not capable of assuming command of the military, get rid of the captain whose authority offends him; he then boldly reverses his perspective, advising this same captain, "infallibly exposed to the bite of ingratitude," to forestall the action of the prince, either in leaving the army on his own initiative after the victory, or in making sure he has the backing of his troops in toppling the established power. This analysis, which again renders visible the logic of political conduct, in recalling the need for being either all good or all bad, teaches the true reason why the Roman Republic did not know the vice of ingratitude. We are told that the conflict was not in fact between the political and the military authority but was secretly structured between the military leaders. Rome, turned toward war, had a great many citizens capable of assuming command, so none was indispensable and each feared the jealousy of the others: "their number even served to hold them mutually in check. They maintained their integrity so carefully, they were so fearful of giving the least umbrage, lest they give the people grounds for suspecting them of ambition that, having arrived at the dictatorship, the surest way to glory in that situation was to promptly abdicate." Considering this commentary, formulated at the end of Chapter 30, we must concede that the comments on gratitude and ingratitude were just window-dressing. The important thing is not to assess the goodness of the Romans; we must simply explore up close the efficacy of a system that made it necessary for them to *appear* good. The same principles definitively govern the conduct of men; but whereas, in certain cases, ambition reacts openly to ambition, in others the play of generalized suspicion disarms it, to the point where external constraint—as we are instructed in Chapter 31—loses to a great extent its reason for being, and the differences between individuals can be tolerated without great danger.

But scarcely have we arrived at that conclusion when the analysis of an episode apparently introduced to show the liberality of the Romans forces us to discover its limitation. In Chapter 32, titled "Neither a Republic nor a Prince Should Defer When It Is a Question of Providing for the Needs of Their Subjects," we learn that shortly after the eviction of the Tarquins, when Rome was facing foreign aggression, the senate urgently took economic measures intended to win over the plebs, fearing that it might prefer the return of the tyranny to war. The event is exploited to reveal the imprudence of the senate, which only decided to make concessions to the people under the pressure of the circumstances, and risked seeing its ruse revealed. Now, the criticism deserves our attention for more reasons than one: indeed, the issue is no longer the goodness of the Romans, but that of the dominant class; and the latter appears mendacious. The reference made once more to the politics of the prince no longer supports a comparison between two regimes, but discreetly signals the close relationship between two kinds of oppression. The allusion to the danger of a reestablishment of the tyranny confirms that the new government did not have the support of the people. Finally, and especially, perhaps, the regime proves to be better at defusing conflicts that risk pitting the state power against private citizens than at resolving those arising from class division. Remembering the preceding argument, we must admit that the generosity normally shown toward military leaders contrasts with the reluctance to satisfy the demands of the plebs.

Now these first indications clarify the structure of the discourse from Chapter 33 on. They prompt us to find—beneath the appearance of a commentary that is discontinuous, attached to particular events— the thread of a discussion that ties the question of authority in the republic ever more tightly to that of the class conflict. Machiavelli returns in Chapter 33 to the threat posed to the state by the acquisition of individual power. In analyzing the events that favored Cosimo de' Medici's enterprise, the success of which he compares to that of Caesar, he limits himself to showing that where corruption has set in, it is better to temporize than to confront the ambitious individual head on, in hopes that his scheme will fail or self-destruct, or at least succeed more slowly. But he says nothing of the relationship between tyranny and the development of social conflict. His obvious intention is to stress, by contrast, the merits of the dictatorship that gave the Romans the ability to concentrate authority in the hands of one citizen to face a perilous situation. His analysis of that institution leaves no doubt about the sincerity of his purpose: the dictatorship is in his view the only way for a republic to offset its natural deficiencies. "The cities organized into republics," he writes, "cannot think without that institution to get out of the most formidable crises. The pace of government in a republic is normally too slow. No council, no magistrate can do anything for themselves, and all having almost always a mutual need for one another, it happens that when all these wills must be united, the remedies are dangerously late, whereas it is a case of evils that require immediate ones. Hence all republics must have a similar institution in their constitution." Thus those who blame Rome for having established such an authority, because it risks engendering a tyranny and because Caesar used it as a springboard to his power, misunderstand its function entirely. If it is true that the dictatorship degenerated as soon as, under the influence of corruption, its power was left too long to a few citizens, it was in its original form the opposite of tyranny, in the sense that it borrowed its effectiveness from tyranny in order to turn it against tyranny within the framework of the law. Recalling the conclusion of Chapter 16, which recommended for a corrupt republic the reorientation of the constitution toward the monarchic principle, the reader may even think that it presents the ideal formula for a regime that internalizes this principle before it is too late, without giving up anything with respect to its constitution. Such was its nature, Machiavelli observes, that the supreme magistrate held only a temporary power, and he could not "order anything that altered the form of the government, or decreased the authority of the senate or of the people, or destroyed the ancient constitution or established a new one." With it, the Romans discovered a *solution* to the problems confronted by all the cities who rigorously subordinate the authority of persons to the law, since within the setting of the law itself accommodation is made for the institution of an extraordinary situation requiring the immediate and sovereign decision of the political actor. The law covers its own transgression rather than being subjected to it in a brutal violation that risks destroying it.

This praise of the dictatorship contains more than one lesson, however. It is already significant that the institution presents itself as a response improvised under the pressure of a danger from without. It is after having denounced the error of the Florentines, who reinforced the power of Cosimo by a clumsy condemnation to exile, that the writer imputes to the neighboring states of Rome an analogous mistake, reproaching them for having forced Rome to create the most effective instrument of its power by a premature coalition. Now, if we must for the moment forgo scrutinizing the strange comparison Machiavelli makes between the individual who aspired to make himself the tyrant of Florence and the republic that attempted to build its empire, we should at least take note of the fact that the creation of the dictatorship is neither the result of the Romans' goodness nor that of the wisdom of their first legislators. It is contingent, or, more precisely, it arose from the correct interpretation of events. Although its significance is universal, its truth is not deduced from the nature of the republican regime; or in any case it is merely a deduction after the fact, the artifice that was wanting, that was required by its lack—a lack that had to be experienced in order for the formula of its fulfillment to become manifest.

To this hypothesis the commentary brings an essential complement by stressing the specific weakness of the republican regime, which proves incapable, because of the practice of assemblies and, in general, of the sharing of authority, of addressing extraordinary circumstances with decisiveness and speed. Such a judgment shatters the image of a regime that is intrinsically good. It destroys our faith in the purity of the origins and forbids our confounding evolution and corruption. Considering that the dictatorship supervened in the course of conflicts, as a parry invented in response to the attack of adversaries, and that it offered a solution to the problem of the internal economy of power, we should conceive of a new relationship between form and accident—or, as we might say in a language that is not, however, Machiavelli's—between structure and history. The principle that ensures the identity of form—or of what in Machiavelli's discourse is referred to as *ordine*—proves to be not itself accidental, but inseparable from accident. It affords us a fleeting insight into a development that can be sufficiently accounted for neither in terms of chance nor of essential necessity.

That the theory of politics implies a theory of history—we were already convinced of it, it is true, on reading the first chapters of the work. But, besides the fact that the path of discovery is necessarily long and difficult, and that the reader must return several times to the starting point to make sure of the rigor of the movement, the analysis of the dictatorship has the merit of allowing him to discover on the basis of a particular phenomenon a truth of interpretation that he risked assessing wrongly in grasping it only in its generality. It has another merit. Being introduced in the course of a discussion that bears on the conflicts between governmental power and ambitious citizens, it momentarily holds at a distance—while at the same time preparing us to receive—the question of class struggle.

The comprehension of this question goes hand in hand with the critique of the common representation of corruption opened up in Chapter 34. Up to this point, the author had spoken of the development of the Roman Republic in terms that allowed one to imagine that corruption coincided with a loosening of the ties uniting citizens to the state. In affirming that the young republic had known no subversive enterprise, he exploited the credulity of his reader and based his arguments equally on the conviction that a regime becomes corrupt when the ambition of private citizens ceases to recede before the public interest. The appreciation of the dictatorship encourages us to forge new categories with which to interpret the history of the republic, but does not yet confront that conviction head on. In reality, it attacks it at the root: in appearance, it lets the earlier problematic subsist. Now the work of interpretation accomplished in the subsequent eight chapters leads, on the contrary, to a conclusion that demolishes that earlier problematic. It is not that the discourse openly assumes a different perspective, or that henceforth it exposes its intention unreservedly. The displacement of its object is at first scarcely perceptible, since one sees the praise of the dictatorship call up as its corollary the critique of the Decemvirate. Through an adroit transition, the writer declares that he is obliged to demonstrate the following: "Why the Creation of the Decemviri in Rome Was Harmful to that Republic in Spite of Their Having Been Appointed by the Free Suffrage of the People." We are tempted to glean nothing from his argument but a confirmation of the preceding theses, to admit with him that all the bounds normally imposed on the authority of dictators were abolished in this circumstance. "The new magistrates annulled the consuls and the tribunes;

they were given the right to make laws and to act in general as if they were the Roman people. Left alone, without consuls, without tribunes, without there being any appeal to the people, without supervision, they were able easily in the second year of their existence, urged on by the ambition of Appius, to abuse their power." Thus the case under consideration brings us the proof *a contrario* of the solution discovered with the dictatorship. Nothing as yet is said about the social conflicts that were at the origin of the Decemvirate. The latter bears the sign of a tragic error, and the wickedness of a citizen appears to be responsible for the attempted takeover of the Republic by force. However, the episode of the Decemvirate adds a discreet disclaimer to the first comments, which assured the reader of the Romans' perfect attachment to freedom during the happy days of the flowering of the regime. Those who have read Livy remember that according to his hypotheses scarcely half a century separates the creation of the first dictator from that of the Decemviri. Moreover, the conclusion of the chapter announces a subsequent reexamination of the episode in terms that cast a totally new light on the phenomenon of corruption: "It is not sufficient here that the material is not corrupted," Machiavelli observes, "because in a very short while absolute authority succeeds in corrupting it by means of friends and partisans. And it does not do him any harm to be poor and without family ties, because riches and other favors immediately come in the train of power."

It is impossible at present to limit oneself to the idea that when the populace is healthy the republic is in security. We would be wrong to imagine that matter determines the form of institutions; the very distinction between matter and form proves to be rather an illusion: there are not on one side good institutions and on the other good citizens. The two terms are always taken simultaneously in a history. The conduct of men is determined at once according to objective possibilities configured by circumstances, and rules or obligations imposed on them by institutions, and the latter are elaborated and modified according to the relations developed by the actors, engaged as they are in factual conduct. Hence it is vain to impute corruption to the vices of individuals or of the political regime: these are no more than signs. What defines it at the most profound level is a concatenation of *responses*, the expressions of which are individual or collective, that end up forming a system to the point of obliterating the desire for freedom. And there are intimations that these responses are always possible, that they are merely put aside, or deferred by the good responses given to the political problem. Machiavelli further insinuates that wealth and favors already existed in 450 B.C., ready to be mobilized in the service of tyranny. Now, these brief remarks will receive all their cogency eight chapters later, when he titles the last argument of the discussion, "How Easily Men May Be Corrupted." Then he will establish that the nature of individuals is changed without difficulty into its opposite (*facilmente gli uomini si corrompono, e fannosi diventare di contraria natura*), and that a good citizen is transformed into an abject oppressor (*mutò i suoi buoni costumi in pessimi*). But he designates, in the interval, the social force that ensures the metamorphosis of the City: the Grandees, and the most vital part of that class, its youth.

On the other hand, in Chapter 35, the analysis of corruption does not proceed to its end point. Moreover, it is remarkable that the critique of the goodness of the Romans is immediately mitigated, in the following chapter, by praise for their modesty. There, Machiavelli points out that the citizens who have been given the highest employments must not scorn the lesser ones, and recalls that in Rome that law was in force. The remark is well timed to oppose the eventual reticence of the reader. How can the reader reproach him for scorning virtue, seeing him contrast favorably the Roman conception of honor, which is completely devoted to the service of the state, to that of the Venetians, who do not tolerate the sacrifice of private ambition to the service of the state? But the way that has been opened up with the commentary on the Decemvirate is immediately rejoined in Chapter 37, the object of which is, according to its title, to show "What Troubles Were Engendered in Rome by the Agrarian Law and to What Degree of Trouble One Gives Rise in a Republic by Passing a Law That Is Too Retroactive and Goes Against an Ancient Custom of the City." Under cover of this first argument, the discourse will persuade us of a twofold truth: on the one hand that the image of corruption masks the reality of the class struggle, that this struggle is ineluctable and that the degeneration of the state is the result of a powerlessness of the dominant class to set a limit to its ambition and to compromise with the demands of the people; on the other hand, that the Roman Republic confronted the same difficulties as the Republic of Florence and that, despite the indisputable superiority of the former (which is obvious, judging on the basis of power acquired and the exceptional duration of the regime of freedom), they were the theater of the same errors.

This truth, of course, is one that must be discovered through the reading of a commentary that remains discontinuous; but there can be no doubt about the writer's intention, once we have recognized the theme that organizes the many arguments of the discussion. In an initial moment, the analysis of the troubles brought about by the Agrarian Law reveals the fundamental conflict between the nobility and the people and what was fundamentally at stake: land ownership. Machiavelli refuses at the beginning of the chapter to take sides on the rightfulness of this law and asserts in conclusion that the intention of the Gracchi was more praiseworthy than was their prudence, because they precipitated the fall of the republic in trying to correct its abuses, thus failing to recognize the advantages of temporizing. But these two points of repair are far from circumscribing the movement of the analysis, which brings out once more the commonly recognized opposition between the desire for acquisition and the fear of losing. And after having momentarily suggested the responsibility of the plebs in the city's troubles, it concentrates on denouncing that of the nobles, to the point of founding once again the thesis advanced in the first few chapters: "But the quarrels arising from the Agrarian Law took three hundred years to lead to Rome's enslavement; which would have taken place much sooner if the people had not found in that law and in other vying objectives the wherewithal to always keep the nobles in check." Moreover, availing himself of his own examination of the Agrarian Law, the author for the first time designates the driving force of the nobles' ambition, making the appetite for goods the deepest motivation for their conduct. "It is also clear from this that men esteem property more than honors (*più la roba che gli onori*). For when it is a question of honors, Roman nobility always gave in without extraordinary outrage to the plebs. But when it was a question of possessions, the nobles showed as much obstinacy in defending them as the plebs had recourse to find an outlet for its appetite in the extraordinary means we have mentioned above."

This stage having been accomplished, Chapter 38 teaches that "weak republics are irresolute and cannot make decisions and if they on occasion take a side, it is more imposed by necessity than chosen." Now, neither the requirements of chronology, nor the obvious concatenation of the arguments authorize this development. It appears all the more disconcerting as we see the author arguing from examples (one taken from Roman history, the three others supplied by the quarrels of Florence with Cesare Borgia, and then with France, over Pisa and Arezzo) that concern a state's foreign policy. But the theme treated informs us of the secret progress of the discussion taking place: one must be able to yield to others when the need for concession is known, without waiting to be forced or for the occasion to be lost; that is, to choose the lesser evil in a timely fashion. This recommendation is inspired by the principle underlying the criticism of the politics of the Gracchi. The direction they decided upon, as established in the preceding chapter, was ill-conceived (*è partito male considerato*): it was procrastination that would have been in order. For the same reason, the refusal to choose a side when that is necessary, and inopportune temporizing, are to be condemned. It suffices to shift that complementary proposition from the setting of external to internal politics and to replace the actor *republic* with that of *dominating class* to discover its significance. Moreover, another sign persuades us of the author's intent: Machiavelli praises the Roman senate for having allowed the subject-cities to arm themselves at the approach of the enemy, when it was itself lacking means to protect it, and to have thus chosen the lesser evil. In doing so, he leads us to think that nobility was more capable of recognizing the necessity of concession in the theater of war than in the arena of civil conflict. But above all, he draws attention to the closest place in which this double theater must be installed, in dedicating two-thirds of his analysis to Florentine examples. On the politics of the dominant class in Florence he is silent, but leaves it to his reader to fill that silence by denouncing the misery of its diplomacy.

The comparison thus adumbrated is seen in a new light in Chapter 39, titled "The Same Accidents Are Often Found to Happen to Different Peoples." The opening observations are so important that we must this time consider them more important than the examples apparently chosen to illustrate them. Machiavelli does not limit himself to commenting on the terms of the chapter title: he reduces them to the primary terms—desires and humors—of his political problematic, to teach us that Florence and Rome live the same history. "He who considers things of the present and of antiquity," he writes, "easily discovers that in all cities and among all peoples, there are the same desires and the same humors, and that they have always been the same. Thus it is easy for the attentive observer of things past to foresee those of the future in each state and to find remedies that have already been used by the Ancients, or, if none are found that have been used, to conceive new ones based on the resemblance of events [*accidenti*]. But because these observations are neglected or not understood by the reader, or if they are understood by him, are not known to those who govern, the result is that the same troubles recur in every epoch." This judgment merits careful consideration. The essential, as I understand it, is not the repetition of events (which is only approximate), but the logic that underlies it and that may be discovered, once we recognize the permanence of the desires and humors. The events are often the same, the desires and humors, always. Political action, linked as it is to foresight, requires, *here and now*, either (with respect to events that have already occurred) a solution that has already been found, or (with respect to novel events) an original solution, but in any case a specific response that conforms to the general givens of the political problem. History, then, must be thought beneath the twofold ensign of identity and difference. The identity of the social constitution is concealed beneath the illusion of the difference of times; but that illusion is inscribed in time by engendering the real repetition of troubles. The destruction of the illusion gives the power to break the cycle of repetition, by relating the event to the effects of desire and humor. However, the destruction in theory of the illusion is not its destruction in act. Its hold is greatest in the place of government. The political actor is the most exposed to allowing himself to be traversed by desire and humor, in misunderstanding what makes him act. While those who misunderstand the identity prove to be the agents of repetition, those who reveal it turn out to be the agents of historical creation.

Nevertheless, however great may be the intrinsic interest of these considerations, it is still more important to understand their strategic function at this stage of the discourse. The preceding chapter, as we have just observed, brought out the difference in the behavior of the patriciate toward the foreign adversary and toward the class adversary, at the same time as the opposition between Roman politics and Florentine politics. The following chapter reexamines the episode of the Decemvirate and the coup d'état of Appius, its head, in showing for the first time that they were a consequence of the class struggle. At the point of juncture of the two chapters, Machiavelli is careful to establish that the same history runs through all societies. Thus we are invited to interpret, as good readers of things past and present, an event that shows the resemblance of the Roman Republic and the Florentine Republic, makes us reject the naïve idea of an opposition of nature between them, and bears a current political lesson. But we must note that the facts reported show the blindness of all the actors caught up in the intrigue: their intelligibility comes from the Machiavellian interpretation, and the lesson to be derived from it, it seems reasonable to believe, is original.

Here are the main lines of the story. The conflict between the nobles and the people had been sharpened in Rome to such a point that it became necessary to charge a small number of citizens with the task of proposing new laws. The sudden demagogy of Appius, known previously for his disdain for the people, won him the support of the latter. After the first year, during which the Decemviri kept within the framework of legality, their renewal made them the masters of the state, and Appius, confident in his absolute authority, turned against the plebs, gave free reign to the insolence of the nobles, and instituted a tyranny whose recklessness nearly delivered Rome to its enemies. Finally, his attempted rape of a young Roman woman brought about a popular movement that put an end to the adventure. Onto this story Machiavelli grafts a commentary structured, from the beginning of the chapter, in such a way as to feature the mistakes committed by the three parties in confrontation with one another: the nobles, the people, and their aspiring tyrant. The analysis of these mistakes seems intended to reveal once again the logic of political action. But this time it is not tied to abstract terms (the prince preoccupied with keeping his power and the military leader forced into aggression to defend himself), as in Chapter 30; it proves to be based on class antagonism—the position of the tyrant being itself determined by the relation established with one or the other group. The writer persuades us of this logic by espousing the point of view of the knowing subject, detached from his object. Thus he declares at the beginning that his study is of importance "just as much to those who wish to maintain the freedom of a republic as to those whose project it is to subjugate it," and he apparently limits himself to the pointing out of errors. In following him, he announces, "one will see many errors made by the senate and the plebs to the detriment of freedom and many errors made by Appius, the head of the Decemvirate, to the detriment of that tyranny that he had proposed to establish in Rome."

There is no doubt that, in favor of this perspective, he leads us to the conclusion that I have already stated by anticipation: the Roman Republic, like all republics, carried within itself from the start the germ of tyranny; corruption does not come from a perversion of mores, but designates, as a permanent possibility, one mode of denouement of the class conflict. In discovering that if Appius had had an understanding of the political game his tyranny could have lasted, we lose faith in the stability of the institutions of the young republic and are prepared to give a favorable reception to the teachings of Chapter 42. But this conclusion closes only a part of the argument. It is not for nothing that Machiavelli concentrates on assessing the errors of the actors and affirms that we should learn from them. We cannot fail to observe that the main thrust of his critique is directed at Appius, to the point of subsequently devoting a short chapter to him: "To jump from modesty (*umiltà*) to pride, from kindness (*pietà*) to cruelty without passing through the necessary transitions is as imprudent as it is useless." His failure, we learn, is the price of his ignorance of the social bases of tyranny: while tyranny can find support only in the people, he thought he could rely on the nobility, forgetting that only a fraction of it was prone to identify itself with his cause and that the Grandees have generally too much ambition and grim determination to be content with the honors and wealth meted out by a tyrant; further, he overlooked the fact that in a politics of violence it is necessary for the one who exerts force to be more powerful than the one who undergoes it (*a volere con violenza tenere una cosa, bisogna che sia più potente chi sforza che chi è sforzato*). To this error is added that of showing his hand—that is, of not being able to conceal his move to the camp of the nobility from the eyes of the people at the opportune moment. The writer's insistence on reasoning from the point of view of the tyrant certainly accentuates the neutrality of the approach he makes a point of stating at the beginning of the analysis. It forces us to silence our preferences and only retain the truth of the judgment on the fate of a republic, a judgment that is founded on completely different premises. But it also responds to a twofold motivation. The thesis advanced in the preceding chapter, according to which the same events occur in different cities, authorizes our thinking that the just appreciation of the attempted enterprise of Appius allows us to understand the mechanism of the establishment of tyranny in a modern republic. It suggests that the power of the Medici, itself incapable of being based on the people and of detaching itself from the oligarchy, does not understand the laws of the political game and prompts us to wonder about its solidity. Now, this last observation is of such a nature as to clarify the critique of the errors of the people's party and the aristocratic one, which Machiavelli summarizes in the last lines of the chapter in a cruel metaphor: "men, as king Ferdinand used to say, often behave like certain little birds of prey, who have such a strong desire to pursue their prey according to their natural penchant that they do not notice the bigger bird above them who is about to devour them." The example of the coup d'état of Appius seems well chosen to designate the Florentine scene in 1512, in which the actors blindly tear each other apart while the tyrant swoops down on them. But we must not be too quick to draw satisfaction from the writer's reticence to draw a lesson from the event in favor of freedom. The fact that he first emphasizes the politics of the tyrant does not prevent him from then proceeding to analyze those of the defenders of the republican regime. Now, it is a fact that he deprives us of the promised lesson. In the body of the chapter, he limits himself to denouncing the excess of the desire for freedom that brought the people to Appius's side from hatred of the consuls, and the excessive desire to command that won the nobles over to him from hatred of the tribunes. Doubtless it is only in appearance that he maintains the equilibrium, since he stresses the insolence of the patrician youth and the gravest mistake of the senate, which, despite the advice of its most prudent members, did not resolve, when a last opportunity had been given them, to depose the Decemviri legally. But he does not draw any explicit consequence from his critique: the impression that predominates, reinforced by the metaphor of the birds of prey, is that of a reciprocal blindness. At the end of Chapter 42, the question of what to do to save a republic when civil conflict has thrown it into a crisis thus remains in suspense—just as did the question, at the end of Chapter 16, of whether it is possible to eliminate corruption by either pacific or violent means.

Attentive to this twofold question, we are disposed to await the response of the rest of the discourse. We must recognize, however, that such a response is not given to us in any straightforward way. But at least we are not disappointed at discovering that the last eighteen chapters of the book are ordered in a way that corresponds to that expectation. Machiavelli does not satisfy that expectation, but maintains it. He pursues the critique of the behavior of the people and the nobles, brings out the asymmetry of the positions of the classes, and gives us an intimation of the place and nature of authority. Simultaneously, he reopens the possibility, at least in theory, of a political reform in Florence, while at the same time pursuing the inchoate comparison between the ancient republic and the modern one.

From the consequences resulting from the creation and fall of the Decemvirate, the writer—at the beginning of what appears to me to be the last part of the book—draws the matter of three chapters, the first two of which direct our attention to the nature of the dominated class. The reader is first brought to notice that the Roman people, which had earlier distinguished itself by its military *virtù* and would later do so to an even greater degree, gives no sign of this when subjected to the tyranny of Appius. "The Roman armies, always victorious under the consuls, are always beaten under the Decemviri." From that observation we must conclude, following the teaching condensed in the title of the chapter, that only "those who fight for their own glory are good and faithful soldiers." But this judgment implicitly contains another: the conduct of the people is determined by the relationship it maintains with the authority that commands it. Therefore it seems futile to attribute courage or cowardice to it, as if it were a question of natural traits. This is an important teaching since a new example is immediately provided, this time in order to prove that when force is on its side, the people shows itself to be, in the absence of authority, incapable of devising its modalities of action. Such is the commentary advanced in Chapter 44 of the examination of the uprising provoked by the tyranny of Appius. The people, we learn, having withdrawn to the Sacred Mount, remain without initiative; the senate only reestablishes relations with it in inviting it to elect tribunes who will represent it; when the people make their demand known, it is that the Decemviri be handed over to them, in the declared intention of burning them alive; and they then receive a political lesson from two senators who have been delegated to them, who advise them to first recover their rights without announcing their revenge, and to take it later, when they get the chance. Upbraiding the plebeians, Machiavelli points out "how stupid and imprudent" it is to ask for something and then to say immediately: "I will do such and such a wrong thing with it." "Be content," he adds, "to obtain a weapon from someone without saying I intend to kill you with it, since, once you have it in your hand, you will be able to satisfy your desire." Discovering this commentary, we are persuaded that the people do not have political savvy, involving guile and calculation. The author's intent seems all the more certain since when we consult Livy's version of the story, we must confess that the contrast established between the plebs' innocence and the senator's guile is an invention of Machiavelli. Three chapters later, under cover of the argument meant to establish that men, though susceptible to error about things in general, do not make mistakes about particulars, it is again demonstrated that despite their relentless determination to fight the patricians, the people are incapable of taking advantage of the occasion to elect candidates from their own ranks to the consulship, and vote for candidates from the dominant class. In Chapter 27, we also learn from an example borrowed from the recent history of Florence that when representatives of the people enter the highest offices of the state, they immediately undergo a change of thinking and behavior, and take as their model those whom they hitherto opposed. Now, although the writer presents these turnabouts as a sign of wisdom, what we come away from his argument with is the idea that the people are devoid of the knowledge and expression of their own power. They thus appear as the agent of the desire for freedom, the bearer of a protest that holds the ambition of the nobles in respect and forces power to prudence; but at the same time, as a Subject that never has authority, whose vocation it is to submit to the authority of men accustomed to having it, or to give it to those of its members who are prepared to exert it within the confines of the space occupied by the dominant class.

This assessment founds an argument that becomes continually more refined until the end of the first book: the people, despite their widespread image, are not the force that puts the republic in danger. Assuredly they are credulous and susceptible to being co-opted by the ambitious, but their success is a consequence of the failure of governments in power who have not been able to win their confidence. Certainly they are unreliable when a crisis convulses the state, but that is because the institutions and magistrates are discredited to the point of dashing any hopes of change. On the other hand, as long as they are enlightened and rendered capable of developing a well-informed opinion, their participation in public affairs goes in the direction of the best decision. And even at those moments when they are moved to extreme acts, the intervention of a man of *virtù* can still put an end to this turmoil. In any event, their behavior depends on that of the men who hold political responsibilities. Considered as a mass of individuals, they have the same qualities and defects as every other human collectivity, but considered as a class, they do not make mistakes; for they are not the knowing subject; the knowledge they have is engendered from the twofold relation instituted with law and authority, and they remain ever caught up in sensible experience, tied to perception and divination—a knowledge of appearances and portents—whereas the knowledge possessed by those who govern, or more generally by the members of the dominant class, implies calculation and foresight. Thus only the dominant class makes mistakes, for its members, who are in a position to maneuver in the interests of their private ambition, are inclined to ignore the imperatives of the preservation of the state. Hence the political action that is justly founded is the one that takes class difference into account—not the one that pretends to be brought to bear from a point that is at a distance from the adversaries, for beneath that fiction it would remain within the limits of the dominant interest, but the one that, in taking up an authority that can only be located at a distance from the people, seeks its direction in popular consensus, that is, bears testimony to the desire for freedom. Freedom alone can keep the two halves of the social body from collapsing inward onto one another, from shutting down the swirling movement of appetite and fear, and thus maintain the division between civil society and the state.

The interpretation of the character of the people, already adumbrated in the three chapters I have referred to, continues in Chapter 53, which claims to establish "that a people often desires its ruin, fooled by a false good appearance; and that it is often affected by great expectations and magnificent promises." This argument, supported by Roman, Greek, and Florentine examples, would seem to confirm the view of those who accuse the dominated class of thoughtlessness and blindness. But already, while the writer brings out, in terms well chosen to please conservatives, the propensity of the people for giving in to the seduction of demagogues, he elucidates their relation to authority. After having observed that the people, frequently fooled by false appearances, desire their own ruin, he immediately adds: "if what is good and what is evil is not inculcated by someone in whom it has confidence, republics are exposed to the greatest dangers." And then he goes a step further: "But when by chance the people have confidence in no one, which happens sometimes when they have been deceived, either by events or by men, the state must perish." Thus the critique of the behavior of the populace turns out to be inseparable from the critique of the behavior of the directors of the city. It makes one begin to think that the author proceeds toward his adversary as he thinks a capable politician must proceed with respect to the ambitious citizen: *he cuts the ground from under his feet,* by preempting the arguments that might be seductive, and by redirecting them so as to serve his own cause. The transfer that is carried out from the question of the people to that of authority is reinforced in Chapter 54, in which we see "how powerful the authority of a grave man is in restraining an excited multitude." It does not escape us then that in substituting the term *multitude* for that of *people*, Machiavelli again uses the language of the conservatives the better to combat the thesis they maintain. Then placing himself beneath the authority of Livy, and asserting that "the populace is strong (*gagliarda*) collectively, but individually weak," he espouses the common opinion that the multitude shows its cowardice the moment it feels the fear of punishment, but uses the argument to suggest that therefore there is no reason to fear its outbursts, and establishes, in passing, that when the outbursts are provoked by the loss of freedom, or by the love of a prince who is still alive, the people are fearsome. The support sought in the tradition turns out to prepare the most daring movement to break away from it, since in the following chapter, which the author dares to title "The Multitude Is Wiser and More Constant than a Prince," he attacks "our Livy and all the historians" head on. Such here is the ostentation with which he claims novelty for his remarks in which he announced, in the first lines of the Proem, the discovery of an unknown continent. "As for me," he writes, "I do not know whether, in wanting to defend a cause that all the historians, as I have said, have opposed, I will conquer a rugged land (*provincia*) and encounter so much difficulty there that I will have to abandon it shamefully or laboriously maintain it. But in any event, as for me, I do not judge, nor will I ever judge it to be a fault to advance reasons in defending an opinion (*con le ragioni*), as long as one does not resort to either authority or force."

How can we not recognize, then, that the same necessity commands discourse to establish the truth of democracy and to win its own freedom of movement with the destruction of established opinion? Machiavelli lets it be understood that there is, beyond political thinking—shrewd and calculating—a thinking politics that makes common cause with the people's desire for freedom; like the latter, though at a distance from its action, it brings into play the question of the being of the city: a question that is veiled in the place occupied by the prince and the prince's discourse. This thought is not a class thought, the thought that gives expression to the people's demands; it is not subservient to the image of the goodness of the people or the wickedness of the Grandees. It does not deny the function of authority, nor does it fail to recognize the place in which it is exerted. It looks into class division, the division of class desire, and the history in virtue of which the unity of a city is instituted as a result of the division. A thinking politics, it does not think *about* politics, detached as such thinking would be from its object; if that were the case, looking down from above on the conflict of the classes and claiming to determine their nature, it would again be the thought of the prince; what thinking politics thinks is what it discovers in the interpretation of the dominant discourse that is being held on politics, under the authority of Livy and of all the historians, in a reading of this discourse as political discourse. Moreover, the chapter we are now discussing leaves no doubt about its being such a reading, since in its conclusion it gives us the motivation of the antidemocratic thesis. After having rejected one by one the arguments discrediting the role of the people, he adds: "but the opinion that is unfavorable to the people is born of the circumstance that everyone speaks evil of them fearlessly and freely, even when living under their power; one speaks of princes with the greatest trepidation and the greatest reserve." Thus we can no longer think that Livy makes an erroneous assessment; his judgment proves servile with respect to the *principi*—who are not only monarchs, but by and large directors of a city, the *principi* of the Roman or the Florentine republics.

But we must also understand that, far more than Livy, it is the contemporaries preoccupied with seeking support from the great Authors who are being challenged. When Machiavelli rejects recourse to authority or force in the discussion and declares that one must supply one's own reasons in defense of one's opinions, he is elucidating for his readers the way the visible power of the directors and the invisible power of the dominant discourse work together.

To the teachings of Chapter 58, which can be rightly considered the most important of the last part of the book, the two following ones appear to add a complement. In contriving to make a new substitution of terms, however, with the replacement of *multitude* by *republic,* the writer again imperceptibly shifts the object of the discourse. The thesis that a republic is more faithful than a prince in its alliances—based on the three-fold observation that both are equally forced not to respect treaties dictated by force, that the republic is slower to decide on a change of sides, and that the people loathe openly disloyal undertakings—results in the obliteration of the scandal of suggested opposition between the princes, conceived of as directors of the city, and the dominated class, or at least in the diminishing of its importance by the introduction of an argument whose good realist and good moral tenor collaborate in the service of an apparently neutral judgment on the behavior of the state. This thesis is also a preparation to accept the last depiction of Rome, in which the virtue of the regime coincides with the power of the people. The Roman Republic, whose merit, according to the title of the chapter, was to admit citizens to the consulate and other offices without age limits, turns out, according to the text of this chapter, to have been elevated to the dignity of a model, because it had been forced by its plebs to open them to all, without distinction of family origin. That the last words of the writer at the end of the first book are to associate the virtue of youth with that of the democracy and the state enamored of glory is well suited to remind us that he is speaking in a city the decline of which is linked to political conservatism and the domination of the older generation.

Such, then, is the truth that must be heard in order to understand the just terms of a political action that may reverse the current sweeping the modern republic, the city of Florence, toward an irremediable decadence. No one will conceive of the means of doing this, we are told, unless he recognizes the necessity of seeking the basis of his enterprise in the people. Change comes at this price. But over the nature and means of such an action Machiavelli casts a veil. In the last chapters, just before establishing that the people united are powerful and before issuing the warning that when they fight to restore freedom their force is formidable, the writer remarks, in a fragment at first blush obscure, "that great changes that take place in a city or a province are preceded by signs that allow them to be prognosticated or announced by men." He then evokes Savonarola's predictions before the entry of Charles VIII into Italy and the visions of those who had perceived men fighting in the air. Then he reminds the reader that lightning struck the palace before the fall of Soderini and compares these events to the warning that a plebeian thought he heard on the eve of the attack of the Gauls on Rome. I wonder whether he is insinuating that some extraordinary sign is presently announcing a change. Is he seriously hypothesizing that the air is peopled with intelligences endowed with compassion for men? These strange words are elucidated when we read Chapter 58, which, as said earlier, is entirely devoted to praising the multitude. In it, the author compares the voice of the people to that of God, and, repeating the words used a little earlier, expresses his amazement at predictions so accurate, if we take him at his word, that the people seem to possess the occult virtue of predicting their own good and ill fortune. Thus it is confirmed that there are two kinds of knowledge: one that comes from the understanding, and seems peculiar to members of the dominant class, or to those who hold their authority from them; and the other, which is sensible knowledge, as manifested in perception and the imagination. The latter belongs to the people. And in remarking that knowledge is thus twofold, it must be admitted that in the very place where the people are not enlightened, not put in a good position to judge, it possesses instead, thanks to the perception of what is close to it, the power to *divine*. What it divines is the weakness of power; it is, in Florence, the weakness of the government of Soderini, on the eve of Spanish aggression; and at present perhaps, that of the Medici government; but what it also divines, as was taught in the last chapter of *The Prince*, is the strength of the one who comes to overturn the established order. It would be a mistake to think that the mass is absent by cowardice in a crisis; it *feels* the political void when there is no one to inspire confidence, but it also feels the new path on which a man of *virtù* has set out. And this latter must never despair of winning the support that the preceding government lacked.

We would do well to be especially attentive to this remark because among the last eight chapters of the book, the only two that apparently break the thread of the discussion are the one that I have just mentioned, dedicated to the theme of divination, and the preceding one, Chapter 55, whose subject is announced in the title: "How Easy It Is to Manage Everything in a City in Which the Populace Is Not Yet Corrupt; Where Equality Reigns, One Cannot Set Up a Princedom; Where There Is No Equality, One Cannot Create a Republic." Remembering that the author has already shown that corruption and inequality are linked, and struck by his judgment of the French monarchy, which here is denounced as a corrupt state, while elsewhere it is praised for the good organization of its laws, we are first tempted to retain, from the analysis, the rigorous opposition established between a regime based on the power of the nobility and a regime that does not tolerate distinctions of birth. This opposition, supported by the examples of the upright republics in Germany and the Italian princedoms, appears to shed new light on the difference between the forms of government—formerly obscured by similar traits of the various forms of domination—and thus to constitute a last stage in the direction of the definition of a democratic republic. Moreover, the critique of the way of life of the "gentry" indirectly brings out the meaning of a regime of inequality. Indeed, Machiavelli declares that he is naming certain ones of "those who live in the laziness of income from their estates, and in abundance, without having to worry about cultivating the land or any other work that is necessary to life." He judges them, for this reason alone, to be harmful in any state, but especially so when they control castles and command subjects; those of them who reign in the Papal States and the kingdom of Naples, in Romagna and Lombardy are denounced as totally hostile to any civil life (*al tutto inimici d'ogni civilità*). Thus we are told that equality reigns only where work is considered as the sole source of distinction, and that it is from the universally recognized value of work that the common relation of individuals, of whatever class, to the laws of the city is derived. But however useful these observations may be, their function in the last part of the book remains doubtful, as long as we have not weighed the practical conclusion drawn from them by the author. Under pretense of neutrality, as if it only mattered to him to bring to bear the necessity of adapting the political regime to the social conditions, he draws attention to the givens of the Florentine problem, underlining the chances of a democratic reform and implicitly denouncing the aberration it would be for the Medici to attempt to initiate a princedom. "Our argument is borne out by the case of Tuscany," he writes, "where three republics—Florence, Sienna, and Lucca—can be seen to have coexisted in a small space for a long time; and the other cities of that province, which are subject to them, have shown in their spirit and their type of institutions that they have retained their freedom and want to continue to do so. This is because in that province there are no castles or lords, and very few gentry, if any; on the contrary, what reigns there is such a great equality that a man who is prudent and well versed in the institutions of antiquity could easily introduce a civil mode of life there (*uno vivere civile*)."

This declaration gives to the analysis of Roman democracy all its political significance. True, it merely preserves the chance of a reform; but in order for us to appreciate its full significance we must recall that the Machiavellian discourse constantly has as one of its key elements the difference between Florence and Rome. Now we have already seen, reading Chapter 39, that the two states were faced with the same difficulties, and carried within them at all times the same mortal germs. Looking back, now that we are assured of having followed the thread constituted by the analysis of the people to the end of the book, to consider the six chapters devoted to the politics of the dominant class, we discover that they not only bring out—as in Chapters 47 and 48—the cleverness of its members to maneuver the plebs and keep for themselves the initiative of action in all cases: they also show their tendency to satisfy, just as did the upper Florentine bourgeoisie, their private interest and ambition to the detriment of the public good. Whether it is a question of the censors whose vengeance against a dictator shows an imperfection in the constitution, or of the consuls whose personal rivalry put the state for a short time in peril, the comparison is necessary between the faults of the ancient republic and those of the modern one, which are manifested in the behavior of their dominant class. But it is a fact that the author only suggests that comparison in accompanying it with—or having it followed by—examples or commentaries that forbid our forgetting the opposition between two styles of conduct and institutions. If, in Chapter 44, he reproaches Savonarola for his error in refusing conspirators of the Medici faction the right (according to a law he had contributed to getting passed) of an appeal to the people, and the patricians for refusing the former Decemviri that same right after their imprisonment, he goes on to observe, four chapters later, that Rome's constitution had the incomparable merit of normally allowing those sentenced to death this recourse. If he condemns the danger to the Roman Republic of having allowed a wild rash of declarations against an endless list of citizens in the immediate aftermath of the Decemvirate, thus setting a precedent for the purge following Savonarola's fall, he immediately quotes an example that brings out the initiative of a tribune, and suggests that where the people had representation, legality could easily be reestablished. If he points out the insolence of the censors who were outraged at their term of office being shortened, the conclusion of the chapter recalls the superiority of the Roman Republic over that of Florence by having the reader observe, "If Rome, which had instituted laws for itself, using men of such wisdom and talent in doing so, had been forced everyday by unforeseen events to create new institutions to maintain its freedom, there is nothing astonishing in the fact that other cities whose beginnings were so full of disorder should find such difficulties that they can never be set right." So committed is he to destroying the reader's adherence to a crude image of identity or opposition between the present and the past that in this same fragment he seems to exclude any chance of regeneration for the republic of Florence. "It is not astonishing," he points out, "that the states that began in servitude feel, I do not say the difficulty, but the impossibility of constituting themselves in such a way as to be able to live both free and untroubled. As we see from what has occurred in the city of Florence . . ."—going so far as to add: "It has continued thus for two centuries for which we have reliable records, without ever having a state such as to truly merit the name of republic." Now, such commentaries cannot but arouse, at a distance, our astonishment before this proposition of Chapter 55, according to which it is not only possible, but easy for a reformer who is able to interpret the history of Rome to set up a popular regime in Tuscany.

Thus Machiavelli's sinuous discourse, which forces itself to take up alternately antagonistic positions in order to liberate—from the dominant representation of the people and the Grandees, the republic and the princedom, antiquity and modernity—the meaning of class difference, regime difference and differences in the times, proves by the same necessity engaged in delivering the meaning of a task, inscribed *here* and *now*. The movement of knowledge carries the movement of the liberation of action. Of the latter we can only say at this stage of our reading that it tends to establish the position of the political Subject in a republic.

But if we have been able to find a sign of this position in the last section of the book, at the heart of the argument that makes of the people the guarantor of authority, we must turn back once more to examine another sign that we have just passed over in silence as we were examining the chapters devoted to the nature of the dominant class. Indeed, the thread of the argument is broken on two occasions, as it is, moreover, in the last part. In Chapters 46 and 52, Machiavelli draws attention to the means employed by an ambitious citizen to seize power, and he inquires into the possibility of opposing him. Both passages make us suspect a ruse, so noticeable is the gap between the declared intention and the actual course of the analysis. In the first, after having announced a general reflection on the effects of ambition, and then, with the help of a citation from Livy, shown the concatenation of aggressive acts brought about by the aggression of the nobles and that of the people, and the fear they inflict on each other, the writer suddenly detaches himself from the adumbrated interpretation—which we cannot believe is his own—to transpose the terminology to the relations between a citizen engaged in extending his power in the City and the men already in place. Then the logic of fear is seen in a new light: it turns out that the ambitious man, once having attained a certain degree of prestige, frightens the municipal authorities who come under his sphere of influence; the recommended solution is to make laws that will make it possible, at the appropriate moment, to prevent a citizen from winning the favor of the people through largesse. The argument is conventional enough to make us expect another conclusion. Now in the second chapter under consideration, Machiavelli suggests other means of action that retain our attention more, because they are applied to the example already given in Chapter 33 of Cosimo de' Medici and especially to that of Soderini. This time, the title does indeed announce the subject of the chapter: "To Repress the Excesses and Dangers of an Ambitious Man Who Is on the Ascendant in a Republic, There Is No More Certain Way, Nor Any That Causes Less Scandal, Than to Forestall Him in the Ways by Which He Expects to Arrive at That Power." We learn, first of all, that there was something better that could have been done before Cosimo's ascent than to seek his assassination or to temporize: those governing should have sought from the people the support they lacked, and that the ambitious one had been able to obtain. This teaching subsequently proves to be the basis of the critique directed against Soderini's adversaries at the beginning of his government, just as much as the basis of his own policy toward those who, by hatred for factionalism, attempted to discredit him with the people and joined the Medici party. The image that comes across is of a bourgeoisie frightened out of its wits, each faction of which has in fact no choice but to inflict fear on the adversary in order to free itself from fear—a circle by virtue of which the logic of behavior should issue in madness, as Machiavelli leads us to believe, ironically advancing that all that Soderini could have done to defend himself from his adversaries would have been to join the Medici party himself . . . The meaning of Livy's thought is thus completely subverted: that fear produces fear is not the sign of a state in which the people and the nobility do not want to yield to one another; it is that of the state in which the people are absent qua historical actor, and in which the primary fear conceived by the dominant class at the thought of the people's intervention in the political scene condemns it within its own camp to the revolving door of fear and ambition.

It is true that, on first reading, these two chapters do not reveal their meaning to us. It is in discovering later the role played by the people in a republic, the foundation it gives to the reformer's authority, that we can measure the scope of the allusion to the crisis that cost Florence its freedom and Soderini his power. But once we have gotten to the end of the book we understand why the critique of Soderini's powerlessness to overcome the Medici faction is placed in the section dedicated to the analysis of the behavior of the dominant class, and why the evocation of a reformer for whom it would be possible to reestablish the republic has its place in the section dedicated to the analysis of the behavior of the people. If the place of the dominant class is that of decision and force, and the place of the people that of irresponsibility and weakness, the authority that is necessarily implanted in the former only finds its meaning by enrooting itself in the other. We have a right to expect the assemblage of these still disjointed elements to move toward clarification as we continue to accompany the reading of Machiavelli with things past and present. There is no doubt that the question *what should we do* is tied to the question *what should we think*.

9

War, and the Difference of Times

The second book of *The Discourses*, according to the last lines of its introduction, proposes to show what political deliberations determined how the Romans extended their empire. But the reading of the first book has fully persuaded us that the object of the discourse was not transparent, and that its author required of those who would understand it a patient labor of interpretation. Furthermore, this introduction, in renewing the appeal to imitation formulated at the beginning of the work, and in adding reservations and specifications that clarify its purport, suggest that the analysis already carried out and the one awaiting us share similar concerns. That the author now returns to the point of origin of the discourse, to modify the character of its presentation to the reader, is in my view an indication that the part of the journey completed allows him to address his readers in new terms, but also that the remarks advanced should orient them in the discussion about to begin.

Machiavelli seemingly justifies the position he has taken of recommending the imitation of the Romans, and the better to convince us of the legitimacy of his enterprise he refuses to yield to the ordinary tendency that favors the past over the present. After having pointed out the reasons both psychological and political for the enterprise, and the hold that the image of ancient times has on minds, he espouses the idea that the world does not change through its variations, that it is always the seat of the same virtues and the same evils, and that it is merely the locus of good and evil that shifts, and asserts that the truth of judgment on the past depends on the position of the observer. He declares that he is convinced, on the basis of this relativism, that in contrast with an inhabitant of the German republics, who has every right to be satisfied with the present political life, the Italian is well inspired to seek, from the depths of his misery, a model in classical times. He finds, for previously exposed illusions, a new explanation that indirectly testifies to his resolve to free himself of them, and in the conclusion he repeats the call for imitation on the part of the young generation. But if we take a closer look, the argument that has been developed under the auspices of justification proves to sustain a twofold critique of the idealization of the past and of conservatism, which has a value in itself, because it tends to detach the present readers—for the first time identified as *giovani*—from all poles of established authority.

Already the proposition stated in the middle of the introduction to the second book, "that the world has always been in the same state and that in it there has always been as much good as evil," and the thesis following therefrom, of a periodic migration of *virtù*, have as a consequence the breaking of the spell that the image of Rome has cast on the men of that time. Mindful of the states that have before or after Rome been the depositaries of *virtù*, we cannot ascribe to that image the timeless status of *the good society*. And if we are to credit the contemporary republics of Germany with the qualities that Rome seemed to have a monopoly on, we cannot very well continue to reason within the opposition between ancient and modern. It is therefore impossible to grant to imitation in politics the same function it has in the sciences and the arts, as the introduction to the first book seemed to insinuate. Knowledge of the Roman model does not have its expected place in the space circumscribed by the humanist tradition. Now, the judgment of Machiavelli here is all the more worthy of our attention in that we have every reason to assume that he is not very concerned about its truth. Indeed, one must have forgotten everything about his positive assessment of the Roman Republic to think that its merits are the same as those of the Medes or the Persians, or that they may now be shared equally with the Turks and the Germans. Such a judgment is only proffered in view of its effect. Furthermore, its function is revealed in connection with other considerations in this introduction. "All men," the author observes at the beginning, "are so keen on what existed in the past that not only do they boast of the days they only know through the writers of the past, but when they get old we hear them praising what they remember having seen in their youth (*ma quelle ancora che, sendo già vecchi, si ricordano nella loro giovanezza avere vedute*)." With this declaration, he introduces two critiques of the idealization of the past that at first seem disconnected. According to the first, it appears that we do not know the full truth about the things of the past, dependent as we are on the accounts of writers who were among history's winners, and thus tried to hide the events of their era that did not reflect honorably on them. Machiavelli remarks that we are wrong in giving credence to their testimonies, for they not only inflate the exploits of the victors, but also exaggerate the resistance of their adversaries in order to increase their own merit. Though he is careful not to mention Livy, how can we not question the validity of his commentary and the credulity of his readers, since a little earlier, at the end of Book 1, we saw his opinion rejected, along with that of "many other writers" whose calumny of the people was imputed to their fear of the princes? Moreover, considering that a large portion of Book 2 is devoted to the examination of the military actions of the Romans and their adversaries, the allusion to the exaggerations of the writers prompts us to accept the announced analyses with circum-spection. But whether or not our suspicions are well founded, we must recognize that the subjection to the great Authors and their political conformism gives us one of the causes of the idealization of the past. The second critique, on the other hand, should be placed at a different level, since it seems to question a general trait of human nature: the propensity to praise the past and denigrate the present, we are led to understand, is a result of the vicissitudes of desire; we have no reason to hate what is past, because hatred is born of envy or fear, two emotions that presuppose our relation to a present object we must know everything about, whence the impossibility of separating the displeasure from our action or vision in the present.

No doubt this critique may inspire some reservations. Is it not true that men believe the accounts of historians who praise princes and dis-credit the people as a result of envy and fear that they conceive in the present? Is it not true that there is transference of emotions aroused by a present object onto a past one? The fact is that what is blurred at this level of reasoning is the political motivation of idealization. A little later, it even disappears entirely, as in the last part of the introduction to Book 2. Machiavelli, after having returned to his critique, detaches himself from any particular consideration and assesses: "Moreover, the desires of man are insatiable; it is his nature to be able and to want to desire every-thing; it is not within his power to acquire everything. From this comes a continual discontent on his part, and disgust with what he possesses; this is what makes him blame the present, praise the past, desire the future, and all of this for no rational motive." But we already know that univer-sal truths, well suited to please the humanist reader, often hide other, downright subversive ones; and we have also learned to recognize, in the breaks in an argument, the signs of an intention. Thus we cannot fail to notice that the considerations on the function age plays in the idealiza-tion of the past, introduced after a digression on the constancy of good and evil in history, add an essential complement to the critique of author-ity. Dexterous in presenting these ideas as if they had no other justifica-tion than to disarm a potential objection to the idea that men praise the past without having a true knowledge of it, Machiavelli suggests a relation between the power of the appetites, the desire for knowledge and the de-sire for action that carries unmistakable significance for politics:

> But to return to our subject, men err when they decide which is better, the present or the past, given that they do not have as good a knowledge of the one as the other; the judgment of old people about what they saw in their youth, and that they have observed and known well, would

seem not to be equally subject to error. This remark would be accurate if men kept the same power of judgment and the same appetites, but they change; and although the times do not really change, they cannot appear the same to men who have different appetites, different pleasures and a different way of seeing things. We lose much of our physical strength with age, and we gain in prudence and judgment; what seems bearable or good to us in our youth appears bad or unbearable; we should only blame our judgment for this; instead we blame the times.

The truth of Machiavelli's critique is subtly introduced through the art with which he plays on the word *giudizio*. First introduced in favor of those who age and increase in knowledge, it is in a sense turned against them, to mark their failure. The reader must first understand that men lose in strength and appetite what they gain in judgment and prudence, then, that at the very moment when they improve, judgment loses the power to relate to what is. He must thus understand that there is a lesser knowledge, increasingly more capable in the rules of its exercise, and a greater knowledge, linked to the reception of time. But this distinction is only clarified when we recognize the positivity of desire, since the fall of judgment, beneath the appearance of its progress, goes hand in hand with that of the appetites that are the lot of youth and link it to its era. Desire, far from being summed up in the experience of a dissatisfaction that bars access to reality and is only fulfilled in the illusion of the good past, turns out to be at the origin of knowledge and action, in which there surges forth, as meaning and task, the present of history.

In discovering this argument, we must admit that the introduction makes a general case against conservatism. What it condemns is intellectual conservatism based on submission to the writers that have been unduly elevated as guarantors of the truth of the past; it is the conservatism of class, based on submission to the princes and all the victorious powers; it is the conservatism of age based on the rejection of change and disdain for the times being lived by the young generation—three interrelated forms of political conservatism. But we do not forget that at the center of this trial there remains the question of Rome. Indeed, it is doubtless to bring out that question that Machiavelli has us avoid the trap of idealization, and makes that interrogation the property of those who desire to know what is and to act *here and now*. Nowhere, up to this point, has he designated his adversaries more clearly: they are those who reflect all the vices of modern society, "those who sit *pro tribunali* [in judgment], who command everyone and want to be adored," those who embody the victorious powers of the day and expect writers to persuade posterity of their glory. Nowhere, till now, has he designated more

clearly his interlocutors. They are those who whose youth has given them
the audacity to open their eyes to the past and the present. He signs a pact
with them, against the masters of power and illusion. Defending the right
to elevate the history of Rome above that of his own day, he concludes:

> But the thing is so obvious to all eyes that I will not hesitate to say boldly
> what I think of those days and of these, in order to encourage in the
> young who read my writings the desire to flee the latter and imitate the
> former, whenever chance gives them the opportunity (*acciocché gli animi
> de' giovani che questi mia scritti leggeranno, possino fuggire questi, e prepararsi
> ad imitar quegli, qualunque volta la fortuna ne dessi loro occasione*).

Book 2, in the light of its introduction, allows us to make out another
purpose than that of presenting the military and diplomatic politics of
the Romans as exemplary. True, that presentation furnishes a manifest
framework for the argument. The author lays out the principles that were
behind the conquest of Tuscany and Italy and guaranteed the security
of the Empire. He describes the procedures used to conduct a war, the
organization of the armies, and the role assigned to the infantry, at the
expense of the artillery and the cavalry. But that analysis is accompanied
by important considerations that take up most of the book and tell a
different story. We are given a new assessment of the actions of Rome in
Italy, and of its effects felt in the present; and the image conveyed of the
model is such that it prevents Florentine readers from identifying with
the Romans. Furthermore, the example of Rome is constantly associated
with that of its enemies, to such a degree that the latter becomes a privileged reference. The problem of conquest is increasingly linked to that
of the resistance of weak states. Simultaneously, the recent history of Florence—and particularly the event that cost Florentines their freedom—
emerges to the surface of the commentary. Far from being able to treat
the arguments advanced as digressions, we are led by their convergence
to wonder about the relation between the knowledge of Rome's past
and the critique of its present representation, on the one hand, and the
search for a new direction in the present conditions of Italian politics on
the other.

Book 1 had already persuaded us that, in order to be inspired by
the politics of the Romans, it was necessary to lose faith in the goodness
of the men who built free institutions. But if a Florentine reader was
still tempted to imagine that the contemporary republics, despite their
imperfection, instilled the heritage of the work of the ancients, now he
must recognize his error and recognize his debt differently. The praise

Machiavelli gives the Roman Republic for the second time, at the beginning of Book 2, consists in commentaries that, spread through the first thirteen chapters, no longer authorize belief in the felicitous filiation of Florence and Rome. Florence is no longer accused of having betrayed the mission Rome allegedly bequeathed to it; Rome proves to be the origin of the corruption of modern Italy. It is true that the writer does not condemn it; quite to the contrary, his praise of Rome is unfailing. He affirms at the beginning that most of the writers, who include Plutarch and Livy, are wrong in ascribing the success of its enterprises to the protection of fortune, and that it would never have benefited from favorable opportunities if its *virtù* had not given it the power to take advantage of them. And this judgment does not appear modified in Chapter 29, in the examination of the mistakes leading to the victory of the Gauls, but for being reconstituted and better founded in political terms at the end of the work. But such is the definition of that *virtù* and its effects that it appears to be exerted only at the expense of other peoples, in extinguishing all other *virtù* in its path, and in the wake of its history. Already in Chapter 2, apparently devoted to showing what strength the adversaries of Rome brought to bear in defending their freedom, the author brings out the Republic's destructive work. It is remarkable that this teaching is balanced by an apology of freedom well suited to win the approval of his republican readers. Inquiring into what motivates peoples to defend their freedom with such passion, he answers: "Experience shows that cities have never increased their wealth and power unless they were independent." Then, after having recalled the rise of Athens and Rome after the expulsion of their tyrants, he establishes a contrast without nuances between republics and princedoms, asserting that in the former only the general good is sought, while in the latter the interest of the prince is most often in opposition to that of the state. He goes so far as to maintain, on the authority of Xenophon, that conquests are in the case of the republic for the benefit of all, while in the princedom they serve only the personal interests of the monarch. His intent is doubtless also to convince us of the link between freedom and violence, since several examples are then produced to prove that peoples take "extraordinary vengeance on those who have robbed them of their freedom." But nevertheless the profession of faith in favor of the republic is especially intended to make the scandalous uncovering of the ravages accomplished by Rome more palatable. Indeed, at the beginning of the chapter, depicting Italy on the eve of Roman conquest, he observes: "Also, instead of one sole country that can boast today of possessing free cities, the ancient times show us a great many peoples enjoying freedom." And in the second part, after having tried the case of the Christian religion, the effect of which was to destroy men's faith in either force or freedom, he abruptly explains the disaffection of the moderns with respect to the republican regime and the loss of love for freedom by the action of Rome. "But, as for me, I am more inclined to believe that the reason for that state of affairs derives from the fact that the Roman Empire, its arms, its greatness, have extinguished all the republics and all the forms of civil life (*ancora che io creda più tosto essere cagione di questo, che lo Imperio romano con le sue arme e sua grandezza spense tutte le republiche e tutti e' viveri civili*)." A judgment that he reinforced a bit later, by asserting that of all the servitudes the harshest is the one that subjects you to a republic—a judgment that strikes its final, and most fearsome blow when, resuming the comparison between the politics of a republic and that of a prince, he makes it serve the opposite end: "The goal of a republic," he says, "is to weaken and enervate all the other bodies to increase and strengthen its own. A prince who makes you his subject does not do this, unless he is a barbarian, a destroyer of all civil life, as are the Oriental princes."

This assertion is all the more jarring to the reader, since the attack launched a moment earlier against Christianity may well have seemed to him to be the height of daring and to furnish, coming from an author who had already condemned its misdeeds, the interpretation to be expected from the decadence of the moderns. Did he not get to the root of the fundamental difference in eras by opposing the *ethos* of the ancients to that of the moderns, the taste for the glories of the world (*l'onore del mondo*), on the one hand, and on the other the concern for "the truth and the true way of life" (*la verità e la vera via*), the present religion that elevates humility and contemplation above action, that places "the sovereign good in humility, abjection, and contempt for things human," and the old one, that placed it "in the greatness of soul, physical strength, and all the qualities that make for the greatest forcefulness in men"? The sudden disqualification of this argument is a coup de théâtre. From the idea of a break in history, we must return to that of its continuity, and recognize that the forces that were at work to produce the greatness of Rome led to the dissolution of *vivere civile* in Italy. As for this conclusion, it is not certain, by the way, that we should give it our full credence. Like the thesis of a periodic migration of *virtù*, it has more force in its effect than in its intrinsic truth. Its power, as I said earlier, is to destroy the identification of the Florentine Republic with its Roman ancestor. The fact is, it enjoins the reader to renounce the pleasure of the reading of history—that pleasure that is enough for the readers of the day, as the introduction to Book 1 already observed, and that requires the demotion of the real to the level of the imaginary. It teaches him that knowledge of the past requires the work of disenchantment, and that such knowledge is not different from knowledge of the present, as long as it no longer avoids what is unpleasant, as the introduction to Book 2 insinuated. In the same vein, perhaps one should even give careful consideration to the relation, due to their association in the same passage, between the critique of Christianity and that of Rome. Do not the former directly, and the latter indirectly, bear on escape from the present world? Are we not to understand that there is, in addition to the religion of Christ, to which a part of the Florentines have given their faith, and which Savonarola was able to exploit for a short time in the name of *verità* and the *vera via,* a different religion—occult in this case, the work of the humanists, who reduced the imagination to the limits of human history only to open up a new illusory heaven in that space, in the name of Rome? It is understandable that Rome would be more difficult to attack directly if its adepts were recruited in the camp of young republicans enamored of freedom, the very group the writer makes his privileged interlocutors.

As for Machiavelli's intention, at least, there can be little doubt, as we see him proceed to expose the means by which Rome built its empire. *Crescit interea Roma Albae ruinis* [Meanwhile Rome grows from the ruins of Alba]: Livy's formula, which opens and closes Chapter 3, is exploited to convince us that the politics of welcoming foreigners, practiced by Rome, obeyed the same principles as the politics of violence that prompted it to raze enemy towns and deport their population to its territory. A conquest *per amore o per forza* [by love or force], the alternative is vain, we discover, if it is true that it is by one and the other path that the republic methodically realized its plan to take power. Chapter 4, however, makes mendacity its main arm; it applies itself to giving allied cities the illusion of freedom, and retains the right of decision-making and the ability to give orders, in order to lead them imperceptibly toward servitude: "All the companions," it is brought to our notice, "that she [Rome] had made throughout Italy, which in many ways lived in a sort of equality with her, except that she had kept for herself the seat of the empire and the conduct of enterprises, without being aware of it, fell under her yoke and labored and shed their blood on her behalf." Such appears to be Rome's strategy: to act in such a way that they only become aware of the lie (*inganno*) under which they have lived when it is no longer time for them to find a remedy. Chapter 9 specifies that Rome took advantage of the opportunities offered when it did not deliberately provoke a war. Thus, observing its actions, there is no reason to distinguish, as the manifest argument at first leads one to suppose, between deliberate and chance wars. Finally, the glorious republic is, in Chapter 13, implicitly defined as a tyrant. There, proposing to demonstrate that to rise from low to high fortune, ruse (*fraude*) can accomplish more than force, the writer covers himself once more with the authority of Xenophon, claims that he teaches the necessity of deception (*questa necessità dello ingannare*) in his life of Cyrus, then daringly replaces the example of the great king with that of the Milanese tyrant Giovanni Galeazzo, and then, even more daringly, with that of the victorious republics, and finally declares of Rome: "There was not at its beginnings a greater lie that it could have used than to have provided itself, according to the ways already mentioned, with companions (*compani*); for under this name it made slaves of the Latins and other neighboring peoples." *Inganno, fraude*, both terms are repeated to qualify a policy, the nature of which Livy himself, as we are told in passing, suggested, using a Latin praetor as his spokesman (*E che sia vero che i Latini si movessono per avere conosciuto questo inganno, lo dimostra Tito Livio nella bocca di Annio Setino pretore latino . . .*).

Now, while Machiavelli's discourse applies itself to detach the reader from the *good image* of Rome, it draws attention, in this first part of the Book, to the position held by the Tuscans before the Roman conquests. It does so in Chapter 3, under the pretext of examining the various means at the disposal of a republic to grow. This examination surely has its own justification, and one might even welcome the distinguishing of three types of conquest, intended to bring out the superiority of the Romans over the Tuscans, who created leagues, and over the Athenians and the Spartans, who transformed the conquered peoples into subjects. But we cannot fail to notice that the position of the ancient Tuscans has a symbolic value. Although we must wait until we have analyzed the work in its entirety before seeking information from the historians about the relationship the Florentines maintained with the first inhabitants of their land, we cannot doubt that it had particular affective charge. Moreover, we must remark that Machiavelli applies himself to recalling the *virtù* of the ancient Tuscans and to showing that they were victims of the Roman lie. Furthermore, it appears, despite praise for the efficacy of Roman policy, that they are worthy of being held up as a model for the contemporary republics. Indeed, after having boasted about the path followed by the Romans, "all the more admirable by the fact that no one had traced out the route for them in advance, and no one trod it after them," and having condemned those who ignored their example, the author adds: "And if the imitation of the Romans has appeared difficult, that of the ancient Tuscans should not appear as much so, especially to today's Tuscans." Thus the filiation of the ancient and the modern Tuscany is suggested, while the destructive work of the Roman Republic is exposed. "Their state (that of the ancient Tuscans) was for a long time secure and glorious in its dominion and its arms and highly praised for its mores and religion. But its strength and glory, first diminished by the Gauls, were destroyed by the Romans, and to such a degree that although only two thousand years ago they were a powerful republic, hardly a memory of it remains." Does this mean that the Florentine reader is being called upon to transfer the identification he once had with the Romans to the ancient Tuscans? That seems doubtful, if only because of the sole remark that there remains almost no trace of them. But that remark proves to command the argument of the following chapter, devoted to demonstrating that the Romans strove to destroy all vestiges of Tuscan power, to the point of letting no more than the name remain. In this chapter, titled "That the Changes of Religion and Language in Conjunction with the Disasters of Floods and Plagues Erase the Memory of Things," I am particularly inclined to seek an indication of what is at stake in the discourse because it presents itself as a digression, and such a procedure has already turned out to be at the service of a truth that is difficult to make heard.

Indeed, the argument is one that destabilizes at the deepest level the Roman referent and the Tuscan referent and all *real* referents of history. Beginning by refuting the objection made to philosophers who have maintained the thesis of the eternity of the world, Machiavelli points out that the limits of collective memory cannot surround the true duration of human history, for the twofold reason that that memory is censored whenever a new religion and a new language supervene, and that natural catastrophes interrupt the course of civilization. Doubtless it is important to remark that his response does not imply that he subscribes to the thesis of the eternity of the world: it is immediately abandoned, as its goal is apparently only to introduce a discussion on the truth of the testimonies of antiquity and the legitimacy of the relationship that men have with the past *here* and *now*. Nor does it seem necessary to dwell on the idea, advanced in the last part of the chapter, that nature uses scourges to purge itself and thus challenge the small number of people it has allowed to subsist to mend their ways. The demonstration that arouses our attention rests primarily on the hypothesis that the behavior of Christians toward paganism informs us about that of all the new religions with respect to the ways of life and beliefs they have succeeded in supplanting. Observing that the Christians "have destroyed all the institutions, all the ceremonies, and wiped out even the slightest memory of the former theology," we have every right to assume that paganism has acted similarly toward the religion established before it. But that hypothesis has a built-in reservation, regarding the action of Christianity: this last has not been able to develop all its consequences, due to the subsistence of Latin. It was therefore not able to destroy, as it resolutely tried to do, all the vestiges of antiquity, differing in this from paganism and all those religions that come along "two or three times every five or six thousand years," and that deliberately extinguish the memory of the eras preceding them. From this argument the following conclusion seems to be deduced: "Tuscany was . . . once powerful, full of religion and *virtù*. It had its customs and its own language. All that has been extinguished by Roman might, so that, as has been said, all that remains is the memory of the name." But no less instructive is the commentary elicited by the observation of the catastrophes that break the thread of collective memory. Speaking of floods as being the greatest and most universal scourge, the author notes that those who escape its ravages are coarse mountain-dwellers (*uomini tutti montanari e rozzi*) who, having no knowledge of antiquity, cannot transmit it to their descendants. "And if," he adds, "some man who has knowledge has taken refuge among them in order to make a reputation and name for himself, he hides his knowledge and alters it as he likes, so that he only transmits to his successors what he wanted to write about it and nothing else." Thus, by this last remark, the first idea of censorship arbitrarily applied by whoever happens to be in power at the time is reintroduced.

We must already recognize that the effect of this analysis is to open up, in history, a depth and darkness such that any possibility of fastening onto an originary political form is precluded. Of course no one could place Rome at the beginning of time. But such was the representation of classical and Christian authors that Rome offered an ideal mastery of the unfolding of human societies, leaving no more than fantasies to subsist at its outer limits—such as the imaginary reconstruction of fifty thousand years in Diodorus Siculus's *History* (to which Machiavelli opportunely alludes), which did not jeopardize the commonly recognized theoretical space. Thus the identification of the Florentine Republic with the Roman Republic could benefit from that space to inscribe the latter as the *good society* within it. Machiavelli breaks such a logic, not, certainly, by the simple hypothesis that a past is hidden within the folds of Roman society, nor even by the hypothesis that there is, beyond all visible history, an invisible history from which the visible one emerged, but in suggesting that the object of our knowledge is imposed on us by virtue of an action peculiar to it—the action of an elaborate lie, of the concerted destruction of the traces of its advent. The idea is far more fruitful than that of a periodic migration of *virtù*, which, allowing us to suppose that the Good had chosen domicile in various places before taking shelter with the Romans, did not go beyond the limits of a realist conception of history, and had no other consequence than to engender a form of relativism. At present, the reader must not only admit that there are other objects of admiration than Rome—a conviction not necessarily invalidating the investing of his desire in the privileged figure of a state that is related to the modern republic: Rome detaches itself from that figure—decidedly losing the quality of a thing that is real, visible, offered to the pleasure of reading—to manifest itself as a Subject constituting itself in keeping with the representation it wishes to give itself, and by means of the dissimulation of its genesis, as the Subject of a discourse that can only be understood by deciphering the signs of its intentionality. Along these same lines, we can venture to compare Rome to the authors who, like Livy, Plutarch, and "most of the historians," censor the signs of the discourse of the Other—the discourse of the dominated, always dangerous—in order to tend their own glory. A legitimate comparison, if we thematize the role that is implicitly assigned to interpretation in the fragment with which we are presently concerned. Machiavelli observes, on the one hand, that antiquity would be nothing to us if Christianity had not had the need to preserve Latin to make it the vehicle of the new law. The continued existence of the language of the Romans, of their texts, thus proves to furnish the matter for a reconstruction of the history that is censored by the moderns. It is apparently thanks to the play that is instituted within the movement of destruction and conservation of the ancient discourse that the possibility of a knowledge of history is born. Rome survives not just from the brute fact of the presence of the writings transmitted in the language; it survives the signs of the operation that represses its testimony, though it does not have the means to annul it. But on the other hand—it is suggested to us—the true reading of these writings and of the history to which they refer is only possible on the condition that we are attentive to the analogous operation that intended in them, and in it, to destroy the Other. The author Rome, like the author Livy, only gives herself up to us in the labor of interpretation, a labor that not only must be carried out on both these authors simultaneously, but is only carried out through a questioning of the present movement of the erasure of antiquity. Clearly we cannot grasp, on the basis of this sole commentary, the full extent of Machiavelli's undertaking, since, as we have already intuited in passing, a singular question arises, in the Christian world, upon the examination of the apparent restoration of the ancient culture, the Roman model, and the pure Latin language. This question brings the relation of humanism to Christianity into play. But at this stage of the discourse, we must be content with locating the adumbrated opposition between interpretation and identification. The moment there is a denunciation of the work accomplished by Rome at the expense of the freedom of the ancient and modern Tuscans, Rome is demoted to a lower level than the place it occupied in the imagination of a republican reader, losing its status as a real object. We can understand, therefore, why it would be futile to transfer to the peoples that Rome subjugated the feelings for which it had been blamed. Nor is it any more possible to assign a status to these peoples in a history per se. They themselves can only be thought in relation to an interpretation. When the writer concludes that all that remains of ancient Tuscany is the name, we are to understand that its religion, its *virtù*, and its language furnish us with no more than a symbolic reference.

It would be unwarranted to conclude from this that the Roman and Tuscan facts disappear beneath fiction. The truth that must once more be recognized is that the facts only speak in contact with one another, that is, when converted into signs; reality appears at their intersection, in the symbolic texture of discourse. We would in fact fall precisely into the realm of fiction if we tried to grasp them within the limits of their definition, removing them from the work of interpretation and investing the reality in them. Of these facts that mobilize the reader's realist faith, the most tempting are surely facts of origin. Thus the writer, by casting doubt on them in this fifth chapter, teaches us how to hear his own discourse. The fact is that, not only is that discourse fated like any other to engender the realist illusion, but it runs the greater risk of being falsified, the moment it claims a *discovery*. Discourse is constantly exposed to the danger, which no discourse has the power to avoid, of allowing its discovery to be reduced to that of a real object, which would somehow be made visible thanks to it, but exist outside of it, visible in principle in the present, the past, and the future. Thus, when Machiavelli suggests that what we take as a beginning is perhaps the effect of our ignorance and of the travesty of a borrowing on the part of the supposed founder, he draws our attention to the status of all the statements that confer on Rome or its legislators the position of the beginning. If I am not mistaken, the brief commentary that the universal scourge of the flood elicits from him has a precise function in the service of this intent. By pointing out that the survivors are most often coarse mountain-dwellers, unaware of what took place before them, he brings back to mind for us the previously portrayed image of the coarse and ignorant Romans, derided by Numa; adding that the enlightened man, having remained in their midst, probably hides his knowledge of the past and presents himself as an innovator, he makes us think that this Numa and Romulus himself were perhaps crafty imitators, or more generally that Rome—which surely did not simply emerge from the waters, yet appears to be born out of nothingness and to invent its history—secretly exploited a heritage. Still more specifically, the remark brings to mind the judgment made about the foreign policy of the Romans in the preceding chapter. As we took particular note, that policy appeared "all the more admirable by the fact that no one had traced out the route for them in advance, and no one trod it after them." Now we must come to the persuasion, not of course of the falsity of such a statement, but of the impossibility of perceiving the creation of the Romans independently of that of the discourse that names it.

Book 2, let us recall, is presented as a commentary on the facts in which the policy followed by the Romans to build their empire is illustrated. Such an image, I have said, does not stand up to a rapid examination of the text. It seems more reliable to understand it as a discourse on war—or more broadly, on power relations between states. But having progressed through the reading of the first chapters, we must admit that if such is indeed its object, it is not immediately accessible. The understanding of war presupposes the elucidation of the relationship we maintain with the image of Rome and a challenging of the reality of history, which we only know through doubtful narrations and a doubtful reading of them, since, for one thing, these narrations bear the mark of a twofold twist, being in the service of the victorious powers and of the dominant religion, and for another, we are ourselves subject to the perspective imposed on us by our situation in the Christian world. This means that the discourse on war has its ground outside the theoretical space circumscribed by the analysis of the conflicts between states and of the strategies of the protagonists in the diplomatic and military play of forces. Or yet again, it means that while it is about war, it must at the same time become a discourse of what gives itself out as discourse on war.

In admitting this, we do violence to the natural disposition that inclines us to believe that the object war is sufficient unto itself, that is, that it owes nothing to the discourse men conduct about it. Moreover, that disposition is illustrated in the assertion commonly spread about that when arms come into play, the word is reduced to silence . . . Discourse on war: we are tempted to understand this as a discourse on the thing itself, analogous to all those discourses that, under the auspices of science, focus on the nature of living or inanimate beings—with their behavior and relations. There is no doubt that we can expect considerations on the justice or injustice of war from a writer, or considerations on the function of war in general in ordering the world; but when we do we do not have in mind the idea that things affect the behavior of the actors or the character of the military operations under study. War being a universal phenomenon that we know through extremely varied testimonies, testimonies of which we sometimes have a sensible experience, it seems legitimate to want to gather all sorts of observations in order to sift out, by examining successes and errors, the principles of a strategy of the actors, though only on the condition of making them relative to the state of the technology used during various eras, and to the nature of the combatants engaged in the conflict. Such a disposition thus prompts us to organize the analyses of Book 2 on the basis of the *positive* lesson it affords us on war. The examples it borrows from the history of the Romans is justified, it seems, by the observation of their success and the attempt to formulate universal rules on the basis of a confrontation with other ancient and modern examples. We may make the objection to his demonstration that technological changes (the modern use of artillery in particular) make the Roman practice of warfare obsolete. But since it turns out that the author, far from being unaware of that objection, proposes to counter it, we are inclined to accredit his project, on the sole condition that the facts produced justify it.

In Chapter 4, Machiavelli compares the various types of conquest; in Chapter 6, he explains "how the Romans went about conducting a war"; they made it "short and hard," which is to say that they acted with rapidity and committed all their forces. In Chapter 7, he describes the advantages they derived from the implantation of colonists on the conquered territories: these last held the conquered at bay and beneath their surveillance. They were disposed to fight in defense of the conquered lands and remained sufficiently poor to escape the dangers of corruption. In Chapter 10, he shows that money is not the sinews of war and that the Romans never counted on it to successfully carry out their enterprises. In Chapter 11, he denounces the peril of alliances made with princes whose reputations one imagines sufficient to discourage an aggressor. In Chapter 12 he discusses the comparative merits, in a defensive strategy, of combat outside the borders as opposed to in the heart of the country. In Chapters 17–19, he examines the organization of armies on the ground and the power of various armies—artillery, cavalry, and infantry. All these analyses do seem to be placed beneath the jurisdiction of an empirical science; the lesson is drawn from the comparison of examples: the authority of the Romans is itself established in relation to the failings of their adversaries, or of other strategists of antiquity, and especially of the moderns.

Now we no longer have any doubt, at present, that we must resist this appearance. The critique of the idealization of the past at the beginning of the book, the warning that knowledge comes from interpretation, and the displacement of the good image of Rome, followed by the muffled attack against the identification of the Florentines with the Romans, oblige us to reject the "realist" status of such analyses. But for all that, there is no reason to think that the judgments stated are devoid of truth in their author's view, and that he is only using them to serve a hidden intention. Their repetition and their coherence attest, on the contrary, to his conviction. But that truth is not empirical, and is not the result of the addition of punctual facts that are in agreement because of their common virtue of being true. It is as a result of that truth that the choice of examples, the possibility of their substitution, and the concatenation of judgments are determined, and we can only relate to them because we ourselves want to discover the meaning of the question obfuscated by the moderns (and the reason for the obfuscation is indifferent): What does war teach us about the fundamental meaning of politics and history?

As a matter of fact, if we are attentive to what is said in the first chapter, we find ourselves already directed toward this question, though we may think we are on the solid terrain of the analysis of the Roman phenomenon. Machiavelli, as I have pointed out, asserts, contrary to Plutarch, Livy, and the general view, that Rome's power is not the result of fortune, but the work of its *virtù;* he suggests that the series of the Republic's successes implies a logic of political decision, just as does the series of mistakes made by the moderns. This must already forbid the reader's throwing himself on the statements relating to the conduct of the war, the strategy of aggression and defense, or the superiority of the infantry, as if they immediately delivered up their meaning. As long as we have not learned the principle governing their articulation in the service of the uncovering of that logic, we can only assign them the value of an opinion—in the best of cases, an accurate one . . . But this makes that initial declaration that we are instructed by the reading of the first book all the more demanding. Indeed, that book has already persuaded us that the institutions of the republic and the actions of men within the city are only intelligible once we have discovered how the effects of the division of classes and of class desire are organized. We have understood that the *cause* of the greatness of the regime depends on the relation that the republic establishes with the division that founds it—that is, it depends on the tacit decision (the origin of which cannot be imputed to some legislator) to give free expression to the conflict, to leave an outlet for the humors to course through the social body, carrying aggression and love of freedom at the same time. We have also understood that it is one and the same task to decipher the logic that subtends the history of Rome and that of the modern republic, and that it only allows itself to be known by a critique of the politically dominant discourse, which at once conserves and destroys the ancient reference: conserving it in a representation that destroys it. Thus we learned that the discovery of the social division is necessarily linked to that of the temporal difference, which is masked beneath the illusion of a difference in the times. Thus, seeking in the second book the cause of Roman power, we must go beyond the definition of the empirical rules of military and diplomatic politics; we can only investigate that cause by putting in question the relationship

that the Romans—taken this time in the sense of their common identity as a people—entertain with the outside world. In a general way, we
can only find meaning in the facts inscribed in the field of war by asking
ourselves what new thing it has taught us that had escaped us in reading
the class conflict.

Now this demand that we make of the discourse—that it challenges
us to make of it—receives a preliminary response in Chapter 8. That
chapter, the object of which—if we are to believe its title—is to explain
"The Reason Why the Peoples Leave Their Own Country and Flood Foreign Ones," or—if we are to believe its first lines—to discourse on the
fundamental distinction between two types of war, presents itself, like
Chapter 5, as a digression that is not, according to the author, foreign to
its subject matter. Not only do the two chapters, by the expedient of digression, set us on the path of interpretation, but, apparently separated
though they are by prosaic considerations on the Roman practice of war,
they are rigorously interlocked with one another. A sign, which we would
be wrong in not paying heed to, is there to alert us to this interconnectedness: invasion is treated as a flood. Indeed, what are we to understand,
if not that there is a break in the political space (the space-world of politics) just as there is a break in historical time; that the traits of both, being
without assignable limits, are also eccentric to any point of repair, as if
disjointed by the blow of the scourge.

Machiavelli, in this eighth chapter, sets up an opposition between
wars dictated by the ambition of a prince or of a republic, and those
imposed on a people by the need for survival. It does not escape us that
by this approach he modifies the conclusion that we were ready to draw
from his appreciation of the Roman conquests. That is in fact the meaning at first reading. We remained under the impression made on us by
the cruel judgment formulated in Chapter 2: the war of Rome, and in a
general sense that of victorious republics, had turned out to be the most
terrifying of all, wars of destruction beyond what princes would prose-
cute, unless they are exterminators of all civil life, like the despots of the
Orient. Now, we learn at this point that these wars are of the minor variety
of war. Far more dreadful is the war conducted by a people forced to flee
its country, under the threat of famine, the plague, or foreign aggression,
and who invades new lands with women and children, not with the intention of dominating their inhabitants, but to settle in their place. That war,
we are told, is the cruelest and most terrifying: *crudelissima e paventosis-
sima*. It would be a mistake to believe that the argument is intended to
soften the traits of the Roman conqueror. The example that is introduced
to reinforce it shows that it has a different purpose. The writer finds a
model for the second variant of war in Moses. The figure of the oriental

despot is replaced by that of the just exterminator. It is impossible to mis-understand the meaning of the example, even though it is seen to satisfy the author's sacrilegious penchant. The scourge-war is presented as a just war, the one into which men are forced by necessity and that owes noth-ing to the desire to dominate the other. And it is impossible to misunder-stand the meaning of the movement of interpretation that has its point of departure in the second chapter. Indeed, we will recall that Machiavelli formulated an initial opposition between the war of the prince, whose conquests profit no one but himself, and that of the republics, in the service of the public good, before advancing a second opposition, which reversed its terms, at the spectacle of the destruction brought about by good regimes: the distinction between the just and the unjust was already becoming clouded. The third link in that chain is supplied in Chapter 8, which completes its erasure. The work is accomplished thanks to the evocation of Moses, but also by the virtue of that implacable remark that the victims of the invasion-flood, if they escape the scourge in time, will in turn inflict on another people their own scourge.

War perceived as a natural cataclysm makes us discover something other than the universal clash of appetites; it reveals the impossibility of containing the space-world of politics within the limits of reason. It re-veals that impossibility the moment there is a felt necessity to think the origin of war and of states in the diversity of times and places. Indeed, we cannot truly assess Machiavelli's thought if we fail to recognize the strength of the movement that spreads out the world's expanse as one sole space—freeing it of any particular domain from whose perspective of the border between human and barbaric lands would be drawn, eras-ing any center of perspective, and thereby defining it as *one* in its par-titioning. Undergoing the experience of this movement, the Jews, the Vandals, the Egyptians, the Romans, and the Greeks—named here and there—peoples present and past, are, all hierarchy abolished, taken up in the plot of universal history, a plot whose guiding thread is destruc-tion. But then it is not the explicit distinction between wars of ambition and wars of survival, or that of the just and the unjust war, that must hold our attention. These distinctions are at the service of the production of the case-limit of the scourge-war, which is the only one of such a nature as to clarify the origin of war: an origin that is not named when we have named the motivations of the actors, but only when we have named the principle of the constitution of political society, in the gross and non-localizable division between the being-people (whatever its dimensions, its regime, the principle of its cohesion) and the world of the outside. This division is not the empirical one of states, each of which has its sur-vival and power interests and which clash because they are implicated in the same game, but founding that empirical division, the division of the very being of the political for each society, the gathering together of which is made by the experience of a radical alterity, of the pure indetermination of the *outside*, and in exposure to death.

That division, which becomes visible in war, is not of the same nature as the internal division of the political society, the terms of which relate immediately to each other and are instituted as different, non-substitutable, by the cleavage of desire that traverses both of them, and the effects of which are organized in the institution of a common political identity. The struggle between states is not a variant of the universal competition for the dominant position, of which the class struggle would furnish another variant, and that of individuals a third—logically the first. Even if it is true that conflicts between state powers are expressed as a desire to dominate, we can only conceive of such struggles in terms of an initial, originary break—a rupture that gave rise to the political society. Thus, the political society was formed by separation from an all-encompassing human race—a humanity differentiated of course into societies relatively far or near, friendly or hostile, or even known or unknown—but, whatever its determinates, seen as a husk of otherness, and as such, identified with nature.

This rupture—can we not say that it is, when transposed into the space of the human world, the break between nature and culture? At least we have the right to judge, following Machiavelli, that it is immutable and outside history. A people can absorb or subjugate or exterminate other peoples: it does not cease abutting its outer limit: the latter is indifferent to the degree of power; it is the same for the immense empire occupied in extending its borders and the small city that has no other power than that of defending itself against the aggression of the conquerors, the same for ancient Persia and the modern towns of Germany. It is not a factual limit; but neither is it reducible to the symbolic limit separating the dominator from the dominated and at the same time uniting them, which is at once the trace of the division and the indivision of desire, and that, as such, is at the basis of a history, and shifts without disappearing in the institution of a city—as is seen in Rome, in the separation between the state and civil society, or in the organs of state authority, such as the tribunate and the consulate, for example. What is true within the city—that the fate of the state is directly put in play by the effects of the social division and that order and disorder are engendered from the same movement—is devoid of meaning outside its space: in that of the world, there is neither order nor disorder, and no historical logic; nothing but the accidental modifications brought about by the intermingling of peoples, the displacement of empires, and new distributions of forces only the aftershocks of which can have meaning in the milieu of the *Polis*.

Now it is in order to confront that limit—the crude, sterile, indomitable division between the being of the city and its outside, the ultimate alterity of the *natural*, in all the modalities that are condensed in the image of the flood—that a state—so it is suggested to us—can rise to the principle of the decision that will govern its actions vis-à-vis the other states and will give it a position of power, whatever its size and strength. The knowledge of the *necessity*, that of the ineluctability of the processes that operate to some degree beyond history, as a consequence of the variations of population (as Machiavelli points out), of natural cataclysms or acts of aggression of other states, or of their victims become aggressors—in sum, that of the ineluctability of accidents that come from the political society's exposure to the outside—is reflected in a series of *necessary* operations, or a logic of action.

That truth—the first book prepared us to understand it. In Chapter 6, as we will recall, the writer on several occasions contrasted the project of a state determined to expand, and accepting the risk, to that end, of civil conflict, with that of a state resolved to maintain itself and setting itself up in such a way as to eliminate internal disturbances. Of this last, he first decided that it offered the better model: *il vero vivere politico e la vera quiete d'una città*. But he then immediately reversed that judgment. "But," he said, "since all things human are in movement, and cannot remain firm, they must rise or fall, and to many things to which reason does not lead you, necessity leads you" (*e a molte cose che la ragione non t'induce, t'induce la necessità*). Thus he distinguished two types of knowledge: (1) master-knowledge (which is, by the way, associated with the power of the Spartan oligarchy), assured of containing, from principle to consequences, the order of the real, and (2) a form of knowledge stemming from the experience of its limit—over which no one has control, since it was born in Rome in the play of conflict—knowledge of necessity or—and this is the same thing—knowledge of the unstable, which consents to supervene in the movement of history.

Now, with this text in mind, we are in a better position to understand the articulation of the relation of a society with its internal division and the one it maintains with its division from the outside. These two divisions do not fit neatly atop one another, yet each can only be known through the other. The power of a society to receive the class struggle, as Machiavelli gave us to understand on several occasions in Book 1, is linked to the choice of a politics turned toward the outside; the power it has to give meaning to this choice—to find the necessary concatenation of the decision—comes to it from the free expression of internal conflict, which not only is of such a nature as to ensure the adhesion of the totality of the citizens to the enterprise of the state, to associate them with its fate, but makes it possible to free political decision from the illusion of a mastery of knowledge, to make it confront division, and carry within its heart the limit of death to its reflection. Again, we would be wrong to imagine a symmetry of relations. Machiavelli does say that the politics of conquest forced the Roman patriarchy to make concessions to the plebs, and that the plebs were able to make the satisfaction of their demands the condition of their participation in the war, but he does not say that the Romans' knowledge of necessity was a condition of the recognition of internal conflict. He cannot think it, for that would be to make a subject of this knowledge appear, whereas it is without subject, and those who become its agents can only do so from their position in a divided city. It is true, as we have just recalled, that he distinguishes between the states that can do without the support of the people and mask the division, in keeping with their project of conservation, and those that constitute themselves as conquering republics. But that division, we must again recall, is no sooner made than it is denied: the states that are in fact involved in maintaining themselves live in ignorance of political logic, and only make this choice because the behavior of the dominant in it is determined by fear of the dominated. The relation that society maintains with its inner division governs the relation it maintains with its outer division. It is only from the former division that history emerges. Moreover, as I have already suggested, victorious behavior is not in itself the sign of a just relation with the outer division. Conquest is another example-limit which is well suited to convince the reader of the impossibility of conservation and to decry the illusion of the mastery of a political form, but, limiting ourselves to the case of the Romans alone, we must admit that conquest does not give us the meaning of the general decision that puts them in a position to conceive their military and diplomatic actions. It is not for nothing that Machiavelli stresses, in Chapter 8, that the Roman Republic had to reject three invasions, that is to say, to face three of those "cruelest and most terrifying" wars that befall peoples like natural cataclysms. Its *virtù* proves linked to its power of defense just as much as to its power of aggression.

What, then, is the truth taught by the phenomenon of war, which the moderns cover up by destroying the memory of antiquity? We are better prepared to answer that question. And first, to eliminate the answer that jumps out at us at first sight, the one the moderns are ready to adopt as their own, whatever use they may put it to, with the intention of not seeing beyond it. It is impossible not to go beyond that simple idea that power makes the greatness of man, and that the ancients believed in it, while they themselves depreciate it. Machiavelli assuredly says this—and that they prefer the *verità e la vera via* to the glory of the world, contemplation to the vigor of the soul and the body and—this is more important to us—that at present we have lost, along with our taste for violence, our taste for freedom. But when he mocks the *vera via* he uses the vocabulary of bigots, to the point of borrowing the words of their master, Savonarola; but we would be very silly, for all that, to lend him the language of Thrasymachus. And when he associates violence with freedom, he is simply foreshadowing a forthcoming development. The argumentation concerns only a fraction of Christians, then—the ones who reduce the terms of politics and war to the principles of the Gospel, speak of good and bad governments, just and unjust wars, and, under the cover of morality, preach obedience to the established powers and the virtue of custom. But those who plunge the state into conquest, maneuver within it to establish their dominance and flaunt their realism in politics—these are also Christians; they are the representatives of the Christian ethos, even if they do not believe in the Gospel—or only believe in it during mass— and no less effective agents of the destruction of the Roman ethos. If they have lost the meaning of power, it is not for lack of using force but, we should rather think, because their enterprises, without greatness and without rigor, at the service of immediate profit, are deserted by the decisiveness that lived within the Romans and endowed their undertakings with the quality of an historical work. And if such is their condition, if they are barred access to reality, it is because they hide from themselves the fact that political society exists only from its division and has strength only in finding in its results the possibility of relating to the world of the outside; because they hide from themselves the fact that society rests entirely on itself, that its foundation is given in its history, in the movement of temporal difference that accompanies that of the social division; and because they flee before the thought that the world is *one*, and one only for those who sustain within it the experience of transcendence. Believers or unbelievers, it matters little: theirs is the Christian ethos, since they hide from themselves the fact that everything plays itself out in the space and time of this world, that is, all on the basis of nothing and in view of nothing, all for human glory, in the suspense of death; it is theirs, since they hold in reserve the illusion that something is not put into play in history, since they abstract power and knowledge, without even giving it the name God, from the work of the division.

Must we not say, then, that the relation of the moderns with antiquity and with reality as such—the Christian lie—can truly be thought only at the level of the metapolitical? In a sense, we must. The dissimulation

of the temporal difference, of the internal division of the political society, of its division from the world of the outside which is constitutive of
the space of the world—we cannot conceptualize that dissimulation as a
factual conduct, the opposite of which would be that other factual conduct manifested by the Romans. It is originary, like the division, for this
last always bears the possibility of being covered over; it can occur in the
field of the visible only qua covered over, and there is no knowledge that
exceeds its orbit. One can only locate the movement that keeps open the
question of power and knowledge by the experiencing of its work. And
this movement itself manifests itself only to those who grasp its trace in
the discourse of dissimulation. It is in the critique of the Christian discourse that it is named—a discourse that does not succeed in obliterating
the term that is "other," and of which it has become the negation and
thus leads to its reversal; a reversal that condemns itself, in ordering itself
around a central cleavage between the beyond and the here below to exhibit, at a distance from the place in which it operates, the division it is busy
veiling. In such a way that the truth of Rome is not in Rome, since it consists
in the reversal of this discourse and cannot divest itself of the temporal difference. But saying that, we must immediately recognize that the register
of the metapolitical does not break with the register of the political, that it
is impossible to convert the metaphysical elaboration of the moderns into
a fact of origin, since it does not allow itself to be disassociated from the
project of the dominant classes to exclude the people from the affairs of
the City, since the discourse that claims to repair the internal breach in society is in the service of the desire of the *principi* of the republic.

The truth taught by the phenomena of war and that is covered over
by the moderns, be they believers or unbelievers, moralists or realists,
is therefore the selfsame one we glimpsed when examining the internal organization of the City. The discourse of war and the discourse of
politics are but one. And if we wish to rid ourselves of any final doubt
on this subject, we may proceed directly from Chapter 8 to Chapter 30,
one of the very last of the book, in which Machiavelli puts modern states
on trial—republics and monarchies blended into one. There, after having recalled that Florence, not only at present, but at the moment of its
greatest splendor, has never ensured its security otherwise than by pur-
chasing it with gold, he writes: "It is not only the Florentines who have
lived from that dastardliness (*viltà*), but the Venetians, and the king of
France, who lives by paying tribute, in such a great kingdom, to the Swiss
and the king of England. And all this comes from the fact that they have
disarmed their people and, both this king and the ones I have named,
have preferred to enjoy the present advantages (*godersi un presente utile*)
in having the power to pillage their peoples, and that they have wished to

flee a more imagined than real danger rather than work to firm up their security and obtain the happiness of their states forever."

This thirtieth chapter appears to me to occupy the place of a conclusion in more ways than one: it reformulates the opposition between ancient and modern states and gives us the principle of political power; it evokes once again, in its last lines, the intervention of a reformer who would be able, *here* and *now*, to draw the lessons of the past; and especially it reverses the thesis of the omnipotence of fortune, advanced a moment earlier under the authority of Livy, thus reconnecting with the book's opening remarks.

In thus discovering what is at stake in interpretation, we are now in a position of being able to relate all the analyses that, on a superficial reading, seem to flow from empirical investigation, that is, from a comparison between ancient and modern facts, to their foundation; and at the same time the rigor of their interconnectedness beneath the rambling appearance comes to light, for we understand that it answers to the need to undo modern discourse, to unveil the principles that underlie the diversity of its statements in the double register of moralism and political realism.

In Chapter 10, after having shown Rome's ability to seize every occasion that can serve its ambition, Machiavelli for the first time brings out the agent of Roman power. Rising in opposition to the common opinion that would make money the sinews of war, he affirms that it is good soldiers that make the military power of the state. Now, the truth of his argument would escape us if we wanted to assess it within the limits of the commentary elicited by the examples he gives. What Machiavelli passes over in silence here, but will say in Chapter 30, is that those who believe in the power of money have closed themselves up in that illusion because they have disarmed their people the better to loot them. Thus he presents as a specific error what is in fact the result of a deliberate policy of the dominant class. He himself is reasoning under the cover of political realism, in pointing out that the affection of his subjects does not give a prince true protection any more than does money; and he pretends to stick with the terms of good sense when he observes that gold does not make good troops, but that good troops make it possible to find gold. Only the interpretation he gives of Livy's thought on this point is such as to alert us to the double meaning of his analysis. The final remark that Livy is a better witness than anyone else of the truth of his thesis, by omitting any mention of money in a fragment in which he enumerates the three factors necessary for military victory, sheds light on Machiavelli's own way of proceeding. Drawing attention to the fact that Livy mentions, as conditions of success, "many good soldiers, prudent leaders, and good fortune," he leads the reader to observe that he himself speaks neither of the function of the leaders nor of the intervention of fortune, and that in place of *many soldiers* he writes *good soldiers*. By his own silence, he thus makes it possible for us to deduce that the object of his critique of money is different from Livy's.

The same intention informs the discussion conducted in Chapter 12, the object of which is to determine whether it is better for one who is threatened by an act of aggression to take the war to enemy territory or to await the adversary and wage it on home ground. The examination of the reasons invoked in favor of one or the other thesis only appears to remain within the precinct of military strategy. What turns out to be the deciding factor in making the best choice escapes the argumentation of the experts in warfare. The defensive capacity of the state depends on the relationship between the head of government and the people; if he can count on the armed resistance of the citizens, his strength is at its height in the country itself, where it can draw from them the largest group of fighters and mobilize their resources to face the invader. But the political truth of this conclusion is not spelled out; it suffices for the author to state the alternative of an armed or a disarmed people to keep us within the axis of his interpretation. Like Chapter 10, Chapter 12 claims, then, to bring out a necessity of action that is unrecognizable by those who pride themselves in reasoning in terms of power relations. In the first case it is shown that strength is not defined by an objective criterion—that of the financial resources at the state's disposal—and in the second, that strength does not depend on the position of the protagonists engaged in the conflict, as the partisans of defense or offense naïvely believe. And we can have no doubt as to the critical relevance of the demonstration, considering that these two chapters are, moreover, separated by an argument [Chapter 11] establishing the ineluctability of power relations. Under the pretext of denouncing the imprudence involved in seeking the alliance of a prince who has more reputation than strength, Machiavelli lets his reader know the terrain on which he stands and that on which the strategists of the politics of war imagine they occupy. Pointing out that the Sidicines were wrong to count on the help of the Campanians who were unable to defend themselves, he says three times that the latter brought them *magis nomen quam praesidium* [more notoriety than protection], to convey that the nature of his discourse is the distinction between imaginary strength and real strength.

But we have yet to learn that the power of distinguishing between these two is linked to that of knowing and confronting the risk of death. That is the lesson of Chapter 14, the apparent purpose of which is to show that men are often wrong in believing that pride can be disarmed by patience. Here Machiavelli is not sharing a psychological observation with us; he not only wants to convince us that the necessity of awaiting the aggressor on one's own ground—which he has just discussed—is not a corollary of the principle of temporization, that art so dear to the Florentine sages. His goal is to show the impossibility of escaping war, once the other is committed to it. In decrying the vanity of concessions made to mollify him, which, he says, have no other effect than to ruin the prestige of the state and to encourage the aggressor, he makes manifest the *limit*, according to which politics must be thought. This limit does not appear in the space of power relations, as the latter is normally thought of, since, we are told, the manifest resolve to fight on the part of him who at the outset disposes of less strength can upset the game, hold the adversary at bay, or attract the participation of a third party. It is rather knowledge of the ordeal in which the fate of the state is brought into play that gives access to reality, that is, governs the knowledge of power relations. Having thus located the object of the discussion, we can easily understand the function of the following chapter, which contains a general indictment of indecision. To know the real strength, to know the ineluctable limit confronted by the state, is at the same time to acquire the power of decision. Machiavelli gives this to be understood by showing the danger of deliberation, when it is important to take the initiative of battle, or choose sides clearly in a conflict between two foreign powers that calls for intervention on one side or the other, or else a declaration of neutrality. But the character of the analysis is such that the principle remains implicit: the author continues to speak the language of realism, but applies himself to making it say what it normally does not say. By the way he denounces, in passing, the faltering politics of the Florentine leaders, he allows his critical intention to transpire, but his demonstration is conducted, from the beginning of the chapter, in such a way that it appears to be established on the same premises as those of his adversaries. Thus, in insisting heavily on the opposition between the vain word and the effective act, he pretends to occupy the position of a military leader on the battlefield, at a distance from the chatter of the politicians. Nevertheless, the rigorous concatenation of the arguments in the three chapters under our consideration persuades us that, beyond the use of language and the action of arms, the position of the Subject is determined by the knowledge of the basis of politics.

This conviction is reinforced by the reading of the three following chapters, devoted to demonstrating the superiority of the organization of the Roman army over the modern Italian armies, and the superiority of the infantry over other arms. Indeed, nowhere does Machiavelli lay greater claim to the competency of a leader; his analysis seems of a strictly technical nature, and one might believe that it is satisfied with being just that, were one to come upon this text without knowing the beginning of the book. The military lesson formulated here, however, only takes on its truth by the function it fulfills in the general problematics of the discourse.

A first sign, at the beginning of Chapter 16, prompts us to wonder about the writer's purpose in the discussion he takes up. Before describing the composition of the Roman armies and bringing out their excellence in keeping with the declared intention of the fragment, Machiavelli draws the reader's attention to the war between the Romans and the Latins during the consulate of Torquatus and Decius. The comparison he sets up between their two armies seems merely intended to stress their common superiority over the modern armies. But in seeking the reasons for the Roman victory, after having observed that "all things were equal between the two adversaries"—discipline, *virtù*, ferocity in combat, number of soldiers—he says that according to Livy the reason resides in the valor of the heads of the Roman army; and a moment later, he finds in the exploits accomplished by the two Roman consuls at once the sign of chance (*sorte*) and that of their *virtù*. This opinion is such as to arouse our suspicion, since we had noticed on reading Chapter 9 that Machiavelli used with Livy the same approach that he attributed to Livy in his critique of money, that is, he mentioned neither the role of fortune nor that of the leaders. Now our suspicion is rewarded on discovering that two chapters later, as the demonstration touches on the excellence of the infantry, he brings the Romans and the Latins back on stage (true, it is in the context of a different war) to teach this time that if the former won, it was because they transformed their cavalry into foot soldiers in the middle of the battle. Again, this initiative seems due to the virtue of the leaders. But in the same fragment, the account of another battle whose adversary is not mentioned—a deliberate omission, I believe, intended to let it be thought that he could be either Latin or Samnite—makes it possible to establish that in one circumstance in which the heads of the two warring armies were killed at the beginning of the fighting, the soldiers were very well capable of acting on their own, and finding their way to victory in the same recourse to the infantry.

It is therefore not doubtful that the transfer of the discussion to the technical field retains the same issues at stake. The infantry now occupies the place reserved in Chapter 10 for the "good soldiers," who are themselves, as we have noted, representative of the people, conceived in its difference from the dominant class. It must be understood that the power of the army rests on the foot soldiers, capable of moving in all directions, as we are told, and of forming a group if they are for a moment put to flight, and of huddling together to form a solid fighting mass, just as the power of the republic rests with the people, who we know allow for the expression and confrontation of all opinions, and that they can, if the governors have not weakened their confidence, save the state in the greatest perils and that, in sum, they give the City its identity. And doubtless we must also understand that the cavalry, assigned as it is to one sole type of conception and operation, essentially divided into particular units and founded on the division of each unit into knight and mount, represents the position of the dominant class, once and for all defined by its enterprise of domination, broken up among its members, each of which pursues his own interest, and founded on the division within each one between the public and the private person. The intelligence of the true arm of war is not drawn from the comparison of brute facts, which would illustrate the merits of the infantry; it proceeds from the knowledge of the agent which is at the source of political power. And, reciprocally, the error made on the choice of arms is not engendered in the space of technology; it is the result of a misunderstanding of the nature of that agent, and, more profoundly, of the avidity of the modern *principi* [princes]. To admit this, one must overturn the apparent economy of the argument and bring back to the center what appears at its periphery; thus, one must detach the brief assessment of the strategy of the condottieri, who, in Chapter 18, find themselves insinuated in the course of the long discussion relative to the advantages of the infantry, to bring out the focus of the analysis.

"And of all the mistakes made by the Italian princes who subjected Italy to the domination of foreigners," writes Machiavelli, "the greatest is doubtless to have held the infantry of small account and given all their attention to the cavalry: the cause of this disorder was the result of the ill will of the condottieri and the ignorance of the rulers. The Italian militia, for the last twenty-five years, having been made up entirely of men without states, simple soldiers of fortune, was only concerned with ways to make itself feared because of its arms by sovereigns who were not armed at all. As it was difficult for them to pay a large number of foot soldiers, and as they had no subjects to furnish them with an army, and since a small number of foot soldiers would not have made them fearsome, they thought up the idea of having a cavalry." There, the writer, as he had managed on several other occasions, induces the reader to slip from one perspective to another. First he speaks of the ill will of the condottieri and the ignorance of the rulers, hiding the reason, and then, without transition, initiates a political interpretation whose conclusion we are left to draw on our own. In this particular case, he marks the division that has developed between the military and the political, and associates it with the role played by money in war; with the remark that princes without arms pay armed men who have no subjects, he forces us to recognize that the current discredit of the infantry can be deduced from that role; he leaves it up to us to connect the present argument with the one in Chapter 10, that is, to conclude that *money has come to occupy in modern societies the place left empty by the people.* But in the same light we see the outline of another chain of elements that can be substituted into the same analysis: the condottieri, whom one is tempted to hold responsible for the corruption of the military institutions, themselves only exist because of the absence of the real agent of power; they thus occupy the position of the imaginary force that had already been identified with money. Not only must we admit that their strategy is determined by the necessity in which they find themselves of getting paid; the value of that strategy imposes itself, like the value of money to the imagination of the *principi*—to the dominant opinion, in a general sense—by the virtue it has to make appear in things a guarantee of power. Now, the critique in the preceding chapter of the modern use of artillery tended to assign to it the same status by a different route. Machiavelli did not deny the factual importance of cannons in combat, since he even thought that, being of great value in offensive war, they would have greatly helped the Romans, who were mainly engaged in attacking; his main purpose was to denounce the illusion of an arm that would be detached from men and would decide the outcome of the war all by itself. He imputed this illusion to the dominant opinion, and says that it reaches its highest degree with the belief that "one will no longer be able to engage in hand-to-hand combat and war will be conducted entirely with artillery." Observing in passing that a good infantry, if it charges the enemy, does not let it use the cannon, and that if the enemy has placed it out in front of itself, the infantry can capture it, he was using the argument already advanced in Chapter 10: money does not make good soldiers, but good soldiers "make" money.

Artillery is, along with the strategy of the condottieri, and money, a figure of the modern *imaginaire*. But it represents that imagination in another respect as well. It furnishes the discourse of war—the reigning discourse—the materialized proof of the difference of times, or, in other words, it is that "something" that reveals, within the real, difference, and at the same time, as Machiavelli says in his own language, makes imitation impossible. On the strength of this proof, we understand, men are content with admiring the *virtù* of the Romans, without reflecting that the way of being of the latter puts into question their own. Thus it is understandable that the writer should do his best to destroy that proof; in doing so, he destroys that other feature of the modern *imaginaire*,[1] the difference of times. True, he destroys at the same time the *virtù* of the

Romans, to the extent that it is perceived as a property—that property possessed, according to Livy, by the condottieri, if we are to believe the first lines of Chapter 16, which opens the discussion on the technique of arms.

Now, in making ourselves attentive to the double function filled by artillery in the *imaginaire*, we are led back to the relation between the social division and the temporal difference. As a guarantee of power, installed in reality, in the absence of the true agent of power, artillery is a link in the series of elements that cover over the social division. As proof of the difference of times, a manifest attribute of the moderns, it is a link in the series of elements that cover over the temporal difference. Indeed, the temporal difference is no more able than is the social one to emerge into the field of the visible. And as I have just suggested, these are two symmetrical illusions (which are compatible, by the way) that make modern artillery and ancient *virtù* the sign of difference. Machiavelli does not, for his part, name the temporal difference; he brings forth what the modern discourse on war excludes, *here* and *now*, as the past; he reveals the movement of that exclusion: thus he produces a difference between the moderns and the Romans, but he not only displaces the terms, when he submits to our reflection that the people are in the latter case the agent of power while in the former its access to power is barred—or, in military terms, that in the latter case the infantry is the real force and in the former the artillery the imaginary one; this difference is insinuated in the obliteration of the difference posited in the present as real, as that of the present and the past. It is not thinkable outside of the work of obliteration. Only in this work is a passage toward the new open, and knowledge and action brought into play.

To know the function given by the moderns to artillery makes it possible to read the meaning of the function of the Roman infantry: it even makes it possible to discover that in the ancient wars there was an equivalent of artillery, the elephants and the chariots. This reading does not spring forth from the text constituted by Roman war, and even less from the one consisting in the ancient wars; rather this text or these texts become legible on the basis of the critique of the experience of the moderns, and, for example, in light of the victory of the Swiss against the French in 1513, when they had neither cannons nor knights—an experience that itself presupposes interpretation. Machiavelli contrasts the tactics of the Romans, who do not hesitate when danger is at its highest point to convert their cavalry into infantry, to those of the Latins and Samnites, peoples who are themselves organized into republics; he also contrasts these tactics to those of Hannibal, one of the most experienced war leaders of antiquity; thus he obliges us to circumscribe an already singular form of behavior within the ancient world to relate it to a principle that is not visible in the empirical field of military operations and is only ultimately intelligible in relation to its opposite, that is, once the systematic denigration of money and power has been grasped. It must also be observed that the virtue of his interpretation is to detach the reader as much from the limits of modern warfare, as practiced at the beginning of the sixteenth century, as from ancient warfare, because while he is determined to produce the most accurate critique of the use of artillery and cavalry in offensive and defensive operations, he suggests that beyond the technological changes a truth about war stands unchanged: that it is the combatant that decides the outcome, and not the arm taken separately from him, however fearsome it may be.

The thread of this analysis, now that we have grasped it, is not difficult to recognize in later stages of the discourse. Two chapters further on, Machiavelli critiques mercenary and auxiliary arms: the former having been implicitly conducted apropos of the *condotta* system, it is the latter that receives his attention, that is, the critique of troops sent by an ally, the command of which remains in his hands, and the upkeep at his expense. It is significant that Machiavelli offers no modern example to support his thesis—though Italian politics would have supplied him with numerous ones—and reasons only on the basis of Capua which had fallen prey to Roman legions assigned to its defense. Besides drawing attention to a sedition that tarnishes, in passing, the image of Roman discipline, the facts reported are the most suitable for demonstrating how the decision to seek assurance in the power of a third party leads to the ineluctable consequence of servitude, since in the case of Capua the action of this third, the Roman Republic, was not deliberate, and Rome was itself the victim of the force it had detached from itself. Thus we learn that he who finds himself put in a position of power is necessarily driven to act in the interests of his own power: a truth that furnishes, in sum, a symbolic equivalent of the one we had already grasped in the analysis of the *condotta*. The condottieri—imaginary guarantors of the power of princes, a force detached like the legions of Capua from the orbit of the state—elaborated the only strategy that was in keeping with their interests by making the cavalry the principle of warfare; they inscribe within the real the results of the failure of the state; in obliterating their origin, they make the political focus of strategy invisible and "produce" the necessity of the cavalry.

But it is doubtless in Chapter 24, with the critique of fortresses, that the analysis of the imaginary forms of modern politics culminates. For the fortress condenses all the illusions of security, erected as it is to protect a city from foreign aggression, either to keep watch over conquered territories and to supply means of defense in case of an eventual uprising, or to furnish a prince with protection from his own people. Decrying these illusions, Machiavelli invites his reader to assemble and consider in one panorama the military policy of the state and the politics of power within it. This does not mean that they are identical. And we are not permitted to forget that the state can be in a situation in which it is necessary to destroy the adversary—an inconceivable position in domestic politics, in which power, to whatever violence it may have to resort in extreme situations, must always seek the consent of the governed. But the same principle regulates the use of power: the prince's folly is to think it can be inscribed in things; that there is some shelter from which no enemy, either from within or without, can drive him, whereas power in fact lies in the way the relation to the Other works itself out. Not only does the fortress not protect him: the fortress assumed to be impregnable cannot hold out for even a day before the conjunction of foreign aggression and an internal revolt; but in making domination visible—as we learn from the example of the Sforza—it crystallizes the hatred of men; in that example, the imaginary force materialized in the fortress signals the absence of the Subject—not only the exclusion of the people from power, but the destitution of the prince beneath the apparatus of coercion. Now this last critique moves us toward the conclusion of Chapter 30. While it brings a last link to the analysis, the fortress best reveals the relation between the imaginary guarantee of power and the modern position of domination. It is not for nothing that Machiavelli attacks, at the beginning of the chapter, the *sages* of his day (*questi savi de' nostri tempi*), then, a few lines later, the *princes* of his day (*principi de' nostri tempi*), gathering beneath the same heading those who claim knowledge and those who, monarchs or masters of state in a republic, pretend to power. He counters them with the experience of the Romans (*il modo del procedere de' Romani*): he leads us back to the origin of the process in which were engendered the function of money, of the strategy of the condottieri, of artillery, of the great protective power, by re-explaining the first choice of the dominant ones in all the modern regimes. He uses the figure of Sforza, the representative of a tyranny exerted by the urbane bourgeois of Florence, to suggest the interrelatedness of the *principi,* Florentine or Milanese. In perceiving this, we should doubtless confess that the modern discourse, the Christian discourse on war, is, in its center, the discourse of the dominant ones, and remember that the critique of the *imaginaire* began in the second chapter with that of the superterrestrial world.

As I have pointed out, the thread of the discourse I have tried to grasp is apparently broken on several occasions. Beginning with Chapter 16, devoted to the organization of Roman armies, two arguments are inter-twined; one of them, which has just been examined, tends to expose the results of the distinction between imaginary and real force with respect to military institutions and collective representations of power, and the other to do the same with respect to the action of states or their represen-tatives in foreign and domestic politics. In the service of the same goal, both being meant to bring out the logic of the choices that are dictated by the involvement of the people in public life, or its exclusion, they also separate, more secretly, to present two sides of modern discourse. Indeed, if we restrict ourselves to the first argument, we must conclude that the projection of power at a distance from its true agent into institutions that ensure its reality is translated at the level of behaviors by the search for se-curity at the cost of the least risk. That this conclusion is legitimate there is no reason to doubt: the function assigned to money, to the strategy of the *condotta* (contract), to artillery and to fortresses, if it is only intelligible in relation to the way the City is constituted, has its parallel equivalent in the psychology of the political actors. When Machiavelli makes fun of the sages of his time, he is decrying at once their false science and their cowardice. But we have already seen that the modern discourse is twofold; if it turns out to be regulated at one polarity by the illusion of security, the result of a fear of putting power in play, it is governed at the other by the delirium of presumption. There is no justification, on the basis of the mark it has made on the *pricipati*, for reducing it to the level of psy-chology. Rather we should construe this as meaning that the same cause is at the origin of a politics that has been diminished, turned away from historical creation, caught up in the illusion of material power and in a politics of adventure, carried away by dreams of grandeur, and incapable of knowing the impossible. It is also a failure to recognize the internal division of the City and its external division, the exclusion of the people from the play of power, which causes power to imagine that it is at the beginning of politics, and disposes of the mastery of the decision. In con-sidering the first side of the modern discourse, we discover the imaginary force detached from men, inscribed in things; in considering the second, we find it merged with the person or posture of the governing entity. Or, in other words, in considering the first, the authorities [*pouvoir*] *have* power [*puissance*]—money, artillery, military competence, the armies bought from a protector, fortresses; in considering the second, they *are* power: the delirium of presumption furnishes the discourse of that illu-sion. Thus there is no reason to be surprised that the two threads cross, as they are the weave of the same chain; and one sole desire is revealed, inscribed on two registers of discourse.

Although the mode of interpretation has seemed to me to be de-

finitively open by the end of the first part of the book, it is the critique
of fortresses, in Chapter 24, that clarifies in my view the articulation of
these two arguments and invites us to seek the detail of their development. Indeed in its last section, where we find demonstrations of the
futility of fortresses conducted for the purpose of stopping an eventual
invader, Machiavelli asserts that a good army will never be stopped by
them, and that in the absence of forces resolved to do battle with it in
open country, it will advance without worrying about leaving behind it
positions difficult to occupy. This observation is well suited to remind us
of a fragment from the first book, in which the author associated, to our
astonishment, a critique of the same type, that of the temerity of a Roman king who had put his entire fortune on the line without bringing all
his forces to bear. In reminding us that the error of putting the destiny
of the state in the hands of the three Horaces resembles one ordinarily
committed when basing one's security on the defense of narrow passages
between mountains, he gave us a key to his interpretation that we could
not immediately grasp, because we did not understand that the meaning of modern discourse was at stake: adventurism and the belief in the
material signs of power [*puissance*] turned out to be the recto and verso
of the same politics. Alerted by that reminiscence, we become sensitive to
the interrelated series of critiques that will shadow those we have already
found. In the section of the three chapters on the strategy of the Romans,
we had neglected long considerations on the ordering of armies engaged
in combat. These considerations, at first reading, appear indeed to bear
strictly on military tactics. Machiavelli shows us the in-depth panoply of
the Roman army along three lines, the ranks being respectively spaced in
such a way that the orderly retreat of the first corps of combat can take
place into the second, that of the second into third, in the eventuality
of a failure of the first, then the second offensive. To this distribution of
combatants he contrasts that of the moderns, who decide on the deploy-
ment of combatants in just one line, on a vast front, and thus deny themselves the maneuverability of retreat and attack, or, more precisely, the
combination in offense of the twofold movement offense and defense.
We now appreciate the symbolic value of that argument, with its memory
of King Tullus. No doubt Machiavelli does not say that the captains of his
day risk their whole fortune without bringing their entire force into play;
he is content to remark that the battle that requires the intervention of
the third Roman line gave birth to a proverb, the Italian translation of
which is: *nos abbiamo messa l'ultima posta* (we have placed our last stake)
and concludes with the error of the moderns, who only give their troops
one (. . . *faccino correre una medesima fortuna*); but the image of gambling
and luck suffices to instruct us. It matters little that the entire body of

soldiers is engaged in a battle; the illusion of Tullus is repeated, since the whole game is played once and for all, and the actor is entirely exposed. The configuration of a space without depth, in which the combatant has nothing behind him, is associated in this chapter with that of a time flattened out, reduced to the dimension of pure present and an action gone with the wind, incapable of reflecting on itself—as is the Roman offensive in the defensive that allows for the doubling back of the two first lines—and it commands at the same time the configuration of a power that is itself without foundation. The reader of Machiavelli need not fear advancing too far on the terrain of interpretation, for the writer supplies him, three chapters later, with an analysis whose object is apparently totally different and has an analogous teaching. Is it too much to say that he can rejoice in finding this cover? After having tried the case of the strategy of the condottieri and decried the imaginary function of the artillery, Machiavelli demonstrates—according to the very terms of the title given to Chapter 19—"that conquests in the republics that are not well ordered (*ordinate*) and do not act according to the example of Roman *virtù* cause their ruin, not their greatness." Nothing, apparently, justifies this remark intercalated between the critique of the artillery and that of mercenary and auxiliary armies, and introduced, moreover, by further praise of the infantry. Its necessity is established with respect to the preceding argument: to organize an army for combat (*ordinare una zuffa*) or a republic (*ordinare una republica*) for the purpose of conquest is to respond to the requirement of relating an action to its foundation. To fail to recognize this is to yield to adventurism. The modern conqueror makes the mistake of carrying his domination too far; like the soldier, in doing so he has nothing behind him; he is tempted by the easiest enterprise, "but to expand one's dominion without strengthening one's military position at the same time is to go to one's downfall. Indeed, it is not strengthening one's position to become impoverished by wars and even by victories, since the conquests cost more than they produce." By ignoring the depth of space, in advancing without cover, he turns out to be incapable of disengaging himself from the horizon of the present, of foreseeing at once the effects of the conquest and the conditions involved in maintaining it. And from that twofold error we may deduce once again the image of authority [*pouvoir*] cut off from the sources of strength [*puissance*], the author tells us, an authority that can no longer increase the number of citizens—that is, receive the positive effects of discord—put the acquired wealth at the disposal of the public treasury, keep the state rich and the citizens poor. The analogy seems even more rigorous if we note that, under the sign of conquest, as previously beneath that of the offensive, the necessary combination of attack and defense is revealed. It is true that Machiavelli again brings out the ineluctability of conquest, and his commentary, inspired by the example of the republics of Germany, which are at once well organized and focused solely on maintaining themselves within their acquired territories, takes pains to relate the success of their politics to their exceptional geographical and political situation. But by observing that aggression is universal and that he who would prefer to do nothing but resist would soon find himself prompted, against his original desire, to expand, he already subordinates the question of conquest to the more general one of war. Then, by directing the essence of his critique on the fanciful enterprises of Florence and Venice, without sparing Rome, who, he says, nearly fell as a result of Capua, he weakens the prestige of the conquering state and in the end leaves his reader with the impression that all that matters is the problem of real force.

Now, knowing the meaning of this twofold argument, we are in a position of being able to determine the direction of the analysis, as it apparently changes paths, with the examination of the state and the peoples it has subjected. Recalling, under the pretext of exploiting the lesson of the events at Capua, the methods employed by Rome to ensure its hold on the other cities, the author presents to us in Chapter 21 the contrast between two modes of domination: one invisible to those subjected to it, "though it may bear on them with a certain weight," the other visible on a daily basis and constantly making servitude intolerable. When we discover the merits of the first strategy, which feigns to respect the subjects' liberty, we must also confess that it is more advantageous for an ambitious state to wait until a neighbor places itself voluntarily under its protection than to arouse its hatred by letting its project of conquest come to light. This argument, which at first seems to favor the use of guile rather than of brute force, proves to be at the service of an even less visible intention, as is borne out by the direction the discussion takes up until Chapter 26, and the relation it maintains with the critique of fortresses, a symbol of visible domination. Indeed, Chapter 22 makes fun of the calculations of Pope Leo X, whom one might justifiably suppose to be chosen as a representative of the modern spirit, or, more precisely, that he is among the *savi de' nostri tempi*. This time, the analysis forbids stopping at an apology for guile in itself. Chapter 23 establishes that the Romans, differing here from the Florentines, chose frankly between a politics of repression and one of confidence when called upon to face the rebellion of a subjugated city: all duplicitous solutions are expressly condemned. Finally, at the end of Chapter 24, which points out and condemns the danger of fortresses as much from the point of view of domination as from that of resistance, Machiavelli condemns the politics of the Latins and the Veiians, that is, the peoples who were in a position of resistance, by showing that they erred in overtly trying to take advantage of Rome's domestic dissentions and did nothing more than unite the Republic against the foreigner, instead of limiting themselves to conducting war from a distance (*la Guerra discosto*); invisible action proves to be as necessary to the dominated as to the dominant.

By grouping in one sole reading the five chapters under consideration, we see that they have in common a challenge to the function of representation in politics, and that they suggest, in various ways, that the powerlessness of authority to take into account the image he gives of himself, or that the other gives of him to a third or that he gives himself by the action of a third, derives from the same presumption. Rome maintains its empire over the subjected peoples or succeeds in dominating them because it knows how to project the image of the protector. Florence succeeds in obtaining the same result in Pistoia, while it fails in its relations with the other Tuscan cities; but its success is exceptional and its failure normal, for, as its conduct toward Sienna teaches, it does not know the effect that its visible maneuvers have on others. Leo X chooses neutrality when the king of France vies with the Swiss for the duchy of Milan, convinced by learned calculation that once the battle had been fought and both adversaries weakened, he will easily overcome the winner and be the spoiler. He is blinded by the delirium of presumption. He sees himself left the glorious master of Lombardy and arbiter of all Italy (*e così verrebbe con sua gloria a rimanere signore di Lombardia, ed arbitro di tutta Italia*). His mistake is to overlook the fact that the balance of power is modified by the winner's victorious image; thus he can do nothing but flee once France has won the battle . . . Rome chooses repression, when it is its only means of reestablishing its authority; Florence, on the other hand, thinks itself dishonored by the thought of razing Arezzo after its insurrection; by presumption, it thinks it is released from the need to bring its power to bear; blinded by the image of its own authority, it is incapable of seeing the image it presents to the Aretines when it uses violence and humiliations that exasperate it, without, however, reducing them to a state in which they are incapable of avenging themselves; in so doing, Florence yields to the same delusions of grandeur as it does when it pretends, by open maneuvers, to exploit the divisions within a city, without seeing that it is being watched, and that by such conduct it succeeds only in restoring unity to its adversaries. These ploys *without depth* are best illustrated by the conduct of the Veiians who go so far as to defy Rome, without understanding that the image of the aggressor restores to Rome a self-image that the bitterness of the civil conflict had jeopardized.

Such, then, is the guiding thread running through the second book, from Chapter 16 on: a soldier, a conqueror, a power, that has nothing behind itself, and that acts in plain view, in the flattened out space and time imposed upon it by its being uprooted from the space and time that is interior to the City; a politics that, whatever its means—force or trickery—proves to be intent on its goal, deprived of its representation, and of the representation of its representation, which alone would be capable of giving it its own depth and thus offering it the circumvolution necessary for intrusion into the space and time of the Other—that intrusion that commands at once domination, subversion, and alliance . . .

But still we must locate the function of the alternative Machiavelli formulates in Chapter 23, for, tied as it appears to be to the particular political choice required by the rebellion of a subjected people, it can be detached from it in order to confront us with the general problem of the decision. That function—we have already recognized it in Chapter 14 and understood that it was the effect of a limit, given in the division of the inside and the outside of the City. Here we learn that to fail to understand the alternative—to abandon oneself to the hope of a compromise or *via del mezzo*—is the same thing as to yield to the illusion of omnipotence. The Florentines show themselves incapable of rising to the conception of an external [or foreign] politics because they reject the idea that a decision ever puts the destiny of the state at stake; this refusal is at the service of their belief in its invulnerability. According to Machiavelli's interpretation, their implicit theory of conduct maintains that the prince would fall if he razed a city, because in doing so he would be revealing that he does not have the means to dominate it; but—to continue with the author's interpretation—such a theory, which invokes the honor of the prince, is constructed in order to suppress the fear that his authority could be affected by the Other. The false image of the honor of the prince would, on this view, dissimulate the test of necessity, which is that of death.

Now, we must mention forthwith the echo of this critique four chapters later. There, Machiavelli draws our attention to the event that provoked the collapse of the Florentine Republic a few years earlier and the restoration of the tyranny of the Medici. That event, mentioned among others aimed at showing that "princes and prudent republics must be content with winning, for usually not to be content with that causes their downfall," undoubtedly has a particular status in the interpretation: it designates not only to Florentine readers the death of their liberty; it also shows the tangible effects of the modern discourse on war and how the failure to distinguish between alternative and necessity is paid for *here* and *now*. We are reminded that the Spanish invader having been momentarily brought to a standstill before the gates of Prato—a small city constituting the last fort capable of stopping him on the road to Florence—the government thought it could reject the conditions of peace that had been offered it. By such a refusal, it aroused the fury of the adversary, lost Prato, and, overwhelmed by fear, did not even consider organizing the defense of Florence. Machiavelli maintains, in this connection, that they had to accept paying a tribute to the Spanish and abandon the French alliance—two requirements presented by the ambassadors of Ramon Cardona—since the life of the republic had been spared (*il popolo . . . rimanendo vivo*). And, noting that such a deal constituted a victory for the Florentines, he comments on the decision adopted in terms reminiscent of the problem of a game of chance: "They should not—even if they had the possibility of a greater victory, or the certainty of one—have left things to the discretion of fortune and staked their last bet on it, a bet no one makes if he is prudent, unless driven to it by necessity." The Florentine government thus appears in the image of the soldier who has nothing behind him, and bets his whole fortune at one time, for lack of retreat lines. The folly of that conduct is, moreover, contrasted with the prudence of Hannibal, who, on his return to Carthage after sixteen years of glory in Italy, finds the city reduced to the limits of its own walls and without any other power than its army; "knowing that it was, for his country, the last stake, he was unwilling to risk it before having tried another remedy; he does not blush to ask for peace . . . Peace having been refused, he did not want to omit doing battle, even if he should lose, judging that he could still win, or lacking that, lose gloriously." In the decision of the Florentine government we find condensed all the traits of the modern discourse on war, but they are also explained in such a way as to leave no doubt about the author's thought. The government's presumption is shown by its vain hope in a greater victory, its idea of honor that blinds it to necessity, and finally its inability to conduct the war. This presumption is driven by the illusion of omnipotence. As opposed to Hannibal, who knows the peace-war alternative, and understands what an ultimate gamble really means, the Florentines know neither how to wage war nor how to make peace, and they play their last card without realizing that it is in fact the last one, that is, as if death were not taken into account. On observing this, we understand that victory in war is not at all the same thing as real success in confronting the enemy. The writer purposely stresses the fact that the Florentines had victory in their hands in yielding to the Spanish ultimatum, that is, in accepting a half-defeat. We discover at the same time that knowledge of what is necessary does not exclude concession; furthermore, the critique of compromise in theory founds the legitimacy of the practice of compromise: it is in saving ourselves from the false lure of a *via del mezzo* that we obtain the power to come to terms with an adversary. The teaching of Chapter 27 thus completes that of Chapter 23: the logic of the decision is detached from the empirical level on which we normally perceive the diversity of political choices, whereas it allows us to assign to this level the true significance of every choice; before this logic, the coherence of the Florentine politics is fully revealed, because the extraordinary thing about the decision made on the eve of the disaster of Prato is that it reveals the necessary reversal of a politics of cowardice into one of presumption. While one might be tempted to impute to the psychology of the actor the meaningless response he gives to the adversary, it must be admitted that it is within the norm of the lack of understanding that secretly organizes the behavior of an authority without real power: the practice of least risk, neutrality, opportunism, a mercenary politics that makes money the basis of diplomacy and war, finds its necessary complement and ending in 1512 in the sudden and mad temerity of a government that, faced with a limit-situation, invokes the honor of the City, refuses to pay the price of independence, and the moment it must do battle takes flight.

But Machiavelli's way of introducing his critique of the government of Florence is no less remarkable than the lesson it teaches. Beginning with Chapter 26, the discourse is organized around the question of the word, as it was organized in the preceding chapters around that of the representation. That these two questions share a privileged link we could have anticipated, in observing that invisible domination and invisible conquest was mediated among the Romans by the word. Machiavelli had not failed to point out that Rome's greatest cleverness was to call the peoples they subjugated *compani*. In Chapter 23, which formulated the alternative of repression or confidence, he quoted Camillus's words before the senate, but above all he related at length the dialogue between the senators and some citizens of Privernum who had come to implore the indulgence of Rome after the revolt of their city. This dialogue, the only one related in the book, not only concluded with a verdict of clemency, but it displayed the quality and reciprocal effects of words on the part of both parties. In Machiavelli's view, we are compelled to agree that if at times words are vain and only actions effective, in other circumstances the word [*parole*] affects history: through it, the Privernates are saved and, so it appears, the Romans obtain their security. It also turns out that the Romans—who were certainly not naïve, and knew that the given word [*parole*] could be retracted if need be—did not neglect the virtue of words and their binding power. Now, in Chapter 26, the writer claims to demonstrate that "insults and invectives arouse hatred for those who use them without bringing them anything useful"; he further specifies his purpose in the first lines of the text, in observing that it is a sign of great prudence to abstain from wounding someone by words, for the threat puts the other on his guard, and the wound arouses hatred which calls for vengeance. This argument is, at first sight, one of those that disconcert: drawn from the preceding chapter, which denounced, on the strength of the example of the Veiians, the vanity of open maneuvers intended to take advantage of the dissentions of a city, it seems to reduce the analysis to the level of the anecdotal. At most it prompts the reader to recognize the similarity of behavior that may be observed within and without the city, since both the examples adduced to denounce the negative effect of offensive language bring the consul Valerius Corvinus on stage—he who, after having quelled the rebellion of Capua, issued edicts imposing severe sentences on those who might be tempted to insult the soldiers compromised in that affair, and Tiberius Gracchus who, having armed some slaves to fight against Hannibal, decreed the pain of death against anyone who scoffed at their slavery. But we must assume that it is in fact the status of the word [*parole*] that interests him, on discovering that Chapter 27—the one that gives us a definitive lesson on the weakness of the Florentine Republic—begins with a new critique of the offensive word: "The use of disparaging words toward an enemy," he says, "is most often the result of the insolence aroused by victory or the false hope of victory." This time we have a different reason for surprise: all the examples brought to bear in support of this judgment are limited to presenting erroneous decisions, dictated by presumption, that make an actor, rather than accept the lesser evil, resume hostilities to his detriment. Nothing is said about how the decisions were announced. Now, the same argument furnishes the matter of Chapter 28, the particular interest of which is to challenge the glorious Roman Republic. Machiavelli makes us recognize the error Rome itself committed in not punishing the three ambassadors it had sent to the Gauls, to dissuade them from attacking Clusium. The ambassadors, according to Livy, joined the Tuscans and threw themselves into the battle. Not only did the senate not honor the Gauls' complaint, but it did not fear to elevate the ambassadors to the rank of consular tribune. Thus we understand that the substitution of a hostile action in the place of an expected word [*parole*] has the same effect as an offensive word or the turning down of a reasonable proposition. It becomes clear that the ambassadors, the three Fabii, did not deliver the message they were supposed to deliver, and that they behaved, in the author's own words, "as men who were better at acting than speaking" (*più atti a fare che a dire*); this last detail confirms that those who believe the word is vain not only err, but do not know what the [spoken] word [*parole*] is. But we also understand something else; for it proves that the silence with which Rome meets the complaint of the Gauls, and Rome's other action, which is not even directed toward them—the appointment of the guilty to the highest rank of the state—is far more serious than the silence and action of the ambassadors. In order to have us appreciate the precise significance of this, Machiavelli exploits another example, of which he expressly says that there is none other more true and more beautiful (*non ci è il più bello ne il più vero esemplo . . .*), and that, as he points out at the end of his commentary, is "completely similar to that of the Romans and worthy of the attention of all who govern." Now, this example is not only remarkable because once again it identifies the Roman Republic with a tyrant, in this case Philip of Macedon, but also because it teaches once more that the events that involve the relationship between states sometimes elicit the same analysis as those that take place inside the City. Such, at any rate, is the first lesson we draw from the comparison. Pausanias, a young nobleman in the court of Philip, after having been raped by someone close to the prince, whose advances he had rejected, and, worse yet, delivered to the abuse of his friends, demands redress in vain. Not only are his pleas unanswered, but the aggressor is elevated to the rank of governor by Philip, and Pausanias, transferring his hatred against Philip, murders him. But the most important thing here is to configure the scenario appropriate to making the truth of the Roman example manifest.

Three protagonists are put on stage: the victim, the culprit, and the third party, who has authority over the culprit. The culprit is deprived of the science of the word; incapable of convincing or of seducing, he violates the *ius gentium*, Machiavelli points out, or a *giovane bello e nobile;* the authority covers the crime with his silence, and takes a measure that, without doing wrong to the victim, gives its stamp of approval to this silence by an action through distance; the victim does not avenge himself on the culprit but on the one who does not answer him; silence fulfills the function of the offending word, which for the nonce was replaced by the lack of the expected word. There is no better way Machiavelli could have suggested that the status of the word cannot be conceived, if we remain in the register of the empirical word and of the distinction between the empirical action and the empirical word. In identifying the word with silence—which is not the lack of the word, a sheer deficiency displayed by the stupid men of war, the three Fabii—but which reveals the intimate efficacy of the word [*parole*], the weight of its message, he brings out the symbolic dimension of war. There is no more beautiful nor truer example, nor, I will add, more at the heart of the political, than that of a private citizen who is privately subjected to violence and humiliation, but who thinks to take vengeance on the aggressor, makes the infraction public, and only himself becomes an aggressor when the material injury has become a legal one. It teaches that all action is shaped by the contours of legitimacy; it decries the stupidity of the modern experts of war, who, after the image of the three Fabii, are fully confident in their knowledge once they have taken into account the combinations of force and clandestine contrivances. Now, this teaching prompts us to return to the function of representation in war and politics. When we asserted that domination and conquest require, on the part of the actor, knowledge of the image he gives of himself along with knowledge of the self-image projected by others, we remained within the limits of the description of the relation between two adversaries, and only partially elucidated its foundation in linking it to the relation between the governing power and the people. It now proves to be the case that power's access to representation is tied to its access to the word, that is, to the symbolic function that is assigned to it of being, qua third party, the agent of the law. How can we overlook the fact that the examples of Chapter 27 bring three adversaries on stage? This scenario refers to that of the conflict that is played out within the city between the prince, the people, and the Grandees. And we must understand—by recalling the analysis of *The Prince*—that the prince is not only a third force, detached in fact from the two former ones in their struggle with each other (as the wily Pope whose greatest cleverness is to be the spoiler imagines)—but that he arises out of a division, that of the state and civil society, which is not simply added to the division between classes, but transposes it into a new register, or represents a kind of reflection of it, and in this sense instigates the symbolic order of politics.

It remains true that the incapacity of the state to take full measure of the function of representation in politics is to be explained on the basis of the position occupied by the power within it, that is, on the basis of the misunderstanding of its relation to the people. But that relation, we must not forget, is not dual; it is mediated by the one it has with the dominant class: a power that covers with its silence the aggression committed by the Grandees against the plebs arouses hatred against itself and exposes itself to the danger of being overthrown. While it is true that the weakness of a state comes from its being cut off from its real source of power, it is also true that this power can only be manifested indirectly, thanks to the repression of the appetites of the Grandees and the mediating function of a language in which the principle of domination and that of the law are conjoined.

From this analysis it can by no means be concluded that the relations between the states are regulated in the same way as the relations between the protagonists in the drama that is the internal history of the city. Indeed, if there is a *ius gentium*, no authority can be its guarantor. The notion of a universal right, we understand, absolutely does not erase the fact of the limit experienced by every political society in its own place, that is, the fact of the division between inside and outside. Indeed, the error would be to imagine that as a consequence of that limit the Other is reduced to the definition of a force that one appropriates or to which one must submit; the error would be to conceive anew the limit in an empirical space in which the states are given to the observer in coexistence and competition. Quite to the contrary, one must recognize that from the impossibility for each state to master the space of the world, from the confrontation of each with the threat of death, threat borne by the stranger, from the enormity that is the junction with the Other, there surges forth the anonymous reference to the Law—a reference without which the internal organization of the city would fall apart. The same reason, in this sense, is behind the fact of there being, for a state, a relation to necessity and a relation to the Law; the power to rise to the logic of the Decision that sets in motion the ordeal of the alternative and power of submitting to the imperative of the *ius gentium.* The same reason is behind the fact that Soderini does not know the stakes of the negotiation with the Spanish and Rome does not know that of its dialogue with the Gauls. And the same reason dictates that the Gauls are for the Romans the agents of the implacable war that Chapter 8 led us to understand had the function of a natural cataclysm; that is, they are messengers of death, and they are those who come to them to press the claim of the *ius gentium* and to remind the greatest power of the day of the dangers of denying it.

Machiavelli's analysis, as we have already pointed out, comes to its conclusion in Chapter 30, which joins the truth of politics to that of war, in teaching that at the origin of the powerlessness of the modern states and the falsity of the dominant discourse lies the choice of the princes who disarmed their people the better to pillage them and assuage their present appetite. But it is worth observing that this conclusion does not close the book. In the following chapter, the writer reconsiders, from a different perspective, the mistakes of the princes who allow themselves to be blinded by a vain hope—mistakes the most remarkable of which was illustrated by the Florentine government's refusal of the Spanish ultimatum of 1512. Though the event is not brought up here, we cannot consider it off-limits to think that the theme of the discussion, "How Perilous It Is to Put Confidence in the Exiled," is well suited to lead us back to it, since the exiled of the Medici clan were on the side of the Spanish who were preparing to attack Florence. Once again the argument is presented as a digression—a digression that justifies itself, moreover, by a digression in Livy himself. Now, we know how dangerous it is to give credence to remarks that are outside the main topic (*fuora del presupposito*). It is true that to all appearances it is not possible to transfer to the Florentine scene the plot of the king of Epirus, fooled and eventually murdered by

Lucanian exiles with whom he had surrounded himself in hopes that they would help to deliver their country to him. At the most, we can only recall that the Medici had bragged about provoking an uprising in Florence at the approach of the Spanish, and that they had lied. But if we notice that the place of the victim, the king of Epirus, is occupied by Soderini, we are prompted to imagine a different transposition: was not the mad temerity of the latter the result of secret dealings with a fraction of his political adversaries who gave him false information on the situation and the arrangements of the enemy? Might not the delirium of presumption of the head of the Florentine government have a more precise political expression than we supposed if it turned out that the error committed was caused by a faulty understanding of the political conflict within the city? The hypothesis, in the absence of more convincing indications, must be left hanging. But it should be remarked that it has the merit of clarifying the argument of the last two chapters of the book. Under the pretext of showing how the Romans proceeded in occupying lands, Machiavelli brings out the tactics of a combatant who has confidence in mass movement and mass offensive tactics; he depreciates ruse, and particularly of that sort that exploits the complicity of defectors; he critiques the customary practice of attacking towns, observing that it forces the assailant to become immobilized in long and costly sieges. These remarks—and there is no reason, by the way, to doubt that they are faithful to the author's thinking—taken in their literalness, are so lacking in justification at the end of the discourse that it is tempting to connect them with the critique of Soderini's government. Are we not to understand that he did not know the proper rules of political warfare; that he had allowed his view to become clouded by the power of opposing factions, had become bogged down in palace maneuvers, put his confidence in intermediaries resolved to fool him or, because they belonged to the oligarchy, were fated to do so? Are we not meant to see that, like Aratus of Sicyon, who excelled in night attacks conducted by surprise and proved to be pusillanimous in broad daylight, he was able enough to get himself elevated to the level of Gonfalonier for life by his adversaries, to the general astonishment, and cowardly enough to abandon Florence when the aggressor was at the gates of the city? Are we not to understand that he did not know what true strength was, and what true ruse, how to mobilize the mass of combatants and how the ground is taken away from under an adversary's feet by depriving him, through reforms, which are tantamount to so many incursions into his territory, of the arm of demagogy? From this point of view the last example borrowed from Livy is instructive, in which we see a Roman military leader conducting his army across "a new, uncertain, and dangerous territory," without worrying about the senate's authority that, at the same time, forbids the enterprise. Presented to illustrate the observation that the Romans gave their military leaders free rein, he ironically but silently modifies its significance, suggesting that, where authority is affirmed, it is not afraid to sidestep legality and discover new pathways. Fabius, turning a deaf ear to the senate's warning, a man of decision, offers a far better antithesis to Soderini, as sensitive as this last seems to be to all the voices supporting the illusion of his omnipotence.

If we are right, the last four chapters draw the reader toward the point at which the Republic of Florence fell apart. This point is beyond doubt for the Florentine contemporary with Machiavelli the one at which the effects of the Christian discourse on politics and war are revealed most clearly. But the hypothesis must not make us neglect the last contribution Machiavelli makes to the analysis of power. The argument of Chapter 31, when it establishes that a prince cannot entrust himself without danger to exiles, furnishes a new link in the chain of the critique of the [spoken] word. What is denounced, after the insulting word, the presumptive word, the lack of the due word, is listening to the false word—the word of the other who lies to us and to himself. With this link, the analysis moves on to its conclusion, because the illusion of omnipotence now proves to govern all the prince's relations to the word [*parole*]. Whether it be that the prince says more than is necessary—that he talks too much—or that he is silent when he should speak, or that he is prone to listen to the seductive word, it is always vain certainty, vain hope, the lure of mastery, that conceals from him the place he occupies in the symbolic order and that at the same time closes him up in a dual relation in which the other is immediately reduced to his own reflection. But above all, this last metamorphosis of the relation to the word makes it possible to move the illusion from omnipotence to the lack of recognition of the division between inside and outside. Indeed, it must be admitted, upon consideration of the twofold figure of the *sbandito,* the *fuoruscito* [exile, refugee], that a prince cannot trade with impunity on the fact of division and its disappearance. With the case of the defector we see the vanity of a solution that would spare itself the risk of war. As a man of the outside, rejected by his city, *sbandito,* he presents himself to the prince as someone who still belongs to it and can get him into it. As a man who has come from the outside to the prince, *fuoruscito,* he presents himself as being on his side. Because of this ambiguous provenance, he occupies the mythic position of the intermediary; he is the figure of that *via del mezzo* who hides the alternative. It is not the factual use of the defector that matters to Machiavelli; doubtless he approves of the use of men who are traitors to their country if need be, and he knows that a subject wounded in his honor is capable of devoting his efforts to destroying it. If the transfuge and his lying words interest him, it is because they allow him to bring out the defect of a politics that thinks it can elude the necessity of attacking the enemy camp thanks to complicity established with such and such a faction. The fault is that of the Florentine government, which, for example, let itself be hoodwinked in Pisa, through hopes that a false deserter would deliver the gates of the city to it. But it is also the fault of the politician Soderini, who was unable, once he had become the head of state, to choose his side openly and combat his internal enemies head-on. And perhaps it is the fault of all the parties of the Florentine bourgeoisie who dodge the requirement of open conflict and play the stealthy game of guile, fooling each other—unto the downfall of the government.

In taking the full measure of this critique, the argument of Chapter 22 becomes clear. This chapter draws attention to the style of the Roman war, and beyond that to a style of action (that of the war of movement and of the word [*parole*] of alliance), that breaks with the illusion of a materialized power—the symbol of which is the town or the siege—and with that of omnipotence—the symbol of which is the false assurance of the ruse. And we are better able to understand the last image, that of the innovative war leader who does not trust the words of the senators, which are doubtless not mendacious, but are vain, because coming from outside the theater of war and falsely pretending to administer it.

Thus understood, the last three chapters of the book bring a teaching that sheds new light on its entirety. It no longer suffices to understand that the relation of the state to the people is linked to the one it has with the world of the outside; nor that the internal division and the external division are necessarily interrelated, and yet irreducible to one another. The sign of each is discovered in the space governed by the other. The position of the state vis-à-vis other states reappears within the city, as that of the political actor—whether a man or a party—vis-à-vis other actors. Protagonists in a conflict whose outcome is determined by the effects of internal division, by the actual course of the class struggle, these actors are nevertheless strangers to one another, subjected to the test of the limit, confronted with the alternative. Just as, as I have said, the position of the central power vis-à-vis the people reappears in the world of the outside, as that of Might forced to undertake the quest of the consent of the Other and to respect the *ius gentium*.

In the final analysis, the object of Machiavelli's discourse in Book 2 is neither the moral guidance of the power of Rome, nor the difference between ancient and modern warfare; nor is it war in general, nor the relationship between politics and war, nor the Christian discourse on politics and war. For us, its readers, it would be giving in to the illusion of materialized power to want to seize upon these objects and assign them a function of knowledge. But neither can we dispense with the work of discovery and destruction of these objects, and deprive the discourse of its moorings to time and place, and make it speak the timeless language of metaphysics. For thus we would forget that the reading draws on the invisible wellsprings of the experience of the agent's own times and places, and that interpretation is itself activation of temporal difference.

10

Authority and the Political Subject

The history of Rome does not fit, then, into the closed space to which some thought Livy had relegated it. And those who go looking in the Anthology of the Great Classics for the narration of the discourses or exploits of their supposed ancestors, merely distance themselves from that history. They do not know the logic that underlies the events, the institutions, and the actions of the Romans; but if they do not know it, it is because they do not want to; for in deciphering a meaning in the past, they should also seek it in the present. Thus, what is hidden behind the enjoyment they are afforded by exempla and maxims, blending aesthetic pleasure with moral exaltation, is the defeat of knowledge. In Florence, the grandeur of Rome is praised, Livy, Plutarch, and Cicero are quoted, but only to avoid the question posed by the extraordinary ascendency of a republic doomed to class conflict and war. They play with history, they approach the point at which its truth is best recognized, they enjoy the spectacle of it, but only to annul its effects, convert it into myth, wipe away the traces of a human adventure and maintain the grandeur of Florence. Machiavelli ruses with that ruse. He elevates the praise of Rome to its highest level, himself presenting copious examples and maxims; but he mixes in with the most exalted ones less celebrated exempla, attaching to fond recollection other facts, both ancient and modern, and fashions them in such a way as to cause them to lose their luster, detaching them from imaginary constellations in which they had taken on the purity of diamond and the rigidity of inimitable models, taking them back to the milieu in which the thoughts and actions of men were nourished before being transformed into objects of representation.

The knowledge thus opened up to us is not only that of Rome, for as we turn toward that milieu, rending the screen onto which the Florentine, the spectator of his own phantasmagoria, projects the image of the past, reawakening the time when the Roman enterprise was being improvised, unfurling the field of possibilities in which the path of the real is cleared for it, the writer conjures up the properly historical dimension of every society—first and foremost that of the society of his own time.

At the end of Book 2, we are in a better position to appreciate

the Proem placed at the beginning of the work. When, after having announced that he was taking a completely new path, Machiavelli worried
about the weakness of his means and recognized the power of others to
go further, his assurance and his reservations were justly measured. If he
had no doubts about the truth of his undertaking, and yet at the same
time thought it might be better conducted, that is because in his view it
went beyond the reconstitution of the facts or the explanation of their
concatenation. Perhaps he was saying that his intelligence was too weak to
sustain it; perhaps he was too well informed of the things of the present,
too little informed of those of the past; perhaps his efforts were insufficient; but at least the way was opened up through which others would be
able to go forward. Thus he let it be understood that his work was commanded by an idea of history that transcended the order of empirical
knowledge. He suggested in particular that there were other possible
points of departure than his own to think what he wanted to think, and
that reflection on politics and history were not necessarily mediated by
an analysis of the events of Rome or of Livy's text. Of course we must be
wary of attributing to the writer a clear consciousness of the contingency
of his point of departure. The materials he gathers and organizes—he
does not choose them from on high, among other possible ones, as the
best suited to his task; nor does he choose from the arsenal of rhetoric the
most effective procedures for winning over his reader. I have said that his
discourse is structured in such a way as to sow the seeds of doubt in that
reader's mind, to reassure him and unsettle him successively in order to
gradually free him from mythical representations of the past and eventually bring him to admit that all societies are caught up in the same history,
exposed to the same accidents, torn by the same strife, ordered in keeping with choices that, while escaping the will of individuals, bear nonetheless the trace of a human intention. But still, the writer's approach is
tributary to the conditions imposed upon him by his time. The fact that
he must speak of Rome in order to speak of history, and that he relies
on examples to introduce the principles that govern the development
of societies and the action of the political Subject—this is not the result
of a free decision. He diverges from the common way of thinking, but
that divergence is executed in relation to terms that govern up to and
including their opposites. He finesses, as we have noted, with the Other's
knowledge, but that ruse puts him once again in the dependency of those
whom he opposes. His critique, however—though tributary, in its presuppositions, its goals, and the very movements it describes, to the milieu in
which it is carried out—goes beyond and knows it goes beyond its manifest
goal. It does much more than jar a particular representation of the past
and the values recognized by an historically determined society—much

more than shift, within a given field of knowledge, the boundary markers of the traditional itineraries; it leads one to think that which, in all situations, is dissimulated: the difference between a transcendental and an empirical history—between an operating history and a represented one; the difference, consequently, between instituted politics in the form of actual regimes and an instituting politics from which all actual regimes derive. Now, it is indeed in meditating on Rome that Machiavelli thinks that difference, but it is also true that only that thought and no other teaches him to meditate on Rome and that it surpasses all the particular terms that may come along to support it. It is indeed in contingent circumstances that he acquires the power to rise to an idea of history that is not in history, and to an idea of politics that is not political. By virtue of ways of knowing inherited from the past, on the basis of an experience shared with the men of an era, regardless of whatever limitation these conditions may impose upon his mind, the power that has in fact been gained is of such a nature that by other means, in other circumstances, others will be able to make it their own and augment its effect.

What Machiavelli does not say, however, but that we can say in his stead, because it is given to us to be able to observe at once the misadventures to which his oeuvre has been exposed and the newer ways of misreading history, is that, contingency never being abolished, the two possibilities are always given to whoever turns toward politics: to move further forward along the path previously opened, or to seal the opening and enclose knowing [savoir] once again within the limits of empirical knowledge [connaissance] and ideology. This alternative is decided most often in favor of the second option. Thus in *The Discourses* readers denounce the archaism of the Roman model and the use of examples in complete ignorance of their critical function. Attached to the truths of positive science, and more clandestinely to the modern idea of historical reason, they cannot—nor do they wish to—know anything about an analysis of Rome that is unfavorable to all forms of idealization of the past, nor about an interpretation of Livy's narration that strikes out preemptively against all forms of the reduction of meaning to the level assigned to it by exact knowledge [connaissance].

It is true that Machiavelli, in focusing on Roman history, concerns himself with the history of a state whose foundation, fall, and adventures carry dates and figures that stand out in the dimension of the past, but he gives that history a status that forbids our relegating it to the level of a series of empirical facts. In a sense, that history is not in time; it does not fill a portion of universal time in the same way the City once carved out its empire in the space of the world; it does not coincide with the series of events and institutions in which we find its trace, since those events are only connected to one another within a single development by attesting to the genesis of a meaning. On the other hand it would be absurd to say that it is outside time: it only appears thus when, converted into myth, the Florentines make it speak the better to keep silent about their own time—and about the temporality of their own society—or when one invokes a spirit of the State, or perhaps Providence, or Fortune, to assign an occult cause to dark forces one does not wish to confront. But because it does not have its place there either, because we can only think it by discovering, beyond the multiplicity of events and institutions, the relations they have to one another and, beyond these relations, the form in which they are stabilized and tend to remain, and in that form itself the sign of a style of organization and development, a unique design of historicity and socialization, we would not be able to get back to its source without identifying other forms, other styles of existence of the state, without assessing the variations presented by political regimes, more or less corrupt societies, social classes, civil conflict, war—in sum, without interrogating the politics of history in all the known modes of possibility.

This investigation—we would be distorting its nature were we to think it is the response to the need for comparison. True, Rome supplies the framework of empirical givens with which other givens coming from other frameworks can be confronted; but meaning is not generated by a census of differences and similarities seen between series of events and institutions. In a certain way, Rome must give us everything to see *in itself* if we are to be able to see outside its borders the multiplicity of the forms of the state. Roman history only teaches us how to read universal history because we decipher already in its own horizons all the signs of politics, because tyrannies and monarchies are implied in the republic, all the traits of class domination in the patriciate, all the traits of subjection and resistance of the dominated in those of the plebs, all the modalities of war in the elaboration of Roman power; because in the final analysis the forces of cohesion that allow themselves to be discovered are only determined in relation to the forces of dissociation that work on [*travaillent*] the social body, as they do universally.

No doubt what I have just said about Rome should apply to any other state. For if it is true that Rome is not just one historical individual among others—a term the identity of which we could name, in compounding a certain number of empirical characteristics and contrasting it with other terms within a definite spatiotemporal field—then one must recognize for the same reasons that we never encounter pure *individuals*, terms enclosed within the boundaries of one place or period; that every state, because it testifies to a singular elaboration of its conditions of existence, causes us to suppose other courses than its own, allows us to intuit the forbidden or repressed possibilities from which it turns away, and shows, in short, in the factual solution it finds, the universality of the political problem to which it responds. How could the difference between empirical and transcendental history be attached to a moment or a place? No more than Rome does Florence, for example, exist in time. And when we follow, in *The Discourses*, the intertwined accounts of past and present facts, we sometimes think that Florence, no less than Rome, is the milieu that illumines all history. But if it is not necessary, the choice of Rome as point of reference is not accidental either, and it does not suffice even to find its symbolic function in Florentine society to appreciate its full importance. Rome has the virtue of revealing the historical dimension of all society because it is carried by a temporality, of which we find the equivalent nowhere else, because instead of trying to close itself up once and for all within the limits of a constitution, crystallize in the form of a certain social relation, and only be transformed under the brutal outside effect of the event, it makes it a law of its existence to put what it has achieved constantly back in play; because the succession of its enterprises, each of which forces it to risk its security and imagine new means to expand its empire over other states, is articulated with an inner change, a progress in differentiation, the expression and opposition of classes, which forces it simultaneously to invent new institutions, to link the requirement of its conservation with that of an historical creation. Caught up in the irrationality of war and the class struggle, worked by the desires that deepen the division of warring groups and secrete the violence of oppression and protest, or else only work together in aggression and against foreign peoples and conquest, apparently finding equilibrium and power only thanks to a spontaneous selection of accidents, Roman society, in Machiavelli's view, is at the same time that place in which the conditions of a conscious reprise of the collective adventure are instituted, in which the possibility is given for a just measure of action, that is, a test of reality in which means and ends are organized, and in which, for men invested with authority, the function of the political Subject is delineated.

The history of Florence and that of Rome are therefore not symmetrical; the passage from one to the other is not simply that of the negative to the positive and, although they shed mutual light on each other, it is not true that they offer us the same access to truth. The logic that commands the organization and development of the ancient city also commands those of the modern city, but we can only discover it where it is embodied and makes itself visible in the play of determinations of a society occupied with transforming itself, that is to say, in those of a popular and conquering republic, not where it is in hiding, in the obverse of the necessity that precipitates the decadence of the oligarchic

Florentine state. Roman society furnishes the intelligible framework of all the other plans of development because it contains their adumbrations and only forbids their immediate outcome by deferring the conclusions toward which they tend, that is, by transferring to the future the chances held open in the present. It is true that these embryonic sketches of development must be seen translated in the reality of other societies before they can be understood as foreshadowed in Rome; but that reality in itself is mute; to make it speak we must discover—in the peripeteia undergone by modern states, in their defeats and victories, the progress and regression that seems the result of randomness, the fluctuations of power relations—that trace of the defeated meaning of which Rome was the guarantor.

But it is one thing to learn to decipher in the Roman text the universal language of politics, to relate the present to the past and the past to the present, in such a way that they lose their boundaries and melt into one sole history discoverable by a sole body of knowledge, and quite another to try to reactivate that language within a society that has become deaf to it, to manage to make that knowledge *here and now* an arm in the battle of politics. At the end of the second book, we cannot avoid wondering about the practical significance of Machiavelli's discourse. Clearly, as we see him decrying the errors of the Florentines in politics and war, we get the idea that he is prescribing new methods of action; but the critique, though based on specific examples, always uses those particular cases to develop a fundamental opposition. Between Rome and Florence, there is a general difference that dims down the resemblance of their forms of government in such a way that in one setting felicitous measures taken are the exception, and most often the result of chance, while in the other each favorable measure seems to bring on and encourage more of the same, leading to a distinctive style. In one setting, everything conspires to the decline of the body politic, to its being frittered away into factions, to the isolation of those in power and the military weakness of the state, whereas in the other the play of internal divisions and wars, though bearing the same characteristics, tends to reinforce at once the power of each class and of the City. In light of this, how can we believe that the critique of errors presents, as the positive of its negative, the definition of right actions? They form a cortege that cannot be broken. Every time we think we are putting our finger on the ignorance, stupidity, or cowardice of an actor, we must admit that his role is being dictated by others. The present intrigues turn out to be commanded by conventions—the meanings of which escape the consciousness of every individual—that rule out a new style of political interaction. Thus, whatever interest one may take in discovering the effect of these conventions on the actions of the individuals involved and the general course of events, especially the fate of Florence, one must be content with knowing, with tasting, as one reads history, the "savor it contains." Now let us not forget that Machiavelli denounced this pleasure at the beginning of his work, and that he made the desire to "act"—a desire he calls proper to youth—a condition of the search for truth. Is his discourse unfaithful to his first purpose, then, or is the moment to assess its practical significance yet to come?

It is a fact that in the first book there are many passages discrediting the hope for clear-sighted and effective action within a society sunk in repetition, in which the debility of power, the fractionalizing of conflicts, the retreat of each individual to the limitations of personal profit, the subjugating dependency on foreign arms, and the exhausting dreams of grandeur destroy, increasingly with every passing day, the conditions necessary for a revolution. Machiavelli observes in Chapter 18, "The constitution of a state, once one has discovered that it cannot serve, must be changed either all at once or gradually, before everyone perceives its vices. Now, both of these methods are almost equally impossible." On the second hypothesis, he comments, it is doubtful that an individual will suddenly appear who is capable of exposing the evil at its source, and even if he does appear, his advice will not be listened to, so imprisoned are men by custom, rebellious to change, and disinclined to know what is not immediately perceptible by the senses. On the first hypothesis, that the use of violence and the institution of a dictatorship are necessary, it is even more doubtful that a generous and honest man will decide to cross the boundaries of the law, or that an ambitious and wicked man, after having transgressed it, should convert into a loyal servant of the state. This doubt is so strong that no example is given that leaves the reader with any hope. Evoking the case of Romulus, Machiavelli is quick to point out that he would not have been able to turn his authority to good use after his first crimes if the Roman people had already been largely corrupted. In another passage, Florence is the object of an explicit criticism, apparently without recourse. Compared to Rome, which was not spared, despite its original independence, adventures that nearly brought about its downfall, Florence appears incapable of removing the original marks of its servitude and is long doomed to perish from its disorders. It is one of those states that feel "not only difficulty, but an impossibility of being able to live in order and peace." Furthermore, the freedom it proudly displays is but a trompe l'oeil: "It continued thus for two centuries for which we have reliable records, without ever having a state such as to truly merit the name of republic." Such judgments seem to condemn all attempts at reform to failure. It is the judgments of the historian or the philosopher that discredit action in the present. True, the principle of a new politics is proclaimed, and one cannot neglect this under the pretext that no one wants to or is able to bring it about. Thus in Chapter 39—in which the thesis of the permanence of the desires and humors of man is formulated, as well as the further thesis, derived from it, of the perpetual return of the same political ills—the idea that an action founded on the knowledge of history is possible is vigorously asserted. This is the idea that one can make use of the remedies once discovered by the Romans, or invent new ones by the comparison between ancient and modern events. The repetition of the accidents that bring about the downfall of states thus no longer appears as an ineluctable phenomenon; it becomes a result of the ignorance of history. It is, in the writer's judgment, because we neglect to question history that we are incapable of understanding its meaning, or because those who hold power refuse to let themselves be enlightened by men instructed in the things of the past; in other words, it is due to a lack of knowledge that the contemporary societies sink into corruption. In theory, the chances for change have therefore not been lost. But there remains the doubt that in a corrupt society knowledge is ever associated with authority, that a politician can want to be a reformer, and that he can succeed in making himself heard.

It is only toward the end of the first book that the author affirms his conviction that great changes remain possible in Tuscany. "There is such great equality there," he observes, "that it would be very easy for a wise man who knew the constitution of the ancient republics to establish a free government there. But so great has the misfortune of that country been that no one has thus far been found with the power and knowledge to do it" [Chapter 55]. After the stern analysis of the corruption that reigns in Italy, this language is disconcerting. The reader has difficulty in believing that the transformations to be accomplished would not encounter very great obstacles, and that malevolent misfortune alone is all that has deprived Tuscany till now of the means of a renewal. He cannot but recognize that Machiavelli's discourse holds him in a contradiction. One minute the road to reform is open, the next closed. Yet there are certain indications that lead one to think that this is not a hesitation or an alternation between pessimism and optimism. When Machiavelli speaks of the chances that remain open to Tuscany, the remarks occur in a section of the book that evokes, without naming them, recent events, and treats the relation of the people to authority. Two chapters earlier, he notes that the people, often deceived by false appearances of good, desire their own downfall, and immediately specifies: "If what is good and what is bad is not inculcated by someone in whom they [the people] have confidence, the republic is exposed to the greatest dangers, but when chance would have it that the people have faith in no one, which sometimes occurs when in the past they have been deceived either by events or by men, the state must inevitably perish." No mention is made there of the Republic of Florence, but we cannot help remembering the conditions in which that government collapsed: the mass of Florence's humble folk who had hated the Medici did not try to fight off the approaching Spanish; they had lost all confidence in the liberal faction of the republican oligarchy that dominated it and had known too many defeats to continue to believe in the virtue of the military leaders. Now, that observation is followed by another, which shows, on the other hand, how appreciative the people are of a capably applied authority—people in the sense of the mass whose outbursts make the bourgeoisie tremble. His goal is clearly to convince the reader that he must not let himself be obsessed by the fear of popular uprisings. Finally, the democratic thesis is affirmed a little further along in this important chapter, in which the merits of the people are compared to those of princes, and found to be superior. This chapter suggests at once that the danger of a revolt of the mass is less than that of a tyranny, and that the people (that is, the oppressed class), once won over to the laws of a republic that knows how to give them their rightful place, are the real strength of the state. Thus we are prompted to think that a reformer could succeed in his enterprise if he had an understanding of the true relationship that a central power must develop with the people, and the means of establishing it; if he took the risk of breaking with those who have fooled or disappointed him, that is, with the entire bourgeois oligarchy, be it pro- or anti-Medici; and lastly, if he did not hesitate to raise a people's army.

The indications at the end of Book 1 are insufficient, however, to dispel our doubts. And Book 2 raises new doubts when it expresses the hypothesis that the Romans themselves were not the conscious artisans of their history. It is true that at the beginning of this second book the writer strongly denies that Rome's fate was the work of Fortune or the gods, and does not hesitate to criticize the opinion of Plutarch, and of Livy, whom he claims to be his model. Rome created its good luck, he maintains, and every state of comparable *virtù* would have received the same help from circumstances; this *virtù* is attested by the principles of conduct (*l'ordine del procedere*) and extreme prudence (*prudenza grandissima*) of the political actors [Chapter 1]. But in the last section of the book, the analysis of an event, the taking of Rome by the Gauls, brings about an odd reversal of perspectives. We must admit that Fortune blinds the mind of men when she does not want them to oppose her designs. Now Livy's authority is reestablished: on this occasion, an occult power was at work to bring about the fall of the City, and then to restore it; it enlisted the agents necessary to the execution of the plan. Hence prudence does not decide the course of events; it is a quality that may or may not find its application, according to a decree that is impenetrable to our understanding. "All men, we are told, who normally live in great prosperity or great hardship deserve less praise or blame than we think. They will usually be seen in ruin or grandeur by an irresistible facility granted them by Heaven—which either denies or offers them an occasion to practice their *virtù*. That is the way Fortune works: when she wants to carry out a great project, she chooses a man with a spirit and *virtù* such that they allow him to recognize the opportunity offered. Similarly, when she prepares the overthrow of an empire, she places at the top men capable of hastening its downfall. Should there be a person strong enough to put a stop to it, she has him murdered or takes away all means of doing anything useful" [Chapter 29]. Now, if we accept this judgment, how can we expect an understanding of history to guide action? How can we not resign ourselves to weakness, when the means of strength are not in the hands of men? It is true that Machiavelli decides against despair: "I repeat as an incontestable truth, the proofs of which abound in history, that men can second Fortune and not oppose her—spin the threads of her warp, not break them. I do not think that for all that they should give up on themselves. They do not know her goal, and since she works only in dark and unknown ways (*andando quella per vie traverse ed incognite*) there is always hope for them, and from that hope they must draw the strength never to give up, in whatever misfortune or misery they may find themselves" [Chapter 29]. But it is, in sum, ignorance that has become hope's recourse. The Florentines, unable to know anything of the ultimate end Fortune has assigned to them, can keep faith in the future and practice political virtue, in hopes that their path may be reopened. If this conclusion is surprising, it is not that Machiavelli ever gave up limiting man's power and knowledge. But the indetermination he vindicated did not disarm his thought. There was no need to imagine a completely positive pendant opposite it in which consciousness and power coincided. To do so would be to render vain the lessons of history. One might devote oneself to the detailed exploration of the signs of Rome's grandeur and decadence, but they would only be signs. The *virtù* of men and laws would bear witness to a divine intervention. One would stand in wonder before the apogee of freedom in the Roman Republic, in the same way that one is astonished to see, without any knowledge of its cause, fire breaking out by rubbing flint: the miracle would not enlighten us.

In the second book, however, as in the first, Machiavelli forces his reader to let go of the ideas he formulates at first. Returning to the example of the fall of Rome, which he used a moment earlier to show the power of Fortune, he again rejects Livy's view. It is not an accident, he notes, that the Romans were able to regain their freedom without having to pay for it; throughout their history they refused to obtain peace or to acquire territory with money; in every case it was to their institutions that they owed their safety. Grappling with the greatest of dangers, Rome proved itself capable of recovering, because it was a popular and armed republic. Nor was it accidental that the modern states do not have the means to protect themselves in adversity, because their governors "have disarmed their peoples the better to rob them, preferring the enjoyment of an immediate profit to a danger more imaginary than real" [Chapter 30]. Henceforth the reader cannot misunderstand; the fate of Rome after the victory of the Gauls is not at all the one that awaited Florence when it was invaded by the Spanish. In Rome, the dissentions that broke out between the patriarchate and the plebs, after the fall of Veientes, had put the regime in peril, but at least the mass who abandoned the City against the advice of the senate to settle on the rich conquered lands did not leave off bearing arms, so that the combat could resume after the disaster. In Florence, however energetic Machiavelli's efforts to create a people's militia were, its recruitment was too timid and too recent, and the upper bourgeoisie's mistrust of the people too ingrained, for a resistance to be organized. "One can assess by these examples," the author notes, "what a distance there is between the conduct of the present-day republics and those of the Greco-Romans, and also why we see every day these miraculous losses and these miraculous conquests."

Miracolose perdite e miracolosi acquisti: here we see the language of ignorance condemned, and the omnipotence of Fortune, so dear to Livy, once more denounced. One conclusion is inescapable: for those who only take seriously what is perceived by the senses, the event is mysterious; it comes necessarily from elsewhere; is propagated from a point outside the field of visibility; what escapes man's gaze is necessarily beneath another gaze—that of the gods. But for those who know how to pierce through the appearances and recognize a logic in history, the event bears a meaning, and this meaning is prepared in the society that receives it; it has the value of an authorization. Machiavelli does not go so far as to reverse the thesis he was advancing; he does not say that Fortune is a mirage, but at present he speaks of her in terms that forbid our imagining a hidden divinity, whose attribute of arbitrariness would be in charge of shaping the destiny of the states: "For where men have little *virtù*," he writes, "Fortune makes her greatest display. And since she is changeable, states and republics often change, and they will go on changing until someone so fervently imbued with antiquity comes along that he orders things in such a way that fortune does not, every time the sun come round again, have occasion to show what she can do." Such language does not represent an absolute break with tradition. But the moment one resists the charm sustained by the image of Fortune, it is immediately apparent that the perspective has changed fundamentally. Instead of understanding that Fortune is changeable, it is sufficient to admit that it is the name given to change—at least to the sort that takes place unbeknownst to the actors, and as a result of their lack of foresight or their inertia—and we will immediately discover the reestablishment of the idea so strongly stated at the beginning of this book: the Romans are the true artisans of their history.

It is true that the question is then reborn: Are we justified in supposing that a man could deliver Florence from corruption and institute a free state? If we reject the myth of an occult power that would use its talents as it pleases to lose or save states, must we not nevertheless recognize that at any given time, in any given city, the government, the institutions, and the mores determine the chances of individual action? Though we admit that political intelligence can be exercised in all situations, we cannot think that it always operates to the advantage of freedom. The highest level of political intelligence is evident in the prince who, in a country of great corruption, deports whole populations, overturns hierarchies, and imposes *ordini nuovi;* or the one who, like Severus, makes his personal authority a rampart against licentiousness. But those men are tyrants. How could a republican reformer succeed in his undertaking? Has Florence not come to such a point of decadence that knowledge is reduced to powerlessness, competent men disdained or exiled, imbeciles or men mad with ambition borne forward to first place? Did not the Romans— who in the context of the City and of their relations with other peoples understood how to ally prudence with daring, bow to necessity when necessary, or go on to the limits of the possible, and make of even of their errors a resource of their experience—draw their *virtù* from the system that bound them to one another? Did not the best impose their authority at the opportune moment as a result of a form of government that gave rational decision-making its best chance? What happens to rational action and decision-making, on the other hand, where they have the least chance of being recognized as such by a people?

The second book brings no answer, but at least its last chapter furnishes a final indication that we have several reasons to believe introduces us to the intention of the last part of the work. In that chapter, titled, "That the Romans Gave Their Army Commanders a Free Hand," the writer draws our attention to the authority of those who carried out a command in the name of the republic in the field. "Furthermore, an object worthy of consideration," he begins by noting, "is the authority they [the Romans] conferred on the consuls, dictators, and other heads of the army: we see that it was very great, and that the senate only reserved the right to decide upon new wars and to confirm peace treaties. It turned all the rest over to the discretion and power (*nello arbitrio e potesta*) of the consul." Certainly the remark had been made in the first book; but the fact of its being reiterated at this stage of the discourse, that is, at the closing of the second book, is already an indication of its importance. Besides, Machiavelli is not satisfied with asserting that a strong republic, far from keeping the citizens on a leash and seeking security in a generalized mistrust, knows how to encourage initiative and delegate its authority; he gives his thesis a reference that modifies its importance significantly. The example given here introduces a famous consul who will be taken up again later, Fabius, who, after having won one victory over the Tuscans, pursued them, indifferent to the orders of the senate, through new, uncertain, and dangerous country (*in paese nuovo dubbio e pericoloso*), the Ciminian forest. Now, we not only praise the senate for having recognized the fait accompli and forsworn punishing the daring leader; we admire him for having gone ahead without worrying about the interdict. His example does much more than illustrate the argument. The important thing is not that Fabius benefits from an authority the heads of modern armies lack, but the fact that he avails himself of it, and specifically in the given circumstances. The image of penetrating the forbidden forest has a symbolic efficacy stronger than the best constructed reasoning. The praise of transgression draws from that source a singular power. Now the fact that this praise comes to us at the conclusion of a long discourse dedicated to the discipline of the Roman armies has for me the value of an admonition. Perhaps, I say to myself, what is meant is that one can act like a Roman outside Rome, since in Rome itself *virtù* did not always call for obedience, and sometimes required the violation of commands.

Such are the thoughts that preoccupy us and make up our expectations at the threshold of Book 3, the manifest purpose of which is to examine the actions of a certain number of Romans and to show the effect they had had on the development of the republic. That this goal acts as a cover for a substantially different intention—I have very good reasons to make that supposition. Not only do I doubt that Machiavelli's aim is to exalt the civic virtues that his contemporaries venerate—the valor of the leader in combat, the devotion of the magistrate to the public weal, respect for the laws—but I suspect once again that he is not so much interested in the Romans themselves and their behavior as in the status of the political Subject, in the conditions of his advent in the ordered field of the institution. I further suspect that the elucidation of this status commands a reflection on the conditions of political practice *hic et nunc*.

Therefore I am not surprised to find that very little space is devoted in the last part of *The Discourses* to the actions of illustrious men. If we imagine we will find there the narration of great exploits, or portraits à la Plutarch, we will have to be disillusioned. Moreover, it is a fact that a very small number of persons among those mentioned escape the author's critique. Still, we must admit that in the first eighteen chapters, there is hardly any discussion of the role played by private citizens in Rome. The only figure who is depicted by Machiavelli without reservations is Brutus, the founder of the republic. Men like Spurius and Manlius Capitolinus are the enemies of Freedom. Twice we are invited not to overestimate the role of the leaders, whose merits must not make us forget those of the mass of fighters. Furthermore, our attention is drawn to the unjust fate of eminent men in republics, and in Rome itself, when the state feels sheltered from danger. The reading of the third book would be decidedly very disappointing if we were to persist in seeing its subject as the actions of the Romans. It bears another, more hidden one.

We need not wait long to see it appear in the text. The first chapter—the very one that the author concludes with a misleading remark—puts us on the right track. While inviting us to conceptualize the phenomenon of the institution, the relationship between authority and law, it prepares us to recognize the position of the political Subject and the modalities of his insertion into reality. Discoveries that will be phased in, in a first moment, by the analysis of the conduct of Brutus, of the conspirator, and of the military leader in combat, actors in "open" warfare, the imperatives of which reveal those of politics, understood as secret warfare. This introductory chapter dispenses with any prefatory material analogous to that of the first two books, but addresses the reader no less firmly, charging him to perform anew the critique of the principles that attached him to the tradition; it puts his newfound freedom to the test before exposing it to the hostile fire of the last questions. Indeed it is as if this were a new beginning. First, Machiavelli reuses a language he himself has taught us to reject. He feigns to ascribe to history a course regulated by nature. "It is unquestionable," he writes, "that all things of this world have an end to their existence; but those alone run the entire course heaven intended for them whose organization does not get disarranged, but remains so well regulated that it does not change, or only changes to survive, not to perish." Then, in keeping with the teachings of classical philosophy, he observes that human institutions, such as states or churches, exposed as they are, being mixed bodies, to accidents, can only maintain themselves on condition that they be periodically brought back to their origin (*principio*). The intention of change is then deemed legitimate, provided it is for purposes of restoration. The recommended change is one that removes the effects of accident, one in which the difference separating it from the origin is annulled. Of that origin, we are told that it has an intrinsic goodness, and of time, that it is corruption. "And because in the course of time that goodness is corrupted, if something does not intervene to bring that body back to itself, it must perforce perish." But these truths are only advanced to be attacked. And through the breach opened up by the attack there enters the enigma of a political action to be exercised without any guarantee inherent in the order of things, without following a path traced out in nature or commanded by God. An action that would be . . . not instituted, but instituting.

The opposition we have indicated between the two paths that would lead back to the origin—that of extrinsic accident and of intrinsic prudence—already creates a source of ambiguity. To the first path, the writer links the example of the taking of Rome by the Gauls—a fact he has already mentioned on two occasions, but this time he returns to it without bothering to evoke an intervention of Fortune. We are doubtless disposed to admit that on that occasion corruption was wiped out as a result of grave danger: we acquiesce to the image of a threatened people who recover self-awareness and revivify the institutions they had long neglected. But we cannot fail to notice that the accident in itself has no efficacy. The Romans react to the danger by the mobilization of their last energies, the Florentines by flight. The response of the former, as we have learned from an earlier commentary, again testifies to their prudence; thus, it is better to distinguish two levels of prudence rather than to conceive of prudence as the opposite of accidents, and to admit that in some cases prudence allows one to foresee dangerous accidents and in others it is awakened on contact with them.

But the objection is too natural for us not to give further thought to the concept of accident. We then see that Machiavelli assigns a positive function to it after having used it, in keeping with tradition, in a negative acceptation. The accident was corrupting; that fact of its becoming positive is no matter of indifference. Its virtue, we are told, is to awaken men. But was there a time when men did not need to be awakened? Or, if you like, could their awakening [*éveil*] to political life be of a different nature than reawakening [*réveil*]? The first institutions, which one likes to think of as having an intrinsic goodness, just because they are originary— are they not born already beneath the impact of the event? Could it not be in response to a great danger (real or imaginary) that a collectivity gathers together, relates to a common law, and causes the groups and individuals it absorbs to shake off their natural inertia? It is necessary, we recognized, to take the institution back to its origin—back to its origin and back to its essence. But can one think the essence without reference to the conditions of fact in which the relation of man to man occurs? Can the initial distinction between essence and accident be maintained, once we admit that the universal presupposes the existence of the particular as that which must be transcended?

There is one indication that we are not going in the wrong direction as we pursue our interrogation in these terms. After having mentioned extrinsic accidents, Machiavelli suddenly speaks of intrinsic ones. Thus the return to the origin, even though it is pursued beneath the sign of prudence, does not break with contingency. Where there is no external danger, internal danger becomes active. It is impossible to misunderstand, considering the examples invoked. "The institutions that brought life back to Rome," the author notes, "were the law of the tribunes of the people, the law that named censors, and all those that were voted in against ambition and insolence." It is true that they carry the mark of Roman prudence, but they can only be explained in reference to events that threatened the life of the City. They are solutions found to specific problems posed by the actions of a faction or class. We must also recognize that they effect a singular return to the origins. It is no longer a question now of advocating the reestablishment of a primitive order. The virtue of the foundation is regained by the new means. If one can nonetheless speak of a regression or repetition, it is on the condition of specifying that what is involved is a detachment from the instituted—a change, the effect of which is bring about a resurgence of the foremost dimension of the law. The creation of the tribunes of the plebs is an innovation that assumes that there has been a breaking away from the principles in vigor in the early days of Rome. It gives new life to the law by profoundly modifying the established legality; it gives it new life because it bridles the appetites of those who by their own power imperil the unity of the state, because it imposes on the collectivity, as on the first day, a necessity that no one can evade without risking its destruction. This is the truth of the return to the origin: not a return to the past, but, in the present, a response analogous to the one given in the past. In the present: that is, in the singular conditions that are constituted, *here* and *now*, by the power relations between factions and classes, the state of moral practices and also the imperatives arising from conflicts with foreign cities.

The preservation of the law always implies the possibility of a renewal of the laws and, in the long run, requires it. To retain its force, the interdict in which it is announced must be modified, must shift along with the changes in the humors and desires of men, or in keeping with the changing form of threats, emanating from within or without, against the state.

Thus, in the end, only measures that are entirely new, extreme measures, have the power to ensure restoration; taken to the extreme, the requirement of conservation merges with that of change.

That truth—doubtless we had already understood it through reading the first book; but in returning to it, we are led to receive an additional one. For it is the same thing to recognize that the *principio* is not determinable from an empirical point of view—or, in our terminology, that the law transcends all the institutions in which it takes on a specific form—and to discover the place of the political Subject. As long as we consider only the form of institutions, we imagine that they draw their virtue from within themselves, and that they determine the behavior of individuals and groups, to the point of not leaving them any choice but to obey and be good, or to disobey and be criminal. But in criticizing this naïve representation, we realize that the law is nothing outside the relation men develop with it, in the always unique conditions in which they are placed—that it is every bit as much in the dependency on human action as it governs it.

As for the action of the Subject, Machiavelli brings us to a full appreciation of it when he observes that a man can produce the same effect as a new law, that is, bring society back, by the virtue of his example, to its origin. We already knew that in certain conditions only the authority of a prince can hold men beneath a common obedience. But now it is the republic that is being considered, and no longer a corrupted republic, in which the laws have degenerated, but Rome at the time of its greatness. As shown in the examples cited as the text continues, the Romans, who play such a great role in the restoration of the state, strike the imagination of their contemporaries by their abnegation, by the sacrifice of their lives even, in the same way they are struck by the threat of legal sanctions. But they do not attract to themselves, as does a prince, the feelings of the mass—or only do so as mediators, to the extent that they make manifest an order of obligation that transcends the world of private interests. They only inspire fear or love by ensuring the conversion of those feelings into obedience to the principles of which they have become guarantors. It may be said of them that they are the direct support of the law, that they give it life by giving it their faith. Now, on these extreme figures of the authority we may decipher the general relation between the Subject and the law. For if it is true that a society cannot maintain its cohesion and force by the sole fact of the exemplary actions of a few individuals, but rather needs an armature of institutions, it is also true that to remain alive, the laws that regulate them must yet find support in men who do more than just execute its commands, but go beyond the limits of their functions and stand up as spokesmen of the universal to the point of using the laws as instruments. Thus it is with the alternative of authority versus law, as with that of extrinsic accidents versus intrinsic prudence. Barely opposed, the terms are rendered more specific in articulation with each other, to the point that it becomes impossible to conceive of them independently. After having enumerated a few of the institutions whose effect was to bring Rome back to its origin, Machiavelli observes: "These laws, to become revitalized, need the virtue of a citizen who gives his spirited support to seeing that they are respected despite the power of those who transgress them." And the better to convince his reader of the character of the actions that ensure the safety of Rome, the writer quotes a series of examples that, with the exception of the last (which we shall have occasion to revisit) are all those of condemnations directed at the ambitious, at the aspirants of tyranny. It is, he also notes, because it concerned deeds that were "memorable and outside the common order" that men were brought back to the vital principle of the republic. Authority in the republic itself is therefore not circumscribed by any particular law, although its manifest status is assigned to it in the space of the institutions; it is only the distance taken up with respect to them by the subject who assumes authority that gives to the law its own distance with respect to all established legality, or, more properly speaking, reestablishes for the collectivity the relation to the Law that was obliterated in the habituation to laws.

Does this mean, then, that one can define the nature of this relation, or that of authority? Stated in these terms the question is to be rejected, since to wish to answer it would again mean allowing law and authority to fall to the level of the empirical; it would mean to again labor under the illusion of a supposed real in itself, in which action would find its determination; it would mean, while intending to define the political Subject, eliminating the trace of its advent. The way Machiavelli destroys that lure prevents our erring, provided we read him aright. Irony consumes the belief already ready to feast on good examples. Once the Romans have been praised for the vigor with which they were able to strike the enemies of freedom, the author quotes, in support of his thesis, "those who governed the state of Florence from 1434 to 1494," whose opinion was that it was necessary every five years to "take over the state again" (*repigliare lo stato*), that is, he clarifies, to "renew that terror and fear that they were able to inspire in all minds at the moment they had taken over." These wise men, whom it is not good to name, are, as everyone knows, the Medici or their servants; for them, to take over—or retake over—the state, meant to wrest from Florence its freedom . . . A second time, after having named the heroes who by their example, and without means of constraint, reanimated the *virtù* of the earliest times in

Rome, he observes that sects (*sette*) undergo the same necessity as states, and that it is owing to Saint Dominic and Saint Francis that Christianity could be brought back to its origin. His commentary, then, leaves no doubt about the value he attaches to such a renovation: "The new orders they established were so powerful that they prevented religion's being lost by the licentiousness of the prelates and heads of religion: these orders are kept in poverty and have enough influence with the people by means of the confession [and by predication], to persuade them that it is bad to speak badly of those who govern badly (*come egli è male dir male del male*) and that it is good and useful to be obedient to them and leave it to God alone to chastise them for their errors. Thus those scoundrels, with no fear of a chastisement in which they have not the slightest belief or that they do not see coming continue to do so much evil. This renewal has thus preserved and continues to preserve this religion."

With this last remark the critical movement of the introduction to the last part of the work culminates. It is totally insufficient—it is no longer sufficient—to cast aside the image of a state whose primitive form is supposed to have borne the principle of its preservation, to reject the division between Being and Time, to give up, consequently, identifying change with corruption, to admit the requirement of a continuous foundation, and to link this to the freedom of the political Subject. Still, we must conclude that this leg of the journey leaves us at a distance from the truth. We decipher a meaning in the politics of the ancient governors of Florence or in the exemplary actions of Dominic and Francis, but the truth is not given with the enterprise of the Medici, no more than it is with that, far vaster, of the Roman Church. We know that, on the contrary, both turn away from it; and it is precisely by knowing this that we know them *in truth*—once we have identified the power of the Medici as a tyranny, and understood that the political life suffocated by him would have been able—or could still—revive, and Florence simultaneously grow, rather than condemn itself to wasting away; once we have taken stock of the effects of the reign of God on present humanity, and recognized beneath the mask the modern figure of despotism. That knowledge is nourished by the knowledge of history, and especially the knowledge of the republics of antiquity; it delivers us from the hold of the institutions to which we are subject and forces us to reformulate the meaning of law and authority. The renewal brought about by the Dominicans and the Franciscans has preserved and continues to preserve religion, observes Machiavelli; that action allows us to get a glimpse of one of the paths through which the transcendence of the law is reestablished; it reemerges from the faded laws of religion by the virtue of men whose despoliation inspires a sacred terror in the people; such is their authority that the particular again fades away before the universal. But what universal? Shall we say that the definition cannot be given, that the law can only be named in the relationship that men establish with it? But how can we forget that in this relationship the meaning of their relations with the world comes into play? That the experience of the law is that of themselves, of life and of death, of the bond between man and man, of their power over things, in sum, and of the limitations of that power? If one thinks, then, that the Christian religion suffocates freedom in man, how can one not consider its preservation worse than its degradation? And if one stresses the authority of those who bring it back to life, why not hope for its downfall rather than glorify it? And if one wishes to work to reestablish the dimension of the universal oneself, how can one not be aware of the daring and dimensions of the task, how not recognize that one must do more than take a few steps outside the existing laws, that one must challenge man's relation to law itself, and advance to the farthest reaches of transgression?

Instructed by the reading of the first two books, we doubted in approaching the third that its object could be to relate the deeds of famous men and show their felicitous effects on Rome's development. This doubt was well founded, as what we find, in meditating on the examples from the first chapter, is that such an object would be fictive. The most brilliant acts are mute if we do not know how they are actions. Not only is it vain to hold them up as models, since they arise from unique conditions, since past and present cannot be superimposed, but even in considering them in the times during which they were carried out, without leaving the scene of empirical history, the one on which Livy places us, we cannot say what authorizes their being abstracted from the continuum of facts and having a particular reality conferred upon them. We may marvel, of course, at the exploit of Camillus in the wake of the Gallic invasion, but in the same way we are enchanted with the prodigious accomplishment of the runner at Marathon. There is no doubt but that we may admire the extraordinary qualities of certain military leaders, but on a par with the heroes of legend. These are merely images with which we satisfy our appetite for the extraordinary . . . Action only becomes the object of knowledge if we dispose of the points of reference allowing us to measure its importance, if we can place it within the field of its coordinates. To think action, and to begin with to determine what an action is, is only possible on condition that we articulate it with the institution, and discover the triple relationship it bears with law, the real, and truth. At that point it is legitimate to consult the history of Rome and seek examples from it. That history is no longer that interweave of facts from which we were going to arbitrarily detach a few samples intended to strike the imagination; it acquires the value of a text in which we read, better than elsewhere, the syntax of a language. The examples are no longer chosen on the basis of their singularity: they are distributed on the basis of the same references; they make us discover and rediscover them; they support our exploration of the possible.

To relate the actions under analysis to one another, to discover in them the variations of the same action—political action—to assess the positions of the Subject—the political Subject—that occur in that action: such is the enterprise whose foundations are set in the first chapter. It justifies the great liberties that will be taken with respect to Livy's account. The use to which Machiavelli puts his examples, the selection of the facts in which he recognizes *actions*, the importance he gives certain actors is governed by the requirement of his own theory. Moreover, in choosing his interpreters on several occasions from among Rome's adversaries, he makes it clearly understood that he is only peripherally interested in the role of individuals in the building of Rome. Better yet: by speaking of facts pertaining to ancient and modern times that have no bearing on that history, and that Livy could not mention, he persuades us that his object transcends the empirical givens of history.

It is therefore not by chance, nor the result of a concession to chronology, that the analyses of the first book open with the case of Brutus, the founder of the republic. With that example, the teaching of the first chapter is immediately concretized, the points of repair of the political action put in place in such a way that it will then become possible to progressively explore the field they delimit; moreover, with that example, a first access to reflection on the most recent events is afforded.

Brutus, as we know, is first of all that man who succeeded in putting an end to the tyranny of the Tarquins by extraordinary means. The king's nephew, the son of a brother whom that king had had assassinated, Brutus succeeded in disarming the monarch's mistrust and in living at his side by feigning madness. Thus, adjudged inoffensive by his entourage, he patiently awaited the propitious occasion for the execution of his revolutionary project. Then, once the republic had been established, he exposed a plot in which his own sons participated, and did not shrink from their condemnation and execution. Machiavelli does not retain the hypothesis (which Livy does envisage) that Brutus struck down the tyrant from vengeance, and he explicitly rejects the hypothesis that he simulated madness in order to preserve his security. His commentary, in the two chapters devoted to him, makes him the republican hero par excellence, the model from which we must learn the requirements confronting the accomplished political Subject. What is remarkable, at first sight, in the portrait of Brutus, is that he combines extreme audacity with extreme prudence, extreme freedom with extreme rigor, the richest imagination with the most thorough and careful thinking, the most affirmative authority with self-effacement before the affairs of the republic. But this is not a question of character traits. It would be vain to admire the coexistence in the same man of apparently contrary qualities if we did not understand the logic governing his actions. The first thing to be understood is that the desire of Brutus engraves itself in reality thanks to an artifice. Since his project is to kill the tyrant and he has no means with which to wage open war (*guerra aperta*), the conspirator cannot do otherwise than craft the conditions for a future operation. The aggression is deferred, and a tactics perfected that will make it possible to act when the adversary exposes himself to danger. The goal does not blind; the impossible is accurately evaluated, pending the possible. But even more important than that exercise of restraint is the choice of the artifice. "No one," notes Machiavelli, "has been judged as able (*prudente*), as wise in any of his successes, as Brutus merited being, by simulating madness." The praise would seem excessive, strange even, if we did not appreciate the precise meaning of the ruse. In passing himself off as a simpleton, Brutus proves that he sees the look of the other on him and composes the only image such as would disarm it. As Machiavelli explains it in the same chapter (Chapter 2), it would be of no help for him—it is of no avail to the man whose quality attracts the attention of the prince—to appear to be without ambition. Even if he really were, he would remain suspect. He would not be believed. His only recourse is therefore to appear such that the adversary cannot perceive him as he should do, because of his own position. Beyond the case of Brutus, we can perceive a warning addressed to those who want to overthrow a regime from the inside: exposed as they are to being struck down before having acted, deprived in the present of the support of the people, their interest is to act with subtlety, to make a show of loyalty until circumstances authorize a takeover by force. We may also think that this warning applies *hic et nunc:* rather than to make a republican declaration of faith under the Medici, it is better to practice deception and make preparations for the future. Perhaps the adversaries of the monarchy should generally speaking come around to the point of view that under oppression "it is appropriate to play the fool like Brutus: something that can very well be done by a madman, praising, speaking of, looking after, and doing things against one's penchant and according to that of the prince." But however it may be about that hypothesis, on which the remainder of the book should shed some light, the praise of the folly of the founding hero has an intrinsic meaning. His ruse best reveals a requirement of action, which may, moreover, call for other means: to take into account, in one's own operation, that of the adversary; to determine the point of view of the other and make one's own indeterminable by him. The chapter on conspiracy [Chapter 6] is devoted to making that requirement fully manifest: it will suffice for the moment to identify what is at stake here, which we have already named: the relation of the subject to the real. This relation is given in the distance taken up by the actor vis-à-vis the present in which his project, and the object of his desire, shine forth, and simultaneously—jointly—in the distance he takes up vis-à-vis himself, by a decentering that allows him to discover the view of the other on states of affairs and on him.

Hence between the power of Brutus to fool the Tarquin, and that of exposing the plot against the young republic, we discover without difficulty a link. Both in attack and in defense, he penetrates the designs of his enemy. If he knows the view of the prince on the conspirator, he also knows that of the conspirator when he has become the supporter of the new regime of government and law. But it would be a mistake to reduce this power to the terms of realism. By bringing these two actions together, Machiavelli adds another dimension to Brutus's enterprise. It is not gratuitous, as we noted earlier, that the writer ascribes to him full awareness of the goal to which his action in fact led—the foundation of the republic. Thus, he reminds us that he insisted on the swearing of an oath over Lucretia's corpse "never in the future to suffer anyone to reign in Rome." Brutus, in taking upon himself the task of ousting the king, acts not only as a military leader familiar with the practice of secret war; he commits a transgression of extreme gravity, one that should draw extreme opprobrium on him: he gives the lie to that "golden rule" stated by Tacitus, which is brought to our attention a little further along in the text, that "men must revere the past and submit to the present—desire good princes and tolerate those they have, such as they are." His action, however, serves the reestablishment of the law, which has been violated by the sovereign himself. What is more, this reestablishment implies a profound change in the relationship men previously had with the law, since for them to obey the law and to obey the individual who reigned in its name was one and the same obligation, while henceforth they must commit themselves to rejecting anyone who comes to reign in its name. The paradox is that he for whom authority is not sacred, for whom the law is not inviolable, has the sense of the sacred and respect for the law to the highest degree. Having left for Delphi with the king's sons while he still managed to pass for a simpleton, he appropriates the oracle's response to make the gods favorable to his plan; on the death of Lucretia, he binds his partisans with an oath. But that is a meager paradox compared to this other: that he assumes the highest authority by imposing himself as the guarantor of the new law, and that that law entails the interdiction for any man to become the representative of the law. As a conspirator, Brutus acts as one who covets the place of the prince; the oracle having made it understood that that place would be taken by the one who, upon returning home, would be the first to kiss his mother, he immediately kisses the ground; his power to divine the thoughts of the Tarquin puts him in the position of being able to replace him; but he does not yield to the temptation of reigning. He refuses for himself what he has refused others. Now, when we consider the way he represses the plot against the republic, that action becomes complementary to the preceding one. The fact that he must oppose his sons is not the result of chance. He appears as the one who knows that the new law must be imposed by an example, that is, by the immolation of the transgressor. Machiavelli brings out what is extraordinary in the fact that a man not only sentences his children to death, but is present at their ordeal. That remark, together with the affirmation that such severity was necessary, sheds light on the function of authority. It is suggested that Brutus seized the occasion of the treason of his sons to make his authority stand out. Common sense would be inclined to judge his severity excessive. But it is important to the author that it be so. Brutus is the man of excess: he is not satisfied with slaying an unjust prince, he makes of the prince as such the image of injustice; he is not satisfied with defending the regime against its adversaries; he supports the law with terror; he simulates madness to escape the prince's attention and draws the attention of everyone to himself by desiring to have his sons executed in his presence. It is by this excess that he resembles the prince: his attitude is not dictated by submission to laws; he departs from them, either by breaking them or by punishing transgressors. His action against the adversaries of the republic, the author emphasizes, is of the same nature as that of the prince against the adversaries of tyranny: "Both he who establishes a tyranny and does not kill Brutus, and he who reestablishes freedom in his country and does not immolate his sons, only maintains it for a short time." But that symmetry reveals what is normally unrecognized. It is readily conceded that a prince must use violence at the outset of his reign to discourage subversion, but we like to think that in a republic law dispels violence. That Brutus should want to and have to exterminate his own children is a sign that no institution is sheltered from aggression, that the order of a republic is no more natural than that of a tyranny, that one must always know and avoid danger. Brutus, we said, fools the prince and does not let himself be fooled by his children. He knows the view of the Other on him. He does not let himself be blinded by his desire. He knows that the desire of the prince pressures him to exterminate any man who endangers him. He knows that the desire of those who covet power is to seize it, even when it is forbidden them. But this knowledge is tied to his position with respect to the law. It is because he himself has been a conspirator that he is capable of outsmarting conspirators. And it is because he has understood that with law the principle of transgression is posited that he perceives the desire of the Other, and takes it upon himself to perform a second act of violence in punishing his own sons.

Finally, in order to be cognizant of the full scope of his action, we must ask ourselves why Brutus is self-effacing before the *res publica* [public thing], instead of making it his property, and where he has come by this knowledge of the law that makes him assume authority in apparently opposite situations. Machiavelli does not permit us to ignore this question, though he does not state it. We ask it because we have noticed that he never speaks of the *goodness* of the founder. Not only does he avoid this commentary, but he contrasts the behavior of Brutus with that of the Gonfalonier Soderini, who, in a situation adjudged analogous to his, was lost because of his goodness . . . and his patience. Brutus is not good, no more than he is patient or moderate. True, it is said of him that he sought the means *di opprimere i Re e di liberare la sua patria*—and we may judge that that end is good. But the words that designate it sound strange to our ears. *Opprimere* is most often used to designate the relation of the stronger to the weaker, of victor to vanquished, even of aggressor to victim, and most often of governmental power to the people. And if we remark that the enemy has not only the figure of the Tarquin, but that he is named "the kings," we can say that Brutus gave himself the goal of combating not only the bad prince, but the good prince; not only the prince in place, but those who throughout time covet that place, that he links the defense of freedom to the constant struggle against his enemies, the kings in power. Does he not know in advance that he will have to slaughter his sons? Perhaps it will be said that this end is good, but it must be admitted that it is not the institution of a good state, in the sense in which we commonly conceive of such a state, that is, as a regime from which evil has been banished. The error would be to believe that the execution of the sons of Brutus definitively rids us of threats of aggression. Terror is not repeated in the same terms, but the rule of law is never assured. Recognizing this, we realize that the question we ran up against just now was ill-framed—and that the writer's intention was to lead us to the place in which we now find ourselves. How, he asked in effect, would a good man resolve to break the law and use violence to save the state? How would an ambitious man, who would not hesitate to use such means, refrain from using them to serve his own ends? It supposed a common boundary between war and civil peace, on the one hand; between obedience to law and transgression, on the other. What the example of Brutus teaches us is that civil war is never over and the distance between the Subject and the law never eliminated.

Would we call good the one who knows this, wishes to reduce that distance to its minimum, and war to its least magnitude? But does goodness engender knowledge? It seems rather to blind it, for if being good means, for a man of state, to want the good of the citizens, then that intention is his downfall when the situation requires violence against some portion of them. It also appears that goodness can end up producing the opposite effect of the one attributed to it, that it perverts authority; for in desiring the good of others and in making decisions about it, one may be tempted to take the place of the law and occupy that of the prince. Thus Brutus does not step back before the *res publica* out of goodness, no more than he sets himself up as judge out of evil. Since it is not his security that he is defending when he sacrifices the most precious goods a man has—his honor, first of all, when he is not afraid to appear as an idiot to others—one must agree that he only acts as he does because he believes what he does is right. In Machiavelli's language, one should say that necessity commands his entire enterprise. It is manifested in the way he frees himself from his own interests and dominates his desires. But it is not just a question of that necessity that subjects the individual to the imperative of the law, since he gives a new meaning to that imperative, since the law needs him in order to be affirmed; nor is it only of that logical necessity in virtue of which, the hypothesis being posited (in this case the elimination of the tyrant), the consequences follow ineluctably, since one cannot include the idea of the task that institutes it. That task is necessary because he thinks it as such. As for naming what right is for him, what necessity commanded him "never in the future to suffer anyone to reign in Rome," this cannot be done if we limit ourselves to considering his actions or his words. What is needed to reply is nothing less, perhaps, than the work of Machiavelli . . . Nothing less than a knowledge of history; not the most extended memory of facts, but thought about the meaning that is preserved in their variations.

May it suffice to observe that his task, the true task—Brutus discovers it in a present. Assuming that this present opens up the richest of perspectives to him, we must not forget that there is no perspective without a point of view. The idea that no one must reign in Rome does not become false, no doubt, but it does not have the force of truth if the present does not allow it to be so. This does not mean that the relation of the Subject to truth is subordinate to the relation to reality, that an idea ceases to be true because it is not "realizable," but that the truth of which this idea is in charge, in a certain present, to the point of being that of a task, is invested in another present, in another idea, and another task. That the place of the political Subject is occupied *here* and *now* by Brutus does not mean that it cannot be so elsewhere in a different time by a prince, although Brutus *here* and *now* is in the right [*vérité*] in wanting the death of the prince. The actions of the father of freedom furnish us with an example, and that example takes us to the furthest point of the knowledge of the true task, but it is not really a question of an example. We would miss its meaning if we were to detach it entirely from its contingency. That contingency, moreover—Machiavelli does not let his reader forget about it entirely, because at the end of his praise of Brutus, he returns for two brief chapters on the mistakes committed by the tyrant of Rome before the institution of the republic. This analysis has no justification in the framework of the argument that announced it. If it allows him, in a first phase, to contrast the rational action just described with the irrational action of those who had their power to defend and were incapable of doing so, it is especially intended to recall in his conclusion that when men are well governed they neither seek nor desire any other freedom (*gli uomini, quando sono governati bene, non cercono né vogliono altra libertà*). Indeed, if it appears that Tarquin the Elder and Servius Fulvius committed the error of ignoring the threat brought to bear against their power by the resentment of those from whom it had been taken—if both allowed themselves to be blinded by their functions, in the illusion in one case that the laws protected him, in the other that he had attached the sons of his victim by benefits—in short, if they perished because they were unable to detach themselves from their own position and see themselves through the eyes of their adversary—Tarquin the Superb, for his part, added to that error (did he not let Brutus live in his entourage?) that of flouting the laws and customs and of exciting the hatred of the people. That was the cause of his downfall and the success of a project that Brutus would otherwise not have been able to form, so certain it is, says Machiavelli, that in a well-governed state the rape of Lucretia could have been the occasion of an appeal to the prince against the criminal, but not of an appeal to the people against the prince. To draw from that example the conclusion that a "good" tyranny is not inferior to a good republic, however, would be to fall into another error. That the people desire no other freedom when they know themselves to be well governed does not mean that, when they win such freedom, they will not rise up. And just because the author for a moment praises good princes, the better to support his criticism of the Tarquins, he does not diminish the merits of the Roman Republic. But the fact remains eloquent that the republic would not have come to be without a series of accidents that discredited the tyranny and drew hatred to the name of prince. Nevertheless, the truth for which Brutus was the spokesman, that no one should reign in Rome, is suspended to the contingency of a situation, and when the people want no "other freedom," truth is not given in the form of a conspiracy against the prince. Between Brutus and a prince who knows how to govern, there is no abyss. To occupy the position occupied by Brutus in the political field of action does not entail coinciding with the goal he chose. But he who confines himself to comparing the position of Brutus to that of the prince and thinks to accede in this way to the most subversive element of Machiavelli's thought would again condemn himself to abstraction and be incapable of finding the path on which the author wishes to set him. It does not suffice to admit that in certain situations the people are satisfied with being governed by a prince, and that consequently it is vain to fight to establish a free government; one must also consider the ambiguous cases, that is, those in which revolutionary action is linked to the greatest happenstance, carries the greatest risks, requires the greatest violence. Machiavelli evokes them briefly after having reasoned on conspiracies. If I am right, the indication given in Chapter 7 is rich with meaning. Wondering "how is it that the transition from freedom to slavery and from slavery to freedom sometimes costs much blood, sometimes none," he points out that Brutus did not have to overcome the most difficult obstacles because he benefited from the general consent of the citizens, and thus gives us to understand that in the absence of that support other means must be employed. Clearly he is careful not to praise violent revolutions (*mutazioni*); he asserts to the contrary that one is still gripped with terror upon reading accounts of them, and that they have very dangerous results when carried out by "men motivated by vengeance." But still our attention is drawn to them, and we must recognize that in certain conditions the restoration of freedom can take place against the desire of a part of the people. The commentary does not specify what those conditions are, but a reference to recent events is such as to alert us, and prompts us to wonder if they are not precisely those obtaining in Florence at the time Machiavelli is writing. Comparing the circumstances in which the Tarquins were eliminated in Rome and the Medici in Florence in 1494, the writer suggests that in both cases tyranny had been unanimously opposed; in other words, that the people, all classes intermingled, desired a regime change. He leaves it up to us to notice that at present the civil divisions would not allow anyone who desired to restore freedom to act as Brutus did. The elimination of a master would not suffice. It is in a sea of revenge that one would have to act, countering the violence of those who seized power at the expense of a part of the citizens, a violence against violence in the service of freedom. A detail sustains our interrogation. The author speaks here of the Roman revolution as of a transition from kings to consuls (*mutazione che fe' Roma dai re a' consoli*), a formulation that lessens the scope of the act of Brutus, presented up until this point as the father of freedom. We think of the regime change as having been pacific because it consisted in a shift in power rather than an upheaval of the social order. In comparison, the violent revolution destroys the privileges of the dominant group, or a part of them, and moves to the forefront those hitherto oppressed. Moreover, as we recall the considerations devoted in the first book to regime changes, we have a better appreciation of the alternative between pacific and violent action. In Chapter 26, Machiavelli emphasized the Romans' skill in hiding from the view of the mass the element of novelty in the passage from monarchy to consulate, and then contrasts to that strategy the policy of the founder-tyrant, forced, "since he is a new prince, to organize all things anew, like himself"; to imitate King David, who impoverished the rich and enriched the poor. It now no longer seems that extreme violence is the monopoly of a prince. From freedom to tyranny, as from tyranny to freedom, the variants of action prove to be the same.

What is announced in Chapter 7 still remains veiled. Machiavelli advances with extreme prudence, as he invites his reader to inquire into the chances of a political action of a new genre *hic et nunc*. Therefore we are not surprised at the brevity of his remarks at this stage of the discourse. But it should not escape the attention of the reader that if this chapter is the shortest in Book 3, the preceding one was the longest of the whole work. Now from the fact that the shortest chapter contains an allusion to the most recent events and offers a glimpse at the possibility of a violent change to the benefit of the republic we can perhaps draw a clue to the interpretation of the longest one, the object of which bears no apparent connection with the present situation. The temptation is all the stronger when we consider that Chapters 8 and 9 complete the argument of Chapter 6, and that, in short, Chapter 7, which we have just examined, constitutes an enclave in the section devoted, starting with the analysis of the behavior of Brutus, to the theme of conspiracies.

Let us repeat that this theme is not the one the author intended to treat: his manifest intention is to highlight the role played by certain men in the edification of the Roman Republic. Hence we see him, when he approaches the phenomenon of conspiracies, at pains to present his study as a digression. If we are to take him at his word, the subject only interests him because it brought to mind the series of plots that took the lives of the first tyrants of Rome, and because it seems well to him that he should examine enterprises as dangerous to princes as to their subjects, the result of which was to cause "to perish and be dethroned more sovereigns than have open wars." Further, it is on a reassuring caveat that the chapter opens. Princes must learn "to beware of conspiracies, and their subjects take part in them with more circumspection, or rather be able to live happily under the masters fate has given them." One must take as a golden rule Tacitus's judgment that "men must revere the past and submit to the present—desire good princes and tolerate those they have, such as they are." But these oratorical precautions (and one may wonder whether they are not ironic, since it is quite certain that the apology for Brutus has canceled out their significance) have in any case little weight in comparison with the lengthy and detailed considerations that claim to establish the rules of the conspirator's enterprise. Indeed what transpires from the argument is the care the author takes to prove, from the most varied examples, that failure is the consequence of an error of judgment, and success possible, probable, or ever certain, when the action is conducted with rigor. The conspiracy is broken down according to the phases corresponding to the preparation, execution, and sequels of the crime, and the difficulties attendant on each, analyzed and finally resolved in the right formulation. Just as in the early pages of *The Prince* he brings out the obstacles to be met by the conqueror, and concludes with the ease of the enterprise once the calculation of the means to be employed has been made, similarly, here he insists first on the dangers awaiting the conspirator, in order to be more convincing at the end of the chances of overcoming those dangers. It is impossible, then, to reduce this analysis to the boundaries the author feigns to set for it. But does it just offer him a new opportunity to expose the rational requirements of action, to accredit the representation of politics as a covert war, to unfold beneath one panoramic overview the play of the adversaries, avoiding all moral considerations on the legitimacy of the ends? Such is doubtless its first effect on the reader, that it obliges him to shift from one perspective to another, to abandon the points of repair constituted by his preferences, to bring about a decentering in order to attain the position of the disinterested spectator vis-à-vis the object of knowledge. But however propitious the occasion—the actors appearing here with the simplified traits of the holder of power and his aggressor—it must be admitted that already on several occasions a reversal of perspectives had forced us into objectivity. From the cause of Rome to that of enemy cities, from the cause of the republic to that of the apprentice-tyrant Appius who applied himself to its destruction, from the cause of the state to that of the military leader whose victories won him the favor of the people, from the cause of Brutus, finally, to that of the Tarquins, the slippage tested our power to grasp the intrinsic logic of action independently of the values ordering it with respect to particular ends. What is remarkable about the chapter on conspiracies is not that it repeats the same operation, but rather that, taking advantage of the already familiar procedure, acting this time under the cover of neutrality of knowledge, the author leads us to think action in a new register. Indeed, the positions of the prince and the aggressor, symmetrical at first glance, do not remain so as the chapter advances. The construction of the argument itself is conceived in such a way as to privilege the second to the point of subordinating the first to it. While at the beginning the one engenders only a rapid examination, the other is the object of the most detailed analyses. It is true that the reader will probably think that to learn about the defense at the disposal of the master of power he need only consult *The Prince*. The author himself invites him to do so. "What he has to do [to avoid being hated] we have, moreover, already said, and we shall not speak of it here." But that justification is not convincing, because it is not so much the general politics of the prince that one would expect to be treated as the precise actions he is compelled to take in the struggle against his enemies within the country. If politics is comparable to war, it operates, like war, on two levels, that of global conflict between states, and that of the operations military leaders carry out in the field. Now, it is on this last level that the analysis is placed. The considerations of general politics are implicit. What is central is the examination of the relation of the actors engaged in a battle to hold onto or to win power. It must therefore be deemed significant that the demonstration is organized in keeping with the enterprise of the aggressor. The reader, first called out to weigh the chances of the two adversaries, thus finds himself led to take the project of the latter upon himself—to reason from his point of view. It matters little that we attribute to him the *virtù* of Brutus or a petty ambition—the qualities of the model are unimportant. All that matters is the place he occupies, and that we occupy along with him in imagination. What is occurring without our being aware of it is a transference—onto the character of the conspirator as such. We are shifted to his position, and it is on the basis of this position that we must conceptualize the rationality of the action.

But this movement is not only imposed because it plays the main role and captivates our full attention. What is essential is that it gradually takes on, through numerous descriptions given by the author, the traits of the prince himself. Like him, he only rises to the high level of his enterprise if his desire does not blind him, if he has made an accurate assessment of the feelings of the people, if he is aware of the image he gives of himself to his adversary, and, finally, if he trusts no one. This last trait is decisive. The conspirator may be forced to seek support: he must under no circumstances depend on others. He must be alone, and assume his solitude. This condition allows the accomplished actor in him to be revealed. But the discovery bears a novelty, for the ideal is thus separated from the image of the sovereign. The conspirator is not only the equal of the prince, or his inverted image in the mirror. In contrast to his adversary, he does not represent the law. The moment he attacks the established authority, he transgresses it. He becomes, as they say, an outlaw, and in doing so reveals, beyond its limits, the truth of action. It is true that when Machiavelli spoke of the "new prince," he already evoked the figure of the hero who upsets the established institutions. When he spoke of absolute tyranny, he described an authority that rises above laws or exalts itself as the measure of law. But in focusing on the action connected with the person of the prince we could not fail to conceive of it within the framework of a form of legitimacy, whether instituted or in the process of being instituted. The authority of the prince appeared bound to winning a consensus. But this consensus implied more than obedience to the prince, more than submission to the laws guaranteed by the prince. Linked to the person of the conspirator, action proves to be in the precinct of an authority that does not have *consensus,* and affirms itself by its distance with respect to the law. It is true that the conspirator may just want to take the place of his adversary, but such is not necessarily his project. Neither Brutus nor Pelopidas (whose example is opportunely cited) proposed to take over the tyranny, and in any case the enterprise implies a retreat outside the public space, a refusal to obey that, at the same time that it is addressed to a particular power, casts its author into illegality. It is also true that a future consensus is posited: the aggressor, if he does not enjoy the people's support once the power has been overthrown, would be lost. But in the present this support does not exist. There is no exchange between the actor and the others that would guide him in his conduct. At the moment he acts, whatever conviction he may have of being approved later, he cuts himself off from the social body. The political Subject is thus better revealed in the conspirator than in the prince; for he is the one par excellence who disposes of no outside guarantee, who counts on neither men nor institutions, who has the power of the force of the state and that of custom against him. How is he Subject? Precisely in that he faces the greatest indetermination at the moment that he acts; in that he extricates himself from the hold of the real, the hold of the law, and the hold of his desire to assert the truth of his enterprise. But this is another way of saying that he is subject in that he makes himself the agent of a new path—that he breaks with the order of established things. Furthermore, between conspiracy against the prince and detachment from the past, Machiavelli establishes a link with the opening of the chapter that makes it possible to appreciate what is truly at stake in his analysis. On the authority of Tacitus, as we have noted, he recommends to men to revere the past and submit to the present, to desire good princes and to tolerate the others. The expression, we said, is advanced in order to be contradicted. But it is worthwhile, to appreciate the dimensions of the contradiction, to examine the terms in which it is formulated.

What is overturned is the idea that there is a rightful power and knowledge; that the place of the Subject coincides with that of the prince; that the locus of truth coincides with that of tradition. This overturning presupposes that the internal connection between power and knowledge in the institution in which the two crystallize and become petrified has been grasped. Machiavelli constantly made an effort to detach his reader from tradition, but doubtless nowhere more daringly than in the preface that introduces Book 2. It is there that he dismantles the mechanisms by virtue of which man is irresistibly pushed to revere the past and to submit to it. It is there that he appears best, himself as a conspirator, as he who contests the legitimacy of the great Authors, only approaches them in order to lead his own projects to success, he who proposes to excite in the souls of young people the desire to flee the false models, and to interrogate the past in order to transform the present. The full significance of this critique is now revealed in the remark that submission to the past and to the established power are but one and the same thing. If we called the first belief, the second obedience, we would readily say that the only obedience to the prince is owing to belief in the ineluctability of his function in the order of things, and there is no belief in that order except by virtue of obedience to the commands of power. On the contrary, the knowing Subject and the acting Subject rise up in the criminal search for what has not yet been thought or not yet done—or in the criminal will to draw from the present the material for a new thought or action. But just as emancipation from the Authors—the questioning of the ancient models of life—does not imply the rejection of the heritage—just as they open the path to the knowledge of history—so detachment from the established power does not bring about the denegation of power as such; it causes instead the sudden emergence of a new relation of the political Subject with power. The figure of the thinker and that of the man of politics do not merge with that of the factual conspirator, but from the place of the conspirator light is shed on a veiled dimension of thought and action, in the place where the prince or the author reigns.

In this place, authority tends to be defined in the conjunction of constraint and conservation; what is blocked out, then, or risks being blocked out for he who exerts authority, is the existence of the Other, and change. And simultaneously authority is given in the collective representation beneath the sign of transcendence: it shines immutable beyond its sordid manifestations. However blameworthy the conduct of the prince may appear, his function remains inscribed, to the eyes of the collectivity, in the order of things. From the place of the conspirator, on the other hand, it is manifest that there is no order of things in themselves—that what is so designated cannot be sundered from a factual relation to wills and forces, always open to modification—that the perpetuation of the same is a decoy, behind which lie hidden the alterations of the social body, with its new needs, the new aspirations of the governed, denied. The enterprise of the conspirator (regardless of whether or not he is conscious of his role) reveals that there is no coincidence between the person of the prince, the authority he claims to embody, the power that is supposed to ensure his establishment, and the law he presumes to represent. Even when the act of aggression seems directed solely toward the currently ruling tyrant, it weakens authority as such; for it seems that authority does not reside in its agent, that it is supported by those who submit to it, and articulated with the real, which it guarantees; it weakens [governmental] power, for that power is revealed as a simple organ of repression, the moment authority is detached from it; it weakens law, for it also seems that law presupposes a collective faith and that although it sets limits to men's desire, it cannot be removed from the hold of that faith without turning into fraudulence.

It is true that these reflections seem to apply only to conspiracies against a prince; but in a republic, the attempt to overthrow power should not take on the same meaning; the place of the conspirator should not open up the same perspective, since in that case no one takes all authority on himself, and there is a distinction in principle between the various areas of political competency. Now, it is a fact that Machiavelli treats this last case at the end of his chapter as if it were not fundamentally different from the first. He again takes up the point of view of the governing entities and that of their aggressor, as if scientific objectivity alone made it necessary to specify the methods of defense and attack in the second hypothesis. In this way, he pushes to the limits the subversive movement that would transform our representation of the political Subject and allows us a glimpse of the practical stakes of his analysis. What he brings us to discover is that despite appearances the republican regime tends to become petrified through the same process as does the monarchy; that it incites the governing entity to identify itself with power, authority, and law, to the point of becoming blinded to its task; that the political Subject must assert itself in the critique of that identification and in the freedom of transgression. The audacity of the writer may be gauged, once again, by the number of precautions with which he begins by enveloping his procedure. Thus, he advances at the outset that conspiracies can only come about in a corrupt republic: "In a healthy republic," he notes, "in which there is no place for evil to take hold, such projects cannot come to anyone's mind" [Chapter 6]. This observation is contradicted a few pages later, when, in considering the enterprises of two ambitious men— Spurius Manlius, a rich demagogue who attempted to corrupt the people by a distribution of wheat, and Manlius Capitolinus, a glorious general jealous of the success of Camillus—Machiavelli tells us that the republic, at the time of its greatest power, was already exposed to conspiracies. These examples show, then, that the healthy regime and the corrupt one differ only in that, in the one, it is possible to strike the conspirators at the first signs of a plot, while in the other they are allowed to acquire the means of acting; that in the one, the people are unanimous in support- ing the defenders of the law, while in the other they are too divided for a timely intervention against the conspirators. But, in the first moment, the praise of the republic that does not give a foothold to evil gives the reader a token of faithfulness to the common opinion. Furthermore, the argument is skillfully split into two parts in such a way that the analysis of the conspiracies seems to end with innocuous advice offered to princes and the directors of republics, while it goes on in the ensuing chapters to bring the reader, with another critique of the politics of Soderini, into contact with the most recent events. What that dichotomy masks specifi- cally is the passage from the position of the conspirator to that of the reformer, or, in a more general way, the transfer of the specific qualities of the conspirator to the figure of the political Subject.

The examples of Spurius and Manlius, which constitute the subject matter of Chapter 8, not only bring us proof that republics are always exposed to the threat of conspirators; nor do they just allow the analysis that was broken off in Chapter 6 to be resumed and one of its last propo- sitions to be modified: their interest is that they bring out the double relationship of political man with the real and his desire, and link the problem of the Subject with that of the state. At the first stage, Manlius and Spurius are blamed for not having understood that "in a corrupt republic the means of achieving glory are not the same as in a republic that is not politically dead." The error denounced here is "not to have observed one's time and conformed to it." But that error seems at first inevitable. From a comparison between these unfortunate ambitious men and Marius and Sulla, it would be unwarranted to conclude, despite the appearances, that the success of the latter is based on an accurate assess- ment of the situation; the truth, borrowed from Livy, is rather that they were well served by the circumstances. "If Manlius had been born in the time of Marius and Sulla, when hearts were already corrupted, and when he would have been able to direct them in keeping with his ambition, he would have had the same success as Marius, Sulla, and all those who aspired since to tyranny. Similarly, if Marius and Sulla had been born in the time of Manlius, their schemes would equally have been crushed . . ." But this judgment is immediately corrected, since after having admitted that Manlius would have been considered a man rare and worthy of being passed down to posterity, if chance had had him born in a corrupt state, Machiavelli rehabilitates knowledge in asserting that "all those who wish to make some change in the government of a republic, whether in favor of freedom or of tyranny, must attentively examine the state in which that republic finds itself and judge accordingly the difficulty of their enterprise." The call for such an examination presupposes that the individual can resist his penchant and govern his action instead of letting himself be carried along by the circumstances. It is true that the example of Brutus had already persuaded us of that; but the new formulation of the problem is sufficiently general to replace the figure of the unscrupulous man of ambition with that of the politician devoted to the cause of the state. Indeed, what is said of the first comes to apply to the second. And the same reasoning applies that, from the observation of an ineluctable determination on the part of the actor, leads to the idea that once it has been recognized, it can be mastered. The starting point of the following chapter is now this universal truth: "The man who least errs and encounters success is the one whose procedure encounters favorable circumstances, but then as always he does nothing but obey the force of nature" [Chapter 9]. The example that sustains that truth is that of a consul admired for his prudence—not that of an apprentice tyrant, but of a Roman whom the wise men of Florence flatter themselves in thinking they imitate when they try to avoid a battle with their adversaries: Fabius Cunctator. This Fabius is not the intrepid general who infringes on the orders of the senate by dashing off in pursuit of the Etruscans in the Cimina Forest; his merit is to have been able to break Hannibal's impetuosity through skillful maneuvers that avoided a head-on confrontation that would have been dangerous for the Romans. Machiavelli does not hesitate to speak of this glorious leader in the same terms he had used a moment earlier in discussing Marius and Sulla. Asserting that his successes were the result of a felicitous encounter between his character and the circumstances, that "had he been a king in Rome," that is, not under the control of the collectivity, he would not have failed to bring about the ruin of the state by his obstinacy in persevering in the same strategy, he prompts the reader to appreciate the conflict between the opposing forces of the rigidity of human nature and the requirements of change; and at the same time he destroys the credibility of the naïve idea of the good model. We discover that Fabius's prudence is not intrinsically good; it only has value in specific conditions. This critique is immediately applied to Soderini, whose delaying tactics were effective as long as the circumstances required them, then were his downfall when it was necessary to take the risk of combat. But Machiavelli adds only the following. "Two things are opposed to our ability to change: first, we cannot resist the penchant of our nature; second, a man for whom a certain way of acting has always succeeded perfectly will never admit that he must act otherwise." Thus he brings us to consider that the omnipotence of nature and habit is impossible to overcome. We must therefore conclude that Soderini did what it was permitted for him to do, given the nature of his temperament and the conditions of the times: his prudence was his ruin after having carried him to the head of the state, just as the daring of Julius II would have been his downfall had circumstances required of him a different style of action. What is remarkable is that the same conclusion is valid for both the state and the individual. When Machiavelli decries the danger that Fabius's prudence could have caused the Roman state, he praises the merits of the republican regime, whose superiority consists in its being able to profit from various characters: "Rome was a republic that gave birth to citizens of all sorts of character, and just as it produced a Fabius, excellent when the war had to be drawn out, similarly, it produced a Scipio when it was time to conquer." But a moment later the praise is annulled. After having noted that individuals are prisoners to nature and custom, the writer adds: "This also explains the fall of cities, because the republics do not change their institutions with the times, as we have shown. It is true that they have the excuse that, in order to make them resolve to do so, times must come that completely convulse them, and they cannot be saved by one man alone modifying his behavior." On these terms, voluntary change would seem to be inconceivable. The inertia of the individual would be such that it would be vain to imagine any modification on his part that would make it possible for him to face new necessities and, for example, to save the state. The inertia of the state, on this account, is such that any new action would be powerless to transform its institutions in an opportune manner. But as we have already observed, Machiavelli only speaks in these terms to abandon them. Fatalism, once again, is only introduced to be rejected.

If we analyze the example of Fabius more closely, as the next chapter invites us to do, we must admit that his prudence, although it responds to his temperament, was based on an accurate assessment of the power relations that had momentarily been established between the Romans and the Carthaginians. The delaying tactics of the consul were justified by the fact that his troops were strong enough, despite the threat they were under, to discourage an attack by the adversary; by keeping him at a distance, the Roman troops unnerved him, wore him down, and made good use of the time gained. The reflection on the past is not limited, then, to teaching the meeting between character and situation: it also teaches the reasons for success or failure. And at the same time, it reveals in the present the error of those who imitate without understanding. Thus truth is established at two levels: it is a fact that certain men give the best of themselves in circumstances that are the most propitious to the manifestation of their genius; the strategy of Fabius confronted with Hannibal is an example of this. But this example might be understood in the following way. The man of action, instructed by history, can know the limitations of his penchant and free himself from it. Similarly, he may judge the nature of the situation and try to adapt to it. Manlius and Spurius let themselves be carried away by their ambition and they failed where Marius and Sulla later succeeded. Livy is not wrong in noting that the times decide on the outcome of their enterprise. But he only sets forth a half-truth, because this very judgment itself modifies the givens of the action; it founds a political knowledge, it opens us to the understanding of the present. Not only do the contemporary men of state lack this knowledge, not only do they fail to take advantage of the lessons of the past, not only do they abandon themselves to their penchants, but they fortify themselves in their errors by making the wrong use of ancient models. This misunderstanding is not a character trait. When we disclose it, we must rather agree that it feeds a fear that disguises itself in the prestige of prudence, and beneath that cover, contributes to the shaping of character. We would be wrong to believe that the governing entities in place resemble Fabius, and that they fail at the moment of the greatest danger, like Soderini, because they are prisoners of their nature. The defeat of this last is the sign of a general powerlessness to take risks and more precisely to confront conflict. Machiavelli is content to note here that their weakness derives from the fact that they have preferred to abandon the conduct of the war to others. But we know that this choice is of a political nature, and that they have done so because they feared arming the people. What is certain is that this policy leads them to limit the power of their military leaders and to contain their enterprises within the strictest boundaries. "When these cowardly princes or effeminate republics," notes the author, "send out one of their generals, the wisest council they think they can give him is never to venture to do battle . . . They think they are imitating in this the prudence of the great Fabius." This last remark completes the process of reversing the first perspective. Roman prudence proves to be an alibi for the contemporaries, but also a decoy. The reason why a Soderini falls, bringing down the entire republic with him, is not just because his temperament and his habits do not allow him to "break with a politics of humility and patience." That reason is the one he gives himself when comparing himself to Fabius. In reality he never understood what was behind the virtue of Fabius; he could not understand, because he understood nothing of politics, which presupposes winning over the support of the people.

In his remarks on Fabius, Scipio, and Hannibal, Machiavelli does not cease speaking of the Gonfalonier Soderini, without mentioning him by name; in critiquing the thesis that it is advantageous to avoid combat, he is attacking the Gonfalonier who, because he had wanted, up until the last moment, to elude the trial his internal enemies were preparing for him, finally lost without a fight.

Soderini, we are told, thought to imitate Fabius and temporize, although he did not have reliable troops; all he could have done was imitate Hannibal, who, when assailed by Scipio and knowing he could not long count on his troops, threw himself into battle. "A commander who has an army massed together and sees that for lack of money or friends he cannot keep it long in the field, is completely mad if he does not put his fortune to the test before his army has to be disbanded; for if he waits, he is sure to lose, while if he tries, he might win" [Chapter 10]. It would be futile to raise the objection that Hannibal lost. Indeed, what the commander or the politician must consider "is that if he must lose a battle, he must at least save his glory; and it is certain that there is far more glory in being defeated in doing battle than for some other reason." Now, the consequences of Soderini's action speak for themselves: both battle and glory were lost. "No one will dispute the fact that Hannibal was a master in the art of war," notes Machiavelli. He leaves it to the reader to add: no one will argue that Soderini was a master in the art of politics. But the critique of the Gonfalonier becomes more specific in the last lines of Chapter 10, though always through a third person. After having observed that Scipio had taken over vast territories in Africa and that Hannibal, even if he had not been attacked, could not keep the war going for a long time, the writer concludes that a military leader who wants to penetrate enemy territory is all the less in a position to avoid battle. Forced to advance, he cannot turn away when the enemy comes to confront him, and if he lays siege to a town he is even more bound to fight. These rather discordant and troublesome propositions (since Hannibal was not in enemy country when he did battle with Scipio) become clearer when we consider the politics of the Gonfalonier before the fall of the republic. Indeed there is no doubt that he had ventured onto the territories of the enemy within by imposing reforms on Florence—reforms contrary to the interests of the upper bourgeoisie; doubtless in Machiavelli's mind the positions of the dominant class were so strong that it was necessary to take the greatest risks and push the offensive to the very end or expect to be overthrown; nor is there any doubt that the reaction would have struck Soderini even if the Spanish had not conducted their armies before Prato, and that there was no worse solution than the one he chose: to provoke the adversary without having gathered the means to win or "to engage one's entire fortune without bringing to bear all one's forces."

In exploiting the example of Hannibal beyond what the historical givens allow, the writer draws our attention to the role he has it play. If he criticizes the model of Fabius and replaces is with that of the Carthaginian leader (of which there will be much further discussion later), it is not solely with the intention of denouncing the weakness of the governing parties of his day, of recalling its causes, and of showing its consequences in Florence. Fabius was the loyal servant of Rome, and Rome imposed its law over immense territories; Hannibal was an aggressor who claimed he would overthrow the Roman Empire at the head of a ragtag army: between one and the other there is the same difference as between the prince and the conspirator.

Thus is accomplished, with the secret identification made between a Florentine leader and the most daring adversary of the power of Rome, the movement that, beginning with a critique of the natural order and established laws, promoting change to the level of historical necessity, detaches the political Subject from the position of the prince and links authority to the revolutionary enterprise.

At least the initial stage of this movement is accomplished. Reflection on the status of the Subject and of action is now articulated with a reflection on the present so rigorously that we are now compelled to think the problem of political theory and that of *hic et nunc* practice as one sole problem. But as for this problem, it is also important to explore its terms, in order to move knowledge closer to the particular, that is, to the point at which the desire to know is at the same time the desire to act.

The path followed by Machiavelli in the first ten chapters of Book 3 is followed by two points of repair that indicate what is at issue in his enterprise: the name Soderini is linked to it. First, he compares him to Brutus: It was, as we will recall, to reproach him for not having recognized the necessity, after having been put in power, of striking down his own partisans. The Gonfalonier appears, then, as a leader paralyzed by the fear of having to overstep legality to defend the new government. Second, his example is invoked with respect to that of Fabius, then secretly contrasted with that of Hannibal, and what he is reproached for is not having been able, at the moment of greatest danger, to take the risk of total war against his domestic enemies. His fault is no longer that of having remained a prisoner of legality; it is of having refused to put himself at the head of a conspiracy to change the government. These two criticisms attack his powerlessness to preserve or to transform the Florentine Republic. In a sense they constitute a verification of the theoretical analysis, but they are more than that: they point to the place where the requirement of theory is born. But we still know almost nothing of the direction of the reformatory or revolutionary action that would ensure the preservation or the restoration of the republic on new foundations. We can only hope, in continuing our inquiry, to encounter a new sign that would let us know we are not on the wrong path. The fact is that such a sign suddenly springs up twenty chapters later when the Gonfalonier is summoned to appear for a third time, and judged, in the name of the Bible, in terms that give us a glimpse into the dimensions of the social upheaval of which he was to make himself the instigator. This return to the present conditions of action prompt us to think that the analyses preceding it—the long considerations touching on the strategy of the military chief in combat and the nature of his authority—have an immediate political significance, and that the same reflection is pursued from the beginning of the book along a variety of pathways.

The reader, having seen the author examine military operations, compare the strategies used on various occasions, weigh the respective merits of the general and the troops, inquire into the best forms of command, draw his examples now from the Romans, now from their adversaries, might be surprised at first reading that such a subject should be focused on at this stage of the discourse, since it had its place in Book 2, and does not correspond to the declared intention of Book 3. But the comparison between open war and conspiracy has opened our eyes. That all that has been said about war is of such a nature as to shed light on politics—that much we are prepared to admit. Furthermore, had we any lingering doubts, Chapter 11, the one that introduces a new argument, would put an end to them. Its object is to show, if we are to believe its title, that "He who has many foes to combat may succeed in overcoming them, even though he is weaker than they, if he can withstand their first attack." In point of fact it is rather a question of emphasizing the freedom to maneuver enjoyed by a state that, having been able to temporize when faced with a coalition of adversaries, may succeed in detaching one of them from their camp and thus modify the balance of power in its favor. Now, the analysis is conducted in such a way that the political problem and the military one prove analogous. Indeed, Machiavelli begins by speaking of the ploys of Appius Claudius, who, to protect the senate and Roman nobility from the protests of the tribunes, strove to break up the solidarity of the latter whenever a proposition collided with the interests of the dominant class; then, without transition, he evokes the policy of

Venice facing the coalitions organized against it (a policy that was skillful in 1484 and clumsy in 1508), and finally returns to the tactics of the Roman senators. In thus compelling the reader to accompany him in this movement of thought, he is tacitly asking him to transfer the reflection he will apply to the domain of war to that of politics. But perhaps we should retain something more from the argument. On this occasion, he praises the wisdom of Appius and seems to embrace the party of the dominant class (not without cynicism, however, since he remarks in passing that among the tribunes there was always a possible turncoat—frightened, corruptible, or a friend of the public good); now such praise cannot fail to disarm his adversaries and divide them at the very moment when they are about to take a dangerous path. On the other hand, he is making himself the accomplice of the reader who is disposed to follow him: he is warning him that his future comments will have to be deciphered.

If I understand this caveat, the question discussed in Chapter 11 can itself be related to the present. Although the author makes no allusion to the recent conflicts that have rent the Republic of Florence, we have every right to assume that the leader Soderini, discussed a little earlier, is once more the intended figure. The fact is, he was unable to elaborate a strategy against his adversaries when there was still time. To the coalition that the main factions of the upper bourgeoisie marshaled against him, he did not manage to respond with a maneuver that would break up their unity. But between the great families there remained sharp rivalries; between the Piagnoni, the Arrabiati, and the partisans of the Medici too many quarrels had arisen for the momentary alliance to be solid. True, this is a mere hypothesis; but Chapter 12 lends it uncommon weight, because it deepens the vague, inchoate critique with the idea of necessity, and this time it contains a precise reference to the events that brought on the fall of the republican regime. Here Machiavelli asserts "that a skillful general must put his soldiers in the necessity of fighting, and offer those of the enemy every means of dispensing with it." The idea is not new, but reformulated at the right moment to complete the preceding argument. Looking at the two chapters together, we see that indeed they destroy the commonly widespread thesis according to which the relationship between relative powers rigorously decides the outcome of a confrontation. That thesis feeds fatalism; it leads one to suppose that in a given situation one sole outcome is possible—that the political crisis in Florence would necessarily be resolved by the downfall of the republic and capitulation to the Spanish. It implies two errors; for one thing, it is not true that the actor who is in the weaker position is condemned to failure: this is only the case if the opposing force is able to maintain itself through time, if it does not encounter obstacles that break it up; for another, to hold to an objective estimation would be tantamount to mis-understanding the nature of forces, because what constitutes the power of a combatant is not only the magnitude of the numbers and the arms, but also the awareness of what is at stake. Now, judging in this way, the problem of military or political action becomes more complex. To sup-pose that the difference in the stakes of a battle is a factual given would be to fall back into objectivism. That difference only has a brute effect when the adversaries allow themselves to be immediately determined by the situation; but if one, instructed on that effect, can control it, giving his troops the sense that the stakes are loftier than it seems to them—if he can make those of the adversary make them seem less so . . . , in sum, if he can put his own troops in contact with the necessity of fighting and persuade the others that they risk nothing in laying down their arms, the balance of power is modified. The examples chosen skillfully support this critique. Indeed, when we consider the wars of conquest led by Florence and formerly by Rome, it appears at first that the power of the combatant is multiplied when he has the conviction he is fighting for his life or his freedom. In the contemporary era, Florence experiences that truth to its detriment. "Surrounded by free towns [Florence] had far more difficulty in winning than did Venice," because the latter was pitted against more powerful neighbors, but whose peoples were accustomed to the domina-tion of a prince. In antiquity, the Samnites, the Volsci, and the Aequi give us the spectacle of cities fiercely determined to defend their indepen-dence against the Roman conqueror. But these observations offer us no more than a half-truth. The comparison between Rome and Florence also teaches us that Rome disposed of generals skillful enough to make its adversaries believe that they would save their lives by surrendering, while Florence, threatened by the invader, was cowardly enough to believe in the promises of peace that were made to it. Now, this judgment, if we remember the object of the chapter, calls for a political interpretation. Once it has been observed that Florentines had neither the virtue of the Romans when they attempted to conquer, nor that of the Samnites, when their freedom was endangered, the problem becomes knowing what could be done in 1512 to put the Florentines in a position of being obliged to fight—what initiative would have to be taken to make manifest the importance of what was at stake and make the war a matter of life and death—a struggle such that the cause of freedom became a vital issue. No general spoke to the Florentines using the sort of language Machia-velli attributes to the Samnite leader Claudius Pontius. "*Justum est bellum quibus necessarium et pia arma quibus nisi in armis spes est*" [War is just to those for whom it is necessary, and the resort to arms righteous to those for whom no other hope remains]. If no one spoke in this way, it may be because there was no one to listen—that it was pointless to call for war when the troops were lacking. Soderini could not speak like Claudius Pontius, because this last (does the author not take care to point it out?) shared with his soldiers the idea that necessity put them in a position to be victorious. But perhaps he needed to find a means to make himself heard, and if the Florentines were not disposed to defend themselves, he needed to act in such a way that they felt obliged, or suddenly acquired the desire, to do so. It is not rash to think that Machiavelli has the most acute interest in this problem. Furthermore, we have good reason to believe that he does not lose sight of it: twenty chapters later he examines "the means certain people have used to create an obstacle to a peace proposal" (*quali modi hanno tenuti alcuni a turbare una pace*). We then learn that "to deprive a people or a prince of all desire to reach an agreement, there is certainly no more efficient or more durable way than to induce them to commit some atrocious crime (*grave scelleratezza*) against the one with whom you want to keep them from becoming reconciled." The examples that support this thesis do not prompt us, it is true, to make a connection with the situation of Florence. But it is doubtless important that this connection not be explicit. Indeed it must not be, if Machiavelli dissimulates a much more scandalous truth than the one he expresses in this passage; if that truth, in the eyes of some, is the most criminal one there could be. We must follow him step by step if we are to discover it. But if we remain attentive to our problem we will not have to wait long to perceive the first signs of a response. Immediately after having underscored the role played by necessity in war, and the use a skillful general can make of it, our author asks a question the necessity of which, at this point in the discourse, is doubtful at the very least: Who should inspire most confidence, a good general who has a bad army, or a good army commanded by a bad general? Further, that question seems badly formulated and the writer no sooner brings it up than he lets it drop. He counters Livy's assertion that "the Roman Republic owed its aggrandizement less to the valor of its soldiers than to that of its generals" [Chapter 13] first with: "We see in many passages of his history soldiers without a general give remarkable proof of their valor, and show after the death of the consuls more discipline and courage than before." But no sooner has he thus rehabilitated the troops than he agrees, with Caesar, that neither a good army led by a bad general nor a good general leading a bad army are of much use. Furthermore, once the terms of the question have been changed, the uncertainty remains. The author, having asked himself whether it is easier for a skillful leader to form a good army than it is for the latter to form a good leader, concludes that "these things seem . . . equal on both sides." The only positive truth that seems to emerge from the discussion is that one must doubly praise leaders who were able to prove their merits both in the face of the enemy and their own army, those who joined to the quality of combatant the capacity to form soldiers. The least I can say is that such a conclusion, taken literally, is of little significance. I find it perplexing . . . It takes on an entirely different stature, however, if we articulate it with a preceding discussion—if we reestablish, beneath the mask of the general, the figure of the politician, and substitute the people for the army.

Thus the argument can be reconstituted in two movements. First, the thesis of those who claim to represent an aristocratic conception of politics is rejected. It is an error to believe, we are told, that the virtues of the people depend on those of the governing parties; a civilized people is capable of acting with wisdom, even when those who direct them make mistakes; the only thing is, when the people themselves are corrupt, a man of *virtù* does not suffice to put them back on the right track. This first moment contains nothing that Machiavelli has not already asserted: it merely paves the way for the second. Indeed, it is only on condition that we reject the conventional image of the authority of the governing party that we can receive the idea of a political enterprise of an entirely new nature. This idea itself only slips into the hollow of an artificial opposition whose terms remain subservient to the Tradition: Is there a better chance that a good governor can inspire virtue in the people or that a good people can form a good governor? The unsaid is that a leader can bring about the arising of a new mass, a mass that the adversary did not take into account, and thus change the basis of the regime. As for this unsaid, the examples of Tiberius Sempronius Gracchus, Pelopidas, and Epaminondas lead us toward it.

The praise of the military leader/founder, disconcerting at first sight, thus proves to be precisely motivated. What a political leader in Florence could have done in a crisis in which the support of the bourgeoisie was absent was to seek support among those who were ordinarily excluded from political activity, in the oppressed social strata—the only ones capable of fighting when they discover that their emancipation is in the offing. His endeavor would be the equivalent of that of Gracchus, who, to reinforce the Roman army, was charged with arming a great quantity of slaves, and succeeded in transforming them into "excellent troops"; or the equivalent of that Pelopidas and Epaminondas who, after having freed the fatherland from the yoke of tyranny "soon made Theban peasants into intrepid soldiers." It should also be pointed out that these examples are the best suited to ensure the passage from the military to the political, since they exhibit the necessity that commanded victory: the slaves knew that by doing battle with Mithridates they were fighting for their emancipation—with the Thebans, their newfound independence. Thus they best reveal the intentions of the writer, as well: to fight against the Spanish and prevent the return of the Medici, an appeal had to be launched for men who were determined to defend their own cause: the plebs had to be mobilized.

But the figure of the military leader/founder, fleetingly evoked, now disappears. Machiavelli underscores, in the following chapter, the importance taken on by stratagems in warfare; then he devotes a lengthy development to demonstrating that the military command should not be divided, analyzes the conflicts between the republic and talented heads of armies, and in a particularly dark chapter comments on the opinion of Epaminondas that there is "nothing more worthy of a military leader than to be able to foresee the enemy's designs." In vain would we endeavor to discover a logical necessity in this remark, were we to stick to a literal reading. But the conviction we have acquired that the analysis of war serves as a prop for that of politics prompts us to seek the thought connections kept hidden by the writer. Certain indications immediately *set* us on the right path. After having praised the military leaders that were able to create their own armies, Machiavelli sets himself in Chapter 14 to the task of showing the effect of new inventions and new words spoken in the midst of battle (*le invenzioni nuove, che appariscono nel mezzo della zuffa, e le voci nuove che si odino . . .*). Now, could one dream up a better *invention* than the arming of troops, the appearance of which the enemy did not anticipate? Or newer words than those of a political leader calling out to the oppressed to fight for their freedom? But perhaps it would be thought that these indications speak only to our imagination, were they not accompanied by a very precise reference to the situations just analyzed. Specifically, in the body of the chapter, a stratagem is brought up that was conceived by a Roman dictator: "This dictator, about to do battle with the Gauls, gave arms to all the valets (*gente vile*) who were in his camp, had them mount mules and other beasts of burden, added flags to the arms that he had given them in order to make them look like part of the cavalry, placed them behind a hill and commanded them to come out and show themselves to the enemy when they received the order in the heat of combat. The ploy was perfectly executed and frightened the Gauls so much that they lost the battle."

The affinity between the arming of the valets by Sulpicius, that of the slaves by Sempronius Gracchus, and that of the weak Thebans by Epaminondas and Pelopidas is obvious. In all three cases, the art of the innovation brings out by contrast the deficiency of those in charge during that era and makes it possible to understand the reason for it; the fact is, if the Florentine politicians were and remain powerless to find new ways to ensure the common weal, it is not from lack of imagination, but because they were and remain terrified at the idea of arming men they consider more dangerous than their adversaries, that is, the common people. If they have a crude conception of power relations and attribute their failures to necessity, it is to hide the possibility of change, which they fear above all else. But the example of the muleteers of Sulpicius casts a new light on this change, because it associates invention with stratagems. In the continuation of the text, Machiavelli even uses the word lie (*inganno*), then fiction (*fitto*), to characterize the procedure. Are we not to understand that the example of the Roman slaves or that of the Thebans already attest to this? The first example of the chapter concerns the conduct of a Roman military leader, Quintius; he, seeing a wing of his army fold beneath the shock of the Volsci, "cried out to them to stand firm, because the other wing was victorious." By these words, we learn, he renewed the courage of his soldiers, frightened the enemy, and carried the day. But this model of skill is mentioned only briefly. It serves to introduce another example, a modern one, in which we see the catastrophic effects of a misunderstood remark. Troops improvised by the Oddi to retake Perugia, which was then under the tyranny of the Baglioni, panic when the man charged with breaking the chains that bar access to the streets, hampered in his movements by his fellows pushing behind him, shouts "get back." Both observations concern the psychology of crowds; they teach us that, whether disciplined or not, mobs are mobile, at the mercy of the wind (*vento*). Machiavelli remarks that if the Roman army was ready to turn back as a result of a simple word, troops without discipline were even more so. But he thus establishes that between the two there is but a difference of degree in credulity. His argument is intended to persuade us that the power of the army does not lie chiefly in its technical training, but in the confidence inspired in it by its leaders. "One must [conclude] that discipline is less necessary in the army to teach how to fight in an orderly way than to keep it from breaking ranks at the slightest unforeseen occurrence . . . A good leader must therefore make a special effort to clearly designate those who are to receive his orders and transmit them to others, and train his soldiers to listen only to those spokesmen." Such a conclusion, translated into political terms, destroys the thesis of those who deny the mass the power to act with discipline. It insinuates that one cannot rely on the so-called intrinsic qualities of the mass to assess its conduct, and that what counts is its relation to authority. It is not rash to make the following interpretation. If the Florentines dispersed at the first rumors of the return of the Medici, they might just as well have been able to reach beyond themselves if a skillful leader had chosen the right moment to give them faith in themselves. What appeared in the reading of the preceding chapter is that that faith implies the conviction that one is fighting on one's own behalf. What now comes to light is that it implies confidence in the one or ones who make the image of success shine forth.

But it also appears that confidence is established thanks to inventiveness itself—which contains a mixture of truth and fiction, or more precisely an element of lying. Although Machiavelli is careful not to say anything more specific about lying, the comparison of the examples advanced at the beginning and the end of the chapter allows us to understand his purpose. In the beginning of the chapter, the example of Quintius reveals the necessity of deceiving both one's adversaries and one's partisans. In making others believe that the balance of power is in his favor, the military leader discourages one side and multiplies the energies of the other. But the deception seems innocent and the author avoids even using the term to qualify that felicitous invention; moreover, he does not analyze it. In the second part of the chapter, on the other hand, the examples of felicitous and infelicitous inventions are multiplied, and analyzed according to the relation established in them between truth and fiction, but then it is no longer question of anything but stratagems used against the adversary. It is up to us readers to remember that the leader fools his own troops at the same time as his enemies. Both the examples chosen reveal that where there is nothing but fiction, the stratagem fails. Thus Semiramis, to deceive the king of the Indies, covers his camels with cow and buffalo hides which give them the appearance of elephants: his subterfuge fails. The Fidenates think they can terrify the Romans by having numerous soldiers come out of their city in mid-battle carrying torches at the end of their lances: the dictator Mamercus is undeterred. It is, in both cases, we are told, pure travesty, the vanity of which is evident when compared to the artifice employed by Sulpicius, who gives armaments to men belonging to the lowest classes of society, men who, though not soldiers, can serve as such, and though they have no horses can ride mules. These men are accomplices in the stratagem against the enemy, but they are also its victims to the extent that they are made to play a role they are not equipped to sustain. Though victims, they still have the means with which to fight, and that is why, *seen from afar,* they are troubling. Now, if it is true that this new mass on the battlefield symbolically occupies that of the common man in the City, must we not conclude that the common man cannot be mobilized without being fooled, nor fooled without the fiction being associated with a truth? This assessment would modify that of the preceding, without annulling it. The political man's task in a crisis, like that of the military leader in a situation of extreme danger, we would say, is indeed to depart from ordinary practice, and to raise recruits for combat who feel the necessity of fighting; but to conceive of that task he must understand that fiction does not suffice—a knowledge lacking in the case of Soderini, a demagogue without daring, satisfied with enticing the people with reforms, as did the Fidenates by lighting fire at the ends of their lances—and that revolution does not end oppression and inequality because, like the Thebans content with their independence, like the slaves of Sempronius Gracchus content with their emancipation, the common man, content with his new rights, will continue to obey.

Great, then, must be the knowledge of the true military leader and the true statesman. And he should be doubly praised for correctly assessing the roles of the real and the imaginary. It is, however, the moment in which we discover the entire extent of his role that Machiavelli chooses to declare that it is not necessary for him to possess extraordinary qualities. After having noted in Chapter 15 that it is essential to refuse to divide command between several individuals, that Rome itself came very close to being undone for having broken that rule (that it would have been, had the army had not been saved by the valor of its foot-soldiers), he asserts that it is better to place a man *di communale prudenzia* than two *valentissimi* leaders at the head of an expedition. To tell the truth, we already knew that the author of a great enterprise must be the sole person to decide the direction of things, and that he must count on no one. It is doubtless important to recall at this moment in the discourse that authority is not a quality of the person, that it is given in the relation established with the specific area in which the action is carried out. But perhaps there is a specific motive for directing our attention to the man *di communale prudenzia*. We learn in the following chapter why it often comes about that a republic divides command. Rather than to confide it to someone who has proven his merits, it is tempted to get rid of him and divide command between those who are the most skillful in winning its favors. This is the way Florence acted: it removed Antonio Giacomini, the only military leader who since 1494 had shown the right way to command, from participating in the war against Pisa. "He cannot even find a place among the three commissioners chosen to conduct the siege." That this trait is not accidental—Machiavelli leaves no doubt on this point. It is, in his view, a rule that men choose demagogues the moment they are no longer forced by circumstances, that is, as a result of danger, to seek true merit. One might perhaps dream of remedying this evil. One might imagine a republic that remains in such a state of poverty that corruption has no hold on it, or one that lives at all times amid conflicts, so that true merit is always honored. History teaches (Rome first and foremost) that, having attained to a certain degree of power, the City suffers from a relaxing of moral standards and turns away from men of talent. That is to say that there is no coincidence between *de jure* and *de facto* authority—or what is more, these two are often inverted. Where there is *de jure* authority, mediocre men rule, whose *de facto* power is masked beneath the insignia of legitimacy: where there is *de facto* authority, where it is asserted outside the laws, there we see men who have won, through trials, a right to command or guide. The image of the character of "ordinary prudence" is well suited to show this opposition. For it is not appropriate to bring up the case of the great man unjustly neglected: to do so would be tantamount to making people think injustice is exceptional, whereas it is part of the nature of democracy that, once freed from the constraints that roused it to its greatest strength, it favors corruption. The analysis thus casts a signal light on the position of the military leader or the politician. If indeed the virtue of the republican government was to ensure the selection of the best men, every conflict between those who hold the power and their adversaries would be a conflict between the law and those who desire to break it; every conspiracy would be a crime against the republic. But if the selection is made in favor of the ambitious, this conflict takes on a different meaning. The opponents are not necessarily in the service of tyranny. They may fight against the disguised tyranny of the entrenched; they are not necessarily disposed to aggression, but sometimes find that they are forced into it, in response to a prior aggression coming from those in power. Hence we are wrong to be surprised at enterprises taken up against the state by men distinguished for their devotion to the public cause; we should rather be surprised at the resignation of those who remain within discipline despite having been subjected to injustice. At the end of Chapter 16 Machiavelli notes the following on Antonio Giacomini. "His patience and integrity must have been extraordinary for him not to have desired to avenge himself, either to the detriment of the state or to the injury of some of his rivals."

This remark indicates the goal in the direction of which the discourse is moving. But the indication is apparently without follow-up. Once again, the writer leads us down indirect byways. In order to follow him, we must read his thought as the other side of his statements, and, when the object of the discourse has shifted, at a distance from them.

Contrary to our expectations, he does not say that a military leader must profit from the ingratitude a corrupt power manifests toward him to turn his arms against it. He says the opposite: that power must deny the military leader whose value it has failed to recognize any new command. But the positive and the negative coincide. We are that much more encouraged to pass from the one to the other since it is the example of Giacomini, an admired military leader, that introduces us to the supposed necessity of getting rid of military leaders who have been provoked to vengeance. The irony is fecund that consists in advising a corrupt republic to get rid of competent men in order to preserve its stability. An irony hidden beneath the mask of realism, but an irony that cannot escape, because the realism here is so equivocal. How is it possible that governors blind enough to confide to ambitious men a command they cannot themselves take up would be sufficiently lucid to know the enemy they have made, foresee his plans, and foil his aggression? How could they have at once so much and so little understanding of their interests? In the conflict that opposes government power and the military leader, is it not to the latter the possibility of realism is given?

The question remains suspended. We have scarcely gotten a glimpse of it and it is already fading away. Here we are, once again transported to the theater of military operations, invited to analyze the behavior of adversaries, each one of whom is confronted with the difficulty of imagining the intention of the other. But this theater is so strange that it makes us wonder about the location at which the discourse places us. The remark that puts us there is immediately modified; its second version is enigmatic. The various examples chosen do not really give us a true illustration: in neither of them does there appear a military leader who is up to the prescribed role . . . That the place of the military leader should remain empty, this is a circumstance that particularly prompts inquiry, since at the same time it circumscribes the highest knowledge. Machiavelli announces: "Nothing (*nessuna cosa*) is more worthy of a captain than to anticipate (*presentire*) the enemy's decisions (*partiti*)." To affirm this, he appeals to the authority of Epaminondas. His name had come up earlier. We know he had the outstanding merit of transforming the Theban peasants into intrepid soldiers. He shared that glory with Pelopidas. But we also know that he distinguished himself from Pelopidas by his taste for knowledge. Plutarch speaks of him as a philosopher general. Thus it is not surprising that he conceived of strategy as an intellectual art: that "to listen to him, nothing could be more necessary and more useful than to know the reasoning and the decisions of the enemy." Machiavelli, who attributes this remark to him, brings out that the good strategist is all the more worthy of praise because knowledge is connected to conjecture. He does not, however, give us any information on the circumstances in which Epaminondas stated this, and there is no trace of it to be found in Plutarch. All we can say is that if Epaminondas is indeed the author of the maxim brought down to us, he applied it first and foremost to the enemy within: his greatest virtue is to have defeated the tyranny in Thebes.

But even more noteworthy is the way the author builds on the expression he has just related. Without discussing it, he replaces it with another one of his own: "It is not so much the enemy's intentions that are difficult to understand as it sometimes is his actions, and not so much those that are carried out at a distance (*discosto*) as those performed at present and in close proximity (*quanto le presenti e le propinque*)." There are several reasons for us to be surprised at this substitution, because, besides the fact that the first expression is so categorical (*nessuna cosa . . .*) as to exclude any correction, it is immediately intelligible—while the second is *prima facie* obscure. What we gain by going from one to the other is not obvious; we apparently lose the familiar idea that knowledge and conjecture are superior to perception. This loss can only be compensated for if we admit that there is, between the two statements, a discrepancy whose meaning is not immediately given—in short, that the second must be interpreted if it is to prove more meaningful than the first. But does this hypothesis not change our relation to the text? The text tells us, in effect, that it is more difficult to see than to foresee, more difficult to grasp the meaning of what is in front of us than to know what lies beyond the appearances. The text, then, tells us something that goes against what we are told by all cultivated people for whom the distinction between the sensible and the intelligible goes without saying. Now, is not this reversal such as to make us stop and think? Indeed, the paradox would cease if instead of translating the proposition as we have done, we esteemed that what the discourse produces, *here and now*, is what it is essential to decipher—that that task is more arduous than the one that would consist in knowing the author's intentions. The paradox would cease if instead of contrasting the supposed appearances of the discourse and the supposed ideas of the author, we conceded that the meaning is in the articulation of the appearances, and not in some other place where we would have to go to find it by conjecture. It is true that we were [in the present task of interpreting Machiavelli's discourses] in doubt about where we were, and true that the military operations appeared to us to refer to political actions, and that we therefore distinguished between a manifest and a hidden discourse. But that distinction is of a different order than the one envisioned by Machiavelli here, since it does not distract us from what is before us, but on the contrary brings us back to it, as to something that must be explored *here* and *now*, as that which is closest and absolutely present.

What we are looking at is the remark of Epaminondas in its supposedly original form, and its modified version; and there are four examples, in groups of two, each group of which contains one reference to events of classical times and one to the present. In the first group, what is at stake is an error committed by one of the adversaries that either costs him his life or comes very close to doing so; in the second group, what is referred to is a twofold error, in which only happenstance decides that the outcome will favor one of the adversaries. The defeat of Brutus and Cassius by Mark Antony is first mentioned to support the statement that "it has quite often happened that, a battle having lasted into the night, the winner thought he lost, and the loser that he won." In that specific case, "the wing led by the first [Brutus] was victorious; Cassius, who didn't know this, seeing himself defeated, thought the whole army had suffered the same fate; despairing of its safety, he killed himself." This first example has the peculiarity of offering the inverse image of a battle, that of Quintius, which had been brought to our attention a little earlier. Quintius, we will recall, seeing that one flank of his army was giving way, reenergized it by shouting out that the other was winning. The merit of Quintius, however, was not in being able to see, but in being able to invent. Machiavelli's point now is that it is more important to see than to invent. But wherein lies the superiority of seeing? To answer, we must first recall that Quintius's example, like those following it that would serve to distinguish between good and bad illusions, seemed to us to be of a political nature. In good illusions, we thought we recognized freedom: half-truth, half-fiction, which the Florentine politician had not been able to make good use of when the occasion permitted it. If that hypothesis is well founded, should we not think that Cassius's error points back to it in a sense, and that what is involved is again a political conflict? Moreover, should we not further assume that the name Brutus is intended to recall the exploit of the first conspirator who founded the republic, and who was able to exploit his victory rather than let it degenerate into defeat? It is a fact that the second Brutus, as opposed to the first, does not know that he is the winner and does not behave as such. As Plutarch notes, the first mistake he makes is to let Antony live. After the death of Caesar, he flees with his co-conspirators to the Capitoline Hill, fearing a popular uprising; then he commits a second error after having regained his rank in the city, in allowing his adversaries to publish Caesar's will, which was favorable to the people. While successful politically with one faction, his conduct shows that he acts as a loser with the other. He is incapable of seeing what is happening before his eyes—the bond that ties the plebs to Caesar and the hatred of himself that has sprung up among the very ones with whom he would like to form an alliance. All his acts prepare a political suicide, because of a lack of knowledge of the play of forces at work—a suicide similar to that of Cassius on the battleground, who was unaware of the defeat suffered by his adversaries in a different part of the battle. An error symmetrical to the first one described above is that of the Swiss in Santa Cecilia, who thought themselves victorious by nightfall, without knowing that the rest of the army had perished or fled; they encouraged the troops of the Holy See and the Spanish to join them, and nearly dragged them down with them in defeat. Thus we discover that an excess of faith is no less dangerous than a lack of faith, and that both failings bespeak a blindness to the situation. Indeed, both defects could be attributed to Marcus Brutus, for if he made the mistake of behaving as if defeated while he had slain the tyrant, was not his initial error to think he was the winner when, placed at the head of a conspiracy, he saw many senators place themselves beneath his authority, but failed to see that the name of Caesar was more powerful than his own? Marcus Brutus is the negative of the great (earlier) Brutus who was able to understand the mood of the populace and strike the enemies of the republic in time; he sins by presumption and by weakness. He has the same defects as Soderini, that other negative of the conspirator-founder. The description Machiavelli gives of his behavior on the eve of the fall of the republic shows him to be at first absurdly overconfident of his authority and bold to the point of refusing the compromise offered him; then, convinced he has lost and giving up the battle even before the enemy attacks, because he is unaware of the untapped power of the populace. Considering that both examples given to us concern the accurate or inaccurate assessment of the ally, it must be said that the true man of politics, who is the homologue the true military leader, is the one who has no illusions about the strength of his partisans. On the opposite extreme, Soderini reports to the wrong regiment, in the sense that he does not see that the bourgeoisie has betrayed him in declaring its loyalty to him, nor does he perceive the strength of the resource he could have found in the common people's support.

Far from lifting the veil enveloping the discourse, the next two examples increase its obscurity. The first portrays a battle between the Romans and the Aequi. The two adversaries had taken refuge on the heights after a long and indecisive battle, and they both beat a retreat after nightfall, each abandoning his camp. Then Tempanius, a simple centurion, "whose valor in this battle, we are told, had saved the Romans from total defeat," took advantage of information obtained from the wounded, pillaged the enemy camp, and won victory for Rome. Now, this version of the episode changes Livy's account considerably, since in the latter it is the Volsci and not the Aequi who are confronted by the Romans, Tempanius is a decurion of the cavalry, and his exploit consists merely in returning safe and sound with the cavalry under his command. Hence we may justifiably assume that Machiavelli wants to highlight the valor of a private in order to bring out in contrast the shortcomings of a consul. If this is indeed the case, his intention is particularly significant in light of the fact that during the period of war with the Volsci, the class war had become particularly intense, and anxious patricians went out of their way to divert it through military expeditions in order to maintain their prerogatives. This intention prompts the reader to recognize that in virtuous Rome salvific leadership did not necessarily reside in the legally empowered. Nor was it to be sought in Machiavelli's contemporary Rome, as it is apparently the purpose of the following example to convince us. In this case the setting is a battle between the Venetians and the Florentines in 1498. The adversaries, we are told, remained facing each other without initiating hostilities, then withdrew—each side unaware of the movements of the other, until the Florentine leaders accidently discovered the retreat of the enemy and charged in pursuit of it, in order to boast of having driven it from Tuscany. The double misapprehension no longer serves to stress the merit of a lowly soldier, but the undistinguished good luck of military braggadocio. If the first episode is based on the vindication of a spirited and forceful plebs, the second offers us a glimpse of the miserable state of Florence, in which the dominant class is misled by its military leaders, and the people devoid of initiative. If the first portrays a bloody battle between adversaries each determined to prevail, the second presents us with nothing more than the fiasco of a battle never fought.

That unfought battle—does it not bring to mind another? Do the circumstances not give us a hint? Did not Florence fall without a fight? And were not the Spanish afraid to attack, after the first resistance put up by Prato, to the point of preparing to abandon the cause of the Medici? Would they have entered Florence if they had not been convinced by defectors that the city was weak? The partisans of the Medici—did they not fear a popular uprising on the eve of the return of their masters? As we recall all this, we should interpret the deeper meaning of the text as follows. Where there is no Tempanius to replace the faltering military leader—where there could be no Tempanius for lack of a democratic government that included the entire people in the life and defense of the city—there were nothing but loud-mouthed braggarts at the head of the military, proclaiming a victory they never won. But perhaps we should go even further in our analogous interpretation, and say that the Medici, restored, hold no more than an illusory power, and that this illusion is based on the blindness of those who believe in their victory. This is a disconcerting proposition, since the conditions are no more present now than they were then for the intervention of a citizen capable of launching a new message and waving the flag of freedom. But it ceases being so disturbing when we recall that Florence did not reach the point, as did Rome or Milan, of the last degree of corruption, and that there are forces within it to sustain a revolutionary undertaking. In recognizing this, we may be able to understand why the place of the military leader remains empty: that task that has been assigned to him and that is most worthy of him is without precedent; it consists in opposing the factions that support the tyranny at the same time as those that dominated a corrupt republic, and in preparing an overthrow such as only a prince can wish for, but the goal of which is to instigate a government of the people. And we may also be able to see why he invokes the dictum of Epaminondas and replaces it with his own. For Epaminondas is the hero of an extraordinary liberation, the most appropriate example to bring home to us what is at stake in the present situation: military leader-philosopher, he brings together the virtue of arms and that of thought. But as great as his exploit was, he was concerned exclusively with freeing his country from foreign domination and tyranny. More subtle is the struggle against one's closest enemy, the one that hides behind emblems of freedom, but has no other care than to exploit the lower classes and reduce them to silence.

That it is more important to understand what is taking place in the present and close by than it is to divine the intentions of the enemy—this enigmatic proposition contains a twofold notification: it directs us to the locus designated by the metaphor, which is at once that of politics and of contemporary history; and it teaches us to scrutinize the relationship that is formed without our knowledge with the other during the very moment we think we are rising by means of conjecture to the highest knowledge: that of future operations. But perhaps we would still miss part of the meaning in limiting ourselves to this notification. The primary function of the Machiavellian remark, we said, is to bring back to the text a look that already ran ahead of future developments. It is to prompt us to a deciphering. Now, what we discover in examining Chapter 18 are not isolated thoughts, nor merely thoughts that have been backed up by other thoughts already brought forward; it is also a *passage* of thoughts that we have reason to believe leads intentionally from what has been said to what is not yet expressed. This passage appears to connect two arguments that have objects in proximity to each other. The first, after having pointed out the unfortunate fate of men of *virtù* in a republic sheltered from danger, concludes with the necessity of not confiding new charges when they have been unjustly treated; the second concerns the way of commanding that must be adopted by a military leader in order not to bring harm to the republic or to himself. The second argument seems to be contained within the limits of four chapters, the purpose of which is circumscribed by the discussion of a judgment of Tacitus and a comparison of the styles of conduct of several military leaders, who are—with the exception of Camillus—opposed in binary pairs. The analysis that takes the form here of a methodical critique of the advantages and disadvantages attaching to a kindly versus a cruel command shows once more the singular position of authority in a republican form of government; but this time within the framework of a vigorous state that struggles to defend itself or to grow. But it is not only by this trait that it shows its novelty. The title of Chapter 19—"Whether Respect for Others is Preferable to Punishment in Controlling the Masses" (*se a reggere une moltitudine e più necessario l'ossequio che la pena*)—clearly indicates the political scope of a subject treated here once more on the basis of military examples. Moreover, the choice of terms around which the question is organized, and the progressive critique of the *bontà* or *humanità* of the leader, are of such a nature as to recall the last part of *The Prince*—which is explicitly referred to here. Thus, we have every reason to believe that the discourse now takes on a new development, which will make it possible to elucidate the function and the task of the political in the republic, just as *The Prince* rose, beginning with Chapter 15, to general considerations on power and authority. Still, however impatient we are to find an answer, prudence requires that we show some restraint in accepting the judgments passed on the military leaders whom the writer summons to define the best style of command. We know that some of these leaders will be discussed later, especially Manlius Torquatus, Machiavelli's praise for whom seems to lend weight to our argument. We also know that other military leaders will come to lend their features to the portrait of the political leader. Lastly, we cannot forget that at the moment when the greatest knowledge was designated, the function of the military leader remained without claimant. Still, the author's intention is clearly visible in the four chapters that lead from the Appius-Quintius to the Manlius-Valerius couple. Quintius and Appius are two consuls who share the command of the Roman armies at a time when the city was torn by the struggle between the plebs and the nobility. Machiavelli specifically states that Appius was the enemy of the people— an ambitious and arrogant patrician. He limits himself to pointing out that his command, hard and cruel, was ineffectual, and sets him in contrast to Quintius, whose qualities were a source of amazement. The first hypothesis introduced is that it is better to be *umano* than *superbo, pietoso* than *crudele.* But that hypothesis is introduced only to be confronted with the judgment of Tacitus, who, "followed in this by many other writers," concluded the opposite: *in multitudine regenda plus poena quam obsequium valet.* A second opposition thus crops up that no longer concerns two different ways of commanding, but two ways of judging the facts: one that is founded on an eloquent but particular example; the other that claims the authority of the knowledge of a famous writer and has the weight of tradition on its side. The treatment Machiavelli gives to this opposition in a first phase is remarkable. He does not decide the issue, but pretends to "respect its terms." His concern, if we are to believe him, is to "save" both opinions. In truth the ruse may run deeper than we are in a position to assess, since the expression attributed to Tacitus seems to have been invented; the only passage in the *Annals* in which *poena* and *obsequium* are contrasted has almost the opposite meaning, since in that passage it is considered preferable to appeal to the respect of the subjects toward the prince, rather than fear of punishment; finally, as for the tradition, it is not attested. Does not Machiavelli substitute his statement for that of Tacitus, and does he not invent his own supporting evidence, just as a moment earlier he replaced Epaminondas? Or would it be preferable to speak in terms of identification rather than ruse? In any case, the announced contradiction is resolved by the remark that one thesis is applicable to republican government and the other to a princedom. "In examining how we can save both these opinions, I say: either you have to govern men who in ordinary life are your equals, or else they are men who are always your subjects. If they are your equals, it is impossible to use punishment entirely, or that severity of which Tacitus speaks. And since in Rome the plebs were as powerful as the bourgeoisie, it was impossible for a citizen who governed them temporarily (*ne diventava principe a tempo*) to treat them with severity and cruelty." Admittedly, this remark is attenuated by an allusion to Manlius Torquatus, whose severity was counterbalanced with an exceptional *virtù*, and by the observation that a prince must never go so far as to arouse hatred. But his conclusion is so clear that at first we do not doubt its sincerity. Our conviction only begins to waver upon reading the following chapter, where examples of the kindness of great military leaders are adduced. The odd thing is not so much that the honesty or generosity of Camillus, Fabricius, or Scipio is manifested in their dealings with their adversaries, and not in the commanding of their own troops. We are more surprised that to confirm his praise, Machiavelli invokes Xenophon and gives as his first model Cyrus, a prince. Now, our surprise is well founded, since a moment later the author contests his first hypothesis by remarking that certain leaders attain the same success by taking opposite tacks. It seems, he then notes, that victory is not the result of the causes just mentioned, and that such procedures make a man neither more fortunate nor more powerful, since the opposite procedures make it possible to attain glory and reputation. This judgment constitutes the subject matter of Chapter 21, and is supported by the examples of Scipio and Hannibal. Thus, at this point in the discourse, the balance remains equal. Recognizing that love and fear are the two main motives in the determination of human actions, we can only admit "that it matters little whether a leader takes one or the other of these two approaches, provided he is a man of great enough *virtù* to make a name for himself among men." The essential thing, therefore, is that the desire to be feared or loved does not blind him, or that, once it has been recognized that man's nature forbids his pursuing a middle path, he proves capable of compensating for an excess by a *virtù* such as that of Scipio or Hannibal.

But the continuation of the commentary sways the balance in Hannibal's favor. We are told that the Roman leader's soldiers and some of his allies rebel for lack of severity on his part, and that he was forced to take cruel measures he would rather have avoided; while, on the other hand, the Carthaginian leader seems to have enjoyed "a very great advantage, admired by all the historians, that of having had, in an army made up of men from so many different nations, neither dissent within their ranks, nor sedition against their leader." At this stage of the argument, the distinction between the commander of a republic and the prince seems to have disappeared, and the model represented by Appius to have won out over the one represented by Quintius. But this is only one stage. Two Roman leaders now replace the preceding couple and lead us toward a conclusion that will completely reverse the original thesis. Their example seems intended to reignite the discussion, since both are presented as endowed, despite their opposite qualities, with the same *virtù*, free of all failings, filled with the same glory. "For not one of their soldiers," writes Machiavelli, "ever shirked battle, or mutinied or failed to comply with the least wish of either of them." The comparison is thus sterling on both sides.

What does it matter, we may persuade ourselves, that the comparison may not be faithful to the reality? If we consult Livy, it seems that Manlius is not of the same caliber as Valerius. The former was consul three times, the latter six; the former won no triumphs, the latter was awarded four of them. The argument requires, no doubt, that their merits seem equal. More noteworthy is the care with which Machiavelli stresses that Manlius was forced by his nature to command with rigor: this commentary will be exploited later. But for the moment, the purpose of the analysis is to establish which of the two's behavior best serves the security of the state. Now, after having observed that the preceptors of the princes tend to favor Valerius, and that Livy speaks of him in the same terms as Xenophon speaks of Cyrus, Machiavelli still does not hesitate to judge Manlius's conduct preferable in a republic. His reason for doing so is that Manlius's command does not win him popularity: it does not win men over to him personally. Devoid of any power that could threaten the government, he does not arouse fears in the senate. On the other hand, even though the conduct of Valerius serves the public good, it would be a cause for alarm in a society already spoiled by corruption, or if a leader of this kind were to hold the position of commander in chief for an extended period. "It will undoubtedly inspire mistrust, and the suspicion will arise that the personal goodwill which, in the course of a prolonged command, a leader inspires in his soldiers, may lead to negative consequences with respect to the public liberty." The final word of the discussion is the opposite of the first: the two terms of the alternative, at first considered with "respect," eventually call for a "cruel" choice. The cruelty of the choice lies in the circumstance that the republic proves to be, despite appearances, the government that imposes severity, or even inhumanity, of command, while the monarchy can accommodate gentleness in the management of men. "I therefore conclude," Machiavelli writes, "that the procedure of Valerius, useful in a prince, is harmful in a citizen—to the state, because it paves the way for tyranny, and to himself, because, making his intentions suspect in the eyes of the fellow citizens, it forces them to take precautions that turn to his disfavor." With this conclusion, the author demolishes the opinion that is favored by a bourgeoisie that claims to be democratic, liberal, and pacific. But it is worth pointing out that the leader obtains security while the state does also, so that their interests coincide. An episode from the history of Venice confirms this thesis *a contrario*. We are told that a citizen who was able to settle a violent dispute in the port, when the public security forces were unable to do so, was thereby judged to be dangerous, and shortly afterward either imprisoned or executed. The example would have us understand that that man of *virtù* had to pay for his imprudence. However noble his intentions may have been, it is not (so he should have reflected) on them that he would be judged, but on the image he gave of his authority. His mistake was to forget that the citizen and the state are always threatened by one another and that consequently certain outstanding services can be considered crimes. The adroit leader, on the other hand, who recognizes in the empowered a potential adversary, and knows he is a potential adversary from their point of view, disarms suspicion by avoiding standing out by excessive popularity. He finds the path to glory in pretending not to seek it.

Such is the truth rendered by the four chapters we have just examined. As we receive it, it must be admitted that it does not pertain to political psychology, and even less to an assessment of the significance of famous Romans. What appears to be confirmed is the conception of a system based on the exclusion of personal power, and consequently on the reciprocal mistrust of the actors; a system organized in such a way that ambition cannot make a career, unless it be by the oblique path of disinterestedness. Such a system creates the possibility of a politics at the service of the public good; not, clearly, because men agree on its definition by nature, but because they cannot coalesce without danger to further personal interests, and because, in sum, obedience to the law turns to their greater advantage. But if we hesitate to adopt this thesis, it is because we cannot forget the reservations it has already encountered. Have we not just been reminded that the success of republican rule is tied to social or historical conditions, and that the city must be kept in poverty or beneath the constant threat of danger from without so that no one can corrupt the people, or so that the people will feel compelled to choose the best governors? Have we not learned that such conditions cannot last long? That the model of Manlius is no longer possible once Rome has drifted into sleepy security, spoiled by wealth and torn asunder by factions? That model is even less conceivable in Florence. It is no doubt important to the author to convey to us that even during periods when the republic has not been spoiled by corruption, the authority of the leader is not measured by the *consensus* of those whom he commands. The importance of this doctrine will be revealed in Chapter 30, where we will read about the errors of Soderini—obsessed, as he proved to be, by his concern to avoid making enemies. But the argument, at this stage of the discourse, does not reveal its full meaning. The comparison between the types of command embodied by Manlius and Valerius is not convincing. For if its manifest goal is to free us from the common representation of the good republican leader and have us recognize the value of violence in the service of law, it also raises objections that go unanswered. The good Manlius is too close to the cruel Hannibal for us to be able to believe he is simply the incarnation of the virtue of the zealous servant of the republic. Even if we admit that he does not behave as one preparing to set up a tyranny, we cannot conclude that he is cut from a different cloth than the prince, because a prince, once in place, no longer continues to curry favor with his subjects either; he must rather fear endearing himself to them, and take refuge behind the law.

The debate about authority in the republic comes only to a provisional conclusion in the passage presently under discussion. There is further evidence of this fact in the entrance of two new personages onto the stage—two outstanding figures, illustrious Romans: Cincinnatus and Camillus. They will, successively, stand in for Manlius. At first their portraits resemble those of the virtuous military leader who discourages his troops from loving him. But Machiavelli soon reveals a motive for their conduct that has nothing to do with virtue. Such is the skillful balancing off of the description he pens to usher in a new truth.

Our author is led to discuss Camillus in order to correct the conclusion he has just drawn from his praise of Manlius. His remarks on Camillus's banishment extend a reservation introduced at the end of Chapter 22. After having extolled, as I recalled earlier, severity of command, Machiavelli suddenly concedes, "It is rare that the private citizen suffers damage from it, unless the hatred that it excites against him is further envenomed by the jealousy that the great renown of his other virtues may inspire." Such is the nature of this concession that, for the time being, the substance of the conclusion does not seem to be put in doubt. The republic, as we are to understand, normally derives advantage from a rigorous authority; if the individual is occasionally not recompensed for his merits, it is because indeed virtue cannot avoid arousing envy. The example of Camillus, however, announced in the last line of the chapter, is introduced for the sole purpose of troubling our conviction. Camillus, presented at the beginning of Chapter 23 as close to Manlius by his way of commanding, at first seems to be a victim of human ungratefulness. But it soon develops that the people had the best reasons to want to get rid of him. In the space of a brief commentary, his image grows tarnished to the point of making his devotion to the republic seem doubtful. This opinion is skillfully prepared by a quotation from Livy: "*Ejus virtutem milites oderant et mirabantur.*" Machiavelli, borrowing this judgment from the historian, leaves him the responsibility of pointing out the hatred Camillus aroused in the army. But having introduced it, he immediately exploits it in a new sense. While Livy stated that the soldiers both hated and admired Camillus's virtue, and thus that the same object both attracted and repelled them, our author would have us understand that they admired his qualities and hated his vices. They admired his vigilance, his skillfulness, his orderliness in arranging and directing all things, and they complained when they saw that he was far more rigorous in punishing than generous in recompensing. It is true that Machiavelli does not use the word "vice" here. But that matters little, since what is in question is not the character of Camillus, but, as we learn from the analysis of his behavior after the victory over the Veientes, his relationship with the plebs. This example reveals what remained hidden in the case of Manlius: the attachment to the authority of a social class. We were ready to agree that a leader should not try to please, that he must find the path to glory at a distance from popularity, that the republican regime encourages such behavior and remains pure as a result. But to speak of the Subject, the law, and the people without saying that the Subject occupies a certain place in the social space, that the law is interconnected with a definite power, and that the people are divided into dominators and dominated, is tantamount to depriving the question of a part of its meaning. Thus, it is insufficient to admire the command of Manlius, or that of Camillus; in addition, we must avoid losing sight of the fact that they are patricians, determined to make their power felt by those whom they command, and to concede none of their wealth to the plebs, who covet it.

It is true that Machiavelli leaves it to the reader to interpret his commentary, but the commentary itself is eloquent. Camillus's determination to deprive the plebs of the spoils of the Veientes and his insolence in displaying his rank are condemned together. "First, he absolutely did not want to share the booty of the Veientes with them, preferring to apply it to public purposes. Second, when he returned to Rome in triumph, he harnessed his chariot to four white horses, which men said was due to his pride, and the desire to make himself the equal of the sun god. Third, he had vowed to dedicate a tenth of the Veientine booty to Apollo, which made him have to take it back from the soldiers, who were already in possession of it." The lack of generosity and overweening pride are not simply character traits: they designate a certain type of behavior of the dominator. As for the first type of behavior, if there is any doubt about it, we need only look back at Chapter 20, in which Camillus was praised for his generosity toward the Falisci. There Machiavelli skillfully stressed the nobleness of the Roman leader's feelings in his relations with an external enemy, and thus prepared us for his later remark, to the effect that they disappeared when it was a question of an internal enemy. Toward the one, he could either give free rein to his generosity, or simulate it in such a way as to defeat him more surely than if he used force. Toward the other, he wanted to do nothing that would increase his power and appear to be a concession. But equally remarkable is the judgment passed on Camillus's pride. The author does not say that he coveted tyranny, but he seizes on this trait to critique the princes who made themselves hateful to their people by their arrogance. The assimilation of Camillus's conduct to that of a prince throughout that passage is even more significant when we consider that already in Chapter 20 he was compared to Cyrus, at that time in a favorable sense. In the present case he is presented as being among those princes who take a line of action "devoid of prudence and reckless," which gratuitously elicits hatred and exposes them to the legitimate fury of their subjects. How, then, are we to be satisfied with the conclusion that the rigorous commander harms no one but himself? However great his talents and his glory may be—a glory that still shines in the eyes of Florentines and imposes moderation on any eventual detractor—we must admit that the republic itself is jeopardized by the intransigence and pride of the patrician leader.

The critique of Camillus remains at a preliminary stage, offset as it immediately is by the encomium of Cincinnatus. In this last we recognize another variant of the Manlius type, and it appears that this one carries no reservations that might temper the reader's unrestricted admiration. Cincinnatus is that leader who normally lives in poverty, cultivates his parcel of land without thinking to pursue a position of command, leaves that occupation when the safety of the state is at stake to take up the position of supreme commander, and relinquishes his functions the moment his task has been accomplished. The first trait recommending itself to us is his refusal to accept the extension of his term of office in circumstances in which the senate wanted to use him to oppose the tribunes who had been reelected by the people. Machiavelli withholds one of the reasons for this refusal, and nor does he say a word about the cause of his poverty. But readers of Livy are aware of the lesson the virtuous leader had learned from life. His son Caeso, one of the most eminent, but also one of the most arrogant young patricians, and the most hated by the plebs, barely escaped a death sentence and fled to Tuscany. He himself was ruined by a fine he had had to pay during the trial and was permanently viewed as suspect by the people. Thus, his modesty was his best protection and chance of safety—and his poverty a consequence of the punishment directed against his son's pride. The fact that the author does not give us the full information furnished by Livy does not eliminate the possibility that he exploits it. It is not by chance, in my view, that he writes in praise of Cincinnatus, after having spoken of the banishment of Camillus: his *virtù* is asserted in response to another banishment—the voluntary exile of Caeso being simply anticipatory, according to his family, to the decision of the tribunal. Nor is it mere chance that, in the following chapters, he writes of the way Rome repressed sedition in subservient states, and the dictator within the City. The portrait of Cincinnatus doubtless appeases the anxiety of certain readers by ostensibly attesting to the loyalty of Machiavelli to the ideal of Roman virtue extolled by tradition. But that is not the only effect it has: it also affords a glimpse, clinging to the positive image, of the image of the young, insolent troublemaker whose provocations must be chastised in order for the republic to be able to maintain itself, and of the image of violence—the dictator whose "royal arm," as Machiavelli will say at the end of Chapter 28, "makes one who has crossed the line return to the fold."

It is true that the reader may be surprised at first that the writer should dedicate a long development here to Rome's external politics. At first reading, a digression of this sort might raise doubts as to the care that went into the composition of *The Discourses*. What is the chapter [26] titled "How Women Have Caused the Downfall of States," doing here, or the following one: "Ways of Restoring Unity in a State. It Is Not True that Disunity Is Necessary to Maintaining Authority in Them"? But once we have found what is at stake in the discussion, our surprise subsides. The author has not abandoned his purpose; he continues to interrogate the position of the political Subject, but after having given it the traits of a military leader, he gives it those of the state. The substitution is made easier for the reader since in the first chapter, the author, under the pretext of disruptions occasioned by women, brings in Aristotle's analyses of conspiracies, as well as his own, in such a way as to lead us by degrees from external to internal affairs—from the relation between master-state and subject-city to the relation between the prince and his aggressor. In such a context, the violence demonstrated by the Romans toward the Ardeatini who were caught up in civil war can only be thought of as referring to the violence that must be employed by the political leader against factions disrupting the republic. The repression of the disorder in Ardea supplies the model that simultaneously underscores the critique of the Republic of Florence toward Pistoia. We understand this to mean that there are circumstances in which ruse is in vain, in which maneuvers that tend to divide enemy parties to impose our authority turn against us—in which, for example, the little sleights of hand of a Soderini turn to the advantage of the adverse factions. It is true that the Gonfalonier is not yet mentioned by name; he will not come back on stage till later. But what has been said of his weakness or his so-called goodness is clear enough for us to be able to compare his attitude toward the partisans of the Medici and the former Savonarolians to that of Florence toward Pistoia. By trying to win over his adversaries and by playing one side against the other, he brought dissention into his own camp, and undermined the basis of his authority to such a degree that he was abandoned by all in the hour of danger. Had he understood what Rome's policy was, and that of the Roman dictator—what they were in reality and not as seen through Florentine ideology—he would not have feared not to appear good. In reality, Rome does not behave as a good power. It acts like a tyrant toward the cities that owe it obedience. Advised of the sedition of Ardea and of the conflict setting the nobility against the people, it hurries forward to intercept the Volscian army that had come to support the plebian clan, encircles it, reduces it to starvation, and then, having triumphed, brings help to the nobles and immediately has the leaders of the sedition executed. Its repression is implacable, but the efficacy of its action is seen in the fact that instead of bringing the divisions of the adversary within its own walls, without resolving them, it avoids the danger of contamination by cauterizing the sickness with fire. Now, what Rome does to the enemy—we find this echoed in the way the dictator represses the factious activity. The goal of Chapter 28 is to convince us of this. Nor does it escape our notice that the example chosen in it—that of a rich merchant previously mentioned, Spurius Melius, who enjoyed a dangerous popularity—is presented in such a way as to give a strong emphasis to the initiative of repression. Machiavelli omits the detail furnished by Livy that arms had been discovered in his domicile and is satisfied with observing that he was put to death for having shown excessive generosity . . . He suggests in this way that violence used against a citizen who poses a threat is legitimate even before the citizen has resorted to it. It is true that here the writer is careful to distinguish between the means by which men acquire popular favor, that he praises ambition that acts in public ways, that is, ensures an outcome through services rendered to the state, while condemning ambition that follows secret itineraries. But one sentence reminds us of the danger incurred by the republic due to men being too desirous of glory: "I say that a republican state cannot endure, nor be governed, in the absence of eminent citizens; but on the other hand, the consideration they earn sometimes leads the state into servitude." Caeso, the most eminent of the young patricians of his day, was a danger to the state; Camillus, whose service was extraordinary both before his banishment and after his return to Rome, also represented such a danger at a certain moment. Can we continue to believe that a character such as that of Manlius is sufficient to ward off that threat? We are beginning to realize that the problem has been deliberately posed in inadequate terms. We are not being asked to choose between a gentle and a harsh command, but rather to examine the link between authority and knowledge. Rome knows how and why its own interests require it to repress. It knows that violence must be the response to the present or potential violence of the adversary. To those who are afraid to use it, Machiavelli suggests that their Roman heroes, such as Manlius, Camillus, and Cincinnatus, were not good by nature; that their devotion to the law was inseparable from the defense of class interests; that there is no formula for being spared the risk of deciding *here and now* who is serving the republic and who working in the direction of its downfall, who by his authority is upholding the law, who subverting it; and finally, that the refusal to strike the adversary is tantamount to accepting one's own undoing.

Now it is after having drawn our attention to the repression in Rome of internal or external enemies that Machiavelli devotes a short chapter [29] to showing that "The Faults of Peoples Come from Their Princes." "*Principi*," he writes. But the use of the term has become sufficiently indeterminate for us to apply it to the directors of a republic as well as to kings or tyrants. The Roman dictator who punishes the ambitious does so with a royal arm, "*con il braccio regio.*"

I see yet another sign of prudence in Machiavelli's justification of this principle (that the sins of the people come from their princes) in his choosing as an example the people of Romagna, whose corruption, before the conquest of Caesar Borgia, was engendered and maintained by the little signors who exploited them. This is because no reader would have been likely to take up their defense. But under cover of that condemnation, I perceive the accentuation of the movement leading from praise for the leader whose virtue lies in his self-effacement before the law to the image of the leader who, by his action, through making himself respected by the people, raises men to the idea of a new task. Any possible doubt about the reality of this movement is removed when we consider the choice of the second example: a pirate leader who succeeds in persuading his followers to free some Roman ambassadors charged with delivering to Delphi a portion of the plunder from Veii. What is being revealed to us is that those in charge have the power to corrupt as well as to awaken men to virtue. Neither good nor evil is anonymous. Thus it is not just the logic of the republican system, the instituted order of the exclusion of personal relations, to which the success of the Roman formula can be attributed. The actions of the empowered, even though they are regulated to some degree, possess their own efficacy. In fact we have already understood this: the analysis of the function of the dictator qua adjudicator/enforcer of justice revealed that there was in the best of regimes some defect in the law that, to be corrected by law, required an excess of authority. We saw that even in times when a salutary insecurity and a salutary poverty still reigned, the threat of corruption was not eliminated, and that good initiatives were needed to correct bad ones. But the light shed on the function of the leader illuminates the chances of a social change thanks to the intervention of a virtuous reformer. For if that function is decisive at a time when the republic functions best, how much more so is it when the restraints that held back its energies are released. In a corrupt regime, true authority is most often thrust aside, but it is all the more required since the ordinary means do not suffice to maintain the reign of law. And he who thinks that the weakness or vilification of the people keep them from desiring a new government forget that the degeneration of their willpower is caused and constantly prolonged by those who direct them.

Thus it is not for no reason that, after having painted a grim picture of Romagna in which there is a corruption that spreads from the dominators to the dominated, and brings it about that at all levels of society "the stronger take it out on the weaker," Machiavelli introduces the example of brigands converted to virtue and describes an action capable of reversing the direction of things. Of the captain respectful of the sacred gift, robbed of his own, Machiavelli goes so far as to say: "Though born in Lipari, this 'prince' behaves like a Roman." He thereby lets it be understood that if a pirate can achieve Roman *virtù*, others who consider themselves civilized should not despair of attaining it as well, and of rallying the people to a just cause. This example is significant for several reasons: being of a nature such as to win the approval of certain readers for the praise it contains for a "good action," it suggests to others that it is not by his generosity that a Camillus differs from a brigand; and finally it suggests that if a man endowed with authority can change wolves into sheep, it is doubtless not impossible for him to change sheep into wolves.

Thus the last stretch is completed along the path leading to the scene of Chapter 30. There is no longer any point, at this stage, in continuing to represent politics in the guise of war: the struggle against the domestic enemy and the foreign one merge. The situation is that in which the state risks the greatest danger. Rome and Florence are simultaneously beneath our gaze. On one hand, Camillus, in response to the redoubtable threat brought to bear on the state by the coalition of all its adversaries, demands that the supreme command be entrusted to it: the very ones who envied his glory stifle their resentment; fear is effective; envy is suppressed in the most effective way: "Each one trembling at that time for himself forgets all ambition and runs to take his place beneath the banner of the great man who he hopes will save him." Camillus is equal to the circumstances; he looks after everything and saves Rome. On the other side we have Soderini, the ruler who cannot quell envy when it does not die down of its own accord. Initially his image is associated with that of Savonarola, the man who first gave the spectacle of powerlessness. He could not defeat his enemies "because he did not possess the requisite authority [he was a monk], and because he was not understood by his own followers. But for all that he was no less vociferous in his indictments of the wise of this world—that is to say, of the envious and the adversaries of his doctrine." But even more blameworthy is the weakness of the Gonfalonier [Soderini], since he held the reins of government in his hands at the moment when the freedom of Florence was at stake. "He counted on time, his goodness, and good luck, and on a few acts of kindness, to overcome such envy: seeing that he was still young he thought he could triumph over the great number of men who opposed him because of envy—without scandal, violence, or tumult. He did not understand that time does not wait, that kindness is not enough, that fortune is fickle, and that wickedness finds no amount of generosity that could satisfy it." The mistake of both reformers is their failure to recognize the danger to the state represented by the envious. Indeed: "If such men live in a corrupt city, in which education has not been able to awaken any generosity within them, it will be impossible for anything to stop them. To attain their ends and satisfy their perversity, they would be willing to accept even the downfall of their fatherland." Or, if Savonarola and Soderini were not entirely unaware of the danger, they were loath to employ the necessary means against it; they hid from the truth that "for that sort of envy there is no other remedy than the death of the envious."

Considering the two responses brought to the political and military crisis confronting a city, the reader discovers what the imitation of the

Romans means to a modern politician. To imitate Camillus is not to act as
Camillus did; it is to find in a new situation the means of combat as adequate as were those used by Camillus; it is even to follow a path apparently
opposed to his, since Camillus, who was then consular tribune, asked the
other tribunes to consent to hand the supreme command over to him,
whereas it would have been appropriate to seize it and exterminate his
rivals. To imitate, in sum, means to invent one's own model; not to govern
according to the established image of good authority, but to decipher
with the help of the past the meaning of a relationship between oneself
and others, the forms of which vary with the singular and therefore always
new conditions of action. In Soderini's case, to save the state did not
require his identifying himself with the savior of the Roman Republic.
When the members of the council swore loyalty to him and to fight to the
death under his command, he did not imagine himself to be in the place
of Camillus. Quite to the contrary, he rejected that identification as a trap
in which the bourgeois of Florence, disguised as Romans, were trying to
catch him, and soon thought rather of Moses, of whom the Bible, "if we
know how to read it," says that he was forced, in order to ensure a future
for his laws and institution, to "have an infinite number of men put to
death (*amazzare infiniti uomini*)."

The third critique of Soderini—the culmination of the discussion
that began in Chapter 19—is organized in the same way as the preceding
ones. First he was compared to Brutus, but a moment later we learned
that his task was far more difficult than that of the founder of the republic, because it did not meet with general approbation. Then, his strategy
was compared with that of the second Fabius, but we then discovered that
it was closer in spirit to that of Hannibal. Now, the example of Camillus
serves to bring out his weakness, but the model invoked is Moses, and
we learn that only the initiative of a bloody mutation could save him and
the state.

But if it is true that Brutus could count on the support of the Roman people, whose valor the Tarquins had not entirely destroyed, Moses,
in his implacable struggle against the enemies of the law, had the support of the Jewish people, forged in trials and battles. As for Fabius and
Camillus, they were at the head of disciplined armies, sometimes capable
of winning even in the absence of their leaders. Last, Hannibal, when he
is brought on stage, has already trained his troops with such *virtù* that he
no longer runs any risk of rebellion. False or true models for a Florentine leader, neither group had to command men who lacked both combat experience and the desire to fight. Machiavelli does not let us lose
sight of this fact. In the following chapter, continuing to praise Camillus, he shows the constancy of his conduct amid personal victories and

defeats, and contrasts him with faint souls, madly presumptuous when fortune favors them, and, at the first reversal, so cowardly as to prefer to flee rather than to defend themselves. But this judgment is immediately corrected by the remark that republics share these virtues and vices, and that they form leaders in their image by the education given to the citizens. Thus, the merits of Camillus are counterbalanced by those of the Roman soldiers, and we must recognize that he would not have been able to win had his army not been well disciplined and exercised in times of both war and peace. Symmetrically, the image of troops without training reduces the leader's power to nothing: "A second Hannibal would fail," we are told, "in commanding such troops." But these reservations cannot, at present, mislead us. Besides the fact that the reference to the Carthaginian leader is ambiguous—because of all the leaders that we have just mentioned, he is the one who, before enjoying the benefit of a combative and loyal army, had had to form it himself—we have not forgotten that Epaminondas converted the Theban peasants into intrepid soldiers, and that Sempronius Gracchus succeeded in mobilizing slaves in the service of Rome. There is doubtless a moment in which the weakness of an improvised army denies its leader any chance of success, but then it is because conditions no longer allow him to introduce new institutions. The observation does not apply to a revolutionary enterprise deliberately taken up. Moreover, we may ask whether, in the most unfavorable cases, it does not remain possible to force men to fight, if not successfully, at least with the energy of a last hope.

The examination at this point in the discourse of ways in which peace may be made impossible [Chapter 32] is well suited to remind us that initiative retains its rights in extreme situations. Specifically, the second episode related is of such a nature as to alert us: In order to deprive their troops, in revolt against Carthage, of all hope of reconciliation, their chiefs, Machiavelli tells us, incited them to murder the Carthaginian ambassador, Hasdrubal. Such a crime is not merely anecdotal, but supports the statement of a general rule: "To deprive a people or a prince of all desire to reach an agreement, there is certainly no more efficient or more durable way than to induce them to commit some atrocious crime against the one with whom you want to keep them from becoming reconciled." Had the rule been applied to Florence, how would it have been translated? We can hardly be surprised to see that on this point our text says not a word. But the reader has only to recall the last days of the Florentine republic to fill in the blanks. No one took the necessary measures to force the people to fight; no massacre, no hostages, but the freeing of the imprisoned Mediceans, due to the insufficient number of guards. Whatever we may think about it, the ignoble choice made by the

Carthaginian captains proves to be symmetrical with the noble choice made by the pirate captain from Lipari. We should also note that the two examples flank that of Moses, the great reformer, who does not hesitate to use the cruelest means to force the envious to respect the law—Moses, who has nothing in common with a good pirate or sinister chiefs of rebel bands, but whose conduct teaches us that the violence of the prince is necessary to the foundation and maintenance of social order. Now this composition allows us to clarify the function performed by Chapter 31. It appears to correct the teaching of the preceding chapter. The nature of the political regime proves so determinative that it reduces the freedom of the individual to nothing; Soderini, as we said, ceases to be an independent actor; a critique of him becomes vain, since no one is adjudged capable—however great his merits—of solving the problem confronting him. But in fact the correction attracts our attention to questions that have become of major importance: Is the revolutionary initiative of a leader possible in the corrupt condition of Florence of the time, and what form should it take? If we stick naïvely to the text, we have to admit that it does more than introduce a reservation: it is incompatible with the preceding argument. Now it is never unintentionally that Machiavelli places the reader in contact with a contradiction. The latter forces us to scrutinize opposite terms in order to discover a meaning that was not immediately apparent. In the case at hand, it forces us to question once again the foundation of collective discipline and the relation of authority to the people. Once again, I say, because this questioning has accompanied the discourse since the beginning of the book—but doubtless in a new perspective, or a form that offers a more direct access to the present situation.

Again, it is on the basis of certain signs that we are able to find the path followed by the author in the last part of his work, from the moment the image of Moses replaces that of Camillus. First of all, the use made of the example of Fabius must focus our attention. This captain, whose effectiveness and glorious transgression was pointed out to us at the end of Book 2, is cited five times, and the entire discourse ends with his praise. We are justified in presuming that he embodies a kind of authority that none of the other Roman leaders—Manlius in particular, who was temporarily held up as a model—is able to represent. Further, we must observe that when Machiavelli mentions him for the first time, it is to specify that his hero advanced into country that was "new, uncertain, and dangerous." Now, this theme of unprecedented action is repeated in several chapters. On one occasion it takes the form of perils to which the leader of a new venture is exposed; on another, we are told of the methods used to combat "a new and fearsome enemy"; on yet another, of the qualities a leader must possess to fight "a new enemy"; and finally, of the usefulness of hunting, in learning how to operate in "unknown" territory. These instances are, in my view, indications that the purpose of the last eighteen chapters of the work is to describe the action of a political subject in dealing with adversaries that the tradition does not allow us to identify, in a situation without historical precedent.

We have no reason to doubt that Camillus's success would not have been possible without the support of a disciplined army. But to conclude that in cases in which such discipline is lacking no undertaking can succeed would be to treat that outcome as a natural given. Now it is precisely this conclusion that Machiavelli begins by rejecting, after having observed that the chiefs can place their troops in a situation in which they must fight to the death. He conducts his refutation in keeping with his usual procedure, initially pretending to accept the common way of seeing things. In a chapter titled, "To Win a Battle the Troops Must Be Inspired with Confidence Both in Themselves and in Their Commander," he first singles out the qualities that ensure harmony within the army, and then stresses the role played by religious feelings among the Romans. But scarcely has he conveyed to us the discourse of a patrician commander who exalted the virtue of religion when an episode from the war with the Praenestines tells us that the soldiers were unmoved by coincidences that might otherwise have seemed to be bad omens. After having put in the mouth of Appius Claudius (how can we not be suspicious of the words of an Appius?) an indictment against the tribunes of the people, who had the audacity to disregard those small matters (*"parva ista," "queste piccole cose"*) that had allowed the ancestors to create the grandeur of the republic, he reminds us that a vain thing (*una cosa vana*) could not dull the manly courage of the troops. Then he goes so far as to maintain that the troops, put in danger by the error of their leader, could overcome the enemy by their own merit. Finally, he mentions the artifice used by Fabius to give confidence to his army when it was preparing to fight "*in paese nuovo incontro a nimici nuovi*": Fabius does not boast of enjoying the favor of the gods, nor does he make the entrails of chickens speak, but after having enumerated all the reasons to hope for victory, declares "that there are others that could be mentioned, but that cannot be communicated without danger." He does not ground his authority in some special science that eludes human understanding, but in his own knowledge.

The example of the intrepid captain who did not hesitate to transgress the orders of the senate and rush headlong into the forbidden forest in pursuit of the Etruscans is of such a nature as to persuade us that in the case of a new action there is no better conduct for a leader, once he has weighed the rational arguments, than to make himself the final arbiter of truth. Now, there can be no doubt about the symbolic value of this example, since Machiavelli immediately moves from the military to the political domain, asking in the following chapter, "What Reports, Rumors, or Opinions Cause the People to Begin to Favor a Particular Citizen: And Whether the People Have Better Judgment Than the Prince in Bestowing Magistracies."

It is true that at first the question seems to have no connection with the preceding considerations. Yet the reservations that the demonstration cannot fail to generate, when one takes into account other passages of the discourse, and the commentaries it introduces, leave no doubt as to the continuity of the argument. The writer claims to establish that the people are better able than a prince to discern the qualities of the men who vie for the highest offices. At first we are tempted to take his words literally. But besides the fact that he has already maintained this at the end of Book 1, by dint of ample argumentation, and that it is not necessary for him to come back to it at the present time, we are surprised that he does not remind us that in periods of security the republican regime favors the ambitious. The perplexity grows as we see him bring up, on the other hand, the example of the second Fabius to prove that the people are attentive to the counsel of competent men, since, if it is true that on one occasion Fabius influenced the vote in favor of a better candidate to the consulship, in at least two others, as we have learned, his warnings were not heard and the rigidity of his character nearly caused the downfall of the republic. Did Machiavelli not note in Book 1 [Chapter 53], "We know what a poor opinion the Roman people formed of him when he tried to persuade them to resist the impetuosity of Hannibal with delaying tactics, and to carry on the war without engaging in battle. In this counsel the people saw only cowardice. They could not understand the usefulness of it, and Fabius could not find enough strong reasons to convince them. The people are so blinded by brilliant illusions . . ."? In recalling this passage, we wonder whether the author himself has ignored it, and is deliberately locking himself up in a contradiction. But we are not left long in doubt, because the following chapter is dedicated to showing the difficulties that besiege a well-informed advisor when the truth he must reveal offends the sensibilities of the people or the prince. There, it is repeated that men are so blind that they only judge the value of advice on the basis of its results. This remark forces us to consider in a new perspective everything that has just been said about the goodness and prudence of the people, and allows us to appreciate its function. It then appears, once again, that the author has introduced a view only to reject it. But we must not neglect what he rejects. It is not, strictly speaking, a democratic view, but rather a view that the "progressive" element of the dominant class forms of democracy: that the people are naturally disposed to rally to the advice of its good leaders, and naturally inclined in the first place to choose them judiciously. That Machiavelli wishes to destabilize this view does not mean that he denies all value to the people and embraces the monarchic or aristocratic view. He directs his harshest criticisms to them. But now it is important for him to reaffirm that one cannot have a novel undertaking depend on an actual *consensus*, and that opinion cannot be truth's ultimate criterion. The way he makes this point is polyvalent. In Chapter 35, he says he only wishes to examine the way an advisor should behave. "The examination of the dangers to which a leader is exposed who takes charge of changes by which many are affected, the difficulty of directing them and bringing them to perfection, and once perfected to maintain them—this would be too broad and difficult subject to be treated here. In reserving that discussion for a more propitious place (*pero riserbandola a luogo più conveniente*), I shall speak only of the dangers incurred by those advising a republic or by those advising a prince to take the lead in some grave and important matter in such a way that for the whole of this advice they may be held responsible." But in fact there will not be a "*luogo più conveniente*" in which the writer will analyze the chances of a novel enterprise. Familiar as we now are with Machiavelli's approach, we have good reason to believe that this artifice is a way of communicating his intention [by preterition], and that he announces precisely what he excludes . . . But it is also true that at this moment, as he alludes to the difficulty in establishing a foundation, Machiavelli is drawing attention to himself—to his former status as secretary of the republic and on his present status, as a writer discoursing on politics.

The observation from which he sets out is that the advisor finds himself in the cruel alternative of either holding his peace, for his own safety, thus betraying his duties toward the state, or of recommending a course of action, and thus incurring the opposition of all who do not agree. Now he experienced this alternative during the former regime, when he was in the service of the government, and he is confronted with it once again in his works, though in a very different way, because he now addresses a public to speak the truth about the present. When he decides that the adviser should neither shut himself up in silence nor risk naming his choice, but rather pretend to examine the various parties with equal serenity, and speak in such a way as to incite others to act in virtue of his own authority, and then when he concludes that if his advice is not followed, at least he will obtain the glory of having seen clearly, even though he was unable to save the state from ruin—what we hear is the making of a case for the figure who was once passionately engaged in a plea for a people's army, and reduced to powerlessness by men entrenched in power, but also an appeal to discover in the continuation of the discourse, beyond the hypotheses serenely analyzed, the politics he advocates. As for that politics, it is understood that its application would fall to others to carry out. When Machiavelli was a civil servant in the republic, the "others" had a definite identity: they were members of the Signoria, the Gonfalonier in particular. But now that the Mediceans had destroyed the republic [of Florence], who were they, if not those whose dream it was to restore freedom—an ill-defined collectivity consisting of young people eager for new things but uncertain about the modalities of action, and a few men in whom hatred of the tyranny in place had not extinguished fear of the poor? It is because he knows the resistance of some of his readers that the writer has to be careful; but it is also because his oeuvre, as the bearer of a certain truth, promises him a glory that is more durable than political success would procure for him, that he resolves to predict the downfall of Florence, on the hypothesis that his discourse is not heard.

Still, in my opinion the decisive question, the examination of which exposes the adviser to great danger, involves the strategy of the republican reformer, at the helm of a new venture, threatened as he is by the greatest of perils since he cannot count on time to bear out the truth of his struggle, but must bring it into play in the action *here and now*. This question, side-stepped the moment it is formulated—I assume that it secretly governs the last part of the discourse. But as a matter fact the question is not entirely new. We would not be able to locate it if we had not already mastered the critique of authority, of discipline, and of the *consensus* in the framework of the republican regime, if the idea of the necessary transgression that must be accomplished by the reformer to reestablish freedom had not imposed itself, if we had not already seen the breadth of the transformation required of his venture in a corrupt society. In a sense, the answer we seek has already been supplied. We have deciphered it in the traits of Brutus, of Fabius and the conspirator, of Hannibal, Sempronius Gracchus and Epaminondas, and Moses, by scrutinizing the conduct of Rome toward subject cities, and the relations the Roman people had with their leaders, and also in researching the reasons for the failure of Soderini or Savonarola. If Machiavelli now takes care to direct our attention toward the difficulties there are in communicating truth, it is not that he has not already traced out the way; but he probably risks offending the sensibilities of his reader most deeply if his discourse turns out to show the milieu and the men to which he is connected: if its impingement on present practice is revealed.

What reinforces my hypothesis is seeing the unanticipated turn taken by the analysis of war after Chapter 35; it is applied to situations in which the enemy is *new,* or the mobilized troops *without experience,* or the places of combat *unknown.* The fact that it opens with a comparison between the armies of classical times and those of modern Italy indicates what is at stake in the discussion, as long as we bear in mind that war offers an equivalent to politics. Indeed, there is no need to point out once again the confusion and cowardice of the moderns in comparison with the discipline of the Romans and the furor of the Gauls, unless it is to give us a sense of what the task of a future leader would be, and to show that he would have to resolve simultaneously the difficulties that the great captains of the past confronted separately: to vanquish, in a new setting, a new enemy, with new troops.

Moreover, the way Machiavelli decries the weakness of the armies of his day is of a nature to clarify his intentions. In Chapter 36, he invokes the authority of Livy to show the difference between good and bad armies, and relates an indictment by Papirius Cursor against undisciplined troops, as if the image depicted by the consul must *a fortiori* apply to the moderns. Now, in this indictment, discipline is understood as respect for the omens and the orders given by the generals. Thus we have good reason to doubt that Machiavelli's thought coincides with that of Papirius or Livy, since we are aware of his reservations about the effectiveness of religion, and of his favorable opinion of Roman soldiers precisely in circumstances in which their leaders fail. This doubt is increased by the circumstance that the head of the cavalry whom Papirius wants punished for having dared to do battle without his orders is Fabius, a figure whose merits we have learned to appreciate on an occasion in which he famously disobeyed orders. Since, according to Livy, Fabius won a brilliant victory over the enemy behind the consul's back, it is difficult for us to believe that the episode discredits him and puts his troops to shame. Our perplexity increases as we consider the example analyzed in the following chapter. There, Manlius, that perfect republican hero, who had just been exalted as a model, and of whom we were repeatedly told that he chose the good path of ambition by winning the people's favor through his exploits in the service of the state, turns out to have committed a serious mistake: with the consul's authorization, he staked the fate of the army on the outcome of single combat with the enemy. His success, we are told, cannot override the truth of the rule "that a good captain must refuse anything that, being of little importance, might have a negative effect on the army"; Machiavelli reminds us once again of the old adage "that it is reckless to engage in a battle in which, without committing all your resources, you stake all your fortune."

That such a mistake should go unrecognized by Livy, whose laudatory commentary is aptly recalled—this deepens the critique of the great author and radically changes our assessment of that "discipline" we were ready to approve a moment earlier, as well as our opinion of that most loyal servant of the state.

But were we to still have hesitations about drawing a meaningful conclusion from what could be reduced to a series of allusions, we cannot close our eyes to a further indication: the introduction into the text at this point of Valerius Corvinus, a captain whose merits had long been compared to those of Manlius, to the former's detriment. No attentive reader can fail to note the change in perspective that takes place before his eyes here. While Manlius is demoted, Valerius is elevated to the highest level. First, the example of Valerius teaches a strategy that, while it may not be the best one, is preferable to that of his rival; he knows that he must prepare his troops to face a new enemy in a new situation. And above all, he possesses, as we are told in Chapter 38, "the qualities a captain needs to win his soldiers' confidence." From the account by Livy presently under discussion, Machiavelli takes pains to excerpt a passage in which the Roman leader invites those in combat under his orders to follow him in his actions rather than to believe his words—to trust his example rather than discipline. And he adds this commentary: "It is not titles that make men illustrious, but men who make titles illustrious," a formula that resonates like a democratic declaration of faith. Still, I do not believe we are meant to conclude on the basis of what has just been said that the judgments previously made of Manlius and Valerius are to be annulled. It is true, no doubt, that in a republic the conduct of one is less dangerous than that of the other. But what is confirmed at present is that there is no conduct that may be called good per se, and that in extraordinary circumstances, when men are confronted with a great danger, only a leader who is able to give them confidence in himself and dispense with the prestige of rank can lead them to victory. Valerius, whose popularity may well have been cause for concern in the senate—and this means in the Roman oligarchy—has the merit of making his troops forget that he is a patrician. In the discourse Livy attributes to him, he goes so far as to declare that he loves the plebs—a remark too striking perhaps to be taken up by Machiavelli as is, but that distinguishes him from most of the Roman leaders, and that Machiavelli would undoubtedly have known. Now, the example of Valerius clearly has political significance: despite appearances, it is not as an army commander that he proves superior to Manlius, but as a democratic leader whose *virtù* is to vouchsafe a venture for which discipline does not offer a sufficient basis. In reflecting on this example, the reader is again led incrementally to abandon the conventional idea of authority; after having recognized the necessity of violence in the service of the republic, upon examination of conduct scrupulously respectful of the law, he recognizes the necessity of an action transcending the established hierarchy, in a situation in which the *consensus* must be revitalized by a reformer.

The situation that requires a commandment of Valerius's type is, as I have said, one in which a new enemy appears. The unanticipated exploitation made of this figure goes hand in hand with a reflection on strategy, which I consequently believe to be concerned with present practice. At the level of appearances, it is true that the problem posed is strictly military, and examined on the basis of examples from the classical world. Nor would there be any reason to seek a modern formulation of the problem, if we accept the statement just made by Machiavelli, that the Italian armies are good for nothing. But so strange is the argument of Chapter 38, so clear the allusions to the error committed by the Florentines during the Spanish aggression, that we have no choice but to reconstruct the part of the discourse that is withheld from us. Why, after having critiqued Manlius, does the author repeat at this point in the discourse that we should not venture to engage in battle without using all our forces, and once again condemn the custom of guarding the narrow passes? Why, after having asserted that a captain "must procure for his soldiers the occasion to measure the strength of the enemy in skirmishes" in order to free them from fear, does he reject that method a moment later, judging it dangerous, and conclude that a prudent leader must avoid any action that might expose his troops to failure and discourage them? Why, after having praised Valerius to the detriment of Manlius, does he then hold Manlius up as an example to the former, for having had the astuteness to accustom his soldiers to the sight of the terrifying Cimbri before the battle? And why does he introduce into the thread of the discussion a critique of those who obstinately refuse to give up what they should concede, rather than opportunely make the sacrifices necessary to their own defense? Of all these questions, the last poses no difficulty. The realism shown by Philip of Macedon, one of the most able strategists of the classical period, or by the Romans when they were in danger—we know that the Florentines were incapable of that, even though their weakness should have made it all the more important for them to use what strength they had wisely and sparingly. This observation can scarcely enlighten us, however, since it is vain to proceed allusively in order to decry an error already explicitly condemned. If it is extremely important, however, to remember this, it is because it designates once more the time and place to which the analysis refers; a time and place that I have already identified, and that correspond to the last battle in which Florence lost its freedom. Now, envisioning it once again, we are in a position to expose the enemy whose newness makes him formidable.

This enemy is not only an external one, the Spanish, who in 1512 march against Prato and threaten Florence, but also and especially an internal one, a part—the Medici partisans—being in the foreign camp, but the rest within the city walls, and made up of the great families of the bourgeoisie who have not ceased fighting against democratic reform, and have put the defense of their own interests ahead of the security of the state. Is this not the adversary who is new and terrifying to the combatants defending the republic, accustomed as they are to fighting against the declared enemies of the regime, the overt partisans of tyranny? Is it not a war against this enemy that requires both the giving up of traditional alliances (that is, those of the moderates, committed to a social politics of compromise) and the avoidance of preliminary compromises (that is, minor reforms), the effect of which would be to discourage the masses if they turned out to be unsuccessful? Is this not the enemy who must be unmasked before the eyes of those who are prepared to support revolutionary action, so that its weakness is revealed to them? Without this interpretation, the Marius example would remain unintelligible. Captain Marius reveals himself as *prudentissimo* in knowing how to dispel the terror that a new enemy arouses in his troops. "He wanted his soldiers, from the cover of their entrenched camp, to see the enemy and become accustomed to looking them in the face, so that the spectacle of a disorderly multitude, hampered by impedimenta, with useless arms or none at all, would reassure them and give them the desire to do battle." As it applies to military operations, this procedure is unusual and one would be hard put to find another case in which it should have been or should be followed. But if we take the position that the troops represent the partisans of the reformer, and the enemy the bourgeoisie, this tactic seems well founded. Indeed it is a Machiavellian truth that the dominant class, when unsupported by the people, is weak; it maintains itself especially by the fear that paralyzes the oppressed; its methods of coercion are limited and ineffectual before a revolt of the masses. The author, in giving voice to that truth, shows the way to be taken by the reformer. But perhaps he is himself taking on the role of Marius, committed as he is in a project of demystification, the goal of which is to convince the new generation of opponents of its chances of success in confronting the illusory strength of those in power.

But let us dwell further on the conclusion of the chapter that skillfully leads back to its introduction. "That wise conduct on the part of the Roman leader [Marius] must be imitated with care by those who do not wish to incur the dangers of which we have spoken above, and act like the Gauls who '*ob rem parvi ponderis trepidi in Tiburtem agrum et in Campaniam transierunt.*'" Those Gauls who flee, frightened by an event of little importance, those Gauls who accept challenging the Romans, staking their fate on the valor of one of their group—those of whom it was said in the preceding chapter that at the beginning of a battle they seem to be worth more than men and at the end less than women—do they not represent the Florentines—modern and effeminate—who left it to Soderini to decide their fate, and provoked the enemy without engaging all their resources, and then disappeared at the first rumor of defeat, because they had not learned to assess the weakness of the dominant class within the city?

The alternative suggested juxtaposes two politics: the old one, that is blind to the nature of the enemy, remains a prisoner of legalism, confined to actions that exclude the intervention of the people; and the new one, the audacity of which is to transgress the law, which has become a rampart of corruption, to denounce and attack those who have made the state into their private thing, and to rally in its service a new mass of combatants. In Chapter 28 we find this politics associated with the appeal launched by Valerius to his troops, as he commits them to battle against a new enemy. Such is his virtue that he attests to the old democratic strain that runs through the new enterprise. But that example itself is only brought up in order to introduce another, the political significance of which we cannot fail to notice: that of Epaminondas and Gracchus, who succeeded in "defeating veteran armies, having plenty of experience, with new armies." The example of these great captains teaches us that a leader will never despair of forming good troops as long as there are enough men. Their success authorizes this conclusion: "A prince who has men and lacks soldiers should blame not their cowardice but his own inertia and lack of foresight," a formula that needs to be translated into the language of politics: a ruler who cannot win support for his power in the people cannot blame them for his failure, but must confess to his own.

But however important this last remark may be, the truth of which is borne out by several earlier declarations to the same effect, the allusion made by Machiavelli on this occasion to the tactics of Gracchus and Epaminondas is particularly meaningful. Those two, he tells us, began to train their troops "by mimic warfare" (*battaglie fitte*), "and accustomed them to obedience and order; then they brought them into the actual fray (*nella vera zuffa*) with great confidence." This remark is deserving of our full attention, as it gradually introduces the argument of the following chapter, the first part of which is devoted to another exercise in simulated combat, hunting, and because, beginning with this analysis, the theme of ruse becomes the predominant theme. Now if we consult Plutarch, it seems that Epaminondas, as opposed to Sempronius Gracchus, did not train recruits in the service of the legitimate power, to prepare them to fight a declared enemy, but, acting under the guise of sporting competitions, he taught Theban youths to dominate in contests against the Spartan occupiers, and applied himself, when they won, to exciting them to rebel. While Pelopidas, having taken refuge in Athens, formed the project of gathering together other banned men to develop a plot against the tyrants, Epaminondas remained in his country, and relying on his poverty to pass unnoticed by the regime, prepared the youth for revolt and created future leaders for a revolutionary war. He did not accustom them to "obedience and order," but to the idea of avenging themselves. Placed in a situation in which the external enemy was not distinct from the internal one, he carried out his operations in such a way as to make his objective undetectable; he caused the young to rise up against their oppressor, by seemingly innocent exercises, being more far-sighted in this than Pelopidas, who counted on the action of one group of conspirators alone to rid the state of tyranny. Now perhaps we call to mind at this point the portrait composed by Plutarch of Thebes's two liberators, and also perhaps consider it to be significant that after having coupled their names in Book 1, Machiavelli chose, unlike the venerable historian, to give pride of place to the leader/philosopher. "Bodily exercises chiefly delighted Pelopidas, learning Epaminondas; and the one spent his spare hours in hunting and the Palaestra, the other in hearing lectures or philosophizing."[1] This opposition is well fashioned to seduce public opinion, but I have good reason to think that Machiavelli does not share it, since he is convinced that force can do nothing without knowledge. This is why I think it more than coincidental that his praise of Epaminondas is followed by his reflections on the relationship between knowledge and practice, and the role of hunting as a simulation of warfare. These remarks introduce Chapter 39, titled: "That a Commander Must Have a Good Knowledge of Places." "Among other things essential to the commander of an army is a knowledge of terrains and of countries, for, unless he has this knowledge, general as well as detailed, no army commander can perform any operation well. Wherefore, just as all sciences demand practice if we desire to attain perfection in them, so this is one that calls for a good deal of practice. And this practice and this detailed knowledge are acquired more by hunting than by any other exercises."[2] This leaves no doubt in the mind of the well-informed reader: Epaminondas, a man of science, had the right idea about the bond between general and particular knowledge, between theory and practice. He was a student of letters and philosophy, and analyzed the conditions in which it was appropriate to act *here and now;* he conceived of a revolution and perfected the exercises that prepared the way for it at one and the same time. In organizing the competitions between Theban and Spartan young men, he taught his partisans to recognize the weakness of the adversary and their own strength in a game that could be seen as analogous to hunting, since it served as training for war, but differed in that the Spartan played the role of the ferocious prey and the point was to make him appear as such in the course of the exercise.

It is true that Machiavelli now speaks of "knowledge of places," and it is not immediately apparent how this ties in with the science of Epaminondas. But perhaps we do not see it because we do not understand what places are being alluded to. Now, have we not acknowledged for some time that war is a symbol of politics, and does Machiavelli not tell us here that hunting represents war? Epaminondas surely has a knowledge of places, because he has learned by the study of past and present deeds, by meditating on the great authors, to recognize the situations in which political actions unfold. He has been able to explore at length, before taking up action in these spheres, the loci of power and conspiracy. We may go a step further. That knowledge—he not only possesses it, but also transmits it, since he will not be satisfied with just stirring up a desire for revenge among the youth, as Plutarch notes: he will take advantage of that excitement to animate them with a desire for learning. Is it not through that activity that he is a great hunter, a master in an art that the good Pelopidas practiced as a physical exercise?

It is true that I give Epaminondas more importance than the text seems to justify, since he is only mentioned briefly at the end of Chapter 38. Moreover, the signs by which I think I can recognize a model in him may be no more than the elaboration of my imagination. But let us consider the praise of hunting that was just now brought to bear on the considerations in Chapter 39 on familiarity with places. That praise cannot fail to make us uncomfortable. Specifically, we must be surprised that at the end of it Machiavelli analyzes at great length an event that brings out the qualities of a Roman captain and has nothing to do with the virtues of hunting. The example is such as to cast doubt on the meaning that was to be attributed to that exercise a moment earlier. Furthermore, the passage that our author excerpts from *The Cyropaedia* in support of his judgment is oddly incomplete. "Xenophon," he writes, "tells us how, when Cyrus was about to attack the king of Armenia, in appointing tasks he reminded those about him that it would be just like one of those hunting expeditions on which they had often accompanied him; and to those whom he sent to form an ambush in the mountains he said that they would be like men going to lay snares in the ridges; and to those who had to scour the countryside that they would be like men who went to rouse a wild beast from its lair so as, after hunting it, to drive it into the nets. This I mention," he goes on to say, "to show that Xenophon supports the view that a hunting expedition is very like a war, and that, consequently, men of standing look on this sport as honorable and necessary."[3] What Machiavelli omits is that on this occasion Cyrus first pretended to be organizing a hunt in order to approach the enemy without arousing suspicion. Now, it is worth remarking that Cyrus was employing ruse, and that his modus operandi draws him closer to that of Epaminondas. He was not using hunting to teach his men the art of war; he was using a game to hide his intentions. We should not let this detail pass, because the authority of Xenophon was already invoked in Book 2, in a passage that we had deemed decisive, to denounce the politics of trickery practiced by the Romans in Italy. That the praise of hunting is borrowed from Xenophon, who was previously held up as the theoretician of ruse—this should put us on notice. We should be particularly attentive to it, because ruse is a dominant theme of the last chapters of this work. Is Machiavelli once more using Xenophon to serve his own ends?

In order to decide the issue, we must remember that earlier he imputed to Xenophon a thesis of success by ruse that the historian/philosopher had not maintained, at least not explicitly, in *The Cyropaedia*. Machiavelli pretended that Xenophon's account made clear an interpretation of politics all by itself. At present he does not deem it necessary to stress the ruse of Cyrus—a ruse that is quite visible, nonetheless—but draws our attention to the function he attributes to hunting. I am tempted to seek in this procedure the sign of further ruse. Again Machiavelli pretends that the relation of a fact is self-sufficient—that, in the case at hand, the presentation of war as hunting, such as portrayed by Cyrus before his officers, was fully eloquent. He does not try to convince his reader with a demonstration, but speaks as if the reader—or a certain reader—understood enough to follow him. Could it be that the reference to the theme of hunting in Xenophon was richer for the reader than any argument concerning the apprenticeship of war and the use of ruse? There is no doubt that it would have been, if he knew the little treatise devoted to that art by the author of *The Cyropaedia*. We know that a Latin translation of the work, *De Venatione*, was in the hands of many readers in Florence at the time when Machiavelli was writing *The Discourses*. In it, Xenophon is not content merely to observe that hunting provides the best training for war. At the end of a long study, dealing with traps, arms, dogs, and wild animals, he sets in opposition to this noble exercise the vile practices of the Sophists. What becomes apparent here as the real issue in the treatise is the education of youth: an issue in the vicinity of which a series of distinctions are organized, between those who care about the welfare of the state, those who criticize educated men and work, and those who like to learn from others and confront the painful trials of virtue: between men who possess the art of deception and those who seek true thought, between those who focus on appearance and utility and personal profit, and those who concentrate on the common good—distinctions that ultimately reveal two categories of hunters: the Sophists, preoccupied with hunting rich young men, and philosophers. Thus we must agree that Xenophon employs, in his own way, the tactic he attributes to Cyrus. He simultaneously makes hunting symbolize philosophy and uses it against his adversaries. And that stratagem in turn sheds light on that of Machiavelli, for does the latter not continue the game by using Xenophon to reach his goal? If his own intent is to incite the young against the lies accredited by the "sages of the times," would he not have us understand by "the knowledge of places and countries" a new knowledge of politics, a "revolutionary" knowledge that stands only on the strength of the exploration of history and the critique of tradition?

In placing himself beneath the twofold authority of Epaminondas and Xenophon, Machiavelli presents himself as possessing the traits of both the captain/philosopher and the politician/philosopher—the founder of an undertaking that allies the science of the general to that of the particular, the objective of which is the truth of all times and places, and the truth of this time and this place. Like Epaminondas, he addresses the young in order to prepare a revolution. Like Xenophon, he is distinct from the modern Sophists in that he does not hunt in order to make them his prey, but to turn them toward knowledge.

We already knew that the young, by their desire to act, tend to be enflamed by the desire for knowledge. It now appears that to achieve this, a series of trials in which they discover their identity, that of the enemy, and the place of confrontation between the two, is assumed. Through his discourse, Machiavelli engages them in simulated contests, in which they must not only show their superiority over the guardians of the tradition, but understand that they constitute a new army, and learn to recognize the traits of their adversary. The stage closest to themselves, on which they can observe the actors playing out their roles, is without a doubt Florence on the eve of the fall of the republic. To have access to the truth of the drama played out there, they must acquire an understanding of history and raise themselves to the level of philosophy, thus being enabled to inspect the situations of the prince and the conspirator, and the public and secret places of corruption. But this drama, in which the signs of a new revolutionary task are to be deciphered, is still a fiction: to master the plot merely empowers them to find their place in present society and to prepare to act when the occasion arises to overthrow the regime.

If I am right, the example our author borrows from Livy, then going on to show in the same chapter [39] how important it is to know the places when you are doing battle in a new country, is elucidated. There is no reason to be surprised that the hero invoked has not learned to hunt. It is not his military ability that matters here, nor is it of any importance that the pursuit of wild animals has or has not prepared him. The tribune Decius lends his traits to the daring politician who, after having avoided the trap in which democracy was about to be caught, escapes the danger to which he was exposed and returns to his place. He lends his features to the captain/philosopher whose art is to assess the present situation in light of past ones, to take a calculated risk, and, once the state has been saved, to end the adventure.

Publius Decius, as Machiavelli relates, served as a tribune under the command of the consul Cornelius, in a war against the Samnites. Having perceived that the Roman army was in a valley where it could easily be closed in, he saw a hill that overlooked access to it and persuaded the consul to let him take it with a detachment. After having thus ensured the passage of the troops, he succeeded the following night in exploring the area, wearing the helmet of a rank and file soldier, and in escaping from the enemy with his soldiers. This twofold success is particularly singled out for our attention. "Therefore anyone who carefully studies the *entirety of this passage*," the author adds, "will see how useful and necessary it is for a captain to know the nature of the places; for, if Decius had not been a prudent man and acquired such knowledge, he would not have been able to see how useful it was to the Roman army to take that hill, nor would he have been able to tell from a distance whether the hill was accessible or not; nor yet, when he had been sent to the top of it and wanted to get back to the consul, would he, with the enemy on all sides, have been able to conjecture with any certainty the way to go and the places that the enemy was guarding."[4] But of the two exploits cited, it is the second we are encouraged to ponder, in order to appreciate Livy's account *in its entirety*. It illustrates the ability of a leader who does not hesitate to do without the outer signs of authority to escape the enemy's notice, and free his men from the greatest danger after having confronted them with it. This leader combines prudence with daring. He is not blinded by vainglory, but only acts to ensure the safety of the army. Moreover, the action he ventures to take is strictly limited to the necessity of the circumstances. The example of Decius clearly contrasts with that of Cyrus, a prince bent on conquest, preoccupied with building up his own strength, but it also balances off that of Epaminondas, by the limits it sets on the operation, and the light it sheds on the *exitus*, the way back. Is this an indication for us to conclude that when the boldest and most innovative action is called for we should free ourselves from the pattern of particular figures, in which the desires of the actors are embedded? Or that the model of the

Theban revolution is all the more solidly founded for having a reassuringly corresponding figure in Roman history? Or that Machiavelli slips his own agenda into the personage of Decius to drop a hint to the young that in his divergence from the tradition he wishes to be their true guardian, and that the new way he opens for them leads to a good destination?

These questions are not vain, since a few chapters further along the name Decius brings them to mind once again. It is true that the historical figure in question this time is no longer the one with whom we have been concerned, but his son: a man also engaged in war with the Samnites, a son who would like to equal his father in glory, but whose courage and daring, to the contrary, serve only to destroy him and endanger the army.

Nevertheless, the episode in which he is the unhappy hero is destined to bring out the prudence of another leader, as able as was the first Decius to combine the concern for victory with that of security: the great Fabius, of whom we know, moreover, that he did not hesitate before the most daring ventures, even if they sometimes made him overstep the limits of legality. Whereas Decius rushed forward at the head of his soldiers, as the author tells us, to meet the enemy, and resolved to sacrifice himself when he saw his troops waver, Fabius, commanding another wing of the army, was content to withstand the impetus of the attack. Only after having learned of the fate of his fellow did he, "zealous to equal him and live," launch all the forces he had saved for the decisive moment, and come away with a brilliant victory. Fabius, like the first Decius, excelled in finding the best solution. The latter divined the intention of the adversary; Fabius added to that skill the ability to divine the enemy's mistakes. Just as he could, upon occasion, neglect the orders he had received and put the established authorities before the fait accompli, he could also, when necessary, defer combat. He no more resembled his descendant—Hannibal's adversary, a temporizer by nature—than did Decius his son. His conduct was not the result of his temperament. He assessed the situation and acted in consequence. He practiced patience when it was necessary. That patience was not good in itself, but praiseworthy in that it could be combined with its opposite. Machiavelli does not leave any doubt about the meaning of his analysis, since in the preceding chapter (44), he showed that we can often achieve by a violent movement and by daring what is not to be had by ordinary means.

The term *impeto* [onrush, impetus], used in the titles of Chapters 44 and 45, prompts us to explore their articulation. The examples chosen, ancient and modern, to thematize one who can force the other's hand and make him conclude an alliance he did not wish to make, recall the action of Fabius, rushing in pursuit of the Etruscans through the Ciminian forest, convinced that the senate could not but approve it, once the victory had been won.

That a leader of such boldness should be so capable of waiting, without giving in to vainglory, and that he should be so skillful in pre-serving his life—there can scarcely be any doubt that Machiavelli had his reasons for bringing this out in the last part of his work. The portrait of Fabius not only brings to mind that of Decius; among these two captains and Valerius, Marius, and Epaminondas, a kinship emerges that owes nothing to their characters or to the nature of their enterprises. Marius accustoms his troops to the sight of the enemy, Valerius engages them in preliminary skirmishes to increase their self-confidence, Epaminondas trains them in simulated combat, Fabius lets the enemy tire himself out during the initial attacks, and Decius moves away from the main part of the army, thus carrying out spatially a detour that others accomplish in time. Some are not afraid to seem lacking in courage; others go so far as to hide the signs of their authority. Their actions share a common pat-tern; but how can we forget that the pattern was first formed for us by the example of [Lucius Junius] Brutus: that conspirator who discovered, in feigning madness, the only way to protect his life from the tyrant, who dishonored himself, patiently awaited the occasion, and was able, once victory had been won, to return to normal. In that chain of identifications we divine the figure of the man who produced them: Machiavelli himself, who endures the new reign of the Medici, and by the roundabout route of *The Discourses* trains the young to withstand the *impeto* of the adversary, to study his physiognomy, to prepare their response, and to commit them-selves to a slow and prudent conspiracy.

The transition from the captain's strategy in combat to that of the political reformer and writer/philosopher is incessant in Book 3. But it is in Chapter 39, as we have seen, that it best reveals itself to our gaze—in that chapter that opens by praising the knowledge of places and ends with the account of the episode in which the Roman army is about to fall into a trap, before being saved by a daring captain. Thus, where Machia-velli gives many signs of the philosophical and revolutionary bearing of the discourse, where he suggests the pact offered to the young against those who have wrongfully seized the emblems of knowledge and law, he also indicates to the reader who is attentive to his message the path leading to a certain place. The narrows in which the consul Cornelius will shut himself up is assuredly intended to lead us elsewhere. Were we to have any doubts about this, it would suffice to convince us to consider the account, given a moment later, of a new episode of the war with the Samnites, and the many examples in the next to last chapter of traps set or avoided. The writer's determination, in the last part of his work, to produce the image of a trap, to describe the diverse situations in which a captain lets himself be taken in by stratagems or succeeds in exposing them, cannot escape our notice. He produces a clever device to give us a glimpse of what he cannot present: the political struggle in which the Republic of Florence founders on the eve of the Spanish aggression. That evocation is necessary, as only an understanding of the conspiracy that destroyed freedom allows the young to appreciate the difficulties of their own conspiracy aimed at restoring it; it alone makes it possible for them to apply the philosophical and political teachings of the author to current history. But cunning must be used to speak of what must not be said because of the danger that would result from denouncing men, families, and factions that are still alive. Here, the cunning is greater than that of the counselor, of whom we were told that to ensure his safety, and avoid betraying the truth, he dispassionately explains the possible courses of action and leaves the other free to decide. One must be content to provide the reader signs that will inform him of the nature of the subject, and leave him free to understand or not understand. Thus, the greatest trick is to introduce the reader to the specified topic by a discourse on trickery; to at once hide and show one's intention by remarks whose overt meaning seems self-sufficient, that is, sufficiently jarring to the common opinion so as not to elicit further surprise, and yet that testify, in the way they are articulated together, to a stratagem. Indeed, how can we be satisfied with the praise of trickery begun with Chapter 40, once we have observed that it contradicts earlier statements, and contradicts itself in the space of a few pages? We must resist the effect produced by certain apparently daring formulas and seek their organizing motif. Machiavelli at the present time claims to limit the use of trickery to the sphere of warfare. The reservation is odd, since he has had us admire that of Brutus and Epaminondas: "I will say only this," he clarifies; "I do not mean that trickery involving breaking your word or the contracts you have made, is glorious; for, although on occasion it may win for you a state or a kingdom, as has been said in an earlier discourse, it will never bring you glory. I am speaking of trickery which is involved in the conduct of a war."[5] But we have not forgotten his interpretation of Xenophon and the commentary on Roman politics. "She [Rome] could not at the start have been more deceitful," he says in Book 2, "than she was in the means she used, as we were saying just now, to acquire companions, since under this title she made them her slaves, as was the case with the Latins and other peoples round about."[6] Again, how could we forget that in his view there is no more reliable means than trickery to rise from a lowly condition to a great fortune? Doubtless Machiavelli took care not to connect tricks or lies to glory, but his examples, whether of Rome or of Cyrus, speak for themselves. We have good reason to suspect he is fooling us at present, since his first assertions are belied in the continuation of the text. It is to a rejection of the alternative between ignominy and glory that he leads us in Chapter 41, when he writes: "When the safety of one's country wholly depends on the decision to be taken, no attention should be paid either to justice or injustice, to kindness or cruelty, or to its being praiseworthy or ignominious. On the contrary, every other consideration being set aside, that alternative should be wholeheartedly adopted which will save the life and preserve the freedom of one's country."[7] It is again to the suggestion that the political leader cannot be wrong in defending the state that he leads us, when he concludes with the French adage "No decision the king makes can be shameful."[8] Ultimately Machiavelli reverses his earlier statement about keeping the sworn word in Chapter 42, which is devoted to defending the position "That Promises Extracted by Force Ought Not to Be Kept," an argument that finds its crowning touch in the proposition that "forced promises affecting a nation will, in fact, always be broken when the force in question is removed, and this without shame to those who break them."[9]

Here we could no doubt again conclude—considering the successive divergences between the propositions—that the author, faithful to his principle, is attempting to dislodge his readers progressively from a commonly held view. But in this case the procedure does not lead to any new teaching. At the conclusion of the analysis, nothing has been advanced that was not known previously. The discourse on ruse thus reminds us of the one Cyrus conducts on hunting before his officers; it accompanies a movement in the direction of the objective; Machiavelli, like Cyrus, speaks of and approaches his goal. The indication of this movement is given to us as much by the hypothesis introduced (that of an extraordinary situation in which the destiny of the state is at stake) as by the example in relation to which all the considerations on ruse are organized. As I pointed out previously, he presented us for the second time with the Roman army pitted against the Samnites, and rushing headlong into a trap. But there was no Decius in that case to warn it of the danger in time. We are told [Chapter 40] that the Romans, fooled by the enemy disguised as herdsmen, proceeded to let themselves be closed up in the Caudine Forks, where they were taken prisoner by the enemy.

But such is the account of the event that it immediately reveals the mistake committed by the Samnites after their success and the just response of the Romans, in a situation in which they seemed doomed. While the Samnite leader imprudently gave his prisoners the alternative of either passing under the yoke in promising peace or of being massacred, the Roman leaders were able to accept dishonorable conditions to save the army. Moreover, once back in Rome, their consul persuaded the senate to violate the commitments they had made by sacrificing, along with him, only those officers who had compromised themselves. Thus the example offers us the image of a fraud and a counter-fraud, of a trickster and a tricked who switch positions. Now, doubtless most of the elements of the scenario need not be taken into account, since Machiavelli manages to have us come upon them in other scenarios. The narrows of the Caudine Fork in which Lentulus and Postumius were trapped resemble those into which the consul Cornelius ventured; the soldiers disguised as herdsmen reappear in the first example in the next to last chapter; the false information reappears in the last example, in which the Florentines are victims of a Pisan; the image of a deceived deceiver reappears in the same passage; while the appeal by Lentulus not to sacrifice his soldiers' lives to the army's honor finds its homologue in the attitude of Fabius, who let his unfortunate fellow officer sacrifice himself rather than run a needless risk. The only element for which we do not find an equivalent counterpart is the fraud committed by the consul, in making a promise he did not keep. But apropos of him, after having observed that one could break the agreements to which the nation had been committed without dishonoring oneself, Machiavelli adds the following commentary. "Everywhere in history one comes across examples of this of one kind or another, and everyone is aware that it happens also at the present day."[10] Even if the remark seems to apply only to the politics of princes, it calls upon the reader to change the focus of his attention to present events.

But we are sensitive, even more than to that call, to the figuration of a situation in which all means must be employed to escape the traps set by the adversary and to save the freedom of the state. Of all the criticisms addressed to the former rulers of Florence, there is one in particular that we cannot forget: they were imprudently resolved to continue the war against Spain, at a time when necessity demanded prudence and compromise. In Book 2, Machiavelli cited the example of Hannibal, who had not been ashamed to ask for peace with the Romans, courageous and experienced in warfare though he was, contrasting him with the presumption of those [Florentines] who refused a negotiation after the first battle of Prato. The analysis of the behavior of the Romans after their defeat makes us clearly understand that the propositions formulated by the viceroy [of Spain] should have been accepted, that it would have been a matter of little importance to promise to pay tribute, to break the alliance with France, even to furnish political guarantees by the eviction of Soderini, so much did political necessity require the winning of time to organize revenge. But the comparison suggested between the realism of some [the Romans] and the insane vanity of others [the Florentines] again only leads us on to examine a situation whose political physiognomy has only been revealed to us momentarily. I suspect that the mistakes made by both the Samnites and the Romans must shed light on the conduct of the Florentine rulers. Among these mistakes, there is one on which our author insists, and that he has already attributed to the Florentines: that of choosing "the middle path," rather than either pardoning or exterminating—of stirring up the desire for vengeance by the use of offensive means. This was the error of the Florentines when faced with the rebels of Arezzo, as we are now told. This was the error of the Samnites before the Roman army. The comparison would be without meaning if we limited ourselves to considering the foreign affairs of Florence. But it acquires a meaning if, as we have already supposed, the most dangerous enemies of the republic were, in 1512, within the city.

Those who openly plotted in favor of the Medici—were they not for a moment at the mercy of the republicans? Some were imprisoned upon the news of the invasion of Tuscany. But that measure was not effective, since during the last days of the regime, as the author points out in a letter, "the fear rose to such a pitch that the men charged with guarding the palace and other gates of the city abandoned them and left them absolutely undefended, thus putting the seigneury in the position of having to release a great many citizens that they had closed up in the palace for a few days for suspicion of friendship with the Medici."[11] Had not Machiavelli already suggested that when we want to force a people to fight and make peace impossible we must compel it commit some great crime? On this occasion, the "middle path" chosen by the government proved to be useless. We may conclude that it is once again being condemned. But were the partisans of the Medici true enemies within the gates? Their opinions were known, their conspiracy visible. More dangerous by far were surely those who pretended to back the government. And there was no one to expose them. Does not the episode of the Samnite ruse bring us valuable insight into the behavior of these adversaries? The soldiers disguised as herdsmen who fool the Romans—do they not represent the bourgeoisie of Florence, who flaunt their devotion to a government they abhor? So might one well imagine, in light of the conditions under which the first Spanish ultimatum was rejected. Then, Soderini convened the council and proudly declared that he held his charge by the will of the people alone, that he would not give it up even if all the kings of the earth were united in ordering him to do so, but that he was prepared to resign if the assembly so desired. Though he had many adversaries, no one opposed him. His resignation was unanimously rejected, and all offered to defend him even if it meant putting their lives in danger. Soderini, taken in by this show of support, and thinking he was safe on the home front, imprudently committed himself to the policy of resistance.[12]

Would it be going too far to think that he was rushing toward a trap deliberately set for him? It is true that we are not in a position to identify the false herdsmen. But if we consult the account given by our author in the letter we have been citing (addressed to someone whose rank and name, however, required prudence on Machiavelli's part), certain facts make it appear that misinformation was not without effect on the Gonfalonier's attitude. While the Spanish met with an initial defeat at Prato, Soderini, we learn, did not listen to the advice of sage counselors and refused the terms of the compromise proposed by the Spanish viceroy, on the basis of misleading information about the weakness of the enemy, their supposed starvation, and the firmness of the defenders of Prato (*referito le cose degli spagnoli deboli, allegando che si morieno di fame e che Prato era per tenersi*). Then, once the news that Prato had been taken was out, he remained confident, relying on "I know not what chimera of his own" (*confidatosi in su certe sue vane openioni*).[13] Now, we must remember the judgment made in Chapter 30, in a point in the discourse in which Machiavelli crudely recommends the physical elimination of the envious, and mentions Soderini's weakness: "Should such men [the envious] have been used to living in a corrupt city in which education has not done them any good, it is impossible for any misfortune to convert them to a better state of mind. Rather would they see their country ruined than to fail to obtain their ends and satisfy their perverse mentality."[14]

What double game was being played in the council, as the Spanish army approached? What was being plotted between enemy factions behind Soderini's back? To what means did the "envious" resort to achieve their ends, at the very moment when they made a show of presenting a united front in face of the imminent danger? We do not know. But given the facts that the fall of Prato was enough to put an end to all resistance, that Soderini himself, without Florentine arms even coming into play, without being deposed by an assembly, by simple pressure from his entourage, consented to flee, and given that that Ridolfi, his successor, the head of the Optimates party, after his firm declaration in favor of the republican regime, stepped aside so quickly before the Medici, it is not difficult to discern the signs of an ambush prepared long in advance, and of collusion between the conniving partisans of the Medici and the so-called defenders of freedom.

The scenario of the ambush in which a captain is induced by skillful men to abandon all suspicion—we may assume that it is particularly edifying, since Machiavelli presents it for the second time in the penultimate chapter of the work. The repetition stands out all the more, the analysis being spare, and arbitrarily excerpted from Livy's narrative. This time, the Samnites are replaced by the Etruscans: Fulvius, a Roman army lieutenant, is charged with the command of the camp in the absence of the consul, who has been recalled to Rome for a religious ceremony. The enemy's stratagem consists in sending soldiers disguised as herdsmen with their animals. On this occasion, the Roman leader wins out, seeing through the adversary's trickery instead of being taken in: the trickster is exposed. Perhaps it is relevant that to note that this leader is not the normal consul who has authority but a replacement. The latter proves skilled in identifying the enemy beneath his disguise, while his superior is busy deciphering the signs of divine power in the entrails of chickens. Has not Machiavelli already noted that it is more worthy of a captain to see what is happening before his eyes than to divine the intentions of the enemy, to interpret his present and closest actions rather than those performed at a distance? It is indeed the merit of the lieutenant to be at the right place, while the consul is elsewhere—to interrogate the visible, while the other vainly searches the invisible. This indication is all the less likely to go unnoticed, since our author has curiously modified Livy's text in this case. In the latter, instead of there being a consul involved, it is a dictator, and there is nothing about his being absent to take part in a religious ceremony. He is back in the Roman camp when the incident in question takes place, and he is the one who leads the attack on the Etruscans. As for Lieutenant Fulvius, it is indeed his scouts who discover the identity of the herdsmen (noticing that they do not sound like herdsmen), but he himself does no more than command an outpost: he does not replace the dictator at the head of the camp. We would have to say that such an error betrays an intention. In Machiavelli's version, Fulvius takes on traits that bring him closer to Decius and Fabius. Like the former, he is able to interpret what the consul does not see, or has put himself in a position such that he is unable to see; like the latter, he is victorious unbeknownst to the leader, who has been detained in Rome for a religious ceremony. All three are heroes who have had to replace a failing authority. But should we not assume that the error was made to attract the notice of an attentive reader? Such an assumption is not unwarranted, in view of the fact that the rule stated in the title of the chapter [48] introduced by the commentary on Fulvius's exploit: "When you see an Enemy make a big Mistake, you should think that it conceals some Trickery."

Thus we are brought back to the idea that the author is disguising his thought, and prompted to wonder how he is tricking us. Of course he is not our enemy, but have we not already said that he trains his readers in simulated combat? Now, it suffices to be on our guard to notice the oddity of the two other examples in this chapter. The first reminds us of the taking of Rome by the Gauls, an event to which the writer devoted considerable space, at a point in his discourse in which he was about to set up an opposition between the Roman state, capable of recovering even when it was about to fall, and the modern state, unable to recover from adverse fortune because it does not have popular support. This opposition, which is subsequently integrated into the opposition between men whom destiny shapes in such a way as to conform to the nature of the two states, such as a Camillus as opposed to a Soderini, will take on its full significance with the collapse of the Republic of Florence. For the time being, we are only told that the Gauls, after having defeated the Romans on the Allia, marched toward Rome, that they found the gates of the city open and unguarded, and spent a day and a night without going any further, for fear of falling into a trap. Then, there follows on this brief account the relation of an episode in which the Florentines are seen to have been cruelly mocked by a false refugee from Pisa. While they were laying siege to that city, we are told, they made a deal with one of its citizens, Alfonso di Mutolo, who promised to place one of the gates at their disposal. "In order to appear faithful to his promise, Mutolo returned several times afterwards to confer on the matter with the deputies of the army commissioners; but rather than to go there secretly, he did so openly and in the company of several Pisans, whom he left a little to one side when speaking with the Florentines. The presence of the latter should have given him away, because it was not credible that he would have dared deal so openly in an affair of this sort if he were doing so in good faith."[15] Our author adds that the Florentines were blinded in this case by their desire to take Pisa. What the text conceals, while at the same time designating it, is the same object that constituted the focus of the chapters dedicated to the ruse of the Samnites. Rome beckons toward Florence. Like the Romans, "its inhabitants charged with guarding the palace and other gates of the city abandoned them and left them absolutely undefended." Furthermore, once the Medici had returned and the government been changed, the nobles hesitated to obey the order of the viceroy who was in a hurry to restore Lorenzo's regime, because despite their victory they were so surprised at the inertia of the people and fearful of a sudden revolt. Machiavelli leaves it to the reader to interpret the signs he leaves in the text. He either does not name Florence, and that is when he signifies it, or else speaks of it by name, but in using an event different from the one [ostensibly] related. He brings about a twofold displacement in space and time to dissimulate and get his thought across. But is that thought not dangerous? We have already wondered, in examining the Samnite ruse: Who—in Florence—were the enemies disguised as herdsmen? What was the false information disseminated? What was the double game organized unbeknownst to the Gonfalonier? The question returns, insistent, laden with the memory of the ambiguous figure of Mutulo, that Pisan who came to offer his services to the enemy the better to destroy him. There would be no reason to be surprised at Machiavelli's caution if Mutulo—or the Mutulos he has in mind—bore the names of the most illustrious names in the city of Florence. Do we dare go so far as to ask whether Soderini himself, derided in the end, did not think he could fool his adversaries by means of some somber and secret bargaining? Do we not know, furthermore, that he speculated on the election of his father to the papacy? Machiavelli writes to him shortly after his fall: "I know you well, and I know what compass guided your crossing. As reprehensible as it is, however, I cannot condemn it, since I see to what port it has led you, and what hopes it allows you to nourish."[16] Language all the more bitter for being preceded by what the author has just declared: "I am reduced to not being surprised at anything and to confessing that neither reading nor action has taught me to savor what men do and the way they do it." Although it is risky to imagine a somber ruse on the part of Soderini, the hypothesis cannot be ruled out.

In the stories Machiavelli composes and arranges as he pleases, a play on identification transpires. The writer not only constantly puts one subject in place of another; he particularly uses peoples or states to designate men. His use of the Etruscans, at the beginning of his chapter, to speak of a failed ruse, must particularly catch our attention. Their role becomes clearer when we recall what was said about them in one of the last chapters: Chapter 43. After having enumerated various situations in which the Florentines were made fools of by the Germans and the French, Machiavelli observes here that the Etruscans had the same bad experience with the Gauls, and concludes that the example of the ancient Tuscans and Florentines proves the unchanging nature of the character of the *franciosi*. This judgment is not to be put in doubt, but it governs another: that the old and the new Tuscans themselves are similar. The title of the chapter, "That Men Who Are Born in the Same Province Keep Over Time More or Less the Same Nature," flows from the end of the argument devoted to the necessity of ruse, for which the episode at Caudium had supplied the specific subject matter. Re-reading it now, after a close examination of the next to last chapter, it seems to prepare the identification that takes place there between the Etruscans and the Florentines. But this identification is itself only one link in the chain that stretches out before us. In Chapter 44, Machiavelli pursues his critique of the Etruscans, under the pretext of establishing that boldness and furor often accomplish what cannot be attained by ordinary means; we see how their hand was forced by the Samnites who put them in the position of having to take up arms against Rome, which they had constantly refused to do previously. The tactic of Julius II and Gaston de Foix is then cited as an example, with the same intention; but there is no mention of the Florentines. Nevertheless, the similarity of their behavior to that of the Etruscans is striking. We know that their hand, too, was always forced by their allies. Now, while we are still under the influence of the judgment about the resemblance, maintained in the course of history, between peoples established in the same territory, Chapter 45—the object of which is to examine whether it is more advantageous first to withstand the impetus of the enemy's attack and then attack them more forcefully later or to begin the battle with full fury—brings two Roman captains onto the stage, one of whom is the great Fabius. On the value of his example we have already shed some light; but now we are in a position to locate the slippage that has taken place from the representation of peoples to that of men. Having set out from a comparison between the French and the Gauls, between the barbarians and the Germans, between the Etruscans and the Florentines, we are imperceptibly transitioned to substituting a comparison between individuals, to bring us to the question of Chapter 46, titled "How It Happens That in a City a Family Retains the Same Customs for a Long Time." The subject of this chapter has taken the place of the one first proposed to us.[17] It is true that for the moment only Roman families are discussed; it is for the Florentine reader to transfer the observations suggested by the history of Rome to his own milieu. But the task is made easier for him, for the author's language speaks volumes. First he gives us to understand that it is not just between one city and another that there is a diversity of institutions and customs, some engendering rude men, others effeminate ones, but also that in the same city, the same difference is to be seen between family and family. Then, after having given the example of the Manlius type, rude and stubborn, the Publicola type, benevolent and attached to the people, and the Appius sort, ambitious and inimical to the plebs, and after having sought the cause of these resemblances not in consanguinity but in education, he suddenly brings his findings to bear on the character of Appius, and concludes: "What goodness and what humanity was shown by the great bulk of the citizens, and how ready they were to obey the laws of their country and the auspices."[18] We cannot but transpose this assessment, and in two ways. Considering the recent past, how can we be surprised, if in Rome itself there was such repugnance at chastising the ambition of the most odious patricians, that in Florence the Republic was powerless to defend itself from their equivalents? And in considering the future, how can one not prepare to oppose those whom one has known for a long time to be bent on destroying all civil liberty?

In Rome, it is true that men resisted the efforts of the factious. Among them was Fabius, of whom we are told that he earned the appellation Maximus for having succeeded, when he was censor, in allocating the families that caused the disorders to four tribes, so that, contained within such tight constituency boundaries, they could not corrupt all Rome. A measure that was not without its costs, for Livy relates that those families, recently granted city rights, were, for Appius Claudius, the strongest supporters against the regime, and that Fabius's reform cut the ground from under him. In Florence, on the other hand, there was never anyone to put a stop to corruption. We presume that the "good republicans" were only good at opposing the petty stratagems of their enemies with ones of their own. Like the Etruscans vis-à-vis the Romans, they traded on the naïveté of the enemy; like Florence vis-à-vis Pisa, they took part in pitiful dealings to get what only a resolute and daring politics could have obtained.

What Machiavelli ultimately teaches the young, desirous of action and knowledge, is to identify their enemies—beyond those who fight openly, those in the guise of herdsmen. He summons them to be persuaded that politics is war, and that like war it is not decided exclusively by the direct clash of armies.

His last remarks on Rome are enlightening in the extreme on this topic. The panoply of plots of which Rome was the theater is depicted in such a way that, in a first phase, we are prompted to give ourselves over to our original faith in the "goodness" of the model republic. And its effect is all the more striking in that we have not forgotten the opinions of Book 1 [Chapter 28]. Machiavelli wrote: "Whoever reads of the doings of republics will find in all of them some sort of ingratitude in the way in which they deal with their citizens, but in Rome will find less than in Athens, and perhaps than in any other republic. If one inquires how this comes about in the case of Rome and Athens, I believe that it was due to Rome's having less ground for mistrusting her citizens than had Athens. For in Rome one sees that from the expulsion of the kings to the time of Sulla and Marius, she was never deprived of liberty by any of her citizens so that in her case there was no great reason to be suspicious of them, and, in consequence, rashly to give them offense."[19] Now he asserts [Chapter 49]: "As we have remarked several times, in every large city there inevitably occur unfortunate incidents which call for the physician, and the more important the incidents the wiser should be the physician one looks for. If there was any city in which such incidents occurred, it was in Rome, where they were both curious and unexpected. For instance, on one occasion all the ladies of Rome . . . Another instance was the conspiracy of the Bacchanals . . ."[20] And also: "Even if the greatness of that republic and its power of administration were not betokened in a thousand other ways, it is to be seen in the nature of the punishment inflicted on the evil-doer."[21] But however dark such a picture may be, it is only drawn up to introduce another: that of the corruption that secretly undermines states. The visible conspiracies that run through the history of Rome are only recalled at the end of the volume in order to encourage us to conclude that they are almost nothing compared to the invisible conspirators. "Although maladies of this kind do great harm to a republic," Machiavelli observes, "they are not fatal, for there is generally time to correct them. But there is no time as a rule when they affect the state, and, unless some wise man corrects them, the city is ruined."[22]

Such is the art of politics that the young are to learn. The art of detecting hotbeds of corruption in the various places in which they occur. The art of upholding laws despite those who surreptitiously oppose them with their private power, and of rising up against laws when they have become a shelter for private power. The art of restoring public power through reform or revolution. Although an understanding of history alone gives us the power of effective political action, although the figures of Brutus, Fabius, and Epaminondas enlighten the task, that art itself lies in invention, and it is always at the heart of an unprecedented situation, facing new enemies, that its practice must be renewed.

Part 5

The Oeuvre, Ideology, and Interpretation

Our reader, if he has been willing to follow us to the end of our analyses of *The Prince* and *The Discourses* has probably ceased expecting us to extricate ourselves from them to produce that pure intelligibility that would normally be promised him and presented as "the thought" of Machiavelli. The tie that binds us to the oeuvre is such that we cannot break it and say what it has not said and would constitute—freed at last from the murkiness of discourse—its essence. To break that bond, we would need a new support, enabling us to lean on some established meanings that we had previously succeeded in extracting—meanings that would now lend themselves to a further and final reductive operation. But meanings do not permit of being unraveled from the discursive weave, and if we contemplate securing them in this way we are left with a message drained of all vitality; if we press on to extract a quintessential meaning, what remains is lackluster knowledge—a knowledge so harshly won from the living language of the author, so fatally rescued from his inner turmoil, that, all ebullience bypassed, we are baffled that so much effort of writing and reading should have been expended for the sole purpose of perpetuating the mediocre formulation of a chain of reasoning.

Ever are we returned to the discourse of the oeuvre. What it imparts cleaves to what it suggests, and our understanding is augmented by our power to speak—which it simultaneously awakens in us. There is no point at which we can cease interrogating the text, no point at which, by virtue of a new distance, we are in a position to withdraw from that strange relationship that transforms us—once the interpretation has begun—into the other of that discourse, and the other of its author as well, now the inhabitant of our own discourse. There is no space within which these two discourses cease to intercept each other, to be inside each other—in which it would be possible to become the reader of one's own reading and to attain, like a person pulling the ladder up behind him once the goal has been reached, to the place of pure epistemological subject. And, now that I have considered it, what could such an ultimate distance possibly be? It would be the banishment of all distance from the discourse of the oeuvre. The idea, beyond the sway of the text, is sufficient unto itself; verbal differentiation is swept aside, and Machiavelli's thought is thought by a thought that presents it only to pass through it and radiate as pure light. Distance, on the other hand, is engendered by the experience of reading, when the writer's words swerve into those of the reader, when the movement brought about by the text's attraction turns us away from it. We think, by joining the other, to merge with the intention that moves him or her to speak, and then find ourselves borne away by an intention that enlists all the resources of our language, drawing from the roots of our own history and fashioning new forms for its own perpetuation. We were totally taken up with understanding, with echoing the work, but (surprise!) it is ourselves that we echo. What was intended as response becomes appeal, eliciting its own response—and thus we ultimately become incapable of distinguishing our own thoughts from the ones we are interpreting. But as for what constitutes the distance, we must accept our not knowing, admit to ourselves that this ignorance subtends the relation and that in our desire to dissipate it—to define our position in relation to that of the other—we lose the memory of the oeuvre and our own collaboration in it; we trade the experience of interrogation for the illusion of knowledge, and fall headlong into fictive entities: a thought devoid of "difference,"[1] a language after language, a world divorced from the commerce of subjects. At the conclusion of interpretation, when the answer is sundered from the question (and it matters little whether the answer is expressed in the form of a question), we touch ideas as a dreamer does his images. They are presented on a set from which we are excluded, ordered in a discourse such that we are unaware that it is still discourse—that it abolishes the divisions that sustain the vigilant word. Indeed, as in the dream, the omnipotence of thought—as was so well brought out by Freud—is attested by the fact that the resistance of being evaporates before it, and every place is occupied at once: that of the author, of the reader, our own, that of past and future. But it is in reappropriating what allowed it to emerge from the dream and protects it at every moment from falling back into the irenic state by converting the principles of its inner structure into positive authority—and at the same time projecting them outside itself, as its object—that thought achieves its ends. Taking full possession of language, thought ceases to forget itself in it, and realizes its totalitarian ambition. At this point the logic that becomes the guarantor of thought's victory is in the service of the intention that was accomplished against it in the dream. From the state in which all thoughts are joined in their unconsciousness of contradiction to the state in which all thoughts are articulated according to the affirmation of non-contradiction, the reversal is so complete that their functions are preserved. The completed interpretation thus restores to one pole of the activity of the mind the *imaginaire*[2] that was engendered at the other pole. The fact that this restoration is possible is doubtless only to be understood as meaning that we must recognize, already at the level of the dream, an interpretation: the elaboration of a discourse, the purpose of which is to overcome the indetermination of an experience that does not in itself permit of being conveyed through intelligible speech. But here we must be content with designating the limit to which the analysis of the work owes its incompleteness. This limit is not an obstacle that obstructs knowledge at a given point of its pursuit. It is interior to knowledge: it is its condition. It is impossible to establish a relationship with the discourse of the oeuvre without being caught in it—impossible to interrogate this discourse without the questions rebounding on us. The work of thinking from which meaning emerges entails that we abandon the distinction between the questioning subject and the object of the question, or, as we put it previously, the determination, in the singular conversation instituted by reading, of the "real" distance between *one* and *the other*. That distance—we can never assess it completely: it is rather it that assesses us. It is in the time of the conversation that it is regulated; or, better yet, the conversation constitutes that distance; it underlies and organizes the interplay of speaking and understanding in which the two focal points of the discourse are differentiated. Within the uncertainty in which it places us in our attempt to find the real position of an author and a reader, it maintains itself as the power of an infinite exchange of thoughts.

The circumstance that interpretation lives from its limit, that it is predestined to incompleteness, and that it should engender an endless labor—all derive from the same necessity. I am never done hearing/understanding,[3] being unable to rid myself of the Machiavellian word and to reduce it to the matter of a pure message; I am never done learning the discourse it causes me to speak; as long as I remain turned toward Machiavelli, and true to the goal of interpretation, the words of the one keep on asking for those of the other. Only tiredness or a certain wearing out of the passion that sustained the relationship, or the attraction to something else that has become stronger, determines the end moment.

But that moment itself—we would be deluding ourselves were we to ascribe it to the contingency of personal motives. To what new fantasy would we be yielding were we to imagine, in the absence of such personal motives, the uninterrupted pursuit of the enterprise, a questioning that this time would end only with the event over which the interpreter has no control, to which he can assign no place in the time of his life—since it is the event that ends it. The illusion of incompletion, although perhaps all of us have allowed ourselves to be taken in by it for a time, is the cover beneath which the illusion of completion lies. When we abandon ourselves to it, it is the discourse of the oeuvre that comes once again to serve as a rampart against the intrusion of the third party. Sheltered by it, the attempt to stave off the ultimate insecurity that comes with the exercise of speech, with the ever-renewed though unthinkable difference between the one and the other, reappears. For if it is true that, on this view, this difference seems accepted and to have become the instigator of an endless conversation, if its reabsorbing into a universal knowledge can be denounced as illusory, if a "plural speech," to use Blanchot's expression,[4] is affirmed, at the same time it is secretly denied that *someone* interprets, and becomes, though we cannot know the place from which he speaks, the support for the relation, betraying through each of his gestures an identity, furnishing an articulation of the plural for which he is, whether knowingly or not, answerable. Now, what is meant by his being answerable, if not that from his discourse there necessarily falls the *said*—not that mass of things said, none of which is truly posited, but the said that, being in a sense behind things said, has the weight of a name. What does that mean, if not that discourse necessarily ends with that fall? True, the interpretation always postpones the end, since despite what an interpreter may accomplish, the interpretation always gives rise to fresh endeavors, and these may rightly be considered branches of the same tree. But whatever we may learn from them—these works—in uncovering the schemas governing them, their limits remain visible in the field they cover. The more they instruct us, the less we can dissolve them into an anonymous discourse. As soon as they cease functioning as signs, and the truth of what is said comes into play, they make us come to grips with a singular speech. It is only in a sense that interpretation, thus extended to the time of history, dissolves the identity of the interpreters; in another sense, interpretation lives only thanks to the diversity of historical time. Its movement presupposes the continuous fall of a discourse, the deferral from book to book of an end that can only be moved because it has been posited. In trying to ignore this, in maintaining, for example, that each person fades away before his or her statements, we would be making do with a half truth—a half truth that, because it gives itself out as the whole truth, would turn into a lie, since it would conceal the imprint always left by a Subject on discourse, and the circumstance that there is— at the locus in which meaning is determined, in which an interpretation is required, a knot impossible to undo, binding the word to knowledge.

This is what determines the odd condition of the interpreter. He forgets himself in the desire to let the other speak, but he must come back from that self-forgetfulness and hear himself speak, then give up knowing what belongs to him and what to the other, taking care not to obliterate that difference in the fiction of a pure thought that would imagine itself detached from both, then confront the trial of the interminable and find in incompletion his word's measure; and then at the end understand that that measure . . . it is not the fact of incompletion that bestows it, but the fact that it is contingent on his relation to incompletion, to which he secretly owes the origin of his enterprise and which gives him his identity. It is in sustaining this relation that he says his name—though still unbeknownst to himself—by the fact that beneath that identity a question removed from any definitive answer is pronounced: a question that lives from his self-effacement, no doubt, but in which it is he himself and no other who has abandoned himself, and in which the enigmatic trace of his disappearance will be preserved.

In this respect, the interpreter cannot be distinguished from the writer. If the one confronts the impossibility of finishing his project otherwise than by a suspension in which that impossibility is maintained, is it not the case that the other (the interpreter), has defined himself through that trial, placing his discourse beneath the sign of the interminable, ensuring it on the basis of its limit, dedicating himself to the passion of incompletion? Is it not the oeuvre that sets interpretation's destiny—the oeuvre, which was produced by a discourse held in suspense, by the exercise of a saying[5] indefinitely in search of itself, occupied with consummating its break with the world given in experience? That break engenders the necessity of a movement without end, exceeding every particular operation of knowledge; the necessity of a detour that cannot lead us back to the object, because it is from having experienced the constraint of deviating from it that the saying was initially launched, and it cannot, without losing itself, go back to it, and yield once again to its prestige, lending it the traits of intelligibility. In that break, the idea did not at some point break away from matter: rather the break constitutes the work of the oeuvre.[6] And if, in the course of that work, the oeuvre is sundered from the writer, on the other hand no product stands detached from the work that produced it, and the thought that is thought in thinking can never be sundered from the thinking that traced it out. Similarly, interpretation cannot respond to the attraction of the oeuvre unless it gives up focusing on it as an object, and becomes similar to it: it is in consenting to the same abeyance of discourse that interpretation receives from the oeuvre its own destiny as oeuvre.

But how could the discourse of the oeuvre command at a distance that of the interpretation, if it did not involve it in its own exercise? The fact is, it traces it out at the same time as it calls it forth. The writer's word lives only from being heard/understood, only rejoins itself because it is divided; because the separation of *the one* from *the other* is constantly re-enacted in its space, and in such a way that it does not suffice, in order to conceptualize it, to intuit two poles within the same subject, one being that of speaking and the other of listening/understanding. We must go a step further, and recognize that speech emanates from hearing/understanding, just as does hearing/understanding from speech. Expression and impression belong to the same movement. To formulate this by saying that the writer is his own reader would be to impoverish the experience—although that formulation does have the virtue of suggesting a distance internal to the subject. It refers us too quickly to that second reading that comes back to meet the *already written*, when this last, be it a sentence or a book, is offered to the stranger's gaze, putting its author in the same position as any other reader. What is more, it would hide from us a part of the experience, since we would still have to understand why the "other" reader cannot fully occupy his position without becoming a writer/interpreter. But there is a first reading that is implied in the writing, which performs the gathering back of the signs at the very moment of their escape. With that first reading, duality no longer suffers the fiction of separate terms; the opposition between passive and active is erased. We are tempted to say that at one and the same time the writer writes from his own dictation and deciphers what is written. But this would constitute two ways of missing the meaning of the event, since it is the same one who hears/understands himself and who speaks to himself, and since he has always begun to hear/understand before speaking, and to speak before hearing/understanding . . . Now, when we are attentive to this incessant division of the word, the difference interior to the subject becomes ungraspable. And although the latter difference gives us the key to the passage of the word toward the outside, although it relates the possibility of communication to the first possibility of an exteriority and of a relation of self to self, we must preserve the ungraspable element of it in order to interrogate the relation of the writer to the "other" reader. For it does not suffice to recognize that the place of the other is already blocked out in the space of the discourse of the oeuvre, and that, in short, that space is open to its reader; it must also be admitted that such a place is undeterminable, and that the moment we make it our own (despite the power we gain of a new distance), we are caught up in the game of the divided word, a word that we can not only hear but that speaks in us, and in doing so incites the word—a word that is in turn simultaneously proffered and heard, always insufficient or in excess, since it necessarily makes us slip from one of its poles to the other.

It is doubtless the nature of all discourse to produce such indetermination. But discourse is normally occupied with overcoming it. It is practiced at the price of conventions that lead one to suppose that an adequation is possible between what it said and what is understood; it is developed according to the modality of affirmation—even when it takes on the negative, dubitative, or interrogative form—so that the meaning is deposited and fixed within the limits of the statement, and the illusion of a coincidence between the interior other and the foreign other is preserved. Under these conditions, the division between speaking and listening is obliterated, at the price of the introduction of a schism between a "conscious" and an "unconscious" of the word. The writer's discourse does not entirely escape this fate: even it cannot avoid the movement of affirmation. Thus, it is always possible to take by surprise the one who conducts the discourse if one can expose the function of closure of his statement, and to understand what he has applied himself to not understanding. But what makes its singularity and changes it into discourse of the oeuvre is that it does not adapt to the stability of things said, that it lives from the refusal of their limits, welcomes the incessant lability of the word, in which the positions of the one and the other are blurred, and that it allows itself to be displaced by "difference" rather than claiming to submit to it. In the register in which this discourse is situated, interrogation takes the place of affirmation. At one and the same time it deprives the word of the measure that would allow it to find a response in the object, it forces the word to exert itself to no avail, that is, to give up the product in which a value of meaning would be allowed to define itself, and it forbids its flowing back to the pole of the one who speaks or the one who hears/understands. An action that stems from the same necessity: the sacrifice of the object does not go without that of the Subject; the movement by which the word turns away from the meaning given in experience does not go without the one that opens it to its own absence. In interrogation, the articulation of language with that from which it becomes language, as that of *someone* with *some other*, does not allow itself to be undone. Affirmation and interpellation, which presuppose the same relation measured from the outside, are also suspended; and, with this suspension, the distinction between the space of the oeuvre and that of the world is also suspended, as well as that of the writer and the interpreter; with this elision, the dimension of the interminable is instituted.

The works of Machiavelli are among those that invite us the most imperiously to scrutinize what constitutes the singularity of the discourse of the oeuvre, for if it is true that the oeuvre is always governed by interrogation and exercised by the passion of incompletion, with *The Prince* and *The Discourses* the signs of that passion are deliberately multiplied. The enterprise is conducted in such a way as to postpone, from term to term—to the point of making the expectation vain—a truth that would seal the discourse and create the fiction of an adequation between thought and what it thinks, a coinciding between he who writes and he who reads.

It is precisely here—where one might expect Machiavelli's discourse to be the most exposed to the requirement of affirmation and interrogation, here where it is attempting to disclose the meaning of things given as present—that the necessity of the detour to which it is subjected, and the impossibility of its reaching a conclusion, are best circumscribed. For indeed, while his discourse seems to turn toward the most recent events, those that were decisive in shaping the fate of the Republic of Florence, focusing on exposing the causes of its collapse, Machiavelli turns out to be involved in a labyrinth of questions from which no exit can be sought. It is true that this route leads toward a kind of knowledge; but the knowledge only unfolds at the price of a deletion of what was first presented as its subject matter; its delineation follows the erasure of what is proposed, time after time, to replace the given. Nowhere can the discourse gather itself and come to closure, outside the experience in which things are given, obliterated, preserved in the discourse only in the form of their cancellation—a form in which the necessary movement of interrogation is initiated for the Subject.

Thus *The Discourses* take on an apparently limited question, phenomena localized in time and space—the military defeat of Prato and the resignation of Soderini's government—then transgress the limits of that question in such a way that the event ceases being an object of knowledge as such; in such a way that, though never disappearing from the horizon, it governs the possibility of the reading of history.

The analysis establishes that the republican regime collapsed because it was incapable of resisting the Spanish invader with an efficient defense system, and that such a system could not rely on mercenary armies commanded by condottieri; only the Florentine people, if it had been prepared for war and mobilized, would have been able to resist that enemy—a foe not inclined to support a protracted and costly operation. Thus the defeat of Florence seems to be attributable to the decadence of the military institutions. Knowing their defects, we can understand how the City, despite its ample resources, had over a long period of time become weakened financially and psychologically by endless wars, and eventually lost the means and the will to resist aggressors. A people no longer having the taste or the experience for arms, or confidence in its military leaders, must, it seems, pay for its lapses with the loss of its freedoms. That argument, however, is insufficient. Ignorance of the art of war is itself the result of a political system in which power seeks security at the price of disarming its people. The military institutions in vigor in Florence proceed from a choice that was made by the dominant sector of the bourgeoisie and maintained day after day, according to which the enemy within—the social strata that was menacing by their demands—was adjudged more dangerous than the external one. In observing the situation, it must be admitted that the masters of the Florentine Republic were no different, in this respect, than the princes who, throughout Italy, as well as beyond its borders, preferred to entrust the defense of the state to mercenaries rather than increase the power of the people. But how can the analysis stop at this point? The case of the Florentine regime cannot be assimilated to that of princedoms, in which the power is by definition kept out of the hands of the people. Although democracy obtains in Florence within strict limits, and the power of an oligarchy is asserted in the economic positions occupied by a few great families, in the experience they have gleaned over a long period in managing public affairs, and in the institutional mechanisms guaranteeing them privileged access to the main public offices, it is a fact that public life includes a large number of citizens from the middle or lower bourgeoisie. Now, while it is true that the dominant strata have the most at stake in maintaining a military system that leaves the population as a whole unarmed, one cannot ignore the help they get from a portion of those whom they try to keep away from the sources of power. Their responsibility in the weakening of the regime must be brought out: despite their efforts to increase their representation within the government and the assemblies, despite the advantages they succeeded in securing during the time of Savonarola and Soderini, they demonstrated their inability to assert a policy that would bring about popular support for the state and the army. Their mentality was in the image of the dominant group, so that the conflicts pitting them against the hegemony, if they did not become blunted to the point of embracing the rivalries of the oligarchic factions, were powerless to bring about a general reform of the system. Thus, far from the divisions—the *desunione* so demonized by the politicians of Florence—being evil in themselves, they suffered from remaining at the level of personal political interests, group solidarity, and quarrels over prestige, without being able to attain the depth of class struggle—without being able to bring about that dialectic of demand and concession that produced the power of conquering republics. That such a dialectic was in fact creative—it suffices to consider the history of the young Roman Republic to be convinced of it. Hence it is by the examination of the conflict between the patricians and the plebs that the process of decadence of the Republic of Florence is to be elucidated. It is true that what one discovers is that the mores and behavior of the people are shaped by those who dominate them and that it took the patrician's choosing the path of war and directing its ambition toward combat for the plebs to be able to give free rein to its desires and have its voice heard. But that is only a partial truth, since we also see the dominant class bent on defending its privileges, turning to war as a diversion from class struggle, and forced into concessions rather than arriving at them by a free assessment of their advantages. The *virtù* of the people finds no more than conditions of possibility in a situation in which its sacrifices and collaboration are sought after; and it, in turn, influences the political life of the City, partially determining the choices of the dominant class. The Roman example illustrates this: the weakness of the regime, in Florence, is not just the result of the nature of the oligarchy that constantly ignored the necessity for a state claiming power to win a base of popular support in order to survive. The petty bourgeoisie itself appears to have been an accomplice in the defeat of the regime, in that it tried to reconcile rather than oppose, feared the lower strata of the population in the same way that the Grandees feared the people as a whole, placed its own security in the position of least risk, made the "middle path" its political ideal, and was incapable of conceiving of a danger that could not be surmounted by diplomatic intrigue and money. It is futile to claim to be able to account for its subjection solely on the basis of the constraints placed upon it. Class relations are of course power relations, but these involve the representation each group has of the other; they are, more specifically, a product of the illusions the dominated hold about power, the virtue of past models, and the strength and experience of the men holding the first ranks in society. To get to the root of these illusions is therefore to reach the deepest recesses of Florentine conservatism from which the tyranny sprang.

The causes of the degeneration of the Republic of Florence elude, then, the order of political phenomena in the narrower sense of the term, just as a moment ago they did the order of military phenomena. What we need to examine is rather that set of beliefs that underlie man's relations with law and authority; with the past and the future, with things of the world and death, separating, for him, what is permitted and what forbidden, the possible and the impossible, good and evil; and since at the center of these beliefs we find, as the focal point of their animation and reproduction, religion, it is Christianity that becomes the privileged object of the analysis. In the stamp with which it marks the men of the time, and particularly Florence, which never ceased desiring to be the city of Saint John, we can catch sight of all the signs of degradation of the political body. The belief in one God, whose decrees regulate the fate of humanity, maintains submission to the established laws and the authority that comes to support them. Taken to the extreme, it accredits all the terrestrial figures of despotism. The conviction that no change within the limits of this world counts for anything in view of the true life and that glory and acquired goods are vain discourages initiative and turns imagination back to the prestigious models of the past, by the very fact of dispossessing it of the future. Hope in a personal salvation, sought in prayer, undermines the taste for risk-taking and the confidence formerly derived from the trials of combat; and, making man cowardly and effeminate, it accustoms him to defeat. Thus there emanates from Christianity a conservatism, and with it the inability to check the forces that work naturally toward the dissolution of the City. But the fact is that in order to evaluate the effect of Christianity accurately we must have an idea of the effect brought about by other religions. Paganism in ancient Rome offers the other term of the comparison. In examining it, we see how a religion can invade the life of a society without smothering it. We know from reading Livy that Roman paganism was exploited by the patriciate for its own interests and that there as well it reinforced conservatism; in cultivating the credulity of the people, it doubtless enchained the latter to the party of its masters. But it did not weigh on spirits to the point of shielding power from the demands of the lower classes. It contained elements necessary to accommodate the desire for glory, and, better yet, the wherewithal to allow itself to be circumvented by those whose daring prompted them to outstanding feats. Now such an analysis shifts the focus of the analysis, because although it brings out a difference between modern religion and that of the classical times, it also informs us that all religion, whatever its inspiration, plays within society the role that men—that is, the collective and individual protagonists of the political drama—give it. With the critique of Christianity, then, we do not reach the fundamental causes, but merely read a general manner of being in keeping with which the mores of an age are ordered. Therefore there remains the question of whether, in its primitive form, Christianity might not give rise to a different interpretation, inspire other beliefs and other relationships. Thus analysis requires that we examine beneath one sole gaze (where they clearly differ in virtue of the nature of the regime being considered—in Rome or in Florence) these two socio-historical types, in which institutions, practices, and beliefs are fashioned in such a way as to make political virtue and the development of the state possible or impossible. To the problem posed by the collapse of the Republic of Florence in 1512, the answer can no longer be sought at the level of the military, political, or religious phenomena *stricto sensu*, though we are on the right track in following them. That answer is to be deciphered in the reading of history, in which there transpires through the course of events the choices made by the actors—individuals or classes—and the mute logic interconnecting them; choices that are never absolutely imputable to individuals, since they only decide within the framework of what their situation gives them to know or puts them in a position to do—choices that remain implicit for the social classes, for it is most often through praxis that they are made, without emerging into the realm of representation—but choices in which we can distinguish such and such a singular elaboration of the universal givens of social life, such and such an anonymous intention that governs random events.

To answer, in this sense, is to work toward revealing answers that are already given, though not formulated, by men in places and times in which fortune has placed them, along with the question that is at the beginning of every political society. But consequently it is also to discover the means by which these answers are obfuscated—how the knowledge that would endanger the solutions that have been worked out is repressed. It is to devote oneself to exploring the artifices that make the discourse a society holds about itself credible, and by means of which it gives itself the substitute of a knowledge. Vain is the belief that the reading of history is self-evident—that it suffices to compare the development of the Roman Republic with that of the Florentine Republic to know the causes of the rapid expansion of the former and the decadence of the latter. In order for history to speak, for the comparison to instruct us, it must be sundered from the function it performs within the *here* and *now* of the collective discourse, especially when the recounting of the deeds of the Romans conceals the tasks of the present. But the critique of the representation of the past—the critique of the image of Rome—cannot bring a simple complement to the analysis; for while it is based on such critiques—while the interpretation of history and politics contains as one of its moments that of the illusions that men, the contemporaries, cherish with respect to the past—it is equally true that access to knowledge is governed by the destruction of those illusions, by a liberation from the collective discourse against which, but also on the basis of which, the discourse of the oeuvre is instituted. Not only is it necessary for the oeuvre, if it is to make itself understood, to undo ties that bind thought to the *imaginaire:* that operation gives the oeuvre the power to understand itself, that is, to generate itself. Far from this being a partial, limited task, within the general enterprise of knowledge, it is, in a sense, knowledge in its entirety that is subordinate to it. In order to undo the fallacious answers elaborated in the collective discourse, we need to have an idea of the question they elude, and, to awaken that question, we must have located the signs in the equivocations, the slippage, the gaps, the contradictions in this discourse. Thus it is impossible to set a limit to the movement of the analysis: it is even impossible to discern one object that would be the present and another that would be the past, one object that would be the representation and another that would be the real, or to separate the operation of the negation from that of the affirmation.

The discourse of the oeuvre, as we were saying, follows the path of an endless detour. Let us now recognize that that path is not linear, and that the moment we propose to trace it out from a fixed point (in this case the political crisis of 1512), we must once again yield to fictive entities, imagining a chain of arguments, or at best a circular procedure, while at every moment the word of the oeuvre is inscribed in several registers at once, opening up an expanding space in which the divisions of ordinary language are blurred. If the event focused on in discourse slips away, if discourse can only keep up with it by referral from word to word, and undergoes the challenge of a distance ever displaced toward the future, it is because it ceases, once questioned, to represent anything *given* and as such to represent anything said, sealed beneath the commentary of the actors, of the stories portraying it, and of that story to the second power, which is that of the historian, in order to allow the dimension of the advent to surge forth within the social field, to render the temporal difference readable within the internal play of its articulations; to open up, through its indetermination, the question of the future. The event loses its limits within empirical space and time, and, along with them, the punctual, visible, and calculable relationships it bears to other events, as it withdraws behind what it *gives*. What it gives is what, if it were lacking, would be kept secret, and the very thing that disguises it in the present, and at the same time a word [*parole*] that, because it takes the event up, is open, multiple, diffuse; it is all that the discourse of the oeuvre unfurls, a place in which we would seek in vain an enumeration of causes, a layering of hypotheses including the near and the far, or the orderly determinations of an objective form of knowledge. But if something of the event is lost in the discourse of the oeuvre that it frees up, the oeuvre in its entirety refers us to it. In the analysis of the civil divisions in Florence of military and political institutions, of religion and more generally of ideology, and in the analysis of ancient Rome, the reflections on history and the nature of political societies, the direct or indirect critique of the philosophical tradition, there remains, at the horizon, the adventure in which the republic founders. It is not only that we continue to get glimpses of it beneath repeated allusions, or that it is suddenly recalled, here and there, along the byways of a development intended to obscure it—for example, that the figure of Soderini, the key personage in the defeat, can be divined through the portrait of Brutus or of the two Fabii, or of Epaminondas, or that Livy's episode of the soldiers disguised as shepherds evokes the traps set to catch the Gonfalonier, or yet again that the theoretical justification of a radical and cruel solution in extreme situations signals the failure and mediocrity of the defenders of the regime in 1512—the recent event is preserved in that it does not cease commanding the relation with the readers whose fate has been marked by it. It gives the discourse the power of fixing them in the place where the desire to know and to act converge; or it provides a décor in which the interrogation of history can unfold while being dovetailed with a provocation to action. Undoubtedly what has happened is, however close to the present, irreversible, and it is indeed as such that it becomes graspable. We may even say that in a sense what is taught in the discourse is the necessity of the convergence of the signs in which the event is announced. If, for example, the analysis of the politics of Soderini implies the hypothesis of means of action different from his, nothing authorizes our thinking that he had the option of using them. When Machiavelli ironically notes that his salvation might have been possible had he been willing to betray the regime at the right moment, but that his past and his character forbade his doing so, or when he reminds us that Fortune places at the head of states the men it needs to elevate or debase them, he is tacitly denouncing the vanity of a reconstruction that introduces a trait that the conditions under consideration ruled out. In Florence, the dominant group, the bourgeoisie as a whole, being what it is, its institutions and mentality reaching the degree of corruption we know them for, it seems that the defeat of the body politic was inevitable the moment it was exposed to military attack. But to detect the modalities through which the inevitable supervenes is at the same time to discover those that exclude the possibility of a political creativity, or, in Machiavelli's way of speaking, the invention of *ordini nuovi*. Now, such a discovery re-engenders many hypotheses. It cannot omit the exploration of the variants that mark out the place of the possible, until retaining that of an imaginary Soderini, heir to Moses or Brutus, but these hypotheses are not inscribed within a science of retrospection. The crossed-out possible, though it is revealed alongside a series of variants that are localizable in empirical history, does not itself have an empirical status; with it what is named is, as we were saying, the dimension of the advent, a relation to the present that subtends all of history. The movement toward the recent past event, because it frees up the present within it, places the reader whose fate has been affected by it within the opening toward what is coming; it is the power of the quickening of the possible *here* and *now*. But how are we to believe that the last word of the discourse of the oeuvre is a call to action? It can no more assign to others the position of actor and circumscribe, within the empirical, the path to a possible future, than it can refashion the recent past into the object of an affirmation. Thus it is not a sign of contradiction that the word of Machiavelli oscillates at the moment of designating the future. Nothing new can come out of Florence, he would have us to understand, yet it would suffice for one man to come who combined authority with knowledge for the destiny of the City to be changed. Then: such a man cannot appear on the stage of a corrupt society; if he were to do so, his call would not be heard; if he knew the ways by which power could be won, he would not wish to use them if he possessed any humanness; if he had the inclination for that, he would not be good; and finally: if the passion of the founder were stronger in him than any consideration of good and evil, the price of the violence to be paid would be so high that we would have good reason to be doubtful of our hopes . . . In this indecisive word it is not the alternation of optimism and pessimism that is marked, or the division between thought and desire; the possible penetrates it without being assigned a place, haunting the contiguous world without being demoted to a modality of the real. Moreover, it is of little importance for us to know whether Machiavelli believes—and if so, to what degree— in the providential intervention of a reformer, or even for us to assess the role he confers on individuals in history. The word the oeuvre draws from him is dedicated to producing the rolling of the possible around the impossible as soon as it has broken with the objective determination of time. It produces it in an affirmation that is immediately destroyed, in an interpellation forthwith annulled. Its effect is that something is said—without remaining; or something is announced without being stamped with the weight of a said. In the language in which the objective determination of time reigns, possibility itself must be objective and as such circumscribed by the conditions fashioned into a statement; nothing of the subject uttering the statement should be taken into account in the representation, or the effect of his position must be neutralized by calculation; the borders of the possible must correspond to the lines of the actual, so to speak. But this language presents itself as true only on the condition that we ignore the conventions that hide the exercise of the word, its mode of advent to itself; and it pays for its artifice with the obliteration of the temporal difference. While the principle of noncontradiction is erected as the law of thought, in order to avoid the overlapping of the possible and the impossible, the future is reduced to the figure of a past that would not yet be past, the not-known pushed back to the limits of an unknown, the measure of which is provided by the known. By contrast, the discourse of the oeuvre is concerned with the temporal difference and the difference, internal to knowledge, between knowledge and non-knowledge. With it, the historical possible is not defined at the point where the exercise of knowledge masters its own limit and reserves the field of its future activities; it reveals itself to be lodged in the hollow of history—history, the very thing that covers it up and bears the negation of it *here* and *now*—an ungraspable to one who aims at it in order to make of it a second real or give it the figure of the future, but quasi-sensible in interrogation, to the degree that it is not lack of knowledge, does not stand at the border of the already known, but tests out Being in relation to what is not yet. If, in *The Discourses,* a possible is announced and then canceled out, it is not because the bond with the real suddenly gives way beneath the impetus of desire; the corruption of the City is not of the order of the real, while revolution would be a chimera, since that corruption is only visible on the condition of interrogating the temporality of human societies—since the same interrogation envelops the question of the corruption, conservation, and foundation of the state, that of the relationship of the Subject to the law, and that of transgression. The truth is just that corruption appears in the signs of the withering away of the body politic, and that its consequences, increasingly visible, are described as ever more compelling; but its "reality" is not given in the signs that men collect and that are engraved in their existence to the point of being illustrated in the configuration of their acts; what is given covers over the continuous, invisible elaboration of social relations, of which no individual or group taken in isolation is the author, and the meaning of which is instituted partly without anyone being aware of it, but in which all are implicated. The relation to the real is the relation to the work that society performs on itself, by which it shows and hides itself, but, in this sense, it is the relation to the possible, to its own possible, such as, *here* and *now*, the trace of it remains at the seams of the instituted. As for this possible, the Machiavellian discourse does not establish it in advancing the image of a reformer who would suddenly crop up and overturn the rules of the current political game. It is the wing-beat of the word, a "maybe,"—insinuated then withdrawn—that makes it flutter and elude our grasp. It would be vain to claim to bring it down to the level of prediction: it does not coincide with the hypothesis of change that would accompany that of repetition, does not settle down in the margin of the probable to indicate the chance of happy accident; it gives sustenance to waiting. This is not to say that it is the object of a waiting; rather it frees waiting from anything that might be an object of expectation, from anything that might be able to satisfy it, while at the same time revealing waiting to itself. For what is opened in the waiting, *here* and *now*, is what is sifted through in the whole inquiry into the political society and into history. The strength to sustain *here* and *now* what is not yet—what may be—is conquered in the movement that unseals the representation of the past and brings back to the light of day the paths of the historical advent, the meanderings of the question buried beneath the answers of the given. Between waiting and questioning, thought follows an indecisive movement, for it is by dint of facing in the present what is beyond its grasp, and yet from which it cannot turn away, that it gains access to the historical dimension per se, and it is in order to discover that dimension that it gives up providing features to the possible. The moment waiting is demoted to prediction, interrogation dies; once interrogation is detached from waiting, it falls into the illusion of a knowledge of history, and that is when the future disappears and leaves us dumbstruck before the fact. But this means that the discourse of the oeuvre does not open up a passageway to what it speaks of, which remains under its inspection, nor does it establish with its reader a relation in the bounds of which it can remain. To whatever the locus on which it sets its sights, it cannot relate otherwise than by abandoning it. To the Other to whom it is addressed, it has nothing to offer that would free it from the task of reopening, there where it is situated, the question of the possible in its double necessity: What to think? What to do?

When the interpreter fixes his attention on the drama that unfolded in the days when Florence lost its freedoms, he is tempted to believe that Machiavelli's entire analysis is invested in it. The effect is similar when he examines, in *The Prince,* the extraordinary adventure that for a moment made Borgia become the new man of Italy. But he must also see the other side of the coin. The defeat of the republic, Borgia's enterprise—these only have the power of making history legible. Their function is to offer a feasible pathway of exploration through an inherently unlimited interrogation. He has every right to forget these specifics. When he allows himself to be taken up by that interrogation, when he is freed from the close horizon drawn by the discourse to the point that Florentine or Italian references lose their privilege in his eyes, he is tempted to define the domain of the oeuvre as that of the pure intelligibility of history. But here again he must give up, because the word as addressed to him as reader, which thereby shapes his role, is addressed to him in such a way as to assign him to a place, to a time, in order to awaken him to the possible, to excite in him the anticipation of what is not yet. His power of understanding is linked to that disposition of expectation, which is given by the oeuvre. But it is in vain that we would try to measure that disposition on the basis of the imagining of things to come and on the basis of the desire to act *here* and *now;* it is articulated with these last, but is different from them. The near future is also a metaphor at the service of a nameless future. It is in this capacity that it maintains its power over a reader foreign to the images and desires of the Florentine of the *Cinquecento;* in this capacity that, having been removed from that milieu, it continues to sustain expectation. Through it we are attracted, or so we think, to the present of the discourse; we understand it as it understood itself, ignorant of what was going to happen; we return it to the living of whom and for whom it spoke. But if this is the case, if its designated absence is deepened by an incessant absence, it is because the interrogation of the entire discourse has carved out within its limits the place—forever free—of the future as the place of non-knowledge.

This interrogation, therefore, as it extends over the analysis of the facts pertaining to classical antiquity and the constitution of political societies—we can no longer conceive of it as a detour in the knowledge of what is said, *here* and *now*, at the heart of the recent past, revealing the possibilities specific to Florence; nor can we abstract it from the space–time to which it is bound. It proves to inaugurate a relation to the present that cannot be grasped by the "natural" experience of time. In terms of that experience, there is a present in its *time* and *place* that is the time and place of the Machiavellian discourse—a present, moreover, that is not distinguishable from that of Machiavelli the writer, and the living readers of his day. That present has a temporal thickness, which includes the years during which the writer expresses himself, his recent past and his immediate future. True, its limits are indefinable. The things that make the recent past seem present are not just the events whose effects are prolonged as far as the immediate future, but also that which, being kept in the memory of the living, is responsible for affecting their relation to that future. What makes the immediate future is not only given in the formulation of the tasks, problems, and unknowns accompanying the present play of praxis and expression; it is also the imagination of the future. But natural experience does not get bogged down in these difficulties; it chooses as present an extent of time with vague frontiers, which it imagines to move imperceptibly along with it, in keeping with a central point given by the position of a living person. But it cannot remain content with this configuration of a present in which everything designated has the same degree of presence and in which its matter would thereby become inexhaustible. Accordingly, it corrects itself, recognizing that the present is only such by its sense of the present, in virtue of an opposition of a mental order between the old and the new. Such is the representation that commands the apprehension of the historical: the possibility of installing oneself in a space–time, in Machiavelli's Florence, of getting back into his present, is ensured by that opposition, which at the same time ensures a continuity of meaning, or a pure presence preserved in meaning through the passage of time.

Now such a representation is undone in the work of the oeuvre. In the oeuvre, the present, in its time and place, does not coincide with the space–time based on the position of the writer and his living readers, but neither is it revealed by the articulation of the new with the old. The paradox, with respect to natural experience, is that this present is determined at the very moment it is undetermined; or rather, its determination is rigorously governed by its indetermination. What makes it legible is what deprives it of figures, or makes it impossible to represent by figures, and hence incommensurable—not without limits, but outside of limits. From this upheaval we forge yet another image, considering that the distinction between things given as past and things given as present merge indistinctly. It is a fact that the words and deeds of the Romans invade the stage of Florentine politics, that light is cast on the latter as the episodes of Rome's class struggle and those of Florence merge. It is a fact, for example, that the deeds of Soderini, pulled away from a first-level immediacy, generated in the present, are then articulated with those of the actors of the past, and that they rise and become fixed by piercing the space of the possible provided them by the latter; that with the evocation of Brutus, of the two Fabii, of Hannibal, and of Epaminondas, the depth of the field in which the Gonfalonier stands is revealed, its own movement taking on life in such a way that the distance between a here and an elsewhere, a now and a past time vanishes, and we are anchored in that here and that now by drifting into an indeterminate time and place. But the image is deceptive, because in truth the difference of times and places is erased without being destroyed. Erased, so to speak, from one page of history, its form is traced on a copy, as a result of the very act of erasure, so that the upsurge of the present is always accompanied by the unfolding of space–times. The work [ouvrage] of discourse is rather as follows: it makes the difference in time invisible, but it unveils temporal difference, a difference whose terms do not exist prior to it, so that they are nothing outside of it—itself unlocalizable, though everywhere and always operative, and maintaining that strange relation with difference in time such that it is produced by the very erasure of difference in time. In vain would we try to define temporal difference in terms of the relation established between modern Florence and ancient Rome, or between those two moments of the history of Florence as fixed, for example, by the fall of the tyranny of the Medici and the fall of the Republic of Soderini; it cannot be measured in terms of points of repair in an objective universe. Yet with temporal difference that relation, those points of repair, are not abolished: temporal difference is not detached from the universe in which they appear. It is true that ancient Rome escapes representation in the discourse of the oeuvre: the latter dissolves it as a term given in natural experience, or (which is the same thing) it dissolves the tie between what is given as present and what is given as past. But temporal difference, which the discourse of the oeuvre frees from difference in time, passes through Rome and Florence, and within Rome, and within Florence, via space–times, always through a *here* and an *elsewhere*, a *now* and an *earlier time;* it necessarily implies that something takes place, has taken place, although the place is erased as soon as it is indicated. If a way of access is opened to the history of Rome, that history is not Roman; history is not Spartan or Athenian, Venetian or Florentine, French or Spanish . . . Yet it does not take on the status of the atemporal. How can we put it? History is nothing when the references to times and places are removed, nothing but the differentiation between space–times. What we said about the event—that it loses its limits the moment we cease apprehending it as something *given* in the story, and that it then *gives* the dimension of advent, and that nevertheless it is by this dimension that it comes into its ownness, conquering its place and date—this must be extended to all the figures in the socio-historical field, and repeated with respect to all institutions, groups, and states whose historicity is revealed the moment they break up as terms of an objective universe. But again, we must go beyond that last image. Both the extent and the meaning of the break brought about by the discourse of the oeuvre with the natural experience of time would elude us, if we limited ourselves to registering the movement that erases the difference and maintains it in its erasure, or its result, which is, with the destitution of the things given as present and the things given as past, the institution of the present in its date and time, *here* and *now,* and by the same token in the past and elsewhere. As long as the origin of this movement, and, strictly speaking, the cause of this effect, remain disguised, there is the risk of letting temporal difference relapse to the level of representation—of finding in it a new—merely more sophisticated—version of difference in time; of configuring, in short, under the rubric of a metaphysics of the "advent," the image of a difference between temporalities. There remains the risk of reestablishing terms that, though they become ever so ephemeral and are broken down into other differential units, still remain *in themselves*. Indeed, such is the hold that the natural experience of time has on us that it always makes us forget the word [*parole*] that convulses it, the interrogative word that alone has the power to separate the subject from the world given in representation, to afford access to what is given as well as to what is not given—an opening that is the incessant work of the destitution of the object, of the "unclosing" of representation, and that cannot close back onto anything that might come to take the place of the erased given. Let us understand that the temporal difference ceases to be a copy of difference in time the moment it proves to be inseparable from the advent of the question in which the assurance of difference in time is undone. It is not because a discourse brings Roman protagonists onto the Florentine stage and mixes things said about the past with things said about the present that it destabilizes the points of repair of the real; it is because it bears through them the question of what constitutes the past and the present; it is not because it attacks the representation of Rome that it changes the Florentine's relationship with Rome, but because it frees the question of Rome from representation. That question does not have an object that would be Rome; it envelops, as question, Florence, the modern state and the ancient state, and all the forms of political society. But however extensive the domain it makes its own, that domain is not its object, either. As question, it lives from its *écart* from the object, and it brings the temporal difference forth from out of this incessant *écart*, in the movement of its own differentiation. It brings it forth, then, to the degree that it is held by it, that it withstands the trial of its own attachment to the present, through the continual deflagration of the *here* and *now*, in a space and time that are in tatters. Actually, it is not with the discourse of the oeuvre that the lack of distinction between the present and the past originates, as we have perhaps risked giving the impression. They are indistinct in natural experience, even when natural experience tends to disguise this fact from itself. The representation common to things both past and present bears the assurance of their difference, but as the representation of the past it is as present as is the representation of the present. For the Florentine, Rome is in the past, but at the same time its image is perhaps what is most present in the present; we must not even say that it haunts the present: it inhabits it. The image that the Florentine reflects back onto himself, in which his identity as a Florentine is preserved, contains that of the Roman. No doubt the representation forgets itself in the object, but that forgetfulness is produced; in a sense it is the work of the representation. Now it is to this work that interrogation returns, in the movement that unseals the object; it is by opening what was sealed and concealed that it clears a path to the possible. But nothing of what is generated in interrogation—what is said of Rome, Florence, history and political society—can be posited, can stand on its own, deprived of the movement that carries it within the opening of interrogation. Thus temporal difference, as it spreads out opposite the Rome–Florence difference, remains implicated in the question that opens the representation of Rome. Machiavelli, with his interrogation, does not place his contemporaries before a difference that they were unaware of; he sends them from the experience of difference in time to a difference of all objective differences, in deepening that experience in such a way that it ceases to be what it is, and turns out to be what it is not. By one sole act the given past and present lose their form, and natural experience breaks in two and enters into contact with itself, in virtue of its being pulled in opposite directions, in virtue of the impossibility into which it has been thrust of forgetting itself in things, that is, of forgetting itself qua experience of things. There are not two operations, one of which would impinge on representation, decrying the shallowness of its content, and the other the tie between the Subject and representation, since representation implies as such a constitution of the object qua object; there is the indivisible work of the modification of experience and of the decomposition of its products. And as for this work, we must not allow ourselves to imagine that it imposes itself from the outside on natural experience and the world given in it. Where would it come from, if it could lord it over natural experience as if it were matter to be modified? If natural experience were unable to bring forth interrogation, how would it open up to it?

What seems odd is that interrogation only finds its pathway as the result of a break with natural experience, and that it is preoccupied with that break as long as it remains faithful to itself, although it is impossible for it to conceive of it. But if it wanted to do so, it would immediately go astray, and the discourse would once again fall into the grip of that experience. What seems odd is that the movement that frees it from natural experience cannot define its space outside of it. But this paradox only disconcerts to the extent that we assign natural experience a reality and limits it does not have, or that we borrow from it, in order to define it, the norms from which we sought to free ourselves. On the other hand, interrogation draws sustenance from the paradox, since the moment it decries natural experience, it awakens what slumbers within it, at once reveals how it gets carried away into the objects in which it forgets itself, and the drifting away into representation that accompanies it; surprises the refutations it inflicts on itself, and the impossibility for it to close itself up in the passion for the real—since in order to think it, it must give up rejoining it from another shore of being, discover itself hidden down inside it as its secret, bind itself to that part of itself, necessarily having stolen off yet ever imminent, without which nothing is given.

Whence the fact that the discourse of the oeuvre, in its interrogative vocation, does not apply itself to cutting its ties with the instituted forms of discourse (which it deprives of their assurance in order to deliver them up to a pure present in which they would converse with one another without knowing it) in order to formulate that present, and what the new is, and what the old. As for this present, it does not grasp it, it only beckons toward it as to the latent, in a word [parole] that itself experiences and brings into play that latency, by accepting its own inner split, the constant distortion between said and understood, the interplay of covert and overt, the impossibility of its own completion. As for the new, appearances not-withstanding, the language of the oeuvre does not concern itself with it except to dissipate its lure. Whatever is thus designated, in every era, is precisely the camouflage of the unutterable, the way to ignore the temporal difference by giving it form and figure. One reads the new in signs; one circumscribes it, cultivates it to find in it a guarantee of the fullness of the present, to confirm the substance of history that would be perceptible in it as in its oeuvre. An open future is supposedly granted it, while in fact it has already been given a name, and it is hypocritically used to bar the passage of what is not yet. But the thrust of the oeuvre of human history is not to be identified by images formed of the old and the new; it is rather in casting them aside, in losing faith in the new, in freeing the question of time from the natural experience of the succession of times, that some measure of the historical advent lets itself be captured in a language—a language that itself can be understood only by preserving its latency: the language of the work of thought.

What remains latent in this language, in the antechamber of the word [*parole*] but always beyond its grasp—how are we to believe that it is within the interpreter's purview to name it? To suppose he has this power would be to attribute to the latent the consistency of something positive, eluding the grasp of the author of the discourse, but graspable by another. Far from giving interpretation the possession of its object, such a hypothesis would be its downfall: either it would have to claim for its own discourse a transparency it denies to that of the writer, and admit that it is power-less to found the distinction, or it would have to admit that both are of the same nature, that it itself bears, inscribed on the obverse of its statements, a reality that escapes it and will only be readable by a third party, and imagine in this third party the same fracture, and sink down into the aporia of relativism. True assurance is won by the interpreter who allows himself to be guided by the question that does the work of the oeuvre, when he consents in its wake to the loss of bearings of natural experience, when that loss becomes his own work, when it entails the loss of his own position in relation to the discourse of the oeuvre, and in relation to what it speaks of, when a place of the oeuvre shows itself to him beyond the framework in which it appeared as something given, and when his word [*parole*]—the interrogative word—is inscribed in the absence of a last text.

The question doing the work of the oeuvre calls out to us the very moment it makes us give up the illusion of an intelligible object given in the discourse, and the illusion of the reality of the socio-historical field in which it is inscribed or to which it points. But freed from this twofold illusion, the question constitutes the interpreter, in assigning him or her a twofold position: it has the power to involve in the discourse a reader who is situated at a distance from the space–time from which it emerged; it has the power to well up within him or her, isolated from the matter that nourished it, cut off from the desire it aroused in the Florence of the Medici, just after the crisis of the regime. Assuming that the question finds one of its formulations in this remark on *The Prince* that Machiavelli made to a friend—"[w]hat a principality is, how they are acquired, how they are held, why they are lost"[7]—surely it can still be understood, when the horizons of Italian politics have disappeared, along with the memory of the instability of the city-states during the *Cinquecento.* It is also true, however, that in order to understand the question we must go to meet it in the discourse in which it arises as a question. The wording we have given of it not only has the fault of being too general; at most it merely indicates what is at stake from a distance, or part of what is at stake. What gives it life is the movement in which the word [*parole*] is put in question, a movement we cannot ally ourselves to except on the condition that we remain as close as possible to its trace, that we reconnoiter the passage that is opened up in a here and now. Although we understand the question at a distance from the space–time in which it appeared, it draws us toward it, inviting us to a proximity that is the resource of that distance. The division of the interpreter into a close and a distant reader is never resolved. Within him or her, there is a perennial impulse to hear what was intended to be heard by the men living in the space–time in which the writer's word was written, and that word always yields to the necessity of hearing what pierces that space–time and is addressed to the Other-at-a-distance whose position accommodates to an indefinite number of space–times. If this incessant interplay that accompanies reading may seem a scandal to those who anxiously cling to the points of repair of natural experience, they must nonetheless extend its limits, recognizing that the interpreter's situation falls within the ambit of the word [*parole*] in the discourse of the oeuvre; for that word extends to and includes his situation even at the cost of an incessant bifurcation of expression and understanding. It includes an unlocalizable, or drifting, Other, who is always on the hither side or beyond any coordinate that would pinpoint him; the blur of the position of the reader is prefigured in its exercise. In vain does he attempt to stay close to this word, or to turn his distance from it to his advantage: he is denied the ability to gauge either distance. But the scandal not only makes the properties of space and time of the oeuvre perceptible: one would be precipitous in ascribing an end to them with the sole thought that the interrogation of the reader who is close and that of the reader who is at a distance are interrelated, or that they can be merged. The experience of reading turns out to be even more disconcerting when we explore the ways in which the interrogation of the remote reader and the proximate one are distinct in interpretation, and we wonder whether the two can be maintained within the same register.

Moving along these paths, we approach the question of the locus of the oeuvre from a new angle, which cannot be distinguished from that of interpretation. That question arises, once we have put aside the double illusion of its inscription in the field of the intelligible and the historically perceptible. And from a new angle, we encounter the question of the time of the word [*parole*], that is, the question of its relation to incompleteness. The question arises, once we admit that the interrogative word lives from the erasure of the object and the deferment of the end. Both questions [that of the locus of the oeuvre and of the register of the interpretation] are conjoined before the increasing numbers of vanishing points of interpretation.

Machiavelli's interrogation—how would we be able to speak about it, or speak it, we, readers from a distance, remote readers, if it did not govern the play of questions produced in the discourse? How would we keep his interrogation in mind at the time of the interpretation, if the oeuvre were not the memory of itself at the time of its advent? He who abstains from answering seems to indicate his own failing or that of Machiavelli—for the writer himself raises suspicions because nowhere does he give us the origin of his questioning. Were we to limit ourselves to seeking it in *The Prince*, the remark confided to Vettori could not meet our expectations.

Che cosa è principato? The expression does not let itself be immediately understood. True, it contains a question the object of which is designated as the *principato*, but neither the nature of the object nor that of the question is immediately decipherable in that expression: *Che cosa è principato?* Is it the type of state whose distinctive trait is government by one sole individual, the monarchy? Is it the power of the prince? Or is it, for example, as an eminent translator does not hesitate to propose, sovereignty?[8] Should we say that the first hypothesis is the only acceptable one, since, from the first lines on, the work contrasts *principati* and *republiche*? But the development of the expression authorizes us to retain the second interpretation, for no sooner has the author added "how many types there are," than he specifies, "how they are acquired, how they are kept, and why they are lost." Now this is not an enumeration of new distinct questions, since, as the work states at the beginning, it is by understanding how power (*imperio*) is acquired that one is capable of distinguishing the *principati.* As for the third hypothesis, while it must be excluded if we consider the literal meaning of the text, it becomes pertinent the moment the analysis whose object is the *principato* is extended to include all forms of monarchic, oligarchic, or democratic power. The question we have just expressed in the form, "What is the *principato?*" as contained in the question "*Che cosa è principato?*" because it does not find a satisfactory answer, opens up another: Why does Machiavelli question in such a way that the object of his question is given in an indecisive representation?

To question in this way is at the same time to wonder where the writer is speaking from, given that he is casting doubt on the distinctions accredited by the Tradition—distinctions the reader was in the habit of trusting. More specifically, to question in this way is to be surprised at the absence of excepted considerations that the question thus posed leaves aside: all reference to a nature of political society and the function of its government. The first question, then, far from allowing itself to be grasped in its object, expands to become the question of the being of the question. We were quite right to say that the meaning of the question is not immediately apparent. Let us now go on to recognize that in order to decipher it we must take up the quest for its origin, by making the effort to understand how it is designated in the discourse. Rather than attempting to apprehend it from the outset, we must let it be developed until we get to the bottom of it. Of course we are not so naïve as to expect to find it in the form of a statement, though there is no reason not to expect it to be best revealed in the words chosen by the writer. Nor do we assume that it is given in an ultimate question, hidden away somewhere in a discourse, or even at the end. In our view, if it is worthy of its appellation of question-origin, that is not because we would obtain, by knowing it, the power to attach all questions to a first link, but by the virtue it has of drawing us in each of them toward its being as question. In this sense it is at the bottom of the first question, as it is of the last. Whatever the entrance the discourse offers us, it is recognizable by the same call.

Now, our reading of Machiavelli has been such that we are now tempted to attach the question-origin to a term that the author, without having abstained from pronouncing it, has not himself detached from the discourse to make it into the manifest support of its genealogy: *principio.* The question that is heard from below all the others, addressing itself through the proximate reader to the remote one, dissociating them from one another—we would like to designate it as that of the foundation or (to give the term its own mission), of the foundation-beginning, which confronts us with the principle of the political society and of the action of the Subject operating within it. In doing so, we would furnish a response, defend the author and his interpreter against the suspicion of failure.

Perhaps that response is not useless; but after a moment's scrutiny, we must admit that it may lead to odd consequences. There is scarcely any need to repeat that the question of the *principio* in Machiavelli's oeuvre sets aside all knowledge of what it is. It is in this that it is a question-origin, which nourishes the word [*parole*] without the question-origin being able to exhaust it. Its power is to stimulate thoughts that have not yet been thought. That is why we would cease to understand it, were we to give way to the illusion of a negative response, quite as much as if we were to fall into the illusion of a positive one. The question of the foundation inhabits every particular question, but none of them would survive if it itself sank away into the pure and simple destruction of its object.

Already in the first chapters of *The Prince*, in which the question of the foundation disappears as soon as it appears, we are set on the right path. The reduction of politics to the field of power relations, the rejection of all guarantee inscribed in a natural order or providential plan, the assertion that the new prince can trust no one but himself—these are all soon accompanied by statements about the greatness of historical creation (the establishment of *ordini nuovi*), and the excellence of the founders—statements that rule out a retreat to the limits of positive knowledge. In vain would we claim to find in the actions of the great legislators referenced in Chapter 6 nothing more than an outstanding case of the fecundity of the calculation of relative strength. Beside the fact that nothing is adduced to furnish a demonstration of this, the meaning of their enterprise no longer finds its measure in the logic of the operations that appeared earlier to give the definition of the conquest of power. The phenomenon of foundation, located in empirical history, opens us to the enigma of the foundation of the state. And we are all the more felicitously attracted to empirical history in this matter in that with the example of Savonarola (the republican reformer), combined with those of Romulus, Theseus, and Moses, the truth of the foundation cannot be limited to the moment of the birth of the political body; it is also decipherable at every stage of its development and in the different forms it acquires. At the same time, the impossibility of our knowing exactly what is contained in the concept of *ordini nuovi*, as well as that of *virtù*, and those of *principe* and *principato*, reveals the depth of that enigma. At one and the same time the stays that lent political thought its assurance— the distinction between power and regime, just and unjust states, legitimate and illegitimate princes, licit and illicit (or desirable versus necessary) endeavors—are removed, and a new principle of truth is suggested, without being brought entirely into the light. But the first questions of *The Prince* are only set forth in their true light with the proposition from Chapter 9: "In all cities one finds these two different dispositions which are born of the circumstance that the people desire not to be ruled or oppressed by the Grandees, and the Grandees desire to command and oppress the people." This proposition tips the scales of Machiavelli's analysis in the direction of the interrogative dimension that is its true nature. Moreover, for the interpreter who gathers his readings of *The Prince* and *The Discourses* into one sole reading, this proposition appears necessarily implied in each of its moments: the interrogation on the *principio* proves to be indissociable from the discovery of an originary division in the social body. But to fully appreciate what that division brings into play, we must recognize that it resists all attempts to annul it in contact with its cause or its effect. As for what can define the locus of its cause, we believe we find it in human nature. The universality of class conflict, we are tempted to think, can only be recognized on the basis of a representation of man as a desiderative being, an animal tethered to specific appetites for power, honor, and wealth. This representation alone would appear to be able to explain why the accidents of the war of all against all engender everywhere the coalition of the stronger or more fortunate on one hand, and that of the destitute on the other—a division set up between the social positions of the dominant and the dominated. It would also herald the possibility of a power that would avail itself of the adversaries' fear and the natural regulation of the appetites it engenders, in order both to carve out a space of its own, at a distance from the classes, and to embody the principle of common utility. But the argument is unsustainable, and it would be an error to seek in the animality of man the origin of the constitution of the social body. Although Machiavelli does not refrain from asserting that the creator of *ordini nuovi* must assume that all men are wicked, and despite the frequency of his trenchant formulations in *The Prince* and *The Discourses* that can be seized upon by the reader seeking a definition of human nature, these judgments cannot furnish a conclusive referent for his analysis; their meaning does not let itself be abstracted from the role they play in the critique of the values accredited by Tradition, and in the unveiling of the pact between the prince and the people. Particularly unintelligible would be the idea that the prince must arm his subjects, seek security not in fortresses but in the confidence he inspires, sustain his own power with that of the people, and that he can find safety when external dangers put him at their mercy, if we had to abide by judgments of this type; for example, the famous remark in Chapter 19: "Because this is to be asserted in general of men, that they are ungrateful, fickle, false, cowardly, covetous." Yet such an idea is not only essential to Machiavelli's political intention, so much so that without it the work *The Prince* would collapse (whereas it would retain all its meaning were we to leave out a few comments on human wickedness), it cannot even be thought, unless we recognize a relationship of man to his desire and to law, a power exerted on him by the *imaginaire*,[9] and an openness to authority, which are accounted for by the conventional representation of a nature of man. Truths that are not of the order of what is merely read between the lines: we find them both in *The Discourses* and *The Prince*, although in the second work analysis brings them to their fullest expression. In both, the desire of man, implied in universal class conflict, proves to be irreducible to the appetite for power, wealth, and honor. Since man's desire includes the refusal of commandment and oppression, we must recognize that no object can furnish an effective measure for it—that it detaches the subject from any particular position and binds him to an infinite requirement. That requirement seems to be of such a nature that satisfaction cannot be obtained by one without it being reborn in another; or that, beyond eventual redistribution of property, prestige, or power, the same force of negativity is maintained. Only such a requirement makes it possible to understand that the multiple oppositions of interest are ordered according to a fundamental division—that despite the established degrees in the possession or dispossession of societal goods, there is necessarily a split of the collectivity into two halves, and the impossibility of their reunification. For between the desire of the people not to be commanded and oppressed, and the desire to command and oppress, there is no conceivable negotiation: what causes one causes the other, by the very fact that they exclude each other; the subject that emerges at one pole of desire encounters at the other end his twin in abolishing himself in it. In a sense, far from revealing to us a positive reality of man, perceptible in the signs of animal appetite, the analysis of desire reveals beyond the phenomenon of social antagonism a primordial duality; it teaches us that there is in what is called human nature the wherewithal to conceptualize not only the struggle and instability that accompanies all forms of society, but the gap between the particular and the universal, between laws as defined in the instituted systems of obligations, in which a general relation of forces is crystallized at each moment, and Law, such as it is given, transcending all actual systems. Consequently, the idea of the animality of man ceases to become banalized in the image of the condition of the human species, in that of a passage from man's animal state to his social one, to nourish instead the question of a difference internal to the being of man, or, in the colloquial terms of *The Prince*, of a dual, man-beast nature that constitutes his socio-historical existence. It is true that *The Discourses* offer us, at the beginning, a reconstruction of the genesis of the first societies, but let us recall that this is merely a paraphrase of Polybius; and, far more striking than the conventional description of a pre-social past is the way the author uses it, the distance he immediately takes up with respect to the historic/mythical account, devoting himself instead to the relation between desire and law in the Roman Republic. In the guise of a question about the role played by the dominant and the dominated in the preservation of the law, the interrogation regarding the basis of the law achieves its rigor by being pursued in relation to the dialectic of class desire. How so? Not because it would justify our seeking, in the desire not to be oppressed, the inception of law, since after all this desire arises in a locus in which the division of classes is already operative, and along with it institutions that legitimate the established relation, so that the dimension of law is already given and the only question to be explored is where it is hidden and where revealed, or, more precisely, where it is lost and where kept. But rather because, as we get to know the instability of the Grandees, the fictional nature of an order of rules sustained by the natural play of appetites is revealed, the conjunction of the infinite requirement of the people and the transcendence of law elucidated, and the impossibility of affording the latter its own space, freed from desire, demonstrated. And at the same time the function of the theses that assign grounding in human nature to the division of classes is revealed. For the paradox suggested in *The Discourses* is that those who pretend to find in the universal bite of appetite the reason for social strife and instability exploit that image to insinuate that the overcoming of the passions comes from satisfaction, that respect for the laws has become inseparable from the status of men who possess wealth, power, and honors, and that class conflict is the sole work, if not the invention, of a coalition of malcontents and the envious. And correlatively, that paradox is such that we must go so far as to recognize the break in the continuum of desire, the movement that carries one to the appropriation of the goods of others, and the movement that annuls it, to admit that there are no common borders between its reign and that of law; that the latter, in the incessant play of its advances and relapses, remains beneath the power of this double movement, and that nothing affords an escape from the division of classes. Indeed, when Machiavelli points out, in examining the young Roman Republic, that "in every republic there are two different dispositions, that of the populace and that of the upper class and . . . all legislation favorable to liberty is brought about by the clash between them,"[10] he leaves no doubt as to his thought: order is not instituted in the break with disorder but is articulated with an ongoing disorder; peaceful harmony is a decoy, under the cover of which oppression seeks to appease the protests that force it to reveal its true identity and thus endanger it. Let us understand that the laws favorable to freedom are not just laws among other laws; moreover, as is shown by the analysis of regimes that stifle popular demonstrations, the existence of law always presupposes, with an implicit disavowal of the use of force, the recognition of the desire of the oppressed. But, in their fixed setting, the power of the Grandees and the powerlessness of the people cause the social relation to become petrified and the political body, in the absence of artifices to preserve it from foreign threat, to disintegrate. But as long as law retains its vitality, that is, as long as it gives men power to enlarge the field of their action, it passes on into new institutions favoring freedom, and this passage is opened up to it by class conflict. Thus, far from imagining that the "natural" struggle of men must be abolished in the state of freedom, or continue only to manifest the ineradicable effects of animality at the outer limits of properly human relations, we must ascribe the entirety of historical creation to it. Or, more strictly speaking, we must abandon the idea of a natural struggle per se, read the nature of man in the social relation, and articulate the question of the basis of class division with that of historical change.

Furthermore, with this interrogation, with the analysis of appetite, it is at once the phenomenon of class division and that of dissimulation that Machiavelli makes us capable of subjecting to ratiocination. Indeed, the latter would remain unintelligible, if we believed human conduct to be explicable solely on the basis of self-interest. It is true that *The Prince*, in particular, stresses its efficacy: men, it is asserted, covet all that would give them profit, and fear all that would negatively affect their security; they look no further than to the immediate objective, scintillating with advantage; their lack of faith and their instability come from an attachment to the ever-changing objects of appetite or fear. Yet this is only a half-truth, with which *The Prince* cannot be satisfied. As we will recall, it is through the analysis of the means at the disposal of a prince to institute and maintain his authority that the universal propensity of peoples to live from illusion is revealed. Now, we would search in vain to reduce that propensity to the result of simplemindedness, even if it is true that the search for what is immediately useful makes one blind to its consequences, or that hopefulness overrides calculation. Illusion is not just a failure of knowledge; it has its own knowledge. For the prince's subjects, it covers the desire not to know—to know nothing of the motivations of his politics, nor of what governs their own conduct, nor of the function of the state in society. Their wish is that the prince should appear good, his intentions noble, and that he should dispense the signs of majesty of the state, and—since other signs are always there to contradict those signs—that he should lie. It is, then, to judge with their eyes rather than their hands, and to see good colors rather than the outline of things. How can this desire be related to appetite, if not by destroying the first definition to include the hunger for representation? If not by concluding that the imperative of conservation itself, so widely held to be primary, includes the need to incorporate the image of the Other, since every time the prince is able to wear the mask well, men are ready to abandon their possessions and lose their lives to defend him, whatever his follies may be? While *The Prince* does no more than give an outline of the analysis of the function of the *imaginaire* in social life, *The Discourses* develop that analysis in all its ramifications, examining politics, religion, and war. Authority, whether of the gods, the senators, or military leaders, or the state, proves to be founded on the power of representation. The skill of the priest in making the entrails of the chicken speak, that of the head of the military in pretending to know more than he does, that of the consul in invoking the good of the state—their common referencing of examples from the past only have the power to distract men from the idea of profit or imminent danger because they correspond to their expectations. And if it is true that these expectations are always associated with deliverance from fear, it is not so much in response to an actual threat that they arise, but from a refusal to confront the indetermination or the contradiction in things, from the hope for an ultimate reality in which each of us would be granted his or her identity. This is specifically the lesson to be learned from the beginning of Book 3, in which there is an affirmation of the need for a periodic return of the institution (whether political or religious) to its *principio*. There, the virtue of this return is linked to an armed takeover that inspires terror. But if the exemplary punishments of the lawbreakers furnish a preliminary illustration, the acts that bespeak a sovereign detachment of the hero with respect to his possessions or his life immediately appear, and with no less efficacy; then, with the analysis of the case of Brutus and that of conspiracies, the meaning of the armed takeover may imply either transgression or defense of the established order. What restores the institution is, then, what gives back to it "*quella reputazione ch'egli aveva ne' suoi principii,*" that is, restores its image at a distance from the behavior that obtained in it, ruled by the play of appetite. Fear is not a consequence of the image, determined by the visible signs of the power inscribed in it; it merges with the trial of transcendence, with the discovery of a different reality, incommensurable, hidden from the knowledge of immediate goals; fear of the punishment proclaimed by the legislator, or of the exorbitant call contained in the crime committed by the conspirator as the sacrifice accomplished by the hero, it is always at the same time its opposite, transport to the place in which there is a necessity without motive, an object—army, church, or state—that excludes the contingency of the subject, a pure atemporal *principio*. Thus we understand why the way of return to the founding of the state suffers no definition—neither that founding of being localized in empirical history, or even of being related to its valor. The *principio* of the institution cannot be dissociated from the powers of the *imaginaire*. It is impossible to determine the origin, the order of the founding and of the beginning, without including in it the representation of the origin. It is impossible to fix it in time, since it does not coincide with the event, since it merely manifests itself in it, in the relationship men form to it, and since there is, in a sense, antecedence of the image before the fact. It is impossible even to distinguish, by the sign alone, the part of illusion from the part of truth, since, by alienation in the image, men rid themselves of, or take on, a freedom to act and think—they always do both at the same time, but either to their advantage or to their detriment. With the same faith they place themselves under the power of a despotic prince, or a despotic God, or roll back the limits of necessity.

Now it is the same thing to think the power of representation in the institution and to think the break in the continuum of desire implied by the rending of society into antagonistic classes; to read the contradiction of a re-connecting of the desire to have and the desire to be, which constitute, respectively, the essence of the desire of the Grandees and that of the desire of the people, and to read the ever-reenacted enterprise of the figuration of a social identity in which difference is abolished: the projection of a natural community into the Army or the Church, into Rome or Florence. To discover beneath the fact of appetite the break of desire is, in fact, to forbid oneself to suppose that there is *real* separation between its two poles, unless it is to let it fall back once again to the level of nature; it is necessarily to agree that it relates to itself across separation, and that this relation can be manifested only in the form of a representation. It would be vain to pretend to reduce the desire of the Grandees to what constitutes its essence: in the experience of the instability of possessions and power, it proves to be unsustainable, carrying within itself its opposite, the desire to be, at the same time that it attacks it in the other, and is condemned to emerge with the self-image of an effectively present totality, a "social nature" in agreement with itself at a deep level. Nor is it a simple lie or a simple ruse if the dominant class denies the rift, even though its self-interest commands it to do so. It thus testifies to the impossibility, in which its desire places it, of assuming the simple position of owner/oppressor. From its point of view, the institution is a substance in which its internal conflict as well as its conflict with the other is dissolved. Similarly, it is impossible to make the desire of the populace coincide with the principle that constitutes it: the populace itself coincides with its opposite; to the extent that it is pure negativity, that it bears the infinite demand "not to be commanded, oppressed," and experiences the impossibility of its goal, it in turn proves to be unsustainable, riveted to the desire to have, at the same time that it discovers it in the other, and is condemned to emerge with a self-image in which the substitute for what is withheld from it is offered. Hence it is not just as a result of deception, though its destitute condition does predispose it to credulity, that the dominated class puts its faith in the institutions of the city. It thus nourishes its desire to exist from the imaginary possessions supplied to it by the social emblems; it satisfies that desire through iden- tification with the position of the other that it lacks. Doubtless the success of the operation is always threatened, since, at the same time, the focal point of conflict remains; thus in response to oppression the people may become alienated from the institutions, and even in times of relative calm its relation to them is ambiguous. But as long as the possibility is provided for it to believe in the sovereign images, that is, in its own image as citizen or subject, soldier, churchgoer, it weaves from its place the veil that hides the division of classes, to the point of becoming an accomplice to the deception practiced by the Grandees or the prince.

Such an analysis, we must further specify, does not lead to the the- sis of a generalized lie, engendered by the imposture of desire. It is true that at the center of the political society there is the division into classes, which we cannot attribute to anything that we may seize upon to make it into a simple consequence, inscribing it in a natural order; and it is true that the desire discovered in it, not at the bottom of it, but as it were the movement of the division, proves to thrive on deception. Involved in the latter are all the postures of the political Subject, identifiable in the figure of the institution, the group, and the individual. But we must take care not to apply to imposture a criterion that it does not tolerate, which presupposes, for it to be judged, a known passage of being and non-being denied by its discovery. In calling imposture by its name, we are immedi- ately obliged to distinguish between that which is on the hither side of all postures, commands their variations, the holds of the *imaginaire*, but also its releases, and that which, in each one of them, in the acquired position held up as being the natural one, is the lie. Otherwise, we would have to conclude that the desire of the Grandees and that of the people are equivalent, as are the republic and the monarchy, despotism and limited power, or popular army and mercenary army, or Christianity and pagan- ism. Now, Machiavelli never authorizes this hypothesis. Although the de- sire not to be oppressed coexists in the people with its opposite, although history shows the passage from the position of the oppressed to that of the oppressor, we must not cease in our effort to find in the people—and let us not forget this—the condition for an openness of the social body to a history, the possibility offered to that social body for new organs, which not only prolong its life, but overturn the primitive givens of the political play—the principle of a deliverance from the repetition to which the appetites of the dominant class, when they flourish freely without bounds, enchain. In the position of the people, imposture shows itself in the desire for emblems that hide its oppression from it, in the desire for a just prince who loosens the grip of the Grandees, imposing his own, and in the desire of the priest in possession of knowledge on last things, who forbids "speaking evil of evil" in Christianity, and in all religions to wish for the death of the prince, and even in the desire for a power that would be in the hands of the powerless. But the desire not to be oppressed undoes imposture, despite its incessant reestablishment, for it is always at its highest point, wherever the position seems attained, wherever the established laws are called laws of nature, or wealth, honor, and power go beyond expectations, that is, in the place occupied by the dominant class. Desire to be and negativity in act, it is through it in fact that the being of society gives itself in excess over all given reality.

Let us understand one further thing. Just as one cannot determine desire on the basis of its imposture, without cutting oneself off from the relation in which the imposture can be attained, nor limit oneself to naming either its division or its indivision without excluding the ability to discover the one in the other, similarly, if we wanted to stop at the mere idea of the abyss of society, we would make it impossible for ourselves to give an account of the experience of the subject who is rooted in it; and if we were to speak only of a final fission of society, we would be forgetting that in the meaninglessness of the patching together of the extremities of desire the sign remains of the cloth that has been rent and that the very veil that hides the tear is woven on the same loom. Machiavelli's analysis does not end with an artificialist conception of the political institution that would associate the function of the *imaginaire* with that of the instrument. It does not authorize our concluding, for example, that the state is a simple means used by the classes to untie the knot of their conflict and attain common goals, nor that it is a simple product of the joint illusions of the people and the Grandees, effective in masking their internal contradictions. Not only does each thesis, taken separately, turn out to be unsuccessful, but with their combinations we remain unable to understand why in one passage the instrument is reduced to its narrowest range of application, and may be said to wear out more rapidly than it serves, in another, illusion clouds the actors to the point where the body politic, doomed to inertia, degenerates, and in yet another, still beneath the cover of illusion, and still by recourse to the mediation of a power "above classes," a *vivere civile* is instituted, a historical creation launched.

This question would be yet again misunderstood were we to envisage, as the final object of analysis, the structure of the political field as ordered along the lines of the division of classes—to decipher—beyond the diversity of regimes, constitutions specific to each of them, arrangements instituted in the praxis that concretizes them—the constants of the field in which class desire, law, power, and authority interrelate; for while that reading must be carried out, it remains subordinate to the requirement of conceptualizing a distinction that is not on its plane, and in which the truth of politics as well as that of the discourse of politics are at stake. It is true that, in *The Prince*, no objective criterion limits the figure of a regime in conformity with the essence of the city; no example has the function of producing a model whose universal application would be undeniable. It is true that we are led to seek, on the basis of privileged variants, the orderly game of authorities that command the social organization and political syntax of political action. But the imposed necessity of exploring this game, of detecting the structural fault lines, forces us at once to recognize within the historical material expressions—manifest in the institution, collective behavior, or the behavior of prince—in which are revealed what we must indeed call, without forgetting the contradictions that work it, an agreement of society with itself, a response that in fact measures up to the level of the question asked. These expressions are not considered felicitous because they indicate, for example, the success of an enterprise (we know that Machiavelli treated accidental successes with disdain), but because they are seen as the result of a just interpretation, because through them the language of politics is spoken as it should be: it is heard/understood at a distance from the specific occasion. Just as it is certain that the traits considered to be expressive do not make up a repertoire from which the prince might draw whatever seems to him to tally with the needs of the moment, that none of them admits of a literal imitation, and that they presuppose, in order to be appreciated, the intelligence of the principles that govern them—so would it be vain to make them into simple signs of a structure and to hypostatize the latter, in the belief that a knowledge of it would engender a mastery of political techniques. What the prince gains in interrogating history is his own power of expression; what he learns from the interpretations implied in the institutions or behavior patterns of the past is to be able, like an interpreter, to decipher himself: it is the task of reinterpretation, applied to a new text that has been given to him to read. Or, since we must always bear in mind that the prince is the son of the Machiavellian word, that he inhabits no figure far or near of the past or the future, that in his name there are condensed all the traits of the politician, and that his vocation is always the new; let us say rather that he furnishes us with the guarantee of the Being of history, of a meaning to be brought out of all known expression, that it extends up to and including non-meaning, defies capture, but denounces the untrue.

This guarantee—it is Rome that constitutes it in *The Discourses,* and still more effectively so than the prince, for not only does interrogation no longer seem suspended to the examination of the position of the governing figure in the sociopolitical field, the analysis of class division and class desire becomes central, and along with it the relation of the subject to law, the difference between regimes in which these relations are institutionally inscribed, and that of historical societies, and societies bogged down in repetition, receive elucidation (and these are all truths that were merely adumbrated in *The Prince*), but the critique of the *imaginaire* becomes twofold, bearing simultaneously on the institutions of Rome and the function of representation of Rome in the political consciousness of the Florentines. Indeed, it is by means of this twofold treatment that the ambiguity is dispelled. The Machiavellian discourse proves to be something other than a discourse on the division of class and of class desire, on the institution and illusion. A discourse on the object whose foundation has been hidden away, it wins its legitimacy by giving voice to a discourse buried within collective life, which only emerges piecemeal, and whose lies always require a half-silence; that is, it is legitimated by becoming the interpreter of unavowed interpretations; or, since the latter are necessarily couched in the language given to the writer, by becoming the self-interpreter of the discourse that society holds about itself. In this exercise, of course, the writer loses the apparent guarantee procured by the rule of objectivity. He cannot pretend to produce statements that are acceptable to all his readers, at least to those who apply to themselves the same rule, since he discovers in the other that foreign other who is associated with his internal other, the access to knowledge barred by representation and to be forced open by an interpretation that is self-interpretation. He is condemned, therefore, and condemns himself, to an indirect communication, tied to the awakening of a consciousness that imitates his own, at a distance. But in doing so he wins the evidence, the only one that has been promised him, of a relation of society to itself. For in the experience of a language in which the possibility of interpretation emerges from the work of occultation, there is given *in it* that of a social space sensitive to itself, in which classes, institutions, the individual actors are not external to one another, assignable to the function that would define their place in a network of oppositions, closed up in the conduct of dissimulation; they are open to one another—and each one open to himself by all the distance that the presence of the others unfolds within him—engaged in the process of a mutual deciphering that is at the same time the adventure of their common differentiation and their common modification. Through that experience, the thought that the desire of the people contains within itself that of the Grandees, and vice versa, or that the state is nourished by the joint illusions of the dominated and the dominant, or that law itself interweaves the history of their passion—that thought is delivered from the artificialist conception, from the fiction of a universe in which there are nothing but effective or ineffective lies, in discovering at one and the same time its place of birth in the desire of the other and the measure of its power in the exercise of its reflection, in its action of disenchantment. The assurance that collective life bears the ongoing occultation of the work of desire and the continuous possibility of a dis-occultation is interrelated with the assurance that there is, in the spoken word, with the subjection of the collective language, implicated in the work of occlusion of thought, the resource for an opening to truth.

For us readers, when the movement of self-interpretation that sustains the discourse of the oeuvre becomes perceptible, when it is marked by the movement it elicits within us, the interrogation on the *principio* turns out to be the question of the basis of politics and of the basis of political thought. These two questions, though indissociable from each other, are not indistinguishable. How could we say that the foundation of politics is thought, or vice versa? The strange thing is that when we ask what the foundation of the state, of class division, of class desire are, and while we free ourselves from any image of a soil in which to discover their roots, we are irresistibly led to forget the question of the foundation of thought, so much so that the latter loses all weight, is rejected from the circuit of collective life, and Machiavelli's discourse, or any other, seems superfluous, and not to inhabit the world in which "politics" are pursued. And the strange thing is that when we wonder what the foundation of thought is, and have given up seeking it in an ultimate idea, we are no less irresistibly inclined to detach ourselves from the phenomena that give politics its specificity, and it is no longer the being of the state or of the social classes or of class desire that nourishes the interrogation but the being of the word [*parole*]. To these two currents it is only certain that we cannot give ourselves over without being returned from the waters of one to those of the other. But it is also true that the impossibility of standing in the opening between one question and the other charges the enigma of the foundation with a new attraction, in making it speak in contact with the division between the being of thought and that of the world.

When we ask ourselves what, for Machiavelli, constitutes the foundation of politics, we are confronted with the idea of an ultimate division, in the sense that it does not cease repeating its dividing with the shifting of terms. It is division of classes, division of class desire, or, if we would leave the causal side for that of the effect, division between state and society, division between the desire of the prince and collective desire . . . But the question of the foundation is not annulled in the experience of division; rather it makes itself heard with increasing strength, like that of instauration. In the instauration of the authority of the prince, or of the authority of Rome, the sign of foundation is legible. But in such a way as to receive division, to open themselves up to the play of differentiation of terms, in giving free rein to the work of conflict, the prince or Rome show themselves capable of founding an enterprise—of opening a passage to history. Such is the indetermination connected with foundation that it is always possible to blind oneself in such a way as to read the justification of the arbitrary in it, to maintain that the prince is free to do whatever he likes, provided he wins power and security. This illusion presupposes the replacement of indetermination by a negation that is nothing but the obverse of the affirmation of foundation, and it reestablishes it hypocritically, moreover, in the disguise of the appetite of the stronger. On the other hand, Machiavelli only forces his reader to recognize the arbitrary in order to invalidate the very thing he believes in, only to aggravate the lack of guarantee, to the point where the political enterprise is seen to be self-supporting, in a movement that rests on nothing and has no other assurance than its in-determination. In doing so, he even forbids our conceiving of the final division as a division that, despite the shifting of its terms, is objective: that division proves to be irreducible, but no more "last" than the articulation that binds what is divided. Nor does he authorize our thinking that the law is born of the break of desire, no more than that the state engenders the division of classes. What is engendered is the relation of men to the Law, or the relation of men to the state, such as is specified in a regime of freedom, monarchy, or lawlessness. The question of the *principio* necessarily entails that of division, we said, but it must also be understood that there never is, in the final analysis, a place of cause and a place of effect, even though we can articulate the causes with the effects—and that in the slippage of terms, the space of the *principio* is indicated, or that of the continuous return of society to itself, as is attested by the necessity of the continuous return to the *principio*. In this connection, it becomes decidedly vain to imagine that this question has a circumscribed place in Machiavellian discourse—that it occupies, as we have run the risk of leading the reader to think, the position of the final question. Perhaps it would be preferable to say that it furnishes a means of finding, in every question, that which, beyond its object, gives it its being as question—that, beneath the term *principio*, there is revealed the passage leading from one question to the next, similarly to the way in

Marx's oeuvre, the term communism, or in Plato's *Republic,* the idea of the Good, perform an analogous function.

Now it is true that, thinking of it this way, we cannot unravel it from the question of the foundation of the thought of politics, such as it is given in the oeuvre. For it is the same necessity that causes us to read the absence of an external guarantee in the political work and in the work of thought. And it is the same necessity that makes us discover the enigma of instauration and of division, the foundation internal to the enterprise, in society and in the oeuvre. It is also true that in discovering a collective discourse implicated in the Machiavellian discourse, and the link between interpretation and self-interpretation, we are carried to the junction of the theoretical and the practical. The possibility offered us, readers from a distance, of letting ourselves be turned toward politics and Machiavellian thought is part of the exchange that takes place between what is part of the question of politics and what is part of the question of the oeuvre. What is more, we could follow the channels of that exchange by examining the modification of our relation to politics and to thought in the work of reading. For desire, the *imaginaire,* law, and authority—we discover these in the experience of thinking itself quite as much as in the field it opens up for us, in what is not strictly speaking thought, but rather ensures its exercise: the desire to know, the relation to the norms of a logical discourse, the relation to authors-guarantors of instituted truths, including the strategy of conservation/transgression that under-girds the reader's conquest. But it is also true that the distance separating thought from what it thinks is never abolished, and that, at the same time that the distinction between an *inside* and an *outside* of the oeuvre is obliterated, it remains impossible to forget the distinction, that the question of foundation remains twofold, and that, for us, what is initiated in the experience of division under the rubric of power turns out to be of a different order than what is initiated in the same experience under the rubric of knowledge.

Now under this last rubric it is the whole dialectic of instauration that is inverted, for instauration only operates within the oeuvre by rejecting the institution, by departing from the rule of the living—people, Grandees, or prince—a departure that is the inscription of desire in space–time. Of course we must recognize that the reflective work [*oeuvre de pensée*] cannot fail to acquire the status of an institution. The moment it becomes a reference, the moment it is hidden beneath accredited representations in space–times and those representations are transmitted— the moment they are charged with nourishing the collective language, the work acquires the properties assigned to it by its insertion into the political space. A power is attached to it, a constraint emanates from it,

a process of legitimation is developed on contact with it, of which it becomes both the object and the agent. Let us even agree that if it meets
this fate, it is because its discourse lends itself to it. This is the case not
only because it uses signs others may take over, but because it secretes
the *imaginaire* in the work of the word [*travail de la parole*]. But thought
only makes its oeuvre, only remakes itself in the interpretation that is
the oeuvre of the oeuvre, on the condition that it withdraw before the
attraction of representation, that it distance knowledge from the possession of the object, or yet again by its resolution to keep the place of the
end vacant, to preserve, in interrogation, the form of a non-power. The
thought of politics only does its work of thought [*oeuvre de pensée*] on the
condition of its not being political thought, of experiencing its desire as
the desire to think. It is in the conquest of that extreme possibility (as we
are discovering) that it succeeds in delivering—in the field of politics, in
the field of history, in the natural experience that is already articulated,
already thought, politically—the unsaid, the un-thought, through which
there are politics, history, natural experience, incessant *écart* between
being and representation. Thus, we cannot detach the tie it offers us to
its being qua thought to what it thinks. The paradox, however, is that its
enterprise designates at the same time the difference between thought
and the things to which thought affords access. It is not simply that there
is more in politics and history than is thinkable about them, or more in
thought than what politics and history mobilize in the way of thoughts.
The point is, we are unable to occupy a position from which we can
dominate all the relations with being, that being only reveals itself in
virtue of an entanglement of the one who is—of a being assigned to a
place—a place that, though remaining itself invisible, is always revealed
by its resistance to what is different. Hence we cannot reduce the question
of the foundation of politics to that of the foundation of the thought of
politics. But again we must not forget how this paradox comes to us. It
is through the work that it gets a name. The only experience we have of
the thought of politics is where its work is accomplished. The question
of the foundation does not admit of being posed as that of thought in
general, or rather only admits of being posed as such within the space
of the oeuvre—just as (as we have said) the question of the foundation
of politics can only be posed within the political work [*ouvrage*], [with
its] classes, institutions, and state. We can no more embrace the field of
political thought with our mental gaze—take an independent measure
of it—than we can master the relationship it maintains with politics. The
only assurance we are given of what it is is the one brought about by our
experience of the instauration in its oeuvre. But it does not suffice to
admit that this experience puts us face to face with the adventure of our

own oeuvre; again this one, which we have referred to as oeuvre of the oeuvre [work of the work] testifies, despite its filiation, to the articulation of the question of the foundation/beginning with the question of a recommencement. In vain the interpreter would like to limit this recommencement to the task with which he has been charged, of speaking from his own position, to say what word [*parole*] is inaugurated in the oeuvre. It does not suffice to admit that the interrogation lets itself be received by him alone who redoes it; he must also confront its contingency, give up the idea of inscribing it in a general interrogation, of gathering together—as if they were part of one sole tree—Machiavellian questions and those of other oeuvres that might reinforce them or that they might reinforce, agree that the oeuvre rests on itself, that the relation of incompletion for which he, the interpreter, wishes to be the support, is marked in the singular orbit of the oeuvre, and that it is the same necessity that attaches us to it and that makes us respond to the requirement of thinking what has not yet been thought—not what is lacking in the Machiavellian thinker, for in a sense what he lacks still belongs to him, but *that which puts thinking back to work*. This requirement gives the interpreter a glimpse of the unsuspected limit of his enterprise. For whatever he may say of the foundation of politics and of the foundation of the discourse of the oeuvre, of the twofold question in which they are revealed, for him, reader from a distance, who claims to deliver it from the space–time in which it was born, a reservation accompanies it: in the ledger that awaits being opened, the thought of politics can be preserved only at the cost of a break with Machiavellian thought . . .

In running up against this limitation, the interpreter remains voiceless, because what puts thinking back to work eludes him. At least he can hope that what eludes him is not entirely alien to him, if it is true that the relationship with works of the past belongs to the experience of the present and that he has worked to modify it. After all, he could hardly ask for more than to be in league with the task of instauration, when he sets out on the modest path of restoration. In the relationship that he establishes with the discourse of Machiavelli, what is he in search of if not help in sketching out, in one place, a self-interpretation of the present collective discourse, incapable as he is of conducting it on a larger front, and without mediator? His enterprise is necessarily condemned to remain in suspense.

Such a conclusion reintroduces, in an unexpected way, the question of the temporality of the oeuvre. When the interrogation—as we, the remote readers, freed from the socio-historical horizons of the Machiavellian discourse, are conducting it—comes to the point of denouncing its own contingency, it challenges us to be aware of its singular inscription and to turn our attention from our voice to that of the proximate reader—the contemporary of Machiavelli. It is the same necessity that prompts us to glance at the question of foundation outside the field of interpretation, dissuading us from pursuing it, and that brings us back within the borders of a *place* in history in which the discourse of the oeuvre has its origin. It is not that we imagined we could explain Machiavelli's interpretation by deciphering its inscription—we have broken with that illusion, which would make it impossible to understand why it still speaks within the remote reader—but because the temporal difference that we are once again experiencing, by the obliteration of the difference in time, by the transference of the interrogation outside empirical space–times implies, as we have already said in a different context, the double encounter of a past present and a present still to come. In reality, the proximate reader has never ceased being mobilized by the discourse; it is only the artifice of analysis that demands that we mark his return to the scene. Neither practice nor logic authorizes our subordinating his position to that of the remote reader, or vice versa. The difference in position is produced by the same reading; or let us say, rather, it is produced in the same interrogation, since it is by the interrogation that the remote reader wins his place. Both their paths cross so necessarily that we were obliged, in exploring the last question, to mention the function played by the critique of the representation of Rome in an analysis of the social *imaginaire*. Furthermore, we thought ourselves justified in asserting that this critique put both the problematic of *The Prince* and that of *The Discourses* in their true light, that it delivered Machiavelli's thought from equivocation, in rejecting an artificialist conception of the institution, and founded the distinction between the collective and the interpretive discourse. In doing so, we betrayed our involvement in a past present— letting ourselves be touched by a word [*parole*] that made itself present by manifesting and revealing within itself the very singular language of men situated in a space–time. It is true that we would not be able to appreciate what is at stake in the analysis of Rome, if the analysis of politics and history did not forbid our reading it as the simple desire for a return to the virtue of the classical model. But neither would it be possible to know the truth of that virtue if the critique of the Florentine representation of the Roman past did not show it being wrested from the powers of the *imaginaire*. Thus, when we ask what question makes us the proximate reader, and how by that question a locus of the oeuvre is designated, the image of Rome is at the center of our research. Yet in scrutinizing that image, all we find is a privileged sign of the relation that the discourse of the oeuvre establishes with the discourse that society conducts on itself. The question wins its assurance there, but its root is lacking. As for that root, we seek it in what we do not hesitate at present to call—postponing for the moment further specification of the meaning of that term—ideology. It is in recognizing the form of its ascendancy that the inscription becomes manifest for us. If we wish to designate the ultimate question that guides the proximate reader and makes it possible to interconnect all questions concerning the space–time of the discourse, we are tempted to say that it is the question of the focus of Florentine ideology.

Still, we must admit that in order to let itself be discovered in the oeuvre, this question requires that we go outside it, and gather from the testimonies of contemporaries or the documents of the historian what we need to blaze our trail. Assuredly we would remain disarmed, if we were ignorant of the regime changes that have, since the beginning of the *Quattrocento,* caused the City to go from the republic to the tyranny of Cosimo and Lorenzo, and of its last avatar under the reign of Piero to a new republic, first inspired by Savonarola, then, he having been executed, directed by Soderini, the Gonfalonier for life, until finally the domination of the Medici was reestablished. These points of repair, however indispensable, would themselves be of little help, were we uninformed about the divisions internal to the bourgeoisie, of the deep divide separating the lower classes from the various strata of the bourgeoisie and the power of a small number of great families who perpetuate themselves despite constitutional upheavals and transformations of political power. This knowledge is required in a general way, to illuminate the background of the set on which the Machiavellian personae move and their plots unfold, and more precisely, to allow us to identify here and there the intention of the discourse; not only to explain the involuntary connotation of a word that conveys a commonly felt experience of the era, but also to detect that deliberate hint that calls for the reader's active complicity. Thus, how could we assess, in *The Discourses,* the significance of the repeated allusions to the treason and trickery surrounding Soderini on the eve of his downfall, if the historian did not make us capable of deciphering on that occasion a privileged episode in the struggle between classes and among factions? We must, for example, know that the creation of the office of Gonfalonier for life—a measure without precedent in the history of the republic—and the election of Soderini were the result of a compromise between conservatives and reformers, that the political conflict was crystallized, since the overthrow of Piero in 1494, in the form of a debate concerning a narrow government under the direct control of the oligarchy, or a broad government, open to representatives of the middle strata of the petty bourgeoisie; that already Savonarola's failure did not have as its sole origin a revolt against intolerance, or the fear his personal authority inspired, but that it was brought on by the resolute opposition of the conservatives to his attempt to democratize the regime; that, after the execution of Savonarola, and faced with the impossibility of an immediate restoration of the oligarchy, part of that group began to dream of the prerogatives of the Medici, while the rest put their hopes in a strong and stable executive, capable of giving a monopoly on decision-making back to the great families; lastly, that the Gonfalonier, foiling the expectations invested in him, despite his fortune and social origins, refrained from calling the secret councils reserved for the upper bourgeoisie, and attempted, through tax reform, to lessen fiscal inequality. With this information the conduct of the upper bourgeoisie in the 1512 crisis is elucidated, and we can assess the naïveté of the statesman who imagined patriotism to be stronger than class interest. We may now find it less disconcerting that an alliance developed between the declared partisans of the Medici, the conservative clan opposed to Soderini's government, and its internal opposition, preoccupied with opposing all reform projects, maneuvering to keep the most important magistracies, and attracting into its orbit a part of the representatives of the lower and middle bourgeoisie. Their conflict, however great, proves to be subordinate to the need to prevent the political promotion of the *populo minuto*. This need was manifested in the repeated crises that punctuate the history of Florence, not just since the fall of Piero, not just since the beginning of the *Quattrocento,* but since the time when the upper bourgeoisie wrested political power from the nobility, and the latter had to insinuate itself into its ranks to retain some power. Through the divisions, the changes that affect its composition, one constant may be found, such that these divisions, these changes themselves, while they cause its instability, seem always to work toward its survival. Torn between ancient nobles and authentic bourgeois, between Ghibellines and Guelphs, between old Florentines and recent citizens, between nouveaux riches and heirs, between interest groups primarily connected with industry and large-scale commerce, with the bank and real estate—broken up according to family alliances, modified by the eruption into its midst of new elements, impossible to exclude from public life over the long haul, or, on the other hand, by the elimination of families fallen victim to political repression or the accidents of fortune, the oligarchy still has the strength to perpetuate itself. When it must yield some of its political privileges—as it appears to do in the last part of the *Trecento,* or in the aftermath of the fall of Piero—it succeeds in seducing or corrupting the new men who people the councils and obtain a part of the magistracies; when these intestine quarrels reach a degree that is no longer compatible with democracy, of however limited a nature, and simultaneously the demonstrations of the *populo minuto* become a threat, it welcomes the rule of personal power; and then, to the detriment of one faction, but to the common benefit, the network of family ties offers the channel for a new form of political expression, mobilizing in favor of a massive realignment under the domination of the Medici. This we need to learn, and to recognize consequently that there is no deep division between the regime of the republican type and that of the tyrannical type in Florence, that in spite of an undeniable difference—the major effect of which is that in one case certain stakes of the political conflict are visible, spark a general interest for the public thing [*res publica*], sustain both protest against and adhesion to institutions, while in the other they are masked, power draws away to secrecy, ignorance and fear discourage the hope of the vast majority and tend to corrupt morality—it is always a small minority who make the state their property, isolate themselves from the people, and by some artifice or another seek security in holding onto acquired positions. There is no question but that to assess the strength of the oligarchy we must seek its basis in the economic system, and that it is a great help for us to discover how the phenomenon of the concentration of capital, singularly advanced in Florence, is accompanied by a cooperative organization that puts handworkers and tradesmen in a position of direct dependence on the industrialists, the negotiators who control import and export, and the bankers—powerful roles that are, moreover, often played by the same individuals.[11]

The illusion would only be to expect, from information given by the historian, a response to the question that involves us in Machiavelli's discourse as his proximate reader. All that we gain by way of knowledge acquired by outside reading increases our sensitivity to the word of the oeuvre; a documentation as complex as you like may be developed to increase our power of comprehension, but it does not create it. Were we to abandon ourselves to the enjoyment of historical knowledge, that comprehension would be destroyed, for then we would grasp nothing in the discourse beyond informative statements, capable of enriching our representation of the political history of Florence, or, if indeed they are the object of our interest, of becoming more fully decipherable by their insertion into a larger set of signs. But as for Machiavelli's discourse itself, in trying to consign it to the status of object and to find within it the elements of a construction that could then be combined with those provided by testimonies or statistical documentation, we would cease to inhabit it, to make ourselves the support of its word, that is, to let it produce itself within us. Paradoxically, the effort of filling in the hollows of the "understood" would dull the keenness of our harkening, honed by lack. Furthermore, we cannot forget that if we must go beyond the confines of the discourse of the oeuvre in order to establish its historical context, it is still within its precincts that the ways leading out of it are adumbrated;

only if we let ourselves to be guided by it can we avoid going astray in our attempts at external contextualization. Indeed, within the discourse a language other than its own may be discovered, in which the experience of men situated in a particular space–time is expressed; the discourse reveals it in letting it be heard, and in that process makes itself heard as well. Now, sure as it is that this language can be better understood by us when we have carefully examined the conditions of the experience that nourishes it, just as surely would it be futile to suppose that examining those conditions can give us the meaning of that experience. From the richest analyses of the economic, social, and political phenomena, we cannot deduce the language in which the relations obtaining between groups and individuals are determined; or, since I have tendered the concept of experience, let me say that it would be naïve to imagine it as being defined outside the language in which it is spoken, to conceive of a real *in itself*, an order of mute things atop which the order of said things, the former's reflection, would be superimposed. In the same way, the space–time opened up by the discourse does not constitute an empirical district that we could survey from on high as if we were free of all attachment. It is impossible for us to reach a pure description of the articulations of these sectors that would be supplied by the economic categories determinative of production and exchange, classes, factions, the state, and the ensuing collective discourses, and the singular oeuvre of the political writer. As soon as we become the reader of such a writer, we find ourselves inscribed, not in a world that would be given independently to objective knowledge, but in a language, an experience, the identity of which is in question. It is due to our involvement in it that we are prompted to receive the information capable of sustaining the question; that question regulates the demand we address to the historian, without ever authorizing us to seek an ultimate, conclusive text, in which the naked truth would appear. If it is true that collective discourses exist outside the oeuvre and consequently that we must multiply our chances of understanding them by exiting its space, it is no less true that it is by the work [*travail*] of the oeuvre that their kinship and governing intention, always disguised in their exercise, is revealed, and that ultimately there is no external criterion of reality we can hold onto, nothing that frees us from the risk of interpretation—or since, as we have said, interpretation is self-interpretation, as much so in the writer's discourse as in our own—no word in contact with space–time that obliterates the Subject. This means that the position of the proximate reader contains the same paradox as that of the remote one. The latter must give up installing Machiavellian thought in a circumscription of the intelligible; he does not have free access to the field of the transcendental; the discourse sends him back to the enigma of a double origin, to its birthplace and to that of the interpreter. Similarly, the proximate reader only reaches the space-time of the production of the discourse in depriving himself of the way to determine it, in experiencing a bond impossible to undo between the discourse of the oeuvre and the collective discourse, between what he understands from it and what makes it speak. The distinction between the empirical and the transcendental organizes the space of the reading through and through, whatever our position may be, but in such a way that we are never before two regions, of which we could take possession one after the other; the transcendental, whether in proximity or at a distance, is instituted as a dimension of experience each time the Subject verifies his or her interwovenness in the word, in history, in the being to which he or she is related.

Again, we would not have gauged in its entirety the question linked to the position of the proximate reader if we limited ourselves to maintaining that Machiavelli's discourse makes itself heard in giving him to understand in its own space a discourse that is "other" and in challenging him to inhabit the history he is interrogating in contact with that differentiation. A part of the movement we accomplish in the conquest of that position would remain hidden. Here we must repeat that if in the course of reading we are introduced into the interior of the discourse, it is because the discourse has the power to open itself to another, that it already contains him, that the word of the oeuvre can be joined in the experience of an irreducible distance, that it can be heard, separated from itself, and that it is through one and the same experience that it engenders its reader or engenders itself through him or her. But we cannot stop at this slippage from the position of an "other" exterior to an "other" interior. We must also be attentive to the polarization that is effectuated in the movement of the word, due to its being intended for a third party. A new relation between inner and outer is thus unveiled. For that other is also chosen by the word [parole]; and surely it cannot coincide with any individual determined in the empirical field; but still, somehow, *somewhere*, visible or invisible, *someone* is its respondent. To that someone the word is given to be understood, at the same time as it understands itself; it is in turning toward that someone, aiming at him or her in a place, that the word wins the power to move outside the field in which it was unaware of itself into a discourse "other," and thanks to this displacement to know the latter. Thus the moment we discover ourselves to be interwoven in the oeuvre, we not only slip into the position of the inner other—a position, moreover, that it is impossible to occupy, whose indetermination forces us to speak in turn and to accept, therefore, to move outside the space of the discourse—we not only enter into a relationship with a discourse "other," from which the discourse of the writer segregates—a relationship from which we could not dream of separating ourselves, of dominating its terms, since our interpretation is caught up in it, we find ourselves sent back to the place of the respondent, put in the necessity of identifying it, and of insinuating ourselves into it, without however ceasing to know it to be elsewhere. Now what we said about the collective discourse—it is appropriate that we repeat it with reference to the respondent: it is in the reading of Machiavelli that we encounter it; it is on the condition that we find its trace within the oeuvre that it becomes possible to follow it thanks to the investigations of the historian.

What is the locus of the ideology from which the collective discourses draw in the space–time in which the oeuvre is written? Is it not, we asked, the ultimate question that installs us in the position of the proximate reader? Who is called upon to support the requirement and the work of detection of this locus? Is it not, we now ask, the question that governs access to the ultimate question?

Both *The Prince* and *The Discourses* seemed to us to be intended for those who have at once a desire to know and to act. It is by being based on such a desire and by exciting it that they lead some readers to understand what to others is unacceptable, and must even protect themselves, by the use of allusion, from their suspicions. Specifically, we must concede that *The Prince*, despite a dedication offered to Lorenzo de Medici, was not written for his adherents. In the recommendation made to the prince to free himself from the faction that brought him to power, in the repeated criticism of the insolence of the Grandees, what is conveyed is rather an agreement with the adversaries of the Medici faction. A strange agreement, apparently, since the author offers his services to Lorenzo, after having invested his hopes in Giuliano. But there is no trace of servility in that affair, as we observed. Machiavelli pretends to designate to Lorenzo the place of the *new prince*, a place that proves to have been announced in the past, provided we know how to interpret it, but a place occupied by no one, implying a radical break with tradition, a political invention, and revealing, moreover, a relation of the Subject to the real—whether he is a monarch, a military captain, or a head of the republic—such that no factual actor could cause it not to remain forever future. If we suppose that Lorenzo is one of those to whom it has been given to understand, it is certain that in order to represent the respondent, he has to deprive himself of the attributes that demarcate his "natural" position of prince. If we suppose that Lorenzo was incapable of understanding, that Machiavelli was mistaken about his resources, we should merely surmise that he hid other readers from him for which the discourse was intended. But then it is not a matter of indifference to learn that that interlocutor was twenty-four years old when *The Prince* was dedicated to him, that both he and Giuliano had been driven out of Florence in their childhood or adolescence, with the fall of Piero, and since then remained at a distance from the political scene—in short, that they took up a heritage, appeared as new men, *perhaps* sheltered from the corruption engendered by the struggle between factions, *perhaps* disposed to draw the lesson from the double failure of the republican regime and the tyrannical one in Florence. We cannot know what faith Machiavelli put in Lorenzo: at least we cannot doubt that if he dreamed of making him his reader, it was to entrust him with the task of a reformer and to steer him clear of the prejudices that had blinded the Florentine directors—those of recent as well as those of a more remote past. Also, it is important to examine the figure of the only Italian prince the work proposes to him as a model, not that Machiavelli is unaware of his shortcomings, but in the conviction that with him the possibility was opened up in Italy for an overturning of the rules of the political game: Borgia, whose adventure, we may venture to say, supplies him with privileged support for his project of *The Prince*. The personage presented first as fortune's fondling, then as the incarnation of *virtù*, was less than twenty years old when he undertook the conquest of Romagna, subduing, by force of arms, the miserable little tyrants who reigned only to torment their subjects and who made Florence tremble. Should we not also see in his example Machiavelli's attraction to the audacity of the new arrivals, for whom the book of the world was not yet written? There is nothing, including Borgia's failure, that does not underline his function in the work. So what if in the end he was undone by Fortune or failed to foresee his change of fate? His project has the wherewithal to carry the word [*parole*] to its encounter with knowledge and action, while the victories won by that lucky, vulgar figure, Julius II, are judged with coldness.

As for the appreciation of Machiavelli the man for Borgia, we may still have our doubts, and the same applies to the hopes he invested in Lorenzo. His embassy reports do not authorize our asserting that he recognized, during his lifetime, except perhaps at the outset of his enterprise, the genius ascribed to him in *The Prince*. But his transfiguration in the discourse of the oeuvre is eloquent. That discourse takes him over, making him into *someone* who is endlessly fascinated with hearing about the Medici, or Savonarola, or Soderini, or the conservatives who plotted against the democratic regime and always, when faced with foreign powers, took the route of least risk, temporization, and deal-making through treaties. The interlocutor called upon to understand does not belong to the category of men who have held, or continue to hold, the highest position, or of the sages of the era (*i savi dei nostri tempi*), or of all those who think themselves skillful or virtuous in seeking the security of the state in the maintaining of acquired positions. He is assumed to have the freedom to be receptive to forbidden thoughts; for example, that in politics so-called good deeds prove to be as harmful as evil ones; for example, that the Grandees, in all regimes, are animated by a passion to dominate and oppress, or that the religion of Christ accustoms men to slavery—but he is also assumed to have the freedom to refuse the satisfactions consisting in a mixture of cynicism and morality, since the critique is aimed at those who make a virtue of "enjoying the advantages of the times." And there is confidence in his desire to learn from history to find the principles of political action, since no recipe is given to him, and he is called upon to arrive at an interpretation of the present and his own position within it. Ultimately it is of little importance whether this interlocutor does or does not hold a rank that would open to him the career of a prince; he is not defined as such by reason of the actual authority he exercises or may claim, but is designated in the symbolic register as representing, in time, the break separating what has been from what is not yet, and in space the social separation between the closed space of the representatives of a regime, class, or faction, and the open space of the political subject for whom the relation to the *Polis* modifies the relation to the institution or the group. In a sense, we identify him with the symbol of youth. We catch a passing glimpse in that work of *a different kindred soul*, living in the space–time of the word, without respect for the values of the City, capable of overturning the idols, breaking the rules of politics, in flagrant opposition to the established order, placing his faith in the completely original, expecting something of the future, and thus the bearer of the chance of a new practice and a new thought.

A privileged indication of the role allotted to youth in Machiavelli's thought may be found in the penultimate chapter of *The Prince*, in a passage in which the author, abandoning strictly political analysis, rises to general considerations on the respective powers of *virtù* and *fortune*. The reader who focuses on the first term to the exclusion of the second will miss the novelty of the observation. The language in which it is framed is that of Tradition. Indeed, enrooted in the patrimony of Florentine thought is the idea that man has no control over destiny, and yet that it is by bringing to bear all the resources of willpower and knowledge that he earns his dignity as subject, and ceases being the plaything of powers transcending him. Alberti had already introduced this theme in similar terms in the preamble to his treatise *Della Famiglia;* it was at the center of the teaching of the masters of the *Quattrocento,* and taken up again as a leitmotif of philosophic-political discourse.[12] Moreover, the association of the Christian God with the pagan Fortuna does nothing more, up till this point, than signal a common disposition to translate the Roman idiom and the modern one into one another. But, as we will recall, the opinion introduced at the end of the chapter is of a different scope, at a distance from the rhetorical statement maintaining the comparison of the river with Fortune. "But, on the whole, I judge impetuosity to be better than caution; for Fortune is a woman, and if you wish to master her, you must strike and beat her, and you will see that she allows herself to be more easily vanquished by the rash and the violent than by those who proceed more slowly and coldly. And therefore, as a woman, she ever favors youth more than age, for youth is less cautious and more energetic, and commands Fortune with greater audacity." Through the amatory metaphor a new idea of the relation of the Subject to the world finds expression. It is impossible, in this framework, to maintain the Christian version of the myth of Fortune; but neither is it possible to maintain the Stoic version of it: man does not define his domain at the limits of the supernatural by the sole effort of liberation from the passions and ignorance; his power is bound to desire; what escapes him is at once outside him and within; it describes at once his space of death and of life; all that can respond to the failing of his being is the excess of the act. And in that moment, the figure of choice in which the trait of desire is inscribed is distinguished from the figure of the sage—whom we like to think has learned to master himself at the same time as mastering others—and corresponds rather to that of the *giovani*, whose daring is not compromised by calculation, but pushes the limits of the possible beyond the real.

To say that the Machiavellian word is in league with the new generation does not mean, of course, that that generation does not undergo the ascendency of the dominant ideas, or that it is detached from social groups and parties; we should rather assume that its most ambitious members are themselves prisoners of representations that they energetically oppose and that they are not all in the same place. Nor are we surprised that the complicity with them is not based on an agreement of opinion, that on the contrary it excludes, in most cases, a clear-cut political relation, and that it necessarily involves the destruction of their common belief in the formula "a good regime." The discourse is addressed to the young, without espousing the hopes that motivate them *here* and *now*— aware that their desire for knowledge, if it receives an impetus from the desire to act, is constantly threatened by the latter to be changed into its opposite. It can only make them its respondent on the condition that it attract them to the place in which it is itself engendered—that it summon them to interpret themselves through it. Thus, in a sense, its strongest tie is woven in a work of disenchantment. But we would be mistaken in imagining that the discourse is the master of the relation, in the sense that whatever knowledge it contains would require no more than to be communicated to an other, apparently intended to educate by its privileged receptivity to new things. It is also true that the discourse is to be understood through the *giovani*—that with their position an *écart* between the possible and the real is given in space–time, a gap between desire and authority, in which the word gains assurance through its own liberation from the dominant representations.

If *The Prince* already affords us a glimpse of the figure of the kindred soul, his lineaments become clearer and his identity more specific in *The Discourses*. Nowhere more clearly than in the Proem to the second book, let us remember, is the call to the *giovani* formulated. At the moment when the knowledge of history and especially of Roman institutions is given its basis on a critique of the idealization of the past, the author gives us an outline of a general trial of conservatism, the underlying motif of which is the contrasting of old age and youth. Decrying the prejudice that values the past more than the present, and thus placing his praise of Rome beneath the sign of demystification, he repeatedly shows how the illusion comes from intellectual conservatism, based on submission to the ancient authors, and from political conservatism, based on submission to the powerful of the era, but finds its ultimate cause in the powerlessness of men who are aging to deal with the weakening of their desires. It is in naming that ultimate cause that he reveals the limit of judgment (*giudizio*), in the sense of the exercise of the understanding, connects the relation to knowledge with the relation to desire, and proclaims his alliance with youth. "But the matter being so manifest that everyone sees it," he concludes, "I shall be bold in saying openly what I think of those times and of our own, so that the minds of young men who read my writings may desire to imitate the one and turn away from the others, whenever fortune gives them the opportunity for so doing." (*acciocché gli animi de'giovani che questi mia scritti leggeranno, possino fuggire questi, e prepararsi ad imitar quegli, qualunque volta la fortuna ne dessi loro occasione*). Yet if, in this fragment, the image of the interlocutor is visible, it is only half revealed; the intention becomes clearer in other ones, in which it is shown only to the reader favorably disposed toward grasping it, and recognizing it as his or her own. Then the complicity is reinforced by allusion, and culminates in the vast metaphor in which we see combined, around the central theme of the knowledge of places and the experience of hunting, the face of Epaminondas and Xenophon, that of the young Thebans called to learn about revolution through mock combat and that of the young Athenians called to learn philosophy through trials of ruse. To the desire for knowledge, Machiavelli opens the path of mediations that connects it to its ends; for the desire to act, he sets the stakes, which are conspiracies and plots against those who hold the power and bring about the ruin of the people and the state. Thus, the pact concluded with the *giovani* proves to be tied to the conquest of a *vivere civile* or a *vivere libero* that only the institutions of a republic make possible. It is, we discover, this kindred soul inspired by the passion for freedom that he addresses, and through him that he is to be understood, in the entire span of the discourses, even up to and including the affirmation of the role of the founder/prince or of the superiority of a monarchy guided by *virtù* over a corrupt republic. That this kindred spirit already inhabited *The Prince*—to convince ourselves of this we have but to observe that all that is said in this first work has its place, or can find its place, in the second. It is true that the possibility—glimpsed—of a change under the impetus of Lorenzo, has the effect of placing in full light the figure of a young pretender to tyranny. But to him the discourse already lets it be known that the monarchic experiment only acquires a meaning when it appropriates the experience of the republican regime; thus, it uses a language that the young republican Florentine is called upon to make his own. The fact that once the image of Lorenzo has been put aside, Machiavelli dedicates *The Discourses* to simple citizens, Cosimo Rucellai and Zanobi Buondelmonti, does not mean that he has changed his interlocutor. It is already for men like them that he was speaking previously, and, furthermore, he does not cease maintaining the position that particular circumstances require extraordinary authority. Flattering himself for breaking with the current usage to which writers yield by ambition and cupidity, he declares in his dedication that he does not wish to address his second work to a prince, but to give it to those who by their qualities would be worthy to be princes. The turn of phrase is eloquent, because it does not cancel the prince's prerogative in principle, while at the same time excluding him in fact. It still allows us to imagine that, given the right accidents of history, the impossible becoming possible, a man who combined the knowledge of politics with authority would be able to accomplish the tasks of the present day in fulfilling the monarchic function—a hypothesis we know will be amply developed in the body of the work. There is no reason to think that the idea of the prince has, in *The Discourses*, a destiny any different than in *The Prince*. In both, the reader is invited, by reason of his attachment to freedom itself, to conceive of the merits of an action that would initiate a government of one; in both cases he must break with the traditional representation of a difference of essence between the republic and the monarchy. But that break takes place from the place in which democratic values are recognized, from a place where the image of a free Rome stimulates the imagination—that is to say, from the locus of republican thought.

The kindred spirit, perceptible in the reading—we are inclined to specify his identity in the light of historical information. Still, we should bear in mind that such information alone would be unable to found an interpretation. It teaches us that *The Discourses* were communicated by their author to a circle frequented by numerous young Florentines; but after all there were not only young people present in the Oricellari Gardens; and the listeners were not exclusively of the republican persuasion. What is more, it must not be overlooked that among Machiavelli's close friends there were some who were as far as possible from being revolutionaries, such as Vettori, who was no doubt the first reader of *The Prince*, and Francesco Guicciardini, to whom *The Discourses* gave the occasion for an important critical commentary. Also, we realize that we are seeking historical evidence to confirm a conviction we acquired in reading Machiavelli. And in fact that evidence is overwhelming. It is important to discover that in the company of a very young host, Cosimo Rucellai, confined to his home by an illness (he would die before the end of the circle's discussions), the future organizers of the conspiracy of 1522 against Cardinal Giulio Medici were assembled: the poet Luigi Alamanni, Zanobi Buondelmonti, a collaborator of Machiavelli in the days when he had official functions, two of the Diaceto brothers, and Battista Della Palla, who were all condemned to exile or execution as a result of their conspiracy. Although we may assume that Machiavelli, despite his being the object of a denunciation, was not involved in the enterprise, we may reasonably suppose that he had their ear when composing his portrait of Brutus, when treating conspiracy as a privileged sort of political action, or when, stressing the role of young citizens in the Roman Republic, he drew attention to the daring acts of Fabius at the beginning of his career, or gave as an example the secret pact concluded between Epaminondas and the youths of Thebes . . . We may imagine a factual complicity with some of his listeners, receptive to his allusions, his irony, the wink of the lecturer who leaves nothing material for spies to use against him, as opposed to others, who may have been attracted by the subtlety of his analyses, but were disinclined to appreciate direct praise of subversion and reassured by the clamorous statements in favor of the order of the day. We also divine a half-hidden teaching that, combining a philosophical requirement with a practical intention, wished to persuade the reader of the vanity of a political battle that lacked a reflection on history.

Furthermore, the hypothesis is enriched by the discovery that some fifteen years earlier, the Oricellari Gardens were known to be a stronghold of antidemocratic opposition.[13] Between 1502 and 1506, the master of the house, Bernardo Rucellai, Cosimo's uncle, had assembled, in the same place where Machiavelli spoke, the most resolute adversaries of Soderini's reforms—both, as it seems, to set up the nucleus for a restoration of the Medici and to found in theory the theses of political conservatism. Rucellai, the brother-in-law of Lorenzo the Magnificent, one of the latter's intimate confidants and charged with important diplomatic missions under his reign, appears as the oligarchy's main spokesman toward him. He plays a dominant role in the eviction of Piero, who was accused of wanting to govern alone, disdaining the advice of the upper bourgeoisie; then, as an enemy of Savonarola, whose democratic convictions worry him, we see him maneuvering skillfully, after his fall, to reconcile the great families compromised under his rule and threatened with the repression that was beginning to strike the *piagnoni* clan, with the victors, recent opponents denounced as *arrabiati*, classical conservatives, above all bent on reestablishing a "*governo stretto*"—both sides being factions closely allied by their positions of fortune and ancestry. At the creation of the lifetime office of Gonfalonier that puts Soderini at the head of the state, Bernardo becomes the leader of the hard-line faction of the oligarchy; hostile to any compromise with the partisans of a broad government, he distances himself from the majority of conservatives who dream of changing the nature of the regime by participating in it and concentrates on regrouping the malcontents. In the circle he then organizes, his role is that of an intellectual leader of the opposition. In his view, an aristocratic government associated with the monarchic principle defines the best regime. Based on the experience of the first years of Lorenzo's reign, his thesis derives its authority from the Ancients, is nourished by the confrontation of the past with the present, contrasts the misery of the latter with the glory of the former, and holds up Rome as a model. Moreover, if it is true that Bernardo is the author of a commentary on Livy, we may surmise that the memory of his teaching and of his convictions would have made him a particularly effective bogeyman in the gardens that Machiavelli frequented. Reading his *Discourses* to young Florentines enthusiastic for change, Machiavelli not only took the place of a political adversary, but he developed vis-à-vis the missing master a counter-teaching, wrested Rome and Livy from the imposture of the conservative interpretation, condemned at once the servility and ignorance of the older generation, and let it be understood that history did not accredit the titles of the Medici, but testified to the superiority of democracy, that the Law was not in the keeping of the Grandees, but in that of the people, and that the restoration of the state sometimes requires insurrection against the established order.

The fact that Rucellai supplies a reference point in situating the opposition between the old and the new generation, however, does not authorize our concentrating all the traits of the dominant ideology in him. We may assume that he served as a target, not only because he best embodied the conservative position, but because he gave it added weight by endowing it with a philosophy of history; we may further assume that Machiavelli's young listeners were freer to condemn Rucellai's political actions than to free themselves from that philosophy, or at least to criticize the historical interpretation that supported it. But on that hypothesis it remains to be understood why the democratic convictions of some were able to harmonize with the representation of antiquity, and particularly that of Rome, which was held by the supporters of the aristocracy. Whatever the truth may be, the analyses of *The Discourses* do not permit us to think that conservatism was reduced in Machiavelli's mind to the limits of a social group—however powerful it might be—committed to preserving its political domination. If it is true that the critical enterprise of *The Discourses* becomes clearer when we scrutinize the role of intellectual mentor played by Rucellai, we must nonetheless bear in mind that that critical undertaking encompasses all aspects of the political tradition, and that democratic thought is preserved within it only at the cost of the abandonment or profound alteration of the ideas that constituted its legacy at the time. The shadow of Rucellai haunts the Oricellari Gardens, but alongside it that of his great adversaries, Soderini and Savonarola, the political figures who tried to wrest from the oligarchy a portion of its power. To the young Florentines who were not reconciled with the present tyranny Machiavelli taught that the fight against the Medici must include a break from the theory and practice of the parties that prepared the way for them, and that mounting an opposition requires a new idea of politics. He denied them the solace of a nostalgia that fed their aversion to the present. This step was all the more necessary in view of the pending crisis of 1527, which would clearly demonstrate that the divisions persisting under earlier regimes were still smoldering. Although the great fear aroused by the defeat at Prato threw the entire bourgeoisie into the arms of the Medici, the former oppositions persisted in the party of the people—the former *piagnoni* remained fervent adepts of a moral reform, and a segment of the oligarchy remained reticent before any government that reduced its prerogatives. The call to know the causes of the fall of the republican regime was at the same time a call to discover, *here* and *now*, the signs of the repetition of the political pattern, and the sources of its sustenance, the cohesion of a practice and a language beyond divided opinions and actual antagonisms.

Now at the same time that it teaches us to navigate the mental topography of the *giovani*, the discourse of the oeuvre reveals that of the guardians of an ideology. Of the latter the signs are already identifiable in *The Prince*, once we become sensitized to the movement of the word [*parole*] that at once installs us in the positions of a discourse that is *other*, makes them untenable and shows, by the passage from one to the other, the necessity of their articulation.

The rational strategy, first held up as a model—and by this I mean a politics based on the calculation of powers—reveals, as we will recall, its limitations once a prediction of the results of the action of a subject motivated by his or her desire replaces the idea of a precise view of the given power relations in the present field of action, and once, at the same time, the idea of a stability of acquired positions is replaced by that of their instability. A discourse that is *other* may be caught sight of in the image of a mastery of uncertainties within the bounds of a short span of time, such as that of the *savi de' nostri tempi*, satisfied with "taking advantage of the times." With the definition of a political reality rigorously measured in terms of operations of winning and holding onto power, there is a collapse of the foundations of the state such as it appears in the workings of Providence, natural harmony or the concord of human wills; again, a discourse that is *other* may be seen, specifically designated as that of Savonarola, literally reversed through paraphrase, which blends together the civic and the religious spirit. Finally, the reinsertion of power into society, upon the examination of class relations, and the central function assigned to authority—at the very moment when a task for the prince, inscribed in the social constitution, is revived—requires of us to think politics beneath the twofold sign of the exorbitance of desire and the power of the *imaginaire;* a discourse *other* again announces itself, attached to the conception of the good government and the natural virtues of the prince, as that of the humanists nourished on Cicero and Aristotle.

Now the analysis does more than designate *other* discourses by antithesis: a technical/rationalist discourse that makes judgments about the enjoyment of present advantages, a Christian discourse that places moral virtue and the renunciation of worldly possessions at the origin of Florentine patriotism, a humanist discourse, which entrusts to the prudence and moderation of the governor the care of maintaining the hierarchy of the functions inscribed in the social body. These discourses prove, despite their heterogeneity, to communicate with one another, to organize themselves as moments of one sole political discourse, occupied as they are with creating the image of a fixed order of things, with hiding class divisions, the division of the ruling power and civil society, and temporal difference. Already, in considering their ultimate referent, an affinity is unveiled—which in one is called necessity, in another Fortune, in a third God. Now, from one term to the other, although they do not have the same meaning, a shift without collision is possible: Necessity, Fortune,

and God have the power to change into one another in order to circumscribe the unknowable, to give it once and for all its due, to banish it from
the place in which it would be dangerous to read it, that is in the lack
of an institution, the enormity of the desire to dominate, the *imaginaire*
of the prince. But more determined is the agreement in the elaboration
of a political mythology, the invariable themes of which are the agreement between the citizens, the intrinsic good of past institutions, the
dangers of change, the status quo in the relations between states, and
the virtues of the happy medium, of the lesser risk, and procrastination.
In discovering, upon reading *The Prince,* the affinities between different,
apparently antagonistic positions, we are induced to think that, if they
are occupied by certain men, they could not be absolutely distinguished
in each, but must, in order for the collective discourse to retain its effect
of dissimulation, be combined to various degrees. Interpretation—as we
have pointed out—not only reveals a discourse *other;* in forcing it to say
itself, when it was content with a half silence, it makes audible its inability
to say itself entirely—the necessity in which the interlocutor of such a
discourse finds himself of always borrowing a part of his arguments from
others. Thus it is that the rationalist/technical discourse seems to us to
be condemned to self-destruction, if it draws its ultimate consequences,
that is, if it continues until it comes out on the abyss that yawns before
the critique of the foundation of the state. It makes politics into calculation, and is quick to eliminate all considerations that might trouble the
logic of self-interest, but on the condition of providing for itself the ir-
removable point of reference, of converting the present traits of the social institution and the historical field into natural givens, of excluding a
relativity of perspectives that would dispossess the dominant class of the
legitimacy of its operations. A condition it keeps quiet about, one that it
even hides for the most part from itself, and in the end fulfills only hypocritically, by reintroducing the idea of a providential order or an essence
of the social body, in virtue of which the exercise of reason—or even
cynicism—knows its rightful limitations. Again, thus it is that the Christian discourse proves to be unsustainable, as a political discourse, and
that it cannot deduce from faith in the next world the norms for action
in this world, and that it must make its peace with rationalist/technical
discourse, and, no less hypocritically than the latter, reintroduce the necessities of political calculation and accept reasons of state, going so far
as to go along with the iron rule of tyranny. Similarly, we see the humanist
discourse forced—in order to uphold the idea of a society in agreement
with itself, in conformity with its nature, and the idea of a good government guided by prudence—to adopt the prosaic maneuvers of the bour-

geois, given over to factional compromise and the arrangements of a diplomacy of evasion and to giving credence to the trivial realism of the technicians of politics.

The Prince reveals a society closed in upon itself, or—since the people are always in the image of the one directing it—a dominant class totally caught up in preserving the advantages it has acquired and in sidestepping all risk of change. The discourse of that class is devoted to ensuring the perpetuity of its institutions and the power of Florence in the world. Before the new generation, a threefold illusion is exposed and condemned—that the leaders of Florence are masters of political science, that the city enjoys the benefit of the special protection of Providence, and that it is the keeper of the grand legacy of the classical age. At the same time, its inner workings are revealed: the denial of the effects of the oligarchic system, which eats away at the political rights of the people and forbids their bearing arms; the denial of the schism between bourgeois and citizen, which undermines the state; and the denial of the latter's ineluctable subservience in the not too distant future by the great powers, with their massive armies. Now, what we hear in *The Prince* becomes even clearer in *The Discourses*, so that the Florentine language proves to be entirely bound to the representation of Rome. With this last work, we are prompted to place the humanist discourse at the center of the ideology, though we are always obliged to locate its articulation with the Christian or the rationalist / technical one, and to scrutinize its function in the economy of Florentine thought.

Thus, it is the work of interpretation that the oeuvre requires the reader to accomplish—the latter being obliged, in order to read it, to decipher what the oeuvre itself designates as a present, hidden text, a text to be established and then revealed. It is the experience of the differentiation of two discourses, which brings us into the space–time of *Cinquecento* Florence, then makes us shift from the inside of the oeuvre to the outside: a shift that would be inconceivable if that work were not open to the outside, and if that outside did not always remain bound to its form of access . . .

What is the relationship between Machiavelli's discourse and that of his contemporaries or immediate predecessors? The question cannot be asked in forgetfulness of its origin, which presupposes our involvement in the oeuvre. Otherwise it immediately becomes lost in the search for similarities and differences, influences undergone or exerted, in which the freedom of knowledge comes at the price of the disappearance of what is at stake for us. On the other hand, that personal stake does not cease soliciting us, when we seek in documents furnished by the historian signs of the text that the oeuvre gives us to read, when the exploration

of the space–time proves to be of service in deciphering them. This is
why we take particular interest in the political debates of the Florentines over the affairs of the city. We possess precious information about
these debates in the form of Machiavelli's correspondence, his private
letters, his reports to the seigneury, the announcements or instructions
to which they respond, and the commentaries to which they give rise. But
even more telling are the protocols of the meetings in which, between
1494 and 1512, the main questions of foreign and domestic policy are
discussed. Through them, beyond the obvious differences of opinion,
a common set of representations, or the system of reference for what
we have been calling a collective discourse, is adumbrated.[14] Indeed, although these meetings, called at the request of the Gonfalonier or of
a governmental authority, and termed *Consulte* or *Pratiche*, were often
limited to a small number of individuals distinguished by their rank and
fortune, we understand that they could also assemble several hundred
citizens. This was the case in the days of Soderini, when the *Pratiche strette*
(narrow *Pratiche*) which played along with the oligarchy and offered it
the advantage of a pressure group, were systematically sidelined by the
Pratiche larghe, which reinforced the democratic base of the regime. At
these meetings, the Florentines gave their opinion on the legislative bills
or measures that committed the state's foreign policy. It is true that they
were deprived of voting rights and decision-making power. But since the
councils of the Republic—the Great Council (*Consiglio Maggiore*) and the
Council of Eighty, in which the political authority was concentrated—
voted and made decisions without discussion, it is in familiarizing ourselves with the nature of their debates that we can best get an idea of the
collective ways of envisioning things. Now the protocols, according to
Felix Gilbert's analyses, unquestionably reconstitute traces of that *other*
discourse intimated in *The Prince* and *The Discourses*. The *Consulte* were
called upon to give their opinion on the orientation of foreign policy: the
crucial question concerned the French alliance, a guarantee of powerful
protection, but one that made an enemy of the emperor and dangerously
isolated Florence from the rest of Italy; on that occasion the ability of the
Florentine bourgeois in calculating the profits and liabilities of an initiative was demonstrated. The risk of an intervention on the part of the king
of France in the eventuality of a reversal of alliances was evaluated, the
intentions of the Italian states sounded; later, when the need to renew
diplomatic relations with Spain was recognized, the advantages and disadvantages of doing so were reevaluated with respect to the French alliance. When Pisa was about to yield before the Florentine armies, the final
attack was postponed, as the calculation of the risks involved outweighed
the fulfillment of the undertaking. It was recommended that France and

Spain be consulted, in the conviction that the status quo could not be modified at any one point without being sure of the consequences, or that—according the expression used in the report—"things being as they are in Italy, Pisa could not be acquired without the assent of two kings."[15] Moreover, the sizing up of situations involved consideration of the interests of the merchants, threatened as they were in their possessions or their persons—in France, if the king became hostile, or in Rome, Naples, or England, if Pope Alexander VI or Julius II were to launch an angry interdict. Past masters in the art of the hypothesis, the Florentines seem to have been equally adept at temporizing. As our analyst of the protocols notes, "The need for postponement, delay, for gaining time forms a constant theme in the discussions of foreign affairs . . . In discussing the relations with other powers, the advice most frequently given is to '*godere il beneficio del tempo*.'"[16] This expression, criticized by Machiavelli, attests to an unshakable faith in the advantages of patience and prudence, and is rooted in the circumstance that "the Florentines did not believe that they could direct or control the developments in foreign policy." Their sole objective was not to be overtaken by events and, in the case of a conflict, to be on the winning side. This generalized way of thinking brought on fear of making decisions, and is best expressed by the motto "*Deliberarsi al certo nelle cose incerte fa sempre pericolo*" (to seek certainty in things uncertain is always dangerous).[17] It seemed to them that the information received was never full enough to warrant a decision. Thus, in response to their ambassadors' urgent appeals when they were put on the spot by foreign princes, the Florentines always gave dilatory counsel; further, in the midst of the war against Pisa, the warning given to the military leaders is reminiscent of the style of the instructions given to diplomats: "*Non si mettino al pericolo o sanza grande necessità o manifesta victoria*" (Let one not put oneself in danger without necessity or certain victory).[18] The principles of political or military action find their best formulation in maxims of the type: "*le cose che possono giovare e non nuocere sono da fare*" (the things that can be useful and not harmful should be done); or yet again, "*i savii hanno il meno male in luogo di bene*" (for the wise, the lesser evil takes the place of the good).[19] As far as warfare was concerned, the Florentines were only willing to undertake it on the condition that it was parceled out into small risks against which they were leveraged by paying tribute to the great powers. Their conception of diplomacy was reduced to maneuvers intended to secure their neutrality or preserve, according to the accredited expression, *la via del mezzo.*

Doubtless it will suffice to observe the actual conduct of the Florentine government in Italian and European affairs to isolate its constants: an ongoing attempt to maintain the balance of power, lack of initiative, stalling tactics in facing the initiative of others, and the use of money as a privileged means in diplomacy and war. Along these same lines, the *Consulte* documents are useful in revealing that such practices were in harmony with the mentality of a large number of citizens, including all the categories of the bourgeoisie. But their greatest merit is to convey the most recent topics of political discourse, and their efficacy lies in their giving us a good command of the way the social order was seen in the Florentine Republic. According to Felix Gilbert's commentaries, these topics were both distinct and varied. After having furnished examples of discussion raised by foreign politics, our historian points out that the judgments expressed are claimed to have been reached by the power of reason. Rejecting desire, which blinds the Subject to the nature and means of his enterprise, the "rational" argument appears to find its explicit basis in the idea of the stability of human nature, or, in more modern terms, in that of a psycho-political determinism that guarantees the repetition of the same sequences of cause and effect; it prides itself in the exercise of explanation and prediction, and in the statement of maxims that have the function of subsuming particular cases under eternal truths; they are attested in a constant recourse to experience, in the analysis of facts taken from the history of Venice, a modern state known for the capable execution of its enterprises, or from that of Florence itself—specifically during the days of its resistance to the conquests of Gian Galeazzo Visconti, on which occasion it was able to save its independence, and, as one was fond of repeating, that of all Italy. Yet the importance given to examples from antiquity, coupled with the invocation of philosophers or historians who gave them authority, testify to a different pole of the collective discourse. It is from the history of Rome, as Gilbert alerts us, that the Florentines think they can read off the meaning of present conduct and events. If the discussion turned to the reestablishment of the *Dieci di Balia*, an organization that would reinforce government authority, it was recalled that the Romans placed themselves under the command of a dictator during the critical periods. Was it a question of what the fate of the former partisans of Savonarola should be? The actions of Caesar were evoked, who refused to seize the opportunity of finding out, by reading the correspondence of the defeated Pompey, the names of those Romans who had been compromised. The quoting of classical authors to support declarations that did not exceed the exercise of good sense became increasingly frequent. Aristotle's *Politics*, in particular, would be used to illustrate arguments stressing the importance of economic and military phenomena in the life of Florence. So strong was the argument from authority that it appears to have overcome confidence in logic and factual proof, though the two were not incompatible and classical culture sustained the prestige of reason. But it must also be noted that the reference to antiquity, and particularly Roman antiquity, coexisted with another, which was equally active. According to our analyst, there were two sources of inspiration for the political discourse: the classical literature and the Christian, the latter's authority being of equal weight. Indeed, if it is undoubtedly the case that religious feelings were exalted under Savonarola's influence, their roots in the distant past may be discerned, and they remain active after the failure of the monk who for a time managed to exploit them so effectively. At the time of Machiavelli, a portion of the bourgeoisie was still persuaded that the Lord bestowed favor upon the City of Saint Giovanni; before the danger it faced, they would evoke the past trials with which it had been afflicted in order that it might redeem itself of its sins. In the glorious resistance once mounted against Milanese despotism—an episode often pointed to as proof of the political prudence of erstwhile leaders and also as a sign of the resemblance between Rome and Florence—they discerned a miracle performed by Providence. Now of course the discourse of Christian inspiration has its own norms; it is presumed to inspire certain judgments favoring the respect of treaties that have been made, or opposing decisions that would sully the honor of Florence; one can well imagine those who speak that language being in conflict with the cynical wing of the *Pratiche* who, for example, after a complaint had been lodged by the Republic of Lucca, a victim of extortion committed on its territory by Florentines, coldly recommended responding with lies and kind words, while at the same time encouraging aggression and larceny; and who, having been consulted on the appropriate fate for a military leader suspected of treason, esteemed proof to be a matter of indifference, and their concern over his great renown sufficient grounds for condemning him. Still, it appears that religious convictions upheld argumentation based on reason. As the reading of Machiavelli leads one to suppose, the same men who vindicated the art of political calculation justified their tergiversation, their lack of foresight, or their failures by invoking a supernatural power, which they were also wont to call God or Fortuna, or both at the same time. And one always sees, in the name of a Christian or classical instruction, or of the power of reason, the establishment of a common ethics of action and of a common representation of the social order. Just as in foreign policy the Florentines conducted one sole discourse committed, despite the diversity of its application, to maintaining their faith in the stability of the position they had acquired within the contemporary system of forces and in the virtue of the least risk, so in domestic affairs they were at one in vaunting the excellence of the basis of their political regime, in holding up as the supreme value unity among its citizens, and praise for the principle of moderation. What was ancient was adjudged good. The projects of reform themselves were not appraised on the basis of their efficacy, but according to their faithfulness to the original model of the constitution. Discredit weighed on any initiative in the direction of change; the same formula was repeated year after year to justify conservatism: "*Ogni mutatione togli reputatione alla citta*" (all change takes away from the reputation of the city).[20] Such was the fear aroused by the *ordini nuovi* that the creation of the *Consiglio maggiore* at the time of Savonarola was itself presented as the instrument of a restoration of the "*antico vivere popolare.*" As Gilbert also notes, the position of the democrats did not differ in this respect from that of the aristocrats; both praised the virtue of the ancient order, while at the very same time under its cover they devoted their efforts to bringing about changes that were in agreement with their interests. Serving the language of conservatism, the three major points of reference we distinguished were efficiently mobilized: if the principles were to be preserved or restored, it was either because experience taught the dangers of innovation, or because they had been laid down by God, or because they were handed down by ancient Rome. Now, this language had as its main function to conceal conflict. However sharp the latter may have become in fact, it seems to have been essential not to call it by its name, not to let the face of conflicting factions appear, even though the nature of the antagonistic groups and of the vested interests separating them was unmistakable. Thus all declared themselves to be defenders of the common cause, promoting freedom, equality, and justice, and opponents of tyranny. The fiction of unification was maintained by means of an agreement on the ultimate goals of the state as defined at its inception, so that the expression of discord was limited to the interpretation of legal rights. All agreed that the law must guarantee citizens their rightful participation in public duties and honors: debate was restricted to the definition of that participation, the criteria for citizenship, and the extent of political responsibilities. The greatest danger was unanimously agreed to be discord, and since that was incessant, great efforts were made to deny its causes, and to impute it to private ambition, the egotism of individuals who were by nature unmindful of the common weal. Their coalitions and the evil effects the "*sette*" [political parties] on the City were condemned, leaving it to be supposed that their dissolution would restore to the state the original truth of an association of each with all. Endlessly it is repeated that the "*concordia della citta*" or the "*unione*" between the citizens must be reestablished, in the pompous conviction that all the present difficulties would find their resolution in the reconciliation between Florentines. In order to accomplish this, commissions of arbitration were sometimes set up with the charge of examining the cause of quarrels and proposing remedies; priests were sometimes called upon to preach love of the City; and the example of the Romans was always there to project the image of the citizen's devotion to the *res publica*.

As we examine the debates of the *Pratiche*, the critical force of Machiavelli's oeuvre is constantly attested. The work proves to bear a *counter-discourse* that overturns the positions of the other, as it undertakes to establish that every society is torn by class conflict, that union is an illusion, the power of the City subordinate to the creation of *ordini nuovi*, the need to restore the *principio* bound to that of a continuous foundation, the opposition "republic versus tyranny" relative to the relation between power and the people, the efficacy of the law dependent upon the initiative of the Subject, and security both within and without acquired at very great risk. But then again, we must recognize that the discourse overturned is at the same time produced. In ideology, the ultimate theses are not stated; all the propositions are, on the contrary, arranged in such a way as to prohibit the thought of the fracture of the social space and the fracture of time—which are camouflaged by the political order. It is in critical discourse that the object and function of the prohibition, at the same time as the discordance of the collective discourse—its internal fractures—are exposed, revealing traces of the avoided. Along these same lines, *The Prince* and *The Discourses* do not give their readers new theses, contradicting those that are commonly shared; rather, they merely open thought to a power of interpretation to which it previously had no access, being barred by the exclusion of the ultimate theses from the field of discourse. But although it is true that this liberating action is incommensurate with the socio-historical conditions in which it is exercised and with the effects it engenders, since interpretation exceeds the limits of a specific ideology, it is rigorously commanded by the requirement of this deciphering, in which a specific mode of elaboration of the political experience is attested.

At the heart of that elaboration we must situate the representation of classical antiquity, or more precisely that of Rome, the dispenser of the most eloquent signs of the space–time of the collective discourse and of the discourse of the oeuvre. It is not just that Rome inspires in a most singular way the language of the Florentines of the beginning of the *Cinquecento,* making it incomparable with that of their contemporaries, regardless of the fervor of the latter's elites in reading Greek and Latin; in the economy of ideology, Rome has a special function in that it both furnishes a source of authority for political expression and a *stage* on which history has already been enacted—a scenario capable of accommodating various texts—those of Aristotle, of Cicero, of classical as well as Christian authors—and in which heroes can exchange places, Cato with Caesar, for example. With this representation, the properly mythical dimension of ideology becomes manifest. Indeed, it allows us to discover in Florentine society, in conjunction with the experience of a remembered, reconstructed time—a time articulated according to the requirements of knowledge—the vision of a past "outside of time" immediately related to the actual present in such a way as to make the latter seem a second-rate copy—a past containing in an eminent mode the meaning of current behavior and events, and disposing of a symbolic efficacy all the more rich for being a condensation of the diverse images of a republican and an imperial Rome, a Rome that is classical as well as Christian—a Rome capable, in short, of supplying the needs of both aristocratic and democratic discourse, and of discourse both rationalist and religious. Of course, as I have indicated, the Rome myth accounts for only a part of the meaning of ideology; it contributes only to its formation, and constitutes only a privileged element of it. But it must now be admitted that its action varied with the socio-political conditions. Thus, the Medici regime, during the period when Machiavelli composed his works, was no more favorable to its public expression than were the days of Cosimo and Lorenzo. We should not be surprised at this: the disappearance of the oligarchy before the power of a family, and the expulsion of the members of the petty bourgeoisie from politics makes the ardor of a Bernardo Rucellai for things Roman of little consequence, and that of the reformers positively dangerous. By and large, when the apparatus of domination is reinforced, and the participation of the people in public affairs disappears, the work of ideology is reduced to narrower confines. But what is true of official political discourse is not true of the discourse of those in opposition: the latter are tempted to borrow the motifs of their hopes or of their projects from the depleted or forbidden font of the language that was freely spoken in bygone days. They revivify words no longer in current use, words that shine forth for being rejected by the faction in power, without asking themselves whether these same words were not in complicity with other words, other images that had beguiled the preceding generation and delivered them over to the tutelage of that faction. Hypnotized by the virtues of the past, they turn once again toward the stage on which the scenes that had so fascinated their fathers were played out. They will make the Roman heroes whom their fathers made speak speak anew, and exult in the image of a double repetition.

This movement—we can only imagine it by listening to Machiavelli's discourse. He is predominantly the one who allows us to recognize the function of the mythical Rome, through the critique of it he conducts in *The Discourses*. But we cannot be content with just finding the signs of it in the interregnum of the Medici. Those signs refer us to an older elaboration, revealing a different space–time, toward which the Florentines turned in debating the affairs of the Republic in the days of Savonarola and Soderini. The collective references of Machiavelli's contemporaries to the classical authors and the deeds of the Romans cannot in themselves explain the extent and insistence of Machiavelli's critique. To account for that phenomenon, we must uncover the source of its inspiration, and get back to the repetition, following it back to its initial moment. Now, that moment was undoubtedly during the period that begins in the last decades of the *Trecento* and ends with the advent of Cosimo. At that time a profound change in the scientific, literary, and political discourse took place. Humanism acquired a new place in the City, on the basis of which an ideology was engendered. That ideology, in turn, quietly and discreetly transmitted in the shadows of the Medici reign, was not to be extinguished, and would determine the language of the Florentines after the restoration of the republic.

The discussions of the *Pratiche* frequently refer to this period, invoking the great event that brought glory to the city. The victorious resistance to Gian Galeazzo Visconti, as we observed, following Gilbert, furnishes an outstanding example of the political intelligence of the "sages" who once governed the republic, of the Roman virtue possessed by the Florentines of those days, and of the divine protection of which they were the beneficiaries. But we were unable to appreciate the function of that reference, as long as we remained ignorant of the ideological upheaval that provoked or precipitated the war against Milan. What the historians reveal to us—preeminently Hans Baron, to whom we owe the fruitful study of what he calls "civic humanism"[21]—is, on this occasion, the formation of a new representation of the role of Florence in Italy, of its past history and its relation to Rome. The republic speaks a language that distinguishes it during this time from the other states. It presents its struggle against Visconti as that of freedom against despotism, formulates before all Italy a historical alternative, and claims a universal mission, convinced as it is that its own defense coincides with that of all the peoples attached to their independence and ready to rise up against oppression. It claims to read in its own past the episodes of one sole venture, as if the war against the tyrant of Verona, Martino della Scala, during the first third of the *Trecento*, the uprising against the duke of Athens, the conflict with Gregory V, and the resistance to the imperialism of Milan are part of the same undertaking in the name of freedom. It declares itself to be the heir to Rome, claims to owe it its foundation at a time when corruption had not yet spoiled Rome beneath the yoke of the Caesars. This language dominates particularly the writings and discourse of Collucio

Salutati, who was doubtless the first to speak it at the end of the *Trecento*, and, through his functions as chancellor of the republic, the most apt at spreading its use. With him, as Eugenio Garin remarks, humanistic teachings extend beyond the university walls and find their seat of choice in the Palazzo dei Signori.[22] The idea of a renascence of knowledge, based on the methodical study of ancient authors, the return to the letter of the texts, the repudiation of the authority argument, and the critical research of thought models became indissociable from the image of a free system of government attached to universal values and holding in trust the legacy of the accomplishments of the Roman Republic. The same necessity seems to govern the historical and the philological efforts directed toward reestablishing the authenticity of facts and texts that earlier generations had betrayed or misunderstood, and toward discovering the true principles of politics, as they were inscribed in classical times in the "good government," the exempla of civic virtue and reason rightly conducted. Thus is confirmed the twofold conviction that the truth of politics is to be found in the exercise of humanist thought, provided it is practiced with rigor, and that the task of knowledge conquers its own authenticity of being in the service of politics: the critique of tyrannical regimes is deduced from a knowledge of history and classical philosophy, but at the same time the image of the kind of science that is cultivated in isolation, that is, with indifference to public affairs, is discredited. Between the conduct of the tradesman whose private enrichment enhances the prosperity of the City, that of the citizen who takes part in assemblies or holds a position in the magistracy, and that of the humanist who translates and comments on the texts of the Ancients, the lines of demarcation tend to fade away. Economic activity, scientific activity, and political activity, subjected to the same model of rationality, are placed beneath the common emblem of service to the state and the apprenticeship of freedom.

But we must recognize that the preceding representation inspires a way of doing things. Salutati himself, who first attained notoriety by his work as a humanist outside of Florence, endowed the function of chancellor of the republic with a responsibility it did not have prior to him, and became a political figure of the first order; at the same time, he acquired an important economic position, directing business and important speculative ventures. Leonardo Bruni, who succeeded him at the chancellery, presented the same traits. Both, at least, were originally "intellectuals," and both were new citizens (*novi cives*) who used their culture to acquire wealth and power. But more significant are the cases of the other humanists, whom historians—in this case Lauro Martines—have shown to belong for the most part to the great Florentine families, to hold key positions in high finance or banking, and to occupy the main public offices.[23] When we see the great number of works produced in the space of about forty years, we cannot doubt the cohesion of political humanism, nor the change realized with respect to the preceding generations, the most illustrious representatives of which were Petrarch and Boccaccio. As for the themes that inspire Salutati's conception—they are elaborated in the historical or philosophical works, broadly distributed among the bourgeoisie. It is Cino Rinuccini, who, in his *Risponsiva alla Invettiva di Messer Antonio Lusco*—a Milanese humanist in the service of Visconti—furnishes a new interpretation of the history of Florence, relates the episodes of its battle for Italian freedom, and composes exemplary biographies of citizens, in which for the first time tradesmen, military leaders, and writers are associated with one another. It is Gregorio Dati who, analyzing Florence's recent conflict with Milan, shows that the former's victory was certain, despite its military weakness, because of the superiority of its economic resources, its diplomatic strategy, and its moral strength, exposes a necessary connection between capitalist practice, political rationality, and democratic values, and compares the position of Florence to that of Rome before Hannibal. It is Vergerio, Salutati's disciple, who pursues, in opposition to Petrarch, the rehabilitation of Cicero, that theoretician of political commitment and adversary of Caesar, and decries in the clemency of the prince who was admired by his predecessors the signs of the degradation of law and the corruption of the regime. And it is Buonaccorso da Montemagno who, in his *Disputatio de nobilitate*—a work that would become exceptionally successful both in Western Europe and in Italy—attacks the privilege of birth, sees true nobility in plebeian work and the love of knowledge, praises nature for giving the same chances of success to all men, and discerns in devotion to the republic the highest level of morality.

No one is more deserving of our inquisitive attention than Leonardo Bruni, who, for his functions, the extent of his literary production, and the influence he had on his contemporaries, proved to be the major voice of political humanism, the inspired intellectual leader toward whom the Florentines turned after the fall of the Medici; then, once the republic was defeated, the beacon of the opponents of the new regime, who came to draw from his teaching motivations and arguments in order to found their resistance to tyranny. In considering the main themes of his oeuvre, it would be difficult not to hypothesize that he is par excellence the holder of the *other* discourse that Machiavelli intimates to his readers. Besides the fact that he brings Salutati's ideas to consummate expression, his actions appear to be the most effective in precipitating the identification of the Florentine with the Roman of the republican period. In the wake of Salutati, and also, it is true, of a few rare writers of the *Trecento*, such as Ptolemy da Lucca and Petrarch, he praises the excellence of the institutions that Rome was able to create to protect itself from the dangers of tyranny, but he was the first to base his convictions on a principle that suffers no compromise with the praise of the imperial monarch. While Petrarch, inflamed by Cola di Rienzo, had subsequently forgotten his justification of the republic and the chants of *Africa* that vaunted the freedom of the days of Scipio, and while Salutati himself had reversed his position by writing a *De Tyranno* that contained a justification of Caesar, Bruni tied political authority so fundamentally to the mores of the people that the opposition between free and oppressive governments became irreconcilable. The *virtus romana* has its roots in the way of life of the citizens, considered to be constitutive of all their social relations, to such a degree that it could not survive the loss of their political responsibility. The assessment of the circumstances in which Caesar's power took hold and the appreciation of his work appear secondary, compared to the decline of civic life that necessarily follows the installation of the tyrant. So strong is the condemnation of the tyrant that it implies the rehabilitation of Brutus, whom Dante, in Bruni's view, seized upon as upon a symbolic figure when he plunged him into the infernal regions, using him as the prototypical lawbreaker, but who in reality meted out a legitimate punishment to the hijacker of Rome's freedom. Now Bruni, appealing to his contemporaries to break away from the long tradition of attachment to imperial Rome, directing them away from the medieval dream of a universal monarchy that would carry on the spirit of the Caesars, declaring a historical hiatus between the era of corruption and that of healthy institutions, relocates the foundation of the modern state back to the time that the emperors had plunged into oblivion. He develops a new version of the origin of Florence, at variance with the one accredited since the beginning of the *Duecento* (as attested by the *Cronica de origine civitatis*, written around 1225, from which the Villani would borrow a century later), that attributed the foundation of the city to Caesar's legions, engaged in the pursuit of Catilina in the siege of Fiesole.[24] Moving the event back to the period in which Sulla became involved in the civil war, he claims to establish that it was the veterans of his army who created a colony at the foot of Fiesole, and consequently that the blood of the free citizens of Rome flows in the veins of the modern Florentines; that the filiation of the two republics is not an idealist abstraction, but rather attested in reality. No less important than that thesis, which is defended in the *Laudatio florentinae urbis*, are the supplements it occasions in his *Historia populi florentini* and the *Oratio funebris* devoted to the Ferrarese general Nanni degli Strozzi. There, probably in order to offer a restructuring that would satisfy the new conditions of a state that had expanded to comprise most of Tuscany, the author praises the ancient Etruscan cities, citadels of governments that were free before the Roman conquest, and then goes so far as to assert—once more, against a tradition devoted to contrasting the descendants of Fiesole with those of Rome—the twofold Etruscan and Roman influence that produced the specific greatness of Florence and its vocation, to embody freedom in Italy. No other document, perhaps, better condenses the ideas of political humanism at its highest point than this *Oratio*, given in 1428, twenty-five years after the *Laudatio*. Bruni, as Hans Baron notes,[25] clearly taking his inspiration from Pericles, who had succeeded in converting his eulogy of the victims of the Peloponnesian war into a panegyric of Athens, seized the occasion of hailing the memory of a former general of the republic to sing the praises of Florence, the depositary in his view of the ancient legacy. After the example of his illustrious model, he makes Florence a mentor for the neighboring peoples, and recognizes her as the center of contemporary culture—the point from which the *studia humanitatis,* political freedom, and equality emanate. There the democratic ideal is affirmed in terms that forbid its being reduced to the definition of a collectively exerted power. It is true that in the *forma popularis* the excellence of the constitution is pointed out. But the virtue of the Florentine regime is not just to make the appropriation of the state's power by a citizen impossible; the author no longer limits himself to seeking the guarantee of democracy in the institution of the Priorate (which allots the supreme authority to nine peers, renewable every two months), in the framework of judicial provisions ensuring the equality of citizens before the law, or in the abolition of the privileges formerly held by feudal nobility. The new idea is that men are recognized in Florence as having equal rights to win public honor, that they are spurred on to a noble competition for the advancement of their standing, and that their energies are greatly enhanced by their aspirations—as a result of which the entire social body is strengthened by their enterprises and their equality.

Finally, it is impossible to exaggerate the importance taken on in Bruni's democratic theory by the project of a restoration of the communal militia. It is true that traces of this motif are to be found throughout the *Trecento,* particularly in the form of specific criticisms voiced by Petrarch and Boccaccio aimed at the use of mercenary soldiers and condottieri. That institution elicited such strong charges and provoked such outrage during the campaigns of the republic that around 1370, according to the historian Bayley, it lost the favor of public opinion.[26] Denounced for its lack of effectiveness, it receives the continual condemnation of the humanists, who base their view on the authority of Aristotle and the example of the Romans—beginning with the censure of Salutati. But already for him, and especially for Bruni, who in 1422 devotes an entire work, *De militia*, to the examination of military institutions, the lesson drawn from the Ancients reinforces a view of the political life that binds the virtue of the citizen to that of the soldier. Thus, the critique of Florence's system of defense is based on a critique of a state that would tolerate a division between the private activity of the bourgeois and his public role. The military service proves to guarantee the devotion of the individual to the City, the test by which he identifies himself fully as a political subject. Another of Bruni's works, his *History of the Florentine People*, establishes the correspondence of that view with the practice during the early Commune, when the *status popularis* was in fact based on the *robur populi*, when every neighborhood (*sesto*) of Florence supplied its contingent to the militia, when the same principles governing the selection of the citizens charged with the political responsibility of the city applied to that of its defenders. The new militia, then, appears as the instrument of a political, moral, and military reform that finds its triple justification in the theory of popular government, the model instituted in early Florence, and the Roman experience maintained by the authority of the classical authors.

It seems hardly necessary to stress the relation between Machiavelli's discourse and that of Bruni, or more generally those inspired by political humanism. A methodical comparison between *The Discourses* and the texts elaborated a century earlier would undoubtedly reveal not only a common frame of reference, but the precise play of reminiscences underlying Machiavelli's analysis. With his assessment of Caesar, of the Empire during the time of its glory, and of the virtue of the ancient Tuscans, along with his critique of modern and ancient institutions, we are specifically referred to the terms of a past discussion that was filled with meaning for his contemporaries. Moreover, the relationship is so patent that many historians have alluded to it. But their perspective is such that they limit themselves to pointing out similarities, or, in the thick of what would prove to be an evolution of political thought, differences on particular points. Now, from the writings of the beginning of the *Quattrocento* to the oeuvre of Machiavelli, the distance cannot be measured by the degree of variations of interpretation, or even by a difference of principle. Machiavelli's thought is worked out within the matrix of political humanism, while at the same time it acquires its identity only in detaching itself from it. Surely it is not a rupture, for in a sense that is impossible; from the language the ancient Florentines spoke the work draws its substance; but its work to reopen that language in order to make it speak anew, beyond the discourses already held—to turn back against its established expressions, denouncing the limits within which it had shut itself up, to interpret the implied interpretation, from which it formerly drew its sustenance.

Machiavelli's discourse is similar to Bruni's when it holds up the Roman Republic as a model. But in Bruni this model accredits the representation of a harmonious society, a leading class naturally inclined to wisdom and justice, and a people—all categories merged into one, gathered together within the circle of its laws. In vain would we seek in his model the idea that the struggle between the plebs and the patriciate and the "infinite disorders" it brings about were the driving principle behind the greatness of the state. Rome is but the embodiment of the good government, as defined by the Aristotelian philosophy that recognizes in harmony the sign of the health of the body politic, and assigns the crucial function of moderation to the middle class. By and large, the democratic ideal is sustained by the denial of conflict, so much so that the predominance of the oligarchic element—declared by Bruno with the advent of Cosimo—appears as a simple variant of the Florentine regime. On the opposition between the republic and tyranny, its intransigence is tied to the refusal to recognize that oppression is implicit in every form of government, and that it can be stronger under the cover of a popular constitution than under the reign of a prince. Such is his apology for republican institutions that it confers on them an essential reality, indifferent to the vicissitudes introduced by social struggles and class dominance. By this conduit, formalism joins hands with conservatism: in the Florentine constitution of his day, Bruni limits himself to reading the signs of the permanence of the principles posited at its origin; he praises the present order for its conformity with an ancient order, itself in the image of the original order instituted by the Roman Republic. But perhaps the inspiration of his theory is reflected most faithfully in his conception of the citizen soldier, in which one would be too quickly tempted to find the first version of Machiavelli's ideas. The difference is not that the reform project continues to attest to a desire for restoration: *The Discourses* seem to participate in the same intention. But eloquent on this point is the appeal addressed to the bourgeoisie, who should take on the responsibility conferred on it by its dominant position, recognize that it forms the corps of the guardians of the City, that it groups an order of chivalry possessing emblems, a code of honor, distinguishing itself from the mass of merchants, driven by the base appetite for profit.[27] An aristocracy based on old and new money, the stewards of culture and power, distinct, it is true, from the feudal aristocracy denounced as barbarous—Bruni seeks the model for it in the Roman patriarchate, but omits associating the lower class with the militia. Better yet, he conceives of the latter as the instrument necessary for the "*boni cives*" to protect themselves from the "*infima plebs*," and, just as Salutati had already done, finds in the insurrection of the *Ciompi* in 1379 a case in point to stress the danger to the dominant class of neglecting the power of arms within the city.[28] Now, Machiavelli takes the opposite view when he shows the *principi*—monarchs or oligarchs—as being obsessed by fear of the class enemy, more concerned with keeping it away from arms than in defending the state. As for the project of a people's militia, he only espouses it in changing its function, in removing it from the aristocratic framework to which Bruni kept it confined. He does not broaden its significance, he does not draw from his premises consequences that had not yet been formulated; he reveals that the premises—those in general of humanist thought—are necessarily in agreement with their consequences, that one sole logic prescribes the identification with Rome, the representation of the good government, the denial of class conflict, and the disadvantage of the plebs, and that that logic works to maintain the societal relationships instituted in Florence, and furnishes the oligarchy with the justification of its power. It is doubtless true that his own critique is engendered by conditions that are at the origin of the humanist ideological elaboration. Rome still supplies the general setting in which the edifice of Machiavelli's oeuvre is erected—a setting we may be sure the writer was not at liberty to choose, but that was imposed on him, inscribed within him before he knew it; yet from those conditions, from that setting, he draws the power to free the thought which is a prisoner to the logic of the *imaginaire*. While repeating the appeal to imitate the Romans, he denounces the lure of identification, intimates that the true relation to the past brings us face to face with a new present, that the return to the origin implies the creation of new things; while endorsing the ideas that enjoined the theory of the popular regime, he still denounces the fiction of a natural community and a power that would be its direct expression; he challenges us to think, with the concept of a people, the division into dominators and dominated, and with the concept of Power, the division into the social and the political.

We realize the full import of Machiavelli's undertaking when we become aware that the effectiveness of the political illusion is always bound up with faith in an authority held to be the guarantor of a field of knowledge. We could not fully appreciate the representation of Rome, the ancient authors, their supposed function in the thought of the listeners gathered in the Oricellari Gardens, if we were unaware that they were sustained by the invisible presence of the fathers of freedom, of those who once conducted "true discourse" in Florence. On the other hand, the more carefully we scrutinize this discourse, the closer we get to Machiavelli's oeuvre, the more the initial effort of identification of the Republic of Florence with the Roman Republic is revealed—the more sensitized we become to the identification of the contemporaries of Machiavelli with the masters of political humanism. The audacity of the oeuvre is further accentuated in our view when we find the intention of moving the supposed true discourse into the category of ideological discourse, or, more strictly speaking—since humanism cannot be reduced to ideology, since with it there appears a language that must be reopened—of circumscribing the ideological function of political humanism. But at the same time, the exploration of the discourse of the founders of the *Quatrocento*, into which Machiavelli leads his reader, reveals what is only indicated in the oeuvre through signs, without being said: the political role played by humanism in the service of the Florentine oligarchy, from the aftermath of the counterrevolution that followed the *Ciompi* insurrection to the advent of Cosimo. Indeed, the question of ideology is clarified when it becomes apparent that the moment in which democratic theory was formed is precisely the one in which the haute bourgeoisie possessed its greatest strength, in which it was able to undo the conquests of the *populo minuto;* that the moment in which the humanists made their case for the participation of all the citizens in public affairs is the one in which it was reduced to its narrowest limits; that the praise of the virtues of the middle class went hand in hand with the eviction of its representatives from the judiciary and the assemblies; and lastly that the affirmation of universal values papered over the prosaic management of the interests of the fraction that held the wealth. The complicity of the partisans of the *governo largo* and of the *governo stretto*—to the advantage of the latter—is exposed by observing the traces left in the memory of the bourgeoisie by the 1378 workers' insurrection, and the unprecedented threat against the property of the grand and the petit bourgeois by the *Ciompi*. The ambiguity of the virtue of the founding fathers then appears in the spectacle of their abundant collaboration with Cosimo, a tyrant in fact, though attentive to the preservation of the appearance of freedom; and this applies particularly to the most illustrious among them, Leonardo Bruni, who thus became the most servile.[29]

Such is the path we follow in trying to assume the position of the proximate reader. That path is adumbrated, we have said, in seeking out the ultimate question that implicates us in the space–time in which the oeuvre is produced. Should we now add that it reaches its goal with the discovery of political humanism in the locus of the *other* discourse it offers us? But it would already be an illusion to believe that with it we would possess the ultimate text on which the Machiavellian interpretation is based. That text, as we have seen, presupposes the elaboration of a social experience; it furnishes a response to the question that emerged, in a new and insufferable light, from the conflict of the lower classes with the bourgeoisie, and bears within it a work of expression and of dissimulation that we could not truly appreciate without a better understanding of the changes occurring in Florentine society—and its contextual world—in the last decades of the *Trecento*. Moreover, that text represents a triumph over an earlier one that it annuls or modifies, drawing its justification from the destitution of former beliefs and authorities. Thus, we would have to plumb the depths of the past and locate its surviving results in order to understand the significance of the intervening mutation, and the power it has to capture the collective imagination at a distance from a historical conjuncture. Specifically, we would have to scrutinize the representation of Rome before it was modified by Salutati and his school in order to assess all that is involved in the identification of the Florentine with the Roman. Thus, the search for the ultimate question should not be satisfied to come up with the reference to political humanism; the latter calls for a fresh interrogation. In vain would we try to convince ourselves that in so doing we would be transgressing the limits of an interpretation of Machiavelli. How could we be sure we have understood him correctly, as long as we are not sure of having understood that *other* discourse on the basis of which and in contrast with which his own conquers its personal identity? It is true that in formulating this scruple we risk being precipitated into an infinite regress in the order of antecedents. But that scruple takes on great weight when we ask ourselves whether conflicts that arise at the end of the *Trecento* are not of a different nature from those that arose earlier; whether, during that period, the power of the state does not establish for the first time its supremacy over the other centers of social power—the Guelph party and the Church; whether the bourgeoisie does not acquire full class consciousness at that time, whether humanism does not do much more than modify the traditional representations, whether it does not initiate a language that for the first time is coherent within the framework of politics; in sum, whether ideology is not instituted by subordinating to itself the functions of myth and religion. To embark on such an interrogation, would this not be tantamount to procuring new means of appreciating Machiavelli's oeuvre, recognizing that with it the difference between interpretation and ideology is given in a way that is not only exemplary, but originary?

But it does not suffice to confess that we are still on the threshold of these questions and that in this stopping-place our task reveals its limits. The illusion would be reborn, were we to suppose that by advancing further we could, at another stage, account at last for the position of the proximate reader. Indeed, whatever the progress of our knowledge, it could not empower us to read the difference between ideology and interpretation, if the latter were not already at work in our own experience, and if we did not already make tacit use of it before conceiving of its operation in the past. It is the oeuvre, no doubt, that puts us in the place of the proximate reader. But *we* are the ones it attracts. We join it in the space–time in which it appears from the space–time in which our lives are made, and without ceasing to inhabit the latter. Our place is not that of the young Florentines we imagined gathered in the residence of Rucellai listening to *The Discourses,* since, as I have said, it is by knowing that place that we make ourselves capable of reading. It is the place of an *other,* involved in the work qua *elsewhere,* the presumed reader qua open by the work of thought to the question of its origin. If Machiavelli's discourse can be understood by us as that of interpretation, that is, if through it an *other* discourse is denounced as that of ideology, it is because here, where we are, Rome and its guardians speak to us in other guises, because the image of a truth that has taken *place,* and faith in a "good society," still sustain desire, and because we confront the requirement of freeing ourselves from their grip. The effort of reading an anti-ideological discourse in the oeuvre is thus dependent on a critique of the representations that invest our experience of politics *here and now.* So necessary is that critique that we were obliged, in order to recognize in the oeuvre the difference between interpretation and ideology, to begin by breaking through the ideological barrier that blocks access to it, that is, by rending the fabric of commentary that has come to conceal it. Still, our project suffers not so much from a failure to articulate the reasons for that critique, from leaving in a chiaroscuro the place in which it is formed and in which the fascination with Rome continues to go on. Were it to wish to proceed, it would have to forswear all completion, having taught us that the ideology both within us and without calls for the endless labor of interpretation, that ideology eludes our grasp while tightening its own the very moment we think ourselves on the solid ground of certainty, and finally that interpretation is inseparable from interrogation.

Notes

All notes in brackets are by the translator.

Part 1

1. [An allusion to the poem by Mallarmé, "Un coup de dés n'abolira jamais le hasard."]
2. [See *Correspondance générale de Marcel Proust*, vol. 5 (Paris: Plon, 1930), 222.]

Part 2

1. Toussant Guiraudet, *Oeuvres de Machiavel*, Paris, Year VII (1798–99), preface.
2. Balzac, *La cousine Bette*, in *La Comédie Humaine*, Pléiade VI, 265. [*Cousin Bette* (Oxford, New York: Oxford University Press, 1992), 157.]
3. Tommasini, *La vita e gli scritti di Niccolò Machiavelli*.
4. Panella, *Gli antimachiavellici*, 16.
5. Charbonnel, *La pensée italienne*, 17–23, 28; Thuau, *Raison d'État*, 55–56.
6. Tommasini, *La vita*, vol. I, 14, 21.
7. Benoist, *Le Machiavélisme*, vol. III, 18.
8. Tommasini, *La vita*, vol. I, 14, 21. "*Turc*" and "*mahométan*" are the terms used particularly by Gentillet and Possevin.
9. For example, that is the opinion of Ribadeneira (*De religione et virtutibus principis Christiani Adversus Machiavellum* [Madrid, 1597]); see Chérel, *La pensée de Machiavel en France* (Paris: L'Artisan du Livre, 1935).
10. I. Gentillet, *Discours sur les moyens de bien gouverner et soutenir en bonne paix un royaume ou autre principauté—Contre Machiavel*, Geneva, 1576 (republ. by E. Rathé, Droz, Geneva, 1968), 37.
11. On the role played by Gentillet in the formation of the anti-Machiavellian currents, see Burd, *Il Principe*, 40.
12. Tommasini, *La vita*, vol. I, 40, 5.
13. See especially Villari, *Niccolò Machiavelli e i suoi tempi*, II, 405. Panella, for his part, notes: "no one perceived the pernicious character of his works, neither then nor afterward, for several years" (*Gli antimachiavellici*, 21).

14. E. Meyer, *Machiavelli and the Elizabethan Drama* (New York: B. Franklin, 1969), 5n3.

15. Ambrogio Caterino Politi, *De libris a christiano detestandis et a christianismo eliminandis*, Rome, 1552; Girolamo Osorio, *De nobilitate christiana*, Lisbon, 1542, see Panella, *Gli antimachiavellici*, 26–27.

16. Panella, *Gli antimachiavellici*, 33.

17. L. Febvre, *The Problem of Unbelief in the Sixteenth Century: The Religion of Rabelais*, trans. Beatrice Gottlieb (Cambridge, Mass., and London: Harvard University Press, 1982), 131–45 ("What the Accusation of Atheism Meant in the Sixteenth Century").

18. Ibid., 142.

19. Ibid., 139.

20. Ibid., 142. On Father Garasse, *Doctrine curieuse des beaux esprits de ce temps*, 1623, see Charbonnel, *La pensée italienne*, 35.

21. Namely, Possevin, Ribadeneira, Bosio, Botero; see Panella, *Gli antimachiavellici*, 53 ff.; Croce, *Storia dell'età barocca in Italia*.

22. H. Hauser and A. Renaudet, *Les Débuts de l'âge moderne*, 3rd edition (Paris: 1949), 561–62. Mario Praz writes: "The black legend of Machiavelli springs up in France in the days of Catherine de Médicis, as the coronation of anti-Italianism provoked by the government and the sovereign" (Praz, M. *Machiavelli e gl'Inglese dell' epoca elisabettiana*, Civiltà Moderna, Quaderni no. 2 [Florence: Vallechi Editore, 1930]). See also Chabod, *Del Principe di Niccolò Machiavelli*, nuov. rev. stor., IX, 1925 (republ. with other essays in *Scritti su Machiavelli*, [Turin, 1964], 123–24).

23. Chabod, *Del Principe;* Mario Praz, *Machiavelli e gl'inglese;* Gentillet clearly exploits an argument already very widespread, and that is not justified by his remark, in which he associates the image of Machiavellianism with that of the rapacity of the Italian merchant and financier: "we see with our eyes and touch with our hands the avarice of the Italians, who undermine and ruin us and suck away all our substance and leave us nothing" (*Discours sur les moyens*, 43).

24. R. Tawney, *Religion and the Rise of Capitalism* (New Brunswick, N.J.: Transaction Publishers, 1998), 36–54.

25. E. Meyer finds 395 references to Machiavelli in the Elizabethan theater; M. Praz confirms and completes his information and points out that "Machiavellian" is already used in a generic sense in the *Sempills Ballads* in 1568.

26. For example, *Machiavelli and the Devil*, by Robert Daborne, cited by Meyer, *Machiavelli and the Elizabethan Drama*, 129.

27. Praz, *Machiavelli e gl'inglese*, 2.

28. Ibid.

29. Ibid., 40: "the name Machiavelli and the name Satan became equivalent to such a degree that while the stratagems attributed to Machiavelli were systematically qualified as diabolical, later the stratagems of the devil became Machiavellian."

30. Tawney, *Religion and the Rise of Capitalism*, 22–23.

31. The inscription at the place where the bonfire was set up says: "*quoniam fuerit homo vafer ac subdolus diabolicarum cogitationum faber optimus, cacodaemonis*

auxiliator." [Whereas he was a subtle and sly man, the best craftsman of diabolical ideas, a helper of the Evil Spirit.] See Tommasini, *La Vita*, vol. I, 70n1.

32. As Zuccolo points out at the beginning of the seventeenth century, the theory of "reason of state" is heatedly discussed at all levels of society: "*non pure dai consignieri nelle corti e dai dottori nelle scuole, ma dai barbieri exiando e dagli altri vili artéfici nelle bottighe e nei ritrovi loro*" [not only by the lawyers in the courts and the doctors in the schools, but by the barbers as well and the other lowly artisans in their shops and gathering places], in Croce, *Storia dell'età barocca in Italia*, 77.

33. They write, for example, "Match-evill" or "Matchievell," or "Mach-evill that evill none can match," Praz, *Machiavelli e gl'inglese*, 42–43. The first name Niccolò merges with a nickname for the devil, already widespread, Old Nick. The accusation of Satanism goes so far as to inspire a legend. If we are to believe Gaspar Amico, the peasants of San Casciano say that no one wanted to live in the house in which Machiavelli had written *The Prince*, knowing that the devil had lived and died there. Tommasini, *La vita*, I, 7n1.

34. Croce, *Storia dell'età barocca in Italia*, 11: "*l'abominio delle dottrine e del nome del M divenne un atteggiamento usuale e convenzionale e come di diritto.*" [The loathing of the doctrines and of the name of Machiavelli becomes a usual and customary attitude as if sanctioned by law.] Praz, for his part, notes that: "*M. accenava a diventare una specie di comodo passe-partout per quanto v'era d'odioso nell'arte di governo, anzi addiritura nell'umana in genere.*" [Machiavelli showed signs of becoming a convenient catch-all for whatever was hateful in the art of governing, or better still simply in mankind in general.] *Machiavelli e gl'inglese*, 11.

35. Burd, *Il Principe.*

36. *Lettere di Giovambattista Busini a Benedetto Varchi sopra l'assedio di Firenze* (Florence: Felice Le Monnier, 1860), 84. Cited by Panella, *Gli antimachiavellici*, 16.

37. First meditation.

38. Ibid.

39. Ibid.

40. Second meditation.

Part 3, Chapter 1

I have used *Il Principe* (*The Prince*) and the *Discorsi sopra la Prima Deca di Tito Livio* (*The Discourses on the First Ten Books of Livy*) in the text established by Francesco Flora and Carlo Cordiè, *Tutte le opera di Niccolò Machiavelli* ([no place]: Mondadori, 1949).

The translation of the exerpts quoted is borrowed in part from E. Barincou—who is in turn very faithful to the translation of Gohory (1571) in the case of *The Prince*—and in large part my own. It is important in many instances, particularly in reading *The Discourses*, to try to reconstruct the precise remark in French, which in the hands of many translators is distorted by a concern for elegance and the desire to avoid repetition of terms. Since I have sought to follow Machiavelli's discourse as closely as possible, always mentioning in the course of my commentary the chapter being referred to, I have decided to spare the reader specific citation references.

1. *Machiavelli and His Friends: Their Personal Correspondence*, trans. J. B. Atkinson and David Sices (DeKalb: Northern Illinois University Press, 1996), 262–65. [Trans. modified.]

2. F. Chabod, "Sulla composizione de 'Il Principe' di Niccolò Machiavelli," *Archivum romanticum* XI (1927; republished with other essays in *Scritti su Machiavelli* [Turin: Einaudi, 1964]).

3. R. Ridolfi, *Vita di N.M.* (Rome, 1954). [R. Ridolfi, *The Life of Niccolò Machiavelli*, trans. C. Grayson (London, 1963).]

4. *Toutes les lettres de Machiavel*, prefaced and annotated by Edmond Barincou, preface by Jean Giono, 2 vols. (Paris: Gallimard, 1955), 1:498.

5. Ibid., 1:167.

6. Ibid., 1:331. (On the manner of treating the rebellious populations of the Val di Chiana, p. 503.)

7. Ibid., 2:252–58 (account concerning matters in France, 1510).

8. Ibid., 2:134–41 (report on matters in Germany, 1508).

9. Most of these ideas are condensed in a document from 1503: *Words to be pronounced before the Balia on the need for procuring money*. Ibid., 2:310.

10. This is the first sentence of the chapter: "*Io lascerò indietro el rationare delle republiche, perchè altra volta ne ragionarai a lungo.*"

11. H. Baron, "The *Principe* and the Puzzle of the Date of the *Discorsi*," in *Bibliothèque d'Humanisme et Renaissance* XVIII (Geneva: Droz, 1956), 405–28.

12. These are the witnesses of Filippo de' Nerli, the author of the *Commentari dei fatti civili occorsi dentro la città di Firenze dall' anno 1215 al 1537* (2, Trieste, 1859, 12), and of Jacopo Nardi, the author of the *Istorie della città di Firenze, 1494–1552* (2, Firenze, 1838–1841, 77). Quoted by H. Baron, "The *Principe* and the Puzzle of the Date of the *Discorsi*," 420n1.

13. On the treatises devoted to the government of the prince, see Allan H. Gilbert, *Machiavelli's "Prince" and Its Forerunners* (Durham, N.C.: Duke University Press, 1938).

14. Chapter 3.

15. Chapter 15: "*Ma sendo l'intento mio scrivere cosa utile a chi la intende, mi è parso piu conveniente andare dietro alla verità effectuale della cosa che alla immaginazione di essa.*"

Part 3, Chapter 2

1. The publication date is given by L. J. Walker, *The Discourses of Niccolò Machiavelli* (London: Routledge and Kegan Paul, 1950), 305 (appendix sources). I refer to the edition *Aegidii columnae romani de regimine principum*, Rome, 1607.

2. *Il trattato circa il reggimento e governo della Città di Firenze* (1498) in Mario Ferrara, *Savonarola* (Florence: Olschki, 1952), 189.

3. Alexandre Koyré, *A l'aube de la science classique*, Études galiléennes I, in

Histoire de la pensée, Actualités scientifiques et industrielles (Paris: Hermann Compagnie, 1939), 17.

4. See Ferrara, *Savonarola.* The denunciation of the *tiepidi* is found in the preaching on the psalm *Quam Bonus,* in the sermon *Sopra Giobbe* (p. 274), and in the eighth sermon *Sopra Aggeo,* given one month after the fall of Piero. In the latter, Savonarola underscores the need to create *ordini nuovi.* The call to prayer as the most effective means of saving the city from danger is found most notably in *Il trattato circa il reggimento . . .* (ibid., 208–10).

Part 3, Chapter 4

1. The traits of this author may fruitfully be thought of as modeled on those of Savonarola. Much light is shed on the argument of Chapters 15 and 18 if we compare it with the *Trattato circa il reggimento . . .* ; see Ferrara, *Savonarola,* cited above at 111n2.

2. See the commentary of Burd, *Il Principe,* in the margin of chap. 18, "Cicero: *De officiis,*" I, 11, 34 and I, 13, 41.

3. Egidio Colonna; see Atkinson and Sices, cited 180n1, 1: 2, 7. The discussion on the necessity of being at once loved and feared, moreover, occupies an important place in the Treatise. Compare 2:2, 36: "*Quomodo reges et principes debeant se habere ut amentur a populo et quomodo ut timeantur; et quod licet utrumque sit necessarium, amari tamen plus debent appetere quam temeri.*" Here the author enumerates the qualities that cause princes to be loved and gives first place to those that make them "*benefici et liberales.*" On the necessity of fear it will suffice to repeat that men are not all perfect and that it is appropriate that the prince, in the service of justice, divert them from evil by the threat of punishment.

4. My emphasis.

5. *Il trattato circa il reggimento . . .* , in Ferrara, *Savonarola.*

Part 4, Chapter 9

1. [The term *l'imaginaire,* used as a noun, does not seem to have a precise English equivalent. It concerns the ability of a group or individual to represent the world to themselves with the help of a network of associated images that give it meaning. Although the term obviously bears a relation to *imagination,* it does not share that term's opposition to *reality.* Rather it is to be thought of as part of the process of perception. I therefore retain the French term (in italics) throughout.]

Part 4, Chapter 10

1. [Plutarch, *The Lives of the Noble Grecians and Romans,* trans. J. Dryden, revised A. H. Clough (New York: The Modern Library, 1932), 349.]

2. [Machiavelli, *The Discourses*, ed. B. Crick, trans. L. J. Walker, S.J., rev. B. Richardson (London, New York: Penguin Books, 1970; reprint, 2003), 510. Trans. slightly modified.]

3. [Ibid., 511. Trans. slightly modified.]

4. [Ibid., 512. Trans. modified.]

5. [Ibid., 513. Trans. slightly modified.]

6. [Ibid., 311. Trans. modified.]

7. [Ibid., 515.]

8. [Ibid. Machiavelli's wording is *"perché dicono che il loro re non può patire vergogna in qualunque sua diliberazione."* He appears to echo the French dictum retrieved by Lefort in his translation: *"Le roi ne peut pâtir vergogne"* (See *Le travail de l'oeuvre Machiavel* [Paris: Gallimard, 1972, 1986], 680), which is more literally, "The king cannot suffer shame."]

9. [Ibid., 516. Trans. slightly modified.]

10. [Ibid.]

11. *Toutes les lettres . . .* (Niccolò Machiavelli to Alfonsina Orsini de' Medici), 313.

12. Ibid.

13. *Toutes les lettres . . .* (Niccolò Machiavelli, *Lettere* [Milan, Italy: Feltrinelli, 1961], 225–26.)

14. [Machiavelli, *The Discourses*, 486.]

15. [Machiavelli, *The Discourses*, 524–25. Trans. modified.]

16. *Toutes les lettres . . .* (N. M. to Pier Soderini at Raguse), 326.

17. [This appears to be an allusion to Chapter 43, titled "That Men Who Are Born in the Same Country Display Throughout the Ages Many of the Same Characteristics."]

18. [Machiavelli, *The Discourses*, 523.]

19. [Ibid., 179.]

20. [Ibid., 526.]

21. [Ibid., 526–27.]

22. [Ibid., 527.]

Part 5

1. [I.e., a thought that, forgetful of the circumstance that meaning is generated through a system of differences, considers itself somehow sui generis and absolute. For a fuller account of *différence* (or *différance*), see Jacques Derrida's *Writing and Difference*, trans. Alan Bass (London: Routledge, 2006), which was originally published in 1967. See also his *Speech and Phenomena* and *Of Grammatology*, published the same year.]

2. [The French *imaginaire*, unlike its English cognate, is devoid of the coefficient of reality/unreality; it should not therefore be assimilated to the English "imaginary."]

3. [French "entendre" means both to hear and to understand. When this

"double entendre" plays a crucial role, as it does in the following text, I translate it as hearing/understanding.]

4. Maurice Blanchot, *The Infinite Conversation*, trans. Susan Hanson (Minneapolis: University of Minnesota Press, 1993), 80–82.

5. [The underlying word here is "parole," which Lefort uses in the Saussurean sense of language as it exists and is used personally by the speaking subject. It also has the moral power of binding the subject to his or her verbal expression. In some contexts it will be translated as "word."]

6. [The original title of this book, *Le travail de l'oeuvre Machiavel*, which translates literally as "The work of the work Machiavelli" is developed here in its conceptual context: the "work" (*travail*) being the laborious, fermentative process of interpretive breaking away from the historical matter to produce "Machiavelli."]

7. Martin Coyle, *Niccolò Machiavelli's "The Prince": New Interdisciplinary Essays* (Manchester: Manchester University Press, 1995), 198. [Letter from N. M. to Francesco Vettori, 10 December, 1513, trans. slightly modified.]

8. Edmond Barincou, *Machiavel par lui-même* (Paris: Éditions du Seuil, 1969).

9. [See above, note 2.]

10. [N. M., *The Discourses*, trans. Leslie J. Walker, S.J., rev. (London/New York: Penguin, 2003), 113. [Book 1, Ch. 3.]

11. Our information comes especially from three classic works: F. T. Perrens, *Histoire de Florence depuis la domination des Médicis jusqu'à la chute de la république*, 3 vols. (Paris, 1914); Georges Renard, *Histoire du travail à Florence*, 2 vols. (Paris, 1914); Antonio Anzilotti, *La crisi constitutionale della Repubblica fiorentina* (Florence, 1919–Roma 1969), which contains exceptionally interesting information and analyses on class struggle and factions and the operation of Florentine institutions; also, Piero Pieri, *Il Rinascimento e la crisi militare italiana* (Turin, 1952), which affords invaluable insight into the economic evolution of Florence and its situation at the end of the fifteenth century; Gene A. Brucker, *Florentine Politics and Society, 1343–1378* (Princeton, 1962), which is essential for an understanding of the social structure and dynamics of myriad conflicts in which the political history of the *Quattrocento* and *Cinquecento* is intertwined. On the same period, the work by Niccolò Rodolico, *La Democrazia fiorentina nel suo tramonto* (Bologna, 1905–Roma, 1970), remains essential. Two brief and enlightening studies by M. B. Becker tie in closely with these last works: "The Republican City State in Florence: An Inquiry into Its Origin and Survival," in *Speculum* XXXV, 1960, and "The Novi Cives and Florentine Politics," in *Medieval Studies* XXIV, 1962, Toronto. A remarkable tableau of the political struggle under the republic (1494–1512) is provided by Nicolai Rubinstein, "Politics and Constitution in Florence at the End of the Fifteenth Century," in *Italian Renaissance Studies*, ed. E. F. Jacob (London, 1960). On the events in which Machiavelli was involved, the best study remains the biography by R. Ridolfi, *Vita di N. M.* (Rome, 1954).

12. On the representation of Fortune, see G. Gentile, *Il pensiero italiano del Rinasciamento*, 4th ed., opere XIV (Florence: Sansoni, 1968).

13. See the invaluable study by Felix Gilbert, "Bernardo Rucellai and the

Orti Oricellari: A Study on the Origin of Modern Political Thought," *Journal of the Warburg and Courtauld Institutes* 11 (1948), 103–31. I make broad use of his information at this stage of my argument.

14. It is to Felix Gilbert that we owe the analysis of the protocols of the *Consulte* and *Pratiche* gathered under the republic between 1496 and 1512: "Florentine Political Assumptions in the Period of Savonarola and Soderini," in *Journal of the Warburg and Courtauld Institutes* 20 (1957), 187–214.

15. Ibid., 199. "*Stando le cose come stanno in Italia non si puo havere Pisa sanza due re.*"

16. Ibid., 198.

17. Ibid., 199.

18. Ibid., 200–201.

19. Ibid., 201.

20. Ibid., 211.

21. Hans Baron, *The Crisis of the Early Italian Renaissance: Civic Humanism and Republican Liberty in an Age of Classicism and Tyranny* (Princeton: 1955; 1966). I rely heavily on the information and references of this work.

22. Eugenio Garin, *La cultura filosofica del Rinascimento italiano* (Florence: Sansoni, 1961), 7.

23. Lauro Martines, *The Social World of the Florentine Humanists, 1390–1460* (Princeton, N.J.: Princeton University Press, 1963).

24. On the first version of the origin of Florence and its political function, see, in addition to the work by H. Baron (cited above, note 21), Nicolai Rubinstein, "The Beginnings of Political Thought in Florence: A Study in Mediaeval Historiography," *Journal of the Warburg and Courtauld Institutes* 5 (1942), 198–227.

25. H. Baron, *The Crisis*, 412–14.

26. C. C. Bayley, *War and Society in Renaissance Florence* (Toronto: University of Toronto Press, 1961). This work provides an instructive assessment of the discussions held on Florence's military institutions, summarizing and commenting on the argument of *De militia*, the text of which is published in the appendix.

27. H. Baron, *The Crisis*, 212–13.

28. Ibid., 193. On the insurrection of the *Ciompi* (wool workers), see G. Renard, *Histoire du travail*, cited in note 11 above, and N. Rodolico, *I Ciompi* (Florence: Sansoni, 1945, 2nd ed. 1971).

29. Not only did Leonardo Bruni rally to Cosimo, but he pushed servility so far as to take the initiative of summoning the judges of Sienna to pursue the Florentine exiles who had taken refuge in their city. See E. Garin, *La cultura filosofica*, 22.

Claude Lefort (1924–2010) was one of the most important continental philosophers of the post–World War II era. His work focuses on interpreting the political life of modern society, and his distinctive conception of modern democracy is linked to both historical analysis and a novel form of philosophical reflection.

Michael B. Smith is a professor emeritus of French and philosophy at Berry College in Mount Berry, Georgia.

www.ingramcontent.com/pod-product-compliance
Lightning Source LLC
Chambersburg PA
CBHW022129020426
42334CB00015B/821